Gaming, Wellness, and Technology in the Bold Global Workforce

Vanessa Kenon
The University of Texas at San Antonio, USA

James Bartlett
Old Dominion University, USA

IGI Global
Scientific Publishing
Publishing Tomorrow's Research Today

Vice President of Editorial | Melissa Wagner
Director of Acquisitions | Mikaela Felty
Director of Book Development | Jocelynn Hessler
Production Manager | Mike Brehm
Cover Design | Jose Rosado

Published in the United States of America by
IGI Global Scientific Publishing
701 East Chocolate Avenue
Hershey, PA, 17033, USA
Tel: 717-533-8845
Fax: 717-533-7115
Website: https://www.igi-global.com E-mail: cust@igi-global.com

Library of Congress Cataloging-in-Publication Data

LCCN: 2025028516 (CIP Data Pending)
ISBN13: 9798337353227
Isbn13Softcover: 9798337353234
EISBN13: 9798337353241

British Cataloguing in Publication Data
A Cataloguing in Publication record for this book is available from the British Library.

Table of Contents

Detailed Table of Contents

that incentivize healthy behaviors by collecting health data from wearables are also explored in this paper. Nevertheless, challenges such as data privacy, accuracy, and accessibility remain, specifically among vulnerable communities. It is crucial to address these issues to fully realize wearable technology's potential in reducing chronic disease burdens and revolutionize mental healthcare. Further research is needed to overcome technological, ethical, and socioeconomic barriers, to ensure the successful integration of wearables to enhance public health.

Esports has grown into a global phenomenon that combines competition with professional careers. Esports, otherwise known as electronic gaming, is a multifaceted and exciting form of competitive video game. This highly organized landscape has created a global phenomenon, rapidly growing in popularity worldwide and captivating the attention of millions of players worldwide. This paper explores the health risks and positive aspects associated with the relationship between esports and physical and mental health.

In today's rapidly evolving work environments, remote work has become more than a trend; it is now a mainstay and rising (Ewers & Kangmennaang, 2023). This shift has necessitated a re-evaluation of traditional work paradigms, particularly in the realms of work-life balance and employee wellness. This chapter details the core strategies for thriving in remote work settings by setting boundaries, combating isolation, and fostering supportive corporate cultures. Transitioning from offices to remote work can blur the lines between personal and professional lives (Bella, 2023; Beňo, 2023). This section provides practical advice on how remote workers can effectively delineate these aspects. Remote workers face unique challenges in maintaining their healthy work-life balance, and they must adopt effective strategies to set and uphold boundaries as the foundation of remote work balance and well-being.

We all know that the word is driven by innovative technology and this transformation is towards Artificial Intelligence (AI). AI is the branch of science which deals with machine based on human intelligent and capabilities. These machines are upgrading the lives along with increased efficiency and profitability at low cost. AI is adding more and more value to our daily and professional lives; especially our workplace. In the domain of Learning and Development (L&D), AI is standing with open wings to revolutionize the way employees learn and develop their ability and proficiency. The current scenario for learning and development (L&D) is based on static data and training program. This method is outdated as it often shows failure for fulfilling the individual requirement of the learner, making it difficult to upgrading and reaching the workforce globally. In this chapter the author will discuss the mission and role of AI in L&D processes, factors leading to effective AI-based learning, benefits of AI adoption, challenges and opportunities of transformation of AI in workplace.

Learner analytics is revolutionizing global education by providing valuable insights into student behaviors, performance, and engagement through advanced technologies like artificial intelligence and machine learning. This chapter explores the impact of learner analytics on global learning programs, highlighting its potential to personalize educational experiences, enhance student outcomes, and address diverse learner needs. It examines key aspects such as data collection and management, adaptive learning, and the integration of predictive analytics. Challenges related to data privacy, cultural and contextual differences, and ethical considerations are discussed, alongside emerging trends such as multimodal data integration and the use of augmented and virtual reality. The chapter concludes by emphasizing the importance of ethical data practices and cross-institutional collaboration in optimizing learner analytics to create more inclusive and effective educational environments.

Foreword

In an era defined by rapid globalization and unprecedented technological advancement, the very fabric of the workforce is undergoing a profound transformation. The rise of remote teams, the increasing demand for specialized skills, and the imperative for continuous learning necessitate a paradigm shift in how we approach workplace learning and professional development on a global scale. This book delves into this evolving landscape, offering a timely and comprehensive examination of the challenges and opportunities that lie ahead.

This volume transcends the limitations of traditional textbooks, providing a dynamic platform for leading academics, researchers, and practitioners to share their expertise and insights. The chapters within explore a wide array of critical themes, examining the pivotal role of experiential learning in fostering adaptable and resilient workforces. This book analyzes how diverse pedagogical approaches, from immersive simulations to problem-based learning, can bridge the gap between theory and practice in a global context. It delves into the potential of harnessing the power of technology – from artificial intelligence and virtual reality to microlearning platforms – to enhance learning and development initiatives, demonstrating how innovation can personalize learning experiences and cater to the diverse needs of a global workforce. This exploration extends to the exciting realm of gaming and esports, investigating how these platforms, once primarily associated with leisure, can be leveraged to foster collaboration, cultivate essential skills, and enhance engagement within a global learning environment.

Furthermore, this book acknowledges the complexities of intercultural communication in today's interconnected world. It provides practical strategies for promoting collaboration, understanding, and respect within teams and for fostering effective learning environments. It also addresses the unique needs of a geographically dispersed workforce, offering valuable insights into overcoming the logistical and cultural barriers inherent in a globalized work environment, particularly in managing remote teams and ensuring equitable access to learning opportunities.

This book serves as an invaluable resource not only for academics and researchers seeking to expand their understanding of global workplace learning but also for HR professionals, corporate trainers, and organizational leaders tasked with developing and implementing effective training programs. By fostering a dialogue between theory and practice, this volume aims to equip readers with the knowledge and tools needed to navigate the complexities of the modern workplace and cultivate a future-ready workforce.

More than just a collection of chapters, this book is a call to action, urging us to rethink traditional approaches to workplace learning and embrace innovation, collaboration, and a commitment to lifelong learning as we prepare for the workforce of tomorrow.

This foreword is a product of human-machine teaming. The text has been crafted in partnership with a generative large language model. The machine and I digested the text, and the model iteratively generated text above based on my prompts to capture and convey the sentiment I wanted to provide for you and as you dive into this work. I hope you are inspired to continue to advance workplace learning!

Wendy Walsh, EdD
Chief Learning Officer, USA

Preface

In today's hyperconnected and rapidly evolving world, the global workforce is experiencing profound transformation. The convergence of technology, wellness, and professional learning is reshaping how individuals engage, develop, and thrive across industries. As editors of *Gaming, Wellness, and Technology in the Bold Global Workforce*, we are pleased to present a multidisciplinary volume that explores how emerging innovations and cultural shifts are redefining professional growth and workplace dynamics.

This book emerges at a pivotal moment. As organizations worldwide navigate complex challenges, from digital transformation and talent mobility to employee well-being and remote collaboration, the need for agile, inclusive, and future-ready workforces has never been greater. The COVID-19 pandemic accelerated many of these transitions, underscoring the urgency for reskilling, adaptability, and intentional support systems for learners and workers alike.

Gaming, Wellness, and Technology in the Bold Global Workforce builds on this momentum by examining the intersection of modern workforce trends with forward-thinking strategies in education, training, and technology. The chapters in this volume represent a diverse array of perspectives and expertise, addressing critical themes such as digital accessibility, intercultural communication, experiential learning, learner analytics, and the integration of game-derived skills. Together, they illustrate how thoughtful innovation can empower individuals and organizations to navigate complexity with resilience and vision.

The opening chapter, *Player Epic: Integrating Gaming and Esports into Corporate Strategy*, introduces readers to the transformative role of gaming and esports in contemporary corporate environments. Through compelling case studies and strategic analysis, the chapter demonstrates how gaming-based initiatives can enhance employee wellness, engagement, and productivity. By positioning gaming as more than entertainment—indeed, as a strategic business asset—it reframes how organizations can cultivate motivation and innovation in the modern workforce.

In *Skills Reloaded: Harnessing Esports for Communication and Collaboration Development in College*, the focus shifts to the collegiate level, where esports programs are emerging as powerful incubators for essential workplace competencies. This chapter underscores the ability of esports to nurture communication, time management, and teamwork skills in Generation Z learners, bridging educational theory with workforce readiness and calling attention to the need for assessment tools that align with this evolving learning landscape.

Chapter 3, *Navigating the Global Workforce Through Workplace Learning and Professional Development: Game-Derived Skills as a New Foundational Layer*, examines game-derived skills as critical assets in a digitally transforming world. By categorizing somatic, cognitive, emotional, and social skills developed through gaming, the chapter highlights how these competencies are increasingly relevant in professional settings. With a strong emphasis on equity and access, it challenges conventional notions of workforce training and promotes inclusive models of skill development rooted in play, innovation, and digital engagement.

The role of wellness technology is explored in Chapter 4, *The Pulse of Progress: How Wearable Tech is Shaping the Future of Public Health*, which presents a forward-looking analysis of wearable devices in public health. Through real-time data collection and personalized interventions, wearables are revolutionizing how individuals manage chronic conditions and mental health. The chapter offers a critical lens on data ethics, accessibility, and the socio-economic divides that must be addressed to ensure that these technologies uplift rather than marginalize.

Chapter 5, *Gaming Through the Lens of Public Health: Awareness of eSports Consequences*, offers a nuanced perspective on esports as both a health opportunity and challenge. As competitive gaming becomes a global phenomenon, this chapter interrogates its physical and psychological implications. It emphasizes the importance of balanced participation and informed decision-making, bringing public health considerations into conversations about esports' expanding role in society and the workforce.

In *Maintaining Balance and Wellness in Remote Work*, Chapter 6 delivers timely insights into sustaining well-being in virtual work environments. With remote work now a permanent feature of many industries, the chapter outlines strategies for establishing boundaries, mitigating isolation, and building organizational cultures that support balance. Its practical guidance is essential for both workers and leaders navigating the blurred boundaries of home and professional life.

Chapter 7, *Artificial Intelligence in the Workplace the Future of Learning and Developments*, spotlights the integration of AI into Learning and Development (L&D). It critiques outdated training models and introduces AI-powered approaches that personalize learning at scale, optimize performance, and support global workforce development. The chapter balances promise with realism, exploring both the opportunities and the complexities of adopting AI-driven education in professional contexts.

Optimizing Global Learning Programs Through Learner Analytics, Chapter 8, focuses on how data and analytics are reshaping global education. By analyzing learner behaviors and needs through advanced tools, this chapter reveals the potential to create inclusive, adaptive learning experiences. It also emphasizes ethical considerations and cross-cultural sensitivities, ensuring that innovation does not come at the cost of learner privacy or equity.

Chapter 9, *Navigating Technological Disruption-Strategies for Continuous Professional Development*, turns attention to continuous professional development in a world of accelerating change. It provides a blueprint for upskilling in the face of AI, IoT, and blockchain, advocating for simulations, microcredentials, and virtual training as vital tools. The chapter offers actionable strategies for fostering a culture of lifelong learning that empowers individuals and ensures organizational relevance in a shifting global landscape.

The innovative use of educational escape rooms is featured in Chapter 10, *Expats Escaping Culture Shock: Designing a Game for Intercultural Communication.* This chapter explores how game-based simulations can prepare expatriates for international assignments by enhancing intercultural competence and easing cultural transitions. It provides a practical model for designing gamified learning tools that address the soft skills critical to global workforce success.

Chapter 11, *Digital Accessibility in the Professional Workplace*, confronts the essential need for inclusive design in digital environments. By demystifying legal requirements and offering hands-on accessibility practices, this chapter serves as a practical guide to creating equitable digital spaces. It reinforces the principle that accessibility must be embedded in everyday actions—becoming habit, not afterthought.

Finally, Chapter 12, *Next-Gen Learning: Gamification Strategies for Engaging Diverse Workforces and Advancing DEI*, reimagines how organizations can drive diversity, equity, and inclusion through interactive, gamified learning experiences. By integrating Universal Design for Learning, growth mindset principles, and design thinking, the chapter proposes a scalable, human-centered framework for DEI training. It challenges traditional approaches and offers measurable pathways for creating truly inclusive workplace learning.

We also emphasize the importance of equity, inclusion, and well-being in global professional development. As leaders and educators, we must champion environments that not only prioritize skill acquisition but also cultivate belonging, mental health, and sustainable career growth, especially for underrepresented and marginalized communities.

This volume serves as a resource for a wide range of stakeholders: academic scholars, workplace learning professionals, HR practitioners, graduate students, policymakers, and organizational leaders. Whether you are designing global learning programs, facilitating digital microlearning modules, or championing wellness initiatives in hybrid teams, you will find actionable insights and transformative strategies within these pages.

We are grateful to the contributing authors whose work has enriched this collection with research, innovation, and practical guidance. Their contributions reflect the boldness and creativity required to lead in today's dynamic world of work. It is our hope that this book not only informs but also inspires a renewed commitment to lifelong learning, inclusive leadership, and human-centered innovation. Their willingness to share their expertise and practice has made this volume possible.

We also thank the Career & Technical Education and Workplace Learning SIG of the American Educational Research Association (AERA) for fostering the community where these ideas were first exchanged and expanded. The expansion of eSports and game design is rapidly moving into this research area. We would like to thank Megan Van Petten with the eSports Trade Association and Danielle Rourke with the eSports Research Collaborative with their assistance in the development of the eSports chapters. Our appreciation extends to the authors and editors of The Wiley Handbook of Global Workplace Learning, edited by Vanessa Hammler Kenon and Sunay Vasant Palsole, whose work laid important groundwork for this volume's development.

We would like to acknowledge our colleagues at The University of Texas at San Antonio (UTSA), whose support has been instrumental in bringing this project to life. A special thank you is due to Vice President for Information Management and Technology Kendra Ketchum. This book would not have been possible without her continual support for innovative ideas and her visionary mission to move projects such as this one forward. The staff and students at the UTSA University Technology Solutions Bold Careers Ambassadors and Interns Program, many listed on the following acknowledgements page, have served as an invaluable resource for this work. The interns and ambassadors who worked on this project are a highlight and daily reminder of the reason we show up at institutions worldwide to support and educate the minds of the future.

Work and family balance will always serve as one of the most important components of workplace learning and professional development and it is something vitally important that we as editors value. We could never complete this work without the support of our families. To that end, we would like to give our love and thanks to Michelle Bartlett and Muhsin Kenon as well as our children and grandchildren. As scholars, we spend many weeks teaching, researching and traveling and miss some of the wonderful family experiences, but family is never far away from our thoughts and hearts. That work life balance and love is a part of each page of this work.

James E. Bartlett
Old Dominion University, USA

Vanessa Hammler Kenon
The University of Texas at San Antonio, USA

Acknowledgments

Project Team:

Thomas Cooper, UTS Program Coordinator

Pebby Garner, Project Coordinator

Miles Nau, Project Coordinator Intern

Cristian Aldrete, UTS Program Coordinator

Annu Paavani Chemata Venkata, Technology Specialist & Senior Ambassador

Editorial Board:

James Beeler, Ph.D., Appalachian State University

Kenneth Ducote, Ph.D., Eastbank Collaborative of Charter Schools

Marcus "Esports" Howard, GameDevHQ

Prasanna Kolar, Ph.D., The University of Texas at San Antonio

Tiffany Mfume, Ph.D., Johns Hopkins University

Carrol L. Warren, Ed.D., North Carolina State University

Editorial Interns:

Ahavah Kirwan, UTS Bold Careers Ambassador

Kylie Perez, UTS Bold Careers Intern

Madeline Hernandez, UTS Bold Careers Intern

Ann Sadornas, UTS Bold Careers, Intern

Tiffany Zheng, Technology Specialist

Maria Regina Chapa, Technology Specialist

Hannah Salazar, Technology Specialist

Kathryn Ninke, Technology Specialist

Bidisha Dalai, Technology Specialist

Abhinaya Guduru, Technology Specialist

Atinuke Ajibolade, Technology Specialist

Affiliate Institutions:

The University of Texas at San Antonio, University Technology Solutions

Old Dominion University, Department of Educational Leadership & Workforce Development

Section 1
Global Workplace and Electronic Gaming

Chapter 1
Player Epic:
Integrating Gaming and Esports into Corporate Strategy – Enhancing Wellness, Engagement, and Productivity

Johnny L. Williams
Player Epic Inc., USA

ABSTRACT

This chapter explores the integration of gaming and esports into corporate strategy, focusing on how these elements can enhance employee wellness, engagement, and productivity. It begins by analyzing current trends in corporate wellness and employee engagement, highlighting the need for innovative approaches in the modern workplace. The chapter then examines the growing influence of gaming and esports as cultural and economic forces, discussing their potential applications beyond entertainment. It outlines how gaming can align with corporate objectives, such as promoting wellness, improving productivity, and retaining top talent. Additionally, the chapter provides case studies, including IBM's "Innov8" business simulation game, demonstrating successful implementations of gaming in workplace environments. By the end of this chapter, readers will understand how gaming and esports can be leveraged to create a more dynamic, engaged, and high-performing workforce.

INTRODUCTION

The integration of gaming and esports into corporate environments represents a significant shift in how organizations approach employee wellness, engagement, and professional development. As workplaces evolve and workforce demographics

DOI: 10.4018/979-8-3373-5322-7.ch001

change, traditional approaches to these critical areas often fail to resonate with employees, resulting in low participation rates and limited impact. This chapter explores how gaming and esports can serve as powerful tools for addressing these challenges, offering innovative solutions that align with the preferences and needs of today's workforce.

Gaming and esports offer several advantages in the workplace. They can serve as icebreakers, helping to build relationships and trust among team members. Competitive gaming, in particular, mirrors the dynamics of traditional sports, encouraging teamwork, strategic thinking, and resilience. Moreover, the immersive nature of games can help reduce stress and provide a mental break, which is crucial in today's fast-paced work environments (Goetzel & Ozminkowski, 2020).

This chapter examines the theoretical foundations and practical applications of integrating gaming and esports into corporate strategy, with a focus on enhancing workplace learning and professional development. By exploring case studies, research findings, and best practices, it provides organizations with actionable insights for implementing effective gaming initiatives that drive positive outcomes for both employees and the business.

BACKGROUND

Global Rise of Gaming and Esports

Gaming and esports have experienced unprecedented growth over the past decade, evolving from niche hobbies to mainstream cultural phenomena. Today, there are over 3.34 billion gamers worldwide, and the esports industry is valued at over $1 billion, with millions of fans and participants globally (Newzoo, 2023; Statista, 2023). This rise can be attributed to several factors, including advances in technology, the proliferation of mobile devices, and the growing popularity of online multiplayer games.

Esports, in particular, has emerged as a major force in the entertainment industry, with professional leagues, tournaments, and sponsorships rivaling those of traditional sports. The competitive nature of esports, combined with its global reach, has made it a powerful tool for engagement, particularly among younger audiences. This cultural shift has not gone unnoticed by businesses, many of which are beginning to explore how they can leverage gaming and esports to connect with consumers and employees alike.

The rise of gaming and esports has also been fueled by the increasing integration of gaming into everyday life. Games are no longer just for entertainment; they are used in education, training, and even therapy. This widespread acceptance and integration of gaming into various aspects of life make it a natural fit for the workplace, where it can be used to address some of the most pressing challenges facing businesses today, such as employee engagement, wellness, and team building.

Current State of Corporate Wellness Programs

Corporate wellness programs have become a staple in many organizations, driven by the recognition that employee health and well-being are critical to productivity and job satisfaction. These programs typically include offerings such as health screenings, gym memberships, stress management workshops, and nutritional counseling. While these initiatives have had some success, they often suffer from low participation rates and a lack of engagement (Baicker, Cutler, & Song, 2022).

One of the main challenges with traditional wellness programs is that they are often seen as top-down initiatives, imposed by management rather than driven by employee interest. This can lead to a lack of enthusiasm and participation, which in turn limits the effectiveness of the programs. Additionally, many wellness programs focus primarily on physical health, neglecting the mental and social aspects of well-being that are equally important in today's workplace (Goetzel & Ozminkowski, 2020).

There is a growing recognition that traditional wellness programs need to evolve to meet the changing needs and preferences of the workforce. Employees today are looking for more personalized, engaging, and holistic approaches to wellness, ones that not only address physical health but also mental well-being, social connections, and work-life balance. This is where gaming and esports can play a transformative role (Willis Towers Watson, 2022).

The Growing Need for Innovative Workplace Solutions

As the workforce becomes more diverse and the nature of work continues to evolve, there is an increasing need for innovative solutions that can address the challenges of the modern workplace. Remote work, flexible schedules, and the blurring of lines between work and personal life have created new demands on employees, who must navigate these changes while maintaining productivity and well-being.

In this context, traditional approaches to employee engagement and wellness are no longer sufficient. Companies need to explore new ways to connect with their employees, foster a sense of community, and promote well-being. Gaming and esports offer a unique opportunity to do just that. By tapping into the universal appeal of games and the competitive spirit of esports, companies can create more engaging and effective wellness programs that resonate with employees and drive better outcomes (Statista, 2023).

The need for innovation in corporate wellness is not just about improving employee satisfaction; it's also about staying competitive in a rapidly changing business environment. Companies that can attract and retain top talent, foster a positive work culture, and maintain high levels of employee engagement are more likely to succeed in the long run. Integrating gaming and esports into the workplace is one way to achieve these goals, providing a modern, innovative approach to employee wellness and engagement that aligns with the needs of today's workforce.

PURPOSE AND SCOPE

Defining the Initiative's Goals

The primary goal of this chapter is to explore how gaming and esports can enhance employee wellness, engagement, and collaboration when integrated into corporate strategies. By examining the motivational power of gaming, this chapter aims to demonstrate how organizations can create workplace cultures that promote health, productivity, and a sense of community among employees. This is not just about adding games to the workplace; it's about fundamentally transforming how companies approach employee well-being, learning, and professional development.

The specific objectives of this chapter include:

- **Enhancing Employee Wellness:** Examining how gaming can promote physical activity, reduce stress, and combat the health risks associated with sedentary work environments.
- **Boosting Employee Engagement:** Analyzing how introducing interactive elements into the workplace can strengthen company culture, increase job satisfaction, and reduce turnover.
- **Fostering Teamwork and Collaboration:** Exploring how team-based games and esports competitions can improve communication, collaboration, and camaraderie among employees.
- **Promoting a Competitive Edge:** Investigating how competitive gaming leagues can cultivate a culture of excellence and achievement, mirroring the success of traditional sports in enhancing performance and motivation.
- **Attracting and Retaining Talent:** Examining how innovative approaches to workplace culture can differentiate companies as forward-thinking employers that value work-life balance and employee engagement.

Scope of the Chapter in Terms of Industry Impact and Corporate Culture

This chapter is designed to have broad applicability across various industries and corporate cultures. While industries with younger, tech-savvy workforces may be early adopters, the potential applications extend to a range of sectors, from finance to healthcare, providing versatile tools for enhancing employee well-being and engagement.

The chapter also examines how gaming and esports can create a cultural shift within companies, moving away from traditional, top-down wellness initiatives to more employee-driven, interactive programs. By giving employees the tools to take control of their wellness in a fun and engaging way, companies can foster more positive work environments that are conducive to both personal and professional growth.

In terms of industry impact, the successful integration of gaming and esports into the workplace could set a new standard for corporate wellness programs, inspiring other companies to adopt similar approaches. This could lead to a broader cultural shift, where gaming and esports are recognized not just as entertainment but as valuable tools for improving health, well-being, productivity, and professional development in the workplace.

OVERVIEW OF TRADITIONAL CORPORATE WELLNESS PROGRAMS

Common Practices and Their Limitations

Traditional corporate wellness programs have long been a staple in organizations, offering various initiatives aimed at improving employee health and well-being. These programs typically include offerings such as health screenings, gym memberships, smoking cessation programs, nutritional counseling, and stress management workshops (Baicker, Cutler, & Song, 2022). While these initiatives have had some positive impacts, they often suffer from several limitations.

One of the key limitations is the low participation rate among employees. Many wellness programs are perceived as top-down initiatives that do not necessarily align with employee interests or preferences (Goetzel & Ozminkowski, 2020). This disconnect can lead to a lack of enthusiasm and engagement, resulting in minimal impact on employee health outcomes. Additionally, traditional wellness programs often focus primarily on physical health, neglecting the mental and social aspects of well-being, which are increasingly important in today's workplace.

Case Studies of Successful and Unsuccessful Wellness Programs

A case study of Johnson & Johnson's wellness program is often cited as a success story. The company implemented a comprehensive wellness initiative that included physical fitness programs, stress management, and mental health resources. Over the years, Johnson & Johnson reported significant reductions in healthcare costs and improvements in employee productivity and morale (Henke et al., 2019). This success can be attributed to the program's holistic approach and its ability to engage employees effectively.

IBM's wellness program represents another successful implementation, particularly in its integration of gaming elements. The company developed a platform that gamified health activities, allowing employees to earn points and rewards for participating in wellness initiatives. This approach significantly increased engagement rates and led to measurable improvements in employee health metrics. IBM's success demonstrates how gaming elements can transform traditional wellness programs into more engaging and effective initiatives.

On the other hand, some wellness programs have not achieved the desired outcomes. A notable example is PepsiCo's wellness program, which, despite substantial investment, showed only modest returns. The program was criticized for its narrow focus on physical health and lack of engagement strategies, leading to low participation rates and limited impact on overall employee well-being (Song & Baicker, 2019).

CHALLENGES IN MODERN WORKPLACES

Increasing Sedentary Lifestyles and Related Health Issues

The modern workplace is characterized by increasing sedentary behavior, largely due to the prevalence of desk jobs and reliance on technology. Prolonged sitting has been linked to a range of health issues, including obesity, cardiovascular disease, and musculoskeletal disorders (Tremblay et al., 2017). These health risks are exacerbated by the lack of physical activity, which is common in many work environments.

The challenge for corporate wellness programs is to address these sedentary lifestyles effectively. Traditional interventions, such as encouraging employees to take breaks or participate in fitness programs, often fall short because they do not integrate physical activity into the workday in a meaningful way.

Declining Employee Engagement and Productivity

Employee engagement and productivity are critical to organizational success, yet they are on the decline in many workplaces. Disengaged employees are less likely to be productive, innovative, or committed to their work, which can have a negative impact on business outcomes (Gallup, 2021). Several factors contribute to this decline, including monotonous work environments, lack of recognition, and poor work-life balance.

Traditional wellness programs often fail to address these deeper issues of engagement and motivation. While physical health initiatives are important, they do not necessarily lead to improved job satisfaction or productivity unless they are part of a broader strategy that includes mental and social well-being.

The Rise of Mental Health Concerns in the Workplace

Mental health has become a growing concern in the workplace, with stress, anxiety, and depression on the rise among employees (World Health Organization, 2020). The COVID-19 pandemic has further exacerbated these issues, highlighting the need for comprehensive mental health support within organizations. However, traditional wellness programs often lack the resources or expertise to address mental health effectively, focusing instead on physical health initiatives.

The challenge for modern workplaces is to integrate mental health into their wellness strategies in a way that is both accessible and effective. This requires a shift from reactive to proactive approaches, where mental health is prioritized and supported through a combination of resources, training, and a supportive work environment.

THE ROLE OF TECHNOLOGY IN WELLNESS PROGRAMS

How Technology Is Reshaping Corporate Wellness

Technology has the potential to transform corporate wellness programs by making them more accessible, engaging, and personalized. Wearable devices, mobile apps, and digital platforms can track physical activity, monitor health metrics, and provide real-time feedback to employees (Patel, Asch, & Volpp, 2015). These tools can also facilitate social connections through online communities, challenges, and competitions, which can enhance engagement and motivation.

Moreover, technology allows for the collection and analysis of data, enabling companies to tailor their wellness programs to the specific needs and preferences of their employees. This data-driven approach can lead to more effective interventions and better health outcomes.

Potential for Gaming and Esports to Address These Challenges

Gaming and esports represent a new frontier in corporate wellness, offering innovative solutions to the challenges of sedentary lifestyles, declining engagement, and mental health concerns. Unlike traditional wellness programs, which often struggle to engage employees, gaming and esports have a broad appeal and can provide a fun and interactive way to promote health and well-being (Kato, 2010).

For example, games that encourage physical activity, such as virtual reality fitness programs, can help combat sedentary behavior by making exercise more enjoyable. Esports competitions can foster teamwork and collaboration, improving social connections and engagement among employees. Additionally, gaming has been shown to have potential mental health benefits, such as reducing stress and improving cognitive function, making it a valuable tool for addressing mental health concerns in the workplace (Granic, Lobel, & Engels, 2014).

The integration of technology, gaming, and esports into corporate wellness programs offers a promising way to overcome the limitations of traditional approaches. By leveraging these tools, companies can create more engaging, effective, and holistic wellness programs that address the full spectrum of employee well-being.

ENHANCING EMPLOYEE WELLNESS

Using Gaming to Promote Physical Activity and Mental Well-Being

Gaming has evolved beyond a mere entertainment medium, offering opportunities to enhance physical and mental well-being in the workplace. Games that incorporate physical activity, such as virtual reality (VR) fitness programs and active video games, can encourage employees to move more during the workday, reducing the health risks associated with sedentary lifestyles. Research has shown that these types of games can significantly increase physical activity levels and improve cardiovascular fitness (Staiano & Calvert, 2011).

Specific examples include games like "Beat Saber," a VR rhythm game that involves slashing blocks with virtual sabers, providing a full-body workout while being enjoyable. Another example is "Ring Fit Adventure" for the Nintendo Switch, which combines traditional RPG elements with physical exercises, making fitness more engaging and accessible.

Moreover, gaming can also support mental well-being. Many games are designed to reduce stress and anxiety by providing immersive experiences that allow employees to disconnect from work-related stressors temporarily. For example, mindfulness-based games and apps have been developed to help users manage stress through guided relaxation and meditation practices (Bakker et al., 2018). These games offer a practical, enjoyable way to integrate mental wellness practices into daily routines.

Addressing Health Risks Associated with Sedentary Work

Sedentary work is associated with numerous health risks, including obesity, cardiovascular disease, and musculoskeletal disorders (Tremblay et al., 2017). Incorporating gaming into the workplace can be an effective strategy to counter-act these risks. Active video games, also known as "exergames," require physical movement, which can help break up long periods of sitting and reduce the negative health impacts of a sedentary lifestyle (Gao & Chen, 2014). Additionally, regular participation in these activities can contribute to overall better health outcomes and higher employee productivity.

BOOSTING EMPLOYEE ENGAGEMENT AND SATISFACTION

How Gaming Creates a More Engaging Work Environment

Gaming introduces a fun and interactive element into the workplace that can significantly enhance employee engagement. By incorporating game mechanics such as challenges, rewards, and leaderboards into daily tasks, employees can experience increased motivation and a sense of accomplishment (Hamari, Koivisto, & Sarsa, 2014). This gamification of work processes makes routine tasks more enjoyable and can lead to higher levels of job satisfaction and productivity.

For instance, Deloitte implemented a gamified training program that increased engagement by 50% and reduced the time required to complete technical training by 50% (Meister, 2015). Similarly, Microsoft used a language quality game to improve the localization of Windows 7, resulting in the review of over 500,000 dialogue boxes and the identification of 6,700 bugs, all through voluntary participation by employees (Werbach & Hunter, 2012).

Building a Positive Company Culture Through Shared Gaming Experiences

Shared gaming experiences can foster a sense of community and belonging among employees, contributing to a positive company culture. When employees participate in gaming activities together, they develop stronger social connections and a shared identity, which can enhance team cohesion and collaboration (Tondello et al., 2016). These social bonds extend beyond the gaming context, creating a more supportive and inclusive work environment.

Google, for example, has integrated gaming spaces into its offices, where employees can take breaks and engage in casual gaming sessions. This approach has been credited with fostering creativity, reducing stress, and strengthening relationships among team members (Stewart, 2013). Similarly, Zappos has incorporated gaming elements into its company culture, with regular gaming events and competitions that bring employees together and reinforce the company's values of fun and community.

FOSTERING TEAMWORK AND COLLABORATION

Team-Based Gaming as a Tool for Building Stronger Teams

Team-based gaming provides a unique opportunity for employees to work together toward a common goal, developing essential teamwork skills in the process. When participating in multiplayer games or esports competitions, employees must communicate effectively, coordinate their actions, and leverage each other's strengths to succeed (Barr, 2018). These experiences can translate into improved collaboration and teamwork in the workplace.

For example, Riot Games, the developer of League of Legends, uses its own game to foster teamwork among employees. Regular team-building sessions involve employees forming teams and competing against each other, which helps them develop a better understanding of each other's working styles and strengths (Riot Games, 2019). This approach has been effective in breaking down silos between departments and creating a more collaborative work environment.

Developing Communication and Leadership Skills Through Esports

Esports competitions can be particularly effective in developing communication and leadership skills. In competitive gaming environments, clear and concise communication is essential for success, as team members must coordinate their actions in real-time (Freeman & Wohn, 2017). Additionally, these competitions often require individuals to take on leadership roles, making strategic decisions and guiding their team toward victory.

Cisco has implemented an esports program that focuses on developing these skills among employees. The program includes regular tournaments and training sessions, where employees can practice communication, decision-making, and leadership in a low-stakes environment (Cisco, 2020). Participants have reported improvements in their ability to communicate under pressure and lead diverse teams, skills that have translated into their day-to-day work.

PROMOTING A COMPETITIVE EDGE

Cultivating a Culture of Excellence Through Competitive Gaming

Competitive gaming can foster a culture of excellence within organizations by encouraging employees to strive for continuous improvement and high performance. The competitive nature of esports, with its emphasis on skill development, strategic thinking, and teamwork, mirrors the qualities that drive success in the business world (Wagner, 2006). By participating in competitive gaming, employees can develop a mindset focused on growth and achievement.

SAP, a global software company, has embraced this approach by organizing regular esports tournaments for its employees. These competitions not only provide a fun and engaging activity but also reinforce the company's values of excellence, innovation, and teamwork (SAP, 2021). Employees who participate in these tournaments often report increased motivation and a stronger drive to excel in their professional roles.

Leveraging Esports to Drive Innovation and Problem-Solving

Esports can also be a powerful driver of innovation and problem-solving within organizations. Many competitive games require players to think creatively, adapt to changing circumstances, and develop novel strategies to overcome challenges

(Granic, Lobel, & Engels, 2014). These skills are directly applicable to the workplace, where innovation and effective problem-solving are increasingly important.

IBM has leveraged gaming to foster innovation among its employees through its "Innovation Jam" program, which incorporates game mechanics to encourage creative thinking and collaboration (IBM, 2018). Participants work in teams to develop solutions to complex business problems, with rewards and recognition for the most innovative ideas. This approach has led to the development of numerous patents and new business initiatives, demonstrating the power of gaming to drive innovation.

ATTRACTING AND RETAINING TALENT

How Gaming Initiatives Can Differentiate Employers in the Job Market

In today's competitive job market, companies are constantly seeking ways to differentiate themselves and attract top talent. Innovative gaming and esports initiatives can serve as a powerful recruitment tool, particularly for younger generations who value work environments that are engaging, social, and aligned with their interests (Deloitte, 2020). By highlighting these initiatives in recruitment materials and job descriptions, companies can position themselves as forward-thinking employers who understand the needs and preferences of modern workers.

For example, Activision Blizzard, a leading gaming company, has successfully used its gaming culture to attract talent from diverse backgrounds. The company's emphasis on creativity, collaboration, and fun, as exemplified by its gaming initiatives, has made it an employer of choice in the technology sector (Activision Blizzard, 2021). Similarly, non-gaming companies like Adobe have implemented gaming programs as part of their employee experience, helping them compete for talent with tech giants.

Reducing Turnover Through Increased Job Satisfaction and Engagement

Employee turnover is a significant challenge for many organizations, with the cost of replacing an employee estimated at 1.5 to 2 times their annual salary (Society for Human Resource Management, 2022). Gaming and esports initiatives can help reduce turnover by increasing job satisfaction and engagement, which are key factors in employee retention (Gallup, 2021). When employees feel connected to their workplace and enjoy their work environment, they are less likely to seek opportunities elsewhere.

T-Mobile has reported a 40% reduction in turnover among employees who participate in its gaming and esports programs (T-Mobile, 2020). The company attributes this success to the sense of community and belonging that these programs foster, as well as the increased job satisfaction that comes from having opportunities for fun and social interaction at work. This demonstrates the tangible business benefits of investing in gaming initiatives as part of a comprehensive employee retention strategy.

IMPLEMENTING GAMING AND ESPORTS IN THE WORKPLACE

Strategies for Successful Integration

Implementing gaming and esports in the workplace requires a thoughtful and strategic approach to ensure that these initiatives align with organizational goals and culture. Several key strategies can contribute to successful integration:

- **Start with Clear Objectives:** Define what you hope to achieve through gaming initiatives, whether it's improving employee wellness, enhancing teamwork, or boosting engagement. Having clear objectives will guide the design and implementation of your program.
- **Secure Leadership Support:** Gain buy-in from senior leaders by demonstrating the potential benefits of gaming initiatives, including improved employee well-being, increased productivity, and enhanced collaboration.
- **Involve Employees in the Process:** Conduct surveys or focus groups to understand employee interests and preferences regarding gaming. This participatory approach can increase buy-in and ensure that the program meets employee needs.
- **Start Small and Scale Up:** Begin with pilot programs or small-scale initiatives to test what works in your organization. Use the feedback and results from these pilots to refine your approach before scaling up.
- **Integrate with Existing Programs:** Look for opportunities to incorporate gaming elements into existing wellness, training, or team-building programs, rather than creating entirely new initiatives.

Organizations like Walmart have successfully implemented gaming initiatives by following these strategies. The company started with a small pilot program that used gamification to improve safety training, then expanded to other areas based on positive results (Walmart, 2019). This measured approach allowed for adjustments and refinements along the way, contributing to the program's overall success.

Overcoming Potential Challenges and Resistance

Despite the potential benefits, implementing gaming and esports in the workplace may face challenges and resistance. Common concerns include perceptions that gaming is frivolous or unprofessional, fears about decreased productivity, and worries about exclusion of employees who are not interested in gaming. Addressing these challenges requires a proactive approach:

- **Educate Stakeholders:** Provide information about the benefits of gaming in the workplace, backed by research and case studies. This can help shift perceptions and build understanding.
- **Address Concerns About Productivity:** Set clear boundaries and guidelines for when and how gaming activities take place, ensuring that they do not interfere with core work responsibilities.
- **Ensure Inclusivity:** Design gaming initiatives that appeal to a wide range of employees, including those who may not identify as gamers. Offer various types of games and activities to accommodate different interests and skill levels.
- **Measure and Communicate Results:** Track key metrics related to your objectives, such as participation rates, employee satisfaction, and business outcomes. Share these results with stakeholders to demonstrate the value of your gaming initiatives.

PwC encountered initial resistance when implementing its gamified training program, with some partners concerned about the professionalism of the approach. The company addressed these concerns by sharing research on the effectiveness of game-based learning and conducting a small pilot that demonstrated improved learning outcomes (PwC, 2020). This evidence-based approach helped overcome resistance and gain support for the initiative.

CURATING DIVERSE GAMES FOR WORKPLACE IMPLEMENTATION

Selection Criteria for Appropriate Games

When selecting games for workplace implementation, it's important to consider several criteria to ensure that they align with organizational goals and employee preferences:

- **Accessibility:** Choose games that are easy to learn and play, with low barriers to entry in terms of skill level and technical requirements. Games like "Among Us," "Jackbox Party Pack," and "Rocket League" are popular choices due to their simple mechanics and broad appeal.
- **Inclusivity:** Select games that appeal to a diverse range of employees, regardless of age, gender, or gaming experience. Games like "Mario Kart," "Overcooked," and "Minecraft" have proven successful in workplace settings due to their universal appeal and collaborative nature.
- **Alignment with Objectives:** Ensure that the selected games support your specific objectives, whether it's team building, stress reduction, or physical activity. For team building, cooperative games like "Keep Talking and Nobody Explodes" or "Spaceteam" can be effective, while games like "Just Dance" or "Fitness Boxing" can promote physical activity.
- **Time Commitment:** Consider the time required to play the game, ensuring that it fits within the constraints of the workday. Quick games like "Tetris" or "Words with Friends" can be played during short breaks, while more involved games might be reserved for dedicated team-building sessions.
- **Technical Requirements:** Evaluate the hardware and software needed to play the game, ensuring that it's compatible with existing infrastructure and accessible to all employees. Browser-based games like "skribbl.io" or mobile games like "Wordscapes" require minimal technical setup, making them easy to implement.

Balancing Competitive and Cooperative Gaming Experiences

A well-rounded gaming program should include both competitive and cooperative experiences to cater to different preferences and achieve various objectives:

- **Competitive Games:** Games like "League of Legends," "Counter-Strike: Global Offensive," and "Fortnite" can foster healthy competition and drive performance. These games can be organized into tournaments or leagues, providing structured opportunities for employees to compete individually or in teams.

- **Cooperative Games:** Games like "Portal 2," "Overcooked," and "Left 4 Dead" emphasize collaboration and communication, making them ideal for team-building activities. These games require players to work together toward a common goal, mirroring the collaborative nature of many workplace tasks.
- **Hybrid Approaches:** Some games, like "Rocket League" or "Team Fortress 2," offer both competitive and cooperative elements, allowing for flexibility in how they're implemented. These games can be particularly valuable as they can serve multiple purposes within a gaming program.

Companies like Shopify have successfully balanced competitive and cooperative gaming experiences in their workplace programs. The company hosts regular "Shopify Gaming League" events that feature a mix of competitive tournaments and cooperative play sessions, catering to different employee preferences and fostering both individual excellence and team collaboration (Shopify, 2021).

CASE STUDIES: SUCCESSFUL IMPLEMENTATION OF GAMING IN CORPORATE SETTINGS

IBM's Gaming Initiative for Employee Engagement

IBM has been at the forefront of integrating gaming into its corporate strategy, with a focus on enhancing employee engagement and driving innovation. The company's "IBM Jam" program uses gamification principles to engage employees in collaborative problem-solving and idea generation. During these events, employees from across the organization come together on a digital platform to share ideas, discuss challenges, and develop solutions, with recognition and rewards for top contributors (IBM, 2018).

The results have been impressive, with IBM reporting increased employee engagement, the generation of thousands of innovative ideas, and the development of numerous patents and new business initiatives. The program has also helped break down silos within the organization, fostering collaboration across departments and geographic locations.

IBM has also implemented gaming elements in its onboarding and training programs, using virtual worlds and simulations to create immersive learning experiences. New employees navigate through virtual environments, completing challenges and quests that teach them about the company's culture, policies, and procedures. This approach has led to higher retention of information and increased engagement in the onboarding process (IBM, 2019).

Microsoft's Use of Gaming for Team Building and Skill Development

Microsoft has integrated gaming into its corporate culture as a tool for team building and skill development. The company's "Xbox Academy" program uses gaming sessions to help employees develop skills such as strategic thinking, problem-solving, and teamwork. These sessions are facilitated by trained coaches who guide participants through reflective discussions about how the skills practiced in games can be applied to their work (Microsoft, 2020).

The company also hosts regular gaming tournaments and events, bringing together employees from different departments and levels of the organization. These events serve as informal networking opportunities, helping to build relationships and foster a sense of community. Microsoft has reported improved collaboration and communication among teams that participate in these gaming activities.

Additionally, Microsoft has used gaming to support its diversity and inclusion initiatives. The company's "Gaming for Everyone" program aims to create a more inclusive gaming environment, both within the company and in the broader gaming community. This initiative has helped raise awareness about diversity issues and has contributed to a more inclusive workplace culture (Microsoft, 2021).

MEASURING THE IMPACT OF GAMING INITIATIVES

Key Performance Indicators for Wellness and Engagement

To evaluate the effectiveness of gaming initiatives in the workplace, organizations should track key performance indicators (KPIs) related to wellness and engagement:

- **Participation Rates:** Monitor the percentage of employees who participate in gaming activities, as well as the frequency and duration of their participation. Increasing participation rates over time can indicate growing interest and engagement.
- **Employee Satisfaction:** Use surveys and feedback mechanisms to assess employee satisfaction with gaming initiatives and their overall job satisfaction. Look for correlations between participation in gaming activities and higher satisfaction scores.

- **Health Metrics:** Track relevant health metrics, such as physical activity levels, stress levels, and absenteeism, to evaluate the impact of gaming on employee wellness. Improvements in these metrics can demonstrate the health benefits of gaming initiatives.
- **Team Cohesion:** Assess team dynamics and collaboration through surveys, manager evaluations, or social network analysis. Look for improvements in communication, trust, and cooperation among teams that participate in gaming activities.
- **Productivity and Performance:** Monitor productivity metrics, such as task completion rates, quality of work, and achievement of goals, to determine whether gaming initiatives are contributing to improved performance.

Long-Term Benefits for Organizations and Employees

The long-term benefits of gaming initiatives extend beyond immediate improvements in wellness and engagement:

- **Cultural Transformation:** Over time, gaming initiatives can contribute to a more positive and inclusive organizational culture, characterized by stronger relationships, increased trust, and a greater sense of community.
- **Talent Attraction and Retention:** Organizations with established gaming programs may see improvements in their ability to attract and retain top talent, particularly among younger generations who value engaging and innovative work environments.
- **Innovation and Adaptability:** Regular participation in gaming can foster a culture of innovation and adaptability, as employees become more comfortable with experimentation, risk-taking, and creative problem-solving.
- **Resilience and Well-being:** The stress-reducing and social aspects of gaming can contribute to greater resilience and overall well-being among employees, potentially leading to lower healthcare costs and reduced burnout.

Companies like Accenture have documented these long-term benefits through longitudinal studies of their gaming initiatives. The company found that teams that regularly participated in gaming activities showed a 20% increase in innovation output and a 15% reduction in turnover over a three-year period, compared to teams that did not participate (Accenture, 2022). These findings highlight the substantial return on investment that gaming initiatives can provide when implemented effectively and sustained over time.

FUTURE RESEARCH DIRECTIONS

Emerging Trends in Gaming and Corporate Wellness

As technology continues to evolve and workplace dynamics shift, several emerging trends are likely to shape the future of gaming in corporate settings:

- **Virtual and Augmented Reality:** The increasing accessibility and sophistication of VR and AR technologies will open new possibilities for immersive gaming experiences in the workplace. These technologies can be used for everything from virtual team-building exercises to simulated training scenarios, providing more engaging and effective alternatives to traditional approaches.
- **AI-Powered Personalization:** Artificial intelligence can enable more personalized gaming experiences, tailoring challenges and rewards to individual preferences and needs. This personalization can increase engagement and effectiveness, as employees interact with games that are specifically designed to address their unique wellness goals and learning objectives.
- **Integration with Wearable Technology:** The growing prevalence of wearable devices offers opportunities to integrate real-time health data into gaming experiences. Games that respond to physiological indicators, such as heart rate or stress levels, could provide more targeted wellness interventions and more accurate measurement of outcomes.
- **Cross-Platform and Mobile Gaming:** The rise of cross-platform and mobile gaming makes it easier to implement gaming initiatives that can be accessed anytime, anywhere. This flexibility is particularly important in the context of remote and hybrid work arrangements, where employees may not be physically present in the office.

Potential Areas for Further Study

To advance our understanding of gaming in corporate settings, further research is needed in several key areas:

- **Long-Term Impact:** Longitudinal studies that track the effects of gaming initiatives over extended periods would provide valuable insights into their sustainability and long-term benefits. These studies could examine factors such as employee retention, career progression, and organizational performance.
- **Demographic Differences:** More research is needed to understand how different demographic groups respond to gaming initiatives, including variations

by age, gender, cultural background, and gaming experience. This knowledge would help organizations design more inclusive and effective programs.

- **Integration with Other Wellness Approaches:** Studies exploring the synergies between gaming and other wellness approaches, such as mindfulness practices, physical fitness programs, and mental health interventions, could lead to more comprehensive and effective wellness strategies.
- **Return on Investment:** Rigorous economic analyses of the costs and benefits of gaming initiatives would provide organizations with the data they need to make informed decisions about investing in these programs. These analyses should consider both direct costs (e.g., equipment, software) and indirect benefits (e.g., reduced turnover, increased productivity).

By addressing these research gaps, scholars and practitioners can develop a more nuanced understanding of how gaming can be effectively integrated into corporate wellness programs, ultimately leading to better outcomes for both organizations and employees.

CONCLUSION

The integration of gaming and esports into corporate strategy represents a significant opportunity for organizations to enhance employee wellness, engagement, and professional development. As this chapter has demonstrated, gaming initiatives can address many of the challenges facing modern workplaces, from sedentary lifestyles and declining engagement to mental health concerns and the need for stronger team collaboration.

Traditional corporate wellness programs, while well-intentioned, often fall short in engaging employees and addressing the full spectrum of well-being. Gaming offers a more holistic and engaging approach, one that resonates with employees across demographic groups and provides benefits that extend beyond physical health to include mental, social, and professional dimensions.

The case studies presented in this chapter illustrate the tangible benefits that organizations can achieve through thoughtful implementation of gaming initiatives. Companies like IBM, Microsoft, and others have successfully leveraged gaming to improve employee engagement, foster teamwork, drive innovation, and create more inclusive workplace cultures. Their experiences provide valuable insights and best practices for organizations considering similar approaches.

Looking ahead, the continued evolution of technology and workplace dynamics will create new opportunities for integrating gaming into corporate strategy. Virtual and augmented reality, AI-powered personalization, and integration with wearable technology are just a few of the trends that will shape the future of gaming in the workplace.

For organizations seeking to implement gaming initiatives, the key to success lies in a strategic and thoughtful approach. This includes setting clear objectives, securing leadership support, involving employees in the process, and measuring outcomes to demonstrate value. By following these principles and learning from the experiences of pioneering organizations, companies can harness the power of gaming to create healthier, more engaging, and more productive work environments.

In conclusion, the integration of gaming and esports into corporate strategy is not just a trend but a transformative approach to workplace wellness and engagement. As more organizations recognize the potential of gaming to address their most pressing challenges, we can expect to see continued innovation and adoption in this area, ultimately leading to better outcomes for both employees and organizations.

REFERENCES

Accenture. (2022). *The business value of play: How gaming initiatives drive organizational performance*. Accenture Research.

Activision Blizzard. (2021). *Corporate culture and employee engagement report*. Activision Blizzard, Inc.

Baicker, K., Cutler, D., & Song, Z. (2022). Workplace wellness programs can generate savings. *Health Affairs*, *29*(2), 304–311. DOI: 10.1377/hlthaff.2009.0626 PMID: 20075081

Bakker, D., Kazantzis, N., Rickwood, D., & Rickard, N. (2018). Mental health smartphone apps: Review and evidence-based recommendations for future developments. *JMIR Mental Health*, *5*(1), e7. DOI: 10.2196/mental.4984 PMID: 26932350

Barr, M. (2018). Student attitudes to games-based skills development: Learning from video games in higher education. *Computers in Human Behavior*, *80*, 283–294. DOI: 10.1016/j.chb.2017.11.030

Cisco. (2020). *Esports as a tool for leadership development*. Cisco Systems, Inc.

Deloitte. (2020). *The millennial survey: Understanding the next generation of talent*. Deloitte Touche Tohmatsu Limited.

Freeman, G., & Wohn, D. Y. (2017). Social support in eSports: Building emotional connections with teammates in competitive gaming. *Computers in Human Behavior*, *75*, 23–31.

Gallup. (2021). *State of the global workplace*. Gallup, Inc.

Gao, Z., & Chen, S. (2014). Are field-based exergames useful in preventing childhood obesity? A systematic review. *Obesity Reviews*, *15*(8), 676–691. DOI: 10.1111/obr.12164 PMID: 24602072

Goetzel, R. Z., & Ozminkowski, R. J. (2020). The health and cost benefits of work site health-promotion programs. *Annual Review of Public Health*, *29*(1), 303–323. DOI: 10.1146/annurev.publhealth.29.020907.090930 PMID: 18173386

Granic, I., Lobel, A., & Engels, R. C. (2014). The benefits of playing video games. *The American Psychologist*, *69*(1), 66–78. DOI: 10.1037/a0034857 PMID: 24295515

Hamari, J., Koivisto, J., & Sarsa, H. (2014). Does gamification work? A literature review of empirical studies on gamification. In *Proceedings of the 47th Hawaii International Conference on System Sciences* (pp. 3025-3034). IEEE. DOI: 10.1109/HICSS.2014.377

Henke, R. M., Goetzel, R. Z., McHugh, J., & Isaac, F. (2019). Recent experience in health promotion at Johnson & Johnson: Lower health spending, strong return on investment. *Health Affairs*, *30*(3), 490–499. DOI: 10.1377/hlthaff.2010.0806 PMID: 21383368

IBM. (2018). *Innovation jam: Collaborative problem-solving through gaming*. IBM Corporation.

IBM. (2019). *Virtual onboarding: Using gaming to enhance the employee experience*. IBM Corporation.

Kato, P. M. (2010). Video games in health care: Closing the gap. *Review of General Psychology*, *14*(2), 113–121. DOI: 10.1037/a0019441

Meister, J. C. (2015). *Future of work: Using gamification for human resources*. Forbes Media LLC.

Microsoft. (2020). *Xbox Academy: Gaming for skill development*. Microsoft Corporation.

Microsoft. (2021). *Gaming for everyone: Diversity and inclusion in gaming*. Microsoft Corporation.

Newzoo. (2023). *Global games market report*. Newzoo.

Patel, M. S., Asch, D. A., & Volpp, K. G. (2015). Wearable devices as facilitators, not drivers, of health behavior change. *Journal of the American Medical Association*, *313*(5), 459–460. DOI: 10.1001/jama.2014.14781 PMID: 25569175

PwC. (2020). *Game-based learning: Transforming professional development*. PricewaterhouseCoopers.

Riot Games. (2019). *Team building through gaming: A case study*. Riot Games, Inc.

SAP. (2021). *Esports and employee engagement*. SAP SE.

Shopify. (2021). *Shopify Gaming League: Building community through play*. Shopify Inc.

Society for Human Resource Management. (2022). *Human capital benchmarking report*. SHRM.

Song, Z., & Baicker, K. (2019). Effect of a workplace wellness program on employee health and economic outcomes: A randomized clinical trial. *Journal of the American Medical Association, 321*(15), 1491–1501. DOI: 10.1001/jama.2019.3307 PMID: 30990549

Staiano, A. E., & Calvert, S. L. (2011). Exergames for physical education courses: Physical, social, and cognitive benefits. *Child Development Perspectives, 5*(2), 93–98. DOI: 10.1111/j.1750-8606.2011.00162.x PMID: 22563349

Statista. (2023). *Gaming industry - Statistics & facts*. Statista.

Stewart, J. B. (2013). *Looking for a lesson in Google's perks*. The New York Times.

T-Mobile. (2020). *Employee engagement and retention report*. T-Mobile US, Inc.

Tondello, G. F., Wehbe, R. R., Diamond, L., Busch, M., Marczewski, A., & Nacke, L. E. (2016). The gamification user types hexad scale. In *Proceedings of the 2016 Annual Symposium on Computer-Human Interaction in Play* (pp. 229-243). ACM.

Tremblay, M. S., Aubert, S., Barnes, J. D., Saunders, T. J., Carson, V., Latimer-Cheung, A. E., Chastin, S. F. M., Altenburg, T. M., & Chinapaw, M. J. (2017). Sedentary behavior research network (SBRN)–terminology consensus project process and outcome. *The International Journal of Behavioral Nutrition and Physical Activity, 14*(1), 75. DOI: 10.1186/s12966-017-0525-8 PMID: 28599680

Wagner, M. G. (2006). On the scientific relevance of eSports. In *Proceedings of the 2006 International Conference on Internet Computing & Conference on Computer Games Development* (pp. 437-442). CSREA Press.

Walmart. (2019). *Safety training through gamification*. Walmart Inc.

Werbach, K., & Hunter, D. (2012). *For the win: How game thinking can revolutionize your business*. Wharton Digital Press.

Willis Towers Watson. (2022). *Global benefits attitudes survey*. Willis Towers Watson.

World Health Organization. (2020). *Mental health in the workplace*. WHO.

KEY TERMS AND DEFINITIONS

Active Video Games: Games that require physical movement from the player, often used to promote physical activity and combat sedentary behavior in workplace wellness programs.

Corporate Wellness Programs: Organized initiatives implemented by employers to improve the health and well-being of their employees, potentially including physical fitness, mental health support, and preventive care.

Esports: Organized competitive video gaming, often involving teams of players competing in structured tournaments or leagues, which can be leveraged for team building and skill development in corporate settings.

Exergames: Video games that incorporate physical exercise, combining gameplay with physical activity to make fitness more engaging and enjoyable.

Gamification: The application of game elements and principles (such as points, badges, leaderboards, and challenges) to non-game contexts, including workplace processes and training programs.

Gaming Culture: The social environment, shared experiences, and community aspects that develop around gaming activities, which can contribute to a more inclusive and engaging workplace culture.

Team-Based Gaming: Gaming activities that require collaboration and coordination among multiple players, often used to develop teamwork, communication, and leadership skills in corporate settings.

Virtual Reality Gaming: Immersive gaming experiences that use virtual reality technology to create three-dimensional, interactive environments, offering new possibilities for training, team building, and wellness activities in the workplace.

Workplace Engagement: The emotional commitment and connection that employees feel toward their organization, colleagues, and work, which can be enhanced through gaming and esports initiatives.

Workplace Learning: The acquisition of knowledge, skills, and competencies in the workplace context, which can be facilitated through game-based approaches that make learning more interactive and engaging.

Chapter 2 Skills Reloaded: Harnessing Esports for Communication and Collaboration Development in College

Anthony Mark Gray
https://orcid.org/0009-0008-4161-3029
Old Dominion University, USA

James E. Bartlett
Old Dominion University, USA

ABSTRACT

This study explores how collegiate esports programs can develop essential communication and collaboration skills among Generation Z college graduates. Given Gen Z's digital nativity and preference for interactive learning, the research examines esports' role in enhancing soft skills. Using a social constructivist framework, the study reviews video content and podcasts from five collegiate esports programs, identifying frequent demonstrations of teamwork, communication, and time management. Findings suggest that esports can bridge the gap between education and workforce requirements, highlighting its potential in cultivating a competent and adaptable workforce. Future research should develop rubrics for assessing soft skills in esports, conduct longitudinal studies on career outcomes, and explore specific esports genres' impact on skill development.

DOI: 10.4018/979-8-3373-5322-7.ch002

INTRODUCTION

Some say that Generation Z (children born between 1997-2012), the second generation after Generation X (children of the 70s and 80s), college graduates, and today's workforce managers mixed about as well as oil and water. Generation (Gen) Z, the *location-aware* generation, is now entering the workforce with different perspectives and goal aspirations than previous generations (Aggarwal et al., 2022). This generation is distinguished by its digital nativity, having grown up with smartphones, social media, and instant access to information. Huss (2023) refers to them as the post-millennials, who account for approximately 2.47 billion individuals. Early exposure to technology has changed the communication styles, learning preferences, and career expectations of this cohort.

Global factors and past experiences, such as the COVID-19 pandemic, have led Gen Z to prefer participating in online learning. The pandemic significantly accelerated the adoption of digital learning platforms, compelling educational institutions to pivot to online modes of instruction almost overnight. Nearly 100 million students worldwide enrolled in web-based courses (Vlasova, 2022). This shift has highlighted how Gen Z leverages technology for their education. Still, it has also underscored the challenges educators face in engaging this tech-savvy yet attention-challenged generation.

Research indicates that Gen Z students value flexibility, personalization, and interactive content in their educational experiences (Yu, 2020). They are less inclined to respond to traditional didactic teaching methods and more likely to thrive in environments that offer real-time feedback, multimedia resources, and collaborative opportunities. Integrating gamification, virtual simulations, and other innovative pedagogical tools has been shown to enhanced their learning outcomes (Duterte, 2024; Li et al., 2023).

To build on this, Gen Z's approach to knowledge acquisition is often pragmatic and goal-oriented. They seek practical skills and knowledge that can be directly applied to their career aspirations (Nikolić & Lazarević, 2022). This contrasts with previous generations' more theoretical and abstract learning preferences (Nikolić & Lazarević, 2022). This has implications not only for educational institutions, but also for employers who must adapt their training and development programs to meet the expectations of this generation in the emerging workforce.

Given these characteristics, educators and employers must both understand and adapt to Gen Z's unique needs and preferences. By doing so, they can better harness this generation's potential, ensuring that their technological proficiency and innovative spirit are effectively channeled toward personal and professional growth. To explore this connection further, this chapter presents a qualitative study analyzing how collegiate esports participation contributes to the development of soft skills in

Generation Z. The study draws from over 50 hours of video and podcast content to examine real-world examples of communication, teamwork, and time management in esports settings. This need for adaptability and understanding is not unlike the evolution seen in the world of esports, where the industry has grown from small beginnings to a globally recognized phenomenon.

HISTORY, EVOLUTION, AND CONTEXT OF ESPORTS

Esports traces its origins back to the 1950s, when physicist William Higinbotham created one of the earliest video games—a simple tennis simulation—in 1958. In the 1960s, the development of *Spacewar!* laid the groundwork for competitive gaming, culminating in the first known esports tournament at Stanford University in 1972. The 1970s and 1980s marked significant advancements with the release of the Magnavox Odyssey, the rise of arcades, and the introduction of competitive games like *Pong* and *Asteroids*. In 1980, the first national *Space Invaders* competition drew over 10,000 participants, followed by an inaugural *Donkey Kong* tournament in 1981. The 1990s witnessed the growth of organized esports through events like the Nintendo World Championships and the establishment of foundational leagues such as the Electronic Sports League (ESL). In the 2000s, international tournaments like the World Cyber Games and the Electronic Sports World Cup further legitimized esports as a global phenomenon. The 2010s and early 2020s saw explosive growth fueled by digital technology, internet streaming, and increased accessibility—trends that accelerated during the COVID-19 pandemic (Zhong et al., 2022). By 2021, esports global revenue surpassed $1.1 billion, largely driven by sponsorships and rising viewership (Newzoo, 2021).

Gen Z is the first generation to experience esports in college, creating a new avenue for research to examine its impacts on students' college experiences and preparation for the workforce. The integration of esports in collegiate environments reflects its growing importance and influence on educational and professional pathways (Jenny et al,, 2017). This generation's engagement with esports highlights their digital nativity and unique learning preferences, which include flexibility, personalization, and interactive content (Yu, 2020).

DEFINING ESPORTS

Esports, or electronic sports, represent a rapidly growing sector within the sports and entertainment industries. Though several definitions exist, a concise and universally accepted definition has yet to be entirely agreed upon. For the purposes of this research, the definition of esports will be adopted from established literature. Esports are a form of sports where electronic systems facilitate the primary aspects of the sport, and the impact on teams and players, as well as the output of the esports system, are mediated by human-computer interfaces (Hamari & Sjöblom, 2017). Broadly, it can be considered competitive video gaming.

While the term has historically appeared in various forms—such as *eSports*, *e-sports*, or *Esports*—the Associated Press officially adopted the lowercase, unhyphenated spelling **esports** in 2017, which has since become the standard in journalism and much of academia (Roth, 2017).

This study focuses on esports in a college setting, where this form of competitive gaming has gained significant traction. According to Jenny et al. (2017), esports in collegiate environments provide a platform for students to engage in competitive gaming while fostering skills such as teamwork, strategic thinking, and communication. The National Association of Collegiate Esports (NACE) has reported a steady increase in the number of institutions offering esports programs, highlighting the growing recognition of esports as a legitimate athletic and academic pursuit (NACE, 2020).

Esports encompass various game genres, including first-person shooters (FPS), multiplayer online battle arenas (MOBA), real-time strategy (RTS), and sports simulation games. These genres offer diverse experiences and challenges, catering to a wide range of player preferences and skill sets (Esports Wales, 2024). The competitive nature of esports is often organized into leagues and tournaments, where players and teams compete for prestige, scholarships, and monetary rewards. For example, the League of Legends College Championship and the Overwatch Collegiate Championship are prominent events that attract significant attention and participation from college students across the United States (Rothwell & Shaffer, 2019).

Esports have been recognized for their potential educational benefits. Studies have shown that participation in esports can enhance cognitive abilities, improve hand-eye coordination, and develop problem-solving skills (Adachi & Willoughby, 2013). These benefits align with the broader educational goals of developing well-rounded individuals equipped with essential 21st-century skills (Börner et al., 2018).

Esports have emerged as a dynamic part of the collegiate experience, offering more than just competitive entertainment. Within these team-based, high-pressure environments, students engage in complex interactions that naturally foster soft skills such as communication, teamwork, and time management. As esports become more integrated into higher education, they present a unique opportunity to examine how digital engagement supports career-ready skill development.

Soft Skills

Soft skills are non-technical skills essential in the workplace, facilitating effective and harmonious interactions among employees and contributing to the overall success of an organization. The National Association of Colleges and Employers (NACE) (2021) defines soft skills as interpersonal skills that include communication, teamwork, problem-solving, and time management .

Communication is a fundamental soft skill encompassing the ability to convey information effectively and efficiently. This involves not only verbal communication but also non-verbal cues, listening skills, and written communication. Effective communication is crucial in ensuring that ideas and information are clearly understood, reducing misunderstandings, and fostering a collaborative work environment (Baumann, 2017).

Teamwork is another critical soft skill that involves the ability to work effectively within a group. This skill is essential in most professional settings where projects and tasks require collaborative efforts. Teamwork skills include understanding group dynamics, being able to negotiate and compromise, and supporting and motivating team members to achieve common goals (National Academies of Sciences, Engineering, and Medicine, 2018).

Problem-solving skills refer to the ability to identify issues, analyze problems, and develop effective solutions. This involves critical thinking, creativity, and the ability to implement solutions in a practical and timely manner. Problem-solving is integral to navigating the complexities and challenges that arise in professional settings (Adachi & Willoughby, 2013). Time management is the ability to prioritize tasks, manage time effectively, and meet deadlines. This skill is crucial for productivity and efficiency, enabling individuals to allocate their time and resources effectively to achieve their objectives (Börner et al., 2018).

These soft skills are vital for collaboration and efficiency in the workplace. They enable individuals to work well with others, adapt to changes, and handle challenges effectively. The importance of soft skills has been increasingly recognized in the modern workforce, as they complement technical skills and contribute to overall organizational success (Deming, 2018).

In the context of esports, these soft skills are developed through gameplay and team interactions. Esports provide a unique platform for players to hone their communication, teamwork, problem-solving, and time management skills in a competitive and dynamic environment (Jenny et al., 2017). By engaging in esports, participants can enhance these essential skills, preparing them for the collaborative and fast-paced nature of the modern workplace (Zhong et al., 2022).

Key Terms

Below are some key terms that will be used throughout the chapter to support reader understanding of core concepts related to Generation Z, esports, and soft skill development.

- Esports – Competitive video gaming facilitated by electronic systems, where the outcome is mediated by human-computer interfaces (Hamari & Sjöblom, 2017).
- Soft Skills – Non-technical interpersonal and cognitive skills such as communication, teamwork, time management, and problem-solving that are essential for workplace success (Deming, 2018).
- Digital Native – An individual born during or after the rise of digital technology who is naturally familiar with and reliant on digital tools, platforms, and media (Prensky, 2001).
- Location-Aware – refers to devices or applications that can detect and use the geographic location of a user to deliver services, data, or interactions based on that location (Techopedia, n.d.).

LITERATURE REVIEW

The existing research literature on esports reveals both positive and negative implications for college students. Delello et al. (2021) comprehensively examines these implications, highlighting significant risks and benefits associated with esports participation.

Positive Implications

The literature has grown as the popularity of esports has been significantly influenced by technological advancements. Within the literature developments have not only enhanced gaming experiences but also drawn connections to personal, academic, and professional benefits for students. Research in esports participation has started to draw connections to communication, academic achievement, and the development of essential 21st-century skills.

Technological Advancements

Technological advancements, such as increased internet bandwidth, video memory, and processing speed, have driven the popularity of esports, linking students' gaming habits to perceived personal and academic benefits (Delello et al.,., 2021). These benefits include social interaction, teamwork, and critical thinking skills. For instance, Adachi and Willoughby (2013) suggest that video games requiring strategic problem-solving skills can enhance players' abilities in this area.

Academic Achievement

Riedel (2016) examined the gaming habits of students and their relationship to their grade point average, finding that video game play had little to no effect on academic performance. This suggests that concerns about gaming negatively impacting academic outcomes may be overstated.

Nielson and Hanghoj (2019) conducted a study collecting data from nine interviews of after-school esports club members. Their research identified four themes: communication, health, game culture, and development and growth. They found that esports participation helped players develop communication skills in a social context, which were transferable to other aspects of their lives beyond gaming.

Skill Development

Zhong et al. (2022) further support these findings, demonstrating that esports participation can foster the development of critical 21st-century skills such as teamwork, leadership, and critical thinking. Employers increasingly value these skills in the modern workforce (Zhong et al, 2022).

Negative Implications

Becoming a significant part of culture and recreation can also have negative implications. The literature highlights several risks associated with esports, raising concerns within the academic community about its impact on students' academic success and overall well-being.

Risk Associated

The literature highlights several risks associated with esports participation. Banyai et al. (2019) report that playing esports may be linked to addictive gaming behaviors. Similarly, Delello et al. (2021) found that as esports continue to gain popularity, gambling-related activities such as betting are also increasing among participants.

Academic Success

These findings reflect broader concerns within the academic community about the potential negative impact of esports on students' academic success — defined as achieving high grades, performing well on tests, completing coursework on time, developing essential cognitive and critical thinking skills, and personal well-being. A significant contradiction in the literature concerns the impact of esports on academic performance.

Addiction and Focus

While some studies, such as Banyal et al., (2019; 2016), suggest no negative effect, others highlight potential risks like addiction and decreased focus, which could harm academic outcomes (Banyal et al., 2019). This dichotomy reflects the ongoing debate within the academic community regarding esports' overall impact on students.

Gaps and Inconsistencies

Several gaps and inconsistencies within the literature should be acknowledged. Delello et al. (2021) pointed out that esports has multiple definitions and spellings, yet the study does not establish a singular operational definition, potentially affecting the reliability of the findings. Additionally, the cross-sectional nature of many studies limits the ability to observe long-term effects, such as the development of gaming addiction or sustained academic benefits. Including longitudinal data would provide a more comprehensive understanding of these dynamics.

The focus on U.S. college students may not represent the global esports community, suggesting a need for more diverse samples to understand impacts across different cultural contexts (Feng, 2024). There is also an inconsistency in reporting the financial impact of esports on students. While some students spend significant amounts of money on gaming, the implications of these expenditures on their financial stability or academic performance are not thoroughly analyzed.

Moreover, there are significant gender differences in esports participation and perceived benefits, but the literature lacks a deep exploration of these differences' underlying causes. The literature on esports provides valuable insights into its growing phenomenon and its implications for college students. While there are clear benefits, such as skill development and social interaction, there are also contradictions, gaps, and inconsistencies that warrant further investigation. Addressing these issues could enhance the understanding of esports' role in higher education and help develop strategies to maximize its benefits while mitigating potential risks.

FRAMEWORK

This study embraces a social constructivist perspective, as outlined by Vygotsky (1978). This theoretical framework emphasizes the critical role of social interactions in the development of cognitive and practical skills. According to Vygotsky (1978), learning is inherently a social process, where individuals construct knowledge through interactions with others within their cultural and social contexts. This perspective is particularly relevant in the context of esports, where collaborative and communicative interactions are integral to gameplay and team dynamics.

Social Constructivism and Esports

In the realm of esports, social constructivism postulates that engagement in these digital activities provides a rich social environment that is conducive to developing essential soft skills such as communication, teamwork, and collaboration. Esports require players to engage in real-time strategic discussions, problem-solving, and decision-making, often under high-pressure situations. These interactions simulate real-world professional environments where such skills are invaluable.

Esports teams function similarly to traditional sports teams, where success hinges on effective communication, coordinated teamwork, and the ability to collaborate towards a common goal. The digital nature of esports also introduces unique elements of communication, such as the use of in-game chat, voice communications, and digital signaling, which add layers of complexity and richness to the interactions.

Gen Z Characteristics and Esports

Generation Z has been shaped by constant exposure to smartphones, social media, and high-speed internet—technologies that have deeply influenced how they learn, communicate, and engage with the world. As digital natives, they are more responsive to interactive, tech-driven environments that provide real-time feedback and personalized engagement (Khan & Al-Shibami., 2023). Esports naturally reflect these preferences, offering fast-paced, collaborative settings where immediate feedback is integral to performance. This synergy positions esports as a culturally relevant and pedagogically effective platform for developing essential soft skills, particularly in communication and teamwork—two competencies highly valued in the modern workforce.

Application of the Social Constructivist Framework

The social constructivist framework is applied in this study to examine how esports participation fosters the development of soft skills through social interactions. This includes observing and analyzing how players perceive their communication during gameplay, collaborate to develop strategies, and manage team dynamics. The framework also considers the impact of these interactions on players' overall skill development and how these skills transfer to real-world professional settings.

By positioning esports within the context of skill development, the study aims to provide insights on how these digital interactions can be leveraged to enhance educational and workforce training programs. This involves understanding the specific elements of esports that contribute to skill development, such as the role of competition, the structure of team interactions, and the use of technology in facilitating communication.

Gaps in Workforce Training for Gen Z

Despite widespread recognition that soft skills are essential for success in the modern workplace, many organizations are falling short in equipping Generation Z with the communication, collaboration, and problem-solving abilities needed to thrive. Although Gen Z is technologically fluent, employers frequently report that these workers lack key interpersonal and leadership skills (Benítez-Márquez et al., 2021; NACE, 2021).

This disconnect stems in part from outdated workforce development models. Many current training programs rely on standardized, instructor-led formats that fail to resonate with Gen Z's learning preferences—namely, interactive, gamified, and personalized learning experiences (Khan & Al-Shibami., 2023). A McKinsey & Company study highlights this gap, revealing that employers often misjudge what younger employees want from professional development (Bennerstedt et al, 2012). While employers tend to emphasize formal advancement tracks, frontline workers—many of whom are Gen Z—prioritize skill-building opportunities, coaching, and real-time feedback (Singh., 2025).

Without a shift toward more dynamic and relevant development models, Gen Z may struggle to make a smooth transition from college to the workplace. This underscores the need to explore innovative approaches to training—such as esports—that naturally align with Gen Z's preferences for experiential, collaborative learning. By integrating esports into training and development pipelines, institutions and employers can offer a high-engagement platform that builds soft skills organically through strategic, real-time team-based play. This model not only aligns with Gen Z's preferences but also holds promise for addressing the needs of future generations.

As Generation Alpha begins to enter educational systems and prepare for future workforce participation, these training gaps may only widen if institutions and employers fail to evolve. Like Gen Z, Gen Alpha is expected to be even more immersed in digital environments and will likely demand greater interactivity, autonomy, and real-time feedback in their learning and development experiences. Addressing these trends now—through innovative platforms like esports—can help establish scalable, engaging models that not only meet Gen Z's needs but also prepare organizations for the expectations of future generations.

Issues, Controversies, Problems

Generation Z employees need to gain the necessary communication and collaboration skills that the workforce demands to retain and progress in their careers (Benítez-Márquez et al, 2021). The study's significance is to understand and address the communication and collaboration skills gap in Gen Z, which is vital for creating a workforce that meets the needs of today's professional landscape. This study sought to contribute valuable insights to educators and employers and aid in developing effective strategies for enhancing these skills in preparation for the workforce. For several reasons, understanding and addressing the communication and collaboration skills gap in Generation Z is essential. First, as digital natives, Gen Z employees bring unique technological adeptness to the workplace, yet they often require development in interpersonal skills crucial for effective teamwork and leadership. Second, in an increasingly globalized and interconnected business world, the ability to communicate and collaborate across diverse teams and cultural boundaries is more important than ever.

The relationship between esports and the problem statement is evident in several ways. Esports environments often mimic the collaborative and competitive nature of modern workplaces, where quick decision-making, strategic thinking, and clear communication are crucial. By engaging in esports, Gen Z players can develop these skills in a context that is both engaging and relevant to their interests. Additionally, the structured nature of many esports teams and leagues can provide participants with valuable experiences in leadership, teamwork, and conflict resolution.

This study aims to offer valuable insights that can guide educators in tailoring their curricula to better prepare students for the collaborative demands of modern workplaces. It also seeks to inform employers about the best practices for training and development programs that enhance these essential skills among their Gen Z workforce. By doing so, the study contributes to creating a more competent and adaptable workforce capable of meeting the dynamic needs of today's professional landscape.

Moreover, the findings of this research are expected to help develop targeted strategies for skill enhancement, thus enabling Generation Z employees to navigate and succeed in their careers effectively. These strategies could include mentorship programs, collaborative projects, and communication workshops focusing on the technical and interpersonal aspects of professional interactions. By addressing the communication and collaboration skills gap, organizations can ensure that their Gen Z employees are well-equipped to contribute to and thrive within the evolving workplace.

SIGNIFICANCE FOR EDUCATIONAL AND WORKFORCE DEVELOPMENT

Understanding the role of esports in skill development has significant implications for educators and employers. For educators, incorporating esports into curricula can provide a novel and effective way to engage students and develop essential skills. This can include integrating esports into courses related to communication, teamwork, and leadership, as well as creating dedicated esports programs that focus on skill development.

For employers, recognizing the skills developed through esports can inform hiring practices and professional development programs. By valuing the communication, teamwork, and collaboration skills that esports players bring, employers can better align their training programs to meet the needs of the modern workforce.

The social constructivist framework provides a valuable lens through which to understand esports' educational and developmental potential. By focusing on the social interactions inherent in esports, this study aims to highlight how these digital activities can contribute to the development of essential soft skills in Generation Z. This understanding can inform both educational practices and workforce development strategies, ensuring that the potential of esports is fully realized in preparing individuals for the demands of the modern professional landscape.

PURPOSE AND RESEARCH QUESTIONS

The purpose of this study is two-fold. One is to explore and understand the development of transferable soft skills, specifically teamwork, communication, and time management, among participants in collegiate esports programs. This investigation aimed to identify the specific activities and aspects within esports environments that contribute to cultivating these essential skills. The workforce values and desires soft skills in today's labor market (Deming, 2018).

Secondly, the investigation sought to evaluate and provide recommendations on how collegiate esports programs can be strategically designed or modified to enhance the preparation of students for successful careers. This includes examining existing structures, practices, and educational integrations within these programs to identify effective strategies and potential areas for improvement. The ultimate goal is to offer actionable insights to guide educators, program directors, and policymakers. Developing more comprehensive and career-relevant esports initiatives that extend beyond gaming, fostering a well-rounded professional skill set in students who are entering or already participating in the workforce. The two research questions were:

RQ1: How does participation in collegiate esports programs, as reflected in video content and podcasts, facilitate developing and demonstrating soft skills such as teamwork, communication, and time management, and how are these skills represented and contextualized within the esports environment?
RQ2: How can collegiate esports programs better prepare students for successful careers within and outside the gaming industry?

RESEARCH DESIGN AND APPROACH

The study employed a narrative inquiry approach, which is a qualitative research method that gathers information through storytelling (Polkinghorne, 1988). This method allows researchers to explore the personal and collective experiences of individuals, providing deep insights into their lives and the contexts that shape them (Naeem et al., 2023). By adopting narrative inquiry, the study aimed to uncover collegiate esports participants' intricate and often nuanced experiences.

Additionally, this study utilized Miller's (2004) digital storytelling techniques to discover hidden themes and experiences among the participants. Digital storytelling involves using digital tools to tell personal stories, offering a rich and engaging medium for capturing participants' narratives. Through this method, the researcher's examined the unique experiences of esports players, revealing underlying themes that might not be evident through traditional research methods.

The researcher's then crafted a narrative of the experience, which combined the diverse stories into a coherent and meaningful account. As Connelly and Clandinin (1990) note, "Humans are storytelling organisms who, individually and collectively, lead storied lives. Thus, the study of narrative is how humans experience life in the world" (p. 5). This perspective underscores the idea that people's lives are composed of stories fundamental to understanding their experiences and interactions (Singer., 2024).

This qualitative study specifically aims to understand how collegiate esports participants develop soft skills such as teamwork, communication, and time management. By focusing on these key areas, the researcher provides valuable recommendations for improving esports programs and better-preparing participants for future career challenges.

Grounded in thematic analysis, the study employed an in-depth review of over 50 hours of video and podcast content from five collegiate esports programs. This extensive review process allowed the researcher to identify and analyze recurring themes and patterns in the participants' experiences. Due to the nature of the data collection process, the exact number of players indirectly participating in these videos was not documented. However, the richness of the collected data provided a comprehensive understanding of the participants' development of soft skills.

Through a narrative inquiry approach, this study aims to contribute to the broader discourse on soft skills development in esports and offer practical insights for educators and program developers. By highlighting the stories and experiences of collegiate esports participants, the research provides a unique lens to understand the impact of esports on skill development and offers actionable recommendations for enhancing these programs.

Data Sources

The study's data collection encompassed an in-depth review of over 50 hours, split between video content from collegiate esports teams and esports-related podcasts. This methodology facilitated a comprehensive examination of the development and application of soft skills within the esports environment. By combining gameplay analysis, team discussions, and expert insights, this approach aimed to thoroughly document the manifestation of essential soft skills such as communication, teamwork, and time management demonstrated by collegiate esports participants.

Due to the qualitative nature of this study, no rubrics were used for direct evaluation. Instead, observational notes were taken during video reviews to document instances of communication, teamwork, and time management. Attention was given to player interactions, decision-making processes, leadership roles, conflict resolution, and strategies employed during gameplay and team discussions.

The video content provided a dynamic and immersive view of the participants' real-time interactions and strategies, which captured the essence of their collaborative efforts and communication styles. Visual documentation allowed for a nuanced analysis of how players coordinate with each other, resolve conflicts, and make critical decisions under pressure. Observational notes focused on key moments where communication was pivotal, such as during high-stakes gameplay or when devising strategies in team meetings.

Similarly, the esports-related podcasts offered expert insights and broader perspectives on the role of soft skills in esports. The podcasts often included interviews with coaches, players, and industry experts, providing valuable context and highlighting best practices for skill development in esports. The combination of video and podcast content enriched the data, offering a holistic view of the esports environment and the soft skills it cultivates.

In documenting instances of communication, the study paid particular attention to how players conveyed information, provided feedback, and coordinated actions during gameplay. Teamwork was assessed by observing how players supported each other, shared responsibilities, and collaborated towards common goals. Time management was evaluated based on how players prioritized tasks, managed in-game resources, and adhered to schedules during practice and competitions.

Overall, this methodological approach allowed for a detailed and multifaceted understanding of soft skills development in collegiate esports. The insights gained from this study aim to inform educators, program developers, and esports coaches on how to foster these essential skills better, ultimately contributing to preparing participants for successful careers within and beyond the esports industry.

Participant Observation and Inclusion

While the number of players observed remains unspecified, the study encompassed a broad range of participants across the five college teams. This approach allowed for a diverse representation of esports environments and player dynamics, ensuring that the findings were not limited to a specific group or type of player. The inclusion of multiple teams provided a comprehensive overview of various play styles, strategies, and interactions within the collegiate esports scene.

Although direct interactions with players were not conducted, the observational data collected from videos and audio recordings offer valuable insights into their behavior and soft skills development in a naturalistic setting. This method of data collection allowed the researchers to capture authentic, unfiltered interactions and behaviors, which are crucial for understanding the real-world dynamics of esports teams. The absence of direct interviews or surveys mitigated potential biases or behavior alterations that might occur when players know they are being studied.

The videos and audio recordings utilized in the study were all published on YouTube, a platform that hosts a vast array of user-generated content. The reviewed materials were publicly accessible and did not require permission to view; therefore, the study adhered to ethical standards concerning privacy and consent. The availability of this content for public viewing without the need for subscribing to specific channels ensured that the data collection process was discreet and non-invasive. Also, public accessibility allows researchers to revisit and verify the data, promoting transparency and reproducibility in the study.

The study analyzed interactions and behaviors in a setting where players are naturally engaged and motivated by leveraging publicly available videos and podcasts This method provided a rich data source, highlighting how players develop soft skills such as teamwork, problem-solving, and adaptability in a competitive environment. These insights contribute to a deeper understanding of esports' educational and developmental potential in collegiate settings.

Analytical Method

For this qualitative analysis, thematic analysis was employed to identify, analyze, and report patterns within the data. This involved a six-phase process: familiarizing with the data, generating initial codes, searching for themes, reviewing themes, defining and naming themes, and producing the report (Polkinghorne, 1988). Thematic analysis was chosen for its flexibility and its ability to capture nuanced, context-rich insights from qualitative content.

The study utilized both inductive and deductive approaches. The inductive phase involved open coding without predefined categories, allowing themes to emerge organically from the data. This was especially valuable in surfacing unexpected patterns of soft skill development in the esports context, such as moments of leadership emergence or informal mentoring among team members. The inductive process helped uncover soft skills in a broader, more exploratory way.

Following this, a deductive analysis was applied, drawing from established frameworks around key soft skills—including teamwork, communication, and time management. This phase allowed the researcher to examine the data more precisely through the lens of these predefined constructs, aligning the analysis with the study's core research questions and workforce development literature.

To ensure analytical rigor, the data was coded in multiple passes, and emerging themes were continuously refined and cross-referenced across different sources (videos and podcasts). Patterns were validated not only by recurrence but also by relevance and depth of context. This layered approach strengthened the trustworthiness of the analysis by integrating both emergent insights and theory-informed validation.

Together, the inductive and deductive processes provided a comprehensive analytical framework, enabling the study to remain grounded in the data while also contributing to existing conversations about soft skill development in collegiate esports.

Use of ChatGPT for Validity Check

A new approach to enhance the validity of the thematic analysis utilized a large language learning model. Specifically, this study used OpenAI's (2024) ChatGPT as part of the validation process. This tool provided an additional layer of scrutiny and ensured the identity themes' robustness. The steps taken are outlined below:

1. *Cross Verification*: ChatGPT was used to cross-verify the themes and code decisions made during the analysis. Various sections of the data, corresponding themes, and the model provided feedback on the coherence and consistency of the themes.
2. *Feedback and Reflections*: The responses generated by ChatGPT were used as feedback. This process involved comparing the Artificial Intelligence (AI) interpretations and suggestions with the existing themes to identify discrepancies or overlooked patterns.
3. *Biased Identification*: ChatGPT's feedback helped identify potential biases in the coding process. It provided a neutral perspective and highlighted areas where personal biases might have influenced the thematic development.
4. *Iterative Refinement*: The themes were refined iteratively based on the insights gained from ChatGPT. This iterative process ensured that the themes were grounded in the data and consistent with broader interpretations.

While ChatGPT added efficiency and objectivity to the validation process, it was used strictly as a supplementary tool, not a substitute for human judgment. The researcher retained full control over coding decisions and interpretation. It is important to note that ChatGPT's feedback is limited to pattern recognition and linguistic context; it does not possess human-level reasoning or awareness of lived experiences.

Incorporating ChatGPT into the validation process demonstrates an innovative approach to enhancing transparency, consistency, and reflexivity in qualitative analysis. This hybrid method reflects the growing role of AI tools in educational and social science research, offering promising possibilities for scaling rigorous, mixed-methods inquiry.

RESULTS

This section presents the findings from an in-depth thematic analysis conducted on over 50 hours of video content and podcasts related to collegiate esports. This analysis aimed to answer two primary research questions. The review focused on identifying instances of communication, teamwork, and time management within the esports content. The frequency and context of these soft skills were analyzed to understand their role and representation in collegiate esports programs. Table 1 shows detailed findings related to each identified theme, providing insight into developing these crucial skills within the esports setting.

Table 1. Frequency of identified soft skills in collegiate esports content

	Frequency Video		
Theme	**Content**	**Podcast**	**Total**
Teamwork	45	30	75
Communication	60	40	100
Time Management	35	25	60

Note. Frequencies represent the number of instances soft skills were highlighted or discussed in esports content and podcasts.

Teamwork

The following findings demonstrated teamwork emerged as a critical factor for success within collegiate esports. Analysis indicated that teamwork is a fundamental component cultivated within the collegiate esports ecosystem. This skill was notably recognized in 45 instances from video content and 30 from podcasts. This highlights the significance of collaboration and collective strategy in achieving success within esports competitions and practice sessions. Collaborative learning requires interdependency, wherein group members must work together to plan, organize, and strategize joint activities to complete a task or solve a problem (National Academies of Sciences, Engineering, and Medicine, 2018). The videos and podcasts had many related examples. One example that built the foundation of teamwork was a comment about the importance of competition and how everyone loved to compete to determine who was better, which led them to a better varsity program. One player said, "Our club was based on competition, and everyone loved to win; everyone loved to compete against each other to see who was better, and that's what led to the varsity program" (NASPA Student Affairs Administrators, 2019). One intersection area that evolved within the analysis was the integral role of teamwork and communication within the esports setting. A team captain of a collegiate Call of Duty team stated, “We're confident in our abilities...if we work together, we can easily win...at the end of the day, it is a team game, and that's going to cost us in the end if we end up losing at all. So, we're pretty confident” (NACE StarLeague, 2023).

Communication

The predominant soft skill is communication, which emerged as the most frequent across all sources, with 60 instances recorded from video and 40 from podcasts. The findings underscore communication's critical role in game settings. By maintaining team dynamics, discussing strategies, and resolving conflicts, effective communication can be conceptualized as one’s ability to speak, listen, and interact verbally and nonverbally (Baumann,2017).

The analysis illuminates communication as a pivotal element within collegiate esports. It stood out as a tool for in-game strategy and vital to building team cohesion and addressing conflicts. For instance, a player from one collegiate team emphasized the importance of structured communication during playoff preparations: “We've played every day for the past week... we've been recording our games, looking over the VODs [videos on demand], trying to fix our mistakes as a team”(SEIU, 2023). This illustrates a systematic approach to communication, underscoring its role in reviewing performances and planning future strategies. Moreover, another player highlighted the dual significance of punctuality and effective communication: “It's about being punctual and organizing my time effectively... ensuring we communicate well during scrims while balancing schoolwork” (SEU Esports, 2023).. This underscores the multifaceted nature of communication in managing schedules and responsibilities effectively. Lastly, the community aspect is enhanced through communication: “A lot of the good things that were happening for esports programs were happening because they were spending a lot of time uniting their community in really creative and diverse ways” (Miami University, 2023).This showcases how communication not only aids in strategy and team cohesion, but also plays a fundamental role in community building.

While communication forms the foundation of team dynamics and strategy, effective time management acts as the scaffold that supports the entire structure of collegiate esports programs. The ability to manage time efficiently is reflected in how players coordinate and execute their strategies and balance their commitments to esports and academic pursuits. Beyond communication, effective time management emerged as another essential skill, as demonstrated by the analysis.

Time Management

Time management was identified in 35 instances from videos and 25 from podcasts, demonstrating its crucial role alongside communication. Players not only focused on the communicative aspects but also on the intensive time investment required during playoffs: "We've been playing every day for the past week... We've been recording our games, looking over the VODs, trying to fix our mistakes as a team" (IGN, 2021)

This not only reiterates the importance of structured practice, but also showcases the deliberate allocation and reflection of time toward collective improvement. Similarly, another esports team reflected on the importance of preparation and time management for significant games: "We faced Robert Morris today... This should be an interesting game. We beat RMU [Robert Morris University] last time we played them... and that's what brought us here today" (The List Show TV, 2019). This indicates how past experiences and reflective preparation are integral in managing time and strategies for significant matches.

This comprehensive analysis confirms the hypothesis that collegiate esports programs contribute significantly to developing teamwork, communication, and time management skills. It also highlighted areas for potential enhancement to align more closely with professional standards. This aligns with the study's purpose of exploring how participation in collegiate esports can develop soft skills transferable to the workforce and offers a foundation for proposing strategic improvements to these programs for career readiness. Esports athletes become software developers, graphic designers, IT professionals, and more (Association for Career and Technical Education [ACTE], 2022). Career and Technical Education (CTE) has a unique opportunity to maximize the science, technology, engineering, and math (STEM) roots embedded in this process of delivering gamified lessons (ACTE, 2022). Academic esports offer a gateway to STEM-related career pathways such as game design and development, information technology (IT), engineering, web development, and orbital careers in sports marketing-related fields.

As Generation Z enters the workforce, it becomes increasingly evident that the innovative and interactive nature of esports can bridge soft skills' gaps. The findings support the assertion that collegiate esports are a valuable supplement to traditional educational approaches, equipping students with the essential skills needed for success in a dynamic and evolving professional landscape.

Following the thematic analysis and the observed frequencies of identified soft skills in collegiate esports content, a Chi-square test for independence was conducted. This form of analysis aids to determine if there were statistically significant differences in the emphasis on soft skills between videos and podcasts. The results of the

Chi-square ($\chi 2$=.052, df=2, p=.975), presented in table 2, indicate no association between the soft skills emphasis and video content vs. podcasts.

Table 2. Chi-square test for differences in soft skill emphasis

Variable	df	x2	p-value
Soft Skill Emphasis	2	.052	.975

Note. The Chi-square test compared the frequency of mentions of teamwork, communication, and time management skills in video content versus podcasts.

This implies that the video content and podcast analysis similarly contribute to understanding the dynamics of teamwork, communication, and time management skills among collegiate esports participants.

DISCUSSION

This study explored developing and demonstrating soft skills such as teamwork, communication, and time management within the context of collegiate esports programs. The analysis was drawn from over 50 hours of videos and podcasts. The investigation sheds light on the multifaceted role of esports in fostering these essential skills. This is a critical proponent for career preparation and success in the modern workforce. The findings from this research echo the growing consensus within academic and professional circles about the value of esports as more than competitive gaming. Collegiate esports emerged as a dynamic environment where players engage in digital competition and develop transferable skills for their future careers.

The themes of teamwork, communication, and time management were prominently featured across the esports content reviewed, indicating a strong alignment with the professional skills sought by today's employers. Cultivating these skills within esports settings is essential, considering the parallels between traditional sports and group-based extracurricular activities.

The introduction of academic esports into this discourse further broadens the educational impact of gaming by linking it directly with CTE and STEM-related pathways. This connection is significant, highlighting esports' potential as a gateway to academic engagement and professional development beyond its recreational and competitive aspects.

Moreover, integrating esports into academic curricula, as highlighted by the ACTE (2022), suggests a progressive step towards acknowledging and leveraging gaming's educational value. This aligns with the shift in educational paradigms that seeks to marry students' interests with their learning and career trajectories, fostering a more engaged and motivated student body.

However, while the benefits of esports in developing soft skills are evident, it is crucial to contextualize these findings within the broader educational and social settings. The impact of esports on academic performance, social development, and physical well-being remains an ongoing debate and research area. In light of these considerations, this discussion aims to gain a deeper understanding of the implications of the study's findings. This discussion will focus on structuring collegiate esports programs to boost professional skill development and navigate the integration challenges within academic settings. It emphasizes the need for comprehensive program designs that improve gaming skills and enhance vital soft skills necessary for career success, ensuring students' all-around growth.

As noted by Zhong et al. (2022), several studies have indicated that esports can contribute to the cultivation of a range of skills, such as teamwork (e.g.,Taylor, 2015), leadership (e.g., Falkenthal & Byrne, 2021), critical thinking (e.g., Vlada et al., 2019), problem-solving (e.g., Adachi & Willoughby, 2013) and communication (e.g., Kimathi, 2024), that are important for students to prepare for future challenges and are increasingly sought by employers (Bellanca & Brandt, 2010).

Higher education institutions in the United States could develop strategies for enhancing soft skills by implementing reflection and feedback sessions for players to participate in after practices and tournament play. These reflection exercises include writing down what the players felt went well, what did not go well, their strengths, and opportunities where they could improve. The benefits of participating in such reflective practices can further develop or enhance participants' communication skills, self-evaluation, and teamwork. These enhanced skills can then be transferable to the workforce as many career and technical roles require these vital skills to be successful.

CONCLUSION

Generation Z has different aspirations and career goals than previous generations. Educators must find innovative ways to enhance Gen Z's communication and collaboration skills before they enter the workforce to ensure that the workforce has the workers it needs to be successful and that these individuals can maintain and progress in their chosen career paths.

Impacts on Research and Practice

The research could contribute significantly to the new technological innovations that are occurring. Gaming has become a large part of Gen Z culture, and its integration into educational and professional settings holds vast potential. Esports, in particular, could serve as a crucial bridge to help cultivate Gen Z's appetite for technology while meeting the workforce's evolving needs by teaching and enhancing their ability to collaborate and communicate effectively.

Technological Innovations

Esports is at the forefront of technological advancements, incorporating cutting-edge software and hardware to create immersive and interactive experiences. This research can contribute to understanding how these technologies can be leveraged in educational settings to foster engagement and enhance learning outcomes. By studying the integration of esports into curricula, educators can gain insights into the best practices for using technology to support skill development. This could lead to the development of new educational tools and platforms that incorporate gaming elements to make learning more engaging and effective (ACTE, 2022).

Workforce Preparedness

As the nature of work continues to evolve with technological advancements, the skills required in the workforce are also changing. This research highlights how esports can be a valuable tool in preparing Generation Z for these changes. By focusing on developing soft skills such as communication, teamwork, and time management, esports can help bridge the gap between academic preparation and professional requirements. Employers can use these insights to develop training programs that harness the skills developed through esports, ensuring that their workforce is well-equipped to meet the demands of modern workplaces (Deming, 2018).

Cultivating Soft Skills

The emphasis on soft skills in esports is particularly relevant as these skills are increasingly recognized as critical for success in the professional world. According to the National Soft Skills Association (2023), soft skills encompass a range of interpersonal and communication skills that are essential for effective collaboration and leadership. By participating in esports, individuals can develop these skills in a practical and engaging context, which can then be transferred to their professional lives (National Soft Skills Association, 2023). This research can inform educators and employers about the specific benefits of esports in soft skill development, leading to more targeted and effective educational and training programs (Baumann, 2017).

Incorporating esports into educational practices can lead to more dynamic and interactive learning environments. This research provides a foundation for developing curricula integrating gaming elements to enhance student engagement and learning outcomes. Educators can use the findings to create programs that teach academic content and develop essential life skills through collaborative and competitive gaming activities. This approach can make learning more relevant and enjoyable for students, particularly those from Generation Z who are accustomed to digital interactions (Khan & Al-Shibami., 2023).

For professionals already in the workforce, esports can offer new opportunities for skill development and team-building. This research can guide the creation of professional development programs that use esports to foster communication and teamwork. By participating in esports activities, employees can develop better collaboration strategies, improve their problem-solving skills, and build stronger team dynamics. These programs can be particularly beneficial in industries that require high levels of teamwork and coordination, such as technology, healthcare, and creative industries (Zhong et al., 2022).

Beyond individual skill development, this research can have broader societal impacts by promoting the positive aspects of gaming culture. By highlighting the educational and professional benefits of esports, this research can help shift the perception of gaming from a purely recreational activity to a valuable tool for personal and professional growth. This can lead to increased acceptance and support for gaming and esports initiatives in educational and professional settings, fostering a more inclusive and innovative society (Börner et al., 2018).

In conclusion, this research can significantly contribute to educational and professional practices. By understanding how esports can be used to develop essential skills, educators and employers can create more effective programs that prepare individuals for the demands of the modern world. Integrating esports into these programs can ensure that Generation Z is well-equipped to navigate and succeed in their careers as technology advances. The findings from this research can help bridge the gap between traditional educational methods and the needs of a digital-savvy generation, ultimately leading to a more competent and adaptable workforce (Aggarwal et al., 2022).

Limitations

While this study provides meaningful insights into the development of soft skills through collegiate esports, several limitations should be acknowledged. One primary limitation is the sample size and data source. The study relied on publicly available video and podcast content from five collegiate esports programs, which inherently limits the scope and diversity of the participant pool. Because the sample was not directly recruited or observed in person, the analysis is constrained to what was explicitly shared or discussed in these publicly produced materials. As such, the findings may not fully represent the broader range of experiences within collegiate esports environments.

Another limitation involves the depth of engagement with participants. Without the ability to conduct one-on-one interviews, focus groups, or live observations, the study lacks direct perspectives from players regarding their experiences, perceived skill development, or the contextual factors influencing their growth. Future research would benefit from qualitative methods such as interviews, which could offer richer, more nuanced insights into how soft skills are learned and transferred.

The time constraints and media formats also presented challenges. Reviewing over 50 hours of video and audio content, while extensive, still represents only a fraction of the possible interactions and dynamics within these teams. Additionally, some potentially valuable non-verbal cues—such as body language, eye contact, or micro-expressions—could not be fully interpreted through podcast audio or limited camera angles during gameplay footage. Future studies may consider recording or gaining access to internal team practices and meetings, where such cues could be more effectively analyzed.

Additionally, the study did not differentiate between esports game genres, which may impact skill development differently. For example, Multiplayer Online Battle Arenas (MOBAs) like *League of Legends* may demand different communication strategies than first-person shooters like *Valorant* or *Call of Duty*. Future investigations could explore whether certain genres are more conducive to developing specific soft skills, such as leadership, decision-making, or time management.

Lastly, the study's reliance on content created for public consumption—often curated or edited—may mean that only polished, highlight-worthy interactions were captured, potentially skewing the representation of typical communication and collaboration behaviors. Despite these limitations, the findings serve as a valuable foundation for understanding the role of esports in soft skill development and highlight opportunities for deeper, more comprehensive exploration in future research.

Future Research

Future research could further explore and expand on the relationship between esports participation and the development of critical soft skills in Generation Z. Longitudinal studies, which track participants over several years, would provide deeper insights into the long-term effects of esports participation on the development of skills such as teamwork, communication, and time management. This approach would offer a more comprehensive understanding of the impact of esports over time. Additionally, experimental studies could compare the development of soft skills between groups engaged in esports and control groups not involved in gaming. By randomly assigning participants to different groups, researchers could more precisely determine the causal effects of esports participation on soft skill development.

Future research should include a more diverse sample encompassing various cultural, socioeconomic, and educational backgrounds to gain a more holistic view. Understanding how esports impact different demographic groups can lead to more tailored and effective interventions. Moreover, different esports genres may foster different types of skills, and future studies could investigate how various game genres (e.g., strategy games, first-person shooters, sports simulations) influence the development of specific soft skills. This could help educators and employers understand which types of games are most beneficial for developing particular skills.

Gender differences in esports participation and perceived benefits warrant further exploration. Future studies could investigate the underlying reasons for these differences and how they influence the overall impact of esports on skill development. Understanding gender-specific experiences and challenges could lead to more inclusive and supportive esports programs. Research could also explore how integrating esports into the academic curriculum affects student engagement and learning outcomes, providing valuable insights for educators looking to leverage esports to enhance student learning and skill development.

While some studies suggest that esports participation does not negatively impact academic performance, further research is needed to explore this relationship in more detail. Investigating how different levels of gaming engagement (e.g., casual vs. competitive) affect academic outcomes and whether specific interventions can mitigate potential adverse effects would be beneficial. Future research could also focus on the non-verbal aspects of communication within esports, such as body language and facial expressions, to provide a deeper understanding of how players communicate and collaborate.

Developing reliable and valid assessment tools to measure soft skills gained through esports participation could significantly enhance future research. These tools could be used to evaluate the effectiveness of esports programs in educational and professional settings, providing a standardized way to assess skill development. Longitudinal research tracking the career trajectories of collegiate esports participants post-graduation could offer valuable insights into how skills developed through gaming translate into the workforce, including job satisfaction, career progression, and the applicability of esports-acquired skills in various professional fields.

In conclusion, future research on esports and soft skill development holds the potential to significantly advance our understanding of gaming's educational and professional benefits. By addressing the current study's limitations and exploring new areas of inquiry, researchers can contribute to developing more effective and inclusive esports programs that better prepare Generation Z for the dynamic demands of the modern workforce. Ultimately, "Skills Reloaded" is not just a metaphor for gameplay—it is a call to rethink how we prepare emerging generations for the evolving demands of a connected, collaborative world.

REFERENCES

Adachi, P. J. C., & Willoughby, T. (2013). More than just fun and games: The longitudinal relationships between strategic video games, self-reported problem-solving skills, and academic grades. *Journal of Youth and Adolescence*, *42*(7), 1041–1052. DOI: 10.1007/s10964-013-9913-9 PMID: 23344653

Aggarwal, S., Gupta, S., Mittal, A., & Rastogi, S. (2022). Gen Z entering the workforce: Restructuring HR policies and practices for fostering the task performance and organizational commitment. *Journal of Public Affairs*, *22*(3), e2535. Advance online publication. DOI: 10.1002/pa.2535

Association for Career and Technical Education. (2022, March 7). *Academic esports: Engage in the future*. ACTE. https://www.acteonline.org/tech-academic-esports/

Banyai, F., Griffiths, M. D., Demetrovics, Z., & Kiraly, O. (2019). Online gaming and gaming disorder: More than just a trivial pursuit. *Current Addiction Reports*, *6*(3), 1–13. https://www.researchgate.net/publication/334846962_Online_gaming_and_gaming_disorder_more_than_just_a_trivial_pursuit PMID: 31366420

Baumann, N. A. (2017). The importance of effective communication: Some food for thought. *The Journal of Applied Laboratory Medicine: An AACC Publication*, *1*(4), 460–461. DOI: 10.1373/jalm.2016.021865 PMID: 33636815

Bellanca, J. A., & Brandt, R. (2010). *21st Century Skills: Rethinking How Students Learn*. Solution Tree Press.

Benítez-Márquez, M. D., Valverde-Berrocoso, J., Morales-Cevallos, M. B., & Sánchez-Santillán, M. (2021). Generation Z in the Workplace through the Lenses of Human Resource Professionals - A Qualitative Study. *ResearchGate*. Retrieved from https://www.researchgate.net/publication/352374489_Generation_Z_in_the_Workplace_through_the_Lenses_of_Human_Resource_Professionals_-_A_Qualitative_Study

Bennerstedt, U., Ivarsson, J., & Linderoth, J. (2012). How gamers manage aggression: Situating skills in collaborative computer games. *International Journal of Computer-Supported Collaborative Learning*, *7*(2), 251–269. DOI: 10.1007/s11412-011-9136-6

Börner, K., Scrivner, O., Gallant, M., Ma, S., Liu, X., Chewning, K., Wu, L., & Evans, J. A. (2018). Skill discrepancies between research, education, and jobs reveal the critical need to supply soft skills for the data economy. *Proceedings of the National Academy of Sciences of the United States of America*, *115*(50), 12630–12637. DOI: 10.1073/pnas.1804247115 PMID: 30530667

Connelly, F. M., & Clandinin, D. J. (1990). Stories of Experience and Narrative Inquiry. *Educational Researcher*, *19*(5), 2–14. DOI: 10.3102/0013189X019005002

De Rosa, A. S., Mannarini, T., Gil de Montes, L., Holman, A., Lauri, M. A., Negura, L., & Lubinga, E. (2021). Sensemaking processes and social representations of COVID-19 in multi-voiced public discourse: Illustrative examples of institutional and media communication in ten countries. *Community Psychology in Global Perspective*, *7*(1), 13–53.

Delello, J. A., McWhorter, R. R., Roberts, P., Dockery, H. S., De Giuseppe, T., & Corona, F. (2021). The rise of esports: Insights into the perceived benefits and risks for college students. [IJER]. *International Journal of eSports Research*, *1*(1), 1–19. DOI: 10.4018/IJER.20210101.oa5

Deming, D. J. (2018). *The value of soft skills in the labor market*. National Bureau of Economic Research. https://www.nber.org/reporter/2017number4/value-soft-skills-labor-market

Duterte, J. P. (2024). Technology-Enhanced learning environments: Improving engagement and learning. *International Journal of Research and Innovation in Social Science*, *8*(10), 1305–131. DOI: 10.47772/IJRISS.2024.8100111

Esports Wales. (2024). *Esports Wales set to inspire at BETT 2024*. Esports Wales. https://esportswales.org/esports-wales-set-to-inspire-at-bett-2024/\

Falkenthal, E., & Byrne, A. M. (2021). Distributed leadership in collegiate esports. *Simulation & Gaming*, *52*(2), 185–203. DOI: 10.1177/1046878120958750

Feng, J. (2024). *University students' participation and opinions on esports in China: An empirical research. Asian Journal of Sport History & Culture*. DOI: 10.1080/27690148.2024.2395954

Hamari, J., & Sjöblom, M. (2017). What is eSports and why do people watch it? *Internet Research*, *27*(2), 211–232. DOI: 10.1108/IntR-04-2016-0085

Huss, J. A. (2023). *Gen Z students are filling our online classrooms: Do our teaching methods need a reboot?* InSight: A Journal of Scholarly Teaching, 18, 101-110. https://files.eric.ed.gov/fulltext/EJ1407503.pdf

Jenny, S. E., Manning, R. D., Keiper, M. C., & Olrich, T. W. (2017). Virtual(ly) athletes: Where esports fit within the definition of "sport.". *Quest*, *69*(1), 1–18. DOI: 10.1080/00336297.2016.1144517

Khan, I. A., & Al-Shibami, A. H. (2019). Generation Z's learning preferences: Impact on organizational learning and development-a study conducted in a vocational institute in UAE. *International Journal of Learning and Change, 11*(4), 379–399.

Kimathi, K. (2024). *Strategic Communication in Esports: Predictive analysis and Optimization for team Performance* (Master's thesis, University of Twente).

Li, M., Ma, S., & Shi, Y. (2023). Examining the effectiveness of gamification as a tool promoting teaching and learning in educational settings: A meta-analysis. *Frontiers in Psychology, 14*, 1253549. DOI: 10.3389/fpsyg.2023.1253549 PMID: 37876838

Miami University. (2023, October 14). *Miami University eSports Panel* [Video]. YouTube. https://youtu.be/b2jN8SBQ9Ig

Miller, C. H. (2004). *Digital storytelling: A creator's guide to interactive entertainment*. Focal Press.

NACE StarLeague. (2023, July 22). *Dunwoody Hawks vs Fort Lewis College Skyhawks | COD: Modern Warfare 3 | NACE StarLeague Playoffs* [Video]. YouTube. https://youtu.be/bEoFcijlR78

Naeem, M., Ozuem, W., Howell, K. E., & Ranfagni, S. (2023). A step-by-step process of thematic analysis to develop a conceptual model in qualitative research. *International Journal of Qualitative Methods, 22*, 16094069231205789. Advance online publication. DOI: 10.1177/16094069231205789

National Academies of Sciences, Engineering, and Medicine. (2018). *How people learn II: Learners, contexts, and cultures*. The National Academies Press.

National Association of Colleges and Employers. (2021). *Career readiness defined.* NACE https://www.naceweb.org/docs/default-source/default-document-library/2024/resources/nace-career-readiness-competencies-revised-apr-2024.pdf?sfvrsn=1e695024_3

National Association of Colleges and Employers (NACE). (2021). *NACE Report 2021*. https://www.naceweb.org/about-us/

National Soft Skills Association. (2023). *Research and best practices in soft skills*. National Soft Skills Association. https://www.nationalsoftskills.org

Newzoo. (2021). *Newzoo's global esports & live streaming market report 2021 (free version)*. https://newzoo.com/resources/trend-reports/newzoos-global-esports-live-streaming-market-report-2021-free-version

Nielson, R., & Hanghoj, T. (2019). *Esports skills are people skills*. ResearchGate., DOI: 10.34190/GBL.19.041

Nikolić, J. L., & Lazarević, S. (2022). Employer Branding and Employee Value Proposition for Generation Z in Digital Economy. Marketing (0354-3471), 53(3). OpenAI. (2024). Response generated by ChatGPT (July 21, 2024). https://chat.openai.com/

Polkinghorne, D. (1988). *Narrative knowing and the human sciences*. State University of New York Press.

Prensky, M. (2001). Digital natives, digital immigrants. *On the Horizon*, *9*(5), 1–6. DOI: 10.1108/10748120110424816

Roth, E. (2017, April 6). *It's official: The AP style guide spells it esports, not eSports, e-sports or eSports*. Yahoo! Sports. https://sports.yahoo.com/its-official-the-ap-style-guide-spells-it-esports-not-esports-e-sports-or-esports-233434245.html

Rothwell, G., & Shaffer, M. (2019). eSports in K-12 and Post-Secondary schools. *Education Sciences*, *9*(2), 105. DOI: 10.3390/educsci9020105

Singer, J. A. (2004). Narrative identity and meaning making across the adult lifespan: An introduction. *Journal of Personality*, *72*(3), 437–460. DOI: 10.1111/j.0022-3506.2004.00268.x PMID: 15102034

Singh, R. (2025). Revamping Employee Experience for the Next Generation Workforce. In *Approaching Employee Experience Management With Data Science* (pp. 65–94). IGI Global Scientific Publishing. DOI: 10.4018/979-8-3693-7848-9.ch003

Student Affairs Administrators, N. A. S. P. A. (2019, June 5). *Esports: Promoting student success in and out of the classroom* [Video]. YouTube. https://www.youtube.com/watch?v=FTaJuqV1bJs

Taylor, T. L. (2015). *Raising the stakes: E-sports and the professionalization of computer gaming*. Mit Press.

Techopedia. (n.d.). *What is location-aware?* https://www.techopedia.com/definition/29929/location-aware

The List Show TV. (2019, May 29). *How esports is changing the world* [Video]. YouTube. https://www.youtube.com/watch?v=OAiCjNg3pZY

Vlada, I. P., Galina, A. M., Elena, A. P., & Yuliya, V. M. (2019). Features of mental activity of students-Esport players. *International Journal of Cognitive Research in Science. Engineering and Education*, *7*(2), 67–76.

Vlasova, H. (2022, March 21). *Online education statistics—How COVID-19 changed the way we learn*. Admissionsly. https://admissionsly.com/online-education-statistics/

Vygotsky, L. (1978). *Mind in society*. Harvard University Press.

Yu, E. (2020). Student-inspired optimal online learning design for Generation Z. *The Journal of Educators Online*, *17*(1). https://files.er

Zhong, Y., Guo, K., Su, J., & Chu, S. K. W. (2022). The impact of esports participation on the development of 21st-century skills in youth: A systematic review. *Computers & Education*, *191*, 104640. Advance online publication. DOI: 10.1016/j.compedu.2022.104640

Chapter 3
Navigating the Global Workforce Through Workplace Learning and Professional Development:
Game-Derived Skills as a New Foundational Layer

Christopher H. Slotboom
Gaming@Work, The Netherlands

ABSTRACT

This chapter explores the relationship between video gaming, professional skills, and the evolving landscape of personal development. It begins by examining the digital gap and ongoing digital transformation. A perspective on gaming is presented, focusing on software usage among working adults, and gaming as a participation goal. Core game-derived skills are categorized into somatic, visual, cognitive, emotional, and social skills, highlighting their relevance in enhancing workforce innovation and adaptability. The chapter addresses access and equity in skill development, emphasizing success stories and socio-economic barriers, while considering changing perceptions of gaming. It delves into game development, gaming professionally and esports, presenting leisure and hybrid forms of gaming as vital components of modern life. The chapter concludes by visualizing the Locktree Gaming Quadrant and the Gaming & Esports Pyramid, outlining their implications for future workforce needs and the balance between performance and relaxation in gaming practices.

DOI: 10.4018/979-8-3373-5322-7.ch003

THE DIGITAL GAP

Figure 1. "Tennis for Two" from 1958, the world's first recreational video game

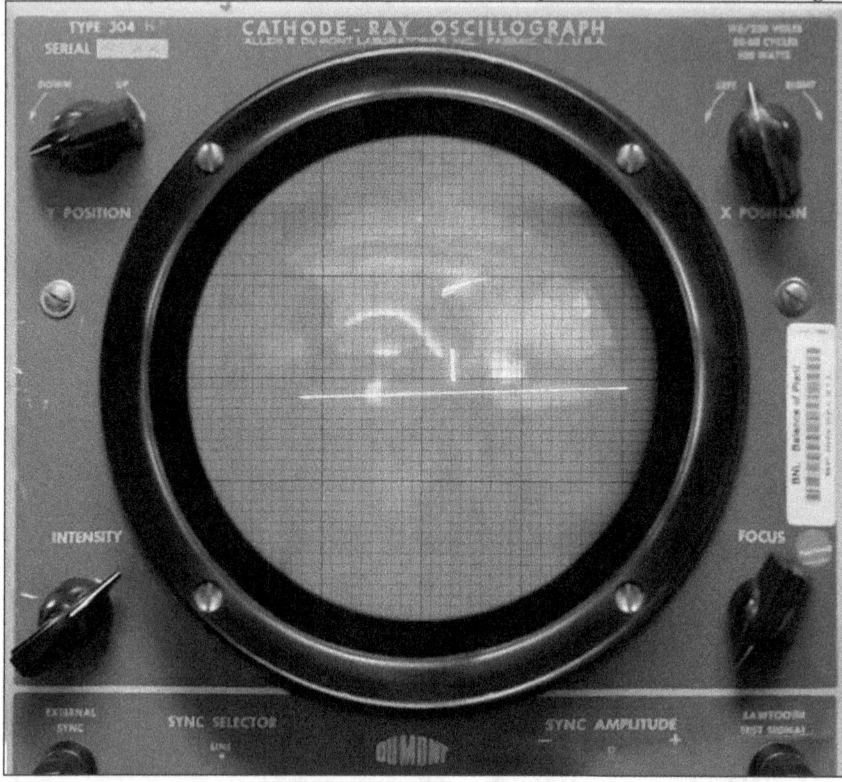

The digital divide, also known as the digital gap, represents the discrepancy between those who have easy access to digital tools and technology, versus those who do not. Globally, 2.6 billion people remain offline as of 2023 (International Telecommunication Union, 2023). Many deeper dimensions of the digital divide, such as digital literacy and the ability to meaningfully engage with technology, remain more difficult to measure or address comprehensively. This gap is a multi-faceted societal issue that encompasses economic, educational, and technological dimensions (Van Dijk, 2020). At its core, the digital gap is not merely about access to devices or internet connectivity (Valdez & Javier, 2021); it also involves the ability to effectively understand the nature of digital tools, participate in digital economies or communities, and leverage digital skills for personal and professional growth. As we continue to evolve in a technology-driven world, bridging this gap becomes increasingly critical to build sustainable and resilient digital societies (United Nations, 2018) with equitable opportunities for all. The digital gap is also visible in healthcare. As chronic conditions and age-related impairments become more prevalent, finding solutions to support physical function, access and independence using digital means is crucial (Saeed & Masters, 2021).

Continued Digital Transformation

Understanding game-derived skills is not merely about validating the benefits of gaming; it's about strategically leveraging these skills to support digital transformation efforts on a societal scale (Kraus, Jones et al., 2021). If you are not familiar with Digital Transformation, an example can be found in the history of Blockbuster (Davis, Todd, & Higgins, 2013). Its business model was lost to history with the rise of Netflix. This new digital company was a completely digital entertainment offering, built on software, is accessed through the internet browser on any medium with many customizable options that support your particular desired use. This type of service uses a completely digital concept as the starting point, instead of a traditional brick and mortar location that moves into a digital space. Many digitally savvy industries, such as high tech, media, and telecom, are still struggling to fully base their business model around digital services. While 89% of large companies globally have a digital and AI transformation underway, they have only captured 31% of the expected revenue lift and 25% of expected cost savings from the effort (Lamarre et al., 2023).

The continued effort of digital transformation is often referred to as digital maturity or digital evolution. This phase involves not just adopting digital tools but fully integrating them into the organizational culture and operations. Companies in this stage focus on continuous innovation, leveraging advanced technologies like artificial intelligence, machine learning, and data analytics to create new business models and enhance customer experiences. They also prioritize agility, resilience, and the ability to rapidly adapt to changing market conditions.

Software Transferable Skills

A promising solution to this digital divide can be found in the concept of game-derived skills (GDS). Game-derived skills are the competencies developed through interacting with video game software, such as strategic thinking, learning, incremental intelligence, teamwork, problem-solving, and STEM-proficiency (Dekker, 2023). These are skills developed through video gaming experiences, which are directly transferable to real-world tasks and challenges, particularly in digital environments. GDS encompass a wide range of competencies, from cognitive and emotional skills to social and even technical abilities in context of 21st century skills. However, research has shown that the extent to which educational domains taught these skills vary considerably (Howard et al., 2021; Siddiq et al., 2016). Recognizing the value of these skills is pivotal, as they form a foundational layer that can help bridge the digital gap.

VIDEO GAMING PERSPECTIVE

Software Usage Among Working Adults

In today's digital age, software has become an integral part of the workplace, significantly influencing productivity, communication, and overall employee engagement. The usage of various software applications ranges from project management tools to collaboration platforms and specialized industry software. According to a recent survey by Statista (2023), approximately 70% of working adults utilize at least five different software tools daily, illustrating the diverse technological ecosystem within modern work environments.

The effective use of software not only enhances operational efficiency but also fosters collaboration among teams, bridging gaps between remote and in-office workers. For instance, tools like *Slack*, *Microsoft Teams*, and *Zoom* have revolutionized how teams communicate, enabling real-time interaction and seamless information sharing. This technological shift supports the concept of a 'hybrid workplace,' where flexibility and adaptability are paramount for both employers and employees.

Moreover, the rise of software usage among working adults aligns with the increasing demand for digital literacy skills. A 2023 report by the World Economic Forum highlights that over 60% of global GDP now depends on digital technologies, underscoring the critical importance of digital proficiency in today's workforce. As digital transformation continues to shape economic growth, developing skills in digital tools has become essential for career advancement. Organizations that invest in upskilling their employees not only boost productivity but also foster greater job satisfaction and improve retention rates. For 49% of employees, the opportunity to learn new skills is a key factor when deciding whether to stay with their employer (PwC, 2024). Specifically in software engineering, Gartner (2024) predicts that 80% of the workforce needs to upskill by 2027 in order to keep up with continuous development.

However, the reliance on software also presents challenges, such as potential burnout from constant connectivity and the need for robust cybersecurity measures to protect sensitive data. Addressing these challenges is essential for creating a sustainable work environment that maximizes the benefits of software while minimizing associated risks.

In conclusion, software usage among working adults is a critical factor in enhancing workplace dynamics. As technology continues to evolve, organizations must adapt by providing the necessary resources and training to empower employees to harness software effectively, ultimately driving organizational success. Video gaming, using game software recreationally, can provide a tool that is currently underdeveloped, even though a substantial amount of people enjoy bi-monthly, up to daily, amounts of use of this software type intrinsically.

Gaming as a Participation Goal

In the past few decades, video gaming (hereafter referred to as 'gaming') has evolved into an incredibly powerful software medium, engaging a significant portion of the global population. Beyond entertainment, video gaming contributes to the development of cognitive abilities and skills, social cohesion, leadership, creativity and social interaction (Dekker & Slotboom, 2023). So, aside from being a source of relaxation, there is a lot to gain from gaming.

As a state-of-the-art form of digital engagement in the 21st century, gaming is incredibly popular among all generations. It has the potential to make a workplace more attractive to both new talent and experienced employees. The use of gaming is also interesting for building relationships with new collaboration partners, investors, clients, or even for finding love.

Eighty percent of all gamers are over the age of 18, with 45 percent identifying as female. More than 90 percent of young people are gamers. In every workplace, there are employees who game to varying degrees.

The concept of lifestyle can be described as a group phenomenon in which groups of individuals consistently share a set of beliefs, display specific behaviors, and express themselves similarly to other members of the party (Dutra, 2021). In relation to playing video games together, this means that a sense of belonging is created. This falls in line with Maslow's Hierarchy of Needs (Maslow, 1954).

Videogames are becoming more significant and influential in contemporary society, demonstrating advanced artistic sophistication with the power of software development. Since the inception of the first video game, Tennis for Two in 1958, **figure 1**, the technology has evolved considerably, now engaging with issues that are also happening in traditional arts, including aesthetics, representation, narrative, emotional engagement, and morality, areas extensively examined in art philosophy. Tavinor (2009) suggests that philosophical aesthetics offers a unique perspective for understanding video games.

Gaming as a Means

Since the 1950s, gaming has evolved from a commercially available leisure activity into a powerful tool for developing essential skills needed in the 21st century. Research indicates that gaming positively impacts cognitive and social skills, which are crucial for performing daily work tasks effectively. By incorporating gaming into workplace training and development programs, companies can enhance employee skills while fostering a more relaxed and engaging atmosphere (Jones et al., 2014; Granic et al., 2014).

The implementation of gaming strategies in the workplace is not limited to skill development. It also encourages team collaboration and problem-solving through interactive and immersive experiences. For instance, multiplayer online games can help improve communication and teamwork as employees learn to strategize and make decisions together. Such experiences can translate to improved cooperation and innovation in real-world projects.

Moreover, a healthy workplace environment is vital for employee well-being and productivity. The World Health Organization (WHO, 2017) indicates that well-designed workspaces can reduce absenteeism and operational costs by up to 27 percent. Understanding ergonomics and creating a supportive environment can significantly mitigate physical complaints among employees (Robertson et al., 2013; Vink, 2009). By integrating gaming elements that promote movement and engagement, companies can also enhance physical well-being, making the workplace more conducive to health and productivity. Additionally, various companies are increasingly leveraging video games and gamification as part of their corporate culture. They use gamified systems to motivate employees, reward achievements, and build a sense of community within the workforce. Research shows that gamification can trigger different emotional responses depending on whether employees are digital natives or digital immigrants, impacting adoption and engagement with new systems (Ebermann et al., 2016). This approach fosters a collaborative ecosystem where technology, software, and technical expertise intertwine, leading to innovative solutions and enhanced performance.

In summary, gaming serves as a multifaceted tool in the workplace, promoting skill development, enhancing team dynamics, and contributing to a healthier work environment. By recognizing the potential of gaming and effectively integrating it into workplace practices, organizations can empower their employees and drive organizational success.

CORE GAME-DERIVED SKILLS

Games can serve as effective tools for building a variety of skills useful in daily life, with numerous positive outcomes achievable through gaming. They are called game-derived skills (GDS), according to Dekker and Slotboom (2023). The specific benefits one gains from gaming depend on the game's content, context and how it is played. However, it is also important to be aware of potential drawbacks.

The difference between analog game-derived skills (skills acquired from offline, non-digital games like board games, card games, and tabletop RPGs) and digital game-derived skills (skills gained from playing video or computer games) lies in the nature of the games themselves, the environments they create, and the ways in which they engage players. While there is considerable overlap in some skill sets, the contexts and modes of engagement in analog and digital games result in different emphases and types of skills developed.

Many of the skills acquired from gaming can be applied directly or indirectly to real-world scenarios (Dekker & Slotboom, 2023). Engaging with different types of games can strengthen various abilities, including social skills, cognitive processing, physical coordination, and emotional resilience. Below is a deeper exploration of the key skills that games can help develop.

Dekker Gaming Skill Overview

To provide a clear and structured understanding of the game-derived skills discussed, the following 'Dekker Gaming Skill Overview' model visually categorizes the various skills and their development through different types of games. This figure serves as a roadmap for the detailed exploration of core game-derived skills in the subsequent sections.

Using the 'Dekker Gaming Skill Overview' model, shown in **figure 2**, provides a structured game-derived skills framework for understanding these in more detail. The model illustrates how different types of skills are developed, categorized into specific domains such as somatic functions, cognitive abilities, emotional regulation, and social interaction and vision. Notably, the model also accounts for common health-related challenges such as insomnia, anxiety, and musculoskeletal complications, highlighting how gaming strategies and interventions can support the management and relief of these issues. This overview will serve as a comprehensive guide to navigating the diverse impact of gaming on skill acquisition.

With this overview as a reference, we can now delve into the specifics of how games influence skill development across different areas, including sustained attention, mental rotation, reading activities, the ability to learn, adaptive regulation and inclusion. This model will guide through the nuances of how various gaming experiences contribute to skill enhancement and real-world applications. With this overview as a reference, we can now delve into the specifics of how games influence skill development across different areas, including sustained attention, mental rotation, reading activities, the ability to learn, adaptive regulation and inclusion. This model will guide through the nuances of how various gaming experiences contribute to skill enhancement and real-world applications.

Figure 2. Dekker video gaming skill overview (DGSO)

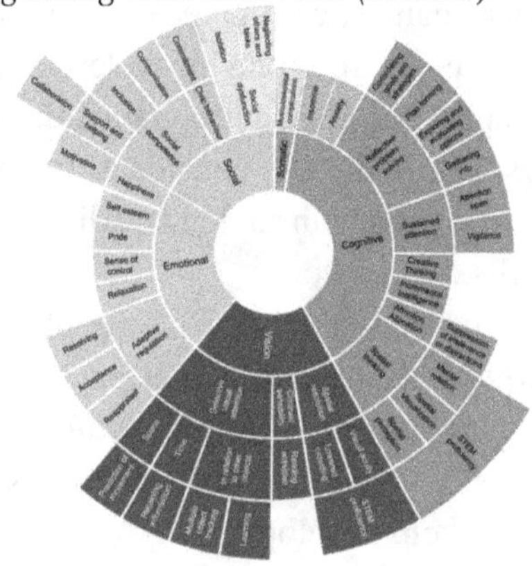

Somatic Game-Derived Skills

Motor Function and Physical Engagement

Analog Games: Analog games enhance fine motor skills, hand-eye coordination, and physical dexterity through activities that involve manipulating physical components. Examples include card manipulation in games like *Bridge*, solving physical puzzles like *Jenga*, and managing miniature pieces in games using *Warhammer*. These activities also require spatial reasoning and handling of various physical components, further developing motor skills and cognitive abilities related to space and object manipulation. There is also an education version of *Warhammer*, that can be used to combine these benefits with creativity.

Digital Games: With the use of controllers, keyboards and other inputs, the hand-eye coordination, reflexes, and fine motor skills related to the digital inputs are improved. 3D printing has been expanding the applicability of inputs by making the input devices even more accessible (Matthews, 2024). Action games and shooters are particularly effective at developing these skills as they demand rapid processing of visual information and precise movements. Games that require quick reflexes also contribute to better motor coordination and reaction time. Additionally, exergaming (a form of blended electronic sports) provides new opportunities to explore and enhance active physical engagement and motor skills. Games like *Zwift* fall into this category. Games are increasingly utilized for fitness training and rehabilitation (Bleakley et al., 2015). Extended gaming sessions, however, can impact physical stamina and ergonomics. Balancing digital activities with physical exercise is crucial for maintaining a healthy lifestyle.

Motor Coordination and Reflexive Decision-Making

Analog Games: Using games, such as card games or physical puzzles, contribute to improved motor coordination and reaction time through the manipulation of physical objects. Activities like card shuffling, puzzle-solving, and managing game pieces enhance hand-eye coordination and fine motor skills. These games often require players to execute precise movements and adjust to dynamic physical environments, which can positively affect overall reaction times.

Digital Games: Especially in action and shooting genres, digital games offer significant benefits for motor coordination and reaction time. Research shows that gamers often have faster reaction times, better sustained attention, and enhanced spatial thinking abilities, such as spatial perception, mental rotation, and spatial visualization (Eichenbaum, 2014; Uttal et al., 2013). These skills are crucial for tasks such as map reading and navigation (van Zoest, 2015). In addition, digital games improve the speed and accuracy of attention allocation, which is beneficial for tasks requiring focus and quick reflexes, such as searching and driving (Hubert-Wallander, Green, & Bavelier, 2010). Through the use of blended electronic sports, exergaming, and other options, there are increasing ways to explore and enhance these skills, while managing health issues shown in **Figure 3**.

Figure 3. Somatic and cognitive game-derived skills

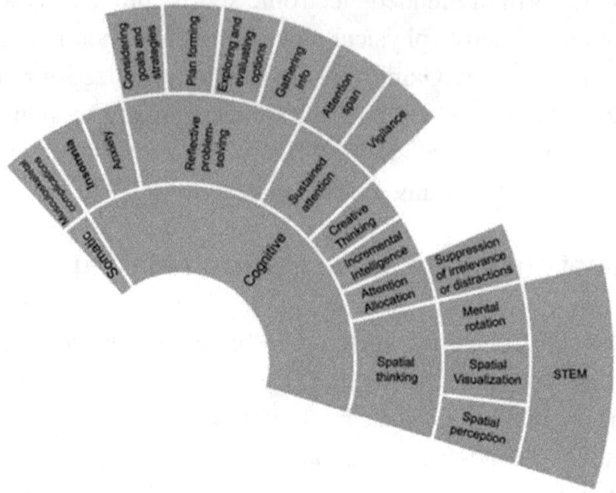

Cognitive Game-Derived Skills

Technical Prowess and Digital Literacy

Analog Games: 'Digital natives' of today think differently (Bennett & Kervin, 2008). It was concluded that there is no need for panic, but the relationship with technology among the younger generation is complex. According to Bawden (2008), digital literacy encompasses a broad set of skills that go beyond technical ability to include critical thinking and the effective use of digital tools. Using (serious) analog games to address this can be a viable way to apply didactic teaching, requiring minimal technical or digital skills. Participants thrive more deeply due to game rules, mechanics, and real-world problem-solving scenarios. An interesting example is Spintronics from science presenter Steve Mould (2022), who demonstrates mechanical circuits without using electricity. Other methods being used outside traditional classroom models include active learning approaches with escape rooms and breakout games (Fotaris & Mastoras, 2019). These are increasingly used in academia as methods for peer-group experiences.

Digital Games: Digital games significantly enhance digital literacy by involving players in understanding interfaces, navigating complex systems, troubleshooting technical issues, and using various game-related software or tools. This is IT-adjacent; however, the core focus is the underlying ability to understand the technological process. Immersive game-based learning environments allow players to engage directly with content, promoting complex problem-solving and strategic thinking which, in turn, enhances cognitive abilities. Educational games designed specifically for learning purposes offer interactive experiences that make complex subjects and processes more accessible and engaging by integrating learning seamlessly into gameplay. Furthermore, multiplayer and online interactions foster collaboration and communication skills. Modding game communities and digital content creation also play a role as a means to increase computational creativity (Grace & Maher, 2021). It allows for players to refine technical skills as they modify game elements and create new content. The use of virtual reality (VR) and augmented reality (AR) within digital games introduces innovative ways to experience and interact with content, expanding digital literacy. These immersive experiences not only improve technical proficiency but also stimulate creativity and innovation among players.

Strategic Evaluation and Plan Forming

Analog Games: Well-known board games like Checkers or Settlers of Catan require long-term strategic planning and a deep understanding of rules and mechanics. Additionally, a longitudinal study using data from the Chinese Longitudinal Healthy Longevity Survey (CLHLS) from 2008 to 2018 found that frequent participation in Mahjong was associated with significantly slower cognitive decline among older adults. The study highlights improvements in domains such as attention, reaction time, calculation, and self-coordination (Zhu et al., 2024). While not designed to measure cognitive abilities explicitly, the findings suggest that analog games can support skills like strategic thinking, pattern recognition, spatial reasoning, and attention to detail. Recent research also indicates that both analog and digital games can effectively train systematic thinking skills, including strategic evaluation and flexible problem-solving, which are essential for complex decision-making (Mitsea et al., 2024)

Digital Games: Real-time decision-making, multitasking, and rapid problem-solving is often involved in digital games as shown in **Figure 3** as well. This is evident in real-time strategy game *StarCraft* (Vinyals et al., 2019), first-person shooter *Call of Duty*, and role-playing games (RPGs) like *The Witcher* and *Horizon: Zero Dawn,* all of which enhance skills related to quick thinking, reflexes, and adaptive strategy. Reflective problem-solving abilities, such as gathering information, evaluating options, formulating plans, and adapting strategies, are often addressed in role-playing, strategy, and puzzle games. This is commonly used in battle royale video games. Open-ended games like *World of Warcraft*, *Pokémon*, *Final Fantasy*, and *Portal* show this as well, because they provide minimal instruction on how to solve in-game challenges (Granic et al., 2014; Prensky, 2012).

Creativity and Innovation

Analog Games: Through storytelling, tabletop RPG's such as *Dungeons & Dragons* provide platforms for players to invent characters, narratives, and scenarios collaboratively. TIME Magazine (2024) celebrated the game's 50th anniversary with a special edition. D&D contains a set of rules with imaginative problem-solving environment with open-ended setting (Sidhu et al., 2024). The use of traditional board games also make it possible to design autism interventions (Atherton et al., 2021) that target specific skills and are used as pedagogical resources.

Digital Games: Games like *Cities: Skylines*, *Factorio*, and *Satisfactory* offer innovative ways to harness creativity through complex systems and building mechanics. *Minecraft* is also an option, a powerful digital tool that nurtures creativity by allowing players to design and build complex worlds, providing an open-ended platform that encourages imaginative problem-solving and innovative thinking (Nebel et al., 2016). *Minecraft* has been shown to support creativity by offering a dynamic, interactive platform that engages users in authentic creating and crafting experiences, which are valuable for assessing and nurturing creative potential (Shaw, 2022).

Vision Game-Derived Skills

Spatial Resolution

Analog Games: Spatial resolution can be improved through analog games like *Tangrams* and *Pentominoes* (Danesi. 2018). These games involve arranging shapes in precise configurations, which enhances a player's ability to mentally visualize spatial relationships. As another example, in *Go*, players must predict how their stones will interact with the grid over time, developing spatial awareness and foresight. These types of games foster spatial thinking, a skill that is essential in fields like architecture, engineering, and robotics, where understanding spatial configurations is crucial.

Digital Games: Digital action video games such as *Valorant* and *Fortnite* offer immersive environments that require players to develop high levels of spatial resolution and multi-object tracking. In these games, players navigate complex terrains, locate targets, and coordinate movements in 3D space, all while managing spatially distributed threats. The ability to rapidly interpret and respond to these dynamic environments sharpens spatial reasoning, which is critical for success in STEM careers. Research shows that these games enhance visual crowding, contrast sensitivity, and visual acuity (Eichenbaum, 2014). Studies by Green and Bavelier (2003), as well as Dye, Green, and Bavelier (2009), demonstrate how action video games improve the ability to perceive visual details in crowded scenes and adapt to varying visual conditions, making them valuable cognitive training tools. Review these skills in **figure 4**.

Figure 4. Vision game-derived skills

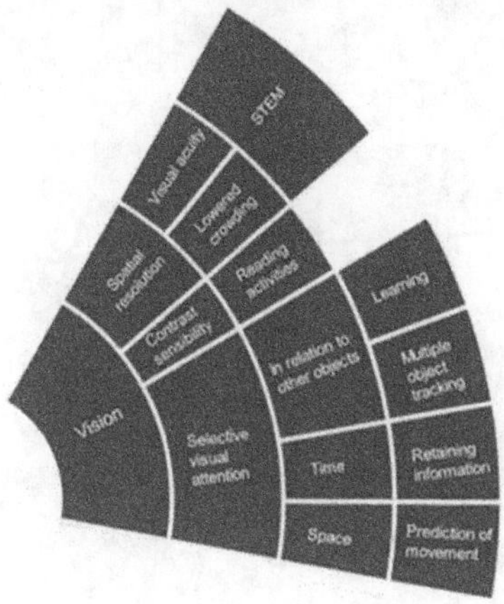

Visual Acuity and Selective Attention

Analog Games: Analog games like *Spot It!* or *Where's Waldo?* challenge players to find specific objects or details within busy visual scenes. In case of *Spot It!*, there is a possible explanation, due to the mathematical relation to geometry (Sengupta, 2016; Lara, 2023). These games require keen visual acuity to distinguish between subtle visual differences and focus on relevant information amidst distractions. The cognitive demand of locating small details or patterns improves selective attention, which is essential for everyday tasks like reading, map navigation, or analyzing visual data in fields like biology or geology.

Digital Games: In digital action games like *PUBG: Battlegrounds* or *Overwatch*, players need to accurately spot enemies and objectives in visually cluttered environments. These games train visual acuity by forcing players to discern small, moving objects at different distances and under varying light conditions. It also induces plasticity (Li et al., 2011). The ability to focus on critical visual cues while ignoring irrelevant stimuli enhances selective attention, a skill applicable in high-pressure tasks such as air traffic control, surgical procedures, or even athletic performance, where rapid decision-making is key.

Figure 5. Emotional game-derived skills

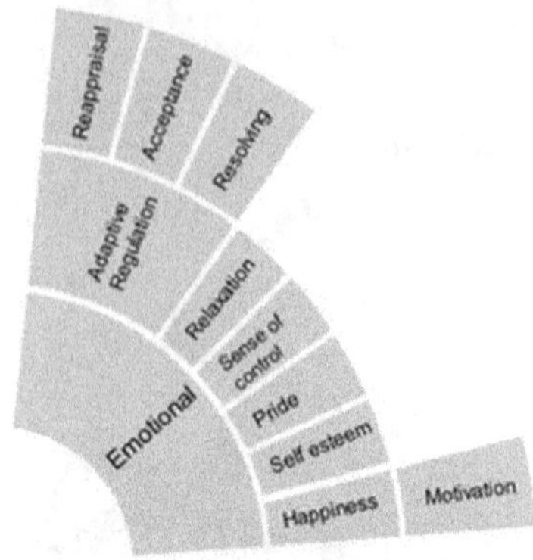

Emotional Game-Derived Skills

Emotion Regulation and Resilience

Analog games: Board games and card games require players to handle their emotions in a social setting. The direct competition and social interaction in analog games teach resilience by exposing players to immediate consequences of their actions and the unpredictability of human opponents. This is useful for emotional competencies, especially during childhood or older adults (Cès et al., 2024).

Digital Games: Managing emotions such as frustration or excitement during gameplay can enhance players' emotional control through real-time interactions and feedback from other players (McGonigal, 2011). Digital games offer a safe environment to experience and regulate a wide range of emotions. The skills are explained in **figure 5**. Features like respawns and retry options allow players to practice resilience by making repeated attempts and recovering quickly from failure. This iterative process helps players learn persistence and adaptability, building resilience in a virtual setting without real-world consequences (Nakamura, 2002; Ferguson, 2015).

Additionally, engaging in gameplay can lead to a state of flow, where players become fully immersed and focused on the task at hand. This state not only enhances emotional engagement but also fosters coping mechanisms for managing setbacks and adapting to new challenges (Granic et al., 2014; Jones et al., 2014).

Mihaly Csikszentmihalyi (1975) introduced a concept of "flow", explained in **figure 6**, as a chart that maps the relationship between challenge and ability. This was part of his broader research on optimal experiences and happiness. The chart illustrates the balance between challenge and ability, highlighting how different levels of each can lead to states such as stress, flow, or boredom.

Figure 6. Concept of "Flow" by Professor Mihaly Csikszentmihalyi

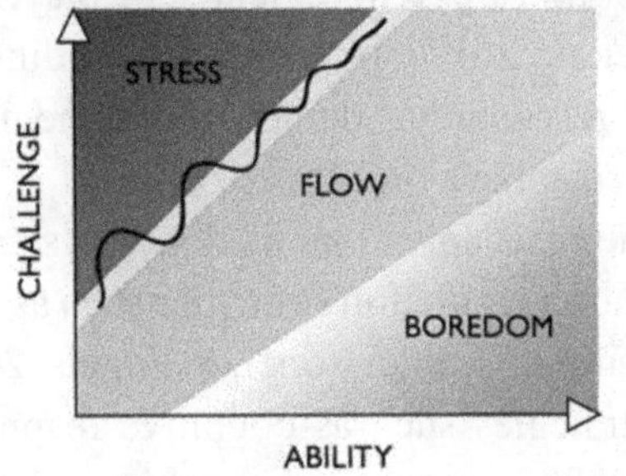

Pride and Self-Esteem

Analog Games: Achievements and victories in analog games can contribute to a sense of pride as players experience success in a tangible, social setting. The social nature of analog games means that feedback and recognition from peers can directly impact players' self-esteem. A game like *The Grizzled* is heightened by its willingness to tackle uncomfortable topics like trauma, discouragement and persistence (Trammell et al., 2017).

Digital Games: Digital games provide opportunities for players to achieve goals and earn rewards that can contribute to a sense of pride. Virtual achievements and leaderboards allow players to experience pride in their accomplishments, often without the immediate social context of analog games (McGonigal, 2011). In digital games, players often receive instant feedback and rewards that can enhance self-esteem. Achievements, progression, and recognition within the game can contribute to a sense of accomplishment and boost confidence in a virtual environment (Fredrickson, 2001). Winning or accomplishing goals in front of others in a cyber environment can enhance feelings of pride and accomplishment (Lafreniere et al., 2013). Successes and positive interactions during digital gameplay can boost confidence and self-worth (Granic et al., 2014).

Reappraisal and Acceptance

Analog Games: Players often need to reframe their strategies and adjust their approaches based on the evolving game situation and opponents' actions. However, when the opponent is one's psychological self, playful mindfulness exercises might apply (Sliwinski et al., 2017). In general, according to Berger et al. (2018), an increasing amount of research has demonstrated the numerous positive effects that play and playfulness can have on life satisfaction.

Digital Games: Game mechanics like feedback systems and in-game rewards help players practice emotion regulation strategies such as reappraisal and problem-solving in a controlled setting (Granic, Lobel, & Engels, 2014). Players can engage in emotion-regulation strategies such as cognitive reappraisal while adapting to in-game feedback and evolving scenarios, as explored in clinical settings (Aldao, Nolen-Hoeksema & Schweizer, 2010). Digital games often provide a space for players to accept failure and quickly try again, thanks to features like respawns and retry options. This virtual setting allows players to practice accepting mistakes and adjusting their approach without real-world implications, which helps them practice cognitive reappraisal in a social context. Additionally, the need to handle both wins an0d losses in front of others reinforces acceptance and adaptability (Granic et al., 2014).

Social Game-Derived Skills

Learning Environments and Feedback

Analog games: In RPGs and board games, immersive learning environments are created through direct human interaction. Feedback in these games is generated by players or a game master, fostering a social and community-driven atmosphere. Players receive real-time responses and guidance from others, which enhances collaboration and communication. The rules are typically explained and enforced through human mediation, requiring players to actively engage with and interpret them. This setup promotes deeper understanding and adaptability, as players negotiate, strategize, and learn from one another's experiences in a dynamic, face-to-face setting.

*Digital Games:*Daniau (2016) and Deterding and Zagal (2018) highlight that advancements in technology have sparked increased interest in using digital role-playing games in education. These games are seen as having significant educational potential compared to other types because they let students engage in various educational scenarios and control avatar characters in fictional settings. Digital games provide structured and immediate feedback through features like scoring systems, achievements, and algorithm-driven responses from non-player characters. This automated feedback is tailored to the player's performance, offering personalized learning experiences. Research shows that such gamified digital environments significantly improve student motivation and learning outcomes, particularly in subjects like mathematics (Fadda et al., 2022). GenAI responses offer even more diversity. Additionally, digital games ensure consistent rule enforcement through programming, which maintains uniformity across sessions. The feedback mechanism helps players quickly grasp the effects of their actions and make necessary adjustments, facilitating accurate tracking of progress and skill development. This approach is particularly effective in delivering a consistent and measurable method of learning and skill acquisition. Moreover, the diverse learning opportunities presented by digital games align well with the principles of multipotentiality, the idea that individuals can thrive in multiple areas of interest and skill. Players can explore various roles, challenges, and genres within these games, encouraging them to experiment with different strategies and problem-solving techniques. For instance, engaging in role-playing games may foster creativity in storytelling, analytical skills through strategic gameplay, and teamwork through collaborative missions. This multifaceted engagement not only broadens an individual's skill set but also helps them discover new passions and interests, showcasing how digital gaming can cultivate a diverse portfolio of skills essential for personal and professional growth.

Interaction

Analog Games: By requiring face-to-face and physical engagement, often occurring in a shared physical space, skills that are derived from analog games are deeply tied to interpersonal communication, negotiation, and social interaction. Players must engage in real-time, direct communication, reading body language, interpreting tone, and managing in-person dynamics. This direct engagement provides rich opportunities to practice social skills, such as discussing strategies and negotiating with others, which enhance social competence and emotional self-regulation. For instance, engaging in behaviors like mock-fights within game settings can improve brain areas involved in social coordination (Pellis & Pellis, 2007). Cooperative analog games that require players to work together can lead to immediate and long-term improvements in prosocial behavior (Gentile et al., 2009) and help bridge social gaps better than solo or competitive play (Velez et al., 2012). Such cooperative play reduces hostility and aggressive thoughts (Granic et al., 2014; Schmierbach, 2010), demonstrating how in-person gaming experiences can enhance social inclusion and communication skills.

Digital Games: Interaction in digital games is often mediated through a screen and can be either synchronous (e.g., online multiplayer games) or asynchronous (e.g., single-player games or turn-based multiplayer games). These games develop skills related to navigating digital interfaces, virtual collaboration, and online communication, which differ from face-to-face interactions. In digital games, players frequently interact with others through text, voice chat, or avatars, discussing strategies and forming alliances. This provides a unique platform to practice and develop social skills, particularly in online environments. Research shows that digital games with cooperative elements, even those involving violence, can foster more helpful behavior than non-violent games (Ewoldson, 2012; Ferguson, 2011). These skills are visible in **figure 7**. As with analog games, cooperative gaming in digital environments also reduces hostility and aggressive thoughts (Granic et al., 2014; Schmierbach, 2010), promoting social competence and inclusion. Additionally, games with civic themes, like "Civilization" and "The Sims," can increase real-world civic engagement, such as voting and participating in protests (Lenhart, 2008), demonstrating that digital gaming can also boost political involvement and social interaction.

Figure 7. Social game-derived skills

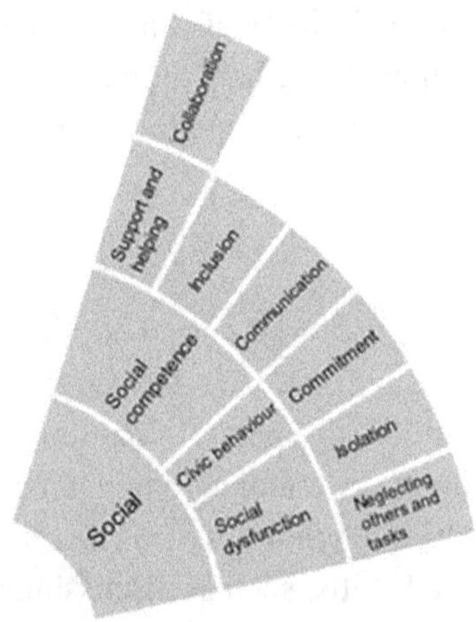

Communication and Emotions

Analog Games: Both verbal and non-verbal communication skills, such as persuasion, empathy, negotiation, and conflict resolution are available. Players engage in direct interaction, which requires them to read social cues, manage in-person relationships, and negotiate in real-time. Managing disagreements and finding solutions in team settings can significantly enhance conflict resolution skills, as players must collaborate and communicate effectively to resolve disputes. RPGs and other narrative-driven analog games involve storytelling and role-playing, which help players understand and empathize with diverse viewpoints and characters. These experiences develop emotional intelligence, active listening, perspective-taking, and managing social dynamics in real-time, as players navigate conflicts and build interpersonal connections.

Digital Games: Digital games focus on developing communication skills like text-based or voice communication in multiplayer settings, digital etiquette, and managing virtual presence. In games with online communities, managing disagreements and finding solutions in team settings enhances conflict resolution and collaboration skills in a virtual context. A significant positive relationship between playing MMOs and social well-being was concluded, irrespective of one's age and/or their casual or immersed gaming patterns (Raith et al., 2021). Furthermore, emotional skills can also be developed through narrative immersion, role-playing, and interacting with virtual characters or avatars, enabling players to understand and empathize with diverse viewpoints. Multiplayer digital games provide opportunities for online collaboration, emotional regulation, and understanding different perspectives, helping to build social and emotional competence. The role-playing aspects of digital games can deepen players' understanding of diverse characters and situations, further enhancing empathy and conflict management skills in digital environments.

Game-Derived Skills Conclusion

In summary, the core game-derived skills encompass a wide array of abilities that extend beyond mere entertainment, impacting various aspects of cognitive, social, and emotional development. Whether through analog or digital games, players can achieve motor coordination, cognitive processing, creativity, spatial resolution, and emotional resilience. These skills are not only valuable within the gaming context, but also translate effectively into real-world scenarios, such as the workplace, aiding in personal and professional growth. If organizations, educational institutions, corporations and non-profit entities are able to leverage these games, then this will have a positive impact on, skills, well-being and productivity.

IMPACT ON WORKFORCE INNOVATION AND ADAPTABILITY

As the digital economy continues to evolve, the nature of work is undergoing rapid transformation. Job roles now increasingly demand skills like strategic thinking, collaboration, and adaptability (Colbert et al., 2016), skills that can be honed through gaming. In a typical gaming environment, adults and children, individuals from diverse backgrounds and life stages come together: a teenager navigating first love, a college student anxious about choosing a major, a sleep-deprived stay-at-home parent, and a war veteran seeking connection (Yee, 2006; Yee, 2014). The skills developed in these dynamic, team-based gaming scenarios, such as effective communication, problem-solving, and emotional intelligence, mirror the competencies required in today's workforce.

Shifts in Hiring Practices

Game-derived skills (GDS) provide a practical foundation for preparing individuals for these ever-changing team environments. For instance, esports professionals display exceptional strategic thinking, computational thinking, quick reflexive decision-making, and seamless team coordination. These are precisely the abilities needed to innovate in the workplace and adapt to emerging technologies like artificial intelligence (AI), machine learning (ML), and big data analytics (Bamela et al., 2022). This alignment between the competencies fostered through gaming and those required in modern work settings underscores the transformative potential of integrating GDS into hiring practices across various sectors.

The integration of GDS into education, healthcare, commercial, public, and non-profit sectors offers innovative pathways for upskilling and reskilling, both of which are crucial in this digital age. By making game-derived skills the foundational layer for understanding technology, organizations can tap into a unique approach to workforce development.

One practical example is the Balloon Analogue Risk Task (BART), a computerized tool that assesses decision-making under uncertainty. Participants earn or lose potential rewards by inflating a virtual balloon, where each additional pump increases both potential earnings and the risk of the balloon bursting (Lejuez et al., 2002). This task is illustrative of how game-based tools can evaluate critical decision-making skills in high-stakes situations, a valuable asset in today's fast-paced work environment. Similar mechanics are found in popular games like *Mario Party 1 and 2*, where a balloon bursting mini-game engages players in balancing risk and reward in an entertaining context.

Game-based assessments are reshaping hiring practices by offering a more engaging and equitable method to evaluate candidates' skills and potential. These assessments, unlike traditional methods, can measure soft skills, reduce bias, and predict job performance through dynamic, interactive experiences. For example, single game-based assessments focus on skills like numeracy, logic, and memory, and are used in various fields ranging from data analysis to digital marketing.

Interactive and job-simulation game-based assessments further enhance the candidate experience by immersing them in work-relevant scenarios, allowing employers to gauge their problem-solving and decision-making abilities in a more realistic context. These tools not only help in identifying the best talent for roles in management, engineering, and healthcare but also emphasize emotional intelligence, which is vital for roles in customer service, sales, and people management.

Ultimately, the use of game-based assessments in hiring reflects a shift towards innovation and adaptability in workforce development, aligning with the demands of a rapidly changing digital economy.

Skills Mapping to Job Roles and Functions

The following overview in **table 1** provides insight into different job roles and how they are relevant to game-derived skills.

Table 1. GDS mapping to job role and function

Game-Derived Skill	Job Role	Industry	Function/Impact
Strategic Thinking	Project Manager	Tech	Developing long-term project plans, managing resources, and adapting strategies to evolving project needs.
Reflexive Decision-Making	Surgeon	Healthcare	Performing precise surgical procedures, making quick decisions in high-pressure situations.
Analytical Skills	Data Analyst	Tech	Analyzing complex data sets, identifying trends, and generating actionable insights for business strategy.
Technical Proficiency	Software Engineer	Tech	Developing, coding, and debugging software applications; staying updated with new technologies.
Digital Literacy	Vocational Teacher	Education	Integrating digital tools into the curriculum, teaching industry-specific software, and staying current with technological advancements.
Spatial Awareness	Architect	Construction/Design	Designing and visualizing architectural plans and spatial layouts; ensuring accurate design implementation.
Adaptive Learning	Customer Service Representative	Retail/Services	Adapting to different customer needs and resolving issues effectively based on interactive training.

continued on following page

Table 1. Continued

Game-Derived Skill	Job Role	Industry	Function/Impact
Teamwork	Military Officer	Military	Coordinating and leading teams in tactical operations, fostering collaboration among team members.
Stress Management	Emergency Response Coordinator	Emergency Services	Managing high-stress situations, making quick decisions, and ensuring effective response to crises.

ACCESS AND EQUITY IN SKILL DEVELOPMENT

Traditional education and training often come with high costs and limited accessibility, especially for marginalized groups (Sissine et al., 2014). In contrast, gaming provides a more inclusive platform for developing skills. Many games are either free or low-cost, offering an interactive and engaging way to learn. Gamification, where game design principles are applied in non-game settings, further broadens access by creating motivating learning environments. However, gamification mechanics are often intertwined with costly organization processes, making them less applicable. For example, gamified educational apps can improve digital skills for those who lack access to conventional educational resources. The effectiveness of educational games in enhancing student engagement is heightened in immersive digital environments (Li et al., 2024). Game-based learning, where the game itself serves as a starting point, could strengthen this effect.

Success Stories

Gaming has emerged as a tool for skill development in communities that have traditionally been underserved by mainstream education systems. Several success stories illustrate the transformative power of gaming for individuals and organizations. For instance, nonprofit organizations like *Games for Change* and *Global Gaming Initiative* use gaming to provide educational outreach in areas such as financial literacy, environmental sustainability, and social justice. In one case, a community center in an economically disadvantaged urban area implemented an esports program that helped students develop digital literacy and teamwork skills, which translated into academic and social improvements (Hall, 2021). Similarly, rural communities have leveraged Game-based learning to close the digital divide, offering students a way to develop technological skills that are essential in today's job market.

In addition, initiatives like *NASEF* (Network of Academic and Scholastic Esports Federation, 2024), which supports scholastic esports programs across North America, Europe, Asia, and beyond, offer an example of how gaming can be used to enhance educational outcomes. By incorporating competitive gaming into school curricula, the alliance helps students develop not only technical gaming skills but also essential soft skills like communication, collaboration, and critical thinking. These programs foster teamwork and create pathways for students to pursue careers in technology and gaming industries.

Depending on the application, a cost-benefit analysis reveals that gaming-based learning can be far more cost-effective than traditional training programs. Traditional education methods often involve significant expenditures, including physical infrastructure, textbooks, and teacher/trainer salaries. By contrast, many digital learning platforms that use intrinsic motivation or reward systems through gamification at a fraction of the cost. For example, platforms like *Kahoot!* and *Duolingo* are either free or offer low-cost subscriptions, making them more accessible to a broader audience. Many casual gaming titles are also offered or low or no cost. Compared to serious game development, utilizing casual games or education versions effectively, the organizational budget can shift from software development to didactic optimization. This affordability can be especially crucial for marginalized communities, where educational resources are limited.

Moreover, the accessibility of various gaming platforms adds another layer of inclusivity. Mobile games, for instance, are widely accessible as smartphones are more integrated into society, even in low-income communities. In contrast, PC or console-based educational games might have higher entry costs due to the need for specialized hardware. However, as internet access and smartphone penetration continue to grow globally, the cost barrier is continually being lowered. Educational apps that integrate game mechanics, such as *Prodigy* or *CodeCombat*, allow users to develop essential skills like mathematics and coding without the prohibitive costs associated with formal schooling.

Socio-Economic Barriers

Platforms in gaming have great potential to break down socio-economic barriers to skill development. Traditional educational resources are often tied to one's location, socio-economic status, and access to physical learning environments, but gaming overcomes these limitations by offering universally accessible and engaging learning environments. In areas where quality education is limited, mobile devices and affordable internet plans enable students to access educational games, helping to level the playing field.

Despite this, challenges remain in certain underserved areas, where access to technology and reliable internet is still an issue. In these cases, partnerships between governments, non-profits, and gaming companies can provide solutions. Programs like *One Laptop per Child* or digital literacy projects in developing countries show how gaming can be used as a tool for both educational and economic advancement.

A key advantage of gaming is its ability to engage learners through interactive experiences. Research indicates that students are more likely to retain knowledge and develop skills in gamified environments where feedback and rewards drive continuous improvement (Li et al., 2024). This is particularly valuable for marginalized groups who face barriers in traditional education, such as racial or gender discrimination. In gaming, success is based on skill and performance, offering a more equitable learning experience.

The Future of Gaming in Marginalized Communities

Looking ahead, the role of gaming in skill development for marginalized communities is poised to expand. The rise of virtual and augmented reality technologies is likely to make gaming even more immersive and educational. These advancements could allow students to gain hands-on experience in fields like architecture, medicine, and engineering areas that have historically been inaccessible to disadvantaged students due to financial or geographical constraints.

In addition, the growing popularity of esports presents new opportunities to integrate gaming into educational curricula. Schools and community centers could offer esports programs that teach both game-specific skills and important soft skills like teamwork, leadership, and strategic thinking. These programs have the potential to level the playing field, providing students from all backgrounds with opportunities to excel and earn scholarships for higher education.

Gaming-based learning also promotes inclusivity by addressing barriers beyond economic ones, such as those related to race, gender, and disability. Esports, for example, can cross racial and gender divides, allowing educators to design inclusive programs that evaluate participants based on skill rather than socio-economic background (Hall, 2021). Additionally, adaptive gaming for learners with disabilities is gaining momentum, allowing a wider range of students to benefit from gamified education.

Conclusion

Gaming offers a unique opportunity to make education and skill development more equitable. By lowering costs, removing socio-economic barriers, and providing engaging and accessible learning environments, gaming has the potential to drive significant social change. As educational institutions, governments, and communities continue to explore and implement game-based learning, the next step is to scale these programs and integrate them into mainstream education. In doing so, the digital divide can be narrowed, giving millions, especially those from marginalized communities, the skills needed to thrive in the digital age.

CHANGING PERCEPTION AROUND GAMING

An important aspect of bridging the digital gap is changing how society perceives the value of skills gained from gaming. Skills like leadership, problem-solving, and empathy, often developed through gaming, are frequently overlooked in traditional educational and professional settings. Many decision-makers, whether they be parents, managers, or policymakers, who may not understand the benefits of gaming, tend to dismiss it as a pastime for children. This is despite the fact that millions of people worldwide have built careers directly or indirectly related to the gaming industry. In fact, the number of individuals enjoying video games as end users now exceeds those engaged with other entertainment sectors combined.

It takes a new way of thinking to understand how a digital creation can have such a profound impact on human life. By recognizing the legitimacy of these game-derived skills, we can better align education and training with the needs of today's digital economy. For many people under 25, digital technology is so deeply integrated into their lives that imagining a world without it is nearly impossible. This idea is reflected in the theory of Shifting Baselines (Burnside, Pauly et al., 1995; Alleway et al., 2023), which suggests that our perceptions of 'normal' are shaped by the environments we grow up in. Alleway and colleagues extended this concept to include broader social and environmental contexts. This deep familiarity with digital technologies fosters adaptability, which is crucial for engaging those who might otherwise feel excluded from digital progress, or in other words, it could leave behind those who are less familiar with these advancements.

Cultural Shifts and Policy Implications

There is still a surprising lack of recognition for gaming as a valid tool for connection and participation, despite research highlighting its importance. International calls emphasize the need for policies that support gaming as part of innovation goals. Efforts have begun to regulate the gaming industry, but the emphasis remains narrow. For example, the EU's *Digital Content Directive* focuses primarily on consumer protection, digital rights, and marketplace fairness (European Parliament & Council of the European Union, 2019). In *Impact of the EU's Digital Content Directive on the Video Games Industry*, policies view games largely as commercial products, rather than as platforms for innovation, civic participation, or skill development. The European Parliament's report *A9-0244/2022* (2022) remarks gaming's dual role as an economic driver and social connector, advocating for harmonized EU policies to address regulatory fragmentation and promote innovation. This contrast reveals a gap between academic research and policy priorities.

Studies, such as those by Mayer (2009), Santo (2021), and Harteveld and Bekebrede (2016), emphasize how gaming can simulate complex policy-making scenarios and engage players with political and social issues in meaningful ways. However, there is a pressing need for policies that recognize and support gaming as a valid component of innovation goals. By integrating gaming into policy frameworks, governments and institutions can foster new pathways for public engagement, improve policy education, and encourage innovative solutions to pressing global challenges.

While the initial costs of gaming technologies can be high, the fast pace of digital change brings new funding opportunities. Solutions like cloud technology and refurbished equipment can help reduce both purchasing and operating costs. Some healthcare providers may still hesitate to accept gaming as a legitimate means of participation, especially since stigmas around gaming persist among older adults. Digital therapeutics (DTx) are slowly becoming more mainstream. DTx company Akili, known for its video game treatment for ADHD, will be acquired for USD 34 million (Grand View Research, 2024). Diabetes and mental health DTx treatments are likely to be imbursed (Lumbreras et al., 2024).

Furthermore, there is a growing acceptance among patients, who see gaming as a valuable way to connect with others, including friends and family. Differences in access to necessary technologies can lead to inequalities in rehabilitation processes. Partnerships with local organizations are helping to improve accessibility and fairness in gaming. However, introducing advanced gaming technologies may present technical challenges and require time to implement. For others, learning to use new tools, like adaptive controllers, can be intimidating and may discourage participation. Moreover, privacy concerns are an ongoing challenge, requiring compliance with established regulations. Finally, the production and use of gaming hardware and software have an ecological impact, making it essential to choose manufacturers that follow environmentally responsible practices. By integrating gaming more closely into societal frameworks, it has the potential to drive societal change at a faster pace, facilitating innovation and expanding avenues for participation and engagement (European Games Developer Federation, 2022).

Results of the Changed Perspective

The shift in perceptions about gaming has significant implications for both individuals and organizations. Digital transformation has reshaped how gaming is utilized, with applications such as esports, serious gaming, gamification, and Game-based learning all playing key roles. Over 3 billion people now see gaming as a major meaningful leisure activity (Newzoo, 2024). Esports, for example, has demonstrated how digital skills can create professional opportunities. Gaming also bridges physical and digital activities, as seen in hybrid sports like exergaming and augmented reality, which enhance traditional sports with sensors and digital environments. Serious games are increasingly used in corporate training to simulate real-world challenges and improve professional skills. Additionally, gamification is widely used in educational and corporate settings to encourage continuous learning and engagement. According to Taborda Mosquera et al. (2021), the growth of video games has accelerated alongside advancements in technology. Gaming across platforms, like the personal computer, console, and mobile, continues to expand with more players joining every year. Organizations such as *Loadout Esports & Gaming* and *Statista* study gaming behaviors and trends, showing how gamers fit into broader consumer markets. For example, 60% of esports fans take gaming seriously enough to play ranked games in Benelux (Loadout Esports & Gaming, personal communication, 2024), and 55% of all U.S. gamers engage with mobile games weekly (Statista, 2024).

Female Gamers: Changing the Narrative

Approximately 45% of gamers worldwide are women (Entertainment Software Association, 2024; Newzoo, 2023), challenging the stereotype that gaming is predominantly a male activity. Acknowledging this diversity is essential for understanding the full landscape of the gaming community. With nearly half of gamers identifying as female, this demographic represents a significant market that gaming companies and developers should consider when crafting content, marketing strategies, and community engagement initiatives. Such awareness can foster more inclusive game design and outreach efforts.

Promoting the involvement of female gamers can encourage other women to participate in gaming, contributing to a more inclusive culture within gaming communities. Greater visibility for female gamers can lead to enhanced representation for women in the gaming industry, providing valuable insights for research on gaming behaviors, preferences, and experiences. Additionally, this representation can influence policy discussions on inclusivity, equity, and fairness within the gaming sector.

Women of diverse backgrounds are also making significant strides in the gaming industry, enriching the community with their diverse contributions. Their participation not only challenges existing stereotypes but also brings unique perspectives and experiences to gaming. Initiatives led by women from this demographic are improving safety, diversity, and career opportunities in the field. This representation is crucial for informing research on gaming behaviors and can shape policies that promote inclusivity and equity in the industry. By enhancing the visibility of women in gaming, there is potential to improve gender equity across various professional sectors.

PLAYING GAMES AND BUILDING GAMES

To differentiate between the various types of gaming, it is important to recognize that video games are software applications. These games are crafted through a blend of simple and complex methodologies, where storylines are created, narrated, and visually represented using computer graphics. Understanding the unique characteristics, purposes, and contexts in which they are used is key to analyzing gaming from the perspective of the end user.

Game development refers to the process of designing and creating these software applications for users. The distinctions between different types of gaming help clarify how each category contributes to the development of game-derived skills and their applications across various settings, ranging from leisure and professional domains to educational and corporate environments. The following section contains an overview that outlines the key differences between several major categories of leisure gaming, competitive gaming, professional gaming, game development and game mechanics outside of games.

Game Development

Similar to other software companies, game development involves the intricate process of designing, creating, testing, and deploying video games. This multifaceted field encompasses various disciplines, including game design, programming, art creation, sound design, and project management. Usually, non-software developers will not easily be able to comprehend this process, as it requires specialized knowledge and skills in each of these areas. Game development transforms creative concepts into interactive experiences through a structured workflow that includes pre-production, production, and post-production phases.

Brief Examples

- Indie Games: Titles like *Celeste* and *Hollow Knight* are examples of games developed by independent studios that often focus on unique gameplay mechanics and storytelling.
- AAA Games: Major franchises such as *The Legend of Zelda: Breath of the Wild* and *Call of Duty* showcase high-budget production values and extensive marketing efforts.
- Mobile Games: Popular mobile titles like *Among Us* and *GenshinImpact* illustrate the trends and innovations within the mobile gaming sector.
- Educational Games: Games like *Minecraft: Education* and *Kahoot!* provide learning experiences while incorporating gameplay mechanics.

Required Investment

High – Developing a game can involve significant financial investment, with costs ranging from a few thousand Dollars for indie games to budgets of millions for AAA titles. Various factors influence these costs, including team size, technology utilized, marketing strategies, and distribution channels. Alongside financial considerations, time investment plays a crucial role in the game development process. Projects can take anywhere from a few months to several years to complete, depending on the complexity and scope of the game. Additionally, development teams typically require access to various resources, including software tools such as *Unity* or *Unreal Engine*, hardware for testing, and potentially a dedicated office space to facilitate collaboration and productivity.

Required Skill

High – The field of game development demands a diverse skill set. Game design involves a deep understanding of gameplay mechanics, storytelling, audio design, and user experience to create engaging gameplay. Programming skills are also essential, with proficiency in languages such as Python, C#, C++, or JavaScript necessary for building game logic and functionality. Game engines, such as *Unity* and *Unreal Engine*, play a pivotal role in this process by providing a framework that integrates various development components, streamlining the creation and management of game assets and mechanics. Many game development organizations leverage their own versions of game engines, which complicates the training of specialists. Furthermore, expertise in art and animation is crucial, requiring skills in graphic design, 3D modeling, and animation, often utilizing tools like *Blender* or *Adobe Creative Suite*. Sound design knowledge is also important, encompassing audio editing and production to create immersive soundscapes and effects. Lastly, effective project management is vital, as it involves coordinating a team, managing timelines, and ensuring that the project remains on track and within budget. In particular, a variety of game development and art tools are essential in the realm of professional gaming. These tools not only enhance the quality of games but also support the competitive standards expected in professional gaming environments, setting the foundation for future discussions on this exciting field.

Leisure Gaming

Leisure gaming refers to casual gaming activities designed for entertainment, relaxation, and fun. Over the past 50 years, software has evolved, affecting gaming through numerous technological innovations in contemporary culture (Shaw, 2015). The resulting video games are played on various platforms, including consoles, PCs, mobile devices, and tabletop setups, and are often intended to provide a stress-free and enjoyable experience. They vary from puzzle, adventure, action, simulation, platformer, card games, board games, and more.

Genres in Casual Gaming

A. Strategy Games: Where players manage armies and resources in real-time to defeat opponents. Strategy and tactics are crucial. Part of its categories are Real-time strategy (RTS), Turn-based strategy (TBS) and Multiplayer Online Battle Arena (MOBA).

B. Shooter Games: Action games where the player views through the character's eyes or over the shoulder and primarily engages in tracking moving targets and clicking the mouse at the right moment to score points. Reaction speed and accuracy are essential. This includes categories like First-Person Shooter (FPS) and Third-Person Shooter (TPS)
C. Fighting Games: Where players engage in one-on-one melee battles or play-fighting, with combinations of attacks and defenses playing a significant role.
D. Racing Games: Games where players control vehicles and compete to achieve the fastest time or first place. Realism and speed are often important, but there are also cross-overs to other genres.
E. Simulation: Games that mimic real-life activities or systems, providing a realistic or semi-realistic experience. This genre can cover a broad range of topics, including managing complex systems, recreating real-world environments, or simulating specific roles or scenarios.
F. Arcade: These games are characterized by their emphasis on quick reflexes and fast-paced gameplay. Arcade games are typically designed for short bursts of play and often include high scores and simple mechanics that are easy to pick up but hard to master. Not to be mistaken with brick-and-mortar arcades, where a physical location is offered for multiple games.
G. Sports Games: Simulations of real or fictional sports. Players participate in sporting events and competitions that mimic rules of the actual sport. They are often recognizable due to realistic graphics and gameplay mechanics, and there are also iterations where management of the sport is more prevalent.
H. Digital Collectible Card Games: These are games where players collect digital cards and strategically use them to defeat opponents. Deck-building and tactics are important. These games often involve strategic play and managing a collection of cards with different abilities and effects.
I. Auto Battler: This is a genre of games where players assemble a team of units that automatically fight against teams of other players. Strategy and positioning are crucial.

Brief Examples

- Casual Mobile Games: Titles like *Candy Crush Saga*, *Angry Birds*, and *Wordfeud* offer easy-to-pick-up gameplay and are ideal for quick sessions. Other examples include *Subway Surfers*, *Farm Heroes Saga*, and *2048*, which also appeal to casual players.
- Tabletop Games: Games such as *Catan* and *Monopoly* provide social interaction and strategic thinking in a physical setting. Additional examples include

Ticket to Ride, which involves building train routes, and *Carcassonne*, a tile-placement game that promotes strategic thinking.

- Casual PC/Console Games: Titles like *Animal Crossing* and *The Sims* provide immersive and relaxing experiences for players. Other examples include *Stardew Valley*, a farming simulation game, and *Minecraft*, which offers a creative sandbox experience. Additionally, high-end games like *Horizon: Zero Dawn*, *Baldur's Gate 3*, and *Hogwarts Legacy* are known for their detailed graphics and engaging storylines.
- Web-Based Games: Games like *Pogo* or *Kongregate* host a variety of casual games that players can enjoy directly in their web browsers, providing easy access to casual gaming without the need for downloads. Recently, TV subscription services such as *Netflix* and *Amazon Prime Video* have begun including casual games in their offerings, allowing subscribers to access a library of games without additional costs, further enhancing the entertainment value of their subscriptions. This integration is made possible by the continuous internet connection of modern television sets, enabling seamless gameplay alongside traditional media content.
- Party Games: Titles such as *Jackbox Party Pack* and *Mario Kart* allow for social interaction and fun in group settings, making them great for gatherings and events.
- Puzzle Games: In addition to *Candy Crush Saga*, other examples include *Tetris*, which challenges players' spatial reasoning, and *Bejeweled*, which involves matching gems to score points.

Required Investment

Low – Casual gaming is highly accessible and affordable, requiring minimal financial investment. Many games are free-to-play or available at a low cost, making them easily obtainable for a wide range of players. Additionally, games often leverage in-app purchases rather than upfront costs, further reducing barriers to entry. Players typically agree to an end-user license agreement that governs software use and monetization.

Required Skill

Low – Due to the breadth of game modes and types, casual gaming requires minimal skill to start, making it ideal for relaxation and entertainment. Many casual games feature tutorial levels, or otherwise intuitive controls and mechanics that scale up along with the game's progression, allowing players of all ages and skill levels to enjoy them without extensive learning curves.

Stakeholders

Game Developers: These are individuals or teams responsible for creating and designing leisure games. They range from large studios to independent developers, focusing on engaging gameplay mechanics, compelling visuals, and user-friendly interfaces.
Publishers: These organizations help distribute and market leisure games. They manage the logistics of getting the games into players' hands, often providing funding for development and marketing strategies to reach target audiences.
Players/Gamers: The end users of casual games who drive demand and influence trends through their preferences and feedback. Players range from casual gamers looking for quick entertainment to more dedicated audiences seeking immersive experiences.
Platform Providers: Companies that provide platforms for casual gaming, such as mobile app stores (*Google Play, Apple App Store*), console manufacturers (*Sony, Microsoft, Nintendo*), and PC gaming platforms (*Steam, Epic Games Store, GOG*). They create ecosystems that facilitate game distribution and user engagement.
Marketing and Advertising Firms: These entities promote leisure games through various channels, helping to build awareness and drive sales. They use targeted marketing strategies to create buzz around new releases.
Content Creators: Streamers, and social media influencers who showcase leisure games to their audiences. They play a significant role in promoting games through gameplay videos, reviews, and live streams, influencing the gaming community's purchasing decisions.

Professional Video Gaming and Esports

Professional gaming and the digital sport called esports have evolved into a significant cultural phenomenon with roots dating back to the 1950s. Early competitive games like *Nim*, *tic-tac-toe*, *OXO*, *checkers*, and *chess* laid the groundwork for what would later become the esports industry. A pivotal moment occurred in 1958 when American physicist and innovator William Higinbotham created "*Tennis for Two*", the first video game that allowed two players to engage in a simulated tennis match on an oscilloscope, marking the beginning of competitive digital gaming.

The 1980s saw a surge in organized competitive gaming, highlighted by Atari's Space Invaders tournament in 1980, which attracted over 10,000 participants. This era also saw the formation of the U.S. National Video Game Team, which toured the country and brought televised competitions to the forefront, gaining recognition in the Guinness Book of Records. In 1990, Nintendo held its first world championship in the United States, further cementing competitive gaming's place in popular culture by rewarding winners with golden game cartridges.

The term "electronic sports" emerged in the 1990s, combining the concepts of electronic media and traditional sports. By 2000, "esports" was officially adopted as a collective term during the founding ceremony of the Korean e-Sports Association by South Korean Minister of Culture, Sports, and Tourism, Park Jie-won. The Associated Press endorsed the term *esports* in 2017, further solidifying its status as a globally recognized term. Countries around the world have adopted variations of the term, reflecting differing cultural perceptions of sport, exercise, and athletic achievement. Ultimately, what it is called matters less than the societal impact and economic goals associated with the sector.

Professional Gaming

Professional gaming encompasses careers where individuals leverage games as software platforms to build their professional lives. This includes a range of activities such as streaming gameplay, creating content, participating in competitive tournaments, and working in various roles within the gaming industry. These careers utilize gaming not just for play but as a medium for income generation and professional development, extending beyond merely playing video games to include roles in content creation, game development, and industry analysis.

Esports

Esports refers to competitive gaming at a professional level in a digital environment (Associated Press, 2017). Similar to traditional competitions, esports involves a regulated structure, skill development, strategy, and teamwork. Players need high levels of hand-eye coordination, reflexive decision-making, and collaboration, while physical fitness supports endurance and overall health during gaming sessions (McNulty et al., 2022). This is further supported by dietary and psychological support, which enhances peak performance and well-being.

According to Migliore (2021), and Jenny and Besombes (2022), esports is viewed as a high-level competitive sport. As a digital sport, esports has become recognized as a professional activity, and its structure mirrors many elements of traditional sports. Due to its wide variety of genres it can be compared to athletics, or with the novelty of snowboarding in the late 20th century. Therefore, esports could be considered a subsection of physical activity in an electronic format, with a focus on cognitive activity. The integration of active motion (or exergaming) with gaming creates a hybrid form, which will be explored further in the next section.

The Knowledge Center for Sport and Exercise and the Dutch Esports Association have developed the "Dutch Esports Ecosystem" infographic (**figure 8**), highlighting primary stakeholders such as Game Publishers, Tournament Organizers, Infrastructure providers (servers, storage, networking), and Teams and Players, along with secondary stakeholders like Knowledge Partners, Finance, Media and Broadcasting, and Societal Institutions such as education. This highlights partnerships between economic and societal institutions, reflecting esports' integration into mainstream frameworks (Branchevereniging Esports Nederland, 2023).

Moreover, Jenny et al. (2024) stress that esports should not be seen as isolated digital entertainment but rather as a complex, multidisciplinary environment merging performance, education, industry, and culture. It further blurs the lines between traditional and digital physical activity, which will be explored in the next section.

Figure 8. Dutch esports ecosystem, by knowledge centre for sport & physical activity

Brief Examples

- Media Streamers and Content Creators (Kaytoue et al., 2012), also known as Influencers, These are individuals who build a following on digital platforms like Twitch (Gandolfi, 2016) or YouTube by streaming their gameplay, creating engaging content, and often monetizing through subscriptions, ads, and sponsorships. They may also excel in areas like video editing, scriptwriting, and voice acting.
- Semi-Professionals are gamers who participate in tournaments and competitions, but do not operate at the highest professional level. They aim for pres-

tige and potential financial rewards, but might not have the same level of support and structure as full-time esports athletes.

- Popular esports titles include "League of Legends," "Dota 2," "Counter-Strike: Global Offensive," and "Overwatch". There are also upcoming esports like "Geoguessr" and "Farming Simulator". The Singapore Olympics in 2023 included esports events, featuring sport simulation games like "Tic Tac Bow" (Archery), highlighting the integration of esports into traditional sports contexts.

Required Investment

High - Professional gaming demands a significant financial investment, encompassing various aspects essential for success. The costs associated with high-performance equipment, such as computers, peripherals (keyboards, mice, headsets), and gaming consoles, can be substantial. Additionally, players often incur expenses for software tooling licenses and game purchases. For the athlete side, training and coaching also represent a considerable financial commitment, with many players investing in professional coaching, mentorship, and practice facilities to enhance their skills. Health and wellness investments, including ergonomic furniture and mental health support, are crucial for maintaining long-term performance. Moreover, players must factor in costs related to participating in events, such as entry fees, travel, and accommodation expenses. Finally, marketing and branding play a vital role, with investments needed for personal branding, merchandise, and sponsorship deals.

Required Skill

High - While initial skill levels in professional gaming can vary significantly, achieving success as an esports athlete requires a combination of high-level technical, cognitive, and physical fitness skills. Players must master game-specific mechanics and strategies to build a prolonged career in competitive gaming. Cognitive skills, including strategic thinking and quick decision-making, are essential during gameplay, while physical skills such as hand-eye coordination and stamina are necessary for enduring long gaming sessions. Similar to mastering other software applications or careers, dedication and commitment to practice are crucial; players must continually refine their skills while balancing gaming with other responsibilities.

It's important to note that various career pathways exist within the broader gaming ecosystem. Esports athletes focus primarily on competing in tournaments and honing their skills in specific games, where each game discipline has unique rules and strategies. In contrast, content creators engage with audiences through platforms like Twitch and YouTube, producing entertaining or informative gameplay videos, live streams, and commentary. Communicating with their audience while also playing the game is a unique trait that requires practice. Their success hinges on their ability to connect with viewers, which often requires skills in video editing, storytelling, and audience engagement. This aligns with early concepts of social TV, where interaction and shared viewing experiences enhance engagement and community-building (Cesar & Geerts, 2011). Game developers, on the other hand, work behind the scenes to create and design the games that athletes and content creators utilize. They must possess strong technical skills in programming, art design, and game mechanics, ensuring that the games are both engaging and functional. Aspiring professionals should recognize the distinct skill sets required for each of these roles to navigate their desired career paths effectively.

Stakeholders

Coaches and Analysts: Professionals who provide strategic guidance, training, and performance analysis for teams and players. They play a vital role in developing player skills, strategies, and teamwork, contributing to the overall success of competitive gaming.

Educational Institutions: Colleges and universities that offer esports programs and scholarships. They help cultivate the next generation of gamers, coaches, and industry professionals by providing training and educational opportunities related to esports.

Fans and Community Members: The audience and supporters of esports, including casual viewers, dedicated fans, and community members. Their engagement, viewership, and participation in discussions shape the popularity and growth of esports.

Game Developers and Publishers: Companies responsible for creating and distributing games; they have a vested interest in the esports ecosystem. Their games serve as the platforms for competitive play, and they often sponsor tournaments and events to enhance community engagement and promote their products.

Infrastructure Providers: Companies that offer the physical and virtual infrastructure necessary for esports events, including servers, networking equipment, and data centers. They ensure reliable performance and connectivity for online gaming and tournaments.

Managed/Cloud Services Hosting Providers: Firms that deliver hosting solutions for games and esports platforms, offering scalable cloud infrastructure to support online gaming, tournaments, and streaming services. They help optimize performance and reduce latency for gamers and viewers.

Media Outlets: News and entertainment platforms that cover esports events, player profiles, and industry trends. They contribute to the visibility and legitimacy of esports in mainstream culture, helping to inform and engage fans.

Professional Players: These individuals compete in tournaments and leagues, often representing teams or organizations. They possess high-level skills and dedication to training and strategy, contributing significantly to the popularity and competitive nature of esports.

Regulatory Bodies and Associations: Organizations that oversee the rules and regulations of competitive gaming, ensuring fairness, integrity, and player protection. They can help legitimize esports as a professional pursuit and promote ethical standards within the industry.

Sponsors and Advertisers: Brands and companies that invest in esports through sponsorships, advertisements, and collaborations. They are essential for funding events, teams, and players, and they help to bridge traditional marketing with the gaming community.

Streaming Platforms: Services like Twitch, YouTube Gaming, and Facebook Gaming facilitate live streaming of esports events and content creation by gamers. They play a crucial role in audience engagement, monetization, and community building for both players and fans.

Tournament Organizers: Entities that plan, host, and manage esports competitions. They create the framework for competitive events, ensuring fair play, organization, and sometimes live broadcasting, which adds to the overall spectacle and audience reach of esports.

HYBRID FORMS OF VIDEO GAMING

In an increasingly digital world, the landscape of gaming has evolved far beyond traditional boundaries, leading to the emergence of hybrid forms of video gaming that blend elements from various genres, platforms and applications. These innovative hybrids redefine what gaming can be, merging the physical with the virtual, and integrating educational, motivational, and competitive components. From exergames that combine physical activity with gaming elements to serious games designed for training and skill development, these hybrids serve diverse purposes, reaching audiences ranging from fitness enthusiasts to corporate trainees. As technology continues to advance, the possibilities for these hybrid gaming forms expand, offering unique opportunities for engagement, learning, and entertainment. This section explores various hybrid gaming types, their definitions, examples, required investments, skills needed, and the stakeholders involved, providing a comprehensive overview of this dynamic field.

Blended Electronic Sports (Exergaming)

Blended electronic sports, often referred to as active video games or exergames, represent a fascinating convergence of traditional active motion and digital tools. These hybrids encompass a variety of activities that integrate the physical aspects of sports with the engaging elements of video games, creating a unique interactive experience. As outlined by Williams and Ayres (2019), blended electronic sports leverage digital interfaces to enhance gameplay, allowing players to engage in physical activity while participating in gaming experiences. Importantly, blended electronic sports typically do not involve complex storylines or character-driven narratives, which are hallmarks of many traditional video games. This melding of genres focuses on physical movement and makes exercise more appealing through the incorporation of game mechanics such as scoring, competition, and rewards. Unlike traditional video games, which often feature intricate storylines and character development, blended electronic sports typically focus on competitive gameplay and skill, moving beyond sedentary gaming to encourage active participation.

Brief Examples

There is something for everyone as several examples illustrate the diversity within blended electronic sports. Augmented Reality (AR) sports games, such as "AR dodgeball" and "AR soccer," exemplify how players can interact with both physical and digital components. In these games, players engage with their immediate environment while also receiving digital feedback, creating a rich and immersive gameplay experience. Exergames further highlight this trend, with popular titles like "Just Dance," "Beat Saber," and "Ring Fit Adventure." These games require players to move their bodies, dance, or engage in fitness routines, making physical exertion an integral part of the gaming experience. By combining the fun and excitement of video gaming with the physical demands of traditional sports, these examples illustrate how blended electronic sports can engage a wider audience, appealing to both gamers and fitness enthusiasts alike.

Required Investment

High – The establishment and operation of blended electronic sports systems demand significant financial investment. The high-tech nature of these hybrid games necessitates substantial resources for advanced digital interfaces, specialized hardware, and cutting-edge integration technology. Players often require high-quality motion sensors, VR headsets, and consoles equipped to handle these intricate games. Furthermore, to ensure a seamless interaction between the physical and digital components, software development and ongoing technical support must be factored into the overall investment. This financial commitment can be a barrier to entry for some individuals and organizations, yet the potential returns in terms of engagement, fitness, and enjoyment can justify these costs for dedicated gamers and fitness centers seeking to innovate their offerings.

Required Skill

Low – One of the appealing aspects of blended electronic sports is their accessibility in terms of skill requirements. Unlike traditional esports, which often necessitate advanced strategies and cognitive skills, the primary skills needed for engaging in these hybrid activities focus on physical coordination and endurance. Players are primarily required to perform active movements, such as running, dancing, or swinging, rather than strategizing complex gameplay. This low skill barrier makes blended electronic sports appealing to a broader audience, including children, casual gamers, and those new to fitness. As a result, these games can serve as an entry point for individuals looking to enhance their physical activity levels while enjoying the social and competitive elements of gaming. The focus on physicality also encourages a sense of achievement through tangible improvements in fitness and coordination, fostering an engaging and motivating experience for players.

Moreover, many end users of blended electronic sports do not necessarily identify as gamers; instead, they may see themselves primarily as individuals engaging in physical fitness or recreational activities. This broader perception allows a diverse audience to enjoy the benefits of blended electronic sports, as they prioritize the physical engagement and social aspects over traditional gaming elements. This redefinition of play ultimately promotes a healthier lifestyle, as players are motivated to engage in physical activity while enjoying the immersive experience of gaming.

Stakeholders

Blended electronic sports, such as exergaming, involve a diverse range of stakeholders who contribute to the ecosystem of these hybrid activities. Players and participants are at the core, engaging in exergaming for fitness, entertainment, or competitive purposes. Game publishers and software developers are essential, as they design and distribute exergames, integrating physical activity with digital interfaces.

Technology and equipment providers play a crucial role, with hardware manufacturers creating the necessary physical equipment and software developers creating the interactive components. Fitness centers and gyms may incorporate exergaming into their offerings, providing new ways for members to exercise, while personal trainers might use these games as part of training programs. Health and wellness organizations also endorse exergaming for its fitness benefits, integrating it into their wellness programs.

Furthermore, educational institutions use exergaming in physical education and health programs, and research institutions study its impact on health and cognitive functions (Chow & Mann, 2023). This practice is not yet widely adopted, but highly encouraged by the WHO. Event organizers host exergaming tournaments and exhibitions, showcasing new technology and providing competitive platforms. Media and marketing agencies promote exergames through various channels, while retailers and online platforms offer the necessary equipment and games to consumers. Finally, regulatory bodies and standards organizations ensure the safety and performance of exergaming equipment and software. Each stakeholder plays a vital role in developing, promoting, and implementing blended electronic sports.

Serious Gaming (Process Simulation)

Serious gaming refers to the use of game-based environments designed for objectives that extend beyond entertainment, employed in educational, corporate, and training contexts to enhance learning and skill development. Unlike traditional games, serious games often diverge from conventional mechanics to specifically simulate real-world scenarios and processes. Their primary purpose is to facilitate practical learning and application, making them valuable tools for teaching, training, and skill-building across various sectors. These games are created with specific goals in mind, such as teaching employees new systems, strategies, or product knowledge, with the primary intent focused on education and skill development rather than leisure. Typically utilized during work hours, serious games aim to improve job performance and achieve better business outcomes while being tailored to meet the specific needs of organizations. Additionally, serious games are integrated into formal training programs designed to impart knowledge, improve skills, or simulate scenarios relevant to employees' roles.

Brief Examples

This includes therapeutic treatment games for children with ADHD. Or hyper realistic training simulations, such as flight simulators, for sectors like aviation and military operations. It is often accompanied with virtual and augmented reality (VR and AR) technology. They are also used as tooling, for instance to generate ecological awareness (Gazis & Katsiri, 2023), simulate the complexities of urban planning from water management perspective. Other examples include learning how to code or understand math problems. **Table 2** shows an overview of organizations using various game mechanics for serious games.

Table 2. Examples of serious gaming

Organization	Key Game Mechanics	Description
Walmart	Virtual Reality (VR) simulations	Walmart uses VR for skills management, training over 1 million employees through immersive simulations, achieving a 22% improvement in performance.
IBM	Interactive simulations	The "IBM Watson Talent" program uses Game-based learning to train employees in AI and data analytics, enhancing analytical skills and decision-making under uncertainty.
Mayo Clinic	VR medical training	Utilizing VR simulations for training, enabling clinicians to perform virtual surgeries and practice emergency responses, enhancing readiness and technical skills.
U.S. Army	Tactical decision-making simulations	The military employs advanced simulation systems to train soldiers in tactical decision-making and combat scenarios, enhancing skills like coordination and situational awareness.
NATO	Cooperative strategy exercises	NATO conducts joint simulation-based games to train military personnel in cooperative strategies and crisis management, enhancing international collaboration and response capabilities.
Maersk	Teaching about drilling operations	Immerses participants in the oil exploration process, teaching them to read earth layers, identify oil reservoirs, and manage drilling operations, all while navigating the complexities of the industry.

Required Investment

High – Developing serious games requires significant financial investment due to various factors. The creation process involves substantial costs related to technology, content development, and ongoing maintenance. Initial investments include hiring skilled professionals such as game designers, developers, artists, and educational experts who can create engaging and effective simulations. Additionally, the costs of hardware, such as servers and VR equipment, can be considerable, particularly when ensuring that the technology can support high levels of interactivity and realism.

Organizations may also need to invest in training staff to effectively use these tools and integrate them into existing educational or training frameworks. Furthermore, the development cycle can be lengthy, requiring continuous iterations based on feedback and technological advancements.

While there are as-a-service models available for serious gaming, which can reduce upfront costs and provide easier access to cutting-edge technology, organizations must still dedicate time and resources to research and iterate on specific scenarios tailored to their unique needs. This research phase is crucial to ensure that the serious games align with the organization's objectives and effectively address the challenges they aim to solve.

Beyond the creation of serious games, organizations often invest in marketing and outreach efforts to ensure that users understand the benefits and functionalities of the tools. While the initial costs may be high, the potential return on investment can be substantial, particularly when serious games lead to improved employee performance, reduced training times, and enhanced learning outcomes.

Required Skill

Low – Users typically need minimal skills to engage with serious gaming educational and training tools, but a certain level of proficiency may enhance their experience and learning outcomes. While the interface of most serious games is designed to be intuitive, allowing these end users to navigate and interact with the content easily, familiarity with basic computer skills is beneficial. Participants are encouraged to possess a foundational understanding of the subject matter being addressed in the game, whether it's a corporate training module or an educational simulation, to maximize their learning potential.

Furthermore, trainers or facilitators often play a critical role in guiding users through the experience, offering assistance and feedback. For more advanced applications, such as those utilizing VR and AR technologies, end users may benefit from a degree of comfort with these platforms, if they have an initial understanding of such technologies. In educational settings, educators may need to develop specific pedagogical skills to effectively integrate serious games into their teaching practices, ensuring that the game aligns with learning objectives and facilitates meaningful engagement. Ultimately, while serious games are designed to be accessible, fostering an environment where participants can effectively learn and apply new skills may require some baseline knowledge and support.

Stakeholders

Software Companies: Game developers play a crucial role in the creation of serious games. These companies design and develop the technology and platforms that facilitate immersive and interactive learning experiences. Collaborating with educational and corporate entities, they focus on building tailored solutions that meet the specific needs of their clients.

Education sector: Educational institutions are significant stakeholders in serious gaming. They utilize these tools to enhance teaching methodologies and offer students immersive learning experiences. By integrating serious games into curricula, schools and universities can provide practical applications of theoretical knowledge, thus preparing students for real-world challenges.

Commercial sector: Corporations of all sizes leverage serious gaming for employee training and development. These organizations incorporate game-based learning to improve employee performance and skills. They invest in serious games to streamline onboarding processes, enhance product knowledge, and develop soft skills, ultimately leading to improved business outcomes.

Government: Agencies and military organizations are key stakeholders in the realm of serious gaming. They employ simulations for training personnel in tactical decision-making, crisis management, and operational planning. In this context, serious games and foresight tools are often used to complement long-term strategic planning efforts. For example, Weigand, Flanagan, Dye, and Jones (2014) emphasize how collaborative foresight methods, including simulation-based scenarios, can enhance strategic thinking and improve decision-making processes in complex, high-stakes environments.

Healthcare Providers: Care organizations utilize serious gaming for training medical professionals. By employing VR and simulation technologies, they prepare clinicians for real-life medical scenarios, thereby improving patient care and enhancing skills in a risk-free environment.

Non-Profit Organizations: Non-profits and NGOs may use serious gaming to raise awareness about social issues or provide educational resources. They may develop games focused on environmental sustainability or public health to engage communities and promote proactive behavior changes.

Game-Based Learning (Digital Learning and Learning Digitally)

Game-based learning (GBL) involves integrating game elements directly into educational content to create an engaging learning experience. The goal of GBL is to motivate and enhance learning outcomes by using interactive and immersive elements. It is a proven way to promote digitalization in the classroom for both teachers and students. By reversing the method and allowing the video game to become the classroom environment, learning becomes interactive, collaborative, and enjoyable. Based on the lesson plan, the engagement can be strengthened even further. When educators harness GBL's full potential, education is truly digitally transformed, going beyond simple digitalization (using digital tools) to completely redefining the learning experience. GBL shifts from using games as tools to using them as an immersive environment in which students engage with educational content directly through gamified systems.

Brief Examples

There are many examples of how game-based learning can be applied in education. Here are a few notable cases:

- Minecraft Education: A version of the popular video game *Minecraft* has been adapted specifically for educational purposes, allowing students to explore virtual worlds while learning subjects such as history, math, and science. By building structures, solving puzzles, and collaborating with peers, students can apply theoretical knowledge in a practical and engaging way. *Microsoft* fully integrated *Minecraft Education* into the IT infrastructure, for a robust support and tools to enhance its utility in classrooms and Learning Management Systems.
- Kahoot!: A quiz-based platform that allows educators to create and share interactive quizzes and games. *Kahoot!* has been used to encourage active participation, making assessments and revision more fun and interactive.
- SimCity EDU: This educational version of the game *SimCity* helps students understand urban planning, environmental management, and decision-making processes. It provides a platform for project-based learning where students apply critical thinking and problem-solving skills.
- Assassin's Creed: Discovery Tour: based on the popular *Assassin's Creed* series, is an excellent example of GBL. *Ubisoft*, the game developer, adapted this historically rich game into an educational tool by creating a special mode that focuses solely on exploring and learning about ancient civilizations, such as Ancient Egypt and Ancient Greece.

These examples highlight how GBL can be integrated into various subjects, from STEM (Science, Technology, Engineering, Mathematics) to humanities, encouraging active participation, collaboration, and problem-solving.

Required Investment

Low – The successful implementation of GBL requires both financial and human resource investment. Educational institutions must invest in software and platforms, which may involve purchasing licenses for GBL tools like *Minecraft: Education*, *Kahoot!*, or custom-built educational games; while some platforms are free, advanced features or full access often come with subscription fees. Additionally, hardware investments are necessary as GBL frequently requires digital devices such as computers, tablets, or VR/AR systems, necessitating upgrades to technological infrastructure to ensure that both students and teachers can efficiently use the required software.

Training and professional development for educators are also crucial, as teachers need to be well-versed in integrating GBL into their curriculum, understanding the specific tools, platforms, and methodologies to enhance learning. Furthermore, incorporating GBL into lesson plans demands significant time and effort from teachers to design, test, and adjust games for educational purposes.

Required Skill

High – Educators need a diverse skill set to implement GBL effectively, encompassing both pedagogical and some basic technical expertise. They must possess high didactic skills, which involve strong pedagogical knowledge to design and implement GBL experiences that align game mechanics with educational objectives and learning outcomes. Technological competence is also crucial; educators should be familiar with digital tools, platforms, and game mechanics to use the software effectively, troubleshoot issues, and guide students through the game environment. Creative thinking is essential for integrating GBL in a manner that is both engaging and educational, including designing challenges, puzzles, or missions that support the lesson's objectives. Additionally, educators need to be adept at assessing students' learning through game-based experiences, which involves tracking progress within the game and using GBL to create formative and summative assessments.

Stakeholders

Several key stakeholders must be involved in the implementation and success of Game-Based Learning:

- Educators: Teachers play the most critical role in designing and implementing GBL into their classrooms. They must also be trained and empowered to take full advantage of the technology.
- Students: The primary beneficiaries of GBL, students engage with the game-based content and provide feedback about their experiences. Their learning outcomes are the ultimate measure of GBL's effectiveness.
- School Administrators: School leaders must support GBL initiatives by providing the necessary infrastructure, resources, and training. Their role includes approving budgets for technology and ensuring the overall strategy aligns with the school's educational goals.
- Parents and Guardians: Parents need to understand and support GBL approaches. Clear communication about how GBL contributes to their children's learning will help gain parental buy-in and may improve the at-home use of educational technology.

- Game Developers and Educational Technologists: These stakeholders are responsible for creating the educational games and platforms that align with the curriculum. Collaboration between educators and developers ensures that the games meet pedagogical standards and effectively serve the learning objectives.
- Policy Makers and Educational Boards: These entities set guidelines and policies that influence how GBL can be implemented in schools. They may provide funding, support research on GBL's efficacy, and create frameworks for integrating digital tools into education.

Gamification (Motivating)

Gamification involves applying game design elements, such as points, badges, leaderboards, to non-game contexts to drive user engagement and motivation. According to Jaramillo-Mediavilla et al. (2024) the integration of these elements and mechanics typical of games in non-recreational environments have a significant impact in enhancing and enriching the learning process. The aim is to make otherwise mundane tasks more enjoyable and rewarding. By incorporating game-like incentives, gamification can boost user interaction, enhance learning (Dichev & Dicheva, 2017), or improve productivity in various settings like sales departments (Woźniak, 2020).

Brief Examples

Gamification often proves more effective than traditional rewards by tapping into intrinsic motivations. It is commonly used in education, business, and other sectors to enhance engagement and effectiveness. In educational apps, game mechanics like quests, challenges, badges, and rewards make subjects such as math, language, and history more engaging, with badges serving as modern equivalents to traditional "gold stars". Video games further support learning through single-player and multiplayer modes, offering puzzles, quizzes, and narrative scenarios that apply knowledge in practical ways. The addition of in-game achievements increase the time investment to interact with the software.

In the business world, gamification helps retain customers by integrating game-like elements into daily routines. For instance, *Fitbit* uses gamification to encourage end users to stay active and make fitness tracking more enjoyable. Key approaches in business include virtualization, seen in language-learning apps and virtual home décor platforms; social comparisons, as with fitness tracking apps like *Nike Run Club*; and tangible rewards, such as those in Starbucks loyalty programs.

A notable example of gamification in public safety is the Radar Speed Sign, illustrated in **figure 9**, which uses visual feedback to encourage drivers to slow down. By displaying the driver's speed in real-time, these signs often flash or change colors when exceeding speed limits, effectively gamifying compliance and promoting safer driving behavior. This approach not only enhances road safety but also engages drivers by appealing to their sense of accountability.

For customer acquisition, businesses might use gamification strategies such as combining virtual experiences with real-world prizes or focusing on self-improvement through social comparison, exemplified by *Team Liquid's Liquid Plus* initiative. This initiative aims to expand fan engagement and community building.

Gamification can also reshape user perceptions by blending virtual elements with social comparisons, aligning with broader business goals. Examples like *Duolingo* and *Tencent Music* illustrate how gamification effectively integrates these elements. Jacobides et al. (2024) provides an overview of various gamification initiatives as well. Find a combined overview in **table 3** below.

Table 3. Expanded Jacobides (2024) overview of gamification initiatives

Organization	Key Elements	Description
Deloitte	Skill-building exercises	Deloitte Pixel engages employees in gamified skill-building and problem-solving activities to foster a culture of innovation and continuous learning.
Duolingo	Scoreboards, rankings, social comparison	Language-learning application that utilizes scoreboards, rankings, community interaction, minigames, and avatars to track progress and motivate engagement.
Facebook	Badges, social comparison	Facebook leverages gamification to reward users with badges based on engagement levels in user-created groups.
Google	Interactive training modules	Google's "G-Suite Training" incorporates game elements to enhance functional mastery of productivity tools, developing strategic thinking and problem-solving skills.
Google News	Badges, social comparison	Google's news aggregator service that presents links to articles based on user preferences, with rewards for engagement.
Nike Run Club	Scoreboards, rankings, social comparison	Fitness application aimed at people who want to improve their running. Users can track their runs and observe progress while engaging with friends for motivation.
Pinduoduo	Virtual gardens, social comparison	Minigame in Pinduoduo's e-commerce application. Each user has a virtual garden, in which purchasing goods on Pinduoduo generates virtual droplets for virtual fruit trees.
Team Liquid	Achievements, points, rewards	By connecting their community online accounts to the Liquid+ platform, various rewards can be gathered while fostering connectivity between fans.
Tencent Music	Scoreboards, rankings, social comparison	Music-streaming platform that has gamified the relationship between artists and their respective fan communities through rankings based on donations received.

Required Investment

The investment required for implementing gamification varies based on the scale and complexity of the application. At a basic level, it includes costs for software development, such as designing and integrating game mechanics into existing platforms or creating new gamified systems, which may involve hiring developers, designers, and project managers. Additionally, technology infrastructure expenses cover server maintenance, data storage, and security to support gamified systems. Content creation costs encompass the development of engaging elements like quests, challenges, and rewards, often requiring content creators, graphic designers, and instructional designers. User experience design investments ensure that gamified elements enhance rather than detract from the user experience, while marketing and promotion expenses involve advertising campaigns, user training, and support. The total investment can range from moderate to high, depending on the depth of gamification and the target audience. Market research suggests that the gamification market is expected to experience significant growth, with a projected compound annual growth rate (CAGR) of approximately 28% through 2030 (Meticulous Research, 2024).

Required Skill

Implementing gamification typically requires a range of skills, initially from basic to moderate, depending on the complexity of the system. At its core, basic gamification can be achieved with a solid understanding of game mechanics and principles, applying these effectively in non-game contexts. Technical skills are also necessary, particularly basic programming to integrate gamified features into existing systems; however, more advanced gamification may require specialized software development expertise. Creative design abilities are essential for crafting engaging and motivating content, such as challenges and rewards, to boost user interaction. Additionally, strong user experience (UX) design skills are crucial to ensure that gamified elements are seamlessly integrated into user interfaces, making them both effective and user-friendly without causing confusion. The success of gamification hinges on balancing organizational goals with the intrinsic motivations of participants. While gamification is often viewed primarily as a tool for extrinsic motivation, its effectiveness depends on aligning game elements with users' intrinsic interests and motivations, thereby creating a more complex system that provides both external rewards and deeper personal resonance.

Stakeholders

- Product Managers: Oversee the development and implementation of gamification strategies, ensuring alignment with business goals and user needs.
- Developers and Designers: Create and integrate gamified elements into platforms or applications, requiring technical and creative expertise.
- Marketing Teams: Promote gamified features and drive user engagement through targeted campaigns and communication strategies.
- End Users: The primary recipients of gamification efforts, whose feedback and engagement levels are crucial for assessing the effectiveness of the gamified elements.
- Business Executives: Provide strategic direction and funding for gamification initiatives, evaluating their impact on organizational goals and ROI.

Figure 9. Radar speed sign that give feedback to drivers on their speed

THE LOCKTREE GAMING QUADRANT

To help organizations identify the most relevant types of gaming for their business needs, whether from an investment or skill requirement perspective, a structured framework is essential. The Locktree Gaming Quadrant categorizes various gaming types based on two key dimensions: the initial skill required from employees and the financial investment necessary for organizations considering gaming-related projects. This framework divides these dimensions into high and low categories, enabling organizations and gamers to determine the most suitable gaming types for specific purposes based on their unique needs and capacities.

Gaming Categories

The following outlines how each gaming category fits into the Locktree Gaming Quadrant:

Quadrant 1: Orange Legendary

Categories:

- o **Esports**
- o **Game Development**
- o **Professional Gaming**

Characteristics:

- **Skill Required:** High – Success in these categories demands advanced skills, including strategic thinking, hand-eye coordination, and often teamwork.
- **Investment Required:** High – These categories require substantial financial investment in high-end equipment, extensive training, and sometimes professional support.

Quadrant 2: Purple Epic

Categories:

- o **Game-Based Learning**

Characteristics:

- **Skill Required:** High – Effective implementation of Game-based learning requires educators to have advanced didactic skills and the ability to integrate educational content with game mechanics.
- **Investment Required:** Low – Utilizing Game-based learning can be cost-effective, especially when leveraging existing games or apps, and does not necessarily require high financial expenditure.

Quadrant 3: Blue Rare

Categories:

- o **Serious Gaming**

- o **Gamification**
- o **Blended Electronic Sports**

Characteristics:

- **Skill Required:** Low – While blended electronic sports can start with little skill levels, achieving success requires perseverance. Serious games and gamification participation typically requires less skill from users but can involve complex design and implementation.
- **Investment Required:** High – Professional gaming and serious games need significant investment in technology and training. Gamification, while involving significant initial setup costs, focuses on enhancing engagement through incentives.

Quadrant 4: Green Uncommon

Categories:

- o **Leisure gaming**

Characteristics:

- **Skill Required:** Low – Leisure games are designed for easy accessibility and relaxation, requiring minimal skill to start.
- **Investment Required:** Low – These games are typically affordable and accessible, often involving minimal or no financial investment beyond the initial purchase or download.

Locktree Gaming Quadrant

The Locktree Gaming Quadrant categorizes various gaming types based on two critical dimensions: skill level and financial investment. These categories help organizations determine the best approach to gaming, whether they are considering employee skill development or financial resource allocation.

To better illustrate this framework, Slotboom (2024, **figure 10**) provides a visual representation of the Locktree Gaming Quadrant, clearly dividing the four categories based on the levels of skill and investment required.

Figure 10. Locktree Gaming Quadrant, by Chris Slotboom, 2024

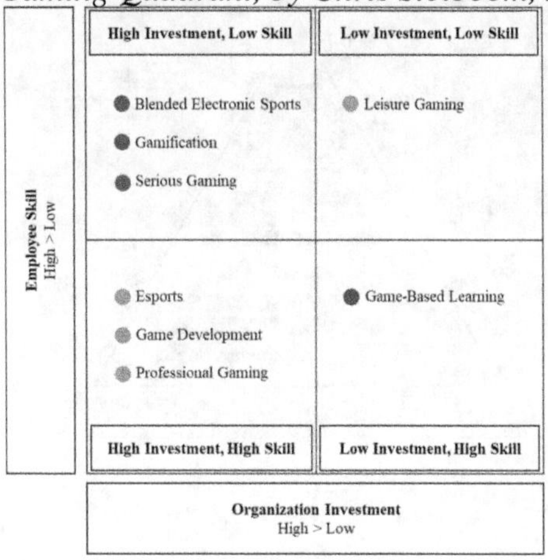

GAMING AND ESPORTS PYRAMID 2024

In order to combine the ecosystem of gaming and esports, an infographic was created by Chris Slotboom (2024), displayed as **figure 11**. The purpose of this infographic below is to provide insight into the different layers of gaming and esports in a clear and concise manner. The pyramid clarifies how gaming contributes to societal and economic value, from sports performance to general well-being, social interaction, professional development and global events, as well as the development of (digital) skills.

The goals include narrowing the digital divide while offering insights into the connection between gaming and digital sports. It aims to emphasize that gaming is not merely a hobby; it fosters essential skills and experiences. Additionally, the initiative seeks to deliver concise information on the various layers and dimensions of the gaming and esports landscape.

Figure 11. Chris Slotboom's gaming & esports pyramid 2024 infographic, 2024

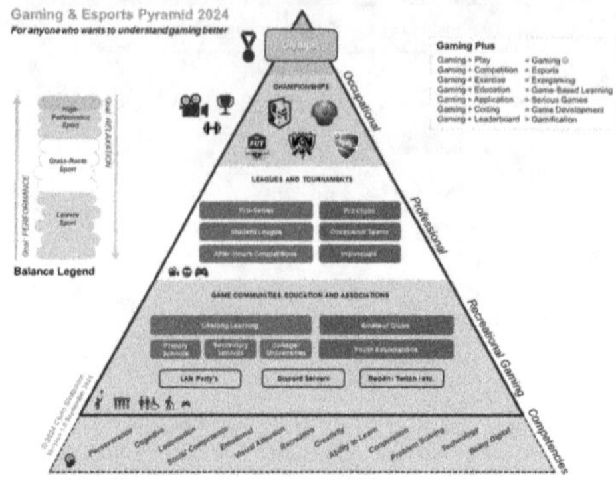

Four Parts of the Infographic

By considering the ecosystem as a pyramid, it allows for stacks of fundamental skills, recreation, professionalism and top performance levels to complement and reinforce each other. The four main parts of the infographic are as follows:

1. Middle: The gaming and esports ecosystem.
2. Under: The skills from gaming.
3. Left: The balance between performance and relaxation.
4. Right: The "Gaming Plus" box.

Ecosystem Pyramid

Let's start with the ecosystem as a pyramid (**figure 12**). See how the layers of fundamental skills, recreation, professionalism and professional level complement and reinforce each other.

Figure 12. Gaming & esports ecosystem pyramid 2024

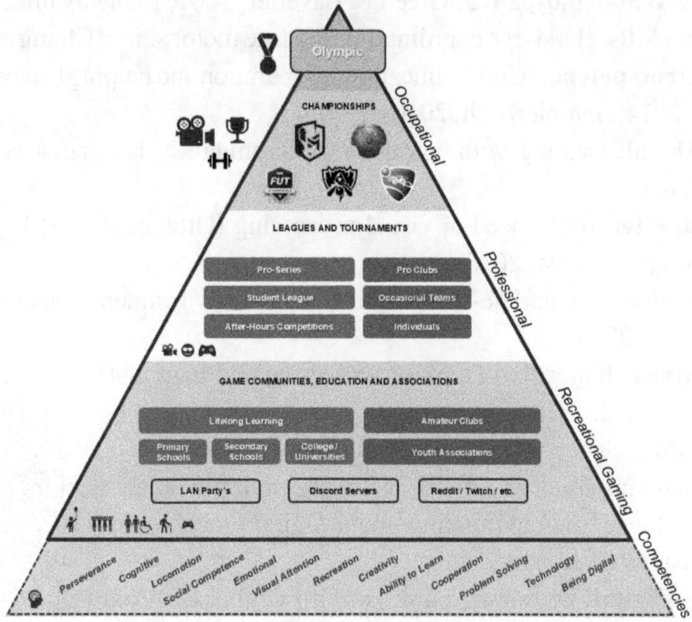

Fundamental Layer

The bottom layer, **figure 13**, concerns the basic skills you gain while gaming, such as problem-solving and strategic thinking. Gaming automatically builds these skills, which helps reduce the digital divide through a broader understanding of technology and the digital world. Read more about this in the study 'Benefits of Recreational Gaming' (Dekker & Slotboom, 2023). Gaming is a specific form of digital interaction that contributes to personal skills, as opposed to purely functional skills that you develop with tools such as Dropbox, Teams, or CRM systems.

Figure 13. Layer 1: Competencies through gaming

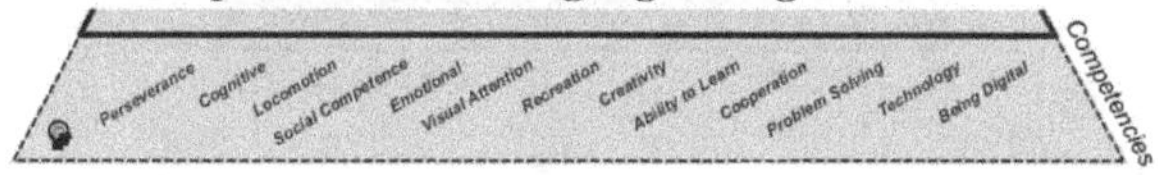

Extensive research shows the benefits of gaming. Here are a number of examples:

Cognitive: Problem-solving and strategic thinking (Bavelier et al., 2011; Adachi & Willoughby, 2013; Green & Bavelier, 2007; Eichenbaum et al., 2014)
Motor skills: Hand-eye coordination and fine motor skills (Chung et al., 2017).
Social competence: Communication, cooperation and helping behavior (Granic et al., 2014; Schmierbach, 2010).
Emotional: Dealing with emotions (McGonigal, 2011) and stress (Jones et al., 2014).
Visual attention: Speed of visual processing (Uttal et al., 2013) and mental rotation (van Zoest, 2015).
Relaxation: Fun and de-stressing in a digital environment (Nakamura, 2002; Ferguson, 2015).
Creativity: Innovative Thinking and Strategic Planning (Jackson et al., 2012; Pasmore et al., 2014).
Learning: Understanding how you learn and acquiring new knowledge/skills (Khesht-Masjedi et al., 2019), including multiple object tracking.
Technology: Logical thinking about digital processes and success in STEM professions (Wai et al., 2010).
Being Digital: Becoming Familiar with Digital Environments (Steinkuehler & Duncan, 2008).

Recreational Layer

Gamers are in diverse social settings such as schools, workplaces, and communities where they share their video game hobbies. This societal layer in **figure 14** emphasizes the social and recreational aspects of gaming, such as bringing generations together through joint gaming activities. Platforms like *Reddit*, *Twitch* and *Discord* also fall under this layer. This differs from teaching with games (game-based learning), in which gaming is used as a means rather than a participation goal.

Figure 14. Layer 2: Recreational gaming

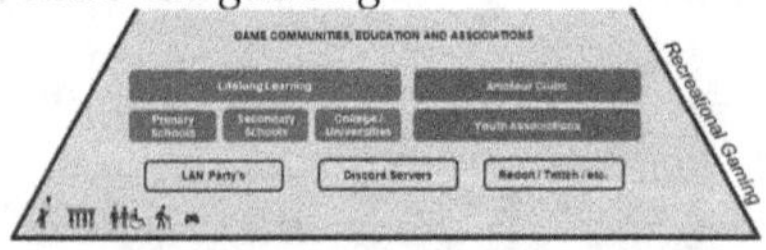

Professional Layer

This tier includes short-term leagues and tournaments in which gamers from different backgrounds showcase their skills and compete against each other. Shown in **figure 15**. These events are often linked to content creation and interact with an audience more than recreational gaming, and can range from local to international levels. This differs from professional gaming as a tester in game development, using (serious) games for marketing and business, or motivating with leaderboards. See the "Gaming Plus" box for more details.

Figure 15. Layer 3: Professional gaming

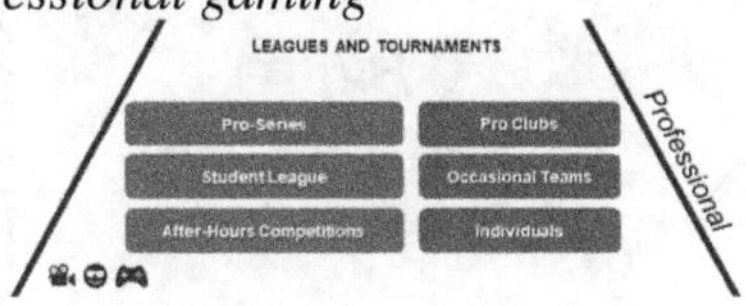

Occupational Layer

This layer (**figure 16**) concerns large, prestigious international events that often attract global attention and represent the highest level of competition. These long-term events follow strict rules and health requirements and constitute the highest level of competition, such as the Olympics. Local tournaments and championships often serve as a stepping stone to these international competitions.

Figure 16. Layer 4: Occupational gaming

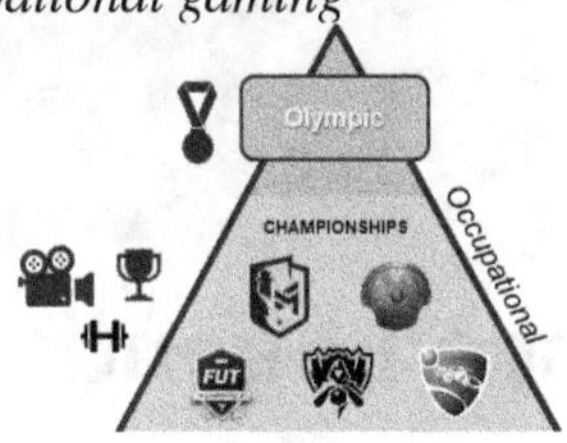

Balance Between Performance and Relaxation

In gaming communities, people mainly play to be together and seek relaxation. The games played are often not competitive, but focused on social interaction or story-based. In a club context, they often play to win and coach to learn more game technique for higher performance and (business) success. Review the balance in **figure 17**.

Figure 17. The Balance Legend

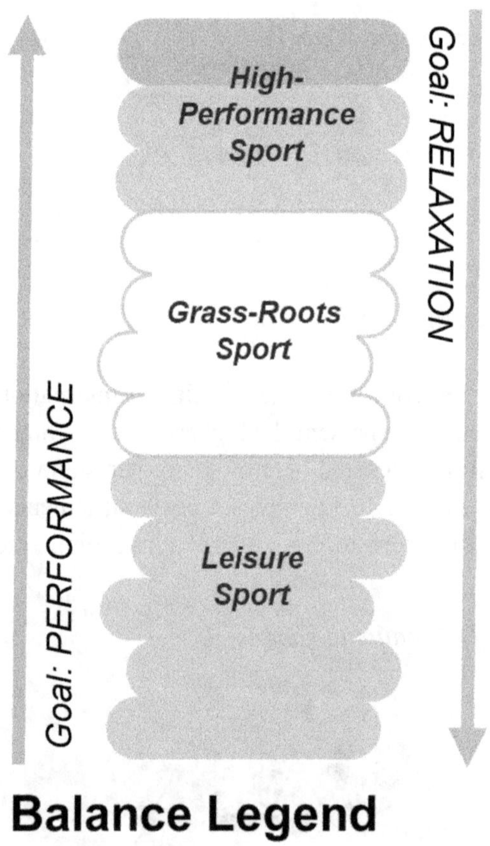

The "Gaming Plus" Box

This is meant to categorize the different ways in which gaming can be combined with other activities and goals. It provides an overview (**figure 18**) of how gaming compares to other disciplines and applications.

Figure 18. Gaming plus box

Gaming Plus

Gaming + Play	= Gaming ☺
Gaming + Competition	= Esports
Gaming + Exercise	= Exergaming
Gaming + Education	= Game-Based Learning
Gaming + Application	= Serious Games
Gaming + Coding	= Game Development
Gaming + Leaderboard	= Gamification

CONCLUSION

To close the digital gap, stakeholders, including policymakers, employers, educators, and community leaders, must embrace game-derived skills, such as problem-solving, strategic thinking, and collaboration, as an essential component of workforce development strategies and digital education. It would be beneficial to integrate these skills into curricula, professional training, or public policy initiatives. By doing so, we can improve access to digital skills training, foster innovation, and ultimately create a more inclusive digital economy and society.

The journey to bridging the digital divide is a collective effort. Understanding and utilizing game-derived skills is a foundational step that can help unlock the potential of individuals across diverse backgrounds, empowering them to participate fully in the digital future. In essence, GDS provide not only a way to better understand the digital world but also to thrive within it, ensuring no one is left behind as we advance into an increasingly digital era of the 22nd century.

REFERENCES

Adachi, P. J. C., & Willoughby, T. (2013). More than just fun and games: The longitudinal relationships between strategic video games, self-reported problem-solving skills, and academic grades. *Journal of Youth and Adolescence*, *42*(7), 1041–1052. DOI: 10.1007/s10964-013-9913-9 PMID: 23344653

Aldao, A., Nolen-Hoeksema, S., & Schweizer, S. (2010). Emotion-regulation strategies across psychopathology: A meta-analytic review. *Clinical Psychology Review*, *30*(2), 217–237. DOI: 10.1016/j.cpr.2009.11.004 PMID: 20015584

Alleway, H. K., Klein, E. S., Cameron, L., Douglass, K., Govia, I., Guell, C., Lim, M., Robin, L., & Thurstan, R. H. (2023). The shifting baseline syndrome as a connective concept for more informed and just responses to global environmental change. *People and Nature*, *5*(4), e10473. Advance online publication. DOI: 10.1002/pan3.10473

Associated Press. (2017). *AP Stylebook 2017*. https://www.apstylebook.com/blog_posts/7

Atherton, G., & Cross, L. (2021). The use of analog and digital games for autism interventions. *Frontiers in Psychology*, *12*, 669734. DOI: 10.3389/fpsyg.2021.669734 PMID: 34447328

Bamela, U., Kumar, S., Lim, W. M., Bamelf, N., & Meyer, N. (2022). Managing the dark side of digitalization in the future of work: A fuzzy TISM approach. *Journal of Innovation & Knowledge*, *7*(4), 100275. DOI: 10.1016/j.jik.2022.100275

Bavelier, D., Green, C. S., Han, D. H., Renshaw, P. F., Merzenich, M. M., & Gentile, D. A. (2011). Brains on video games. *Nature Reviews. Neuroscience*, *12*(12), 763–768. DOI: 10.1038/nrn3135 PMID: 22095065

Bawden, D. (2008). Origins and concepts of digital literacy. In Lankshear, C., & Knobel, M. (Eds.), *Digital literacies: Concepts, policies and practices* (pp. 17–32). Peter Lang.

Berger, P., Bitsch, F., Bröhl, H., & Falkenberg, I. (2018). Play and playfulness in psychiatry: A selective review. *International Journal of Play*, *7*(2), 210–225. DOI: 10.1080/21594937.2017.1383341

Bleakley, C. M., Charles, D., Porter-Armstrong, A., McNeill, M. D., McDonough, S. M., & McCormack, B. (2015). Gaming for health: A systematic review of the physical and cognitive effects of interactive computer games in older adults. *Journal of Applied Gerontology*, *34*(3), NP166–NP189. DOI: 10.1177/0733464812470747 PMID: 24652863

Branchevereniging Esports Nederland. (2023). *Dutch esports ecosystem* [Infographic]. https://www.esportsnederland.com/infographic_esports_nederlandse_ecosysteem

Brunetti, F., Matt, D. T., Bonfanti, A., De Longhi, A., Pedrini, G., & Orzes, G. (2020). Digital transformation challenges: Strategies emerging from a multi-stakeholder approach. *The TQM Journal*, *32*(4), 697–724. DOI: 10.1108/TQM-12-2019-0309

Cès, P., Duflos, M., Tricard, E., Jhean-Larose, S., & Giraudeau, C. (2024). Playing board games to increase emotional competencies in school-age children and older people: A systematic review. *Leisure Sciences*, •••, 1–24. DOI: 10.1080/01490400.2024.2373415

Cesar, P., & Geerts, D. (2011). Past, present, and future of social TV: A categorization. In *Proceedings of the 2011 IEEE Consumer Communications and Networking Conference (CCNC)* (pp. 347–351). IEEE. DOI: 10.1109/CCNC.2011.5766487

Chow, D. H. K., & Mann, S. K. F. (2023). Exergaming and education: A relational model for games selection and evaluation. *Frontiers in Psychology*, *14*, 1197403. Advance online publication. DOI: 10.3389/fpsyg.2023.1197403 PMID: 37484077

Chung, A. T., Lenci, L. T., Wang, K., Collins, T. E., Griess, M. D., Oetting, T. A., & Shriver, E. M. (2017). Effect of fine-motor-skill activities on surgical simulator performance. *Journal of Cataract and Refractive Surgery*, *43*(7), 763–768. https://europepmc.org/article/MED/28823438. DOI: 10.1016/j.jcrs.2017.05.024 PMID: 28823438

Colbert, A., Yee, N., & George, G. (2016). The digital workforce and the workplace of the future. *Academy of Management Journal*, *59*(3), 731–739. DOI: 10.5465/amj.2016.4003

Danesi, M. (2018). *Ahmes' legacy: Puzzles and the mathematical mind*. Springer. DOI: 10.1007/978-3-319-93254-5

Daniau, S. (2016). The transformative potential of role-playing games: From play skills to human skills. *Simulation & Gaming*, *47*(4), 423–444. DOI: 10.1177/1046878116650765

Davis, T., & Higgins, J. (2013). A blockbuster failure: How an outdated business model destroyed a giant. In *Chapter 11 bankruptcy case studies* (Vol. 11). https://ir.law.utk.edu/utk_studlawbankruptcy/11

Dekker, S., & Slotboom, C. (2023). Benefits of recreational gaming. *International Journal of Esports*, *1*(1). https://www.ijesports.org/article/96/html

Deterding, S., & Zagal, J. P. (2018). *Role-Playing Game Studies: Transmedia Foundations*. Routledge., DOI: 10.4324/9781315637532-1

Dichev, C., & Dicheva, D. (2017). Gamifying education: What is known, what is believed, and what remains uncertain: A critical review. *International Journal of Educational Technology in Higher Education, 14*(1), 9. DOI: 10.1186/s41239-017-0042-5

Dutra, M. J. (2021). What is the gaming lifestyle? An exploratory investigation. *Journal of Games, Game Art, and Gamification, 6*(2), 44–55. Advance online publication. DOI: 10.21512/jggag.v6i2.7891

Dye, M. W. G., Green, C. S., & Bavelier, D. (2009). Increasing speed of processing with action video games. *Current Directions in Psychological Science, 18*(6), 321–326. DOI: 10.1111/j.1467-8721.2009.01660.x PMID: 20485453

Ebermann, C., Piccinini, E., Brauer, B., Busse, S., & Kolbe, L. (2016). The impact of gamification-induced emotions on in-car IS adoption – The difference between digital natives and digital immigrants. In *Proceedings of the 49th Hawaii International Conference on System Sciences (HICSS)* (pp. 1307–1316). IEEE. DOI: 10.1109/HICSS.2016.169

Eichenbaum, A. B. (2014). Video games: Play can do serious good. *American Journal of Play, 71*(1), 50–72.

Entertainment Software Association. (2024). *Essential facts about the computer and video game industry*. https://www.theesa.com/wp-content/uploads/2024/05/Essential-Facts-2024-FINAL.pdf

European Games Developer Federation. (2022). *2022 European video games industry insight report*.https://www.egdf.eu/wp-content/uploads/2024/06/2022-European-video-games-industry-insight-report.pdf

European Parliament. (2022). *Report on esports and video games (2022/2027(INI)) [A9-0244/2022]*. Committee on Culture and Education. https://www.europarl.europa.eu/doceo/document/A-9-2022-0244_EN.html

European Parliament & Council of the European Union. (2019). Directive (EU) 2019/770 of 20 May 2019 on certain aspects concerning contracts for the supply of digital content and digital services. *Official Journal of the European Union, L, 136*, 1–27. https://eur-lex.europa.eu/eli/dir/2019/770/oj

Ewoldsen, D. R., Eno, C. A., Okdie, B. M., Velez, J. A., Guadagno, R. E., & DeCoster, J. (2012). Effect of playing violent video games cooperatively or competitively on subsequent cooperative behavior. *Cyberpsychology, Behavior, and Social Networking*, *15*(5), 277–280. DOI: 10.1089/cyber.2011.0308 PMID: 22489544

Fadda, D., Pellegrini, M., Vivanet, G., & Zandonella Callegher, C. (2022). Effects of digital games on student motivation in mathematics: A meta-analysis in K-12. *Journal of Computer Assisted Learning*, *38*(1), 304–325. DOI: 10.1111/jcal.12618

Ferguson, C. J. (2015). Everything in moderation: Moderate use of screens unassociated with child behavior problems. *The Psychiatric Quarterly*, *86*(1), 1–8. DOI: 10.1007/s11126-014-9326-5 PMID: 25270895

Fotaris, P., & Mastoras, T. (2019). Escape rooms for learning: A systematic review. *Educational Technology Research and Development*, *67*(2), 123–145. DOI: 10.1007/s11423-018-9612-5

Gandolfi, E. (2016). To watch or to play, it is in the game: The game culture on Twitch.tv among performers, players, and audiences. *Journal of Gaming & Virtual Worlds*, *8*(1), 63–82. DOI: 10.1386/jgvw.8.1.63_1

Gartner, Inc. (2024, October 3). Gartner says generative AI will require 80 percent of engineering workforce to upskill through 2027 [Press release]. https://www.gartner.com/en/newsroom/press-releases/2024-10-03-gartner-says-generative-ai-will-require-80-percent-of-engineering-workforce-to-upskill-through-2027

Gazis, A., & Katsiri, E. (2023). *Serious games in digital gaming: A comprehensive review of applications, game engines, and advancements*. WSEAS Transactions on Computer Research., DOI: 10.37394/232018.2023.11.2

Gentile, D. A., Anderson, C. A., Yukawa, S., Ihori, N., Saleem, M., Lim, K. M., Shibuya, A., Liau, A. K., Khoo, A., Bushman, B. J., Huesmann, L. R., & Sakamoto, A. (2009). The effects of prosocial video games on prosocial behaviors: International evidence from correlational, longitudinal, and experimental studies. *Personality and Social Psychology Bulletin*, *35*(6), 752–763. DOI: 10.1177/0146167209333045 PMID: 19321812

Grace, K., & Maher, M. (2021). Towards computational co-creation in modding communities. *Proceedings. AAAI Artificial Intelligence and Interactive Digital Entertainment Conference*, *10*(3), 15–20. Advance online publication. DOI: 10.1609/aiide.v10i3.12750

Grand View Research. (2024). *Digital therapeutics market size, share & trends analysis report by product, by application (oncology, respiratory, diabetes), by end-use (patients, providers, payers), by region, and segment forecasts, 2023–2030.* https://www.grandviewresearch.com/industry-analysis/digital-therapeutics-market

Granic, I., Lobel, A., & Engels, R. C. M. E. (2014). The benefits of playing video games. *The American Psychologist*, *69*(1), 66–78. DOI: 10.1037/a0034857 PMID: 24295515

Green, C. S., & Bavelier, D. (2007). Action-video-game experience alters the spatial resolution of vision. *Psychological science, 18(*1), 88-94. https://www.jstor.org/stable/40064582

Green, C. S., & Bavelier, D. (2012). Learning, attentional control, and action video games. *Current Biology*, *22*(6), 197–206. DOI: 10.1016/j.cub.2012.02.012 PMID: 22440805

Hall, M. M. D. (2021). *Fortnite, Screenagers, and Student Resistance: A Correlational Analysis of Video Game Performance and Critical Thinking Levels*. ProQuest Dissertations & Theses, Regent University.

Harteveld, C., & Bekebrede, G. (2016). A frame-reflective discourse analysis of serious games. *Simulation & Gaming*, *47*(5), 632–654. DOI: 10.1177/1046878116662959

Howard, K. S., Tondeur, J., Siddiq, F., & Scherer, R. (2021). Ready, set, go! Profiling teachers' readiness for online teaching in secondary education. *Technology, Pedagogy and Education*, *30*(1), 141–158. DOI: 10.1080/1475939X.2020.1839543

Hubert-Wallander, B., Green, C. S., & Bavelier, D. (2010). Stretching the limits of visual attention: The case of action video games. *Wiley Interdisciplinary Reviews: Cognitive Science*, *1*(1), 1–9. DOI: 10.1002/wcs.44 PMID: 26302012

International Telecommunication Union. (2023). *Universal and meaningful connectivity by 2030.*https://www.itu.int/en/mediacentre/Pages/PR-2023-09-12-universal-and-meaningful-connectivity-by-2030.aspx

Jackson, L. A., Witt, E. A., Games, A. I., Fitzgerald, H. E., von Eye, A., & Zhao, Y. (2012). Information technology use and creativity: Findings from the Children and Technology Project. *Computers in Human Behavior*, *28*(2), 370–376. DOI: 10.1016/j.chb.2011.10.006

Jacobides, M. G., Ma, M. D., Trantopoulos, K., & Vassalos, V. (2024). The business value of gamification. *California Management Review*, *66*(2), 91–107. https://lbsresearch.london.edu/id/eprint/3621/1/jacobides-et-al-2024-the-business-value-of-gamification.pdf. DOI: 10.1177/00081256231218469

Jaramillo-Mediavilla, L., Basantes-Andrade, A., Cabezas-González, M., & Casillas-Martín, S. (2024). Impact of gamification on motivation and academic performance: A systematic review. *Education Sciences*, *14*(6), 639. DOI: 10.3390/educsci14060639

Jenny, S., Gawrysiak, J., & Besombes, N. (2021). Esports.edu: An inventory and analysis of global higher education esports academic programming and curricula. *International Journal of Esports*, *1*(1). https://www.ijesports.org/article/59/html

Jenny, S. E., Besombes, N., Brock, T., Cote, A. C., & Scholz, T. M. (2024). *Routledge handbook of esports*. Taylor & Francis. DOI: 10.4324/9781003410591

Jenny, S. E., Manning, R. D., Keiper, M. C., & Olrich, T. W. (2016). Virtual(ly) athletes: Where eSports fit within the definition of "sport.". *Quest*, *69*(1), 1–18. DOI: 10.1080/00336297.2016.1144517

Jones, C. M., Scholes, L., Johnson, D., Katsikitis, M., & Carras, M. C. (2014). Gaming well: Links between videogames and flourishing mental health. *Frontiers in Psychology*, *5*. Advance online publication. DOI: 10.3389/fpsyg.2014.00260 PMID: 24744743

Kaytoue, M., Silva, A., Cerf, L., Meira, W.Jr, & Raïssi, C. (2012, April). Watch me playing, I am a professional: A first study on video game live streaming. In *Proceedings of the 21st International Conference on World Wide Web* (pp. 1181–1188). DOI: 10.1145/2187980.2188259

Khesht-Masjedi, M. F., Shokrgozar, S., Abdollahi, E., Habibi, B., Asghari, T., Ofoghi, R. S., & Pazhooman, S. (2019). The relationship between gender, age, anxiety, depression, and academic achievement among teenagers. *Journal of Family Medicine and Primary Care*, *8*(3), 799–803. DOI: 10.4103/jfmpc.jfmpc_257_19

Kraus, S., Jones, P., Kailer, N., Weinmann, A., Chaparro-Banegas, N., & Roig-Tierno, N. (2021). Digital transformation: An overview of the current state of the art of research. *SAGE Open*, *11*(3). Advance online publication. DOI: 10.1177/21582440211047576

Lafrenière, M. A., Bureau, J. S., Vallerand, R. J., & Ntoumanis, N. (2013). On passion and moral behavior in achievement settings: The mediating role of pride. *Motivation and Emotion*, *37*(1), 121–133. DOI: 10.1007/s11031-012-9292-7

Lamarre, E., Chheda, S., Riba, M., Genest, V., & Nizam, A. (2023, July 31). The value of digital transformation. *Harvard Business Review*.

Lara, J. S. (2023). Spotting k-TriCaps in SPOT IT! *Senior Projects Spring 2023*, 349. https://digitalcommons.bard.edu/senproj_s2023/349

Lejuez, C. W., Read, J. P., Kahler, C. W., Richards, J. B., Ramsey, S. E., Stuart, G. L., Strong, D. R., & Brown, R. A. (2002). Evaluation of a behavioral measure of risk-taking: The Balloon Analogue Risk Task (BART). *Journal of Experimental Psychology. Applied*, *8*(2), 75–84. DOI: 10.1037/1076-898X.8.2.75 PMID: 12075692

Lenhart, A., Kahne, J., Middaugh, E., Macgill, A. R., Evans, C., & Vitak, J. (2008). *Teens, video games, and civics: Teens' gaming experiences are diverse and include significant social interaction and civic engagement.* Pew Internet & American Life Project. https://files.eric.ed.gov/fulltext/ED525058.pdf

Li, R. W., Ngo, C., Nguyen, J., & Levi, D. M. (2011). Video-game play induces plasticity in the visual system of adults with amblyopia. *PLoS Biology*, *9*(8), e1001135. DOI: 10.1371/journal.pbio.1001135 PMID: 21912514

Li, Y., Chen, D., & Deng, X. (2024). The impact of digital educational games on student's motivation for learning: The mediating effect of learning engagement and the moderating effect of the digital environment. *PLoS One*, *19*(1), e0294350. DOI: 10.1371/journal.pone.0294350 PMID: 38206923

Lumbreras, A. G., Hurwitz, J. T., Liang, X., Schippers, S., Phillip, K., Bhattacharjee, S., Waters, H. C., & Malone, D. C. (2024). Insights into insurance coverage for digital therapeutics: A qualitative study of US payer perspectives. *Journal of Managed Care & Specialty Pharmacy*, *30*(4), 313–320. DOI: 10.18553/jmcp.2024.30.4.313 PMID: 38555623

Maslow, A. H. (1954). *Motivation and personality.* Harpers. https://psycnet.apa.org/record/1955-02233-000

Matthews, D. (n.d.). DIY adaptive gaming: Game control for people with upper limb disabilities (Bachelor's thesis, University of Twente).

Mayer, I. S. (2009). The gaming of policy and the politics of gaming: A review. *Simulation & Gaming*, *40*(6), 825–862. DOI: 10.1177/1046878109346456

McNulty, C., Jenny, S. E., Leis, O., Poulus, D., Sondergeld, P., & Nicholson, M. (2022). Physical exercise and performance in esports players: An initial systematic review. *Journal of Electronic Gaming and Esports*. DOI: 10.1123/jege.2022-0014

Meticulous Research. (2023). *Gamification market by type (structural, content), offering, organization size, deployment mode, application (HRM, CRM, customer engagement), end-use industry (BFSI, retail & e-commerce, education & research), and geography - Global forecast to 2030 (Report ID: MRICT - 104314).* Meticulous Research. https://www.meticulousresearch.com/product/gamification-market-5015

Migliore, L., McGee, C., & Moore, M. N. (2021). *Handbook of esports medicine: Clinical aspects of competitive video gaming*. Springer., DOI: 10.1007/978-3-030-73610-1

Mitsea, E., Drigas, A., & Skianis, C. (2024). Well-being technologies and positive psychology strategies for training metacognition, emotional intelligence and motivation meta-skills in clinical populations: A systematic review. *Psych*, *6*(1), 305–344. DOI: 10.3390/psych6010019

Mould, S. (2022, October 27). *Mechanical circuits: Electronics without electricity* [Video]. YouTube. https://www.youtube.com/watch?v=QrkiJZKJfpY

Nakamura, L. (2002). *Cybertypes: Race, ethnicity, and identity on the Internet*. Routledge. DOI: 10.4324/9780203953365

Network of Academic and Scholastic Esports Federation. (2024). About NASEF. NASEF. https://www.nasef.org/about

Newzoo. (2023). *Global games market report 2023*. https://newzoo.com/resources/trend-reports/newzoo-global-games-market-report-2023-free-version

Newzoo. (2024). *Global games market report 2024*. https://newzoo.com/resources/trend-reports/newzoos-global-games-market-report-2024-free-version

Pasmore, W., Lafferty, K., & Spencer, S. (2014). Developing a leadership strategy: A critical ingredient for organizational success. Center for Creative Leadership, 1-28.

Pauly, D. (1995). Anecdotes and the shifting baseline syndrome of fisheries. *Trends in Ecology & Evolution*, *10*(10), 430. https://hdl.handle.net/20.500.12348/2785. DOI: 10.1016/S0169-5347(00)89171-5 PMID: 21237093

Pellis, S. M., & Pellis, V. C. (2007). Rough-and-tumble play and the development of the social brain. *Current Directions in Psychological Science*, *16*(2), 95–98. DOI: 10.1111/j.1467-8721.2007.00483.x

PwC. (2024). *Global Workforce Hopes and Fears Survey 2024*.https://www.pwc.com/gx/en/issues/workforce/hopes-and-fears.html

Raith, L., Bignill, J., Stavropoulos, V., Millear, P., Allen, A., Stallman, H. M., Mason, J., De Regt, T., Wood, A., & Kannis-Dymand, L. (2021). Massively multiplayer online games and well-being: A systematic literature review. *Frontiers in Psychology*, *12*, 698799. DOI: 10.3389/fpsyg.2021.698799 PMID: 34276523

Robertson, M. M., Ciriello, V. M., & Garabet, A. M. (2013). Office ergonomics training and a sit-stand workstation: Effects on musculoskeletal and visual symptoms and performance of office workers. *Applied Ergonomics*, *44*(1), 73–85. DOI: 10.1016/j.apergo.2012.05.001 PMID: 22727324

Saeed, S. A., & Masters, R. M. (2021). Disparities in health care and the digital divide. *Current Psychiatry Reports*, *23*(9), 61. DOI: 10.1007/s11920-021-01274-4 PMID: 34297202

Santo, R. (2021). Making public policy fun: How political aspects and policy issues are found in video games. *Journal of Political Science Education*, *17*(3), 389–406. DOI: 10.1080/15512169.2019.1696880

Schmierbach, M. (2010). "Killing spree": Exploring the connection between competitive game play and aggressive cognition. *Communication Research*, *37*(2), 256–274. DOI: 10.1177/0093650209356394

Sengupta, D. (2016). *A mathematical analysis of Spot It!*http://deepusengupta.com/projects/mathematical_analysis_spot_it.pdf?i=1

Shaw, A. (2015). *Gaming at the edge: Sexuality and gender at the margins of gamer culture*. University of Minnesota Press., DOI: 10.5749/minnesota/9780816693153.001.0001

Shaw, A. (2022). Creative Minecrafters: Cognitive and personality determinants of creativity, novelty, and usefulness in Minecraft. *Psychology of Aesthetics, Creativity, and the Arts*. Advance online publication. DOI: 10.1037/aca0000310

Siddiq, F., Hatlevik, O. E., Olsen, R. V., Throndsen, I., & Scherer, R. (2016). Taking a future perspective by learning from the past: A systematic review of assessment instruments that aim to measure primary and secondary school students' ICT literacy. *Educational Research Review*, *19*, 58–84. DOI: 10.1016/j.edurev.2016.05.002

Sidhu, P., Carter, M., & Zagal, J. P. (Eds.). (2024). *Fifty years of Dungeons & Dragons*. MIT Press. DOI: 10.7551/mitpress/15175.001.0001

Sissine, M., Segan, R., Taylor, M., Jefferson, B., Borrelli, A., Koehler, M., & Chelvayohan, M. (2014). Cost comparison model: Blended eLearning versus traditional training of community health workers. *Online Journal of Public Health Informatics*, *6*(3). Advance online publication. DOI: 10.5210/ojphi.v6i3.5533 PMID: 25598868

Sliwinski, J., Katsikitis, M., & Jones, C. M. (2017). A review of interactive technologies as support tools for the cultivation of mindfulness. *Mindfulness*, *8*(5), 1150–1159. DOI: 10.1007/s12671-017-0698-x

Slotboom, C. (2024). *Locktree Gaming Quadrant*. Team Locktree.

Slotboom, C. (2024). *The new gaming & esports pyramid 2024*. Team Locktree. https://www.teamlocktree.com/news/business/the-new-gaming-esports-pyramid-2024/

Statista. (2024). *Frequency of using smartphones to play games in the U.S.* Statista. https://www.statista.com/statistics/248892/frequency-of-using-smartphones-to-play-games-in-the-us/

Steinkuehler, C., & Duncan, S. (2008). Scientific habits of mind in virtual worlds. *Journal of Science Education and Technology*, *17*(6), 530–543. DOI: 10.1007/s10956-008-9120-8

Taborda Mosquera, J. P., Arango-López, J., Gutiérrez Vela, F. L., & Padilla Zea, N. (2021). Analyzing effectiveness and fun through metrics applied to pervasive gaming experiences. *Universal Access in the Information Society*, *20*(3), 545–554. DOI: 10.1007/s10209-020-00768-x

Tavinor, G. (2009). *The art of videogames*. Wiley-Blackwell. DOI: 10.1002/9781444310177

Trammell, A., Loring-Albright, G., & Boluk, S. (2017). Mechanics of trauma in *The Grizzled. Analog Game Studies, 4*(1). https://analoggamestudies.org/2017/01/mechanics-of-trauma-in-the-grizzled/

United Nations. (2018). *E-government survey 2018: Gearing e-government to support transformation towards sustainable and resilient societies.*https://publicadministration.un.org/egovkb/en-us/Reports/UN-E-Government-Survey-2018

Uttal, D. H., Meadow, N. G., Tipton, E., Hand, L. L., Alden, A. R., Warren, C., & Newcombe, N. S. (2013). The malleability of spatial skills: A meta-analysis of training studies. *Psychological Bulletin*, *139*(2), 352–402. DOI: 10.1037/a0028446 PMID: 22663761

Valdez, V. B., & Javier, S. P. (2021). Digital divide: From a peripheral to a core issue for all SDGs. In *Reduced inequalities* (pp. 88–101). Springer International Publishing. DOI: 10.1007/978-3-319-95882-8_107

van Dijk, J. (2020). *The digital divide* (2nd ed.). Polity Press.

van Zoest, V. (2015). *Relationship between video gaming and spatial thinking skills of children 8 to 10 years old* (Bachelor's thesis). Wageningen University and Research Centre. https://edepot.wur.nl/351159

Velez, J. A., Mahood, C., Ewoldsen, D. R., & Moyer-Gusé, E. (2012). Ingroup versus outgroup conflict in the context of violent video game play: The effect of cooperation on increased helping and decreased aggression. *Communication Research*, *39*(8), 1–20. DOI: 10.1177/0093650212456202

Video Game Insights. (2024). *Global PC Games Market Report 2024*. https://vginsights.com/assets/reports/VGI_Global_PC_Games_Market_Report_2024.pdf

Vink, P. (2009). *Creating supportive environments for workplace well-being*. CRC Press. https://books.google.nl/books?id=2RYNDgAAQBAJ

Vinyals, O., Babuschkin, I., Czarnecki, W. M., Mathieu, M., Dudzik, A., Chung, J., Choi, D. H., Powell, R., Ewalds, T., Georgiev, P., Oh, J., Horgan, D., Kroiss, M., Danihelka, I., Huang, A., Sifre, L., Cai, T., Agapiou, J. P., Jaderberg, M., & Silver, D. (2019). Grandmaster level in StarCraft II using multi-agent reinforcement learning. *Nature*, *575*(7782), 350–354. Advance online publication. DOI: 10.1038/s41586-019-1724-z PMID: 31666705

Wai, J., Cacchio, M., Putallaz, M., & Makel, M. C. (2010). Sex differences in the right tail of cognitive abilities: A 30 year examination. *Intelligence*, *38*(4), 412–423. DOI: 10.1016/j.intell.2010.04.006

Weigand, K., Flanagan, T., Dye, K., & Jones, P. (2014). Collaborative foresight: Complementing long-horizon strategic planning. *Technological Forecasting and Social Change*, *85*, 134–152. DOI: 10.1016/j.techfore.2013.08.016

Williams, W. M., & Ayres, C. G. (2020). Can active video games improve physical activity in adolescents? A review of RCT. *International Journal of Environmental Research and Public Health*, *17*(2), 669. DOI: 10.3390/ijerph17020669 PMID: 31968642

World Health Organization. (2017). *Protecting workers' health*.https://www.who.int/news-room/fact-sheets/detail/protecting-workers'-health

Woźniak, J. (2020). Gamification for sales incentives. *Contemporary Economics*, *14*(2), 144–161. DOI: 10.5709/ce.1897-9254.337

Yee, N. (2006). Motivations for play in online games. *Cyberpsychology & Behavior*, *9*(6), 772–775. DOI: 10.1089/cpb.2006.9.772 PMID: 17201605

Yee, N. (2014). *The Proteus paradox: How online games and virtual worlds change us—and how they don't*. Yale University Press.

Zhu, L., Wang, Y., Wu, Y., Wilson, A., Zhou, H., Li, N., & Wang, Y. (2024). Longitudinal associations between the frequency of playing Mahjong and cognitive functioning among older people in China: Evidence from CLHLS, 2008–2018. *Frontiers in Public Health*, *12*, 1352433. Advance online publication. DOI: 10.3389/fpubh.2024.1352433 PMID: 38550318

Section 2
Workplace Public and Mental Health

Chapter 4
The Pulse of Progress:
How Wearable Tech is Shaping the Future of Public Health

Ameera Law
The University of Texas at San Antonio, USA

Sebastian Gutierrez
The University of Texas at San Antonio, USA

Keren Asgodom
The University of Texas at San Antonio, USA

Mahrukh Khan
The University of Texas at San Antonio, USA

ABSTRACT

This paper focuses on wearable technologies' integration into management of chronic diseases, support for mental health disorders and health insurance policies. Through the examination of peer-reviewed studies, research found that wearables have potential in promoting healthier habits, improving patient outcomes by collecting real-time data for personalized medicine, and offering interventions for mental health conditions. Considerations of innovative "pay-as-you-live" insurance models that incentivize healthy behaviors by collecting health data from wearables are also explored in this paper. Nevertheless, challenges such as data privacy, accuracy, and accessibility remain, specifically among vulnerable communities. It is crucial to address these issues to fully realize wearable technology's potential in reducing chronic disease burdens and revolutionize mental healthcare. Further research is needed to overcome technological, ethical, and socioeconomic barriers, to ensure the successful integration of wearables to enhance public health.

DOI: 10.4018/979-8-3373-5322-7.ch004

INTRODUCTION

As it has evolved, technology has become the norm in everyday life. No other form of technology is as intertwined with our routine lives as wearable technology. Wearable technology, also called wearables, can best be defined as "integrated analytical units equipped with sensitive physical, chemical, and biological sensors capable of noninvasive and continuous monitoring of vital physiological parameters" (Babu et al., 2023). They can be small electronics, mobile devices, or computers with wireless communication capabilities that can be incorporated into gadgets, accessories, or clothes and worn on the human body (Ometov et al., 2021). Wearables are increasingly becoming more integrated within society and thus the workplace, introducing new conversions about long-term effects on both physical health and mental health and the evolving landscape of health insurance.

The assimilation of wearable technology with mental health initiatives represents a promising frontier, enabling innovative approaches to monitoring and managing conditions. Exploring and understanding the effects of wearables is important because of the possible impact on users' behavior and long-term health outcomes over an extended period. Wearable technology holds immense promise in changing healthcare delivery. By incorporating wearable technology, especially in disadvantaged populations, it will be possible to take advantage of the full capability of this technology to improve public health and lay the foundation for a healthier future and workplace.

What is Wearable Technology?

Wearable technology has revolutionized the world, with its most extreme effects being felt in the healthcare field. It has altered the course of the healthcare industry completely, changing the way we collect data and manage health conditions. There are many types of wearables. These devices span from consumer items like smartwatches and fitness trackers to complex medical devices; however, the impact of these devices is all the same. Wearable technology collects almost instantaneous data on the lives of those who wear it, allowing researchers and health professionals to have a never-before-seen understanding of the overall well-being of the general population. This can especially be seen in recent years as AI has been a remarkable helping hand in the collection of data for wearable technology (Motti, 2019).

The invention that began the new era in healthcare was the pacemaker. In 1950, doctors Wilfred Bigelow and John Callaghan and engineer Jack Hopps came together with the shared goal to prevent "cardiac standstill", better known as cardiac arrest. By 1958, implantable external pacemakers were first attempted (Ward et al., 2018). Though these external pacemakers had limited functionality, it created the foundation for cardiac pacing technology. Because of technological advancements, today's pacemakers are smaller, more adjustable to fit personalized needs, and are far more reliable. Pacemakers created a domino effect, leading to many innovations that would alter the healthcare industry. Using wearable technology, like pacemakers, has become a necessary instrument in healthcare, improving the lives of many.

The evolution in wearable technology within the last two decades has grown due to sensors that monitor vital signs (Pentland, 2004). The progress in sensor technology has allowed for miniaturization and increased connectivity which has been essential in creating high-tech wearable technology. With these advancements, health professionals can tackle more specific health challenges, such as monitoring lifestyle adaptations during pregnancy through wearable sensors, which has led to behavior change interventions through their collection of data (Penders et al., 2015). This collection of data has led to behavior change interventions and resulted in the discovery of new indicators for pregnancy complications.

The continuous development of wearable technology has also helped tremendously with deaf and hearing-impaired individuals. Wearable devices like cochlear implants and hearing aids have made great strides within the deaf and hearing-impaired community and in turn, public health; however, there are still limitations with said devices. These limitations include limited availability within lower-income communities and the ability for the devices to be easily lost due to size. Nonetheless, vibration-based wearable devices have also been a major success for deaf and hearing-impaired individuals. The wearable vibration-based system helps deaf and hearing-impaired individuals recognize sentences using vibrations. The device is meant to be worn on an individual's back and uses a microphone and vibration motor to process speech. The system uses Mel Frequency Cepstral Coefficients (MFCC), preprocessing, and Dynamic Time Warping (DTW) to convert spoken language into vibration patterns (Yağanoğlu, 2021). This piece of wearable technology has become a useful tool for deaf people who might face issues with everyday communication, especially when sign language interpreters are not available. Yağanoğlu (2021) also finds that vibration-based wearable devices are different from traditional hearing aids because they are still successful even in loud environments, which is a common issue with hearing aids.

However, while wearable technology still requires further improvement in chronic disease management, it still offers a practical way to monitor the daily activities of those with chronic diseases. They help in measuring levels of ambulation in said study, which is important in diseases like multiple sclerosis where fatigue is one of the more common symptoms (Chiauzzi et al., 2015). The study showed the success of wearable devices in post-surgical mobility recovery in elderly cardiac surgery patients.

Long Term Effects

One of the more noticeable impacts of wearable technologies is the incredibly large amount of data that wearable technology collects daily (Motti, 2019). It allows for better research surrounding the efficiency of public health interventions and helps improve upon already effective health programs that can now try to target more specific challenges (Motti, 2019).

However, wearable technology does have its limitations with issues such as a lack of accessibility, accuracy problems for people of color (Colvonen et al., 2020), and the lack of studies about the long-term effects radio frequency being emitted from wearable devices are causes for concern (Keykhosravi et al., 2018). Though these concerns must be addressed, it is also vital that the lasting impacts of wearable technology and the data it gathers are studied. The impacts of these devices will continue to cause a ripple effect throughout the healthcare and public health field for generations to come.

The long-term usage of wearable devices can create a massive societal shift for vulnerable communities. An example of this is electroencephalogram (EEG) systems, which record brain activity with small sensors placed over one's head. The EEG system can detect seizures by finding the average wave amplitude, duration, dominant frequency, and power in the main energy zone, then extracted for analysis (Qu,1997). These features detect the onset of a seizure and tell it apart from normal EEG patterns. Once a seizure occurs in a patient, it is remembered within the system. Then the system scans for matches to this pattern, and signals medical professionals of the beginning of a new seizure. Though this system has its limitations because it requires adjustments by the medical staff to avoid false alarms, studies show that the "average false alarm rate was only .02/h." (Qu, 1997). The EEG systems have provided great results in creating early intervention for seizures.

Wearable technology has multiple positive health outcomes, one of which is increased physical activity; a systematic review conducted by Joe et al. (2019), stated an obvious decrease in weight with participants who used wearable devices. Though there were no significant decreases seen in cholesterol levels or blood pressure in the studies reviewed, the study focused on HbA1c levels in older patients with type 2 diabetes, where a large decrease was seen. The review suggests that wearable devices have an important role in health behavior change. However, their direct impact on chronic disease outcomes still requires further investigation since patients with chronic illness need more comprehensive support that changes throughout their disease, meaning wearable technology needs to be more adaptable. For wearable technology to cater to the ever-changing needs of the chronically ill, they must provide better insights to be effective in managing chronic illnesses (Chiauzzi et al., 2015). For this to happen, patient-physician collaboration must be emphasized.

Theoretical Framework of Wearable Technology

The Health Belief Model suggests that individuals are more likely to accept health-related behaviors if they perceive themselves to be susceptible to a health problem, recognize the severity of the issue, believe that doing something to help their health issue would be worth it in the long run, perceive few barriers to, and have enough self-efficacy to persevere (Green & Murphy, 2014). Applying said model to long-term usage of wearable technology suggests that people who realize that wearable devices, like fitness trackers, are valuable tools for improving their health are more likely to use them in their daily routines. This is because consumer wearable devices give people easy-to-read health data and this data can help improve their awareness of their health issues, giving the individual a chance to become aware of their perception of susceptibility or severity. Wearable devices motivate the users by showing them the product of their new healthy behaviors, like weight reduction (Joe et al., 2019). Wearable technology also allows individuals to create reminders and act as cues to actions. Self-efficacy also plays a serious role in getting individuals to use consumer wearable devices. Though the usage of wearable technology cannot give an individual self-efficacy, an individual's self-efficacy can be improved by wearable technology if the individuals create feasible goals.

Similarly, Zahrt et al. (2022), explores the influence of activity adequacy mindsets or AAM and how the use of wearable fitness trackers trickles down into the individual's daily actions and beliefs. AAM are beliefs that individuals have about the health consequences of their physical activity (Zahrt et al., 2022). The study stated that those who received their correct step counts improved their perception of activity adequacy, created a better diet, and improved their mental health. The participants who received inaccurate and deflated step counts had a sense of inadequacy when it came to their physical activity, causing participants to engage in unhealthy eating habits and increased heart rate and blood pressure (Zahrt et al., 2022). This is because the study further highlights the need for truthful feedback, as it proves mindsets can create lasting changes in health behavior. This approach could help wearable technology in the future to create code for improving people's well-being by positively influencing them about their health behaviors.

THE USE OF AI IN WEARABLE TECHNOLOGY

The use of artificial intelligence in all fields of technology has become increasingly prevalent as it has advanced. According to (Chidambaram et al., 2022), "The intersection of large volumes of data and healthcare applications calls for the use of artificial intelligence technology to improve how the data are handled, processed, and used." This is evident in wearable technology because artificial intelligence increases the functionality of wearable devices when it comes to predictive analytics. The usage of artificial intelligence in predictive analytics can be seen within sports medicine. Chidambaram et al. (2022) states that AI analyzes data from sensors to improve their performance, which helps improve post-injury rehabilitation and examine how dire an athlete's injury is. Since the AI system continuously predicts the probability of an injury, it improves the athletes' performance in the game, whether basketball or baseball, and helps improve the overall health of all athletes (Chidambaram et al., 2022). This review touches on the matter that AI has the ability to effortlessly identify patterns and concepts that the average human cannot see.

AI algorithms can process data quicker and on a larger scale than humans, decreasing healthcare professionals' medical errors.. AI further reduces human error in areas such as data entry, sampling, and interpretation (Chidambaram et al., 2022). Because of the AI within wearable devices, the ability to deliver individualized health is strengthened, allowing for the door of possibilities to open for a much more personalized approach to healthcare practices and leading to lasting impacts on public health.

Transparency and Accountability of AI Algorithms

Using AI in health monitoring raises concerns about accountability and transparency. AI systems need to be clear and understandable so users and healthcare professionals can trust the decisions they make. This means explaining how AI algorithms work in a way that non-experts can understand (Al Kuwaiti et al., 2023).

Transparency is especially important in healthcare, where AI decisions can significantly impact patient outcomes. By clearly showing how an AI system arrives at a diagnosis or recommendation, we build trust between patients and doctors. Transparency also helps identify and correct any biases or errors in the AI, ensuring it works effectively and fairly (Bajwa et al., 2021).

Addressing Bias in AI Algorithms

Addressing biases in AI algorithms is crucial to ensure that everyone benefits equitably from AI-enhanced wearables. AI systems learn from vast datasets, which may unfortunately reflect historical injustices. If left unchecked, these biases can perpetuate unfair healthcare outcomes (Ahmed et al., 2022).

To mitigate this issue, AI models should be trained on diverse datasets that encompass various demographic groups and contexts. Incorporating fairness criteria during algorithm development and regularly auditing for bias can help ensure that all user groups receive equal treatment and accurate predictions (Junaid et al., 2022).

Consulting with experts in ethics, social sciences, and medicine is also essential. Their insights can shed light on potential biases and contribute to refining algorithms to minimize unfair impacts (Nahavandi et al., 2022).

Ensuring informed consent and respecting user autonomy are also critical ethical considerations. It is vital that consumers fully understand what data is being collected, how it will be used, and who will have access to it. Providing users with control over their data—such as the ability to review, modify, or restrict access—empowers them and fosters trust in the technology (Bajwa et al., 2021). Taking these steps to increase user-control, will contribute to a more trusting adoption of AI in wearable technology.

Personalized Treatment with Artificial Intelligence

Artificial intelligence (AI) significantly impacts healthcare with data analysis, predictive modeling, and personalized treatment capabilities. When combined with wearable health devices like fitness trackers, smartwatches, and medical monitors, AI greatly enhances health tracking and treatment. These devices, which started as basic fitness trackers, now feature sensors that monitor various physiological characteristics. They send constant data streams that AI algorithms analyze in real-time, enabling personalized health suggestions, predictive analytics, alerts, and instant feedback (Bajwa et al., 2021). AI uses patient data profiles to provide customized recommendations, promoting healthy habits through prompts and reminders (De Ramón Fernández et al., 2022).(AI)

AI-enabled wearables ensure prompt and efficient care by enabling continuous monitoring and flexible therapy for ailments like diabetes or hypertension (Ahmed et al., 2022; Nahavandi et al., 2022). They are also helpful in treating chronic illnesses, providing mental health care, and responding to emergencies (Docles, 2023; Xie et al., 2021). In emergencies, AI can predict seizures and detect falls, speeding up response times and enabling preventive action (Ahuja et al., 2024; Shajari et al., 2023). AI can also analyze mood and stress levels, offering insights and therapeutic treatments to improve mental health management (Al Kuwaiti et al., 2023).

This integration of AI and wearables has the potential to transform healthcare, making it more precise, timely, and personalized. It paves the way for a future where healthcare is proactive, predictive, and tailored to individual needs.

Predicting health occurrences with machine learning algorithms is a significant advancement in preventive medicine. Through the analysis of physiological signs such as heart rate variability, AI can detect potential cardiac events, and thus early intervention and prevention are made possible (Tariq et al., 2023). Similarly, fitness trackers equipped with artificial intelligence (AI) capabilities can monitor a diabetic patient's blood sugar levels and provide personalized, in-the-moment guidance on dietary and medication adjustments (Ahmed et al., 2022). By transforming the system from a reactive to a proactive one, this technology has a significant impact on the field of preventive medicine, which aims to stop illnesses before they fully manifest (Ahmed et al., 2022; Junaid et al., 2022).

AI can also increase patient involvement and adherence to treatment plans. Wearables with AI capabilities can offer personalized therapies for mental health support, remind users to take their prescriptions, and suggest lifestyle modifications. This customized approach reduces the strain for medical staff while also improving patient outcomes by enabling remote monitoring and early intervention (Wilmink et al., 2020).

AI-enhanced wearables are essential for gathering and evaluating vast amounts of health data in research. This data improves our knowledge of a variety of diseases and guides the creation of novel treatment plans. With the ability to continually monitor vital signs, anticipate future health problems, and provide individualized advice for food, exercise, and medication modifications, these gadgets enable people to manage their health more successfully in daily life (Bajwa et al., 2021). As a result, wearable AI technology promotes the treatment and prevention of chronic illnesses, improving quality of life and health outcomes (Ahuja et al., 2024; De Ramón Fernández et al., 2022; Sharma et al., 2022; Yelne et al., 2023).

Furthermore, wearer analytics powered by AI can provide a more in-depth understanding of their general health. AI can identify minute alterations that might portend the emergence of health problems by continually learning from the data gathered. AI-powered wearables are crucial for preventative healthcare because of their constant learning and adaptability (Xie et al., 2021)When managing chronic conditions, where prompt reactions and ongoing monitoring are required, this type of integration is quite helpful. AI-enhanced wearables can assist in the early diagnosis of potential issues and the tailoring of treatment regimens by giving medical personnel access to real-time data and predictive insights This approach prioritizes personalization in healthcare, enabling tailored treatment plans that take into account the unique needs and issues of each patient. (Al Kuwaiti et al., 2023; Baptista et al., 2024; Docles, 2023).

Enhanced Interaction with User

Wearable technology provides highly tailored experiences because artificial intelligence can process large volumes of data and learn from human interactions (Ahmed et al., 2022; Junaid et al., 2022; Nahavandi et al., 2022). These devices allow users to monitor their daily activities, health measurements, and lifestyle choices, while receiving personalized recommendations to support their health goals (Shajari et al., 2023). For instance, a user aiming to get more fitfitter may receive customized training regimens to help them reach their goals and perform at their best (Bajwa et al., 2021). AI can also analyze eating patterns and recommend dietary adjustments to improve overall health. Sleep patterns are a fundamental aspect of human biology and well-being, directly linked to our physical health, mental acuity, emotional stability, and overall quality of life (Tariq et al., 2023). The study of sleep, known as sleep medicine, has revealed the profound impact that sleep patterns—or lack thereof—can have on our daily functions and long-term health outcomes. AI can offer insights and suggestions to enhance sleep hygiene and promote more consistent rest and recovery.

According to a study, "AI algorithms integrated with wearable devices can process and analyze diverse data streams in real-time, enabling personalized health interventions and recommendations" (Ahmed et al., 2022). The improvement of user experience and engagement is a critical component of AI integration in wearable technology. The device's recommendations and comments may be personalized by AI algorithms to better serve the user's needs and make them more applicable. For instance, a wearable with AI capabilities may gradually learn about its user's tastes and behavior to provide personalized recommendations on food, exercise, and sleeping patterns (Ahuja et al., 2024).

This tailored approach promotes a more engaging and participatory experience while helping users adhere to health norms. Users are more likely to follow guidance when they receive feedback and suggestions personalized to their needs and interests, leading to better health outcomes and increased user satisfaction. (Ahmed et al., 2022). For instance, AI can remind users to drink enough water based on their activity level and surrounding conditions. It can also recommend dietary changes if users are not getting enough nutrients from their diet. Such focused interventions can make health management programs much more effective. According to a study published in the Journal of Medical Internet Research, "Personalized feedback from health monitoring devices enhances user engagement and adherence to health guidelines, resulting in improved health outcomes" (Ahmed et al., 2022).

AI may enhance gamification elements like goal-setting and incentive schemes, which would make healthcare more motivating and interesting. As users advance, it may generate activities that change to keep them tough yet doable. For example, AI may adjust the level of fitness exercises according to user performance, making them challenging but manageable (Nahavandi et al., 2022). Incentives can also be tailored to an individual's tastes, which increases participation (Junaid et al., 2022). When users reach health objectives, they may receive virtual badges, points, or even tangible incentives, which they may post on social media to foster a sense of support and community (Gajardo Sánchez et al., 2023).

Gamification in the medical field has already shown encouraging outcomes. For instance, gamified health applications greatly increased patients' adherence to their prescription regimens and promoted healthier lifestyle choices, according to research done in a hospital environment (Smith & Jones et al., 2023). To encourage patients, these applications included features like leaderboards, point systems, and social sharing options. According to Smith and Jones (2023), gamification can improve health management, as seen by the increased satisfaction and engagement that patients reported having with their treatment programs. Hospitals and other healthcare providers may develop more individualized and successful health management programs by combining AI with gamification techniques. This combination may make boring health-related duties fun, which encourages a sustained commitment to good habits.

Wearable AI technology makes for more dynamic and interesting user interfaces. Natural language processing and machine learning enable these gadgets to communicate with consumers in more ways—voice commands and conversational interfaces, for example. Through this engagement, the user and their device may work together to manage health rather than viewing it as a duty. Users may converse with their wearable to better understand their health statistics and ask health-related questions. They can also get immediate feedback, making the user feel more engaged and supported in their journey toward health management with this level of interactivity (Junaid et al., 2022).

Future Challenges and Directions in Wearable AI Technology

Wearable AI technology is a promising field with many exciting new discoveries in store. Research is crucial in the field of integrating AI with other cutting-edge technologies like blockchain and the Internet of Things (IoT). The overall efficacy, interoperability, and data security of health monitoring systems can all be enhanced by this combination (Wilmink et al., 2020). For example, blockchain technology may ensure that only authorized personnel can access health data, providing a transparent and secure means of managing it. When blockchain and AI are used, health data may become more dependable, and secure data interchange between different healthcare institutions can be facilitated (Xie et al., 2021).

It is additionally important to consider the significant energy consumption associated with AI server room maintenance when calculating the power required. AI server rooms need a lot of electricity to power high-performance computer systems and keep the cooling system at the right level to avoid overheating. Sustainability issues arise because of the potential for increased operating expenses and a greater carbon footprint. De Ramón Fernández et al. (2022) discusses how it will be more crucial than ever to discover economical and environmentally friendly ways to power these server rooms as AI technology develops and finds more uses.

The potential for changing healthcare through the integration of AI with wearable health equipment is substantial. AI-enhanced wearables can promote preventative healthcare, improve the treatment of chronic illnesses, and increase patient involvement through continuous, real-time monitoring and tailored interventions. Even if there are still obstacles, continued developments in wearable technology and AI could solve these problems and open new avenues for managing and monitoring health. To fully reap the benefits of wearable health devices driven by AI, ethical, privacy, and scalability problems must be addressed as this sector develops (Bajwa et al., 2021).

A potential concern with wearable technology is the formation of a gap between those who have access to wearable technology and those who do not (Reid et al, 2019). The divide is a product of the high cost of wearable technology and low technology and health literacy rates. In marginalized communities where the access to resources is less than adequate, wearable technology will not be beneficial (Reid et al, 2019). Though this is a more recent concern for wearable technology, this extends further than the devices themselves and touches on the issue of accessible internet and internet-based devices. For wearable technology to be used to its greatest extent basic access to the internet and low-cost computers or smartphones need to be prioritized first.

Another major concern with wearable technology is the way radio frequency transmitters send and receive data. Long-term exposure to radio frequency radiation is a major concern that Keykhosravi et al. (2018) covers in their study. Keykhosravi et al. (2018) suggests that long-term exposure to radio frequency radiation can worsen skin problems such as dermatitis. The study also questions the possible changes in skin cell physiology that can occur, however, it is still being studied as the magnitude of damage correlates closely to the length of exposure.

MENTAL HEALTH AND WELLNESS

Mental health is important for every human being since it helps people perform their everyday activities, deal with stress, make healthy choices, and even their overall health. If a person's mental well-being is compromised, it can disrupt a person performing their daily activities and cause harm to their physical well-being. According to the World Health Organization (2022) about 970 million people around the world were living with a mental disorder in 2019 - the most common mental disorders being anxiety and depressive disorders. And cases keep increasing, showing estimates of a 26% and 28% increase respectively for anxiety and depressive disorders due to the COVID-19 pandemic (World Health Organization, 2022). Depression and anxiety have a significant impact on individuals in terms of lost years due to ill health, especially with depression being a major risk factor for suicide. A person with mental disorders tends to have a shorter lifespan due to health issues correlated to their mental status which makes it imperative to explore possible solutions to mitigate these issues (Ahmed et al., 2023).

Wearable technology offers many advantages, the biggest being its convenience, relieving people from continuously having to hold their smartphones in their hands. Not many people realize that wearable tech may also be utilized to track their mental health, such as in the case of fitness trackers.

Application of Wearables on Mental Health

As technology advances, it has seen widespread adoption in healthcare settings in order to help improve quality and increase the efficiency of care delivered to patients. The adoption has been gradual but with time, wearables have the potential to revolutionize the way mental health can be monitored and managed. According to Gomes et al. (2023), some benefits of wearables are that they can continuously track physiological parameters, such as heart rate and breathing patterns, and behavioral parameters such as sleep quality, physical activity, and social interactions. In addition, it can provide real-time feedback to individuals about their mental health. For example, if a person's heart rate increases, a wearable will alert the person to the presence of stress or anxiety. Wearables can also provide personalized interventions based on the data they collect. For example, a wearable that tracks sleep quality could provide recommendations on how an individual could improve their sleep habits. Lastly, wearables can help medical professionals by enhancing traditional mental health interventions because they can provide real-time data that can help inform treatment decisions (Gomes et al., 2023).

In the following are some examples of how wearables with the combination of mobile apps may help some specific mental disorders.

Stress and Anxiety

Wearables can help identify when a person is experiencing stress and anxiety. While stress is not considered a mental health issue, it is related to mental health and can negatively impact a person's mental health well-being. Acute stress typically does not impose a health burden; however, chronic stress can increase a person's risk of a variety of physical and mental health problems, including anxiety, depression, digestive issues, headaches, muscle tension and pain, heart disease, heart attack, stroke, etc. (American Psychological Association, 2022).

Wearables may help manage anxiety and long-term stress, which may be detrimental to a person. While it cannot treat stress, it can sense different parameters of a person such as heart rate, pulse rate, pupil dilation, skin temperature, and electrodermal activity in the human body. These are usually physiological signals and markers needed to gauge a person's stress level (Alhejaili & Alomainy, 2023). Furthermore, since a person can wear wearables constantly, a person's stress levels can be recorded constantly as they are performing their daily routines or in situations where they experience stress. When the data is recorded, it can be paired with mobile apps related to mental health interventions. In the study by Ponzo et al. (2020), they researched the efficacy and sustained effects of using a mobile app (BioBase) and paired wearable device (BioBeam) for university students in the United Kingdom experiencing levels of anxiety. After a 4-week intervention with the BioBase program, results showed a significantly reduced level of anxiety and an increase in perceived well-being. The effects were sustained at a 2-week follow-up. This study shows that wearables with digital mental health interventions can be helpful when treating stress and anxiety among students (Ponzo et al., 2020). This exemplifies how stress and anxiety can be monitored and how wearables can reshape the way people with stress/anxiety can monitor and manage their symptoms.

Depression

Like anxiety and stress, depression can stunt a person's daily life. Depression is a common mental disorder that can affect all aspects of life, including a person's relationship with their family, friends, and community, or life at school or work. If left untreated, it can lead to other physical or health complications, or worse suicide (World Health Organization, 2023).

While wearables are unable to treat depression, it can, however, sensor data for the detection of different health conditions. Wearables can monitor physiological and behavioral data, including steps, heart rate, energy expenditure, sleep patterns, respiration rate, blood oxygen saturation, skin temperature, and skin conductance, etc. The data on these digital biomarkers can then be used to predict the risk of depression and expand mental health screening across populations (Rykov et al., 2021). In the study by Rykov et al. (2021), they collected data on 267 full-time employees at Nanyang Technological University who wore Fitbit Charge 2 devices (activity trackers) for 14 days consecutively. The participants also completed a health survey which included a screening for depressive symptoms. Through wearables, steps, heart rate, energy expenditure, and sleep data were collected to note the patient's digital biomarkers such as physical activity, sleep patterns, and circadian rhythms. Results showed that participants with a greater variation of nightmare heart rate between 2 AM and 4 AM and between 4 AM and 6 AM and lower regularity of weekday circadian rhythms, showed greater severity of depressive symptoms. However, the author claimed that while the study showed several reliable associations, there are still limitations of digital biomarkers being able to detect depression in the whole sample of working adults (Rykov et al., 2021).

In a review by Sequeira et al. (2020), they focused more on how wearables can help with the diagnosis and prediction of Major Depressive Disorder in children and adolescents (MDD-CA). MDD-CA is a prevalent mental disorder that can greatly harm children if left untreated which is why this review focuses on monitoring, which refers to tracking of signs and symptoms over time, and prediction, which refers to estimating when signs and symptoms will re-emerge in the future. They did a scoping review of peer-reviewed studies about using mobile and wearables to characterize depression in children and/or adolescents and found majority of the studies used smartphone apps to track or monitor depressive symptoms while a few studies used actigraphy which are wristwatch-like devices to help measure an individual's movement, activity, and sleep and wake cycles. Both mobile and wearable technologies have the potential to aid in self-monitoring and objective data collection for monitoring and predicting depressive moods in MDD-CA. However, wearables and mobile data are not yet advanced enough to predict a relapse of MDD-CA (Sequeira et al., 2020).

Although wearables have many functions that could assist one with mental health, they do not treat mental health disorders. Currently, wearables can only monitor and manage symptoms and/or signs and help provide mental solutions by providing easy access to the individual's own data. Having access to their personal data can help them take an active role in their life by making positive changes to their lifestyle and improving their mental health (Alhejaili & Alomainy, 2023).

Types of Wearable Technology in Mental Healthcare

Due to technological advances, many types of wearable devices can be worn on multiple parts of the body and detect or track different biological signals. Wearables can be classified in many ways and one way is by classifying them by what body parts they can be worn on. The wearable devices developed so far have been arranged into three categories: head, limb, and torso wearable devices (Lu et al., 2020).

Head wearable devices include glasses, helmets, headbands, hearing aids, earrings, earphones, and patches (Lu et al., 2020). Examples of head wearables regarding mental health are brain-sensing devices such as MuseTM headband (InteraXon Inc.) or the Lowdown Focus glasses (SmithOptics Inc). These wearables helped reduce stress and anxiety through technology-mediated mindfulness exercises. There is also a wearable forehead electroencephalography (EEG) device called "Mindo-4S Jellyfish" which is used to determine how ketamine can show improvements in EEG depressive signatures (Hickey et al., 2021).

Limb wearable devices include devices worn on the arms, legs, and feet. These are the most common wearables on the market. Most wearables worn on the upper limbs are smartwatches, bracelets, and other accessories used to monitor daily activities and physiological parameters (Lu et al., 2020). Examples of limb wearables are the Apple Watch and Fitbit which track heart rate to detect any physiological responses to stress (Hickey et al., 2021).

Torso wearables mainly include suits, belts, and underwear (Lu et al., 2020). An example is the Vital Jacket which is a medical-grade wearable ECG device and actigraph. The Vital Jacket assesses the impact of stress on cognitive performance in air traffic controllers (Hickey et al., 2021). Another example is the Hexoskin Smart Garment which are sensorized undergarments that can measure heart rate, respiratory rate, and sleep data (Gomes et al., 2023). These are only a few examples of wearables related to mental health that are listed, but there are numerous wearables with more functionalities than the ones listed above.

Challenges with Mental Health Applications

With the many advantages wearables offer, they can improve the way people monitor their mental health conditions. However, no wearables are perfect, posing some challenges such as wearability, data resolution of wearable sensors, power consumption, health safety, security, and privacy.

One of the major challenges with wearables is the tradeoff between the complexity of the computations and the weights of the wearables. The purpose of wearables is to be comfortable enough for users to wear them in their everyday lives without disturbing their normal activities. Considering comfortability, they are typically small, which makes the sensors have lower resolutions compared to non-wearable devices (John Dian et al., 2020). Since they are typically small, designing a wearable that can be low-power consuming yet able to store high amounts of energy while being able to operate for a long period of time is another challenge. With wearables usually reduced to lightweight and less power consuming designs, wearables could potentially be easy hacking targets if it is not designed with good encryption and protection services when collecting data. This is also closely linked with privacy since wearables collect a lot of sensitive data such as vital health signs and location of the users. Without proper encryption services and appropriate privacy policies, people's data could be hacked, which is a breach of privacy (Lu et al., 2020).

Other issues include safety related to health since all wearables use wireless technologies to transmit their sensed data to another node, gateway, or base station. Users are exposed to radio frequency electromagnetic energy from wireless transmission which could pose a safety concern since WHO/International Agency has classified it as possibly carcinogenic to humans (John Dian et al., 2020; U.S. Department of Labor, n.d.). As challenges regarding wearables are navigated, the integration of it into health insurance policies creates room for more conversation, especially with how much must be considered.

INTEGRATION OF EMERGING TECHNOLOGIES IN HEALTHCARE

Chronic diseases are a growing concern worldwide, with nearly 25% of adults suffering from one or more chronic health conditions, thus placing a heavy burden on individuals, families, and healthcare systems (Yi Xie et al., 2021). To enhance public health outcomes, exploring the impact of health insurance policies on the integration and widespread adoption of wearable technology in healthcare plays a crucial role. In this regard, healthcare providers have begun to use wearable devices and recommendation systems to collect data in real time and to manage health conditions based on the generated data (Roy et al., 2018). The use and application of such technology and the corresponding richness of data that it can provide bring the health and care insurance market both potential opportunities and challenges (Spender et al., 2019).

Wearable sensing and information and communication technologies are key enablers driving the transformation of health care delivery toward a new model of connected health (CH) care (Loncar-Turukalo et al., 2019). Traditionally, health insurance has relied on static data when providing patient care and premium determination, but with advancements in wearable technology and information and communication technologies (ICT), health insurance companies are presented with an opportunity to redefine their role from being financiers of healthcare to being active participants in the health and well-being of their policyholders. The advent of these technologies is fundamentally changing the health insurance industry. Given the realities of the COVID-19 world, the health insurance industry is poised at a crossroads of evolution where the industry would become data-intensive and data-driven. (Nayak et al.,2021). Wearable technology can revolutionize the health insurance industry by providing continuous health data for personalized risk assessment, policy pricing, and preventive health measures. Americans are increasingly turning to a variety of quantified self-health and fitness tracking (QSHFT) technologies to learn more about their everyday habits, connect with valued others, and motivate themselves toward healthier behaviors (Brinson & Rutherford, 2020). To complement technology achievements, future work involving all stakeholders providing research evidence on improved care pathways and cost-effectiveness of the CH model is needed (Loncar-Turukalo et al., 2019). Not only does this highlight the growing trend towards personalized medicine but also enables a more proactive management of health, while potentially reducing the overall cost burden on the healthcare system by mitigating risks before evolving into serious health conditions. However, there is hardly any empirical evidence that firmly can confirm or refute the claim that physiolytics devices can attain a lasting health behavior change (Wettler & Wulf, 2020).

Challenges and Barriers in Integration

A major concern with wearable technology is the risk that individuals may potentially be overlooked due to skin color. Colvonen et al. (2020) analyzes these concerns about the accuracy of wearable technology, such as Apple watches and Fitbit, in people with a darker skin tone. Colvonen et al. (2020) states that these devices track health-related metrics such as sleep patterns, physical activity, and heart rate technology, using green light signals. However, the PPG green light technology is less accurate in measuring health metrics in individuals with darker skin.

Maintaining general accessibility, efficiency, and quality of health services for a rapidly aging and less healthy population has become a key challenge of this century (Mettler & Wulf 2020). The integration of wearable technology into insurance policies, particularly those that reward users for healthy behaviors or monitor health metrics for risk assessment, presents promising opportunities for both insurers and insured individuals. But wearables also pose grave privacy risks, with potentially very serious consequences, including a reduction in life chances (Banerjee, Hemphill & Longstreet 2016). Barriers related to privacy and data security, the reliability and standardization of data collected by wearable devices, and economic barriers such as cost, and accessibility raise legitimate concerns for policyholders. Each aspect poses significant challenges that must be addressed for the successful integration of wearable technology into insurance models. Although there are potential solutions for these implementation issues, more innovative work is required for the wide-scale adoption of wearable health technology (Dinh-Le et al., 2019).

Privacy and Data Security

One of the most pressing concerns with the integration of wearable technology into insurance policies is the issue of privacy and data security. As Americans increasingly integrate quantified self-health and fitness tracking (QSHFT) technologies into their lives, the data collected by these devices offer to not only help users live healthier lives, but also present opportunities for interested parties to identify and target them based on their health-related behaviors (Brinson & Rutherford, 2020). Wearable devices collect a vast amount of sensitive health information, including physical activity levels, heart rates, sleep patterns, and sometimes even GPS locations. Companies can gather, and trade data gleaned from smartphone sensors and wearables to learn moods, stress levels, habits, well-being, sleep patterns, exercise, movement, etc. to make credit, insurance, and employment decisions compromising privacy and possibly even resulting in barriers to healthcare (Banerjee, Hemphill & Longstreet, 2016). There is a constant peril that personal data that is collected with physiolytics device may be unconsciously (and/or illegally) accessed by third parties or repurposed for other aims than health and well-being (Wettler & Wulf, 2020). The handling of this data by insurers raises legitimate concerns regarding privacy breaches and unauthorized access to personal health information. Existing policies related to the collection, aggregation, and use of these data do not consistently address and protect individual health privacy concerns (Brinson & Rutherford, 2020). Health insurance companies may require that policyholders share data to participate in coverage or incentive programs.

The value of personal information is often not known when it is collected (i.e., when notice and consent are normally given); also, the relationship between users and processors of personal data has become increasingly complicated, as datasets are combined, transferred, shared, or sold (Banerjee, Hemphill & Longstreet 2016). To safeguard member data, insurers must implement data protection measures against hacking and other forms of cyber threats. Furthermore, there's a need for transparent policies on how this data is used, who has access to it, and how long it is stored. Ensuring data privacy and security is necessary to gain the trust of users and encourage their participation in insurance policies that utilize wearable technology.

Standardized Data

Another significant challenge is the reliability and standardization of data collected by wearable devices. There is a wide variety of wearable technologies available, each using different algorithms and methodologies to track health metrics. Yet, the variability of sensors and lack of consistency of data collection in the wearable context makes it difficult to coordinate and assess quality (Canali et al., 2022). This variance raises concerns about the accuracy and comparability of data collected from different devices. Inaccuracies occur for various reasons and vary according to what is being measured (Spender et al., 2019). For insurers to rely on this data for policy pricing or rewards, there needs to be a standardized framework for data collection and analysis. To achieve accurate recommendations, wearable devices need to apply contemporary data analytics to user data that devices capture and integrate it with other health systems (Roy et al., 2018). Establishing industry-wide standards for wearable health data can ensure that the information used by insurers is accurate, reliable, and consistent across different devices and platforms. Addressing this challenge is crucial for the data collected by wearables to be considered valid and actionable by insurance companies.

Economic Considerations

Economic considerations also present a significant barrier in the widespread integration of wearable technology in insurance policies. In countries with market-oriented healthcare systems, this growth in chronic diseases has led to a continuous rise of health premiums in the past years, making insurance coverage particularly unaffordable to people with low-to-middle-income (Wettler & Wulf, 2020). Considerations such as the initial cost of wearable technology, the cost of data management, and uncertain return on investment affect the successful adoption of wearables. A sensor that relies on exotic materials or technology will be less successful compared to a sensor that is based on existing and inexpensive technology (Devine et al., 2022). High costs of sensors alone could deter insurance companies, even if the costs of sensors weren't applied, the cost of redesigning and manufacturing new devices would still pose a barrier. For many insurers, the risk of manufacturing a wearable device for a specialty application might be undesirable. Regarding economic considerations, it is difficult to sell a specialty sensor designed for a narrow market (Devine et al., 2022). Despite the potential wearable technology has to improve health outcomes and reduce healthcare costs through early intervention, insurers might hesitate to integrate wearables due to the uncertainty of return on investment. The adoption of wearable technology is limited by the marketing perspectives of manufacturers and the cost of data management and analysis requires sophisticated systems. For insurers, this involves investments in infrastructure, software, and skilled personnel. The cost could pose a significant barrier for insurers, especially for smaller companies with limited IT budgets. In terms of financial savings, this consideration is important to understanding barriers to the widespread adoption of wearable technology.

Insurance Policies and Incentives for Wearable Technology

Insurance policies and incentives have become a key component in the adoption and integration of wearable technology within public health systems. These policies have the power to influence consumer behavior and impact how healthcare providers incorporate wearable devices into patient care. According to a study by Soliño-Fernandez et al. (2019):

A total of 997 Americans across 46 states participated in the study. Most of them were 25 to 34 years old (40.22%), 57.27% were female, and 74.52% were white. On average, 69.5% of the respondents were willing to adopt health-insurance use-cases based on wearable devices, though 77.8% of them were concerned about issues related to economic benefits, data privacy and to a lesser extent, technological accuracy.

Research indicates a significant proportion of consumers are willing to share their health and fitness data collected by wearable devices with their insurance providers if it could lead to lower premiums or other financial incentives. Despite the benefits, the collection and use of personal health data through wearable technologies raises privacy concerns, necessitating clear policies and regulations to protect consumer information. Health insurance companies have begun to recognize the potential benefits of wearable technology in promoting healthier lifestyles and managing chronic diseases. As a result, some insurers have started to cover or reimburse for wearable devices. For instance, as noted by Paluch and Tuzovic (2019), John Hancock was one of the first life insurance firms in the USA to offer a free Fitbit device and the potential for a 15 percent reduction in annual premiums for members who meet their target goals. By including coverage for wearable devices, health insurance companies can influence their adoption rates. This is only the first step in health insurance companies incorporating the capabilities of wearable technology into insurance coverage to monitor and encourage healthy behaviors.

To further encourage the adoption and sustained use of wearable technology, many health insurance companies have developed incentive programs that reward policyholders for monitoring and engaging in healthy behaviors. For example, premium discounts, cash rewards, or other incentives are offered to participants who meet certain health goals. Research indicates that financial incentives, such as premium discounts or wellness product vouchers, can significantly increase consumer willingness to adopt wearable devices and engage in healthy behaviors (Soliño-Fernandez et al., 2019). Through well-designed incentive programs, health insurance companies can encourage healthier lifestyles among policyholders and reduce healthcare costs by preventing diseases and health issues. These initiatives by insurance companies support the uptake of wearable health technologies and expand the use of patient-collected data to improve patient health (Dinh-Le et al., 2019). Overall, the adoption rates of wearable technology in the health insurance sector are influenced by coverage policies and incentive programs.

Clinical Impact

Currently, these devices can help patients and providers manage chronic conditions such as diabetes, heart conditions, and chronic pain (Dinh-Le et al., 2019). In chronic disease management, wearable health sensors and systems could improve treatment in early detection diagnosis as well as long-term patient monitoring (Kirk et al., 2018). By using wearable devices to continuously monitor patient health statuses, insurers provide members with early detection of health issues, proactive interventions, and personalized healthcare plans tailored to individual needs. The impact these devices have on the care process, the surgical patient, and the care setting is promising, but further research is needed to establish their clinical efficiency (Kolovos & Petros, 2020).

Innovative Insurance Models Emerging from Wearable Technology Integration

New innovative insurance models, known as "pay-as-you-live" policies, where insurers use wearables to collect data on lifestyle and health metrics to adjust premiums. Health insurance companies can use this model to reward policyholders for their healthy behaviors with lower premiums, reducing the overall costs of healthcare costs (Wiegard et al., 2019). Furthermore, the integration of wearable technology into the health insurance sector has enabled insurers to have a more proactive role on chronic disease management, thereby reducing hospital visits, providing specialized treatment plans, and improving public health. The future design and development of digital technology in this space will rely on continued analysis of best practices, pain points, and potential solutions to mitigate existing challenges (Dinh-Le et al., 2019).

Chronic Disease Management

AI-powered wearables can be especially revolutionary for people managing chronic diseases. Critical health measures, such as blood sugar levels for diabetics or heart rate variability for individuals with cardiovascular diseases, can be continually monitored by these devices (Ahmed et al., 2022; Wilmink et al., 2020). AI algorithms embedded in these wearables analyze real-time data to identify early indicators of potential health problems. This capability enables timely notifications to users or healthcare practitioners, allowing for proactive management of conditions before they worsen (Ahuja et al., 2024). By leveraging AI, wearables not only monitor health metrics but also provide personalized insights and guidance (Junaid et al., 2022). Users can receive tailored instructional information to better understand their conditions and make informed health decisions. This holistic approach enhances disease management, potentially reducing the likelihood of complications and improving overall health outcomes (Tariq et al., 2023).

Chronic conditions including diabetes, high blood pressure, and heart disease pose serious problems for global healthcare systems. A potential way to enhance the management of these illnesses is through wearable technology and artificial intelligence. AI can support timely and tailored interventions, which can aid in the monitoring and management of chronic conditions. Wearables with AI capabilities, for instance, can monitor the vital signs and physical activity of individuals with chronic illnesses, informing both the patients and their medical professionals of any abnormalities that may need to be attended to (Bajwa et al., 2021). AI-enabled continuous glucose monitors can reduce the risk of hyperglycemia and hypoglycemia in diabetes treatment by predicting glucose changes and recommending insulin dosages (Ahmed et al., 2022).

Integration with Healthcare Systems

Wearables with AI capabilities are evolving beyond standalone devices and are increasingly integrated into bigger healthcare systems. The provided link facilitates easy sharing of health information between patients and medical experts, enabling more informed decisions and the creation of customized treatment plans. AI systems, for instance, can evaluate wearable data and electronic health records (EHRs) to offer a comprehensive picture of a patient's health condition (Xie et al., 2021). When managing chronic conditions, where prompt reactions and ongoing monitoring are required, this type of integration is quite helpful. AI-enhanced wearables can assist in the early diagnosis of potential issues and the tailoring of treatment regimens by giving medical personnel access to real-time data and predictive insights (Wilmink et al., 2020). This strategy places a strong emphasis on customization in healthcare, allowing for customized treatment programs that take into account each patient's particular requirements and problems (De Ramón Fernández et al., 2022).

Ethical Considerations

Although wearable health devices have enormous potential advantages from AI, there are also important ethical and privacy issues that require some attention. Wearable technology raises concerns about data security and privacy since it collects and transmits sensitive health information (Sharma et al., 2022). Maintaining user trust requires strong data protection protocols and adherence to laws like the

Health Insurance Portability and Accountability Act (HIPAA) and the General Data Protection Regulation (GDPR) (Nguyen et al., 2020).

As far as data and security go, many personal health data points are collected by wearable technology, such as heart rate, activity level, sleep habits, and even biometric data. Since cloud-based systems are frequently used to analyze and store this data, there is a greater chance of data breaches and illegal access. It is essential to use robust encryption techniques and secure communication protocols to reduce these hazards (Nahavandi et al., 2022). Frequent vulnerability assessments and security audits can assist in locating and addressing any system vulnerabilities (Baptista et al., 2024).

In addition to being required by law, adherence to data privacy laws such as GDPR and HIPAA is essential for gaining user trust. Strict rules on data processing, storage, and transfer are required by GDPR, guaranteeing that personal data is treated with the highest care (Olyanasab & Annabestani, 2024). Similarly, HIPAA emphasizes the value of security and privacy in health data administration and offers rules for safeguarding health information in the US (Junaid et al., 2022).

Legal and Ethical Frameworks

Developing and using AI in wearable health devices should be guided by strong legal and ethical frameworks that prioritize people's rights and well-being. These frameworks should address important issues like consent, data ownership, and privacy. They should also promote principles such as doing good (beneficence), avoiding harm (non-maleficence), and ensuring fairness (Bajwa et al., 2021).

It is important to involve a diverse group of stakeholders, including those from technology, healthcare, law, and ethics, to create comprehensive and practical guidelines. This collaboration ensures that the frameworks are well-rounded and consider different perspectives, ultimately protecting and benefiting everyone involved (Nahavandi et al., 2022).

CONCLUSION

The advent of wearable technology offers innovative solutions in healthcare, particularly in the management of chronic diseases and mental health. Wearable devices range from standard fitness trackers to advanced medical sensors that enable continuous monitoring and management of health conditions, promoting trends toward personalized healthcare. Its capabilities provide real-time insight into physical and psychological states, not only in response to immediate interventions but also in the development of "pay-as-you-live" health insurance policies that incentivize healthier lifestyles.

As the prevalence of wearables steadily increases today, they show promise in enhancing public health outcomes. These innovations have significantly impacted patient data and personal health management, with artificial intelligence further increasing the capability of wearable devices. However, to support the integration of wearable technology into healthcare and insurance systems barriers related to privacy, data accuracy and economic viability must be addressed. This chapter underscores the benefits and existing barriers, highlighting the need for future study to further validate the effectiveness of wearable technology in promoting quality of life.

REFERENCES

Ahmed, A., Aziz, S., Abd-alrazaq, A., Farooq, F., & Sheikh, J. (2022). Overview of Artificial Intelligence–Driven Wearable Devices for Diabetes: Scoping Review. *Journal of Medical Internet Research*, *24*(8), e36010–e36010. DOI: 10.2196/36010 PMID: 35943772

Ahmed, A., Aziz, S., Alzubaidi, M., Schneider, J., Irshaidat, S., Abu Serhan, H., Abd-alrazaq, A. A., Solaiman, B., & Househ, M. (2023). Wearable devices for anxiety & depression: A scoping review. *Computer Methods and Programs in Biomedicine Update*, *3*, 100095. DOI: 10.1016/j.cmpbup.2023.100095 PMID: 36743720

Ahuja, A., Agrawal, S., Acharya, S., Batra, N., & Daiya, V. (2024). Advancements in Wearable Digital Health Technology: A Review of Epilepsy Management. *Cureus*, *16*(3), e57037–e57037. DOI: 10.7759/cureus.57037 PMID: 38681418

Al Kuwaiti, A., Nazer, K., Al-Reedy, A., Al-Shehri, S., Al-Muhanna, A., Subbarayalu, A. V., Al Muhanna, D., & Al-Muhanna, F. A. (2023). A Review of the Role of Artificial Intelligence in Healthcare. *Journal of Personalized Medicine, 13*(6), 951-. https://doi.org/DOI: 10.3390/jpm13060951

Alhejaili, R., & Alomainy, A. (2023). The Use of Wearable Technology in Providing Assistive Solutions for Mental Well-Being. *Sensors (Basel)*, *23*(17), 7378. DOI: 10.3390/s23177378 PMID: 37687834

American Psychological Association. (2022, October 31). How stress affects your health. https://www.apa.org/topics/stress/health

Babu, M., Lautman, Z., Lin, X., Sobota, M. H., & Snyder, M. P. (2023). Wearable Devices: Implications for Precision Medicine and the Future of Health Care. *Annual Review of Medicine*. Advance online publication. DOI: 10.1146/annurev-med-052422-020437 PMID: 37983384

Bajwa, J., Munir, U., Nori, A., & Williams, B. (2021). Artificial intelligence in healthcare: Transforming the practice of medicine. *Future Healthcare Journal*, *8*(2), e188–e194. DOI: 10.7861/fhj.2021-0095 PMID: 34286183

Banerjee, S., Hemphill, T., & Longstreet, P. (2018). [PDF] wearable devices and Healthcare: Data sharing and privacy ... Semantic SCHOLAR. https://www.semanticscholar.org/paper/Wearable-devices-and-healthcare:-Data-sharing-and-Banerjee-Hemphill/93adc384700d2b5ba5a0a76b9287ce16d5dfa351

Baptista, N. T., Dessalles, R., Illner, A.-K., Ville, P., Ribet, L., Anton, P. M., & Durand-Dubief, M. (2024). Harnessing the power of resistant starch: A narrative review of its health impact and processing challenges. *Frontiers in Nutrition*, *11*, 1369950–1369950. DOI: 10.3389/fnut.2024.1369950 PMID: 38571748

Brinson, N. H., & Rutherford, D. N. (2020). Privacy and the quantified self: A review of U.S. health information policy limitations related to wearable technologies. *The Journal of Consumer Affairs*, *54*(4), 1355–1374. DOI: 10.1111/joca.12320

Canali, S. Schiaffonati, V., & Aliverti, A. (2022). Challenges and recommendations for wearable devices in Digital Health: Data Quality, interoperability, health equity, fairness. PLOS Digital Health. https://journals.plos.org/digitalhealth/article?id=10.1371%2Fjournal.pdig.0000104

Chen, K., Zdorova, M., & Nathan-Roberts, D. (2017). Implications of Wearables, Fitness Tracking Services, and Quantified Self on Healthcare. Proceedings of the Human Factors and Ergonomics Society Annual Meeting, 61, 1066 1070.DOI: 10.1177/1541931213601871

Chen, M., Ma, Y., Song, J., Lai, C. F., & Hu, B. (2016). Smart Clothing: Connecting Human with Clouds and Big Data for Sustainable Health Monitoring. *Mobile Networks and Applications*, *21*(5), 825–845. DOI: 10.1007/s11036-016-0745-1

Chiauzzi, E., Rodarte, C., & DasMahapatra, P. (2015). Patient-centered activity monitoring in the self-management of chronic health conditions. *BMC Medicine*, *13*(1), 77. Advance online publication. DOI: 10.1186/s12916-015-0319-2 PMID: 25889598

Chidambaram, S., Maheswaran, Y., Patel, K., Sounderajah, V., Hashimoto, D. A., Seastedt, K. P., Mcgregor, A. H., Markar, S. R., & Darzi, A. (2022). Using Artificial Intelligence-Enhanced Sensing and Wearable Technology in Sports Medicine and Performance Optimisation. *Sensors (Basel)*, *22*(18), 6920. Advance online publication. DOI: 10.3390/s22186920 PMID: 36146263

Colvonen, P. J., DeYoung, P. N., Bosompra, N., & Owens, R. L. (2020). Limiting racial disparities and bias for wearable devices in health science research. *Sleep (Basel)*, *43*(10), zsaa159. Advance online publication. DOI: 10.1093/sleep/zsaa159 PMID: 32893865

De Ramón Fernández, A., Ruiz Fernández, D., Gilart Iglesias, V., & Marcos Jorquera, D. (2022). Analyzing the use of artificial intelligence for the management of chronic obstructive pulmonary disease (COPD). *International Journal of Medical Informatics*, *158*, 104640–104640. DOI: 10.1016/j.ijmedinf.2021.104640 PMID: 34890934

Devine, J. K., Schwartz, L. P., & Hursh, S. R. (2022). Technical, Regulatory, Economic, and Trust Issues Preventing Successful Integration of Sensors into the Mainstream Consumer Wearables Market. National Library of Medicine. https://www.ncbi.nlm.nih.gov/pmc/articles/PMC9002880/

Dinh-Le, C., Chuang, R., Chokshi, S., & Mann, D. (2019). Wearable Health Technology and Electronic Health Record Integration: Scoping Review and Future Directions. *JMIR mHealth and uHealth*, *7*(9), e12861–e12861. DOI: 10.2196/12861 PMID: 31512582

Docles, E. (2023). Healthcare Artificial Intelligence: Transforming the Future of Medicine. *Health Science Journal*, *17*(6), 1–3. DOI: 10.36648/1791-809X.17.6.1033

Edwards, C. (2003). Wearable computing struggles for social acceptance. *IEE Review*, *49*(9), 24–25. https://digital-library.theiet.org/content/journals/10.1049/ir_20030904. DOI: 10.1049/ir:20030904

Farrell, M., Spender, A., Bullen, C., Altmann-Richer, L., Cripps, J., Duffy, R., Falkous, C., Horn, T., Wigzell, J., & Yeap, W. (2018, September 1). Wearables and the internet of things - considerations for the life and health insurance industry. Queen's University Belfast. https://pure.qub.ac.uk/en/publications/wearables-and-the-internet-of-things-considerations-for-the-life-

Gajardo Sánchez, A. D., Murillo-Zamorano, L. R., López-Sánchez, J., & Bueno-Muñoz, C. (2023). Gamification in Health Care Management: Systematic Review of the Literature and Research Agenda. *SAGE Open*, *13*(4), 21582440231218834. Advance online publication. DOI: 10.1177/21582440231218834

Gomes, N., Pato, M., Lourenço, A. R., & Datia, N. (2023). A Survey on Wearable Sensors for Mental Health Monitoring. *Sensors (Basel)*, *23*(3), 1330. DOI: 10.3390/s23031330 PMID: 36772370

Green, E. C., & Murphy, E. M. (2014). *The Health Belief Model*. The Wiley Encyclopedia of Health Psychology., DOI: 10.1002/9781118410868.wbehibs410

Gui, H., & Liu, J. (2018). Latest Progresses in Developing Wearable Monitoring and Therapy Systems for Managing Chronic Diseases. arXiv: Medical Physics. https://doi.org//arXiv.1802.01747DOI: 10.48550

Hickey, B. A., Chalmers, T., Newton, P., Lin, C.-T., Sibbritt, D., McLachlan, C. S., Clifton-Bligh, R., Morley, J., & Lal, S. (2021). Smart Devices and Wearable Technologies to Detect and Monitor Mental Health Conditions and Stress: A Systematic Review. *Sensors (Basel)*, *21*(10), 3461. DOI: 10.3390/s21103461 PMID: 34065620

John Dian, F., Vahidnia, R., & Rahmati, A. (2020). Wearables and the Internet of Things (IoT), Applications, Opportunities, and Challenges: A Survey. *IEEE Access : Practical Innovations, Open Solutions*, *8*, 69200–69211. DOI: 10.1109/ACCESS.2020.2986329

Junaid, S. B., Imam, A. A., Abdulkarim, M., Surakat, Y. A., Balogun, A. O., Kumar, G., Shuaibu, A. N., Garba, A., Sahalu, Y., Mohammed, A., Mohammed, T. Y., Abdulkadir, B. A., Abba, A. A., Iliyasu Kakumi, N. A., & Hashim, A. S. (2022). Recent Advances in Artificial Intelligence and Wearable Sensors in Healthcare Delivery. *Applied Sciences, 12*(20), 10271-. https://doi.org/DOI: 10.3390/app122010271

Kang, H. S., & Exworthy, M. (2022). Wearing the Future—Wearables to Empower Users to Take Greater Responsibility for Their Health and Care: Scoping Review. *JMIR mHealth and uHealth, 10*(7), e35684. Advance online publication. DOI: 10.2196/35684 PMID: 35830222

Keykhosravi, A., Neamatshahi, M., Mahmoodi, R., & Navipour, E. (2018). Radiation Effects of Mobile Phones and Tablets on the Skin: A Systematic Review. *Advances in Medicine*, *2018*, 1–5. Advance online publication. DOI: 10.1155/2018/9242718 PMID: 29850642

Kirk, M. A., Amiri, M., Pirbaglou, M., & Ritvo, P. (2019). Wearable Technology and Physical Activity Behavior Change in Adults With Chronic Cardiometabolic Disease: A Systematic Review and Meta-Analysis. *American Journal of Health Promotion*, *33*(5), 778–791. DOI: 10.1177/0890117118816278 PMID: 30586996

Kolovos, P. (2020). Wearable Technologies in Post-Operative Recovery: Clinical Applications and Positive Impacts. *International Journal of Caring Sciences*, *13*(2), 1474–1479.

Lee, B. C., Ajisafe, T., Vo, T. V., & Xie, J. (2019). Understanding Long-Term Adoption and Usability of Wearable Activity Trackers Among Active Older Adults. Interacción. https://link.springer.com/chapter/10.1007/978-3-030-22012-9_18

Lobelo, F., Kelli, H. M., Tejedor, S. C., Pratt, M., McConnell, M. V., Martin, S. S., & Welk, G. J. (2016). The Wild Wild West: A Framework to Integrate mHealth Software Applications and Wearables to Support Physical Activity Assessment, Counseling and Interventions for Cardiovascular Disease Risk Reduction. *Progress in Cardiovascular Diseases*, *58*(6), 584–594. DOI: 10.1016/j.pcad.2016.02.007 PMID: 26923067

Loncar-Turukalo, T., Zdravevski, E., Machado da Silva, J., Chouvarda, I., & Trajkovik, V. T., Trajkovik, V., Chouvarda, I., Machado da Silva, J., & Zdravevski, E. (2019). Literature on wearable technology for Connected Health: Scoping Review of research trends, advances, and barriers. Journal of medical Internet research. https://pubmed.ncbi.nlm.nih.gov/31489843/

Lu, L., Zhang, J., Xie, Y., Gao, F., Xu, S., Wu, X., & Ye, Z. (2020). Wearable Health Devices in Health Care: Narrative Systematic Review. *JMIR mHealth and uHealth*, *8*(11), e18907. DOI: 10.2196/18907 PMID: 33164904

Mettler, T., & Wulf, J. (2020). Health promotion with physiolytics: What is driving people to subscribe in a data-driven health plan. *PLoS One*, *15*(4), e0231705–e0231705. DOI: 10.1371/journal.pone.0231705 PMID: 32294126

Motti, V. G. (2019). Wearable Health: Opportunities and Challenges. Proceedings of the 13th EAI International Conference on Pervasive Computing Technologies for Healthcare. https://dl.acm.org/doi/10.1145/3329189.3329226

Nahavandi, D., Alizadehsani, R., Khosravi, A., & Acharya, U. R. (2022). Application of artificial intelligence in wearable devices: Opportunities and challenges. *Computer Methods and Programs in Biomedicine*, *213*, 106541–106541. DOI: 10.1016/j.cmpb.2021.106541 PMID: 34837860

Nahavandi, D., Alizadehsani, R., Khosravi, A., & Acharya, U. R. (2022). Application of artificial intelligence in wearable devices: Opportunities and challenges. *Computer Methods and Programs in Biomedicine*, *213*, 106541–106541. DOI: 10.1016/j.cmpb.2021.106541 PMID: 34837860

Nayak, B., & Bhattacharyya, S. S. (2020). The Changing Narrative in the Health Insurance Industry: Wearables Technology in Health Insurance Products and Services for the COVID-19 World. *Journal of Health Management*, *22*(4), 550–558. DOI: 10.1177/0972063420983112

Nguyen, C. T., Bang, H., Manogaran, G., Athota, V., & Tavares, J. M. R. S. (2020). Internet-of-Things (IoT) technologies for healthcare: Opportunities, challenges, and management. In Nguyen, C. T., Bang, H., Manogaran, G., Athota, V., & Tavares, J. M. R. S. (Eds.), *Internet of Things (IoT) Technologies for Healthcare* (pp. 3–24). Springer.

Occupational Safety and Health Administration. (n.d.). Radiofrequency and Microwave Radiation—Health Effects. https://www.osha.gov/radiofrequency-and-microwave-radiation/health-effects

Olyanasab, A., & Annabestani, M. (2024). Leveraging Machine Learning for Personalized Wearable Biomedical Devices: A Review. *Journal of Personalized Medicine, 14*(2), 203-. https://doi.org/DOI: 10.3390/jpm14020203

Ometov, A., Shubina, V., Klus, L., Skibińska, J., Saafi, S., Pascacio, P., Flueratoru, L., Gaibor, D. Q., Chukhno, N., Chukhno, O., Ali, A., Channa, A., Svertoka, E., Qaim, W. B., Casanova-Marqués, R., Holcer, S., Torres-Sospedra, J., Casteleyn, S., Ruggeri, G., & Lohan, E. S. (2021). A Survey on Wearable Technology: History, State-of-the-Art and Current Challenges. *Computer Networks, 193*, 108074. DOI: 10.1016/j.comnet.2021.108074

Padyab, A. M., & Habibipour, A. (2021). Issues and Adoption Barriers in Wearable Technologies. *International Journal of Technology Diffusion, 12*(1), 75–89. https://ideas.repec.org/a/igg/jtd000/v12y2021i1p75-89.html. DOI: 10.4018/IJTD.2021010104

Paluch, S., & Tuzovic, S. (2019). Persuaded self-tracking with wearable technology: Carrot or stick? *Journal of Services Marketing, 33*(4), 436–448. DOI: 10.1108/JSM-03-2018-0091

Penders, J., Altini, M., Hoof, C. V., & Dy, E. (2015). Wearable Sensors for Healthier Pregnancies. *Proceedings of the IEEE, 103*(2), 179–191. DOI: 10.1109/JPROC.2014.2387017

Pentland, A. P. (2004). Healthwear: Medical technology becomes wearable. *Computer, 37*(5), 42–49. https://pubmed.ncbi.nlm.nih.gov/16301769/. DOI: 10.1109/MC.2004.1297238

Ponzo, S., Morelli, D., Kawadler, J. M., Hemmings, N. R., Bird, G., & Plans, D. (2020). Efficacy of the Digital Therapeutic Mobile App BioBase to Reduce Stress and Improve Mental Well-Being Among University Students: Randomized Controlled Trial. *JMIR mHealth and uHealth, 8*(4), e17767. DOI: 10.2196/17767 PMID: 31926063

Reid, C. R., Schall, M. C.Jr, Amick, R. Z., Schiffman, J. M., Lu, M., Smets, M., Moses, H. R., & Porto, R. (2017). Wearable Technologies: How Will We Overcome Barriers to Enhance Worker Performance, Health, And Safety? *Proceedings of the Human Factors and Ergonomics Society Annual Meeting, 61*(1), 1026–1030. DOI: 10.1177/1541931213601740

Roy, S. N., Srivastava, S. K., & Gururajan, R. (2018). Integrating wearable devices and recommendation system: Towards a next generation healthcare service delivery. AIS Electronic Library (AISeL). https://aisel.aisnet.org/jitta/vol19/iss4/2/

Rykov, Y., Thach, T.-Q., Bojic, I., Christopoulos, G., & Car, J. (2021). Digital Biomarkers for Depression Screening With Wearable Devices: Cross-sectional Study With Machine Learning Modeling. *JMIR mHealth and uHealth*, *9*(10), e24872. DOI: 10.2196/24872 PMID: 34694233

Sequeira, L., Perrotta, S., LaGrassa, J., Merikangas, K., Kreindler, D., Kundur, D., Courtney, D., Szatmari, P., Battaglia, M., & Strauss, J. (2020). Mobile and wearable technology for monitoring depressive symptoms in children and adolescents: A scoping review. *Journal of Affective Disorders*, *265*, 314–324. DOI: 10.1016/j.jad.2019.11.156 PMID: 32090755

Shajari, S., Kuruvinashetti, K., Komeili, A., & Sundararaj, U. (2023). The Emergence of AI-Based Wearable Sensors for Digital Health Technology: A Review. *Sensors (Basel, Switzerland)*, *23*(23), 9498-. https://doi.org/DOI: 10.3390/s23239498

Sharma, H. K., Kumar, A., Pant, S., & Ram, M. (2022). Role of Artificial Intelligence, IoT and Blockchain in Smart Healthcare. In *Artificial Intelligence, Blockchain and IoT for Smart Healthcare* (1st ed., pp. 25–36). Routledge. https://doi.org/DOI: 10.1201/9781003333050-3

Soliño-Fernandez, D., Ding, A., Bayro-Kaiser, E., & Ding, E. L. (2019). Willingness to adopt wearable devices with behavioral and economic incentives by health insurance wellness programs: Results of a US cross-sectional survey with multiple consumer health vignettes. *BMC Public Health*, *19*(1), 1649–1649. DOI: 10.1186/s12889-019-7920-9 PMID: 31839006

Tariq, F., Islam, S. M. R., & Mostefaoui, G. K. (2023). Future Challenges in Artificial Intelligence for Smart Healthcare. In *Artificial Intelligence for Disease Diagnosis and Prognosis in Smart Healthcare* (1st ed., Vol. 1, pp. 305–310). CRC Press., DOI: 10.1201/9781003251903-17

Ward, C., Henderson, S. M., & Metcalfe, N. H. (2013). A short history on pacemakers. *International Journal of Cardiology*, *169*(4), 244–248. DOI: 10.1016/j.ijcard.2013.08.093 PMID: 24083883

Wiegard, R., Guhr, N., Krylow, S., & Breitner, M. H. (2019). Analysis of wearable technologies' usage for pay-as-you-live tariffs: Recommendations for insurance companies. *Zeitschrift Für Die Gesamte Versicherungs-Wissenschaft*, *108*(1), 63–88. DOI: 10.1007/s12297-019-00431-2

Wilmink, G., Dupey, K., Alkire, S., Grote, J., Zobel, G., Fillit, H. M., & Movva, S. (2020). Artificial Intelligence–Powered Digital Health Platform and Wearable Devices Improve Outcomes for Older Adults in Assisted Living Communities: Pilot Intervention Study. *JMIR Aging*, *3*(2), e19554–e19554. DOI: 10.2196/19554 PMID: 32723711

World Health Organization. (2022). Mental disorders. https://www.who.int/news-room/fact-sheets/detail/mental-disorders

World Health Organization. (2023). Depressive disorder (depression). https://www.who.int/news-room/fact-sheets/detail/depression

Xie, Y., Lu, L., Gao, F., He, S., Zhao, H., Fang, Y., Yang, J., An, Y., Ye, Z., & Dong, Z. (2021). Integration of Artificial Intelligence, Blockchain, and Wearable Technology for Chronic Disease Management: A New Paradigm in Smart Healthcare. *Current Medical Science*, *41*(6), 1123–1133. DOI: 10.1007/s11596-021-2485-0 PMID: 34950987

Xie, Y., Lu, L., Gao, F., He, S., Zhao, H., Fang, Y., Yang, J., An, Y., Ye, Z., & Dong, Z. (2021). Integration of Artificial Intelligence, Blockchain, and Wearable Technology for Chronic Disease Management: A New Paradigm in Smart Healthcare. *Current Medical Science*, *41*(6), 1123–1133. DOI: 10.1007/s11596-021-2485-0 PMID: 34950987

Yağanoğlu, M. (2021). Real time wearable speech recognition system for deaf persons. *Computers & Electrical Engineering*, *91*, 107026. DOI: 10.1016/j.compeleceng.2021.107026

Yelne, S., Chaudhary, M., Dod, K., Sayyad, A., & Sharma, R. (2023). Harnessing the Power of AI: A Comprehensive Review of Its Impact and Challenges in Nursing Science and Healthcare. *Cureus*, *15*(11), e49252–e49252. DOI: 10.7759/cureus.49252 PMID: 38143615

Zahrt, O. H., Evans, K. M., Murnane, E. L., Santoro, E., Baiocchi, M. T., Landay, J. A., Delp, S. L., & Crum, A. J. (2022). Effects of Wearable Fitness Trackers and Activity Adequacy Mindsets on Affect, Behavior, and Health: Longitudinal Randomized Controlled Trial. *Journal of Medical Internet Research*, *25*, e40529. Advance online publication. DOI: 10.2196/40529 PMID: 36696172

Chapter 5
Gaming Through the Lens of Public Health:
Awareness of Esports Consequences

Kashish Ali
The University of Texas at San Antonio, USA

Autumn Garcia
The University of Texas at San Antonio, USA

Alina Vadsariya
The University of Texas at San Antonio, USA

ABSTRACT

Esports has grown into a global phenomenon that combines competition with professional careers. Esports, otherwise known as electronic gaming, is a multifaceted and exciting form of competitive video game. This highly organized landscape has created a global phenomenon, rapidly growing in popularity worldwide and captivating the attention of millions of players worldwide. This paper explores the health risks and positive aspects associated with the relationship between esports and physical and mental health.

INTRODUCTION

Esports is a form of competitive sports facilitated through electronic systems or otherwise known as video games. This multiplayer form of video gaming is organized in different teams, leagues, and tournaments (Ketelhut et al, 2021). Esports'

DOI: 10.4018/979-8-3373-5322-7.ch005

recent popularity was ignited by the expansive growth in new games, broadcasting sources, and gaming partnerships. Gaming and esports especially gained a popularity boost from the COVID-19 pandemic lockdown when people were strictly confined to their homes and turning to esports as a source of entertainment. People at home were not the only ones battling their boredom with esports; athletes were also playing esports since their seasons were delayed due to the pandemic (Wheless, 2021). Esports has created an international community of players, and it continues to grow at an unprecedented pace. Participating in the fun and exciting realm of esports entails both a plethora of health challenges and benefits. It is crucial to find an equilibrium between the esports gaming and physical and mental health through self-care and collaborative efforts.

ESPORTS AND PHYSICAL HEALTH

Overview

Individuals engaging in esports for competitive video gaming can be presented with multiple physical health effects which can be both beneficial and harmful. Physical health and esports are directly related to one another and individuals can be impacted by this in either ways (Rudolf et al, 2020). This section examines the positive impact it has while also addressing the negative impacts. Nowadays, many esports athletes are prioritizing their physical fitness and engaging in healthier activities such as going to the gym, participating in workout routines, practicing mindfulness and eating healthy. They are doing this to promote physical health and incorporate healthy behaviors in daily life to improve their gaming performance (Seffah et al, 2023). In addition to that, esports require them to interact with other athletes, promoting them to gain essential qualities such as teamwork, leadership, and communication skills giving them confidence within themselves (Sanz-Matesanz et al, 2023). Even if the player is shy and reserved, engaging in esports forces them to communicate as they are often playing against one another instilling confidence and building on teamwork and quick decision making. Furthermore, competitive video gaming often requires accuracy and fast hand and eye movement which improves one's fine motor abilities. Along with that, precision, strategic thinking, and keeping focus are all essential qualities needed in this sport. These activities help one maintain a good cognitive health improving their critical thinking and brain function.

Physical Demands of Esports

There has been controversy around whether esports should be considered a legitimate sport, given that it does not fall under the criteria of a traditional sport. A traditional sport can be defined as a physical activity that is performed individually or with a team. Whereas those who participate in esports do not typically do physical activity and players perform their gaming seated in front of computers or devices. This may not always be the case for esport athletes since there are many games that require certain physical skills for the player to execute the game. In a sport like jump roping, competitive jumpers focus on a variety of techniques and aspects, such as gymnastics and other athletic moves. Acquiring such precise physical skills is done through months to even years of intense training (Hamari and Sjöblom, 2017). In a similar fashion, esports athletes utilize their physical skills through fine motor coordination in gaming. Fine motor skills are movements that involve the use of the small muscles of the hands, fingers, and wrists. These skills refer to the coordination of manipulating objects with precision and intricacy. Examples of fine-motor skills are seen in daily tasks and activities, such as gripping a toothbrush, writing, using utensils and drawing (Jenny, Manning, Keiper, et al., 2016). Gaming can potentially improve fine motor skills through the activities involved in the game. Video games involve precise movements and coordination, such as controlling an avatar to aim at a specific target or to move around an obstacle. A study conducted in 2019 showed that computer games were efficient in improving fine motor skills in children with Down syndrome disorder (Hashemi, Arabameri, 2019). Similar development and enhancement of fine motor skills has been observed in esport players who are often successful in their gaming performance. Because most games require precise coordination, hand-eye coordination is commonly improved in esports players through the constant coordination between the visual input and manual output in the game. Players who engage in fast paced games are also likely to improve their reflexes and reaction times, finger dexterity, and multitasking (Pluss, Novak, Bennett, et al., 2020). However, these skills are enhanced and developed based on the type of game being played, the complexity of the game's course, user experience, and the amount of training completed by the user. Competitive esports gamers spend hours refining their skills and practicing games to strive for perfection.

Sedentary Lifestyle and Health Risks

Sedentary behaviors in the US have exponentially grown during the twentieth and twenty-first century. People have grown more sedentary due to the nature of their jobs, activities, and their level of inactivity. Although esports are beneficial in providing entertainment and a fun opportunity for competition, it has its complicated downsides, such as certain health concerns that can arise due to the sedentary nature of esports. One study revealed that individuals aged 13 and older, typically spend an average of 6.3 hours per week playing video games, and 8.5% of American youth exhibit addiction to video games. This lifestyle of gaming has been associated with physiological problems, such as obesity and increased caloric intake. Based on existing limited research, there is a positive correlation between esports gaming and increased Body Mass Index (BMI) as a result of prolonged screen time and prolonged sitting (Trotter, Coulter, Davis, et al., 2020). While esports itself may not seem to directly cause obesity, especially abdominal obesity, there are several evident aspects that contribute to the relationship between obesity and esports gaming (Turel, 2017). Lack of inactivity can cause a slow metabolism and reduce the amount of calories burned, both which can lead to excessive weight gain. Furthermore, this sedentary nature is also linked to increased caloric intake through over consumption of high caloric foods with large percentages of salt and sugar, or foods of low nutritional value. Many players will often opt for foods and drinks that are unhealthy because they are typically quick and convenient to access without interfering with their gaming activities and schedules (Mao et al, 2021). For example, evidence has shown that older youth are most likely to consume sugary drinks while playing video games than younger individuals. A model proposed that when a user's video game use is high, individuals are more motivated to reach for sweet drinks (Turel, 2017). Video gaming has also been associated with increased alcohol consumption and substance abuse, which can lead to weight gain and contribute to obesity (Trotter, Coulter, Davis, et al., 2020). Poor sleep quality is another indirect variable that links esports gaming to obesity. Video gaming may adversely influence different aspects of sleep quality including duration and efficiency. This can result in irregular sleep patterns, which can lead to hormonal imbalances that affect eating habits. Insufficient sleep is associated with higher levels of the hormone ghrelin, which increases appetite and Studies also suggest that those who play video games right before bedtime are more likely to experience sleep disturbances and poor sleep quality, increasing their likelihood of greater abdominal adiposity (Turel, 2017).

Furthermore, the sedentary nature of esports can cause cardiovascular issues. Since the 1950s, numerous studies have reported that sedentary behavior has a positive correlation with adverse health effects (Ford and Caspersen, 2015). Remaining in sedentary positions for prolonged periods is significantly associated with higher rates and risks for cardiovascular diseases, including hypertension, type 2 diabetes, and atherosclerosis. Regular physical activity is essential for good cardiovascular health because it improves blood circulation and maintains blood pressure and cholesterol levels. As per the Centers for Disease Control and Prevention, it is recommended that adults perform about 150 minutes of physical activity per week to promote their health (Zimmer, Haupt, Heidenreich, et al., 2022). Physical inactivity can lead to fat buildup in your arteries, the blood vessels that carry blood to your organs. With excessive buildup, arteries can get clogged causing disrupted blood flow to the heart and leading to fatal heart implications such as a heart attack or a stroke. Prospective studies have proven that physical inactivity is highly associated with coronary heart disease and strokes (Lippi, Henry, Sanchis-Gomar, 2020).

Musculoskeletal issues are another health concern that affects many competitive esport athletes. Esport athletes constantly enact the same hand movements while gaming, such as clicking or moving the mouse. Without proper rest, these movements can cause strained injuries in the hands, wrists, and fingers, inflicting pain, or conditions like carpal tunnel. A systematic review reported that, "Eleven out of twelve studies demonstrated a negative impact of video game playtime on the musculoskeletal system" (Tholl, Bickmann, Wechsler, 2022). Participants most reported pain in the neck, shoulder, and back. It is evident that excessive video gaming is correlated to musculoskeletal disorders due to the overall effects of prolonged sitting, repetitive movements, and being sedentary.

The negative impact of video gaming on vision health has gradually evolved into a public health issue in recent years. People who spend long hours in front of computer screens for work or leisure are often faced with what is termed as "digital eye strain" or "computer vision syndrome." Video games have been deemed as another culprit behind vision issues because of the continuous use of screen devices. Studies conducted in Southeast Asia, consisting of populations that are addicted to gaming, reported that 19% of the participants had suffered from eye strain. Esports gaming can get intense and lengthy and require players to go long periods of time without taking breaks. Failure to incorporate breaks from looking at a screen can cause eye strain. Blue light exposure is also known to increase eye strain and cause other health issues such as disrupted sleep and circadian rhythms. In extreme cases, constant exposure to blue light without proper care can lead to damaged retinal cells and symptoms of digital eye strain (Mylona, Deres, Dere, et al., 2020). It is vital for esports players to take preventative measures for digital eye strain such as practicing the 20-20-20 rule, in which individuals are advised to take a 20 second break every 20 minutes at something that is at least 20 feet away (Datta, Sehgal, Bhattacharya, et al., 2023). Excessing use of video games can cause one to be isolated from everyone and to neglect their daily activities often resulting in depression and other mental health issues. In addition to that, late night gaming causes irregular sleeping patterns worsening their sleep cycle and mental health.

Sleep Patterns and Esports

The rise of esports has created concern around its influence on sleep efficiency and how it may disrupt sleep patterns. One of the primary ways esports can disrupt sleep patterns is through late-night gaming. It is quite typical for video gamers to spend endless hours in matches or tournaments that can lead late in the night. Tournaments are often populated by people from all parts of the world, which means that a span of multiple time zones are involved amongst the players. This can interfere and cause a misalignment of schedules, causing players to switch up their usual bedtime routines and sacrifice their sleep. Participating in gaming at night can also lead to irregular sleeping patterns which is not good for one's health as it can cause irregular circadian rhythms affecting their quality of sleep and health (et al, 2020). Furthermore, if a person doesn't get enough sleep due to gaming, it can lead to hypertension, obesity, depression,and laziness. Therefore, participating in tournaments during unconventional hours can lead to sleep deprivation, which can ripple into health concerns. Research has linked video games to irregular sleeping habits and poor sleep quality. A study examining the sleep characteristics in esports players showed that their sleepy efficiency was below recommended levels. One potential explanation to this phenomenon amongst esport players is exposure to blue emitted by gaming devices. Blue light from devices is known to influence sleep negatively by suppressing melatonin production and impacting the circadian timing system. Results of this study also showed that esports players who performed better in gaming were those who had spent longer hours sleeping. These results support that gaming performance is influenced by sleep efficiency (Moen, Vatn, Olsen, et al., 2021).

Sleep is necessary for health and well-being in people of all ages. Proper sleep is a necessity for our cognitive functioning, immune system, cardiovascular, and metabolic health. Getting sufficient sleep is not only important for improving health, but also improving overall quality of life. Lack of sleep is associated with a cumulative of sleep disorders and health risks such as cardiovascular disease, obesity, and diabetes. To mitigate these medical concerns, it is imperative for esport players to be mindful of their sleep duration and regularity. Players must take into consideration that their health is more valuable than participating in a late night gaming session. The American Academy of Sleep recommends that adults should get at least 7 hours or more of sleep to improve sleep efficiency and circadian alignment and other aspects of health (Ramar, Malhorta, Carden, et al., 2021).

Managing Physical Health

Esports is more than just a form of video gaming; it is a hobby, a passion, and a profession to people across the world. It is vital for esports players to manage their physical health to enhance their overall well-being and performance and to ensure that they can continue playing safely. The number one way for esports players to improve their health is by incorporating regular exercise into their routines. This can consist of aerobic exercises such as walking, running, or cycling. Due to the sedentary nature of esports, doing any sort of physical activity is better than none. Creating an ergonomic setup is equally important in protecting health, as it minimizes any strain on the back, neck, wrists, and eyes that can occur with prolonged sitting. Ultimately, esports and gaming in general should be enjoyed in a balanced manner. Finding a harmonious balance between gaming and physical activity will reduce the risk of physical issues emerging (Trotter, 2020). A health management model that focuses on health and injury and prevention in esport players was developed for primary care sports medicine physicians to follow when evaluating the health of players. The model of esport physical assessment is curated based on preliminary data and focuses on all aspects associated with esports. After conducting the assessment, primary care physicians will then be able to identify the player's needs and provide further assessment and treatment. Incorporating this health model is particularly useful in maintaining the health of esport players. (DiFrancisco-Donoghue, Balentine, Schmidt, et al., 2019).

ESPORTS AND MENTAL HEALTH

Esports have both positive and negative impacts on individuals mental health, depending on how they engage in sport. When participating with mindfulness and proper balance, this competitive gaming can affect a person's mental health positively. As this sport requires critical thinking, strategic thinking, and quick decision-making, individuals engaging in this activity can sharpen their brain function and cognitive ability. For individuals participating in it after work or school, gaming can provide stress relief allowing them to clear up their minds and decompress from their daily stress and concerns. As individuals interact with people from around the world, for those feeling lonely and hopeless, it can cause a sense of community and belonging giving them an opportunity to make new connections and form friendships. In addition to that, participating and winning in these sports can help boost one's self confidence and self esteem encouraging them to build towards personal development and goals. Although esports has many beneficial qualities contributed towards public health, when not handled properly, it can have many adverse effects on one's mental health.

Mental health and the world where esports and gaming intersect is a growing area of concern and research and draws attention to two important areas: the prevalence of mental health challenges among gamers and the factors that contribute to these challenges. Research has shown a potential link between violent video games and increased aggression in players which suggests that exposure to violent games might indeed lead to heightened aggression (Anderson and Dill, 2000).

As esports can get extremely competitive it can cause high levels of stress and anxiety leading them to get burnt out. They often have the pressure to perform better than everyone and to win, this often affects their sleep cycle and social isolation affecting their mental health (Cai et al, 2022). Moreover, gaming addiction has been shown to interfere with other social responsibilities and can lead to negative psychological outcomes such as anxiety and depression. This addiction often intertwines with the immersive nature of video games, where players become engrossed in virtual worlds, further complicating the psychological aspect (Von der Heiden et al., 2019). However, it is important to note that not all psychological impacts are negative. Multiplayer games could enhance prosocial behavior and teamwork skills, highlighting a positive aspect of gaming on social and cognitive development such as problem-solving, spatial reasoning, and strategic thinking. Video games can provide a platform for mental stimulation and skill development, challenging the prevailing notion that gaming is solely detrimental to mental health (Kimmig et al., 2018).

The prevalence of mental health problems in athletes has emerged as a major concern. A seminal study of gaming addiction revealed that a subset of gamers exhibits addictive behaviors that often coincide with symptoms of anxiety and depression This suggests that a large proportion of gamers may experience mental health problems associated with their gaming habits (Burleigh et al., 2022).

Understanding the factors that contribute to mental illness among gamers is important in order to develop effective interventions and strategies to promote psychological well-being within this community. One of the primary challenges identified by Smith et al. (2022) is the potential for social isolation and loneliness among gamers. Excessive gaming tends to reduce face-to-face contact, as individuals can immerse themselves in their virtual world. This withdrawal from physical social networks can lead to feelings of isolation and loneliness, which are well-documented risk factors for a variety of mental illnesses including lack of motivation, depression, and anxiety (Smith et al. 2022). On the other hand, the online gaming environment also provides opportunities for positive social interaction. Online gaming forums can be virtual meeting places where individuals from different backgrounds can make friends and feel a sense of belonging. These virtual friendships can provide emotional support and companionship, counteracting the negative effects of social isolation that can occur offline (Von der Heiden et al., 2019).

Unique Stressors in Esports

The world of esports is characterized by a unique set of stressors that can greatly affect the mental health of athletes and players. These stressors, from high-pressure and competitive environments to the sedentary lifestyles often associated with gaming, contribute to the mental health illnesses of individuals in this area (Palanichamy, Sharma, Sahu, & Kanchana, 2020).

One of the main sources of stress in esports is the high-pressure competitive environment. Kane and Spradley's (2017) research highlights that the recognition of esports as a legitimate sport has led to intense competition, where there is pressure to consistently maintain a high level of performance while players struggle to excel on the global stage can be overwhelming, causing a lot of stress levels among esports players. Fear of failure and the consequences of dysfunction can increase anxiety and negatively affect mental health (Kane and Spradley, 2017).

Long hours of practice and playing games are another important source of stress in esports. Research reveals that esports players typically spend a lot of time training and competing, with some practicing up to 10 hours a day. This grueling routine can be physically and mentally exhausting, disrupt sleep patterns, and leave a person feeling drained. The relentless pursuit of improvement and the need to stay on top of your game can lead to chronic stress and anxiety. While an arduous practice schedule is necessary for success, it can take a significant toll on psychological well-being (Schary et al., 2022).

Public scrutiny is an inherent aspect of the world of esports. Esports athletes often find themselves in the public eye, with fans and critics watching their every move closely. These constant evaluations can aggravate performance anxiety, as fear of failure becomes more noticeable. The pressure to meet the expectations of fans, sponsors, and organizations can be paralyzing, causing a great deal of stress and psychological strain (Smith et al., 2019).

The lack of physical exercise and a sedentary lifestyle inherent in esports can further exacerbate participants' mental illnesses. Prolonged absence from work and research time can lead to physical health problems such as obesity and musculoskeletal issues. These physical health problems can also negatively impact psychological well-being. Additionally, lack of regular exercise can increase stress and anxiety, as exercise is known to have mood-enhancing effects (Weaver et al., 2009).

The unique stressors within the esports industry, including the high-pressure competitive environment, long hours of practice and play, public scrutiny, and a sedentary lifestyle, contribute significantly to the mental health challenges faced by esports athletes. Recognizing and addressing these stressors is vital for safeguarding the well-being of individuals within the esports community and fostering a healthier and more sustainable esports culture.

Social Isolation and Loneliness

With its vast online communities and virtual networks, the gaming world presents a paradoxical dilemma of social isolation and loneliness. While gamers tend to engage in extensive networking, research shows that these interactions can sometimes contribute to feelings of isolation, underscoring the importance of real-life interactions.

The paradox of online social interaction highlights the complex relationship between virtual interactions in the game world and social relationships in the real world. Online gaming communities can provide a sense of belonging and companionship, with players forming bonds around common interests and experiences. However, these virtual interactions may not entirely replace real-life social interactions. Players may spend excessive amounts of time in the virtual world, resulting in a sense of disconnect between the physical world and real-life relationships (Lemmens, Valkenburg, & Peter, 2011). Additionally, when played obsessively, one might become addicted to competitive gaming causing them to neglect everyone around them and harm their physical and mental health. Examples of these effects include avoiding friends and family, skipping exercise and healthy meals, and experiencing health issues.

The importance of real social interaction cannot be underestimated in the context of mental health. While online interaction can provide support and friendship, it may lack the depth and depth of emotional connection found in face-to-face relationships. Loneliness arises when individuals prioritize virtual connections over real-life ones, leading to feelings of isolation and alienation. Striking a balance between online and offline communication is important for emotional well-being.

Strategies to reduce social isolation among gamers include limiting screen time, prioritizing face-to-face contact, and engaging in social activities other than play. Incorporating physical activity and hobbies into your routine can help combat the sedentary lifestyle associated with gaming and encourage real-world socialization. In addition, open communication with friends and family about play habits, and seeking help when needed, can also be effective in reducing isolation.

Burnout and Overexertion in Gaming

Burnout and overexertion are widespread issues within the gaming community, affecting esports athletes and casual gamers alike. Understanding the concept of sport burnout is important, as it has significant implications for mental health. Furthermore, balancing sport with other social activities and the practice of self-care is important for the well-being of individuals involved in sport.

Understanding burnout in sport includes recognizing the emotional and physical exhaustion that can result from excessive overplay. In sports, it is often the result of a relentless pursuit of success and excellence, resulting in long hours of practice and competition. Gamers and esports players can become mentally drained and physically exhausted, experiencing symptoms such as decreased motivation, emotional exhaustion, and decreased productivity. This state of burnout can severely affect mental health, causing stress, anxiety, and even depression have occurred (Smith et al., 2019).

Balancing gameplay and other social activities is critical to prevent burnout and overexertion. Committing too much time to gaming at the expense of other responsibilities can lead to neglect of real-life responsibilities, such as work, education, and relationships. This imbalance can lead to feelings of burnout and stress growing. Establishing clear boundaries for gaming and other activities, including physical activity and socializing, is essential to maintaining a healthy lifestyle (Saquib et al., 2017).

Self-care practices play an important role in reducing burnout and excessive effort among gamers. Combining regular breaks during gaming sessions with relaxation techniques such as meditation and deep breathing exercises can help relieve stress and emotional exhaustion. Making physical health a priority by exercising and maintaining a balanced diet can also contribute to overall well-being. Additionally, seeking support from friends, family, or mental health professionals when experiencing burnout symptoms is an important step in managing sport-related mental health (Smith et al., 2019).

Burnout and overwork are common issues in gaming, and highly indicative of mental health. Getting under the concept of burnout in play, balancing play with other social activities, and practicing self-care are important to prevent and manage these challenges. It is important to promote gaming about sustainable positive attitudes to promote a comprehensive approach to wellbeing in the play community.

Cyberbullying and Harassment in Gaming

Cyberbullying and harassment have developed as major concerns in the gaming community, contributing to an atmosphere with serious mental health effects for gamers. Cyberbullying is defined as online bullying often associated with harassment, verbal abuse, threats, and emotional discomfort. This often causes a toll on one's mental health leading to lowering their self esteem and confidence. In order to protect mental well-being it is crucial for one to balance competitive gaming with physical activities and to address these potential negative effects early on to prevent it from escalating and causing long lasting detrimental effects. Esports is supposed to be a fun entertaining gaming experience and due to this toxic behavior, it ruins the overall purpose of the game. This discouragement not only has an impact on players' mental health but also reduces their enjoyment of the game. This "virtual world" introduces cyberbullying which if not taken action too early on can be fatal. During these competitive gaming, players may experience excessive bullying, harassment, and verbal abuse from their opponents or peers causing a toll on their mental health. Online toxicity, characterized by behaviors like hate speech, unsportsmanlike conduct, and harassment towards other players is a prevalent concern in the gaming world (Kwak, Blackburn, & Han, 2015). This type of toxicity produces a hostile environment that goes beyond the virtual realm, affecting players' entire gaming experiences and causing increased stress, anxiety, and discomfort among those subjected to toxicity.

Furthermore, online toxicity frequently discourages people from engaging in gaming communities, resulting in a culture of fear and isolation. This discouragement not only has an impact on players' mental health but also reduces their enjoyment of the game. As a result, the impact of online toxicity extends well beyond the immediate gaming and can have long-term consequences for individuals' mental health. The mental health repercussions of cyberbullying in gaming are significant. Victims of cyberbullying face a flood of nasty remarks, insults, and harassment, which can lead to feelings of helplessness poor self-esteem, depression, and extreme action such as suicide. Individuals exposed to cyberbullying in online games showed greater levels of distress, anxiety, and social isolation, according to Kwak et al. (2015). Importantly, the repercussions of cyberbullying may flow over into gamers' offline lives, harming their relationships, academic achievement, and professional functioning. The emotional anguish produced by online abuse can lead to long-term mental health difficulties, stressing the importance of tackling cyberbullying within the gaming community.

Addressing the gravity of cyberbullying is essential, not only to protect individuals from harm but also to create a secure environment for all players. Esports has taken proactive measures to combat this issue by implementing stringent regulations against cyberbullying. The establishment of safer gaming environments is pivotal in alleviating the mental health toll inflicted by cyberbullying and harassment. Collaboration between game creators, platform operators, and the gaming community is vital for creating an atmosphere that encourages polite and inclusive interactions. Kwak et al. (2015) recommended numerous ways to combat online toxicity, including the implementation of reporting mechanisms, community moderation, and penalties for toxic behavior. These measures not only discourage individuals from harassing others but also enable victims to seek help when they are subjected to cyberbullying. Education and awareness programs are critical in combating cyberbullying in gaming. Empowering players with empathy, sportsmanship, and respect may help alter the game culture toward more positive interactions. Furthermore, encouraging inclusiveness and diversity within gaming communities may have a major impact. In order to protect mental well-being it is crucial for one to balance competitive gaming with physical activities and to address these potential negative effects early on to prevent it from escalating and causing long lasting detrimental effects.

Esports and Public Health Awareness

As esports has evolved tremendously in recent years and gained a lot of people's interest, it serves as an excellent platform to spread public health awareness. As many users engaging in competing video gaming are youths, spreading awareness regarding physical health and incorporating healthy practices in the education curriculum can reduce obesity and other physical issues (Yin et al 2020). Furthermore, spreading public health awareness regarding esports amongst people of all ages is necessary as gaming is on a rise amongst all age groups. Embedding esports curriculum in schools and advocating them with vital information about proper nutrition, physical exercise, mental health and the importance of balancing lifestyle can reduce the negative impacts of esports in individuals at a very young age (Riatti et al, 2021). In addition to that, organizing workshops for individuals focusing on different aspects of esports and having guest speakers who have been negatively and positively been impacted by esports educate the participants can also cause awareness. Using esports tournaments as a platform to deliver public health messages to those engaging or watching competitive gaming, can also positively impact one's life and educate them about esports.

As the demand of esports is increasing everyday, it is extremely important to introduce support systems to individuals being impacted by competitive gaming whether physically or mentally. Along with educating the participants, spreading awareness amongst their parents and other family members is also crucial for them to help out their family members and from helping them to astray. The alliance between esports and public health tends to educate and create a healthier lifestyle for all the gamers, transcending the division of real life and virtual world.

CONCLUSION

In conclusion, esports has caused a lot of attention worldwide and has become a niche interest. While esports provides a variety of benefits from cognitive stimulation to abundance of connections, it is important to explore its connection with public health and understanding both the positive and negative aspects. Engaging in esports can be rewarding but getting addicted to this can be harmful to one (Mistry et al, 2023). Although esports provide an exciting multifaceted realm, it also presents a spectrum of potential health hazards that require more awareness. As the esports industry continues to expand and grow at an unprecedented rate, it is vital for players, healthcare professionals, and policyholders to take measures to mitigate these health risks. Understanding and advocating the impact of esports to society and public health is crucial nowadays due to the quick rise of esports. Using esports tournaments as a social platform to educate players and people watching the games about the positive and negative effects of esports can minimize the detrimental effects and promote a healthier lifestyle. Furthermore, implementing initiatives aimed at reducing health risks from gaming can vastly improve and maintain the physical health of esport players. The persistent issue of cyberbullying and harassment, as well as the significance of developing safer gaming environments, was explored. The esports community can assure its continuing development and success by addressing these mental health challenges and establishing a culture of inclusion and well-being. Because esports blur the line between sport and entertainment, recognizing and addressing its mental health concerns becomes critical. By doing so, we can ensure that esports stay a vibrant and genuine cultural phenomenon for many years to come, benefiting both players and fans.

Ultimately, esport players must find a healthy balance between gaming and taking care of their overall health. It is crucial to remember that success in esports does not only come from gaming; the physical and mental health of esports players is just as valuable in successful gaming performances. Interventions must be implemented and encouraged to ensure that esports remain a strong and enjoyable community for all.This article is an appeal for further research by researchers, educators and esports companies to come together to navigate this fascinating but complicated relationship between esports and public health.

REFERENCES

Anderson, C. A., & Dill, K. E. (2000). Video games and aggressive thoughts, feelings, and behavior in the laboratory and in life. Journal of personality and social psychology, 78(4), 772.DOI: 10.25035/jade.02.01.03

Bányai, F., Griffiths, M. D, Király, O., & Demetrovics, Z. (2019). The psychology of esports: A systematic literature review. Journal of gambling studies, 35, 351-365. DOI: 10.25035/jade.02.01.03

Burleigh, T. L., Griffiths, M. D., Sumich, A., Wang, G. Y., Stavropoulos, V., Kannis-Dymand, L., & Kuss, D. J. (2022). Co-Occurrence of Gaming Disorder and Other Potentially Addictive Behaviours between Australia, New Zealand, and the United Kingdom. International Journal of Environmental Research and Public Health, 19(23), 16078–. https://doi.org/DOI: 10.3390/ijerph192316078

Cai, L., Huang, Z., Feng, Q., Chang, X., & Yan, K. (2022). Co-Transformation of Digital Health and eSport in Metaverse: Moderating Effects of Digital Personality on Mental Health in Multiplayer Online Battle Arena (MOBA). *International Journal of Environmental Research and Public Health,* 20(1), 760–. https://doi.org/DOI: 10.3390/ijerph20010760

Choi, C., Hums, M. A., & Bum, C.-H. (2018). Impact of the Family Environment on Juvenile Mental Health:eSports Online Game Addiction and Delinquency. *International Journal of Environmental Research and Public Health, 15*(12), 2850–. https://doi.org/DOI: 10.3390/ijerph15122850

Darvin, L., Vooris, R., & Mahoney, T. (2020). The playing experiences of esport participants: An analysis of treatment discrimination and hostility in esport environments. *Journal of Athlete Development and Experience*, *2*(1). Advance online publication. DOI: 10.25035/jade.02.01.03

Datta, S., Sehgal, S., Bhattacharya, B., & Satgunam, P. N. (2023, May). pattern and associations with asthenopic symptoms. *Indian Journal of Ophthalmology*, *71*(5), 2071–2075. DOI: 10.4103/ijo.IJO_2056_22 PMID: 37203083

DiFrancisco-Donoghue, J., Balentine, J., Schmidt, G., & Zwibel, H. (2019, January). Managing the health of the eSport athlete: An integrated health management model. *BMJ Open Sport & Exercise Medicine*, *5*(1), e000467–e000467. DOI: 10.1136/bmjsem-2018-000467 PMID: 30792883

Drape, J. (2021, December 19). Step Aside, LeBron and Dak, and Make Room for Banjo and Kazooie. *The New York Times*. https://www.nytimes.com/2021/12/19/sports/esports-fans-leagues-games.html

Ford, E. S., & Caspersen, C. J. (2012, October). review of prospective studies. *International Journal of Epidemiology*, *41*(5), 1338–1353. DOI: 10.1093/ije/dys078 PMID: 22634869

Hamari, J., & Sjöblom, M. (2017). *What is eSports and why do people watch it?* Internet.

Hitt, K. (2020, January 31). *Pittsburgh Knights and Coco-Cola partner to help launch Coke Energy*. The Esports Observer. https://esportsobserver.com/pittsburgh-knights-coca-cola-deal

Holden, J. T., Rodenberg, R. M., & Kaburakis, A. (2017). Esports corruption: Gambling, doping, and global governance. *SSRN*, *32*, 236–273. DOI: 10.2139/ssrn.2831718

Internet and Videogaming Addiction on Adolescent Vision: A Review of the Literature. Frontiers in Public Health, 8, 63–63. https://doi.org/DOI: 10.3389/fpubh.2020.00063

J. (2023, July 18). *The Hidden Struggles of Esports: LoL pros in a mental health crisis*. Esports.net. https://www.esports.net/news/industry/hidden-struggles-of-esports-athletes-mental-health-crisis/#:~:text=A%20study%20by%20Psychology%20Today

Kane, D., & Spradley, B. D. (2017). Recognizing ESports as a Sport. *The Sport Journal*.

Kapur, V. K., Olson, E. J., Rosen, C. L., Rowley, J. A., Shelgikar, A. V., & Trotti, L. M. (2021). Sleep is essential to health: An American Academy of Sleep Medicine position statement. *Journal of Clinical Sleep Medicine : JCSM : Official Publication of the American Academy of Sleep Medicine*, *17*(10), 2115–2119. DOI: 10.5664/jcsm.9476 PMID: 34170250

Ketelhut, S., Martin-Niedecken, A. L., Zimmermann, P., & Nigg, C. R. (2021). Physical Activity and Health Promotion in Esports and Gaming-Discussing Unique Opportunities for an Unprecedented Cultural Phenomenon. *Frontiers in Sports and Active Living*, *3*, 693700. DOI: 10.3389/fspor.2021.693700 PMID: 34604743

Kimmig, A.-C. S., Andringa, G., & Derntl, B. (2018). Potential Adverse Effects of Violent Video Gaming: Interpersonal- Affective Traits Are Rather Impaired Than Disinhibition in Young Adults. *Frontiers in Psychology*, *9*, 736–736. DOI: 10.3389/fpsyg.2018.00736 PMID: 29867689

Kwak, H., Blackburn, J., & Han, S. (2015). Exploring Cyberbullying and Other Toxic Behavior in Team Competition Online Games. *Proceedings of the 33rd Annual ACM Conference on Human Factors in Computing Systems*, 3739–3748. DOI: 10.1145/2702123.2702529

Lemmens, J. S., Valkenburg, P. M., & Peter, J. (2011). Psychosocial causes and consequences of pathological gaming. *Computers in Human Behavior*, *27*(1), 144–152. DOI: 10.1016/j.chb.2010.07.015

Mao, E. (2021). The structural characteristics of esports gaming and their behavioral implications for high engagement: A competition perspective and a cross-cultural examination. *Addictive Behaviors*, *123*, 107056. DOI: 10.1016/j.addbeh.2021.107056 PMID: 34332273

Palanichamy, T., Sharma, M. K., Sahu, M., & Kanchana, D. M. (2020). Influence of Esports on stress: A systematic review. *Industrial Psychiatry Journal*, *29*(2), 191. DOI: 10.4103/ipj.ipj_195_20 PMID: 34158701

Pluss, M. A., Novak, A. R., Bennett, K. J. M., Panchuk, D., Coutts, A. J., & Fransen, J. (2023, April). The reliability and validity of mobalytics proving ground as a perceptual-motor skill assessment for esports. *International Journal of Sports Science & Coaching*, *18*(2), 470–479. DOI: 10.1177/17479541221086793

Riatti, P., & Thiel, A. (2021). The societal impact of electronic sport: A scoping review. *German Journal of Exercise and Sport Research*. Advance online publication. DOI: 10.1007/s12662-021-00784-w PMID: 40477796

Rosell Llorens, M. (2017). eSport Gaming: The Rise of a New Sports Practice. *Sport, Ethics and Philosophy*, *11*(4), 464–476. DOI: 10.1080/17511321.2017.1318947

Rudolf, K., Bickmann, P., Froböse, I., Tholl, C., Wechsler, K., & Grieben, C. (1870). K., Bickmann, P., Froböse, I., Tholl, C., Wechsler, K., & Grieben, C. (2020). Demographics and Health Behavior of Video Game and eSports Players in Germany: The eSports Study 2019. *International Journal of Environmental Research and Public Health*, *17*(6), 1870. Advance online publication. DOI: 10.3390/ijerph17061870

Sanz-Matesanz, M., Gea-García, G. M., & Martínez-Aranda, L. M. (2023). Physical and psychological factors related to player's health and performance in esports: A scoping review. *Computers in Human Behavior*, *143*, 107698. DOI: 10.1016/j.chb.2023.107698

Saquib, N., Saquib, J., Wahid, A., Ahmed, A. A., Dhuhayr, H. E., Zaghloul, M. S., Ewid, M., & Al-Mazrou, A. (2017). Video game addiction and psychological distress among expatriate adolescents in Saudi Arabia. *Addictive Behaviors Reports*, *6*, 112–117. DOI: 10.1016/j.abrep.2017.09.003 PMID: 29450245

Schary, D. P., Jenny, S. E., & Koshy, A. (2022). Leveling up esports health: Current status and call to action. *International Journal of Esports*, *3*(3).

Seffah, K. D., Salib, K., Dardari, L., Taha, M., Dahat, P., Toriola, S., Satnarine, T., Zohara, Z., Adelekun, A., Ahmed, A., Gutlapalli, S. D., Patel, D., & Khan, S. (2023). Health Benefits of Esports: A Systematic Review Comparing the Cardiovascular and Mental Health Impacts of Esports. *Cureus*, *15*(6), e40705. DOI: 10.7759/cureus.40705 PMID: 37485153

Smith, M., Sharpe, B., Arumuham, A., & Birch, P. (2022). Examining the Predictors of Mental Ill Health in Esport Competitors. Healthcare (Basel), 10(4), 626–. https://doi.org/DOI: 10.3390/healthcare10040626

Smith, M. J., Birch, P. D., & Bright, D. (2019). Identifying stressors and coping strategies of elite esports competitors. [IJGCMS]. *International Journal of Gaming and Computer-Mediated Simulations*, *11*(2), 22–39. DOI: 10.4018/IJGCMS.2019040102

Tholl, C., Bickmann, P., Wechsler, K., Froböse, I., & Grieben, C. (2022, December). disorders in video gamers – a systematic review. *BMC Musculoskeletal Disorders*, *23*(1), 1–678. DOI: 10.1186/s12891-022-05614-0

Turel, O., Romashkin, A., & Morrison, K. M. (2017, August). A model linking video gaming, sleep quality, sweet drinks consumption and obesity among children and youth. *Clinical Obesity*, *7*(4), 191–198. DOI: 10.1111/cob.12191 PMID: 28320073

Von der Heiden, J. M., Braun, B., Müller, K. W., & Egloff, B. (2019). The association between video gaming and psychological functioning. *Frontiers in Psychology*, *10*, 1731. DOI: 10.3389/fpsyg.2019.01731 PMID: 31402891

Wattanapisit, A., Wattanapisit, S., & Wongsiri, S. (2020). Public Health Perspectives on eSports. *Public health reports (Washington, D.C.: 1974)*, *135*(3), 295–298. https://doi.org/DOI: 10.1177/0033354920912718

Weaver, J. B.III, Mays, D., Sargent Weaver, S., Kannenberg, W., Hopkins, G. L., Eroĝlu, D., & Bernhardt, J. M. (2009). Health-Risk Correlates of Video-Game Playing Among Adults. *American Journal of Preventive Medicine*, *37*(4), 299–305. DOI: 10.1016/j.amepre.2009.06.014 PMID: 19765501

Wheless, E. (2021). The top gaming partnerships of 2021; Gaming and esports got a popularity

Yin, K., Zi, Y., Zhuang, W., Gao, Y., Tong, Y., Song, L., & Liu, Y. (2020). Linking Esports to health risks and benefits: Current knowledge and future research needs. *Journal of Sport and Health Science*, *9*(6), 485–488. DOI: 10.1016/j.jshs.2020.04.006 PMID: 32417192

Chapter 6
Maintaining Balance and Wellness in Remote Work

Michelle Bartlett
https://orcid.org/0000-0001-7719-987X
Old Dominion University, USA

ABSTRACT

In today's rapidly evolving work environments, remote work has become more than a trend; it is now a mainstay and rising (Ewers & Kangmennaang, 2023). This shift has necessitated a re-evaluation of traditional work paradigms, particularly in the realms of work-life balance and employee wellness. This chapter details the core strategies for thriving in remote work settings by setting boundaries, combating isolation, and fostering supportive corporate cultures. Transitioning from offices to remote work can blur the lines between personal and professional lives (Bella, 2023; Beňo, 2023). This section provides practical advice on how remote workers can effectively delineate these aspects. Remote workers face unique challenges in maintaining their healthy work-life balance, and they must adopt effective strategies to set and uphold boundaries as the foundation of remote work balance and well-being.

INTRODUCTION

In today's rapidly evolving work environment, remote work has become more than a trend; it is now a common and rising mode of employment (Ewers & Kangmennaang, 2023). Remote workers in scholarly literature are sometimes referred to as e-workers. Despite ongoing calls from some employers, including governmental agencies, for a return to physical offices, forward-thinking organizations continue to incorporate remote workers into their strategic talent pipeline. This shift has necessitated a re-evaluation of traditional work paradigms, particularly in the realms of

DOI: 10.4018/979-8-3373-5322-7.ch006

work-life balance and employee wellness. This chapter presents the core strategies for thriving in remote work settings by setting boundaries, combating isolation, and fostering supportive corporate cultures. Transitioning from offices housed within an organization's physical location to remote work can blur the lines between personal and professional lives (Bella, 2023; Beňo, 2023). This chapter offers strategic recommendations to help remote workers navigate the unique challenges of maintaining a healthy work-life balance by effectively delineating personal and professional boundaries as a foundation for well-being and success. To navigate these evolving dynamics of the workplace, this chapter offers a comprehensive exploration of strategies that support remote workers in maintaining balance, fostering well-being, and building sustainable routines, beginning with the critical step of setting boundaries.

SETTING BOUNDARIES

Establishing routines helps demarcate the start and end to a workday, a critical component of effective remote work practices. In the absence of traditional environmental cues, such as commuting or transitioning between office spaces, remote workers must adopt intentional strategies to create psychological and physical boundaries between professional and personal domains. These routines not only facilitate cognitive shifts necessary for task engagement and disengagement but also contribute to overall well-being, reduced burnout, and enhanced productivity. This section examines the role of pre- and post-work rituals, particularly the practice of pseudo-commuting, as evidence-based approaches to promoting work-life balance in remote settings.

Creating a Pre-Work and Post-Work Routine

One key approach is to define work hours. Beňo (2023) supported the idea of *pseudo-commuting*; their study defines pseudo-commuting as a habit or ritual that e-workers perform to simulate a traditional commute, creating a mental and physical transition between work and home modes. This practice addresses the challenge of separating these spheres when working remotely. Research has found multiple benefits of pseudo-commuting, including improved work-life balance, reduced work-from-home fatigue, boosted productivity and well-being, enhanced daily structure, and time for mental preparation and decompression (Susilo, 2024). Using a quasi-experimental approach, participants engaged in various pseudo-commuting activities, such as walking, biking, meditating, or creating coffee rituals. Interview data strongly supported pseudo-commuting as an effective tool for balancing work and home life. These practices have been shown to have positive implications for e-workers, employers, and society, potentially leading to increased work engagement, stress recovery, and overall improvements in happiness and health (Beňo, 2023; Susilo, 2024; Tackett & Lemon, 2025).

Setting Clear Work Times

When operating in a remote work environment, the boundaries between professional and personal spaces often become blurred. This lack of clear delineation can result in work activities encroaching upon all hours, potentially leading to excessive labor, mental and physical fatigue, and eventual occupational burnout. Remote workers need to identify the hours in their workdays like they would in traditional office settings. Employees can avoid the common pitfall of overworking by establishing and strictly adhering to specific work hours. Another essential strategy is creating distinct workspaces; setting up home offices conducive to productivity is vital. Employees could physically workspaces from personal spaces to foster mental differentiations between work and leisure time. Well-organized and dedicated workspaces can significantly enhance focus and productivity. Interestingly, research by Chevtaeva et al. (2024) highlights that maintaining well-being in remote settings can also include dynamic strategies such as working while traveling. Through a topological analysis of over 32,000 Instagram posts, their study identified 23 elements that support mental health during remote work trips, suggesting that, under certain conditions, mobility and work are not inherently incompatible. This finding underscores the importance of flexibility and intentional design in remote work environments, whether at home or when traveling. Finally, digital tools can be crucial in separating work and personal lives. Using separate devices or accounts for professional and personal use can help maintain a psychological division between the two spheres. Together, strategies of structured time, defined space, flexible environments, and technological boundaries can support remote workers in achieving sustainable, healthy work-life integration (Allen et al., 2021).

Examples of Using Pseudo-Commuting to Signal the Start of the Workday

- Morning walk or jog around the neighborhood
- Preparing and enjoying a special breakfast or coffee ritual
- 10-15 minutes of meditation or yoga
- Reading a few pages of a book
- Listening to a motivational podcast or upbeat music playlist
- Getting dressed in work attire (even if working from home)
- Writing in a journal or reviewing your daily goals

- Watering plants or tending to a small garden
- Doing a quick workout or stretching routine
- Tidying up your workspace before sitting down to work

Examples of Post-Work Pseudo-Commuting to Signal the End of the Workday

- Write a short list of tasks you have left that you are leaving for the next workday
- Evening walk or bike ride to replicate a *commute* home
- Changing out of work clothes into casual wear
- Preparing and sipping a relaxing tea or beverage
- 10-15 minutes of unwinding meditation or deep breathing exercises
- Closing and putting away work materials or devices
- Engaging in a hobby for a set amount of time (e.g., 30 minutes of painting)
- Calling a friend or family member for a quick chat
- Taking a shower or bath to wash away the workday
- Preparing dinner as a transition to evening activities
- Listening to calming music or a non-work-related podcast

These activities help create clear boundaries between work and personal time, signaling to your brain when it is time to focus on work and when it is time to relax and engage in personal activities.

COMBATING ISOLATION

The Psychological Impact of Remote Work

Remote work has undeniable benefits, but it also introduces unique psychological challenges. Oakman et al.(2021) have shown that remote workers are more susceptible to feelings of isolation, anxiety, and even burnout due to the blurred boundaries between personal and professional lives. Without the regular in-person interactions and support systems available in traditional office settings, remote workers may feel disconnected from their colleagues, leading to a sense of loneliness. Additionally, the constant pressure to remain online and available can increase stress levels, especially if expectations around working hours are unclear. The psychological effects of remote work are multifaceted and can vary depending on individual circumstances, but some key challenges have become widely recognized. One of the most common is the experience of social isolation. Working remotely often eliminates the organic, day-to-day interactions in a traditional office setting, like casual conversations in the hallway or spontaneous brainstorming sessions. This lack of face-to-face interaction can lead to feelings of loneliness, which, over time, may contribute to more severe mental health issues such as anxiety and depression. Employees may feel disconnected from their colleagues and the company culture, reducing their sense of belonging and engagement with their work.

Another significant psychological challenge of remote work is the blurred boundaries between personal and professional lives. This connects back to the concept of setting start and stop times for your day. Many remote workers struggle to *switch off* at the end of the workday without a physical separation between home and office. This constant connectivity can lead to an *always-on* mindset, where employees feel compelled to respond to emails or complete tasks outside regular working hours. Over time, this pressure to be continuously available can lead to increased stress, fatigue, and eventual burnout. Additionally, the lack of structure in the remote work environment can exacerbate overwhelming feelings as the line between work and leisure becomes increasingly indistinct.

Employees and organizations must take proactive steps to address these mental health challenges. Some organizations offer times for networking and off-site meetings for teams to address the issue of isolation. Other companies can play a key role by implementing wellness initiatives designed to support remote workers. For example, offering wellness days can allow employees to rest and recharge, helping prevent burnout before it takes hold. Regular check-ins with managers can also help remote workers feel connected and supported, providing a space to discuss any issues they may be experiencing. Moreover, promoting a culture of openness around mental health is critical. When employees feel they can talk openly about their struggles without fear of judgment or reprisal, they are more likely to seek help when needed. This culture of support can be reinforced by providing resources such as access to counseling services, stress management workshops, or mindfulness training. Also, encouraging team members to set boundaries, such as defining clear working hours and creating dedicated workspace areas, can help them maintain a healthy work-life balance, ultimately reducing stress levels and promoting more sustainable work routines.

Beyond organizational policies, professional development can help employees build skills for self-awareness, resilience, and mental health management. Workshops on stress reduction, emotional intelligence, and remote interpersonal dynamics can strengthen individual coping strategies and promote a shared language around well-being. Employees can adopt practices to protect their mental health. Prioritizing self-care, establishing routines, and seeking social interactions outside of work can help mitigate feelings of isolation. By creating a supportive work environment and encouraging mental health conversations, organizations and employees can work together to ensure that the psychological impacts of remote work are managed effectively, allowing workers to thrive personally and professionally.

Building Effective Remote Work Routines

The foundation of thriving in a remote work environment often lies in establishing structured routines. Without the natural boundaries created by a commute or a physical office, it becomes crucial to create rituals that signal the start and end of the workday. Developing a pre-work routine, whether it is pseudo-commuting, exercising, or simply changing into work clothes, can help remote workers mentally prepare for the day ahead. Similarly, winding down with a post-work routine can reinforce the transition from work to personal time.

The importance of routine in a remote work environment cannot be overstated. Routines provide structure, which helps remote workers maintain a sense of normalcy and control over their workday. In the absence of traditional office cues like commuting or scheduled lunch breaks, it is easy for the day to become unstructured and chaotic. A well-defined routine establishes boundaries and predictability, boosting productivity, enhancing focus, and improving overall well-being. It helps individuals stay on track with tasks, prevents procrastination, and ensures that work does not bleed into personal time, thereby maintaining a healthy work-life balance.

Creating habits that promote productivity begins with a strong morning routine. The act of getting ready for the workday, whether it involves preparing breakfast, exercising, or engaging in a pseudo-commute like a short walk, signals to the brain that the workday is about to start. For some, changing into professional attire, even when working from home, can help set a productive tone and create a mental shift toward work mode. These morning rituals serve as cues that transition workers from home life to the work mindset, making it easier to focus once the workday begins. For others, it may be helpful to schedule the most important tasks during the early hours of the day when energy and focus are often at their peak.

Implementing routines that build in regular breaks throughout the day can be key to maintaining focus. Taking mental breaks can enhance concentration and prevent burnout. These breaks can also serve as opportunities for self-care, whether stretching, meditating, or simply stepping outside for fresh air. Additionally, maintaining a designated workspace at home can enhance productivity. A clear physical distinction between *work* and *home* can reinforce boundaries and allow individuals to disconnect from work mentally when the day is over.

Equally important is having a post-work routine that signals the end of the day. This might involve logging off at a set time, changing into more casual clothes, engaging in a hobby, or spending time with family. A clear end-of-day ritual can help remote workers switch from work mode to personal time, preventing the blurring of boundaries that often leads to burnout. Setting digital boundaries, such as silencing work notifications after hours, can be especially important for those who may feel pressure to be constantly available. Disconnecting from work-related tasks allows employees to recharge and ensures they are better equipped to maintain focus and productivity when they return to work. While individual strategies such as boundary-setting are essential for maintaining work-life balance in remote settings, sustainable success also requires systemic support; thus, organizational culture plays a pivotal role in reinforcing these practices and promoting overall employee well-being.

FOSTERING SUPPORTIVE CORPORATE CULTURES

While individual routines and boundary-setting practices are essential for personal well-being in remote environments, they must be reinforced by organizational structures that promote sustainable work habits. As such, encouraging a supportive corporate culture through thoughtful use of technology, intentional communication, and inclusive engagement strategies becomes critical in shaping a remote workforce that is both productive and resilient.

Technology's Role in Supporting Remote Work Balance

Technology has undoubtedly revolutionized how we work, making remote work possible, efficient, and productive. However, this same technology can blur the lines between work and personal life, leading to a sense of being constantly *on* and available. However, workers can leverage technology to support a healthier work-life balance by intentionally using tools that simplify tasks, set boundaries, and promote time management. One of the key ways to achieve this is by automating routine tasks. Many remote workers spend significant time on repetitive administrative tasks such as scheduling meetings, sending follow-up emails, or managing calendars. By using automation tools like email schedulers, project management platforms, and smart assistants, workers can streamline these tasks and reduce the cognitive load. Automating these functions allows individuals to focus on high-value work while reducing the need to check messages or manage day-to-day details constantly.

In addition to automation, using technology to set clear boundaries around communication is crucial. Platforms like Slack, Microsoft Teams, and email are essential for staying connected remotely. Still, they can also create an expectation of immediate responsiveness, leading to burnout. Workers can protect their work-life balance by taking advantage of features that manage notifications, such as setting *do not disturb* times during off-hours or pausing email alerts after the workday ends. Many communication platforms allow for status updates, enabling employees to signal when they are unavailable or in focus mode, thereby reducing interruptions and helping to create a culture of respect for personal time. To support the effective use of technology, organizations could offer professional development focused on digital literacy, asynchronous communication, and managing remote workflows. By helping employees build these skills, companies can reduce technostress and empower individuals to work more confidently and independently in digital environments. It is also important to define clear communication protocols within teams, such as limiting instant messaging after certain hours or designating specific timeframes for responses to non-urgent requests.

Time-tracking tools can also play an important role in maintaining balance by providing a clear picture of time spent during the workday. Tools like Toggl or RescueTime help remote workers monitor their time on tasks and activities, offering insights that can help prevent overworking. These tools assist in tracking productivity and can also be used to flag when someone is working beyond their regular hours. With these insights, employees can make informed decisions about when to take breaks, stop for the day, and how to structure their time more efficiently. Tracking time can also prevent scope creep, where work gradually expands beyond set hours without clear recognition.

At the organizational level, having clear policies on technology usage is essential to support employees' work-life balance. Policies that limit after-hours emails or support the use of separate devices for work and personal life can help remote workers maintain a psychological boundary between their professional and personal lives. For example, many companies now implement *right to disconnect* policies, which empower employees to log off from work-related communications without fear of repercussions. Encouragement to use separate devices for work and personal activities further reinforces this divide, preventing work tasks from encroaching on personal time. Additionally, organizations should clearly communicate expectations around technology usage, such as response times for messages, and ensure that leadership models these boundaries.

Championing Team Collaboration and Engagement

Remote work environments can make collaboration and engagement more challenging, especially for teams accustomed to in-person dynamics. However, remote teams can stay highly engaged and collaborative with intention and the right strategies. Maintaining and building team cohesion in a remote work environment requires intentional strategies to foster engagement and connection. Regular check-ins are among the most effective ways to keep teams aligned. These check-ins can include daily stand-up meetings, weekly progress reports, or one-on-one sessions with managers. The purpose of these meetings goes beyond just task updates; they provide a platform for team members to connect on a personal level, share challenges, and offer support. Frequent communication helps ensure that everyone remains on the same page, reinforcing a sense of team unity even when physically apart. Video conferencing tools, such as Zoom or Microsoft Teams, offer opportunities for face-to-face interactions that help bridge the gap created by remote work. These moments of virtual interaction remind teams that they are working together towards a common goal, even if they are geographically dispersed.

Another strategy for promoting team cohesion is incorporating virtual team-building exercises into the remote work schedule. Activities like online games, quizzes, or virtual coffee breaks allow team members to interact in a relaxed setting, helping to build rapport and strengthen interpersonal relationships. These exercises do not have to be elaborate; even casual, light-hearted interactions can significantly enhance team bonding. For more structured approaches, companies can host virtual workshops or themed events that engage employees in collaborative problem-solving or skill-building activities. Such exercises promote a culture of teamwork, trust, and collaboration, which is critical to sustaining team morale and a positive working atmosphere. Collaborative tools are also essential in enabling real-time interaction and enhancing engagement. Platforms like Slack, Asana, or Trello allow teams to communicate and collaborate on projects in real time, breaking down the barriers that remote work can sometimes create. These tools facilitate seamless collaboration, with features like shared document editing, file sharing, and integrated task management, ensuring that all team members can contribute equally regardless of location. Real-time collaboration tools reduce the friction of working asynchronously by making it easy for team members to stay informed and contribute to ongoing projects, reinforcing a sense of shared ownership and responsibility. In addition, integrating video chat or voice features into these platforms allows for spontaneous conversations that mimic in-person interactions, enhancing team collaboration and creativity.

Cultivating an inclusive remote culture is another critical element for maintaining team cohesion. It is important that every team member feels connected, valued, and heard, regardless of their role or location. Leaders can create this culture by actively seeking input from all team members during meetings, acknowledging contributions, and celebrating achievements, no matter how small. An inclusive culture also means being mindful of the unique challenges that remote work may present for different individuals, such as time zone differences or personal obligations. Offering flexible work hours or accommodating diverse work preferences can help ensure that all team members feel supported and able to contribute fully. Organizations can create a remote culture where employees feel engaged, valued, and motivated to collaborate by prioritizing inclusivity and open communication.

OVERCOMING COMMON PITFALLS IN REMOTE WORK

Remote work is rife with challenges, such as procrastination, overworking, and lacking motivation. These pitfalls often arise because remote workers must self-regulate their time and effort more than in an office setting. For some, the lack of a structured environment can lead to distractions, while for others, the absence of clear boundaries causes them to work longer hours. To overcome the common pitfalls of remote work, remote workers must adopt effective time management strategies and create boundaries within their work environment. One helpful technique is the Pomodoro method, where workers break their day into focused 25-minute work intervals, followed by 5-minute breaks. This approach prompts sustained concentration while allowing time for regular mental rest. Setting realistic, achievable goals for each day or week can also help remote workers stay focused and motivated, breaking down larger tasks into smaller, manageable milestones.

Additionally, taking regular breaks, whether a short walk, stretching, or a moment away from the screen, can prevent burnout and maintain energy levels throughout the day. Managing workspace distractions is another critical factor; creating a dedicated workspace that minimizes interruptions, setting boundaries with family or housemates, and reducing digital distractions with tools like website blockers can significantly enhance focus. By adopting these strategies, remote workers can maintain high productivity while protecting their well-being in a remote work setting.

ADAPTING REMOTE WORK TO DIVERSE NEEDS AND PREFERENCES

Remote work is not a one-size-fits-all model, and individuals' experiences vary based on their unique personalities, roles, and life circumstances. Extroverts may miss the daily social interactions of the office, while introverts may thrive in solitude. Similarly, parents or caregivers may need additional flexibility to manage work alongside personal responsibilities. Adapting remote work to diverse needs and preferences is crucial for stimulating an inclusive and effective work environment. Flexibility in work hours is one of the most important factors, as it allows employees to manage their responsibilities (such as caregiving or parenting) while still maintaining productivity. Offering flexible schedules can accommodate early risers, night owls, or those in different time zones, ensuring all team members can work during their most productive hours. Additionally, recognizing that individuals have different communication styles is key to building a collaborative remote team. While some may prefer frequent video calls to stay connected, others may thrive with written communication via emails or messaging platforms, which offer more time to process and respond. Professional development that trains team members to understand and navigate these preferences can enhance team cohesion and communication. These sessions can also include strategies for working across time zones, adapting to neurodiverse communication styles, and supporting equity in remote settings. In terms of task management, tools that allow for individual autonomy and team collaboration can cater to diverse work preferences. For instance, project management platforms that offer clear task assignments, deadlines, and status updates help maintain transparency while allowing employees to manage their tasks in a way that suits their workflow. By embracing flexibility and acknowledging the unique needs within a team, organizations can create a remote work environment where all employees feel supported and empowered to perform at their best.

CORPORATE RESPONSIBILITY IN REMOTE WORK

Companies play a pivotal role in setting the tone for a healthy work-life balance in remote settings. Corporate policies must prioritize workers' well-being by ensuring that boundaries are respected and support systems are in place. Corporate leadership plays a critical role in encouraging a healthy work-life balance in remote settings by modeling healthy work habits and setting clear expectations. Leaders can demonstrate this by avoiding after-hours emails and respecting boundaries between work and personal time, signaling to employees that disconnecting is okay. Promoting paid time off and encouraging employees to take breaks helps prevent burnout and emphasizes the importance of rest and recovery. Additionally, establishing clear communication guidelines, such as setting expectations for response times and appropriate hours for contact, ensures that employees are not overwhelmed by the demands of constant connectivity. Providing access to mental health resources, such as counseling services or stress management workshops, is another way leadership can support employee well-being. By developing remote work policies that balance productivity with wellness, leaders can create an environment where employees feel valued and supported. Ultimately, when leaders prioritize well-being and openly embrace these practices, they set the tone for a company culture that respects and promotes work-life balance, ensuring long-term employee satisfaction and productivity. In addition to modeling these practices, organizations can support leaders with professional development opportunities that focus on managing remote teams, modeling well-being, and creating inclusive virtual cultures. Training programs that help leaders set communication norms and recognize signs of employee burnout are essential in reinforcing healthy work environments.

SUSTAINING LONG-TERM REMOTE WORK SUCCESS

While remote work has become necessary for many companies, its long-term success depends on adaptability, continuous improvement, and a focus on sustainability. Sustaining long-term success in remote work requires organizations to remain adaptable and continuously refine their strategies. One key approach is to regularly reassess and update remote work policies based on employee feedback, ensuring that the policies remain aligned with the evolving needs of the workforce. This could involve conducting surveys, holding town halls, or implementing focus groups to understand the challenges and preferences of remote employees. Offering ongoing training for leaders on effectively managing and supporting remote teams is also essential, as remote leadership requires skills different from traditional in-office management. Investing in advanced tools that facilitate seamless collaboration, communication, and well-being (such as project management platforms, mental health apps, or ergonomic home office setups) can significantly enhance long-term productivity and employee satisfaction. Cultivating a results-oriented culture is another critical component; by focusing on the quality of output rather than the number of hours worked, organizations empower employees to manage their time effectively, promoting autonomy and job fulfillment. Ultimately, companies that treat remote work as an evolving practice and are committed to continuous improvement will be better positioned to maintain a productive, engaged, and sustainable remote workforce.

COMBATTING ISOLATION THROUGH BUILDING COMMUNITY IN A REMOTE SETTING

Remote work, while offering flexibility, can lead to feelings of isolation. Leonardi et al. (2023) found that individuals with a higher need for autonomy thrive in remote work settings. Still, more sociable individuals may become less productive due to feelings of isolation. This section proposes innovative solutions to foster connection and community among remote workers with higher social needs. In the realm of remote work, the maintenance of social connections and team cohesion requires creative approaches. One promising method is the introduction of virtual social interactions, such as virtual coffee breaks and online social clubs. These platforms provide avenues for informal interactions among colleagues that replicate the casual conversations in physical office spaces. Such interactions are essential to build rapport and maintain the camaraderie within teams. Equally important are regular team check-ins. These frequent meetings should transcend beyond work-related discussions and serve as platforms for social engagement and morale boosting. The check-ins can foster positive work environments by recognizing team members' efforts and accomplishments. Finally, community building initiatives play vital roles in remote work settings. Team-building activities that can be conducted remotely foster feelings of belonging and teamwork among remote employees. Such initiatives might include virtual team-building exercises or collaborative online projects. These activities enhance team dynamics and contribute to the cohesive and supportive work cultures that are crucial for the well-being and productivity of remote teams.

Can You Resonate With Jordan?

Jordan, a marketing specialist, transitioned to remote work without establishing clear boundaries. They kept their laptop open in the living room, responding to emails at all hours. Jordan's workday began as soon as they woke up and often extended late into the evening. They skipped regular meals, worked through weekends, and rarely took time for themselves or to connect with colleagues. As weeks passed, Jordan felt increasingly isolated and burnt out. Their productivity declined, and they struggled to separate their professional and personal life. The lack of structure and social interaction led to decreased job satisfaction and a sense of disconnection from their team.

Jordan Talked With a Mentor. What Changes Can You See?

Jordan implemented a structured approach to remote work after seeking advice. They created a dedicated office space in a spare room and established a consistent routine. Each morning, Jordan took a 15-minute walk to *commute* to work, followed by a coffee ritual to signal the start of their workday. They scheduled regular virtual coffee breaks with colleagues and joined a weekly online team trivia game. At the end of each day, Jordan closed their laptop, changed out of work clothes, and went for another walk to *commute* home. They also started a virtual book club with coworkers to maintain social connections. By setting clear boundaries and actively developing community, Jordan gradually overcame their feelings of isolation, maintained steady productivity, felt more connected to their team, and achieved a healthier work-life balance in the remote setting.

CULTIVATING A SUPPORTIVE WORK CULTURE

Corporate culture's role is pivotal in supporting remote employees (Pamula & Zalewska-Turzyńska, 2023). This section discusses the necessary cultural shifts and leadership roles that promote healthy work-life balance. Respecting the personal time of remote workers is paramount in today's work environment. Companies must implement strategies that honor the distinctions between work and personal lives, such as setting clear communication guidelines that prevent encroachment into non-working hours. This respect for personal time helps prevent burnout and promotes a healthier work-life balance. Another aspect that requires attention is the underutilization of paid leave. Employers need to advocate for remote workers to take advantage of their leave entitlements. Companies can do this by normalizing time off through internal policies and messages emphasizing the importance of rest and recuperation for long-term productivity and employee well-being. Last of all, the role of leadership is crucial in modeling work-life balance. When leaders practice and prioritize their work-life boundaries, positive examples are set for everyone else. This modeling can influence company cultures and make them more supportive of individual needs by promoting sustainable approaches to work among all employees.

THREE REAL-WORLD APPLICATIONS THROUGH CASE STUDIES

This section grounds these strategies in reality by presenting case studies from various organizations that have successfully navigated the challenges of remote work. Valuable insights can be gained by illustrating work-life balance strategies applied across various industries. Each sector has unique ways of incorporating these practices, from cutting-edge tech companies to mission-driven non-profits. By showcasing a variety of industry examples, we can observe the universal relevance of work-life balances and the distinct approaches that have been adapted to different work cultures and demands. The analyses of the success stories and the lessons learned from these organizations shed light on the practical aspects of implementing work-life strategies. They provide readers with actionable insights and takeaways from real-world challenges and triumphs. These analyses celebrate successes and candidly examine the hurdles to understand what works and what does not comprehensively. Furthermore, examining adaptation strategies reveals how organizations evolve their remote work policies and practices over time. It is a testament to the dynamic nature of remote work environments and the need for continuous improvement. As organizations learn from experience and feedback, they refine their strategies, leading to more effective and sustainable remote work policies that benefit both the company and its employees.

Case One - GitLab: Pioneering All-Remote Work at Scale

GitLab has established itself as a leader in remote work, operating as an all-remote company since its inception in 2011. Their approach to remote work is comprehensive and well-documented, serving as a model for organizations worldwide. One of GitLab's most significant contributions to the remote work movement is its publicly available remote work guide. This extensive resource covers various aspects of remote work, including communication protocols, time management techniques, best practices for virtual meetings, tools and technologies for remote collaboration, and strategies for maintaining work-life balance. The guide is valuable for GitLab employees and other organizations looking to implement or improve their remote work policies. Recognizing the importance of casual interactions in building strong team relationships, GitLab has implemented several initiatives to foster informal communication. These include virtual coffee breaks, which are regular, optional video calls where team members can join for casual conversation; a *Random Room* Slack channel that randomly pairs employees for brief, informal chats; and social hours, which are themed virtual gatherings for team members to socialize and share common interests. These initiatives aim to simulate the spontaneous interactions that typically occur in traditional office settings, helping to build camaraderie and combat feelings of isolation.

To ensure their employees have comfortable and productive work environments, GitLab provides several forms of support. This includes a home office stipend, an allowance for employees to purchase ergonomic furniture and necessary equipment; coworking space reimbursement for employees who prefer to work from local coworking facilities; and an internet and technology allowance to ensure reliable internet connectivity and up-to-date technology. This financial support allows workers to create personalized workspaces that suit their needs and preferences, whether at home or in a shared workspace. GitLab places a strong emphasis on asynchronous communication and thorough documentation. They employ a handbook-first approach, documenting all company policies, processes, and decisions in a comprehensive online handbook. They also prefer asynchronous communication methods to accommodate different time zones and work schedules. Additionally, all meetings are recorded and transcribed for those who cannot attend in real-time. This approach ensures that information is accessible to all team members, regardless of their location or working hours.

While GitLab successfully implemented remote work, it has also faced challenges. These include effective onboarding of new hires in a virtual environment, managing across multiple time zones, and performance management in a remote setting. To address these challenges, GitLab has developed a structured virtual onboarding process, uses tools to visualize team members' time zones, encourages flexible scheduling, and focuses on outcomes rather than hours worked, using OKRs (Objectives and Key Results) to measure performance. GitLab's remote work model has positively impacted employee well-being and productivity. Employees report increased work-life balance due to flexible schedules, reduced commute stress and associated costs, higher job satisfaction and engagement, and improved productivity and focus in personalized work environments.

Questions to Ponder:

1. How might GitLab's approach to remote work need to evolve as the company continues to grow? What new challenges might arise at different scales of operation?
2. In what ways could GitLab's emphasis on asynchronous communication and documentation potentially impact creativity and spontaneous innovation? How might these effects be mitigated?
3. Consider the environmental impact of GitLab's all-remote model. How does it compare to traditional office-based companies in terms of carbon footprint and sustainability?
4. How might GitLab's remote work practices affect employees' sense of company culture and loyalty over the long term? What strategies could maintain a strong organizational identity in a fully distributed team?
5. Reflect on the potential societal impacts if more companies adopted GitLab's all-remote model. How might it affect urban planning, real estate markets, and community structures?
6. Given GitLab's success with remote work, why do you think some companies still resist fully remote models? What factors might make GitLab's approach less suitable for certain industries or organizational structures?
7. How does GitLab's remote performance management approach challenge traditional notions of productivity and work? What are the potential benefits and drawbacks of focusing on outcomes rather than hours worked?
8. Consider the impact of GitLab's remote work model on diversity and inclusion. How might it open up opportunities for a more diverse workforce, and what new challenges might it present to ensure equity and inclusion?

Case Two - Microsoft: Adapting to the New World of Work

Microsoft, a global technology leader with a diverse workforce, has demonstrated remarkable adaptability in changing work dynamics. The company's response to the evolving nature of work, particularly in light of the COVID-19 pandemic, offers valuable insights into how large, established organizations can successfully navigate the transition to remote and hybrid work models while prioritizing employee well-being. In recognition of the shifting landscape, Microsoft introduced more flexible work hours, moving away from the traditional 9-to-5 schedule. This policy change acknowledges the diverse needs of its global workforce, particularly benefiting employees balancing work with family responsibilities or those collaborating across different time zones. By allowing employees to adjust their work hours to suit their circumstances better, Microsoft has taken a significant step towards creating a more inclusive and accommodating work environment. Understanding that remote work can present unique challenges to mental health, Microsoft has substantially expanded its mental health resources and counseling services. These services have been made easily accessible to all employees, regardless of their location or work arrangement. This proactive approach to mental health support demonstrates Microsoft's commitment to the holistic well-being of its workforce, recognizing that employee health extends beyond physical safety to encompass psychological and emotional wellness.

In a novel approach to combating burnout and promoting work-life balance, Microsoft introduced the concept of *wellness days*. Employees can use these days off to focus on their personal well-being, separate from their regular vacation time. This initiative acknowledges the increased stress and potential for burnout in remote work settings, where the lines between work and personal life often blur. By providing this additional time off, specifically for wellness, Microsoft actively encourages its employees to prioritize self-care and maintain a healthy work-life balance. Microsoft's approach to remote work also extends to its technological innovations. The company has leveraged its products, such as Microsoft Teams, to facilitate remote collaboration and communication. Microsoft supports its workforce and contributes to the broader ecosystem of remote work technologies by continually improving these tools based on user feedback and observed needs.

The company has also reimagined its physical office spaces to accommodate a hybrid work model. As employees begin to return to offices, Microsoft has redesigned workspaces to facilitate collaboration and social interaction while maintaining flexibility for those who continue to work remotely part-time. This approach recognizes that the future of work is likely to be a blend of in-person and remote arrangements, requiring adaptable spaces and technologies. Microsoft's leadership has been vocal about the importance of adapting to new work models. CEO Satya Nadella has frequently discussed the company's *hybrid work paradox*, acknowledging the complex balance between the flexibility of remote work and the value of in-person collaboration. This open dialogue about the new work model's challenges and opportunities has helped to shape Microsoft's policies and foster a culture of adaptability. Regarding productivity measurement, Microsoft has shifted focus from traditional metrics to outcomes and impacts. This change aligns with the realities of remote work, where visibility into daily activities is reduced, and emphasizes the importance of results over presence. This outcomes-based approach has required a shift in management style and performance evaluation methods, demonstrating Microsoft's commitment to evolving its work culture.

Questions to Ponder:

1. How might Microsoft's flexible work policies impact team cohesion and company culture in the long term? What strategies could maintain a strong organizational identity in a hybrid work environment?
2. Consider the potential impact of Microsoft's wellness initiatives on employee retention and attraction. How might these policies influence the company's competitive tech job market position?
3. What challenges might arise from Microsoft's shift to an outcomes-based productivity measurement approach? How could this change affect different types of roles within the company?
4. How might Microsoft's remote and hybrid work approach influence its product development and innovation processes? Could there be both positive and negative impacts?
5. Reflect on the potential broader societal impacts if more large corporations adopted policies similar to Microsoft's. How might this affect urban planning, real estate markets, and local economies in tech hubs?
6. How might Microsoft's global presence and diverse workforce influence its remote work policies? What unique challenges and opportunities does this present compared to smaller, more localized companies?
7. Consider the environmental implications of Microsoft's hybrid work model. How might it compare to traditional office-based work and fully remote models regarding sustainability and carbon footprint?
8. How might Microsoft's remote work policies evolve in the coming years? What new challenges or opportunities might emerge as technology and work cultures continue to change?

Case Three - Mozilla a Mission-Driven Non-Profit Example

The Mozilla Foundation is a prominent example of a non-profit organization fully embracing and supporting remote work. As a globally distributed organization, Mozilla has implemented a comprehensive remote work strategy that aligns with its mission of fostering an open and accessible internet. The foundation provides its employees with tangible support for remote work, including stipends for home office setups and monthly internet reimbursements. This financial assistance ensures that all team members, regardless of location, can access the necessary tools and resources to work effectively from home. Mozilla also recognizes the importance of flexibility in a distributed workforce, offering adaptable working hours that accommodate various time zones and personal schedules. This approach supports work-life balance and enables the foundation to tap into a diverse, global talent pool.

Mozilla has developed several initiatives to maintain a strong sense of community and shared purpose among its remote workforces. The foundation regularly organizes virtual team-building activities and all-hands meetings, empowering connection and collaboration across its distributed teams. Recognizing the importance of continuous growth and development, Mozilla provides its employees access to online courses and conferences, encouraging ongoing learning and skill enhancement. The foundation also prioritizes employee well-being through comprehensive wellness programs, which include mental health support and fitness reimbursements. These offerings demonstrate Mozilla's commitment to supporting the professional needs of its remote workers and their personal well-being. By implementing these policies, the Mozilla Foundation exemplifies how non-profit organizations can create a supportive, productive, and engaging remote work environment that aligns with their mission and values.

Food for Thought Discussion Questions:

1. How does Mozilla's approach to remote work reflect and reinforce its mission of fostering an open and accessible internet? In what ways might this alignment between organizational structure and mission benefit Mozilla?
2. Consider Mozilla's potential challenges in maintaining its organizational culture across a distributed workforce. How effective are their virtual team-building and all-hands meetings in addressing these challenges?
3. Mozilla's remote work policy allows them to access a global talent pool. How might this impact the diversity of perspectives within the organization, and how could this diversity potentially influence Mozilla's work and mission?
4. How do you think Mozilla's status as a non-profit organization influences its approach to remote work? Are there aspects of their strategy that might be more challenging for for-profit companies to implement?
5. Reflect on the potential long-term impacts of Mozilla's investment in employee well-being and professional development in a remote setting. How might this affect employee retention, productivity, and overall organizational success?
6. Consider the environmental implications of Mozilla's distributed workforce model. How might this compare to traditional office-based non-profits regarding carbon footprint and sustainability?
7. How might Mozilla's remote work practices influence other non-profit organizations? What potential ripple effects could this have on the broader non-profit sector?

8. Mozilla's remote work policy includes financial support for home office setups and internet costs. How might this approach to equitable access to work resources align with their mission? What challenges might arise in implementing such policies globally?
9. Given Mozilla's focus on internet accessibility, how might their experience with remote work inform their understanding of digital divide issues? How could this insight potentially shape their future initiatives or projects?
10. How do you think Mozilla balances the benefits of asynchronous, flexible work with the need for real-time collaboration in a mission-driven organization? What strategies might they employ to ensure effective teamwork across time zones?

CONCLUDING THOUGHTS ON IMPLEMENTING REMOTE WORK

Implementing remote work policies similar to those mentioned above in other organizations requires a comprehensive approach to prioritizing employee well-being, productivity, and connection. Companies can start by developing a detailed remote work guide covering communication protocols, tools, and best practices for remote collaboration. This guide should be easily accessible and regularly updated. Organizations can implement virtual social activities like scheduled team-building sessions or online chat channels for non-work discussions to foster informal communication and team bonding. Providing support for home office setups through stipends or allowances ensures employees have comfortable and productive work environments. Adopting flexible work hours allows employees to balance their work and personal lives more effectively to ensure that implementing core hours can overlap for necessary collaboration.

Prioritizing mental health and well-being is crucial in a remote work environment. Organizations can partner with mental health providers, offer counseling services, and provide access to wellness resources. Introducing *wellness days* or additional personal days for self-care can help prevent burnout. Recommending regular breaks and time off, including implementing no-meeting days and setting clear expectations about after-hours communication, promotes a healthy work-life balance. Investing in appropriate technology and tools for remote work is essential, as is training managers in effective remote leadership strategies. Equally important is providing ongoing professional development to build employee and manager capacity in remote collaboration, digital etiquette, and self-directed productivity. Regular feedback collection and willingness to adapt policies based on employee needs are key to successful implementation. Finally, creating a culture of trust and focusing on results rather than time spent working can foster autonomy and engagement among remote workers. By thoughtfully implementing these strategies and tailoring them to their specific needs, organizations can create a supportive and productive remote work environment that benefits both employees and the company as a whole.

The Way Forward in Remote Work

The landscape of work has undergone a significant transformation, with remote work becoming a permanent fixture for many organizations. This shift has brought opportunities and challenges, requiring reimagining how we approach work, collaboration, and work-life balance. As we look to the future, it is clear that success in remote work settings will depend on our ability to adapt, innovate, and prioritize well-being alongside productivity. Central to this new paradigm is recognizing that effective remote work goes beyond simply replicating office-based practices in a home environment. It requires a holistic approach that addresses the unique challenges of distributed teams, such as combating isolation, maintaining team cohesion, and establishing clear boundaries between work and personal life. The strategies outlined in this chapter, from pseudo-commuting to virtual team-building activities, provide a foundation for creating healthier, more balanced remote work experiences. Leadership plays a crucial role in shaping the future of remote work. Managers and executives must lead by example, demonstrating trust in their teams while providing clear expectations and support. This involves promoting a culture of open communication, embracing flexibility, and prioritizing outcomes over hours worked. It also means being attentive to the diverse needs of team members and providing the necessary resources and technologies to enable effective remote collaboration. Moving forward, we should focus on creating sustainable remote work environments supporting individual and organizational success. This involves ongoing assessment and adaptation of work practices, investment in technologies that facilitate seamless collaboration, and a commitment to employee well-being. By embracing these principles, organizations can harness the full potential of remote work, creating more resilient, diverse, and productive teams that are prepared to thrive in an increasingly digital and distributed world.

REFERENCES

Allen, T. D., Merlo, K., Lawrence, R. C., Slutsky, J., & Gray, C. E. (2021). Boundary management and work-nonwork balance while working from home. *Applied Psychology, 70*(1), 60–84. DOI: 10.1111/apps.12300

Bella, K. M. J. (2023). The role of flexibility: Balancing work and personal needs. *International Journal of Scientific Research in Modern Science and Technology, 2*(2), 25–30.

Beňo, M. (2023). Re-establishing home and work boundaries by pseudo-commuting whilst working from home. *Central European Business Review, 12*(4), 123–134. DOI: 10.18267/j.cebr.335

Chevtaeva, E., Neuhofer, B., Egger, R., & Rainoldi, M. (2024). Travel while working remotely: A topological data analysis of well-being in remote work trip experiences. *Journal of Travel Research, 63*(2), 466–480. DOI: 10.1177/00472875231151923

Ewers, M., & Kangmennaang, J. (2023). New spaces of inequality with the rise of remote work: Autonomy, technostress, and life disruption. *Applied Geography (Sevenoaks, England), 152*, 152. DOI: 10.1016/j.apgeog.2023.102888

Leonardi, P. M., Parker, S. H., & Shen, R. (2023). How remote work changes the world of work. *Annual Review of Organizational Psychology and Organizational Behavior, 11*(1), 193–221. DOI: 10.1146/annurev-orgpsych-091922-015852

Oakman, J., Kinsman, N., Stuckey, R., Graham, M., & Weale, V. (2020). A rapid review of mental and physical health effects of working at home: How do we optimise health? *BMC Public Health, 20*(1), 1–13. DOI: 10.1186/s12889-020-09875-z PMID: 33256652

Pamula, A., & Zalewska-Turzyńska, M. (2023). Internal communication satisfaction while remote work: The organizational culture perspective. *European Research Studies, 26*(2), 30–48. DOI: 10.35808/ersj/3137

Susilo, T. (2024). The impact of talent management, employee well-being initiatives, and remote work policies on workforce productivity. *The Journal of Academic Science, 1*(2), 81–90.

Tackett, T., & Lemon, L. L. (2025). A balanced approach: Remote employees' experiences with employee engagement and well-being. *Corporate Communications: An International Journal*. Vol. ahead-of-print No. ahead-of-print. https://doi.org/ DOI: 10.1108/CCIJ-08-2024-0154

Section 3
Artificial Intelligence (AI) and Technology Innovation

Chapter 7
Artificial Intelligence in the Workplace: The Future of Learning and Developments

Tarana Afrin Chandel
https://orcid.org/0000-0002-8605-6018
Integral University, India

ABSTRACT

We all know that the word is driven by innovative technology and this transformation is towards Artificial Intelligence (AI). AI is the branch of science which deals with machine based on human intelligent and capabilities. These machines are upgrading the lives along with increased efficiency and profitability at low cost. AI is adding more and more value to our daily and professional lives; especially our workplace. In the domain of Learning and Development (L&D), AI is standing with open wings to revolutionize the way employees learn and develop their ability and proficiency. The current scenario for learning and development (L&D) is based on static data and training program. This method is outdated as it often shows failure for fulfilling the individual requirement of the learner, making it difficult to upgrading and reaching the workforce globally. In this chapter the author will discuss the mission and role of AI in L&D processes, factors leading to effective AI-based learning, benefits of AI adoption, challenges and opportunities of transformation of AI in workplace.

DOI: 10.4018/979-8-3373-5322-7.ch007

INTRODUCTION

The advent of Artificial Intelligence (AI) is rapidly transforming industries across the globe, creating new opportunities and challenges. In the workplace, AI is not only automating routine tasks but is also reshaping how employees learn, develop, and engage with their roles. Since it is no longer a tool for automation, AI is increasingly becoming a strategic partner in reshaping how organizations approach learning and development (L&D). From personalized learning pathways to advanced predictive analytics, AI is becoming an essential tool in workforce development. As companies strive to remain competitive in a fast-changing global economy, they are looking to AI not only to streamline operational tasks but also to enhance employee skills, foster growth, and unlock untapped potential within their teams.

In the traditional model of learning, training programs were often rigid and standardized, offering the same content to all employees regardless of their individual needs or career goals. AI disrupts this approach by enabling personalized learning experiences that adapt to each employee's unique learning style, pace, and aspirations. With AI's ability to analyze vast amounts of data, organizations can now identify skill gaps, predict future learning needs, and create dynamic, tailored development plans for their workforce. Moreover, AI's integration into the workplace extends beyond just individualized learning. It has the power to boost employee engagement, provide real-time feedback, and offer new avenues for collaboration through intelligent tools like chatbots, virtual assistants, and gamified learning environments. These innovations are making learning more accessible, interactive, and motivating for employees at all levels.

However, the rise of AI in learning and development does not come without its challenges. From concerns about data privacy to the ethical implications of AI-driven decision-making, organizations must navigate a complex landscape as they incorporate these technologies into their L&D strategies. Employees, too, may feel apprehensive about how AI will affect their roles and job security, which necessitates thoughtful implementation and transparent communication from leadership. This chapter delves into the transformative role AI plays in the future of workplace learning and development. It explores the key opportunities AI offers for enhancing training programs, improving employee performance along with and organizational growth and shaping career trajectories. At the same time, it addresses the potential challenges and ethical considerations that organizations must tackle as they integrate AI tools into their L&D frameworks. As we look to the future, AI will undoubtedly continue to evolve, driving the next generation of learning and development practices in the workplace.

Background

In the beginning 1950s, there were numerous names in the field of "machines thinking" such as cybernetics, automata theory, and complex information processing (McCorduck, P., 2004). These names suggest many conceptual orientations (John McCarthy, 1956). In 1955, John McCarthy, Assistant Professor of Mathematics at Dartmouth College, planned to arrange a group to explain and build an idea about machines which can think like human brain (John McCarthy, 1956). He suggested the name as 'Artificial Intelligence (AI)' for this new thinking machine. AI was initiated by scientist John McCarthy (T. A. Chandel, 2023). He officially announced this name at Dartmouth Conference in 1956, in front of many organizations, official name of AI existed from 1956 (official birth).

AI is a branch of science and engineering for designing intelligent thinking machines (Mathur, S. et al., 2016). He also defined AI as the simulation of human intelligence in a machine, manufactured to for working accordance to human behavior. Brynjolfsson and McAfee have texted in their book "***The Race against the Machine***" (Brynjolfsson & Andrew, 2012). The task domain of AI is shown in figure 1 (shoeby Mathew, AI, Cetin; 2024)

Marvin Minsky, founder of the MIT AI Lab, wrote in 1992 a novel titled "The Turing Option", i.e. situated in 2023, discussing artificial general intelligence (AGI). Think about it next time you chat with ChatGPT and wonder what the next 30 years might bring (Philippe Delanghe, 2023). Artificial general intelligence (AGI) is based on software programs that allows machines to sense and detect the environment and utilize intelligence learning to take decisions that enhances the possibility of achieving specific aims and objectives (Russell Stuart J., 2021; Rich, Elaine, 2010).

Figure 1. Task performed by AI

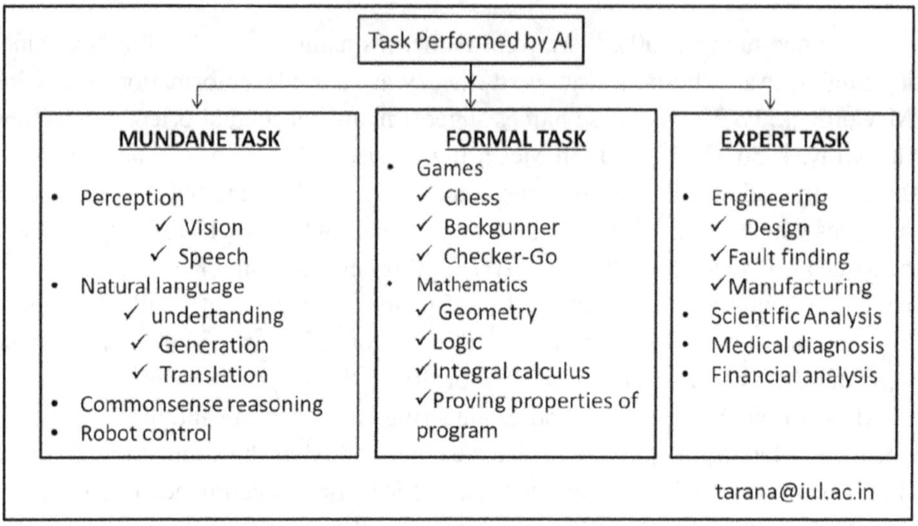

Today, the world is having a significant transformation in their work-style driven by emerging technologies. This emerging technology that is shaping this transformation is the artificial intelligence (AI). This technology is revolutionizing the ways the employees learn and develop their skill in workplace. In today's world, impact of AI on individuals learning experience, content creation and skill development is more conspicuous than traditional approach. Conventional approach of learning and development depend on training programs. This method is outdated today as it doesn't fulfill the requirement of individual learning. Apart of it, providing training to individual person according to their need becomes expensive as well as time-consuming, thus, difficult to reach the workforce globally. AI is a useful tool which can address the challenges and upgrade the effectiveness of L&D action plans. AI is replacing human potential at macroscopic level with intelligent duties. AI is merging with computer science thus producing intelligent machines. With the utility of AI, organization can develop its own learning experience that can customize the learning technique of their employees. It also makes administrative work automated, providing free time for focusing on their strategic initiatives. For institutions and organization, to remain competitive in present changing work environment, it is necessary to update oneself with recent advancement (Marcos Guevara, 2023). AI is a useful tool which can address the challenges and upgrade the effectiveness of L&D action plans. With the utility of AI, organization can develop its own learning experience that can customize the learning technique of their employees. It also makes administrative work automated, providing free time for focusing on their strategic initiatives.

Today, entrepreneurs have experimented on technology intelligence for successful transformation in their organization (Wamba Taguimdje, 2020). Decision and frame makers are now relying on AI, allowing machines to sense and perform in same manner as human has knocked the door of corporate organization with enhanced effectiveness and efficiency (D. Pavitra and B. Surajit, 2019; Dhamja and Bad, 2020). Entrepreneurs have started utilizing AI for optimizing their product value. COVID-19 pandemic, pushed the institutes and organization towards digital pathway of teaching, working and training (Bozkurt and Sharma. 2020).

Beginning of AI in Education

According to Moore's law (Moore, 1998) the development of digital technologies doubled every year. It didn't only enhanced the speed and efficiency of electronics appliances and gadgets exponentially, but also upgraded their operations and performances by adding multiple features. (Nicolae Moroianu, 2023; Jiahong, Weipeng, 2022). Thus, technologies played a vital role in transmuting human perception and execution toward sustainability with the capability to upgrade skill & educate individuals about the ecological footprint., hence, affecting the opinion and action (George et al., 2021; Schroder et al., 2021; Dwivedi et al., 2022). On the other hand, lack in alertness to environment change and correlation with digital innovations, requires implementing green Information Technology curriculum at colleges and university levels to efficiently talk on these challenging issues (Perkins et al., 2018; Marques et al., 2019; Miller J., 2020).

Moreover, the effect of COVID-19 pandemic globally had propelled colleges and research institutions to investigate innovative shortcoming speedily within a limited duration (Tam, El-Azar, 2020), while all the traditional / offline teaching methods were diverted towards online because of lockdown globally (T.A. Chandel, 2023; Sloan, 2020). Due to lockdown, schools and colleges were closed to maintain social distancing and decline the spreading of the diseases, thereby disturbing the learning process globally (UNESCO, 2020; M.A Mallick). Every educational institute followed e-learning platform such as Google classroom, Zoom, WebEx and Skype (Chandel, T.A. 2023). The educational paradigm shifted from traditional teaching system to the online teaching mode (Chandel, T.A. 2023), embracing new innovations in education with open arms (Akimov et al., 2023). As the result, educational infrastructure incorporates the provision of software and applications, nurturing an innovative education paradigm, modeled by machine learning/ human-machine interaction, giving rise to Education 4.0 (Gennari et al., 2023; Chandel, T.A, 2023) is shown in figure 2.

Figure 2. Human-Machine interaction

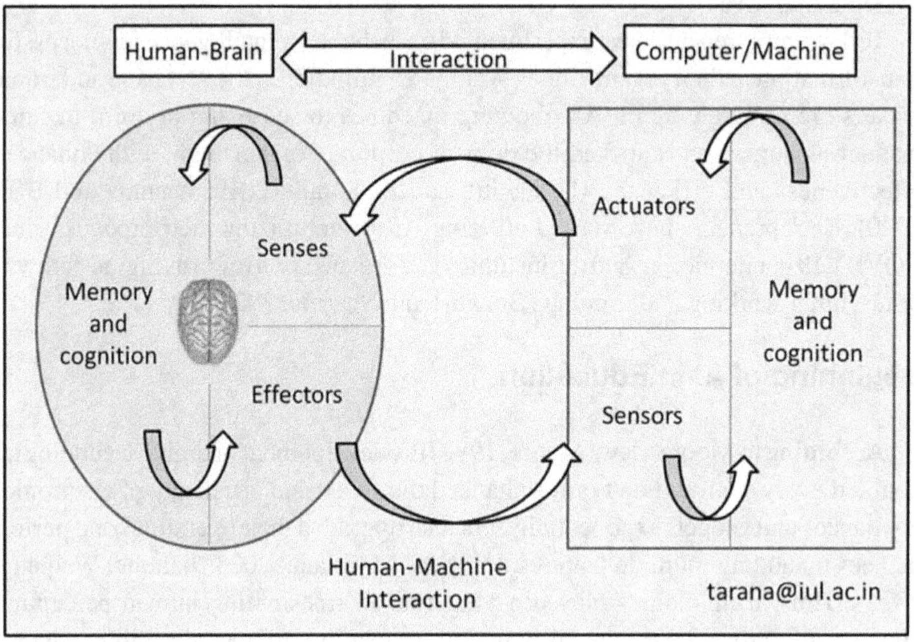

On this basis artificial intelligence has become an interesting discipline for an educators and researchers, having the ability of self-educating (Tahiru, 2021; Lee, Yeo, 2022; Liu et al., 2022; Mizumoto, Eguchi, 2023; Ray, 2023; Wand et al., 2023). As the utility of AI technology in education sector has increased, there has been a continuous growth in the publications in this discipline. Chiu et al (2023) has discovered four major functions executed by AI in education, thus increasing the value of audio and video learning and development, training, evaluation, and administration. They disclosed that AI is a human-machine, that enhances flexibility and interconnect the digital world, and support versatile teaching approaches, enhances teachers' instructional skills, uplift teachers' professional development, come up with automatic assessment, analyse students performances, assess student artefacts for constructive reviews, provides self-convenient service, support accurate decision making. A part of it, it has been revealed that before COVID-19 pandemic, AI tools has already been adopted and used in education system in developed countries such as USA, South Korea, Japan, Hong Kong, Estonia (Tahiru, 2021).

Previous studies also had fragmental contribution toward AI in Education 4.0 and innovative technological expertise. Importance of AI tool in education was emphasised for advance teaching and learning practices (Mollick, E. and Mollick, L., 2023). User-friendly and serviceable AI application can upgrade teacher's skill, increase learning capabilities and support empirical and research-based practices. AI tool such as Chabot's provide golden opportunities in teachers career to elevate their educational expertise (Lee and Yeo, 2022).

Moreover, Jiahong and Weipeng in 2022 examined the effect of AI on children in play group education or having nursery education/ early childhood schooling (ECS). They observed children having conceptual education using AI tools showed considerable change in their emotional behaviour, collaboration within other children with learning and development enhancing their competitive efficiencies. In 2023, Iku-Silan high-lighted in his research has proved identical intelligent learning outcomes along with confident and self-assurance.

RISE OF AI IN L&D

COVID-19 pandemic fast-tracked macro trends such as digital transformation and ever increasing skill gap, propelling one-self and corporates to rethink how to grow them. Living and working individually throughout the crucial time of pandemic, social and economic turmoil has effected individually to prioritise flexibility and achievement. Entrepreneurs are reviewing their business strategies and work frame to fulfil their new demands. Amidst this period, learning and development became a new mandate in making one-self the best.

Our lives are increasingly powered by Artificial intelligence (AI), a silent companion that has been quietly integrated into our world since the early 1960s (Michael Vaughn, 2023). AI in L&D enhances training and development programs in collaborations with organizations, improving personalised learning, decision-making skills virtual guidance and mentoring (Akshay Birje, 2024). AI involves numerous technologies likewise ML, natural language processing, facial recognition, computer vision and robot on your smartphone, and weather forecast on your favourite app, AI and AI-reminiscent processes have seamlessly become an intrinsic part of our daily routines. These innovative technologies empower machine to explore data, identify pattern and make self-decision with the assist of human. The use of AI in L&D has gained popularity due to its personalized, efficient, and data-driven learning experiences. AI has the potential to remodel L&D. With swift development of AI tools, it is understood that organization has the ability to increase the training programs and provide more efficient, novel and productive experiences. According to Asma A Sheikh Co-Founder & Director of Enthral.ai says "***AI enables training and skill development for all learners—from employees to extended enterpris***e" (Akshay Birje, 2024).

In many applications, AI is only a software agent that assists the user or applicants while functioning independently (Michael Vaughn, 2023). It simulates intelligently as human brains would advance to solve a problem. It makes decision on behalf of the observations and data collected from the environment and performs action based on observed data collected, reaching to its desired conclusions or outcomes (Michael Vaughn, 2023).

Today AI is not only a silent agent as said earlier. AI had added more features to perform active roles as chatbot examples are ChatGPT and Bard. These applications can involve human level conversation along with coding and creative content writing. Apart of it image designing tools such as ***Midjourne*y *and Stable Diffusion*** can develop high quality images and art-like pictures from text inputs (Michael Vaughn, 2023).

The rise of AI in L&D has disturbed the corporate L&D operation. Previously, the employs took long time even months to complete their task, but now it can be accomplished within an hour by machine. Resulting, enhanced demand on AI in L&D shifted gradually.AI is prepared to update the skill, moving towards a time ahead where learning can become more personal, efficient and affective.

Role of AI in L&D

The role of AI in L&D is to boost learning and development programs within an organization (Matt Burr, 2024). Some important role of AI in L&D is shown in figure 4, rest are explained in text. Its basic role is shifting towards continuous learning rather than traditional training and learning. It contributes numerous aspects of L&D; examples are personalized learning, decision making on ground collected data, virtual/ online counselling and guidance and many more (shiv Nadar, 2024).

Figure 3. Role of AI in learning and development

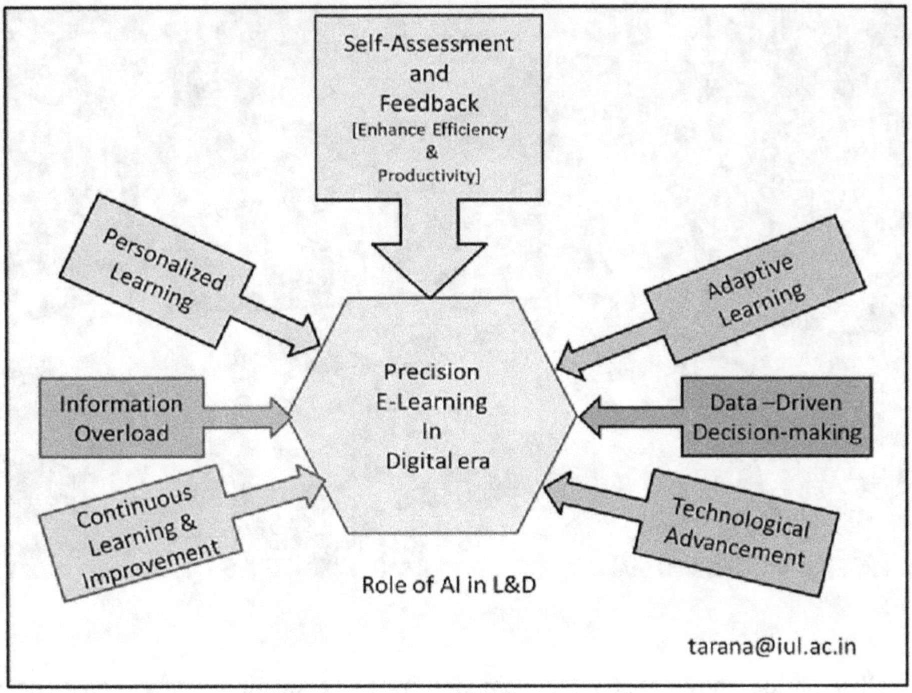

Personalized Learning

Education is the foundation of individual development and community growth, enhancing knowledge and talent of the students for bright future. Personalised knowledge signifies that each and every individual students learning is customised for their needs as shown in figure 5. Personalised learning allows every individual to fulfil their goal through innovative technology, the quality of materials they utilize for learning, speed of their learning. In current digital world, AI plays an important role in increasing educational knowledge. AI enables academicians to personalize their knowledge, to nourish the requirements of the students and strengthening them. An AI algorithm collects the data and analyse each employee about their talents, interest and the way they preferred learning. This method of analysis provides thorough understanding of individual leaners identity. AI boosts personalized learning by analysing huge data of students. With intelligent algorithm AI can analyse students' performance and highlights differed patterns of learning issues or differences in understanding. With these applications, forecast of AI in education is to exceed 10% in between 2023 and 2032 (Sruthi Santhakumar, 2024).

Figure 4. Personalized learning

Observation shows that AI is remodelling the education system. Evidences show that such advancements are shaping the future of education. Ms Anju Wal (Director Principal at Shiv Nadar School Faridabad) also shared; how AI permits more personalizes, qualitative and quantitative teaching, thus enriching the experience of the classroom (Shiv Nadar, 2024). By automating the task repetitively, AI provides spare time for teachers to focus and interact with student's activity and creating effective learning atmosphere. As technology interweaves its path into every individual's lifestyle, educational geography is transforming towards integrity of AI. AI is speedily reshaping the education system especially in personalized learning. (Trigyn technologies, 2023;Meehirr K, 2023). As we are embracing the revolutionary power of AI, the futurity of education hold a grip toward personalize, involving and engaging into potential learning, thus penetrating into new era of education system globally.

Impact of AI-Personalized Learning on Student Outcomes

Researchers constantly highlight the improvements in academic performance when engagements are considered through AI-driven personalized learning (Sruthi Santhakumar,2024). 75% of learners are utilizing AI-driven learning methodology. This field of vision seems encouraging with emerging innovative technology, exploring transformation toward learning process. It is not far away when future of every learner has its own unique way and path to achieve success.

Adaptive Learning

Adaptive learning method use machine learning (ML) and artificial intelligence algorithm to access performance of students or employees based on collected data. Figure 6 shows AI-driven adaptive learning (Mudit Khandelwal, 2022). This information's helps to evaluate the strength and weakness of employees/ students. Adaptive learning platform think about learning style of individuals likewise audio and video learning approach. Students following adaptive learning driven by AI has been observed scoring 62% much more in their test score.

Figure 5. AI-driven adaptive learning

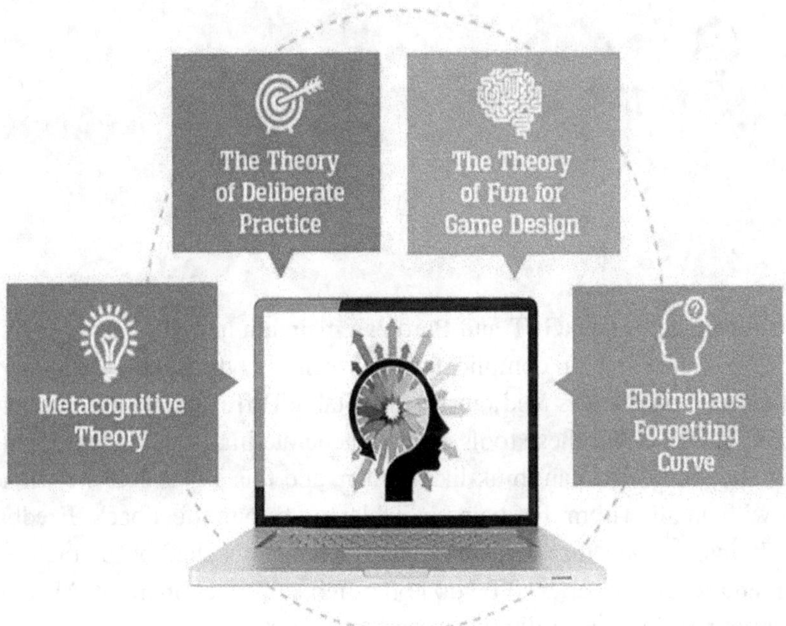

Figure 6 shows comparison between traditional learning and adaptive learning (Claned, 2024). Adaptive learning method increases the engagement of students toward learning. This approach not only boosts the academic career but also develops creativity and creative thinking skills, brainstorming, enhances decision making skills and analytic reasoning's which is essential to succeed in competitive exams. Educational organizations can support meritorious and talented students by providing them resources and tools required to flourish globally. Every individual believe that adaptive learning has lot of potential.

Figure 6. Traditional and adaptive learning

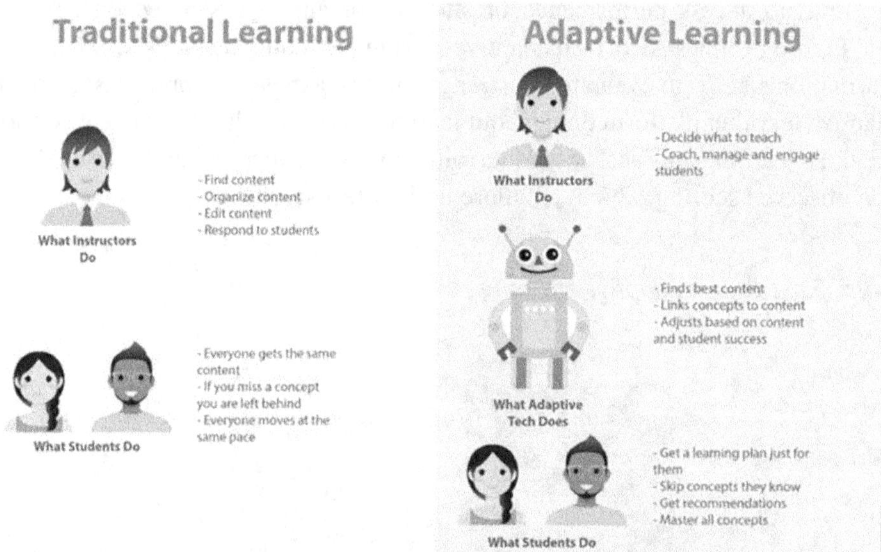

AI chatbot such as ChatGPT and Bard can maintain human dialogue (Michael Vaughn, 2023) and can help complicated task such as coding and creative writing. Some other AI tools such as Midjourney and Stable Diffusion are used to generate high quality image. With these tools one can generate images with text input (Michael Vaughn, 2023). AI can think like human, and this is possible with machine learning with an algorithm that helps in achieving through feedback. Feedback is given by human worker that gives the rating, example is chatbot interaction. Observation and feedback can also be done through self-assessment of AI if coding or programing is done accordingly. Adaptive learning has numerous advantages which are mentioned below:

- It allows learners to be self-focussed and successful. They are free to master themselves software as well as in skills they are untrained.
- It permits learners to study, making their own pace in practicing and reviewing their skills gradually.
- It enhances the efficiency and engagements of learners with activities and lessons they require to improve their skills and experiences.

- It is cost-effective compared to expensive text-books.
- It has proper course structure and learners can study according to course objectives
- It supports the administrators/ faculties in identifying the skill of individual employs/ and students as well.
- It also support faculties as well as an administrator to judging the improvement in the performances by comparing the data collected continuously.

AI-Driven Adaptive Learning with Real-Time Content Streaming

- **AI-Driven Adaptive Learning with Real-Time Content Streaming**

E-learning digital platform provide live streaming content ideas according to their learning needs and performances. With AI-Driven adaptive learning, learner receives personal content blocks containing practical exercises, explanatory text and other materials, assisting in achieving their goals (Shahid Shan,2024).

Here are some different ways, how AI-powered adaptive learning solves educational challenges (Mudit Khandelwal,2022; Shahid Shan,2024)

- **Saves training resources to minimize the budget**:

People learn much faster in AI-driven adaptive learning. It is observed that 97% of learner has found this platform more valuable. Big organization cannot hire trainer for individual employee. Individual trainer of each employee will lead to larger expenses. Adaptive learning minimizes the training cost and enhances the training resources. Software generates appropriate task and related tools after analysing the data for the employee. This innovative technology in education makes provision of the program according to their requirement. It behaves as personal mentor on digital platform

- **Enhances knowledge retention to improve learners' long-lasting skills**

If someone doesn't apply brain for long duration, it shifts towards passive mode. The same behaviour is with the employees. They forget the courses and trained skills provided to them for their future of themselves and organization. AI-driven technology assures that the employees are ready to manage any issue/ business matter happening. AI-driven learning technology continuously analyses and detects the knowledge gaps in employees and suggests appropriate trainings so that employees are always ready to accept the challenges.

- **Boosts learners' engagement to help and create a continuous learning culture**

Traditional training courses would propel all the employees to follow same curriculum structure which doesn't apply for every employee, as different employees have different experience. Thus same training given to all employees is simply waste of time and money. AI-driven adaptive leaning provides training to each employee according to their requirement and experience. Each employee chooses its own path to improve its skills. Each employee can also access its weakness and continuously improve their knowledge thus keeping every one focussed towards their work and activities. Resultantly, every employee enhances its qualification and organizations gets skilled employee.

- **Increases time efficiency to reduce training time**

Traditional education takes 40-60% more time than e-learning. By making provision of AI-driven learning technology in the organization, employee's starts educating themselves accordingly

And enhance their skill efficiently.

- **Performs deep analytics to track training efficiency and learners' performance**

AI tool analyses the data of the employees and provide progress record of the employees in metrics to the training manager.

Efficiency and Productivity

We all know that "Time is Money" in every sector. Precision e-learning and micro learning (i.e. educational strategy that focuses on learning new information in small units) lead towards more efficient learning and high efficiency task performance. Micro education demand is very high amomg corporate sector to optimize employee productivity.

Intelligent Tutoring Systems

AI-driven education tools guide and supports students individually, help them in understanding the area of interest, access learner understanding, identifies difficult areas and provide learning content accordingly.

Individualized Learning Paths/ Facilitating Inclusive Learning

AI-driven educational tools provide individual learning pathways for learner according to their interest, objectives and knowledge. By choosing the curriculum and fulfilling their requirements, AI supports the challenges and optimizes learning environment that strengthens every learner.

Now a day, traditional teaching cannot provide creative, supportive, interactive and inspiring learning environment. Human expertise along with AI leads towards constructive, effective and personalized leaning for everyone.

Predictive Analytics

AI can predict the capabilities of learning difficulties at early stage. Algorithm in machine learning can also predict the challenging areas of students facing during learning and can change the resource to ensure learner continuous to stay on the path towards success.

Data-Driven Insights

AI-driven educational tool collect and assess students data regarding their involvement levels, results and behaviour. By extracting these collected data, educator can keep eye on learner activities and understand them and make personal decision to optimize their learning and experience efficiently.

Continuous Learning and Improvement Through Data Analysis

AI data can analyse the potential to move beyond learner ability thus advising wider education framework. Once educational framework/ strategies are decided through the dataset, institutions can design their curriculum for continuous improvement in overall learning skill of the students

Gamification and Engagement

AI supports learning through riddles/ puzzles and games making it enjoyable and motivates the learning process through challenging and interactive sessions. This approach of leaning, not only engage the learner but also enhance brainstorming.

Assessment and Feedback

With the help of AI, learner can easily assess and evaluate themselves. AI also has automatic grading system featured by AI algorithm which can provide immediate feedback on puzzles/ games, quizzes, and exams. This reduces the load of educator and provides valuable feedback within short time period, aiding the learner for their sustained improvement.

Multimodal Learning

AI technologies drive multiple mode of learning experience through different framework examples are audio and video content, text and other interactive sessions. They allow the student to opts the method of learning they better prefer, making learning more personalised. AI technologies facilitate multimodal learning experiences by incorporating various formats, such as text, audio, video, and interactive elements. This allows students to engage with content in ways that suit their learning preferences, making the educational experience more personalized and engaging.

AI in Talent Management

Talent management is a discipline that utilizes human resource planning to enhance business market values making it possible to reach their business goal (Skills Caravan, 2024). The digital era of AI and automation is remodelling the geography of talent acquisition and management. It has become easy for HR manager to exploit AI based recruiting software, making them ahead from others. AI-driven talent management modernises recruitment process, fulfilling the requirements of candidate talents and provide insight data-driven for stronger decision-making. As organisations welcome this transformation, it is essential to adapt these profound changes for managing human capital among trending workforce globally. AI-Talent management has different models as shown in figure 9 (Skills Caravan, 2024).

Different models of AI-Talent management are mentioned below

- Talent acquisition and analytics
- On-boarding engagement and retention practices
- Learning and development
- Performance management
- Succession planning
- Workforce planning

Figure 7. AI in talent management

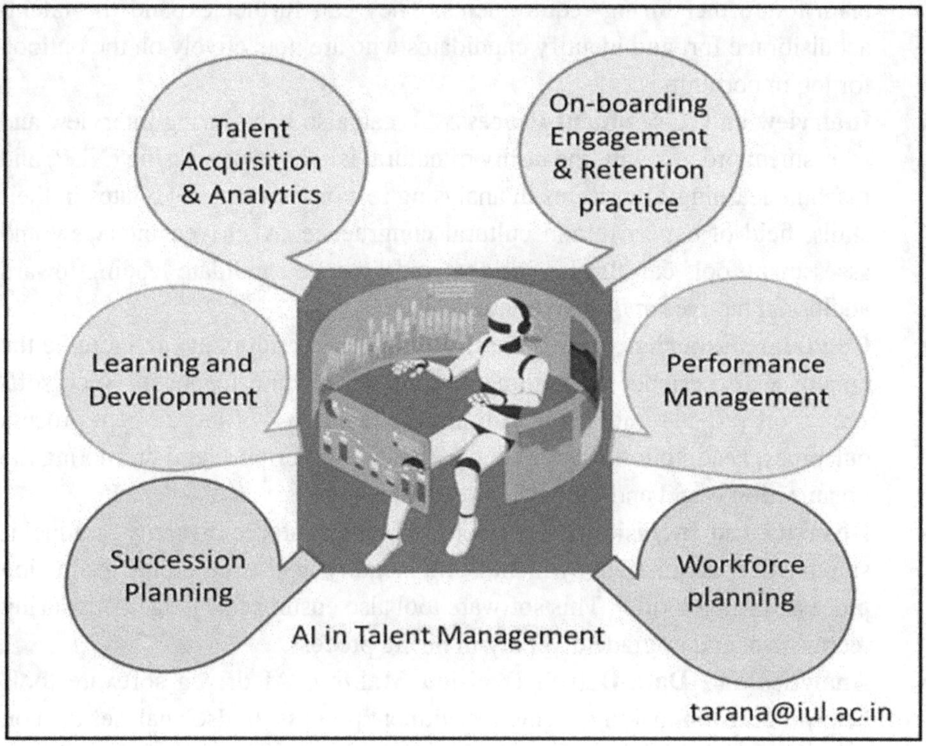

Talent Acquisition and Analytics

Talent acquisitions AI can affect the recruitment policies in the organization, thus supporting modernize employment process. AI plays a vital role in talent acquisitions in the following ways;

- **Resume screening and candidate matching**: AI can analyse curriculum vitae (CV) based on the defined parameters. AI-driven resume scanning tool saves time and energy at initial stage of screening, assuring that screened and selected candidates can be processed for advance evaluation. AI-driven tools can analyse the experience and skills, matching the parameters of the job requirement.
- **Sourcing and Talent Pool Management**: AI-driven tools can identify the skills of the candidate by the analysis of numerous sources of data as profiles available on social media, LinkedIn, online job board and many other professionals' sites. Thus, AI-driven management software's can automatically

identify and select strong candidates, supporting recruitment manage talent team for further hiring requirements. They can further expand the talent-acquisition effort and identify candidates who are not actively on the outlook for job opportunities.

- **Interview and Assessment Process**: AL can also help during interview and assessment process with the utility of natural language processing (NLP) and machine learning-algorithms in analysing response of the candidates in their skills, field of expertise and cultural congruence. AI-driven interview and assessment tools can furnish insights and approve candidate leading toward additional motives and regular assessment
- **Candidate Experience**: AI driven software for recruitment can increase the employees experience by automated routine task and feedback. Such software tools provide interaction within time regardless of recruitment process outcomes, heading toward confident candidate experience and promoting the organization brand and influencing top-talent.
- **Diversity and Inclusion**: AI- driven software reinforce diversity and inclusion in talent acquisition by identifying inequity in CV screening, evaluation processes and job offer. This software tool also ensures fair judgement during recruitment and upgrade diversity in hiring process.
- **Analytics and Data-Driven Decision Making**: AI driven software tools helps in decision making during recruitment process. It also analyses data on hiring metrics such as quality of recruitment, cost per recruitment and time duration within which vacancy has to be filled. This analysis supports the recruiter in making decision and reaching their optimised hiring strategies.

On-Boarding Engagement and Talent Retention Practices

Newly appointed candidates on their first day of joining set a stage of success among other employment with their full mind-set. Innovative technologies support custom learning from the beginning of their journey in their employment for success. AI can supports in the following ways

- **Lighten the administrative burden**

It reduces administrative work with unnecessary paperwork.AI tools can track each and every documents that are read, capture e-signatures once process is completed, thus not required to follow manually.

- **Reduces Productivity Time**

AI-driven learning tools can help the employees in enhancing job-related based learning such as journals or book at the same time doing their assigned task.

- **Allow on boarding to occur 24/7**

AI-driven tools can help newly recruited employees by guiding required on board steps and suggesting next step to to ramp up smartly in their roles.

- **Talent retention**

It is basically the practice of keeping skilled and talented employees in the organization. Employees are valuable assets for an organization and importance of employee increases with time. Retention of employees is essential for organisational growth, thus maintaining healthy relationship among employer and employees. Methods to retain talents are as follows

- Encouraging flexibility at the workplace
- Levelling up the employee engagement strategy
- Creating a program for College graduates
- Providing frequent praise
- Investing in technology
- Eliminating unnecessary barriers in the workplace
- Offering opportunities for professional development
- Nurturing the employees

Learning & Development

This method allows individual leaner to acquire knowledge and develop their skills. Some of the methods such as personalised learning, adaptive learning, content cu-ration and recommendation, assessment and feedback, virtual reality and simulation, learning analytics and insights, employment engagement and motivation

Performance Management

AI-driven recruiting process has great impact on performance management in the organization by simply automating and maximizing many aspects of performance management process.AI can be used for performance management in the following ways

- **Performance Tracking and Analysis**

AI-driven talent management software track and analyse performance data of employees automatically, such as productive and goal outcome along with managers feedback. Performance tracking software tool provide real-time insight into employee performance, identifying their strengths and weakness area for improvement, thus supporting managers in making decision regarding performance evaluation and feedback.

- **Performance Reviews and Feedback**

AI can review performance by analysing performance data and summarizing feedback. This tool can also manage objectives and feedback from the analysis of performance data, thereby, eliminating biasing and assuring justice in evaluation process.

- **Goal Setting and Alignment**

AI tool can assist in aligning performance goal with the analysis of organizational vision and objectives along and departmental mission target along with individual performance records. These data provide a platform with definite real-time achieving goals.

- **Feedback Analysis and Sentiments Analysis**

AI tool can analyse data collected from other sources such as social media, survey of employees, employee's remarks and generate an images of sentiments. This AI sentiment analysing tool supports the manager in gaining employee perception, sentiments, involvement level in activities concern for improvement in their performance.

- **Performance Prediction and Early Warning Systems**

AI- driven tool can use performance data along with other relevant data to find out the future performance and potential performance issues. These data can alert the manager and guide the employee to take relevant time to improve his performance in achieving his goal

- **Recognition and Rewards**

AI tool after analysing the performance of the employee, give recognition and awards depending upon the performance data and fostering the environment of motivation and appreciation

Succession Planning

Even with excellent retention policies, an organization faces some ROI as employee takes decision for retirement. When employees having excellent skills or field expertise leave the organization, creating a large gap and hinder organization success, leaving behind negative involvement amongst the left employees. It is vitally important that organization should have firm succession plans for replacement in order to assure smooth functioning. Thus we can say that succession planning is sensitive part in talent management. AI can support in the following ways

- **Identify flight risk**

Prediction of the escape risk depend upon different parameters such as sentiments of employees, influence of mentor, duration of working at same designation/ position, salary history and potential career on their way ahead. These are some of the factor leading towards predicted rate of attrition.

- **Uncover most capable successors**

Leveraging AI driven data model, analyse the behaviour and leadership quality in the employees who would readily step forward and fulfil the gap of previous successors.

Workforce Planning

Workforce planning means organizational present and future planning in utilizing correct talent in correct job position in achieving planned objectives. AI can be used in many ways to enhance productivity and effectiveness of the workforce planning process. Some of them are mentioned below:

- **Workforce Scenario Planning**

With different AI simulating tools, organization can change the business goals and marketing strategies to regulate the demand, having affective impact on the human resource.

- **Demand Forecasting**

AI-driven software can identify and analyse, previous and contemporary real time data such as production data, consumer demand and sales data for forecasting the workforce demand accurately. Workforce forecast maintains employee shortage or excess.

- **Skill Gap Analysis**

With the help of AI-driven software tools, organization can analyse skill gaps in the workforce, and arrange them accordingly with future business requirements. This can be achieved by providing additional trainings, fulfilling the skill gaps and assuring workforce readiness

- **Workforce Segmentation and Analysis**

Workforce can be segmented based of different factors such as skills and learning experience, work potential and performance and many more. This can be done with AI tools in developing goal objectives for talent acquisition, progress and retention. AI can analyse insight data for the requirement of different segments, supporting organizational workforce planning strategies accordingly.

AI CHALLENGES ON LEARNING AND DEVELOPMENT

Policies and regulations lag much behind for adapting new innovations. With the growth of AI and uncontrollable use of it, organizations should be aware of ethical implementation on working with new technologies especially in the domain mentioned below (Michael Vaughn, 2023; Claned, 2024, Marcos Guevara, 2023):

- Importance of Striving for Unbiased Data
- Intellectual Property (IP) and Data Collection
- Misuse of Personal Information
- Digital gaps
- Ensuring ethical use of AI
- Job loss

Importance of Striving for Unbiased Data

As AI is introduced globally and we incorporate AI in workplace in order to analyse the data available from workforce. These data are analysed through algorithm, achieving the goal in most effective manner. These data serve as the base of AI learning, leading towards either positive or negative outcome of the organization.

An investigation was done by ProPublica in 2016 (Michael Vaughn, 2023) claimed that AI algorithm's utilized by the judges were recommending strict punishment for black race individuals. Resultantly, suggested that algorithm cannot be biased. Rather, they are affected by the data under observation. Thus, concluded that AI data utilized by the judges on training was unfair for minorities.

Data Collection and Intellectual Property (IP)

As, we are aware that organizations never disclose their actual data used for training, rather than providing a broad conceptualized dataset. ChatGPT was trained on 300 billion-word dataset, and Midjourney utilized hundreds of millions of images. For both i.e. ChatGPT and Midjourney got the data from the public domain available online (Michael Vaughn, 2023). Plenty of information's are available online but major issue is copyright. Did these AI tool used legal information's. No clear crystal answer was given by organization behind ChatGPT, while Midjouirney CEO replied that they used the copyright image material. But today both the organization is facing similar legal challenges. Many writers and artist has filed the lawsuit against OpenAI.

Personal Information Misuse

Ethical use of learner data in AI-driven personalised learning system is a major issue. As AI requires numerous data for individual suggestion, personal information's of students are misused, violating rules and policies. Consequently, the ethical ramifications of collecting and analysing student's data should be precisely considered by the mentors and policy makers, ensuring correct laws protects and conserve students' rights and safety.

Ensuring Ethical Use of AI

Another major issue is the chances of algorithm biasing in AI-driven personalised learning. Insufficient design and training of AI-driven algorithm system must be reinforced pre-existing prejudices unintentionally. To ensure AI-driven algorithm is not biased, mentors and developers must keep eye on the algorithm continuously providing safer zone to the students'.

Digital Gaps

For smooth and easy access of AI-driven personalised learning, it is important to minimize digital gap. All the learners may not have computer system or laptops with internet facilities with required speed due to which issues in learning may increase. It is important to solve this issue and ensure that the learners are benefited to some extent by providing proper resources and infrastructure making learning easier.

Job Loss

AI-driven learning and development software and other innovative tools can automate the working task, thus, creating a fear among employees in losing job. Thus organization should invest on training development programs for the security of employee's job.

Organization using AI in L&D

Here are five big business enterprises that are successfully leveraging AI in L&D (Akshay Birje, 2024). These are as follows

- IBM
- Amazon:
- Google
- Microsoft
- McKinsey & Company

IBM

IBM as shown in figure10 has incorporated AI into its L&D for employees for customised learning. By analysing the real time employee's data and interest of their choice, AI driven personalised learning and resources leads towards involvement and participation reaching towards improved learning outcomes. Apart of it, IBM uses AI-driven chatbot for supporting and guiding their emplys instantly inorder to incline the L&D process efficiently.

Amazon

Amazon use AI-driven adaptive learning for individual employees required in their job. AI-driven algorithm analyses employees performance data and suggest personalised skill development and career advancement programs for individuals. This is an exclusive method of L&D, where individual employ can train them and align with their career objectives, leading towards expertise in their field and retention.

Google

Google as shown in figure 12 utilises AI tool for their employees by providing access to the learning resources and opening the windows of opportunity.AI-driven algorithms also analyse employee's concern, liking lack of knowledge and skill, offering different courses, seminars and professionally skilled training, programs. Basic motive behind using AI-driven learning is to promote learning and teamwork through virtual mentoring programs and knowledge-sharing platforms.

Microsoft

Microsoft as shown in figure13 involves AI in L&D strategy to enrich training and techniques. AI leverages deep learning algorithm to examine employee's remarks and performance to highlighting areas for improvement and training accordingly. Microsoft also utilize AI-driven simulators for delivering hands-on-training for enhancing technical skills, thus elevating potential L&D programs.

McKinsey & Company

McKinsey & Company as shown in figure14 utilizes AI in L&D to improve learning and development activities in offices globally. AI-driven problem solver observes learning trend of employees and guide the customised learning path and resources. This enterprise also use AI for social alliances and interchanging information's through virtual societies and learning management system (LMS), thus, maintain the environment of continuous learning and progress.

FUTURE RESEARCH DIRECTIONS

The integration of Artificial Intelligence (AI) into workplace learning and development presents a wide array of future research opportunities aimed at enhancing employee growth, productivity, and organizational adaptability. A significant direction involves the personalization of learning experiences, where AI can tailor training modules based on individual performance data, learning preferences, and career goals. Further research is needed to examine the long-term effectiveness of such adaptive learning systems. Additionally, the role of AI in fostering human-AI collaboration is gaining interest, especially in understanding how AI can support, rather than replace, human mentorship and coaching. Ethical concerns also demand attention, particularly regarding algorithmic bias, data privacy, and transparency in AI-generated learning pathways. Researchers are also exploring the impact of AI on informal and social learning, including how virtual platforms and AI tools influence peer-to-peer knowledge sharing and community engagement. Another emerging area is the use of AI for continuous performance assessment and feedback, which could revolutionize how employees receive support and guidance in real-time. Organizational culture and readiness remain crucial factors in the successful adoption of AI technologies, highlighting the need for studies on leadership, employee trust, and change management. Moreover, the global applicability of AI-enabled learning systems warrants investigation, as cultural and regulatory differences may affect their effectiveness and acceptance. Integrating AI with emerging technologies such as virtual reality (VR), augmented reality (AR), and wearables could further transform training delivery, meriting interdisciplinary research. Lastly, there is a growing need to evaluate the return on investment (ROI) of AI-driven L&D initiatives and to develop robust metrics that link learning outcomes with business performance. As AI continues to evolve, its potential to reshape workplace learning requires ongoing inquiry into both its technical capabilities and human implications.

CONCLUSION

Leveraging AI in personalised learning has transformed education in teaching-learning practices. The current scenario of learning and developments program gives equal opportunities to the entire learner through comprehensive and accessible learning globally. It is essential to ensure that all the ethical consideration are met and providing safeguards to students personal information and rights before using AI in academics. Harnessing full capability of AI in academics requires continual research and an eye for vigilance assuring success and sustainability. Since enough tutors are not available to make learning more specialised, thus AI fulfils the gap in high quality education. Customised learning provides full control on the way of individual learning, making their own pace and convenience. AI can figure out the skill required for target learner.

Employees can also use AI for personalised, adjustable and data-driven learning experiences that fulfil their progress needs. AI has transformed the way of conducting training programs and skill advancement for the employees in the organization. With AI in machine learning (ML), employees can improve their technical skills for better outcomes in their learning journey.

Multiple risk and challenges are linked with AI in L&D such as loosing of job, biasing, copyright related to data information. By adapting best practices such as utilizing correct AI problem solver/ simulators and promoting environment of personalised learning can upgrade employment skill, increase business and efficiency, leading towards organization growth and success. Ultimately, employees and students who do not explore AI in L&D are left behind because technology empowers their competitor's.

The future of L&D lies in using AI. L&D groups or teams should invest their time and capital in exploring generative and sustainable AI-driven tools in order to make employment easier, productive and progressive.

REFERENCES

al Akimov, N. (2023). Components of education 4.0 in open innovation competence frameworks: Systematic review. *Journal of Open Innovation*, *9*(2), 100037. DOI: 10.1016/j.joitmc.2023.100037

Bhatt, P., & Muduli, A. (2023). Artificial intelligence in learning and development: A systematic literature review. *European Journal of Training and Development*, *47*(7/8), 677–694. DOI: 10.1108/EJTD-09-2021-0143

Birje, A. (2024). How AI has transformed the Learning and Development L&D Program, https://www.airmeet.com/hub/blog/how-ai-has-transformed-the-learning-and-development-ld-program/

Bozkurt and Sharma. (2020). Emergency remote teaching in the time of global crisis due to corona virus pandemic. *Asian Journal of Distance Education*, *15*(1), 1–6. DOI: 10.5281/zenodo.3778083

Burr, M. (2024), The Rapidly Evolving Role of L&D in an AI-Powered World, https://nomadiclearning.com/blog/2024/04/the-rapidly-evolving-role-of-l-and-d-in-an-ai-powered-world

Caravan, S. (2024), AI and its Role in Talent Management, https://www.skillscaravan.com/post/ai-and-its-role-in-talent-management#:~:text=AI%20in%20Talent%20Management%20refers,performance%20management%2C%20and%20workforce%20planning

Chandel, T. A. (2022). *Green Entrepreneurship and Sustainable Development" "International Perspectives on Value Creation and Sustainability through Social Entrepreneurship." 173-208*. Global publisher., DOI: 10.4018/978-1-6684-4666-9.ch009

Chandel, T.A.(2022), Green Entrepreneurship and Sustainable Development" "International Perspectives on Value Creation and Sustainability through Social Entrepreneurship.".173-208, IGI Global, chapter DOI: DOI: 10.4018/978-1-6684-4666-9.ch009

Chandel, T.A (2023) Reshape the Sustainable State-of the-Art Development of Smart Cities, e book Convergence of IoT, Blockchain and Computational Intelligence in Smart Cities, 58-82, CRC Press, Taylor & Francis Group, DOI: 10.1201/9781003353034-4

Chandel, T. A. (2023). *Hybrid Energy Storage Systems for Renewable Energy Integration and Application: Artificial Intelligence Applications in Battery Management Systems and Routing Problems in Electric Vehicles*. GI Global., DOI: 10.4018/978-1-6684-8816-4.ch011

Chandel, T. A.. (2023). *Green and Clean Energy: Current Global Scenario, Renewable Energy and AI for sustainable Developments* (Vol. 1-30). CRC Press, Taylor & Francis., DOI: 10.1201/9781003369554-1

Chiu, T. K. F., Xia, Q., Zhou, X., Chai, C. S., & Cheng, M. (2023). Systematic literature review on opportunities, challenges and future research recommendations of artificial intelligence in education. *Journal of Computers and Education: Artificial Intelligence*, *4*, 100118. DOI: 10.1016/j.caeai.2022.100118

Claned, (2024/04/12), The Role of AI in Personalized Learning, https://claned.com/the-role-of-ai-in-personalized-learning/

Delanghe, P. (2023), 1956: The official birth of AI, Generative AI strategy consultant, https://www.linkedin.com/pulse/1956-official-birth-ai-philippe-delanghe-couac/

Dwivedi, Y.K. et al (2022). Climate change and COP26: Are digital technologies and information management part of the problem or the solution? An editorial reflection and call to action. International Journal of Information Management, 63(2022)102456, 1-39 https://doi.org/.DOI: 10.1016/j.ijinfomgt.2021.102456

Gennari, R., Matera, M., Morra, D., Melonio, A., & Rizvi, M. (2023). Design for social digital well-being with young generations: Engage them and make them reflect. *International Journal of Human-Computer Studies*, *173*(103006), 1–21. DOI: 10.1016/j.ijhcs.2023.103006

George, G., Merrill, R. K., & Schillebeeckx, S. J. D. (2021). Digital sustainability and entrepreneurship: How digital innovations are helping tackle climate change and sustainable development. *Entrepreneurship Theory and Practice*, *45*(5), 999–1027. https://commonslibrary.parliament.uk/climate-change-solutions-the-role-oftechnology/. DOI: 10.1177/1042258719899425

Guevara, M. (2023), The future of L&D: How AI is revolutionizing talent development, https://www.chieflearningofficer.com/2023/03/20/the-future-of-ld-how-ai-is-revolutionizing-talent-development/

Jiahong, S., & Weipeng, Y. (2022). Artificial intelligence in early childhood education: A scoping review, Computers and Education: Artificial Intelligence. 2022,100049 DOI: 10.1016/j.caeai.2022.100049

John McCarthy et al. (1955), Dartmouth workshop/Summer Research Project on Artificial Intelligence, held at Dartmouth College, Hanover, New Hampshire, 1-13, http://jmc.stanford.edu/articles/dartmouth/dartmouth.pdf

Khandelwal, M. (2022) AI Based Adaptive Learning, https://www.linkedin.com/pulse/ai-based-adaptive-learning-mudit-khandelwal/

Lee, D., & Yeo, S. (2022). Developing an AI-based chatbot for practicing responsive teaching in mathematics. *Computers & Education*, *191*, 104646. DOI: 10.1016/j.compedu.2022.104646

lUNESCO (2020). Global Education Coalition. COVID-19 Education Response. Retrieved from: https://en.unesco.org/covid19/educationresponse/globalcoalition

Marques, C., Bachega, S. J., & Tavares, D. M. (2019). Framework proposal for the environmental impact assessment of universities in the context of Green IT. *Journal of Cleaner Production*, *241*(118346), 118346. DOI: 10.1016/j.jclepro.2019.118346

Mathur, S., & Modani, U. S. (2016) Smart city a gateway for artificial intelligence in India. *2016 IEEE Student Conference on Electrical, Electronics and Computer Science (SCEECS)*, 1–3 DOI: 10.1109/SCEECS.2016.7509291

Meehirr, K. (2023), How AI Is Personalizing Education for Every Student, https://elearningindustry.com/how-ai-is-personalizing-education-for-every-student

Miller, J. (2020). Climate change solutions: The role of technology, House of Commons Library,

Mizumoto, A., & Eguchi, M. (2023). Exploring the potential of using an AI language model for automated essay scoring. *Research Methods in Applied Linguistics*, *2*(2), 1–13. DOI: 10.1016/j.rmal.2023.100050

Mollick, E., & Mollick, L. (2023). Using AI to Implement Effective Teaching Strategies in Classrooms: Five Strategies, Including Prompts, Wharton School of the University of Pennsylvania & Wharton Interactive, March 16, https://ssrn.com/abstract=4391243

Moore, G. E. (1998). Cramming More Components Onto Integrated Circuits. *Proceedings of the IEEE*, *86*(1), 82–85. DOI: 10.1109/JPROC.1998.658762

Moroianu, N., ... 2023 Artificial Intelligence in Education: a Systematic Review, The 6 th International Conference on Economics and Social Sciences, 906-921 https://www.icess.ase.ro/wp-content/uploads/2024/07/Artificial-Intelligence-in-Education.pdf

Nadar, S. (2024), The Role of AI in Personalized Learning for Students, https://blog.shivnadarfoundation.org/educational-empowerment/the-role-of-ai-in-personalized-learning-for-students/

Pamela McCorduck & Cli Cfe. (2004) Machines Who Think, A K Peters/CRC Press, Second Edition, 2004, https://doi.org/DOI: 10.1201/9780429258985

Perkins, K.M, et al (2018). International perspectives on the pedagogy of climate change. Journal of Cleaner Production, 200, 1043-1052, https://doi.org/. 2018.07.296. DOI: 10.1016/j.jclepro

Ray, P. P. (2023). ChatGPT: A comprehensive review on background, applications, key challenges, bias, ethics, limitations and future scope. *Internet of Things and Cyber-Physical Systems*, *3*, 121–154. DOI: 10.1016/j.iotcps.2023.04.003

Rich, E., Knight, K., & Nair, S. B. (2010). *Artificial Intelligence* (3rd ed.). Tata McGraw Hill India., https://pubhtml5.com/ning/enwh/

McGuire, R. (2021). What Is Adaptive Learning And How Does It Work To Promote Equity In Higher Education?. Everylearnereverywhere. org.

Russell, S. J., & Novig, P. (2021). *Artificial Intelligence: A modern Approach* (4th ed.)., https://en.wikipedia.org/wiki/Artificial_intelligence#CITEREFRussellNorvig2021

Santhakumar, S. (2024), 6 Ways AI is Personalizing Education for Every Student, https://www.quixl.ai/blog/6-ways-ai-is-personalizing-education-for-every-student/

Schroder, A., Prockl, G., & Constantiou, I. (2021). How Digital Platforms with a Social Purpose Trigger Change towards Sustainable Supply Chains, *Proceedings of the 54th Hawaii International Conference on System sciences*, DOI: 10.24251/HICSS.2021.580

Sloan, K. (2020). E-Learning: How the coronavirus has changed education forever. Cybint, retrieved from: https://www.cybintsolutions.com/e-learning-how-the-coronavirus-has-changed-education-forever/

Taguimdje, W.. (2020). Influence of artificial Intelligence on form performance: The business value of AI-based transformation projects. *Business Process Management Journal*, *26*(7), 1893–1924. DOI: 10.1108/BPMJ-10-2019-0411

Tahiru, F. (2021). AI in Education: A Systematic Literature Review [JCIT]. *Journal of Cases on Information Technology*, *23*(1), 1–20. DOI: 10.4018/JCIT.2021010101

Tam, G., & El-Azar, D. (2020). 3 ways the coronavirus pandemic could reshape education. World Economic Forum, https://www.weforum.org/stories/2020/03/3-ways-coronavirus-is-reshaping-education-and-what-changes-might-be-here-to-stay/

Technologies, T. (2023), The role of artificial intelligence in personalized https://www.trigyn.com/insights/role-artificial-intelligence-personalized-learning

Vaughn, M. (2023) The Rise of Artificial Intelligence in L&D: New Opportunities and Challenges, https://www.openlms.net/blog/insights/rise-ai-learning-development-opportunities-challenges/

Wand, X.. (2023). Preparing for AI-enhanced education: Conceptualizing and empirically examining teachers' AI readiness. *Computers in Human Behavior*, *146*, 107796. DOI: 10.1016/j.chb.2023.107798

Chapter 8
Optimizing Global Learning Programs Through Learner Analytics

Mohit Yadav
https://orcid.org/0000-0002-9341-2527
O.P. Jindal Global University, India

Ajay Chandel
https://orcid.org/0000-0002-4585-6406
Lovely Professional University, India

Le Vu Bui
Vietnam National University, Vietnam

ABSTRACT

Learner analytics is revolutionizing global education by providing valuable insights into student behaviors, performance, and engagement through advanced technologies like artificial intelligence and machine learning. This chapter explores the impact of learner analytics on global learning programs, highlighting its potential to personalize educational experiences, enhance student outcomes, and address diverse learner needs. It examines key aspects such as data collection and management, adaptive learning, and the integration of predictive analytics. Challenges related to data privacy, cultural and contextual differences, and ethical considerations are discussed, alongside emerging trends such as multimodal data integration and the use of augmented and virtual reality. The chapter concludes by emphasizing the importance of ethical data practices and cross-institutional collaboration in optimizing

DOI: 10.4018/979-8-3373-5322-7.ch008

learner analytics to create more inclusive and effective educational environments.

INTRODUCTION TO LEARNER ANALYTICS IN GLOBAL LEARNING PROGRAMS

Learner analytics is one aspect that has been well extended into today's education systems and also promises transformative power toward global learning programs. By definition, the core behind learner analytics is the description of data collection, its analysis, and interpretation obtained from the learning behaviours, interactions, and outcomes expressed by the students. This data-driven approach, first of all, should be instrumental in feeding insights that can enhance the entire learning experience and help in personalizing educational content and informing teaching strategies (Blumenstein, 2020). In a more globalized world, in which education crosses borders, cultures, and languages, the application of learner analytics becomes increasingly important. Many global learning programs serve highly diverse and distributed populations. Analytics are needed for deepened insight into student needs, learning habits, and challenges; this will help educators understand how best to address such complexities by offering learning pathways that best meet the unique demands of a global student body (Bronnimann et al., 2018).

Large-scale digital learning platforms have made it possible to collect large volumes of data on the engagement of learners, performance, and progress. Within a global learning environment, where learners can be based in very different time zones and educational contexts, such data is especially valuable. Learner analytics can track participation, highlight patterns of disengagement, and identify struggling students-all in real-time. This enables educators and administrators to intervene early, providing personalized support to help students from different parts of the world achieve better learning outcomes (Cigdem & Öncü, 2023). By analysing how learners from a variety of cultural and linguistic backgrounds engage with course material, institutions can adapt their global learning programs to be more inclusive and accessible. The promise of learner analytics goes beyond improving the experiences of individual students toward improving institutional decision-making. Most of the educational institutions offering global programs must make informed decisions to develop better curriculum design, resource planning, and teaching methodology. Learner analytics provides the necessary tools to analyze learning trends on a macro level by offering insights into pedagogic efficacy and assisting in the optimization of content delivery. For instance, institutions will know which teaching methodology works best in a specific cultural context or which learning resources are most appealing to students from a particular region. This may then be used to tailor educational programs for a better fit of the needs that exist globally among learners (da Silva et al., 2022).

Personalization is yet another critical advantage that learner analytics have on global learning programs. Each student brings a set of unique experiences, skills, and challenges to their learning that learner analytics helps unmask. Learner analytics informs educators in the design of personalized learning plans responsive to individual students' needs (Dawson et al., 2019). Whether it be additional resources for students who are having trouble grasping a concept or advanced materials for students who are excelling the subject, learner analytics can help educators provide deeper learning with much better customized learning experiences. Since, on most international settings, the learners generally face issues of either language barriers or differences in prior knowledge or disparities in educational standards, personalization is considered key to providing equity in education access.

As such, though, learner analytics also presents some challenges in their application within global learning programs. Great care will need to be taken to guarantee that the collection, usage, and sharing of data are appropriately dealt with in terms of privacy, security, and ethics. In fact, this is particularly the case since students may come from various jurisdictions, each having different legislation concerning data protection (Ferguson, 2012). Moreover, educators should possess appropriate competencies to interpret learner data and make sense of it for teaching purposes. Despite of these challenges, one should not take away the opportunities presented to learner analytics in enhancing global learning programs. As digital education continues to grow and scale, leveraging data to optimize the learning experience will be tantamount to global education strategies that will enable better serving of the large, diverse, global student populations (Elias, 2011).

DATA COLLECTION AND MANAGEMENT IN GLOBAL LEARNING PROGRAMS

Data collection and management are some of the key components of using learner analytics effectively within any global learning program. This starts with data collection of various kinds, including demographic data, academic achievement, and engagement metrics, among others; the amount and range of data are wider than in traditional settings due to the diversity of cultural, linguistic, and educational backgrounds of students in a global learning environment (Gasevic et al., 2018). The amount of data generated by the majority of learning management systems and digital platforms supporting global education includes login frequency, interaction time with content, down to complex data, like assessment scores, feedback loops, and collaboration activities. Such data comprises a huge amount of information, which, when properly processed, may lead to insight into how learners approach the material, where they are challenged, and offer possibilities for personalized pathways in learning (Ginda et al., 2019).

This essentially means that it needs to be managed effectively, as such is sure to capture just the right amount of information at the right time, store it, and present it for analysis. Given the global nature of learning today, especially in terms of e-learning, data volume and variety may overwhelm a learning environment, and rigorous data management systems will become imperative. Such systems should handle big volumes of data; sometimes, processing needs to be done in real time (Greller & Drachsler, 2012). They should be agile to store different data types from various sources. Besides, they shall be compliant with international data protection regulations, which might differ considerably among countries. In this regard, any form of data privacy and security is paramount, especially in global programs where sometimes students may fall under different legal frameworks regarding data protection-such as the GDPR by the European Union or other regional set standards. It should be upon the institutions to implement strict policies so they can safeguard sensitive information about students and avoid data breaches that might result in loss of personal privacy (Hernández-de-Menéndez et al., 2022).

Ethical considerations in the collection of data are well considered. This means making sure the student is informed about what data are being collected, for what purposes, and who can have access. This will help maintain transparency in data collection practices, enabling them to create more trust between institutions and learners. In this way, students will be comfortable with their knowledge of exactly how their data are being used. Besides, ethical use of learner data dictates that institutions should not bias data interpretation and ensure resultant decisions thereof are not retrogressive to specific groups of learners, especially in a culturally diverse environment (Hooda & Rana, 2020).

Apart from the ethical and security issues, institutions equally have to grapple with the technical difficulties that arise during integration and aggregation of data emanating from a variety of platforms leveraged during global learning. These include but are not limited to LMS systems, video conferencing facilities, online assessment platforms, and third-party educational apps generating data in various formats. Managing the data effectively calls for consolidating such information into a centralized system that may support comprehensive analysis. It calls for investment in high-level data management technologies able to integrate and organize these varied streams of data and present data in a useful form to educators and administrators (Kasemsap, 2016).

In this way, through effective strategies for collecting and managing data, institutions running global learning programs are enabled to adopt the power of learner analytics for informed decision-making. The ultimate consequence is enhanced learning experiences and further personalization, which bears improved learning outcomes for students from around the world.

LEARNER BEHAVIOR AND ENGAGEMENT INSIGHTS IN GLOBAL LEARNING PROGRAMS

It is important to know how learners' study and engage in order to better optimize learning for global learning programs. Learner analytics provides the tools to deeply analyse the pattern of students interacting-in-depth insights into patterns of behavior-in course materials, instructors, and peers that will inform and shape learning outcomes (Macfadyen et al., 2014). In global programs, where such students could come from different cultural and educational backgrounds, identification of these patterns will assist educators in adapting teaching methods and learning environments to meet varied needs. Similarly, through data analytics, the institution will be able to keep track of key usage indicators like participation rate, time spent on tasks, completion of assignments, and engagement in either discussion forums or collaborative activities. Such information alone is truly instrumental in the identification of at-risk students due to potential disengagement or underperformance, and the formulation of timely interventions to re-engage them (Maseleno et al., 2018).

Engagement insights provide a window into how learners are interacting with course content. A relative degree of active participation could be based on a range of metrics including frequency of logins, duration of online sessions, and clickstream data. These insights enable educators to adapt more flexible approaches toward student engagement in global learning settings where multiple students have to navigate challenges related to time zones, languages, and internet access (Robertson, 2014). For example, it may emerge that learners in one region are very responsive to asynchronous learning models, while others enjoy synchronous activities such as live webinars or group discussions. These insights into behavior allow the institutions to apply different learning strategies, thus providing flexibility and creating a better experience for the learners.

Learner analytics may also highlight useful trends in the type of learning materials that students engage with. In fact, by determining which resources students return to repeatedly, which they spend the most time with, and which are consistently passed over, teachers can get a sense of which materials function best and alter their resources based on that concrete evidence. For instance, when some video lectures are a lot more watched and/or engaged with than others, this could indicate that the topic covered or method of teaching is more in tune or resonates more profoundly with the worldwide community of students. When the materials are less well attended or result in poor performance, then materials can be revised with the purpose of meeting the needs of the learners (Siemens, 2013). The second important advantage when tracking learner behavior involves the identification of patterns of disengagement. Analytics can also identify early warning indicators, such as lower discussion engagement, low rates of assignment submission, or not logging on for an extended period of time. In a global learning environment where students may be facing unique challenges, including technological limitations and outside responsibilities, such interventions are even more important in a timely manner. The educators can then reach out to the students with personalized support, extra resources, or course structuring that is more accommodating. This proactive approach helps avoid dropping out and ensures learners' involvement in the course to the very end (Srinivasa & Kurni, 2021).

Engagement insights are crucial for improving collaboration among learners. Analyses of participation in group activities show the instructor the effectiveness of collaborative learning methods and identify students who require special help when working in groups. Many international learning programs stress the importance of peer learning, and with information on group engagement, an institution can foster substantive interaction among learners from different parts of the world (Blumenstein, 2020).

In other words, insight into learner behavior and engagement becomes quintessential in forming adaptive, student-centered global learning environments. Using such data-driven insights allows educational institutions to better guarantee that each learner receives the best content delivery for maximum satisfaction and, hence, increases better success of the global learning programs.

ADAPTIVE LEARNING AND PERSONALIZATION IN GLOBAL LEARNING PROGRAMS

Among the latest methodologies in education, adaptation, and personalization take a leading position, especially within global learning programs. The cultural, linguistic, and educational diversity of participants in these programs warrant learning systems that focus on individual needs and preferences. It is at this level that adaptive learning, appropriately informed by learner analytics, becomes imperative (Bronnimann et al., 2018). The Adaptive learning systems dynamically adjust content, format, and pace based on vast amounts of learner performance metrics, learning pace, and engagement levels. On the other hand, personalization furthers this adaptive process in which instruction is tailored to meet the unique needs of each student in relation to his or her specific learning goals, preference, and challenges.

One of the most recognizable strengths of adaptive learning in global programs is constructing personalized learning pathways for students. Traditional approaches to education often fail to account for the varied levels of prior knowledge and different learning styles present in a globally diverse student population. That is where adaptive learning platforms step in-they continuously analyze the interaction of students with content, powered by algorithms in machine learning, and adjust themselves (da Silva et al., 2022). Depending on how the student shows mastery or the lack thereof, it might involve either providing higher-level materials for a student showing mastery in given areas or providing additional support through supplemental exercises or alternative explanations for the student in whom such a concept has not taken root. This dynamic adjustment enables every learner to progress further at a pace that enables them to maximize their potential for success (Cigdem & Öncü, 2023).

Application of learner analytics in adaptive learning allows for adjustments in real time. In the event that students work their way through course materials, learner interactions are continuously tracked and insights developed that enable the next best steps. For example, if a student consistently performs poorly on quizzes in a repeated topic, the system would recommend review material, tutorials, or additional practice questions. On the other hand, if a student does exceptionally well in one area but then starts to show some level of disengagement in another area, adaptive learning systems can automatically engage the student further with interesting or relevant content in the area where interest has lagged. Such a high level of personalization ensures that while students' progress academically, they also remain engaged throughout their respective learning journeys (Dawson et al., 2019).

Adaptive learning, therefore, helps to complete the gaps in such global learning programs when students come from different regions, each region facing disparities in the availability of educational resources. Students from regions that may have little or no proper primary education end up having problems with simple concepts, but the other students who come from more technically advanced educational systems would need enrichment activities so they do not get bored. Adaptive learning tools can then detect these gaps early and serve up the right level of challenge for each student, guaranteeing equal opportunities to learn. This also bears relevance in global education programs; where ensuring a level playing field is necessary, whatever the starting point of all students may be (Elias, 2011).

Besides, personalization can go further than academic content, including language, relevance to one's culture, and even learning format. In global settings, there might be preferences on the part of students about the modality through which they want to consume learning content. Some learners might get more from visual aids like videos and infographics, while another group of learners would like reading textual material or taking part in interactive simulations. By analyzing the preference and behavior of learners, a personalized learning system can deliver that content in a format most effective for the students. This is all the more important in the case of any potential language barrier, or students who are not used to certain teaching methods. For instance, an English language course may include multiple language subtitles or supplementary learning material in the learner's mother tongue for clarity (Ferguson, 2012).

In adaptive learning environments, the role of instructors themselves evolves into that of a facilitator or guide. The reality is that through the implementation of learner analytics, instructors will be allowed to learn with great detail what every one of their students has mastered and what they have struggled with to allow them to provide effective feedback. Instead of placing the focus of their instruction at a general middle, teachers can make use of the information produced by adaptive systems to reach in where it is needed to offer extra coaching to those students who need it most. Moreover, this increases the efficiency of the learning process in that there is a greater potential for better interactions among both the students and educators (Gasevic et al., 2018).

Another important aspect of adaptive learning in global programs is that it can embed the feature of lifelong learning. Since the global workforce is increasingly dynamic and fast-paced, workers need to keep on updating their knowledge and acquire new skills. Adaptive learning technologies can support this through constantly updated, personalized learning pathways that evolve as the learner progresses through their career or educational journey. For a global learner, many of whom have to balance education against other commitments such as work, it is flexibility that will be paramount. Learners could engage with content at their own pace, revisit areas of interest, or explore new topics based on emerging needs-all with personalized support (Ginda et al., 2019).

While adaptive learning and personalization have much to offer, there are challenges too. Setting up such systems requires technological infrastructure which may not be available throughout the world (Greller & Drachsler, 2012). Furthermore, there are issues around data security and privacy, in particular about sensitive information concerning learners across different national borders. Ensuring that such systems keep ethical design and implementation in mind will be critical for maintaining the trust of students and academics alike.

Otherwise said, adaptive learning and personalization are bound to revolutionize global learning programs, serving diverse learners' needs one at a time. Supported by learner analytics, institutions can further provide dynamic, responsive learning environments that support growth and foster equitable access of students for enhanced engagement. And as these technologies continue to develop further, their functionality in shaping the future of global education will only continue to expand, helping institutions create more inclusive, personalized, and effective learning experiences around the world (Hernández-de-Menéndez et al., 2022).

CHALLENGES TO IMPLEMENTING LEARNER ANALYTICS IN GLOBAL LEARNING PROGRAMS

While the potential is huge for enhancing Global Learning programs using Learner Analytics, this implementation is fraught with significant challenges that institutions need to be very aware of. These challenges range from technical, ethical, and cultural issues, adding complexity that allows tapping into the full power of the learner data (Bodily et al., 2017).

One of the key challenges in implementing learner analytics has been data privacy and security. Various institutions collect reams of sensitive data in global learning programs, some of which contain personal data, academic performance information, and behavioral insight. Sometimes, this data crosses international borders, hence falling under various legal frameworks and regulations, such as the General Data Protection Regulation European directive and other regional data protection laws (Wilson et al., 2017). Therefore, with so many diverse regulations in place, it becomes quite a challenge for an institution operating in many countries to be in full compliance. Institutions should take effective measures on data security to avoid leakages, hacking, or any unauthorized access with due transparency over collection and usage of learner data. Besides, anonymization of data and the use of encryption methods can reduce risks, but the management of such security protocols across different regions provides its own set of challenges. The most critical challenge pertains to the ethics of using learner data. The power of learner analytics rests in personalizing and adapting learning experiences. This inherently raises fairness and bias issues. The risk exists that algorithms of analysis could unconsciously perpetuate bias, especially in global programs where there is a host of cultural backgrounds. For example, learners from a particular region or background could be unfairly branded based on previous performance or ensuing patterns of use with a biased view of their capacities. Institutions should be cognizant of the risks and make sure that systems of learner analytics are designed in a non-discriminatory, transparent, and inclusive ways to avoid reinforcing stereotypes or disadvantages amongst particular groups of students. Ethical concerns also extend to the use of predictive analytics, where data is used to predict student outcomes. Such predictions, if misused, can lead to labelling students as underperformers and consequently affect their educational opportunities and consequences negatively (Schmitz et al., 2017).

This is exacerbated further by the technical difficulty in implementation of learner analytics. Good systems require the integration of more than a few data sources: LMSs, assessment and testing platforms, video conferencing tools, and other digital learning environments. On global learning programs, these may vary widely based on region or institution, and this complicates efforts to standardize data collection and to ensure interoperability between systems. Beyond that, the volume of data created by global programs is at times impossible for traditional data management systems to handle (Bodily et al., 2017). For that, scalable infrastructure in data would be required. Most of the institutions have either technological or economic insufficiency, particularly those from developing regions, to avail the use of learner analytics systems, which extends the gap between well-resourced and under-resourced institutions (Wilson et al., 2017).

One other closely associated challenge is that with educators' and administrators' skills. Because implementing learner analytics requires not only the right technological tools but the competencies to interpret and act upon the data produced, many educators may lack data analysis competencies or feel overwhelmed with the apparent complexity of the learner analytics systems. In practice, this can lead to underutilization of data, misinterpretation of insights, and thus lower effectiveness of analytics-driven interventions. Overcoming this, the institutions have to invest in professional development and training that prepares educators with knowledge and tools which will enable them to apply learner analytics. Scalability of such trainings across global programs does face logistical challenges and largely in regions where access to educational resources is poor (Schmitz et al., 2017).

Global cultural and contextual diversity also faces some challenges in applying learner analytics in global learning programs. Learning behaviors and patterns of engagement may vary widely depending on the cultural context; approaches that work with one population of learners may prove less effective with another. For example, some populations may be more habituated to traditional forms of learning whereby the lecturer takes most of the talking, and such populations may take time to get accustomed to more interactive or self-directed modes of learning (Bodily et al., 2017). Also, the learner who comes from a region with less exposure to digital literacy will go through an online site differently compared to learners who come from a region with advanced technology. Such are differences that make it difficult for learner analytics systems to find any meaningful or useful information devoid of such diverse cultural and educational contexts the learners span across the globe. Because of that, institutions need to ensure analytics systems are flexible enough to handle such variations and to avoid generalized assumptions on the behavior of learners (Wilson et al., 2017).

Last but not least, the cost involved in setting up learner analytics systems is very high and generally perceived as one of the major deterrents to utilizing the systems in a number of institutions, especially those institutions operating in settings with low resources. Infrastructure required for collecting, storing, and analysing large volumes of data involves skilled personnel who can manage such systems (Schmitz et al., 2017). This is a potential exacerbation of current global inequalities in education-the best-resourced institutions will be able to exploit advanced analytics, leaving the under-resourced behind. What is required therefore is further development via collaboration among governments, educational institutions, and technology providers toward cost-effective solutions that are scalable across a wide range of global contexts (Bodily et al., 2017).

In other words, while learner analytics holds great promise in improving global learning programs, successful implementation of it also needs to meet very significant challenges. Institutions should address issues of data privacy, security, and ethics, alongside technical, cultural, and financial barriers. With an insightful approach, including investment in infrastructures and training, ethical considerations will enable the releasing of the power of Learner Analytics to advance learning outcomes and create more inclusive, personalized global education experiences (Wilson et al., 2017).

CULTURAL AND CONTEXTUAL CONSIDERATIONS IN LEARNER ANALYTICS FOR GLOBAL LEARNING PROGRAMS

Cultural and contextual issues remain very critical in realizing the sustainable and successful implementation of learner analytics in global learning programs. Learners from different parts of the world come from different cultural, linguistic, and socio-economic backgrounds, and these differences influence their approach to and interaction with educational content, technology, and learning environments. Implementation strategies for learner analytics by educational institutions would need to take into account such cultural and contextual variations if analytics-driven interventions are to be effective and inclusive for all learners (Maseleno et al., 2018).

One of the critical considerations of culture in global learning programs is related to differential learning styles and pedagogical traditions around the world. Whereas in some cultures, students would be more familiar with teacher-led or lecture-based approaches where passive learning is almost the order of the day, for example, other systems might stress much more active learning, collaboration, and self-directed study (Robertson, 2014). And, engagement-based, one-size-fits-all learner analytics systems often suffer from invalid measurement of participation or progression across diverse cultural contexts. For example, a more traditional and hierarchical educational culture may result in a learner contributing less in interactive forums or even collaborative projects-not because they are disengaged but because they are unfamiliar or uncomfortable with such modes. Without knowing such contextual factors, learner analytics systems might interpret the latter behavior as disengagement or lack of motivation and thus trigger inappropriate interventions or feedback (Srinivasa & Kurni, 2021).

Another critical issue has to do with linguistic barriers in global learning environments. Global learning programs are usually conducted in a lingua franca, such as English, which may not be their first language for many of its students. This could influence how learners would engage in learning material, take part in discussions, or even complete assignments. For example, non-native-speaking students may require more time to read and process any text-based content, or they may not say much in discussions because they feel far less confident in their speaking of the language (Gasevic et al., 2018). Learner analytics systems that are not cognizant of these differences in language might draw inappropriate inferences from the speed at which learning takes place or may interpret slow responses as a lack of understanding, rather than recognizing language as a potential issue. Consequently, every institution should take into consideration offering multilingual support or alternative assessment accommodations when interpreting data derived from global learners.

While linguistic diversity seems to be a critical factor in approaching global learning programs, socio-economic factors also are another apparent factor. For instance, students hailing from the low-resource sections may have to struggle with poor or no access to dependable internet, poorer technology, or even other pressing liabilities such as working for a living or family responsibilities. Because of these limitations, learners may have less frequency in using online platforms or submitting assignments. Learner analytics systems that track only online engagement metrics, such as logins or time spent on a platform, are at great risk of penalizing students who do not have regular technology access. Such contextual challenges have to be duly recognized by institutions, which would need to modify their analytics frameworks to include offline engagement, flexible learning schedules, or alternative assessment strategies that accord socio-economic disparities. By doing so, they can be assured that learner analytics does not harm the students from less privileged backgrounds (Hernández-de-Menéndez et al., 2022).

Attitudes relating to education, technology, and the handling of privacy are also deeply cultural and tend to vary from region to region. While in some cultures, students may have little objection to providing personal data and to participating in virtual learning environments, in other cultures, concerns about privacy and data security may make them cautious or resistant and thus lower their participation levels. Such cultural attitudes to the sharing of data need to be born in mind when implementing learner analytics systems. Institutions must make crystal clear how learner data are collected, stored, and used, with due regard for data practices consistent with local cultural norms and legal frameworks. For instance, data privacy can be such an issue in certain regions that institutions would have to apply stricter practices of data anonymization or grant more agency to the students on what data is shared (Cigdem & Öncü, 2023).

Then again, there are cultural differences for motivational and reward structures. Some students, in other words, are motivated by end-oriented interests-like becoming a better version of themselves or satisfying their intellectual curiosity-whereas others are often more instrumental, interested in grades or certificates (da Silva et al., 2022). If an analytics system for learners only focuses on metrics related to the performance of academic outcomes, then important alternative signals of learner success that are relevant to other dimensions of learning will remain obscured: say, growth in self-confidence, collaboration competencies, or the ability to communicate across cultures. These softer skills, valued differently across cultures, should be factored into the learner analytics to provide a holistic view of progress and achievement for the learners (Dawson et al., 2019).

Cultural sensitivity is also crucial in the design and implementation of adaptive learning systems. The technologies for adaptive learning rely on data to offer experiences tailored to individual students. However, personalization algorithms, informed by the learning behavior of students from one cultural context, may be irrelevant or less effective for students from another cultural context. For example, an adaptive system developed based on data from Western educational contexts could focus on individual accomplishment and competition, whereas students from a collectivist culture would be more at ease in collaborative, group-oriented learning environments. Institutions shall ensure that adaptive learning algorithms are responsive to diverse cultural learning preferences and will not reinforce the norms of one dominant educational system alone (Dawson et al., 2019).

Finally, learner analytics need to take into consideration regional variations in the accessibility and use of digital technologies. In some parts of the world, students will have less experience with certain digital tools or online learning spaces and might, because of this, approach educational platforms in different ways. Analytics systems that assume high digital literacy will misinterpret these learners' fumbling as uninterested or without aptitude. In reality, the capacity-building or development of digital skills for this student group may be much required prior to their engagement with the content. The institutions may consider offering training or induction programs regarding the digital tools used in learning to help learners from varied regions get accustomed (Gasevic et al., 2018).

Conclusion Learner analytics in global learning programs work effectively along with consideration to culture and context. Systems take into consideration that the learning styles, languages, socio-economic challenges, and cultural attitudes of global learners are different. These provide a basis for institutions on how to provide inclusivity, equity, and effectiveness within systems of learner analytics. This allows a learning environment that is supportive and culturally responsive, meeting the needs of students from all walks of life (Hernández-de-Menéndez et al., 2022).

MEASURING IMPACT AND EFFECTIVENESS IN LEARNER ANALYTICS FOR GLOBAL LEARNING PROGRAMS

Measuring the impact and effectiveness of learner analytics in global learning programs is at once an unwieldy and vital process in ensuring that data-driven interventions and insights from these systems result in pertinent educational outcomes. After all, the highest purpose of learner analytics should be to provide a better learning experience through personalized content, enhanced engagement, and academic success for students (Hooda & Rana, 2020). However, for this to be met, each institution has to have a well-set mechanism of determining short-run and long-run impacts of learner analytics in regard to student performance, retention, and overall satisfaction. The most direct measures in assessing the impact of learner analytics are the metrics derived from academic performance. By comparing student performance before and after the introduction of learner analytics, an institution is able to contextualize the effectiveness of data-driven interventions. As an example, improvement in test scores, completion of assignments, and overall grades may indicate that analytics systems' personalized learning pathways pay off in making students understand course materials better and reach academic goals (Maseleno et al., 2018). Additionally, institutions are able to drill into the discrete data points-such as how the adaptive learning platforms impact student performance in this or that subject or at this or that skill level-to determine which interventions may be more effective for a selected population of students. However, it is very critical to put performance data in context: gains can be because of revised curriculum, instructor engagement, or ancillary support structures (Ginda et al., 2019).

The other critical success indicator of learner analytics is student engagement. Engaged students are likely to persist in their studies, participate in active learning, and perform better academically. The learner analytics systems go further in detail about student engagement by monitoring a range of behaviors such as participation in online discussions, completion of interactive exercises, or time spent on learning platforms. By monitoring these behaviors over time, the institution will be able to see if analytics-driven interventions-including recommendations for personalized content or real-time feedback-lead to sustained engagement. For example, if a learner analytics system identifies those learners who might fall out and then successfully re-engages them with targeted intervention, that should show an outcome that proves its positive effect on student retention and completion of courses (Cigdem & Öncü, 2023). The various trends in the engagement metrics also portray the cultural or contextual factors that enable the institutions to mould their strategies in accordance with the needs of the global learners. Retention rate is another metric of learner analytics. In global learning programs, students are burdened with various challenges regarding access, technology, and socio-economic conditions, and therefore high dropout rates may become a serious issue. Learner analytics may identify early signs of disengagement or academic struggles to enable interventions before students drop out (Maseleno et al., 2018). Comparing retention rates before and after the implementation of learner analytics allows the institution to account for whether these systems actually lower the rate of dropouts and support persistence. Besides, learner analytics can deliver an insight into which type of intervention works best in student retention, such as providing extra academic help, offering flexibility in learning schedules, or simply addressing the technical deterrents (Ginda et al., 2019).

In addition to the problems related to performance and engagement, there is also a requirement for considering the wider educational experience and satisfaction of students. Surveys and feedback from learners serve a place for providing rich, qualitative data on how students perceive the impact of learner analytics on their educational journey. For example, students may indicate that personalized pathways make the content more accessible and relevant to them, or that adaptive learning systems have allowed them time management and learning pace. Besides, the learners' feedback can provide a number of insights on improvement that might be needed regarding technical problems with the analytics platforms or data privacy concerns. Together, qualitative and quantitative data may provide an institution with a deep look at the strengths and weaknesses of its learner analytics, which in turn enables more informed decisions on how to refine and improve systems (da Silva et al., 2022).

Longitudinal studies, on the other hand, are another valuable device of measurement for its long-term impact. While short-term performance and engagement gains are important, true measures of effectiveness rest in the long-term success of students. Institutions can track student outcomes over multiple semesters or years to determine if benefits from learner analytics last over time. For instance, following the trends of students who have gone through their careers with adaptive learning interventions might show whether such systems are supportive of long-term growth, skill mastery, and even workforce readiness. Longitudinal studies could also capture increases in graduation, employability, and lifelong learning practices as a result of the use of learner analytics, since those have become key elements in learners' success for more and more countries facing increasingly competitive and interconnected global pressures. Yet another relevant aspect when assessing the effectiveness of learner analytics is that of the accuracy and equity of the evidence brought forward by such systems (Srinivasa & Kurni, 2021). If these latter are biased by their ways of data collection, algorithms, or interventions, then this skews the results and may well disadvantage certain groups of students. The learner analytics systems would need to be audited regularly by each institution to make certain that the data they collect is representative of a diverse student population participating in global programs and that algorithms are not reinforcing stereotypes or creating inequitable learning experiences. This calls for a commitment to good data ethics, transparency, and continuous scrutiny so that the implications of learner analytics should be positive and equitable for all learners (Dawson et al., 2019).

Scalability and adaptability provide the frame of reference needed for the proper effectiveness of learner analytics. Global learning programs include large and sometimes highly heterogeneous cohorts of learners (Cigdem & Öncü, 2023). Thus, it is essential for learner analytics systems to scale in proportion to the size and diversity of its learners, no matter where they may be in the world or how varied their educational background may be. Institutions need to decide if the learner analytics platform would manage to scale with growing volumes of data, integrate with a number of different learning management systems, and present reliable and consistent results across multiple learning environments. Furthermore, the system should be adaptable to other cultural and contextual factors. Thus, institutions need to consider whether the learner analytics platform is flexible enough to accommodate diverse learning styles, languages, and socio-economic conditions so that this system remains effective in supporting learners worldwide (Dawson et al., 2019).

Therefore, the impact of learner analytics on the effectiveness of the programs offering global learning has to be assessed from an all-rounded perspective: the academic performance by the students, the engagement of students, the retention rates, satisfaction of learners, and outcomes over the long term. Longitudinal studies, ethical audits, and the integration of quantitative and qualitative data will ensure that learner analytics systems meaningfully improve educational outcomes and develop more inclusive, personalized, and effective learning environments for students everywhere (Hooda & Rana, 2020).

FUTURE TRENDS IN LEARNER ANALYTICS

The future of learner analytics, therefore, holds much promise as this learning programs continue to grow and evolve in emerging trends that will continue to further enhance its potential for personalization of learning and improving educational outcomes, making education more accessible. These also reflect increased integration of advanced technologies such as artificial intelligence, machine learning, big data analytics, and adaptive learning systems into frameworks. It is expected that as increasing numbers of larger-scale implementations of learner analytics are adopted worldwide by institutions, focus will increasingly shift toward innovations that can make these systems smarter, more ethical, and best meet the diverse needs of all learners around the globe.

Artificial intelligence and machine learning are possible key trends in the future for learner analytics, enabling much value to be delivered from data analysis in an increasingly sophisticated manner in real-time. Currently, learner analytics systems are highly dependent on data generated through learning management systems and virtual learning platforms. AI will enhance the analytics capability of various data points and deep patterns in the way students behave, perform, and engage (Hooda & Rana, 2020). These systems will further be empowered through AI-powered algorithms in recognizing the needs of learners in real time, giving instantaneous feedback, and offering personalized recommendations. In the future, adaptive learning systems will be able to constantly tailor the learning experience to individual learners based on their learning styles, pace, and preference. With the integration of AI and ML into assessment, there is keen awareness of more nuanced learner behaviors and academic performances that informs educators in constructing more appropriate interventions fitted into the unique circumstances of each learner (Hernández-de-Menéndez et al., 2022).

Another future trend that is going to reshape learner analytics is predictive analytics. Predictive analytics makes use of data from both historical and real-time bases in order to predict future outcomes, such as determining which students are likely to fail or drop out. Such a predictive capability can revolutionize how institutions identify and provide support to struggling students. Instead of being reactive in response to adverse experiences that students may have already faced, predictive analytics can empower educators with prospective guidance on reaching out and support in advance, before issues escalate beyond critical levels. In particular, this could involve early alerts about potential disengagement or academic struggles triggering personalized tutoring, additional resources, or curriculum adjustments. Predictive analytics can also tell a lot about the gains that give valuable insight into long-term success for students and hence help institutions improve their retention rates or reduce dropouts, especially in global programs where learners face various extrinsic challenges (Hernández-de-Menéndez et al., 2022). Data-driven personalization will be even more fanciful and pervasive in the future of learner analytics: the more data collected on a particular student's habits, preferences, and performance, the more personalized learning pathways will be incrementally more accurate and proficiently compelling. In the future, personalization will entail not only an adjustment in the delivery of content to suit individual learning styles but also assessments and assignments, including the pace at which students go through courses (Maseleno et al., 2018). For instance, advanced learner analytics might decide to mine more than just how students perform on assessments. They may also decide to mine how they like to engage with content, such as videos, texts, or interactive exercises. This will create a more learner-centered approach to education, most especially in global learning programs with learners of diverse cultural and educational backgrounds. Personalized learning experiences with consideration to cultural, linguistic, and regional differences will be the bridge to fill up the gap between one-size-fits-all education models and what real needs global learners have.

Another key trend is the increasing emphasis on ethical and responsible use of learner analytics. As data gathering around student behaviors continues to expand, so too will the concerns around data privacy and security. Ethical use will be of greater concern, including the need for learner analytics systems to be transparent, fair, and respectful of student autonomy (Maseleno et al., 2018). This increasingly requires institutions to implement rigid frameworks for data governance, ensuring that the use of student data is responsible and that students themselves are fully informed of how this data is used. In conjunction with this, there will be an increasing need for algorithms which avoid bias and discrimination, particularly in global programs serving students from a diverse set of backgrounds. Algorithmic transparency and inclusivity will help make the algorithms for learner analytics support all students equally and do not reinforce harmful stereotypes or perpetuate inequality. The integration of several data sources will be another influence on the future of learner analytics (Gasevic et al., 2018). Currently, most of the learner analytics systems heavily depend on digital traces within learning platforms, such as login, clicks, and results of assessments. In the future, though, analytics will expand to include multimodal data from video analysis, voice recognition, biometric data, and even emotion tracking. Such advanced data sources will enable a far richer understanding of student engagement and learning behaviors. For example, video analysis can provide insights into tracking facial expressions and body language indicative of student focus and engagement during online lectures, while biometric data might give insight into levels of stress or cognitive load. Aggregating these various streams of data will enable learner analytics systems, in their totality, to convey a far richer understanding of the cognitive and emotional dimensions of learning and, thus allow for interventions that are more precisely targeted at academic needs and the welfare of students' mental health (Ginda et al., 2019).

Increased usage of augmented and virtual realities in education will also impact the future of learner analytics. The reason being that as AR and VR technologies become increasingly part of global learning programs, they will yield a new set of data that can be analyzed to further improve the learning experience (Gasevic et al., 2018). For example, VR environments can track how students interact with 3D simulations, enabling learner analytics systems to understand their problem-solving skills, creativity, and spatial understanding in real time. AR and VR can provide immersion and learning by doing, while analytics collected based on learners' interactions will enable new means of measuring student engagement, skill building, and collaboration in virtual spaces. Integrating AR/VR with learner analytics will unleash more possibilities of experiential learning and also yield more profound insight into precisely how students apply knowledge in practical, real-world settings (Hernández-de-Menéndez et al., 2022).

Lastly, learner analytics will be more cross-institutional and cross-border in collaboration. It follows that with the growing global learning programs, sharing of data, insights, and best practices in learner analytics across institutions will be increased. Universities, education technology companies, and governments can collaborate on the process of building more robust and scalable learner analytics systems that will meet the needs of students from region to region and across different educational contexts. In addition, this would provide standardized frameworks for data collection, privacy, and its ethical usage, therefore providing consistency in the application of learner analytics throughout all global learning environments (Maseleno et al., 2018).

In all, the future of learner analytics has the potential to transform global education through AI, predictive analytics, personalized learning, multimodal data, and ethical data governance. As institutions continue to adopt these advanced technologies, the sophistication, adaptiveness, and ability of learner analytics to address global learners' diverse needs will continue to improve. Educators can only provide such superior learning environments, though, by being ahead of the curve in these trends. This enables them to make learning more inclusive, engaging, and effective-learning atmospheres for students to flourish in a fast-evolving environment (Srinivasa & Kurni, 2021).

CONCLUSION

Learner analytics is certainly an emerging force for change in the field of international education. It holds unparalleled possibilities to enhance the experience of learning, personalize educational content, and meet the varied and emerging needs of students around the world. Educational institutions will be able to plan interventions by integrating advanced technologies of artificial intelligence, machine learning, and big data analytics backed by deeper insight into the behavior and performance of the students. This ability to analyze and act upon data in real time will allow educators to facilitate learning experiences tailored to the individual needs of students, predict the likely impediments that may arise, and hopefully improve student outcomes and overall retention.

However, learner analytics are not implemented without challenges. Data privacy, security, and ethical concerns ought to be dealt with very cautiously to make sure insights arising from analytics are used responsibly and equitably. Equally, institutions will have to navigate the different cultural and contextual differences, making sure that analytics systems will adapt to the diverse backgrounds and learning preferences of the world community of learners. Moreover, with the ever-evolving field of learner analytics, attention needs to go toward addressing the biases and bringing in transparency regarding data practices in order to eliminate discriminations and make the playing field fair in regard to educational opportunities.

A number of emerging trends shape the future of learner analytics, including integration of multimodal data sources, expansion of predictive analytics, and an increased focus on ethical data usage. Advances in augmented and virtual reality are going to open new dimensions for data gathering and processing, further enriching our understanding of the way students engage with content and apply knowledge. Cross-institutional collaboration also plays a crucial role in the advancement of learner analytics, as it enables sharing best practices and advancing standardized frameworks that support global learning environments.

Finally, through learner analytics, educational experiences can be tailored to individual students in ways that are informative, interactive, and more productive. By seizing such opportunities and meeting the associated challenges, educational providers can harness the power of data to fuel innovation, lead improvement in education outcomes, and enable learners of all ages to reach their full potential. In harnessing the full potential of learner analytics, ongoing development should seek to create an enabling and agile educational environment that can meet the emerging needs of students in a dynamic world.

REFERENCES

Blumenstein, M. (2020). Synergies of learning analytics and learning design: A systematic review of student outcomes. *Journal of Learning Analytics*, *7*(3), 13–32. DOI: 10.18608/jla.2020.73.3

Bodily, R., Graham, C. R., & Bush, M. D. (2017). Online learner engagement: Opportunities and challenges with using data analytics. *Educational Technology*, •••, 10–18.

Bronnimann, J., West, D., Huijser, H., & Heath, D. (2018). Applying learning analytics to the scholarship of teaching and learning. *Innovative Higher Education*, *43*(5), 353–367. DOI: 10.1007/s10755-018-9431-5

Cigdem, H., & Öncü, S. (2023). Leveraging Learning Analytics to Improve Student Engagement. In *Perspectives on Learning Analytics for Maximizing Student Outcomes* (pp. 64–88). IGI Global. DOI: 10.4018/978-1-6684-9527-8.ch004

Dawson, S., Joksimovic, S., Poquet, O., & Siemens, G. (2019, March). Increasing the impact of learning analytics. In *Proceedings of the 9th international conference on learning analytics & knowledge* (pp. 446-455). DOI: 10.1145/3303772.3303784

Elias, T. (2011). Learning analytics. *Learning*, *1*, 22.

Ferguson, R. (2012). Learning analytics: Drivers, developments and challenges. *International Journal of Technology Enhanced Learning*, *4*(5-6), 304–317. DOI: 10.1504/IJTEL.2012.051816

Gasevic, D., Paul, P. R. I. N. S. L. O. O., Chen, B., Fan, Y., Rodrigo, M. M., Cobo, C., & Cecilia, A. G. U. E. R. R. E. B. E. R. E. (2018). Learning analytics for the global south.

Ginda, M., Richey, M. C., Cousino, M., & Börner, K. (2019). Visualizing learner engagement, performance, and trajectories to evaluate and optimize online course design. *PLoS One*, *14*(5), e0215964. DOI: 10.1371/journal.pone.0215964 PMID: 31059546

Greller, W., & Drachsler, H. (2012). Translating learning into numbers: A generic framework for learning analytics. *Journal of Educational Technology & Society*, *15*(3), 42–57.

Hernández-de-Menéndez, M., Morales-Menendez, R., Escobar, C. A., & Ramírez Mendoza, R. A. (2022). Learning analytics: State of the art. [IJIDeM]. *International Journal on Interactive Design and Manufacturing, 16*(3), 1209–1230. DOI: 10.1007/s12008-022-00930-0 PMID: 40478020

Hooda, M., & Rana, C. (2020). Learning analytics lens: Improving quality of higher education. *International Journal of Emerging Trends in Engineering Research, 8*(5), 1626–1646. DOI: 10.30534/ijeter/2020/24852020

Kasemsap, K. (2016). The role of learning analytics in global higher education. In *Developing effective educational experiences through learning analytics* (pp. 282–307). IGI Global. DOI: 10.4018/978-1-4666-9983-0.ch012

Macfadyen, L. P., Dawson, S., Pardo, A., & Gašević, D. (2014). Embracing big data in complex educational systems: The learning analytics imperative and the policy challenge. *Research & Practice in Assessment, 9*, 17–28.

Maseleno, A., Sabani, N., Huda, M., Ahmad, R., Jasmi, K. A., & Basiron, B. (2018). Demystifying learning analytics in personalised learning. *IACSIT International Journal of Engineering and Technology, 7*(3), 1124–1129.

Robertson, J. (2014). Learner-Centric Learning Analytics. *Recuperado el, 24.*

Schmitz, M., Van Limbeek, E., Greller, W., Sloep, P., & Drachsler, H. (2017). Opportunities and challenges in using learning analytics in learning design. In *Data Driven Approaches in Digital Education: 12th European Conference on Technology Enhanced Learning, EC-TEL 2017, Tallinn, Estonia, September 12–15, 2017* [Springer International Publishing.]. *Proceedings, 12*, 209–223.

Siemens, G. (2013). Learning analytics: The emergence of a discipline. *The American Behavioral Scientist, 57*(10), 1380–1400. DOI: 10.1177/0002764213498851

Srinivasa, K. G., & Kurni, M. (2021). *A beginner's guide to learning analytics.* Springer.

Wilson, A., Watson, C., Thompson, T. L., Drew, V., & Doyle, S. (2017). Learning analytics: Challenges and limitations. *Teaching in Higher Education, 22*(8), 991–1007. DOI: 10.1080/13562517.2017.1332026

Chapter 9
Navigating Technological Disruption:
Strategies for Continuous Professional Development

Muhammad Usman Tariq
https://orcid.org/0000-0002-7605-3040
Abu Dhabi University, UAE & University College Cork, Ireland

ABSTRACT

This chapter focuses on one of the most important strategies needed to implement technological disruption – constant professional learning. It starts with defining the effects of technological innovations across different sectors and describing the functions of such core technologies as AI, IoT, and blockchain. In the next stage, the problem of difficulties in employees and organizations regarding such shifts is described, with focus made on the gap in skills and lifelong learning. The chapter also delves into the practical measures that can be taken by the professionals as well as the organizations to remain in the market through effective use of internet applications, simulations and use of virtual reality for the professional competencies' development due to which micro credentials and the internet-based certifications have become significant. Furthermore, it focuses on the issue of the culture of innovation and adaptation providing techniques for how such a culture can be developed in an organization.

DOI: 10.4018/979-8-3373-5322-7.ch009

INTRODUCTION

In a world characterised by constant technological evolution, the global workplace is not a stable structure because it continues to reform and requires educational acquisition. Technological development is changing industries in the modern world. For instance, the use of artificial intelligence and machine learning in the analysis of data and decision making has changed. AI systems in the healthcare industry can diagnose diseases with the highest success rates, whereas machine-learning technologies in the finance industry forecast market trends and oversee investment funds. Similarly, the Internet of Things (IoT) is reshaping manufacturing to include smart factories that utilise connected devices to supervise production in real-time. Blockchain, which is associated with digital currencies, is also used in supply chains to securely share data within various industries (Fuller & Epstein, 2023). These advancements are crucial to society, but at the same time come with the following difficulties. These forces industries to transform conventional approaches to business and operations, incorporate new technologies systematically, and cope with the developing lack of skilled labour. As a result of the growing use of automation and AI in businesses' day-to-day activities, there is an increased need for intuitive, creative, and problem-solving skills, and hence the need for constant training (Rad & Arion, 2024). The incorporation of new technologies in the workplace occurs very quickly, and this poses several difficulties for both workers and organisations. Among these critical areas, a lack of skill is pertinent. Consequently, with the advancement of technology, the competencies required for the exploitation of these technologies are also altered. For instance, many IT professionals are fluent in old-generation programming languages, but emerging applications such as AI and data science require IT professionals to train in new languages, such as Python, TensorFlow, and R. Human skills, such as critical thinking, flexibility, and emotional intelligence, are also indispensable (Viltz, 2021).

Managers must also pay a certain price and risk to improve organizational performance by adopting these technologies. Attention to investment in new technologies depends on their cost; in many cases, the integration of new technologies can be very expensive, and it interrupts the business process and decreases efficiency during the period of adaptation to new technologies and tools. In addition, it is challenging to provide a proper shield to these technologies because of the frequent release of new types of vulnerabilities created by these technologies (Rad & Arion, 2024). Thus, maintaining professional relevance for individual professionals is a crucial step and largely depends on how they can manage their personal learning and development processes in the context of new forms and types of technologies. One of the most efficient approaches is the recognition of online learning platforms. Massive platforms, such as Coursera, edX, and LinkedIn Learning, constitute numerous courses on innovative technologies and basic competencies. Such platforms give one the convenience of learning as they want, and when they want, because they are organised in such a manner. That is, a marketing specialist may take courses in digital marketing and data analysis to provide them with strong requirements for the modern market (Viltz, 2021). Simulation and virtual reality (VR) are tools that can be used for training. Virtual reality training offers an actual life experience which is suitable for individuals to practice as if in a real environment. For example, surgeons and other medical staff can train for surgeries using VR simulations, thus improving their mastery in the operations without compromising the life of patients. Likewise, flight simulators can be helpful to pilots in an aspect that allows them to practice the use of such equipment in case of emergencies by practising how they will handle the equipment when faced with pressure (Rad & Arion, 2024).

Mini credentials and online certifications are also coming into focus, as they provide niche learning and certification for skills. Cybersecurity blockchain and AI are just a few of the topics covered by nanodegrees and specialisations offered by platforms such as Udacity and Coursera. Leaders in the field acknowledge these credentials which provide professionals with concrete means of demonstrating their knowledge and dedication to lifelong learning. Promoting an innovative and ongoing culture of professional development is essential for organisations. The application of agile methodologies is a strategy that works well. Iterative development cooperation and continuous improvement are encouraged by agile frameworks such as Scrum and Kanban. Software development teams that employ scrum, for instance, meet on a regular basis for sprint reviews to assess progress, pinpoint obstacles, and modify tactics as necessary. With this strategy, teams are guaranteed to be adaptable and sensitive to shifting needs while also increasing productivity. An additional crucial tactic is to promote cross-functional cooperation (Rad & Arion, 2024). Organisations can attract diverse perspectives and encourage innovation by assembling staff from various departments and specialisations. Cross-functional teams have been effectively implemented by businesses, such as Google and 3M, to spur innovation. For example, a 20 percent time policy permits staff members to dedicate 20 percent of their working hours to projects that deviate from their main duties, which has resulted in the development of ground-breaking products such as Gmail and Google Maps. Organisations must invest in ongoing training and development initiatives to remain competitive. Providing employees with online training workshops and certifications keeps them aware of emerging technologies and market trends. IBM provides a plethora of courses and personalised learning pathways through a learning platform to help staff members grow professionally. In addition to improving employee retention and satisfaction, this investment guarantees that a company has a workforce that is both competent and flexible (Benett and McWhorter, 2021).

Several trends are expected to shape future workplace learning and development. The growing trend in personalising learning experiences through AI and machine learning is noteworthy. To suggest specialised content and learning pathways, AI algorithms can be used to evaluate learners' performance preferences and progress. The implementation of a personalised approach guarantees that employees receive training that is both pertinent and effective, thereby improving their engagement and outcomes. The use of blockchain technology for verification and credentialing has become a new trend. The issuance verification and sharing of professional credentials are made transparent and safe by using blockchain technology. With the help of this technology, hiring procedures can be streamlined, and credential fraud risks can be decreased, giving employers confidence in job candidates' qualifications. Professional development strategies have also been influenced by the growing popularity of remote and hybrid work models. Companies need to offer accessible and adaptable learning opportunities because more workers are working from home. Supporting remote workers and guaranteeing ongoing development requires digital collaboration tools, online workshops, and virtual training programs (Viltz, 2021). A multimodal strategy that blends individual initiatives with organizational support is needed to navigate technological disruptions through ongoing professional development. Professionals may improve their skills and maintain their competitiveness by utilising virtual reality simulations, online learning platforms, and micro-credentials. Companies can cultivate an innovative and adaptable culture by implementing agile approaches, promoting cross-functional cooperation, and allocating resources for ongoing education initiatives. It will be possible for people and organisations to prosper in a rapidly evolving global workplace by anticipating future trends and adjusting to new technologies (Fuller and Epstein 2023).

BACKGROUND

Artificial intelligence, also known as AI, is considered a revolutionary force that leads to changes in most industries, from those that deal with manufacturing to those that offer customer services. As an example, diagnostic systems explain how, in healthcare, AI accurately scans medical images for diagnosis compared to doctors, thereby increasing the chances of the patient's recovery in case of an illness. In finance, the AI algorithm predicts market movements and increases investment efficiency, providing attitudes which are difficult to calculate. Furthermore, the use of AI in customer service is made possible by chatbots communicating quickly and effectively with clients, thereby improving their experience and efficiency (Webster, 2009). The Internet of Things (IoT) is another key technology that disrupts industries with the help of connected objects and exchanges of information. In agriculture, IoT sensors check soil and crop health and trigger the use of proper quantity and quality of water that is required. In manufacturing, IoT predictive maintenance predicts the failure of a machinery system, thereby reducing the number of times machines are offline. Furthermore, the IoT remains a core aspect of smart cities because it applies to traffic control, energy consumption, and security (Panda & Kaur, 2023). Blockchain, which has a decentralised and secure ledger system, has impacted industries which require transparency and avoidance of errors. For instance, in the supply chain, blockchain provides the history of product rights from the point of origin, making it harder to commit fraud and increasing responsibilities. Blockchain plays an important role in the financial industry by enhancing the speed of cross-border payments, eradicating middlemen, and minimising costs. Moreover, there is a field of intellectual property rights, for instance, blockchain records ownership and licencing information, which provides protection to creators in a digital environment (Webster, 2009). Most technologies, such as AI, IoTs, and blockchain, are not merely weapons but agents of the deep transformation of industries all over the world. It intensifies productivity, raises the level of decision-making, and repositions business at a new, higher level of competitiveness and innovation. Implementing these technologies means changing organizational approaches, retraining employees, and considering legislation to take full advantage of these developments in terms of creating the world's future work environment (Fuller & Epstein, 2023; Tariq, 2025).

CHALLENGES POSED BY TECHNOLOGICAL DISRUPTION

Technological advancement is now considered one of the biggest and most promising disruptors and, at the same time, the threat that employees and organizational entities must face while anticipating, planning, implementing, and adapting new technologies in their working environments. First, owing to the general tendencies of the speed of innovative development, one of the most significant obstacles is merely the speed of technological change. AI – IoT – blockchains are examples of technologies that change rapidly; thus, the knowledge base and infrastructure must be updated more often. This is because the rapid advancement in technology exposes the current systems and practices to becoming obsolete, resulting in more frequent replacement and, consequently, training and retraining of human resources (Ra & Maclean, 2021). Further, it is possible to observe that the skill gap appears to be a major challenge. A variety of fields experience a lack of skilled practitioners in new technologies in the current environment. For example, the application of big data experts with experience in artificial intelligence and machine learning is a highly demanding but scarce resource. This lack of skills not only slows technological implementation but also limits the growth of organisations through the creation of new services and the development of competitive advantages in an increasingly digital environment (Panda & Kaur, 2023). Third, there are barriers associated with the culture of an organisation; workers from such a culture will always oppose change. Resistance can also be caused by human factors, such as when employees must deal with new processes which stem from the integration of technology into a company's organizational structure. This resistance can be caused by the perceived threat of losing a job, employees' unwillingness to change, and/or doubts regarding the usefulness of a particular technology. Mitigating this kind of resistance entails the implementation of several change-management strategies, communication of gains, and employee involvement in change processes (Rad & Arion, 2024). Other important issues with security are among the hotly debated issues concerning this issue. Owing to the Internet of Things, which is actively used in organisations, there are more opportunities for cyber-attackers, and cloud computing also has its own threats and reasons for vulnerability (Fuller & Epstein, 2023). Disadvantages are in the form of threats that affect the confidentiality of data and network and identity theft which are detrimental to an organisation's reputation. Managing these risks requires effective cyber security controls, constant surveillance, and constant education of employees regarding the best practices of data protection (Viltz, 2021; Parekh, 2024).

In addition, the cost of acquiring technology and incorporating it into the business is quite high and may be beyond the reach of most firms, especially those of a small size. Hardware, software, and training expenses are costly and can easily cause the company to blow through its budget, especially if the industry is new in terms of profit, or if the market is in a bad economic state. The monetary cost ensures that the implementation of technology is planned and executed according to the organisation's goals and projected revenue on investment (Rad & Arion, 2024). Overall, it can be said that technological disruption brings beneficial changes in the spheres of employees' and organisations' functioning, yet it also poses different problems. To overcome these challenges, it calls for the execution of proactive measures that include learning organizational culture, skill development programs, organizational culture of innovation and adaptability, strengthened cybersecurity, and equal weight to monetary investments as the value offered by technologies. Overcoming these issues allows organisations to utilise new technologies effectively and gain top-line growth for a firm in today's global environment (Fuller and Epstein, 2023).

Strategies for Adapting to Technological Changes

Continuously technological advancements are changing the job markets and redefining the professional roles as well as competencies nowadays. Individual professionals and organisations must proactively adapt to change to remain competitive and relevant. Therefore knowledge, skills and operational efficiency must be improved, which requires the adoption of strategic approaches. This paper explores in an extensive way strategies designed for both individuals and organisations to overcome technological changes successfully.

Strategies for Individual Professionals

As an individual professional, you have to adopt the attitude of proactively working to adapt to technological advancements using a process of continuous learning, collaboration, applying it practically, and being mindful of emerging trends. These strategies mean professionals have a chance to thrive as more and more of work becomes centred around technology. Continuous Learning and Skill Development is one of the best ways for professionals to be relevant. This is a strategy of pursuing those educational opportunities that would improve one's technological skill that is relevant for one's career. This includes signing up for online courses, taking up workshops, getting certified and actively participating in professional development. Access to high quality and modern online learning platforms is available for what they are charging you now for their services which include Artificial Intelligence, Machine Learning, Blockchain and Cybersecurity. Maintaining awareness of these technologies allows professionals to keep updated with the industry needs, match their skill set to these demands and increase their employability and their value in the field (Rad & Arion, 2024).

Additionally, Networking and Collaboration play crucial roles in the professional adaptation process. It helps people make connections within the professional network, join influential business communities, and share ideas, experiences and see what's going on in the industry. Conferences, webinars, and meetups encourage direct communication with peers and industry leaders, which paves way not only for networking but also for practical insights on how new technologies can be applied in the business environment. Collaborative discussions and knowledge exchange help individuals to refine their skills as well as adapt to technological innovations (Gardner, 2017). In addition, a Growth Mindset, which entails an Adaptability and a Flexibility, is necessary to solve and confront technological changes. Professional must always be ready to learn new skills, adapt to the emerging technologies, which tend to change the work practices. Also, studies are there, that showing that those who actively seek out new learning opportunities especially on the basis of the interdisciplinary collaboration are able to do more with the modern technologies. Career advancement depends on being willing to take on new roles, integrate new tools and apply innovative process (Ra & Maclean, 2021). Furthermore, acquiring Hands-on Experience is indispensable for developing proficiency in contemporary technologies. Actively participating in projects that incorporate new tools or techniques enhances practical understanding, fostering confidence and competence. Engaging in activities such as coding challenges, hackathons, innovation initiatives, or experimental projects within one's workplace provides a practical foundation for mastering complex technologies. Practical application is particularly valuable as it transforms theoretical knowledge into tangible skills, thereby increasing the individual's ability to apply cutting-edge solutions effectively (Rad & Arion, 2024; Tariq, 2025).

Equally important is the practice of Monitoring Industry Trends. In an evolving technological landscape, professionals must remain well-informed about developments pertinent to their fields. Reading industry-specific publications, subscribing to technology-oriented blogs, and leveraging social media to access current research and discussions equips individuals with the knowledge necessary to anticipate changes. This approach ensures that professionals can apply best practices, adopt relevant tools, and continuously enhance their skills to remain competitive (Gardner, 2017).

Strategies for Organisations

For organisations aiming to adapt to technological advancements, it is essential to invest in their workforce by supporting employee retraining and reskilling initiatives. Developing a culture of innovation and learning is key to maintaining a competitive edge in an increasingly digital world. A fundamental approach to achieving this is through Skills Assessment and Gap Analysis. Organisations must conduct thorough competency modelling and knowledge audits to identify technological strengths and weaknesses within their workforce. Understanding these gaps enables companies to formulate targeted training programs aligned with overall organisational goals and individual employee career objectives. By mapping current skills against the desired technological competencies, organisations can create comprehensive training strategies that foster employee growth and productivity (Viltz, 2021). Another critical strategy involves Investment in Learning Resources. Providing employees with access to relevant learning materials, such as online courses, workshops, and seminars, is crucial for enhancing their technological capabilities. Collaborating with educational institutions or partnering with e-learning platforms can expand access to specialised training programs tailored to organisational needs. Ensuring that employees have the tools and resources to acquire new knowledge improves overall performance and ensures alignment with technological advancements (Ra & Maclean, 2021).

Furthermore, implementing Internal Training and Mentorship Programs can greatly enhance knowledge transfer and skill acquisition. Structured mentorship arrangements enable experienced professionals to share insights about emerging technologies with less experienced colleagues. Cross-training initiatives further ensure that employees gain a broad understanding of different departmental functions, fostering technological competence and organisational agility (Rad & Arion, 2024). To ensure sustained growth and innovation, organisations must also Promote a Learning Culture. Encouraging curiosity, experimentation, and continual learning among employees promotes adaptability and openness to technological advancements. Recognising and rewarding employees who demonstrate dedication to personal growth and innovation fosters a positive environment conducive to technological progress. Embedding a learning culture within the organisation encourages employees to actively engage with new technologies and apply them effectively to their work (Viltz, 2021).

Additionally, Integration of Technology in Work Processes is essential for embedding technological innovation within daily operations. Organisations should actively implement new tools and methodologies, allowing employees to gain practical experience with emerging technologies. Experimenting with innovative ideas, applying theoretical concepts to real-world projects, and seeking feedback from relevant stakeholders ensures that organisations remain adaptable to technological advancements (Webster, 2009). Effectively adapting to technological changes requires both individuals and organisations to adopt proactive strategies aimed at continuous improvement and innovation. Professionals can enhance their competencies by engaging in continuous learning, collaborating within professional networks, applying knowledge through hands-on experiences, and staying informed about emerging trends. Simultaneously, organisations can achieve sustainable growth by assessing skill gaps, investing in training resources, fostering mentorship, promoting a learning culture, and integrating technology into work processes. By embracing these strategies, professionals and organisations can successfully navigate technological shifts and maintain their relevance and competitiveness in a rapidly evolving global landscape.

ROLE OF EXPERIENTIAL LEARNING IN NAVIGATING DISRUPTION

Teaching and learning by experience are central to managing technological disruption, as this methodology delivers real-life experiences for learners, thus improving their mastery of new technologies. Thus, experiential learning differs from conventional classroom training which involves conceptual acquisition, as it involves bringing people into actual environments where they can apply what they know, solve problems, and learn how to work in a constantly changing world (Turner & Javed, 2023).

Importance of Experiential Learning

Another type of learning is experiential learning, which, unlike traditional learning processes, combines theoretical concepts by applying them in practice. The face-to-face mode of delivery ensures that students grasp the information passed around them in a better way because of their physical involvement in operating emerging technologies (Ra & Maclean, 2021). In objectives of engaging in experiential learning, basic competencies such as critical thinking, problem-solving, and decision-making are developed. When people confront obstacles within the defined parameters, they gain confidence and the ability to efficiently work through technological problems, broadening their capability to master emerging technologies to work on increased rates (Rad & Arion, 2024). The use of technological advancement influences industries and, therefore, professionals outside of one's comfort zone. Such qualities are fostered through experiential learning because learners face different situations and unexpected occurrences. Redesigning ensures that learners apply the methods while acquiring insight into failures and enhances the approach based on the format until they are prepared to succeed in increasingly dynamic fields (Ra & Maclean, 2021). Most emerging technologies in modern society call for integration involving several fields of study. Experiential learning requires collaboration and cooperation with other people, which means that a combination of people with different experiences and knowledge in one team increases the effectiveness of learning and the ability to achieve desired goals. Interdisciplinary undertakings promote creativity and cooperation in the approach to tasks in contrast to the integrated nature of current workplaces (Viltz, 2021). Research has shown that students who engage in learning by experience tend to benefit from retention compared to those who only read or listen. Thus, by utilising new technologies in practical tasks, people strengthen themselves, are able to foresee future trends, and respond to them before they become critical (Webster, 2009; Tariq, 2025).

CASE STUDIES OF SUCCESSFUL EXPERIENTIAL LEARNING PROGRAMS

Google's Engineering Practicum Internship: The Engineering Practicum internship program encompasses the simplest entry-level internship that any undergraduate student can undertake in the software engineering profession and company of choice, in this case, Google. The students operate on the actual projects assigned by senior developers and learn coding, debugging, and software engineering practices. Apart from improving technical skills, this mode of learning affords interns practical experience in the world of technology upon which they can build their careers (Panda & Kaur, 2023).

IBM developed the Digital Nation Africa initiative, where people within the Africa region can take free online courses and be able to take practical on matters pertaining to AI, cloud, blockchain, and cyber security. With such features as modules and labs, learners participate in the practical application of knowledge and skills with various stimuli, which is like real-life training. This program provides learners with employable niches and socioeconomic transformation in Africa's new technology fields to enhance the rate of economic growth and development in Africa (Viltz, 2021). General Electric's FastWorks program is a modification of the Lean Startup which is supported by principles of experiential learning. For example, teams execute creative workshops and more complex projects to design, create, and test a new product offer, new service offering, or a mix of both. The principles of the Fast Works model include fostering a culture of prototyping, feedback from customers, and testing; motivating an entrepreneurial approach to employees; and increasing the speed of obtaining new solutions in the healthcare, aviation, and renewable energy industries (Rad & Arion, 2024). The idea at MIT Media Lab called 'Learning Creative Learning' focuses on ways of learning by doing so through creative projects and their interaction with educational technologies. Groups work on concepts, create interactive media, code physical computing devices, and conduct experiments with tools, including digital fabrication. This learning-by-doing approach cultivates exploration, innovation, and especially peer cooperation and is thus based on building a community of independent learners who accept technology to communicate and create (Panda & Kaur, 2023). Experiential learning is crucial in approaching the era of technological disruption in terms of its effectiveness in providing skills, encouraging flexibility, helping to memorise for a long time, and stimulating creative ideas. Exemplary cases of the implementation of the concept of experiential learning in different fields show its effective use in training professionals for the existing and new conditions facilitated by informational technologies in a rapidly developing world economy (Gardner, 2017). The use of technology in professional development has transformed the world and the way people gain and improve their knowledge in modern society. Through positing technology applications, particularly in the areas of the Internet base, simulations, Virtual Reality (VR), and micro-credentialing, professional learners can personalise their learning based on specified career orientations and market needs (Birla, 2023).

Utilising Online Platforms, Simulations, And Virtual Reality For Skill Development

Many learning sites, such as Coursera, edX, and Linked Learning, are abundant in a wide range of classes and tutorials in several fields in technology, business, and arts. These platforms enable a choice of lesson delivery that can be friendly to employees while ensuring that these professionals receive quality education from some of the best institutions worldwide. For instance, a software developer can take courses in digital expert programming or cybersecurity to bow with advancements and industry standards (Ra & Maclean, 2021). Simulations and VR technology are commonly used to produce real-life simulations to acquire knowledge. Universities and corporations in health, aviation, and production require employees to be virtually trained to master complicated processes, improve decision-making abilities, and avoid possible hazards in real situations. For instance, doctors can practice surgeries or emergency operations in a virtual world and enhance their skills in treating patients, thus increasing the benefits without negative impacts in the real world (Rad & Arion, 2024). Today, in many online classes, individuals find labs and practical exercises after teaching ideas and concepts (Horn, 2017). For example, coding bootcamps use virtual coding platforms where students can write and debug their code, engage with the material through collaborative coding, and even receive feedback from instructors on the spot. Such an approach promotes the acquisition of skills and training for professionals to face test situations that emerge in technology-oriented organisations (Ali, 2023). Digital platforms use the process of algorithms and data analysis to adapt the learning process according to participants' results, interests, and deficiencies. Appropriate courses, projects, and other resources are suggested to users based on the individuals' respective objectives and skills, purely based on machine learning algorithms. This strategy makes learning more enjoyable and efficient and encourages learners to engage in learning because they are attending to their specific needs (Horn, 2017; Tallat et al., 2023).

Role of Micro-Credentials and Online Certifications in Facilitating Continuous Learning

Micro-credentials are tiny certifications called digital badges or nano degrees, which point to a learner possessing certain knowledge or skills developed through online courses, workshops, or practical projects. There is also the issue of micro-credentials that companies such as Udacity and Coursera provide in niches such as data analytics, UX design, and project management. These credentials offer a sign that one has been actively updating one's professional knowledge and skills, increasing the chance of getting a job in today's competitive economy (Rad & Arion, 2024). It is common nowadays to find learning programs where certification is obtainable in steps and can be 'stacked". For instance, Google's IT Support Professional Certificate offered through Coursera comprises several courses that lead to an assessment test. At the end of the program, learners are certified to get a chance to advance in their careers or in the IT support field, as well as be able to specialise in new technologies as they are introduced to the market (Ali, 2023). Most online certifications reflect the set industry standards and are accepted by premier organisations and employers. For example, AWS certifications confirm the knowledge of cloud computing services, whereas PMI certification represents the knowledge of project management with the help of certain methods. Certifications add to the credibility of the professional; they indicate to the employer that the employees are hardworking, dedicated, and follow the changes in evolution within their field (Rad & Arion, 2024). It identifies online certifications as a flexible approach to learning that can be incorporated into working professionals' schedules and career progression plans. Courses are fully flexible, which is an excellent characteristic for learners; they can enrol in certification courses at their convenience, and they have a lot of free time to work because certification courses do not have strict class schedules. Such flexibility is highly suitable for working professionals seeking to acquire additional competencies or switch to other positions without having to leave their jobs (Rachmad, 2021). Thus, the use of technology as a tool in professional development means that people can easily acquire and enhance the important skills that define success in today's world economy. Access to online platforms, simulations, virtual reality, microcredits, and stackable certifications allow organisations and their members to receive personalised and highly immersed learning which helps to improve their knowledge and skills, open new job opportunities, and stay relevant to the labour market. Adopting these technologies helps professionals develop and adapt to the changes that are determined by the technological growth and change of industries (Bozkurt & Paskevicius, 2020).

Fostering a Culture of Innovation and Agility

Fostering a culture of innovation and agility within an organisation is essential to remain competitive in today's dynamic and rapidly changing business environments. By creating an environment that welcomes change and encourages creativity, organisations can build a responsible, adaptable, and proactive workforce that drives growth and innovation (Rachmad, 2021). Establishing a culture of innovation begins with a strong leadership commitment and a clear vision of the organisation's future. Leaders must articulate the importance of innovation, set ambitious but achievable goals, empower employees to experiment with, take calculated risks, and explore ideas. For example, companies like Google and Amazon encourage innovation through initiatives like "20% Time" and "Day One" thinking, in which employees are given time and resources to pursue exciting projects and explore innovative solutions beyond their core responsibilities (Bozkurt & Paskevicius, 2020). Organisations can foster innovation by creating spaces and opportunities for employees to think, collaborate, and imagine freely. Implementing idea management platforms, organising hackathons or innovation challenges, and creating cross-functional teams will promote a diversity of perspectives and stimulate creative thinking. Companies, such as 3M and Apple, are famous for promoting innovation through structured processes that encourage employees to develop new product ideas (Choi & Chung, 2021). Recognising and rewarding innovative ideas and contributions strengthens a culture that values creativity and risk taking. Organisations can create innovation awards, financial incentives, or career advancement opportunities for successful innovation initiatives. For example, companies such as Salesforce celebrate innovation through their Innovation Awards program, which recognises employees and customers who leverage Salesforce technology to drive change and positive business outcomes (Rachmad, 2021). Agile methods and practices: Adopting agile methods, such as Scrum or Kanban, allows teams to respond quickly to changing market needs and customer feedback. Agile frameworks emphasise iterative development, frequent collaboration, and continuous improvement, allowing teams to deliver incremental value and adjust priorities as requirements evolve. Organisations, such as Spotify and Zappos, adopt agile principles to drive innovation, streamline workflows, and improve team productivity (Choi & Chung, 2021; Javed and Arham, 2023).

Encouraging cross-functional collaboration and knowledge sharing improves agility by leveraging diverse perspectives and expertise. Organisations can create multidisciplinary teams to collaboratively work on projects, encouraging innovation through problem solving and collective creativity. For example, companies, such as Airbnb, foster cross-functional collaboration through initiatives that bring together engineers, designers, and marketers to co-create innovative user experiences and solutions (Rachmad, 2021). Developing a flexible workforce requires investing in continuous learning and skill development. Organisations can help employees learn new skills through training programs, workshops, and consulting. By focusing on skills related to emerging technologies and market trends, employees can remain adaptable and drive innovation. Companies, such as Microsoft and IBM, prioritise employee development through personalised learning paths and certifications in cloud computing, AI, and cybersecurity (Chaaban & Du, 2021). Empowering employees to make autonomous decisions promotes agility and responsiveness within the organisation. Leaders must delegate and encourage decentralised decision making, allowing teams to act quickly and seize opportunities. Implementing frameworks such as "empowerment networks" or "decision matrices" clarifies decision authority and accountability, allowing employees to innovate and adapt to changing circumstances. Examples include companies such as Buurtzorg in healthcare and the Haier Group in devices, where decentralised decision making has driven innovation and customer-centric solutions (Bozkurt & Paskevicius, 2020). In short, fostering a culture of innovation and agility requires intentional leadership, an environment that supports creativity, and strategies that enable employees to embrace change and drive continuous improvement. By prioritising innovation, rewarding creativity, adopting agile methods, and nurturing a learning mindset, organisations can nurture an adaptable and resilient workforce. with uncertainty, seizes opportunities, and maintains a competitive advantage in an increasingly complex global market (Rachmad, 2021; Purcell and Lumbreras, 2021).

FUTURE TRENDS IN WORKPLACE LEARNING AND DEVELOPMENT

Forecasting trends in technological advances and preparing for further changes in the requirements of the job market are very important for maintaining current and constant skill enhancement, in addition to maintaining organizational viability. There are regularities due to new technological developments in learning technologies, changes in force and roles, and the need for new authorities in the working world (Narbariya). Artificial Intelligence and Machine Learning: Workplace learning is in revolution as faculty and machine learning are being touted as the key to fit-for-purpose learning environments. They can study students individually, determine their weaknesses, and suggest materials that would be most effective in improving students' performance. For example, players such as Coursera and edX are adopting technology to recommend relevant courses to learners, making the programs more targeted. The transition to learning through AI is effective for continuing education in one's vocation because it is less restrictive to access it and easier to define specific courses for professional growth (Rachmad, 2021; Harney and Collings, 2021).

Virtual and Augmented Reality (VR/AR): VR and AR applications enhance training and development, providing excellent simulation experiences to employees. These technologies make it possible to mimic actual working conditions and thus facilitate the performance of several practices by employees (Minea, 2020). For instance, the health and production sectors employ VR in surgical rehearsals and machinery operations, respectively. As the use of VR/AR technologies grows and becomes cheaper and more accessible, they will be applied more in the professional development of teachers, creating rich, engaging, and highly effective learning experiences that are memorable and improve their abilities (Narbariya). Blockchain for Credentialing: Electronic credentials are one of the revolutionary products of blockchain-based platforms. Blockchain brings about a concrete solution of transforming certifications into a digital format as a way of enhancing security and countering fake certificates. Today, there are examples of using blockchain in education; for instance, learning machines and blockcerts use blockchain for issuing digital diplomas and certificates. This innovation enables employers to easily verify the integrity of the documents provided by the candidates through the hiring process, thereby increasing the employment of deserving candidates and reducing that of those who have forged documents (Choi & Chung, 2021).

Preparing for Skills and Roles of Future Workplaces

Digital Literacy and Technical Skills: In view of these changes, technology becomes a part of the work environment, and thus technical competencies become core competencies of every profession. They will have to be IT literate and familiar with software and hardware systems, data analysis, and protection measures. It is possible to help organisations build their workforce through skill development courses that touch on basic and improved technical skills in information technology best suited to their operations. For example, PwC and Accenture offer sophisticated digital upskilling initiatives to guarantee that their employees are ready to successfully implement change-enhancing technologies (Narbariya). Soft Skills and Emotional Intelligence: The consequences show that the future workplace will value so-called soft skills, including communication, teamwork, flexibility, and self-regulation. In this case, human skills are important for tasks that are normally defined as knowledge work that involve solving problems and creating and communicating with others. The programs that focus on these soft skills, besides the technical ones, will ensure that any employee undergoes preparation that will enable him or her to maintain a mainstream balance in the professional aspects of his or her working life. The idea of values such as teamwork, perseverance, and compassion are achieved in some companies through training that includes characteristics associated with Google, known as "Googliness" (Clarke, 2019).

Lifelong Learning and Continuous Development: As technology advances rapidly, the requirement for continuous learning throughout life increases. Employers and employees must develop the attitude that the lifelong learning process is critical for passing through the curve. This can be supported by the training culture, providing training aids, and embracing training and education among employees. This has adopted by organizations such as IBM through "New Collar" where the emphasize on constant education and training mainly through "Your Learning", IBM's learning management system that consist of myriad of course and development (Narbariya). Therefore, one may conclude that the prospects of workplace learning futures and development are tightly connected to specific applied technologies and changing requirements in the job market. Predicting technological advancements and fostering relevant knowledge of digital tools, cultivating softer skills, encouraging constant learning, and readiness for novel positions and tasks will keep organisations' personnel relevant, adaptive, and successful in the transformation of the workplace. Adopting these trends will not only help the career path of millions of employees but also help organisations succeed in a world that is evolving daily (Clarke, 2019).

CONCLUSION

Mitigating the impact of technology change is not easy, especially today, where there is a continuous creation of new technology tools and advances in existing ones; thus, it is crucial that paralegals engage in continuous professional development. The strategies are as follows: the utilisation of practical, realistic, and experience-based learning, the reliance on technology in skills development, employee culture promotion of innovative and adaptive learning, and the identification of future trends in distinctive learning for employees. Applied field exercises enhance the knowledge and skills concerning the application of new technologies. Based on the specifics of further knowledge and skills enhancement, the use of training in the form of simulations, including virtual ones, as well as interactive laboratories, allows us to obtain relevant experience and develop critical thinking, problem-solving, and professional adaptability (Duignan,2020). Leveraging Technology for Skills Development: The potential rearrangement of controls, as well as the possibilities of experimenting online, in simulations, and virtual reality for learners, vary greatly and can be very learner oriented. Micro-credentials and other online certifications prove competencies in a particular area and offer quantifiable proof of continuing education. In this way, through these technologies, the professional constantly updates to ensure that he is up to the market demand.

Fostering a Culture of Innovation and Agility: For organisations, certain conditions must be fostered to enhance creativity and acceptance of change. Imperative practices include leadership commitment, incentives for innovation, and embracing collaboration together with risk-taking. The use of agile approaches in solving problems and involving employees in the decision-making process contributes to the creation of a flexible labour force. Preparing for Future Trends: Disruptions such as AI, VR, and blockchain are already in the pipeline and preparing for them is beneficial for any organisation and even the individual. Stressing digital competence, interpersonal competencies, and learning continuity security professionals for new occupations and professions, making him or her perpetual. As the dynamics of the workplace continue to change worldwide, this is perhaps the right time to develop strategies that embrace aspects of resilience and flexibility. Management and employees, or any other entity, must develop one that encourages knowledge enhancement and adaptation. This entails the identification of emerging market trends, employee training, and entrepreneurial mindset promotion. Scalability is achieved through the ability to adapt the tactics that are applied, which leads to resilience because the act of failing is carried out with lessons that enable change in strategies in real time. Based on this, the organisation can have a high potential for success or innovation because employees are backed with safe spaces and are allowed a growth mentality when it comes to the unknown or change. Continuous delivery and cross-functional collaboration are promoted to develop greater adaptability to the environment and improve innovation rates (Duignan,2020).

REFERENCES

Ali, M. (2023). Strategic leadership in the digital age: Navigating uncertainty. *Journal of Management & Social Science*, *1*(1), 1–8.

Bennett, E. E., & McWhorter, R. R. (2021). Virtual HRD's role in crisis and the post Covid-19 professional lifeworld: Accelerating skills for digital transformation. *Advances in Developing Human Resources*, *23*(1), 5–25. DOI: 10.1177/1523422320973288

Birla, R. (2023). The Challenges of Media Education in the Digital Era. *Journal of Communication Management (London)*, *2*(04), 281–288.

Bozkurt, A., Jung, I., Xiao, J., Vladimirschi, V., Schuwer, R., Egorov, G., & Paskevicius, M. (2020). A global outlook to the interruption of education due to COVID-19 pandemic: Navigating in a time of uncertainty and crisis. *Asian Journal of Distance Education*, *15*(1), 1–126.

Chaaban, Y., Al-Thani, H., & Du, X. (2021). A narrative inquiry of teacher educators' professional agency, identity renegotiations, and emotional responses amid educational disruption. *Teaching and Teacher Education*, *108*, 103522. DOI: 10.1016/j.tate.2021.103522

Choi, L., & Chung, S. (2021). Navigating online language teaching in uncertain times: Challenges and strategies of EFL educators in creating a sustainable technology-mediated language learning environment. *Sustainability (Basel)*, *13*(14), 7664. DOI: 10.3390/su13147664

Clarke, T. (2019). Creative destruction, technology disruption, and growth. In *Oxford Research Encyclopedia of Economics and Finance*. Oxford University Press. DOI: 10.1093/acrefore/9780190625979.013.393

Duignan, P. A. (2020). Navigating the future of learning: The role of smart technologies. In *Leading educational systems and schools in times of disruption and exponential change: A call for courage, commitment and collaboration* (pp. 125–137). Emerald Publishing Limited. DOI: 10.1108/978-1-83909-850-520201012

Fuller, J., McKittrick, K., Seibel, S., Wilson, J., Dash, V., & Epstein, A. (2023). Unlocking economic prosperity: Career navigation in a time of rapid change.

Gardner, P. (2017). Flourishing in the face of constant disruption: Cultivating the T-professional or adaptive innovator through WIL. In *Work-integrated learning in the 21st century: Global perspectives on the future* (pp. 69–81). Emerald Publishing Limited. DOI: 10.1108/S1479-367920170000032004

Harney, B., & Collings, D. G. (2021). Navigating the shifting landscapes of HRM. *Human Resource Management Review*, *31*(4), 100824. DOI: 10.1016/j.hrmr.2021.100824

Horn, M. B., & Staker, H. (2017). *Blended: Using disruptive innovation to improve schools*. John Wiley & Sons.

Javed, I., & Arham, R. (2023). Technological Disruption and Change Management: Navigating Uncertainty in the Digital Age. *The Management Science Letter*, *1*(01), 65–75.

Minea-Pic, A. (2020). Innovating teachers' professional learning through digital technologies.

Narbariya, S. (n.d.). Navigating the future of work: Challenges and strategies. In *Digital paradigm shift: Unravelling technological disruption in business* (p. 193).

Panda, S., & Kaur, N. (2023). Crafting sustainable careers in a dynamic professional terrain. In Panda, S., & Kaur, N. (Eds.), *Crafting sustainable careers in a dynamic professional terrain* (pp. 77–87).

Parekh, R. (2024). The Future of Business Leadership: Navigating Technological Disruption. *Management Science Research Archives*, *1*(4), 35–46.

Purcell, W. M., & Lumbreras, J. (2021). Higher education and the COVID-19 pandemic: Navigating disruption using the sustainable development goals. *Discover Sustainability*, *2*(1), 6. DOI: 10.1007/s43621-021-00013-2 PMID: 35425919

Ra, S., Jagannathan, S., & Maclean, R. (2021). *Powering a learning society during an age of disruption*. Springer Nature. DOI: 10.1007/978-981-16-0983-1

Rachmad, Y. E. (2021). Disruptive dynamics: Navigating the tech-led business boom. In *Book of the Association for Information Systems Publishing*. Professional Book Atlanta Special Issue.

Rad, D., Roman, A., Runcan, R., Toderici, O., Stoian, C. D., Sinaci, M., & Arion, F. (2024). Adapting to the unseen: Understanding workplace learning disruptions in educational counseling during COVID-19. *Migration Letters : An International Journal of Migration Studies*, *21*(S8), 1236–1255.

Reich, J. (2020). *Failure to disrupt: Why technology alone can't transform education*. Harvard University Press.

Tallat, R., Hawbani, A., Wang, X., Al-Dubai, A., Zhao, L., Liu, Z., & Alsamhi, S. H. (2023). Navigating industry 5.0: A survey of key enabling technologies, trends, challenges, and opportunities. *IEEE Communications Surveys and Tutorials*, *26*(2), 1080–1126. DOI: 10.1109/COMST.2023.3329472

Tariq, M. U. (2025). Revitalizing Pedagogy: Integrating Indigenous Knowledge and Practices Into Higher Education Disciplines. In Kgari-Masondo, M. (Ed.), *Indigenous Teaching Disciplines and Perspectives for Higher Education* (pp. 379–400). IGI Global Scientific Publishing., DOI: 10.4018/979-8-3693-9296-6.ch018

Tariq, M. U. (2025). Innovative Business Models: Integrating Social, Economic, and Environmental Goals in Rural Manufacturing. In Prabhakar, A., Yu, P., & Erokhin, V. (Eds.), *Rural Social Entrepreneurship Development: Network-Based Manufacturing System Model* (pp. 147–174). IGI Global Scientific Publishing., DOI: 10.4018/979-8-3693-7515-0.ch005

Tariq, M. U. (2025). AI and Work-Life Balance: Transforming Employee Wellbeing in the Modern Workplace. In Ahmed, E., Babar, A., Samad, A., Ahmed, R., & Beydoun, G. (Eds.), *Strengthening Human Relations in Organizations With AI* (pp. 85–110). IGI Global Scientific Publishing., DOI: 10.4018/979-8-3693-6507-6.ch004

Tariq, M. U. (2025). AI-Powered Business Process Automation: Revolutionizing Firm Management. In Derbali, A. (Ed.), *AI, Economic Perspectives, and Firm Business Management* (pp. 199–224). IGI Global Scientific Publishing., DOI: 10.4018/979-8-3693-7357-6.ch010

Tariq, M. U. (2025). Navigating Public Administration 5.0: Embracing AI for Smarter Governance. In Wongmahesak, K., Ahmad, J., & Mustanir, A. (Eds.), *Public Governance Practices in the Age of AI* (pp. 167–186). IGI Global Scientific Publishing., DOI: 10.4018/979-8-3693-9286-7.ch008

Turner, M., & Javed, A. (2023). Technological disruption and change management: Navigating uncertainty in the digital age. *The Management Science Letter*, *1*(01), 65–75.

Viltz-Emerson, M. A. (2021). *Forward solutions in digital learning transformation: A study in navigating 21st-century organizational learning for learning & development professionals*. Pepperdine University.

Webster-Wright, A. (2009). Reframing professional development through understanding authentic professional learning. *Review of Educational Research*, *79*(2), 702–739. DOI: 10.3102/0034654308330970

KEY TERMS AND DEFINITIONS

Artificial Intelligence (AI): A technology that enables machines to mimic human intelligence, enhancing decision-making, automation, and predictive analysis across various industries.

Internet of Things (IoT): A network of interconnected devices that collect, exchange, and analyse data in real-time to enhance processes and systems.

Blockchain: A decentralised, secure digital ledger technology used for transparent and tamper-proof record-keeping across various industries.

Machine Learning: A subset of AI that enables systems to learn and improve from experience without being explicitly programmed.

Agile Methodologies: Frameworks promoting iterative development, continuous improvement, and collaboration to enhance adaptability and productivity.

Section 4

Future Perspective on Global Workplace Learning

Chapter 10
Expats Escaping Culture Shock:
Designing a Game for Intercultural Communication

Susanne Weber
https://orcid.org/0009-0004-6490-8314
Institute of Human Resource Education and Management, Germany

Frank Achtenhagen
https://orcid.org/0009-0005-4196-7714
Faculty of Economic Sciences, Göttingen, Germany

ABSTRACT

The world is rapidly changing, with significant impacts on businesses and personal lives. Companies operating globally are increasingly moving parts of their operations abroad. To remain competitive, firms must recruit highly qualified, internationally mobile staff, often referred to as "expatriates" or "expats." However, relocating can lead to culture shock, causing expats to feel disoriented, stressed, and out of place, which can result in poor work performance and costly early returns. Effective human resource management is essential in addressing these challenges. Research shows that preparation and support programs focusing on both logistical ("hard facts") and cultural ("soft facts") aspects are crucial. One innovative solution is to use educational escape rooms (EERs) for training. This chapter outlines how EERs can be designed to address culture shock, offering a blueprint for their creation and assessment. This approach lays the groundwork for similar training tools in other areas, enhancing their effectiveness and applicability.

DOI: 10.4018/979-8-3373-5322-7.ch010

INTRODUCTION

In today's rapidly changing and uncertain world, marked by volatility, anxiety, non-linearity, and incomprehensibility—captured by the "BANI" concept (Cascio, 2020)—organizations are increasingly compelled to adapt their strategies for talent mobility. To remain competitive, businesses must go beyond traditional relocation strategies and embrace new, flexible models for attracting and managing highly qualified, internationally mobile professionals and employees (Bonache et al., 2024). Work itself is no longer confined to specific places, roles, or hierarchical structures. The shift towards a more "borderless" world of work brings human performance into sharper focus, detaching labor from rigid organizational constructs and embedding it within flexible, globally dispersed frameworks.

Hence, global mobility today involves beside sending employees abroad on traditional expatriate assignments a wide spectrum of mobility types including international remote workers, self-initiated movers, digital nomads, project-based international work, and other fluid forms of global engagement (Bozzi, 2024; Krogmann & Zinner, 2023). The trend toward the flexibilization of assignment models has increased due to digitalization and the COVID-19 pandemic (Bozzi, 2024).

Nevertheless, several firms perceive significant challenges in fully transforming to digital work models due to organizational, individual, and technical factors. These include a lack of integration into corporate culture, legal uncertainties, reduced personal interaction, blurred boundaries between work and private life, inadequate or limited access to technological infrastructure, and concerns regarding data security or digital safety (Frick & Marx, 2021). Although there is still much to explore on both the side of digital nomads and that of organizations and management, mobile professionals—whether expats or digital nomads—face numerous challenges (Bozzi, 2024; Frick & Marx, 2021).

The adjustment process to an alien analog workplace or a global virtual workspace can be emotionally and cognitively demanding. Without prior international experience respectively an experience of nomad lifestyle and strong support systems, many global employees report feelings like disoriented, isolated, and anxious (Bozzi, 2024, p. 6; Hensellek & Puchala, 2021, p. 207-208). Although these feelings might arise from different sources (such as the loss of familiar norms, loosing social contacts) they can be characterized by confusion, a sense of alienation or frustration (Ting-Toomey & Chung, 2022; Hensellek & Puchala, 2021). These feelings not only reduce performance but also increase the risk of premature returns for expats or a discontinuation of the nomadism. Early returns or giving up being a nomad can be costly—for the sending firm, in terms of investment and reputation, and for the individuals, who miss out on professional development opportunities and may suffer personal setbacks (Genkova, 2021; Waxin & Brewster, 2024).

To mitigate these issues, expats and nomads alike must manage such cultural differences and must navigate such frustration phases of adjustment applying intercultural communication competence. Here, human resource management plays a central role. Innovative firms are beginning to use AI-driven tools and data analytics to offer tailored relocation and global mobility support. Thereby, the focus is shifting from short-term business outcomes to long-term goals such as innovation, firm culture, and employee development (Flynn et al., 2025). This also means paying more attention to employees' holistic well-being during international assignments or virtual work. It includes both "hard facts" (e.g., bureaucratic assistance, housing, legal aid) and "soft facts" such as cultural training, coaching, and mentoring—elements that have traditionally been undervalued but are crucial to long-term success (Genkova, 2021; Ting-Toomey & Chung, 2022).

The goal is to move away from one-size-fits-all solutions and instead offer a wide range of personalized support using manifold modi of delivery to evoke learning and development processes that promote intercultural competence (including intercultural communication), resilience, satisfaction, and sustained engagement in a globalized work environment (Flynn et al., 2025).

Although digitalization has been widely researched, its impact on expats' daily lives and its connection to global mobility management remain underexplored (Bucher et al., 2024; Hausberg et al., 2019; Wang, Lockett & Zhou, 2024).

In our contribution, we, therefore, suggest to implement a technology-enhanced „Educational Escape Room" (EER) to develop intercultural competence. Therefore, we chose to base the EER on the concept of "cultural shock," as it represents a phase of confusion, alienation and frustration (Ting-Toomey & Chung, 2022) that frequently arises in intercultural and global work contexts and typically constitutes a condition individuals seek to overcome respectively to „escape". Thereby, we are focusing on the format of assigning employees abroad, because this format remains relevant (c.f., Setti et al., 2022; Enatto, 2024).

As EERs are explicitly designed for teaching and learning purposes (Makri et al., 2021; Veldkamp et al., 2020b) they must be constructed in accordance to specific criteria as formulated e.g., by the Evidence-centered game design (ECgD) principles (Mislevy et al., 2014; 2016; Li et al., 2024; Weber et al., 2021a) to reach the intended learning goals by finishing the game (Makri et al., 2021; Veldkamp et al., 2020a, b). Nevertheless, there is a significant need for guidelines to design and implement effective evaluation measures for EERs in practice, particularly those focussing simultaneously on competence-oriented assessments (Fotaris & Mastoras, 2022; Veldkamp et al., 2020b).

With the focus on developing cultural awareness and basic intercultural communication strategies as part of an intercultural competence we designed an EER step by step according to the ECgD. In doing so, we outline exemplarily the experiences of a German expat, Max, who moves to the U.S. for an international project with his firm and experiences culture shock, which he seeks to escape.

Using the concrete example, we illustrate the specific design criteria for initiating the intended learning processes in a blueprint and summarize them abstractly in a "canvas" format to enable transfer to other escape situations and topics, especially occuring in global mobility.

THEORETICAL CONSIDERATIONS

Situation of Expats

Expats are individuals who have temporarily relocated across national borders for work. This group includes "assigned expats", who are sent abroad by their employers, and "self-initiated expats", who independently seek employment in the international labor market, with or without a firm's support (e.g., Stoermer et al., 2024; Tharenou, 2015). The decision to become an expat can be influenced by various factors, such as the prospect of higher income, personal development, career opportunities, or cultural affinities (Knocke & Schuster, 2017; Wittek, 2021). Similarly, firms choose to send or hire expats for complex reasons (Enatto, 2024; Kour & Jyoti, 2022; Setti et al., 2022), including the geographical concentration of industries (e.g., Alfaro & Chen, 2014), the need for foreign workers in aging societies (e.g., Börsch-Supan, 2003), organizational benefits of a diverse workforce (e.g., Nederveen Pieterse et al., 2013), enhanced knowledge transfer and performance or social networks (Wittek, 2021; Escobar Borruel, 2022). Depending on a firm's internationalization strategy, the roles and expectations of expats can vary significantly. For example, an ethnocentric strategy may require expats to transfer parent firm policies to subsidiaries, a polycentric strategy might involve filling management positions with local managers while retaining foreign management styles, and a geocentric strategy could aim to unify the firm under a shared global concept (Lindemann et al., 2013; Wittek, 2021).

Culture Shock

These personal and firm factors shape expats' expectations, motivations, emotions, perceptions, and actions. Regardless of the specific reasons for relocation, the process is highly challenging as expats transition from a familiar environment to an unfamiliar one. In this new and unknown setting, expats often feel overwhelmed, leading to confusion, disorientation, anxiety, loneliness, insecurity, and stress. They may also make cultural missteps, which can hinder their ability to perform efficiently and effectively in their workplaces. Managing cultural differences during the “adjustment” process to the cultural challenges of the host country and alien work environment, experiencing culture shock is highly likely (e.g., Ting-Toomey & Chung, 2022, p. 112; Verghese, 2013).

> *Culture Shock [...] is an intense feeling of not being ‘at home’, a sense of non-belonging, and a sense of being an outsider. In this ‘fish out of water’ environment, the individual’s identity appears to be stripped of all protection. Previously familiar cues and scripts are suddenly inoperable in the new cultural setting (Ting-Toomey & Chung, 2022, p. 112).*

Culture shock typically occurs within the first few weeks after arriving in the host country. Almost all expats experience it, though the degree and intensity vary based on previous experience, personal attitude, and preparation (c.f., Ting-Toomey & Chung, 2022; Verghese, 2013). This phase is the most emotionally intense and challenging for expats, as they often feel consciously incompetent and mentally and emotionally exhausted in various aspects of their lives (Ting-Toomey & Chung, 2022, p. 125). Such stress can lead to either aggressive and hostile behavior or withdrawal. Ting-Toomey and Chung (2022, p. 125) identify three types of expat behavior, or “culture shockers”: (a) the “early returners”, who employ aggressive or passive-aggressive strategies to cope with the “hostile” environment and prematurely return to their home culture; (b) the “time servers”, who do the bare minimum, with little engagement in the host culture, and “serve their time” while looking forward to leaving; and (c) the “participators”, who are committed to adapting optimally, fully engaging with the new cultural setting, and taking advantage of both instrumental and socioemotional learning opportunities in the new environment.

It is essential to note the “presumed similarity paradox”: as Vromans et al. (2013) illustrate, when expats assume a high degree of similarity between their home and host cultures, they often underestimate the differences, leading to more challenging adjustments. This underestimated cultural difference, particularly between e. g., the United States and Germany, is frequently discussed in intercultural training programs (Thomas, 2022, p. 6).

Escaping Culture Shock

To navigate this culture shock phase, expats must work through the adjustment process. Drawing on communication theory, Ting-Toomey and Dorjee (2019) propose the “integrative identity negotiation theory”, which emphasizes the generation of shared meanings. Expats must negotiate three key dimensions: content meaning (e.g., facts and information), relational meaning (e.g., unique relationships, expectations, non-verbal intonations, specific gestures), and identity meaning (e.g., the fulfillment of their identity needs). This negotiation requires “intercultural competence” applying competent "intercultural communication strategies", which, according to Ting-Toomey & Chung (2022, pp. 35–36; 40–44), include several core elements:

- **Awareness:** Understanding and interpreting oneself and others, recognizing cultural differences and similarities.
- **Knowledge:** Grasping the factors shaping intercultural encounters, including history, environment, political and socioeconomic contexts, identity concepts, cultural dimensions, and the phases of adjustment processes, such as culture shock and rebound.
- **Skills and Abilities:** Developing intercultural conflict management techniques, practicing mindful listening and observing, effective questioning, and managing face-work.
- **Responsive Attitudes:** Cultivating open-mindedness, cultural self-awareness, ethnorelative thinking, and empathy.

The context of situational communication and interaction is crucial, encompassing different domains such as work, social relationships, and personal life (Black et al., 1991; Lessle et al., 2024, p. 57). These domains often experience spill-over and cross-over effects (Lessle et al., 2024, p. 68), influenced by the dynamics of the adjustment process with its various phases (e.g., honeymoon, hostility, humor, in-sync), formal and informal settings (e.g., seating arrangements), and the broader social system, which includes history, culture, politics, law, and organizational structure (Ting-Toomey & Chung, 2022, p. 34).

The adjustment process, or "integrative identity negotiation" (Ting-Toomey & Dorjee, 2019), is completed when the interacting partners or groups achieve a mutually shared understanding. This means that the communication and behavior exchanged are considered appropriate (i.e., they align with mutual expectations, shared values, norms, and social roles and exhibit respectful, reflective behavior), effective/efficient (i.e., they foster common ground and yield goal-oriented outcomes), and adaptable (i.e., they reflect an awareness of the counterpart's perspectives, interests, goals, and communication styles, with a willingness to modify one's behavior and goals to suit the interaction) (Ting-Toomey & Chung, 2022, pp. 36–37).

Successful adaptation in this process is marked by the expat feeling understood, respected, and positively valued at both the level of their social identity group and their personal identity (Ting-Toomey & Dorjee, 2019). To navigate this challenging adjustment process, expats must build a network with people from diverse cultural backgrounds, which provides social support and helps avoid the isolation of the so-called "expatriate bubble". While co-nationals or other expats may share similar experiences, interactions with host-nationals offer richer, more varied information and insights (van Bakel, 2019).

Establishing connections with host country nationals is essential for a successful adjustment (van Bakel, 2019; van Bakel et al., 2017, p. 218). Through various types of contact—such as the number of people (size), interdisciplinary contacts (breadth), and deep relationships (depth)—expats can gain different forms of support, including emotional support, social companionship, informational support, and instrumental support. These relationships also help expats build networks and organize their lives (van Bakel et al., 2017, p. 218).

Intercultural Competence

Although (inter)cultural competence (ICC) is defined in various ways, there is broad agreement that it entails „the ability to function effectively across different cultures" (Urgun et al., 2025, p. 2). It refers to the cognitive, emotional, and motivational foundations behind effective behavior in culturally diverse situations (c.f., Blömeke et al., 2015; Shavelson, 2012). Thus, ICC includes awareness (recognizing cultural differences), knowledge (e.g., identity concepts, cultural dimensions), skills (e.g., communication strategies, mindful listening), and attitudes (e.g., open-mindedness, empathy, cultural self-awareness) (Ting-Toomey & Chung, 2022).

Analytically, ICC includes related cognitive and non-cognitive abilities based on personality traits but, simultaneously, situation specific states manifested in realized behavior in real-life situations. The particularly used knowledge, skills and attitudes (states) manifested within a situation-specific behavior are not directly visible, they just can be inferred from observable behavior. Thus, competence refers to real-world performance, either as constituent of the construct or as a validity criterion (Blömeke et al., 2015).

Defining ICC requires analyzing real-world tasks in authentic contexts and identifying the related knowledge, skills, and attitudes. Since no two individuals demonstrate ICC in the same way, it is their behavior in real-life settings that should be assessed and matched against the criterion. Rooted in educational research, ICC emphasizes identifying and developing relevant knowledge, skills and attitudes through targeted interventions and training.

While several definitions of ICC exist, similar concepts like cultural intelligence (CQ) share overlapping components. CQ is defined as the „individual's capability to function and manage effectively in culturally diverse settings (Ang et al., 2007, p. 337) and includes the four dimensions: metacognitive, cognitive, motivational, and behavioral. Like ICC, CQ is considered developable through training and experience (Chao et al., 2017; Setti et al., 2022; Blömeke et al., 2015).

In literature, these two approaches are often distinguished as follows: Cultural intelligence is considered a specific form of intelligence and is based on Sternberg and Detterman's (1986) multi-loci theory of intelligence, comprising the above mentioned four dimensions. Proponents of the cultural intelligence (CQ) approach argue that cultural competence models tend to focus on narrower personality traits (e.g., self-awareness, cognitive flexibility) and pay less attention to situation-specific behavior, while also rarely considering all relevant dimensions and factors at the same time (e.g., Ang & Van Dyne, 2015; Urgun et al., 2025). Advocates of the intercultural competence (ICC) approach criticize the cultural intelligence (CQ) model for emphasizing overly broad intercultural capabilities, rather than focusing on specific, culture-related situations. As a result, they argue, the CQ approach is often too detached from actual situational demands (cf. Blömeke et al., 2015).

In our study, we adopt the ICC approach from an educational perspective, allowing us to design interventions that foster individuals' cultural awareness and intercultural competence including intercultural communication strategies. These interventions are grounded in real-world situations typical of performance demands in specific fields (here: culture shock situations experienced by an expat), aligned with corresponding effective behaviors, and informed by theoretical insights into the phenomenon, which serve as the primary point of reference (see Blömeke et al., 2015; Leutner et al., 2017; Mulder, 2017: Ting-Toomey & Chung, 2022).

Intercultural Training and Support

Studies show that support and training programs are crucial for effectively developing intercultural competence, managing the different phases of cultural adjustment, and enhancing task or job performance (Kraimer et al., 2016; Kour & Jyoti, 2022; Setti et al., 2023). Especially, mixed approaches (such as classroom discussions, instructional material, experiential methods, simulations (incl. games), and reflective journaling) have proven to be most effective (c.f., Urgun et al., 2025, p. 6). In light of evolving work models, HR departments face significant challenges in identifying individual training needs, designing appropriate programs, managing their implementation, and evaluating their impact. New technologies could provide valuable support in meeting these demands (Wang et al., 2024).

With regard to fostering intercultural competence, online and blended learning formats offer promising approaches to address the diverse needs and goals of intercultural training (c.f., Lee, 2010). A variety of digital tools—such as internet-based expatriate platforms, specific social media networks, or online courses, videos, simulations, serious games, virtual and augmented reality, as well as online coaching and mentoring—can be used to design flexible, mobile and engaging learning environments (Kirste & Holtbrügge, 2019; Wang et al., 2024).

These digital formats alone or in combination can target the key goals of intercultural training: affective (e.g., attitudes, emotions), behavioral (e.g., flexibility, social skills), and cognitive outcomes (e.g., cultural knowledge) (Ward, Bochner

& Furnham, 2020). Through the use of diverse modes (synchronous and asynchronous) and formats (digital and analog), expats can be encouraged to actively engage with the host culture, better understand the stages of culture shock, and learn that frustration is a normal part of the adjustment process.

Mentors, coaches, and especially host country nationals play a vital role in this learning ecosystem. They help interpret unfamiliar situations, offer emotional support, build trust, and foster connections between expats, local team members, the firm, and the broader cultural environment (van Bakel, 2019).

In our contribution, we propose exemplarily the use of an EER as a flexible and interactive tool that can be integrated into a firm's on-site, online or blended learning programs.

EERs

> *An educational escape room (EER) can be defined as an instructional method requiring learners to participate in [individual or; Authors according toMakri et al., 2021, p. 4] collaborative playful activities explicitly designed for domain knowledge acquisition, skill development, or behavioural change so that they can accomplish a specific goal (e.g., participants must escape from a physical or virtual room, solve a mystery, find a hidden item, prevent a disaster, break into a vault, etc.) by solving puzzles linked to unambiguous learning objectives in a limited amount of time (Fotaris & Mastoras, 2022, p. 1).*

Studies show that EERs enhance learning by stimulating interest and engagement in the subject matter (López-Pernas et al., 2019; Makri et al., 2021). They generate positive emotions and flow experience (Peleg et al., 2019) and stimulate motivation through competitive elements, varying game levels, and time constraints. By tackling challenging tasks, EERs promote the development of communication skills, creative and critical thinking, problem-solving abilities, leadership skills, and collaboration (Fotaris & Mastoras, 2022; Makri et al., 2021). Additionally, EERs enhance feelings of competence, autonomy, and belonging, positively affecting competence development (Makri et al., 2021; Menon & Romero, 2020; Veldkamp et al., 2020b).

From a learning theory perspective, EERs can be implemented in various ways: (a) Based on cognitivism, EERs can focus on teaching and testing objective knowledge through questions, answers, and problem-solving tasks. Players solve these tasks individually, aiming to learn specific knowledge and develop or refine their cognitive schemata; (b) Based on constructivism, EERs can stimulate higher-order thinking processes, such as creative and critical thinking and problem-solving, to help players construct their own mental models of the phenomena. Depending on the technology, open-ended answers and multiple solutions may be accepted; (c) Based on social constructivism, EERs are often used to solve tasks collaboratively in teams, which enhances both collaboration and communication skills. EERs are often situated within social constructivism (Makri et al., 2021, p. 47).

For an EER to be successful, various design criteria must be considered. However, there are only a few systematically structured approaches in the current literature (Fotaris & Mastoras, 2022; Veldkamp et al., 2020b, p. 1). The prominent approaches by Clarke et al. (2017, p. 78), Makri et al. (2021, pp. 56–57), and Veldkamp et al. (2020b, pp. 5–6) elaborate on didactic design elements for EER, which can be classified according to the game-theoretical perspective (cf. Kapp, 2012; Kapp et al., 2014; Schell, 2020). These elements include *learning features* such as addressees, goals, and content topics, and *game features* such as narratives, tasks/puzzles/quizzes, equipment, setting, and (digital) technologies, as well as briefing, supporting, or debriefing. Additionally, game masters/game leaders monitor and guide the game and intervene in case of problems (Makri et al., 2021, p. 48). Competence *assessment features* and overarching evaluation, as suggested within the ECgD framework by Mislevy et al. (2014; 2016), are also crucial. Moreover, the effectiveness of games in an educational context is determined not only by the individual game components but also by how they are implemented in the learning and training process (cf. van Rosmalen & Westera, 2014) and the extent to which the needs and preferences of the players are met (cf. Larson, 2020).

There is a need to evaluate the use of EERs, establish guidelines for their development and implementation (Jenkin & Fairfurst, 2019), and address the lack of measures for assessing EERs (Fotaris & Mastoras, 2022), including competence-oriented game-based assessments (Aprea & Ifenthaler, 2021; Ifenthaler & Kim, 2019; Li et al., 2024; Weber et al., 2021a, b). Evaluations and assessments are crucial not only for gaining insights into the effectiveness and impact of EERs but also for improving the games themselves.

ECgD

Game-based design and assessment is a challenging task, particularly with a focus on competencies, as it requires simultaneously addressing three different perspectives within the same artifact, namely the EER: the learning, the game, and the assessment features. Mislevy et al. (2016) attempt to integrate these three features within their ECgD approach, summarized in Figure 1 as follows:

1. **Learning Features:** These focus on the target audience, the domain, and the competencies (knowledge, skills, attitudes) that players should acquire, including their quality and level (breadth, depth, flexibility). This involves extensive "domain analysis" and "domain modeling" to identify central domain situations,

big ideas, actions, and challenges. The goal is for players to learn to think and act like individuals in the target domain by performing well in the game.

2. **Game Features:** These provide a set of situations, tasks, and environments designed to prompt players through intended learning processes and to demonstrate the intended competencies through expected and accepted evidence. Game elements such as *mechanics* (e.g., authentic stories, dramatic situations, challenges, rewards, penalties, time limits), *dynamics* (e.g., using skills, recognizing, describing, analyzing, applying, generating, prioritizing, evaluating), and *aesthetics* (e.g., design, layout, sound, sensory experiences) are developed to engage players.
3. **Assessment Features:** These address how to score (scoring scheme) and analyze observed evidence (statistical models). By examining students' responses and connecting them (evidence model) to the intended competence model (student model) and the set game challenges (task model), insight can be gained into players' competencies respectively their thinking and behavior in the specific domain. Assessment can be related to (a) the final learning product at the end of the game (e.g., escaping from the EER in the shortest possible time), (b) the (sub-)tasks completed during the game, and (c) the problem-solving process and strategies employed during the game (e.g., through log files; Bley, 2017; Mislevy et al., 2016, pp. 25–27; Weber et al., 2021a).

Figure 1. Canvas for linking learning, game, and assessment features

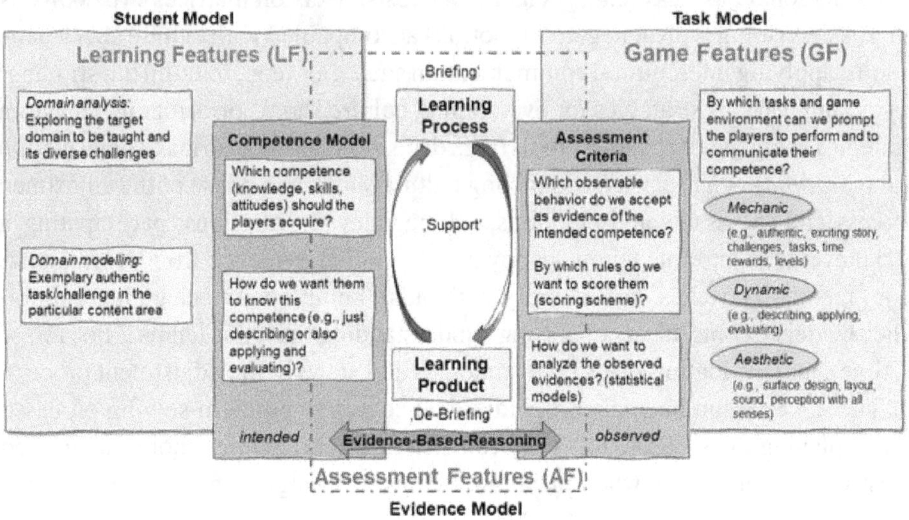

Source: Own depiction

How these abstract, theoretical considerations of the canvas can be translated into concrete, practical game design steps is illustrated in the following blueprint.

BLUEPRINT OF AN EER ON ESCAPING CULTURE SHOCK

Learning Features

To identify learning goals, we conduct a domain analysis of typical situations and challenges expats face. Our blueprint addresses the need for expats (Who is affected?) to engage in a course to develop intercultural communication competence, particularly for managing culture shock (What is the need state?). Culture shock is one of the most challenging phases of the adjustment process that every expat must navigate (What is the problem?). Failing to manage this phase can lead to inefficiency, stress, cultural faux pas, or even costly returns and loss of reputation (Why does it matter?; statement formulated in accordance with Fotaris & Mastoras, 2022, pp. 7–8). Therefore, we focus on strategies for managing and overcoming, respectively "escaping" this phase.

According to Ting-Toomey and Chung (2022), relevant competence facets in such situations include (a) *knowledge* (K) about the adjustment process and its phases, especially culture shock, the rebound phase, culture dimensions and differences (e.g., indulgence vs. restraint), the importance of interactions with host country nationals (including types of contacts and qualities of social support), and typical tools used in international business (e.g., social media posts, decision matrices); (b) *skills* (S) such as describing typical negative emotions accompanied with culture shock using emojis, applying intercultural communication strategies (e.g., mindful questioning), developing various strategies for overcoming culture shock, prioritizing behavioral strategies using typical business tools (e.g., decision-making matrices, social media); and (c) *attitudes* (A) such as recognizing culture shock as a phase of the adjustment process and the associated emotions, asking relevant questions, participating in social events (e.g., table tennis, happy hour), valuing evidence from professionals (e.g., mentors, coaches, host country nationals), being open to changing opinions when evidence contradicts beliefs (e.g., understanding that table tennis is not a waste of time), and evaluating one's own strategies and stage in the adjustment process.

These KSAs can be applied in individual cognitive problem-solving processes (when playing the EER alone). They can also be integrated into more social or co-constructivist processes when playing in teams or engaging in collective learning (e.g., Dochy et al., 2022, pp. 219–221).

To model these competencies with respect to their structure (KSA; cf. Binkley et al., 2012; DeBruijn & Baartman, 2011; Genkova, 2021) and level (recognizing, analyzing, developing new strategies, probing new strategies, evaluating, and reflection) (Anderson & Krathwohl, 2001; Bloom et al., 1956; Gronlund, 2000; Marzano & Kendall, 2007), we formulated a competence matrix (Figure 2). This matrix aligns with the international discussion on competence (cf. Blömeke et al., 2015; Hartig et al., 2008; Leutner et al., 2017; Weber & Achtenhagen, 2017).

Figure 2. Competence structure and levels (student level) with assigned game tasks (task model)

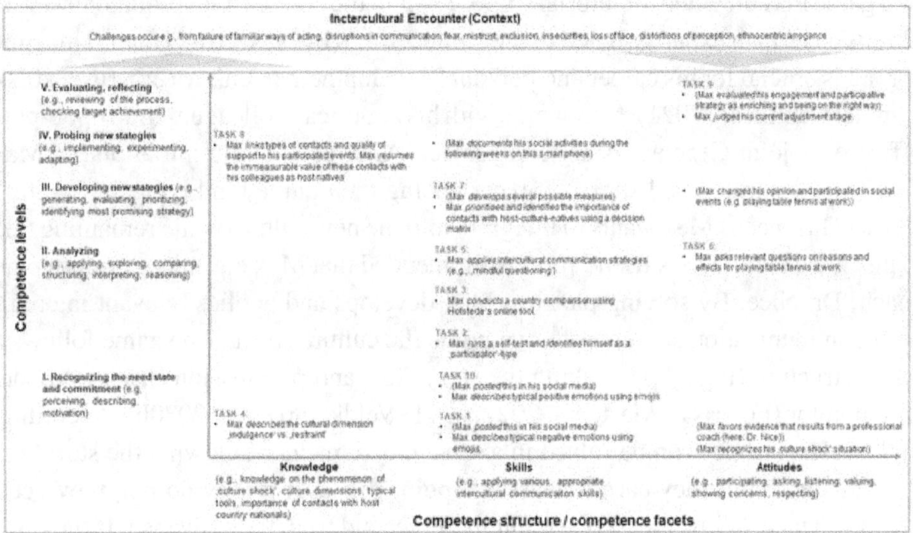

Source: Own depiction

Game Features

Our blueprint focuses on a hybrid EER that combines virtual rooms with quizzes. This approach addresses the common issue of limited time for intercultural preparation courses, offering a cost-effective, mobile course format that can be used flexibly at different times and locations. This is increasingly required in the BANI world (Evseeva et al., 2022). We suggest positioning this EER with its specialized domain-specific content after participants have completed a previous introductory module on the relevant knowledge, skills, and attitudes necessary for handling culture shock situations. The EER aims to allow participants to apply and deepen these competencies (Morrell & Eukel, 2021).

To offer players meaningful game activities, authentic tasks should be chosen that represent a reason for escaping in real situations and require the knowledge, skills, and attitudes (KSAs) to be taught. The individual tasks/puzzles/quizzes should form a cohesive storyline (Fotaris & Mastoras, 2022, p. 11). In our blueprint, we choose a 60-minute EER tackling culture shock, representing a dramatic situation where intercultural communication strategies (KSAs) are necessary to escape this underlying double bind phenomenon.

Within a starting briefing phase of about 10 minutes, the EER player is introduced by a game master, video, or tutorial (Figure 3) into the context. Our protagonist, Max (35), is a German expat assigned to the United States by his German firm. This time abroad is crucial for his career and personal development (Genkova & Kruse, 2020; Zimmermann et al., 2021). Max works with his American colleagues in an open-plan office on a joint German–American project. After an exciting initial phase, Max now feels frustrated and stressed, experiencing the double bind typical of culture shock. This means Max wants to integrate into the new culture while remaining tied to his home culture. His friend Jörg recommended that Max consults a professional coach, Dr. Nice. By solving puzzles, Max develops and applies relevant intercultural communication strategies to overcome the culture shock. The game follows a linear structure (Figure 4), making the story flow and progression easier to model and monitor (Fotaris & Mastoras, 2022, p. 11; Veldkamp et al., 2020b). According to the rules, puzzles can be solved in a self-guided manner following the storyline. Players advance if they earn at least one point per task; if they do not, they get a second chance. With at least one point in the second trial, they advance. If they still earn zero points, they receive a pass card to continue the game (Fotaris & Mastoras, 2022, p. 17). During gameplay, players receive feedback on their current progress via an individualized progress bar. At the end of the EER, a de-briefing phase of about 20 minutes helps players link their experiences to the intended learning goals and the culture shock phenomenon. This phase allows players to make sense of their learning and reflect on how to apply it to real-life situations (Fotaris & Mastoras, 2022, pp. 18–19).

A short teaser is provided to engage players and immerse them in the experience of culture shock (Figure 3).

Figure 3. Teaser for introducing into the "culture shock" situation

Culture Shock Situation

Max, (35) German, has been assigned to the U.S. as an expat by a German company. He works with colleagues in an open-plan office on a joint German-American project.
After an exciting first phase, Max now feels bad:
- He is insecure in his behavior.
- He believes he can no longer think clearly.
- He feels generally disoriented.
- He has the impression that his behavior, his values and his identity are being rejected.
- He generally no longer feels up to the demands of the new work/life situation. ....

What Max expected to be enriching and exciting quickly turns into a source of profound stress and confusion.

Today, Max experienced the following situation at work, which for him was the straw that broke the camel's back: The office is hectic. Colleagues are talking loudly on the phone and two colleagues are playing table tennis in the corner. Max sits at his desk and stares at his laptop. His colleague, Jason, a lively American, joins him.

JASON (*smiles*): *Hey, Max! How's it going?*

MAX (*looks up, stressed*): *I'm trying to get used to the work culture here. But it's different from Germany.*

JASON (*laughs*): *Yes, we have a relaxed atmosphere here. Come on, take a break and play a game of table tennis with us. This is our "brainstorming area". Ideas flow here just like the balls. It's relaxing!*

MAX (*hesitantly*): *I really have a lot to do. In Germany, we don't take breaks so lightly.*

JASON (*shrugging his shoulders*): *It's not just about work here, Max. It's also about having a good time.*

JASON (*obviously uncomprehending*): turns away and goes back to the table tennis.

MAX (*confused; incomprehensible*): continues his work tensely.

Source: Own depiction using ChatGPT for creating the picture

The EER game structure follows one cycle of an individual cognitive problem-solving process, as illustrated in Figure 4. In each step, the EER player encounters game tasks (*mechanics*) that reflect typical challenges of the adjustment process. These tasks are designed to foster the necessary learning processes (*dynamics*) to achieve the intended learning goals and competencies, as detailed in Figure 2. Depending on the available technology, creativity, and target audience, the surface design and layout of the game may vary to engage all senses (*aesthetics*). To balance the difficulty of each task, various difficulty-generating factors must be considered, including cognitive, psychomotoric, and affective taxonomies (Anderson & Krathwohl, 2001; Bloom et al., 1956; Gronlund, 2000; Marzano & Kendall, 2007), as well as types of cognitive load (such as intrinsic, extraneous, germane; van Merrienboer & Kirschner, 2018) to align with the intended competence level taught by the designed tasks and prompts.

Figure 4. Game structure and linked tasks

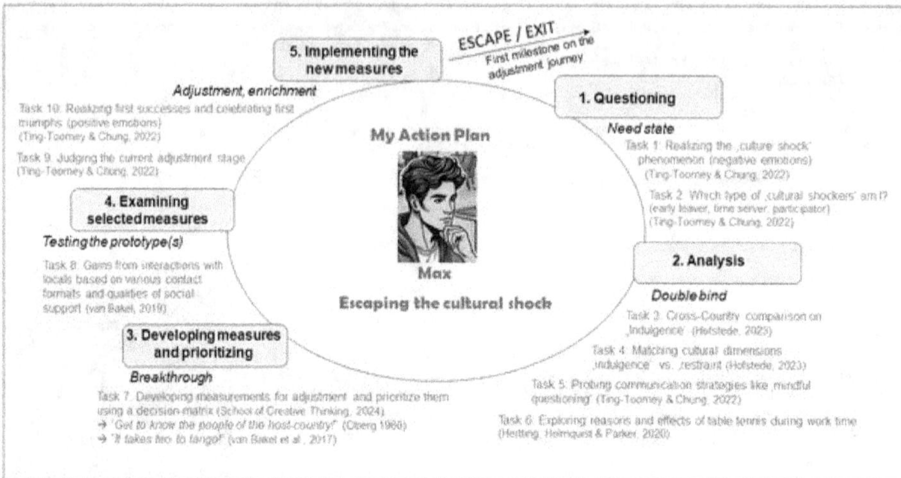

Source: Own depiction in accordance with Dochy et al., 2022, pp. 219–221 (using ChatGPT for creating the picture)

Questioning: The game starts by questioning the current situation. The protagonist, Max, recognizes the onset of culture shock and the accompanying negative emotions. He describes these feelings to his family and friends in a social media post (Figure 5). The accepted correct answers are listed in Table 2 within the Appendix.

Figure 5. Task 1: Social media post (negative emotions)

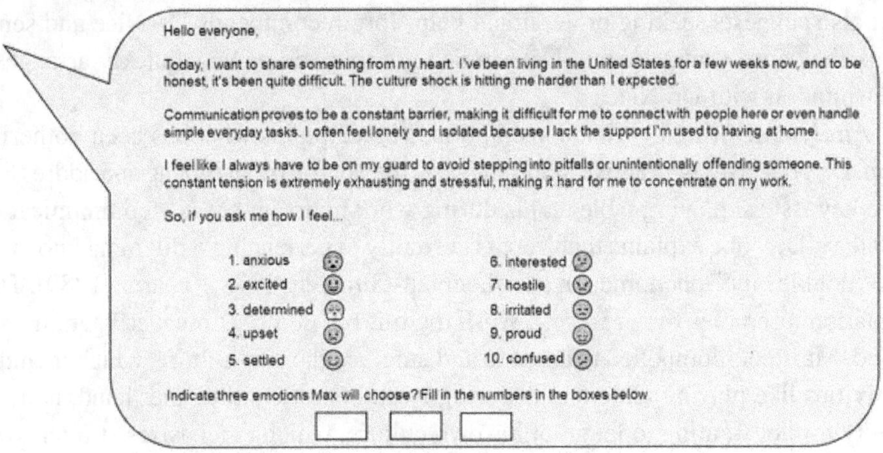

Source: Own depiction using ChatGPT for creating the emojis

Furthermore, he searches the internet and discovers three prototypes of "culture shockers" (early returners, time servers, participators) and various behavioral strategies discussed in several online groups. Max attempts to identify which type of "culture shocker" he is and takes a self-assessment test (Figure 6).

Figure 6. Task 2: "culture shocker" self-test

Self-Test to identify your type of „culture shocker"

1. Expats show genuine interest in understanding and adapting to local customs.
2. Expats show little interest in exploring or understanding the host culture.
3. Expats avoid extracurricular activities or social events.
4. Expats miss deadlines or refuse to participate in group activities.
5. Expats are forming friendships and professional networks that enhance their cultural immersion and learning.
6. Expats participate in cultural events.
7. Expats openly criticize local customs.
8. Expats have a rigid daily routine that involves work and immediate return to their living quarters.
9. Expats avoid social interactions.

Which of the nine behaviors shown can be assigned to the culture shocker type "participator"?

Participators behave as described under number ...

☐ ☐ ☐

Source: Own depiction

At this moment, Max receives a message from his friend Jörg, who has been living in the United States as an expat for a few years. Jörg understands how much Max is struggling, having experienced culture shock himself. He offers to be a mentor but also suggests seeking professional help. Jörg recommends Dr. Nice and sends Max the contact information. Determined not to give up, Max quickly arranges a consultation with Dr. Nice.

Analysis: During his first consultation, Max explains what has been bothering him. Dr. Nice listens attentively and suggests they begin by analyzing and addressing two key issues: playing table tennis during work hours and Max's communication strategy. Dr. Nice explains that Max is currently experiencing a dilemma known as the "double bind" phenomenon (Kirshenblatt-Gimblett, 1978; Zaharna, 1989). This situation resembles the proverb, "Wash my fur, but don't get me wet!" On the one hand, Max feels compelled to adapt to and embrace the new culture, which includes activities like playing table tennis during work hours. On the other hand, he feels guilty for not wanting to let go of his own culture, which emphasizes stricter work discipline and a clear separation between work and leisure.

These conflicting expectations lead to stress and confusion because, no matter Max's decision, he feels as though he is doing something wrong. To help break this double bind, Dr. Nice, acting as a neutral party, initiates meta-communication (Kutz, 2018) to foster awareness and reflection during this second phase of analysis. He suggests that Max compares the United States and Germany using The Culture Factor Group's (2024) country comparison tool (Figure 7). The goal is to identify the most significant cultural differences Max faces. According to this tool, Americans are more likely to prioritize personal pleasure and leisure, while Germans tend to emphasize duty and social norms (Figure 8; The Culture Factor Group, 2024; Hofstede et al., 2010). This finding aligns with Max's experiences and concerns.

Figure 7. Task 3: country comparison between the United States and Germany

Run a country comparison between United States and Germany and upload the graph!
(you can use for example the online tool of The Culture Factor Group (2024): https://www.hofstede-insights.com/country-comparison-tool?countries=germany%2Cunited+states)

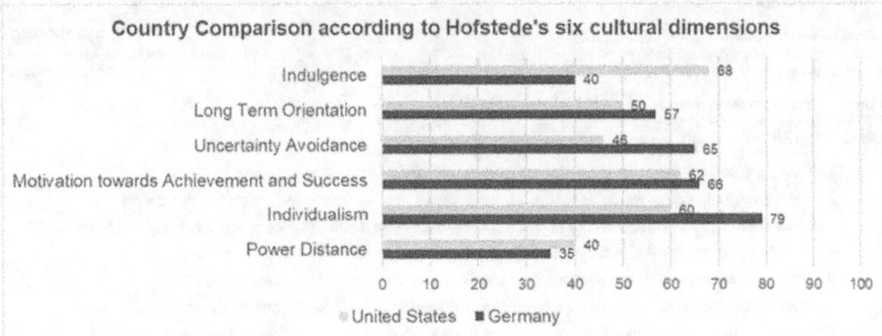

The main difference is ______________________ .

Source: Own depiction

Figure 8. Task 4: main differences between the United States and Germany regarding "indulgence"

Hofstede's indulgence dimension measures the degree to which a society allows the free satisfaction of basic human needs and desires in terms of pleasure and enjoyment.

Complete the cloze text to name the key differences:

(a) Highly indulgent societies emphasize ____________ and ____________, while restrictive societies emphasize ____________ and ____________.

a1_duty
a2_leisure
a3_personal pleasure
a4_social norm

(a) Highly indulgent societies report ____________ and ____________, while restrictive societies tend to report ____________ and ____________.

b1_cynicism
b2_higher level of happiness
b3_optimism
b4_pessimism

Source: Own depiction

At the end of the first meeting, Max agrees with Dr. Nice to explore the reasons behind social and sports activities, especially table tennis, during work hours and their effects. Recognizing that his often overly direct communication strategy has not always been well received by his colleagues, Max plans to work on improving this aspect. He intends to use "mindful questioning" strategies (Figure 9) to guide this exploration.

Figure 9. Task 5: probing communication strategies like "mindful questioning"

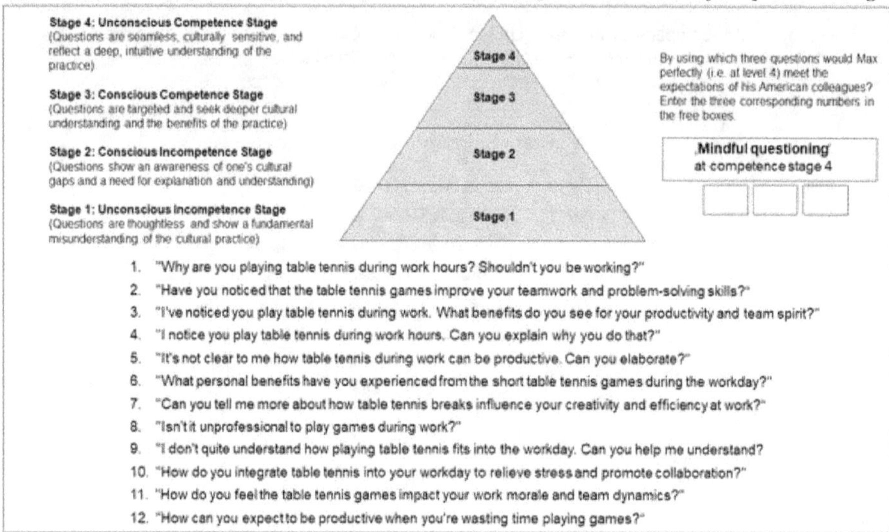

Source: Own depiction in accordance with Ting-Toomey & Chung, 2022

Through mindful questioning, Max eventually uncovers five reasons his colleagues value playing table tennis at work and five examples of their personal experiences. He records these insights on his smartphone, as shown in Figure 10.

Figure 10. Task 6: exploring reasons and effects of table tennis during work time

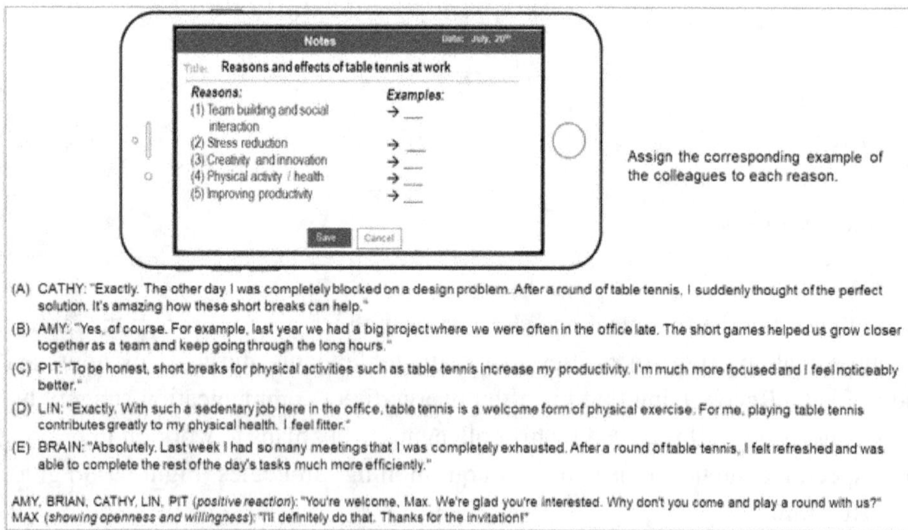

Source: Own depiction

Developing Measures and Prioritizing: A week later, Max meets with Dr. Nice for a second consultation. He shares his experiences with using mindful questioning (Ting-Toomey & Chung, 2022) and discusses the reasons and effects of playing table tennis at work (Hertting et al., 2020), referencing the notes he made on his smartphone. Max is surprised by his colleagues' numerous reasons for playing table tennis during work hours. He must admit that their arguments and examples made him reconsider his stance, ultimately convincing him that table tennis can contribute to productive work. During their discussion, Max and Dr. Nice collaboratively developed a list of strategies Max could use to enhance his adjustment process. Since he cannot implement all strategies at once, Max evaluated and prioritized them based on "feasibility" and "effectiveness," organizing them into a decision matrix (Figure 11).

Figure 11. Task 7: developing means for adjustment and prioritize them using a decision matrix

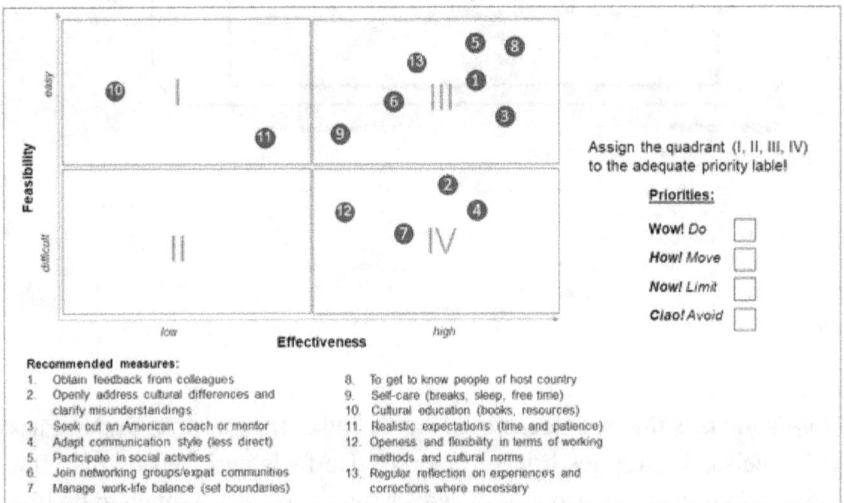

Source: Own depiction in accordance with School of Creative Thinking (2024)

Using the priority matrix, Max decides to get to know his American colleagues better and participate in social events, including table tennis. Dr. Nice supports Max's plan, noting that recent studies reaffirm Oberg's (1960) statement (Genkova & Kruse, 2021; van Bakel et al., 2017, p. 218): "What can you do to get over culture shock as quickly as possible? The answer is to get to know the people of the host country." (Oberg, 1960, p. 182). "It takes two to tango!" (van Bakel et al., 2017).

Examining Selected Measures: The following week, Max notes various activities to which he has been invited and those he has organized for the team. He compiles a list of these activities to prepare for his upcoming meeting with Dr. Nice. During the meeting with Dr. Nice, Max reports on his interactions with colleagues and new acquaintances. Together, they reflect on the types of contacts and social support he has received, and the benefits gained from these various interactions with locals (Figure 12).

Figure 12. Task 8: types of contexts and social support

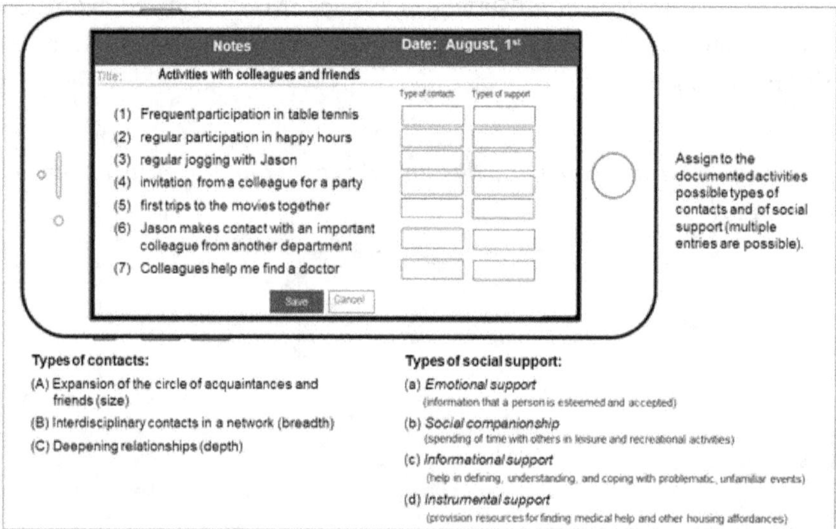

Source: Own depiction

Implementing the New Measures: At the end of this session, Dr. Nice asks Max how he feels. Max replies briefly, “Good!” He feels enriched by his efforts and successes. However, he also acknowledges that there is still much to do to achieve full adjustment (Figure 13).

Figure 13. Task 9: judging the current adjustment stage

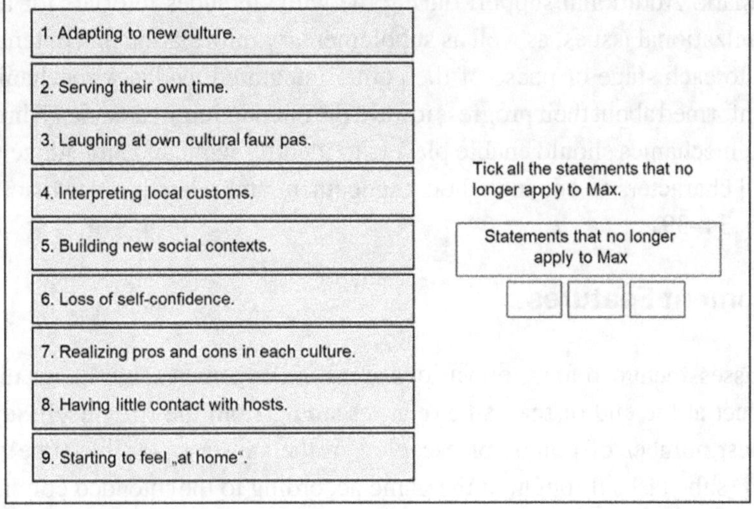

Source: Own depiction

On the way home, Max writes a social media post in which he happily shares his progress, noting how it is gradually helping him to overcome his culture shock (Figure 14).

Figure 14. Task 10: realizing first successes and celebrating first triumphs (positive emotions)

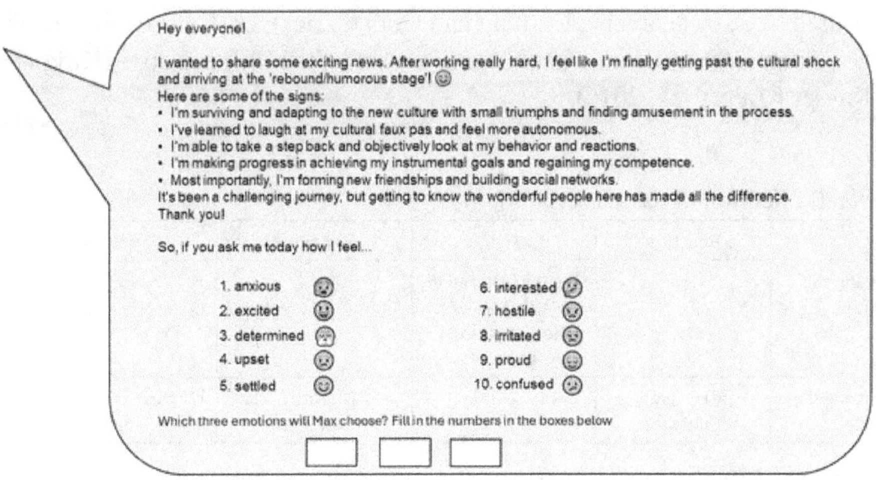

Source: Own depiction using ChatGPT for creating the emojis

The EER can be played individually, aiming to achieve the maximum credits as a benchmark. Additional support during the game includes tutorials for technical and organizational issues, as well as supplementary information on content aspects relevant to each stage or phase of the game. Integrated feedback mechanics keep players informed about their progress toward the intended competencies. Throughout the EER, mechanics should enable players to identify with, and empathize with the story and characters to enhance their engagement and relatedness (Mislevy et al., 2014, pp. 34–39).

Assessment Features

The assessment can focus on various areas of the game (Table 1): (a) the learning product at the end of the game (e.g., escaping from the EER itself, achieving the highest number of points, or escaping in the shortest possible time); (b) the mastered (sub-)tasks throughout the game according to the intended competencies (Figure 2); (c) the problem-solving process and strategies used during the game (e.g., through log files; Bley, 2017; Mislevy et al., 2016, pp. 25–27; Weber et al., 2021a). This is especially relevant for complex game structures that offer non-linear, non-sequential pathways rather than just linear ones (Fotaris & Mastoras, 2022, pp. 15–16; Veldkamp et al., 2020b), where game rules allow for choosing individual pathways or going back and forth; (d) the game, including its delivery and support, is evaluated by participants at the end. Reactions and reflections (e.g., on questions, opinions, impressions, feelings) are gathered during the de-briefing phase, such as through 360-degree surveys; (e) the transfer effects of the degree to which participants apply what they learned during the EER game when back on the job can be measured (e.g., by analyzing learning and work diaries); or (f) the degree to which targeted organizational outcomes occur as a result of the EER initiative (Kirkpatrick & Kayser Kirkpatrick, 2016).

Table 1. Location of assessment

	Reaction	**Learning**	**Behavior**	**Results**
Inside the game		**(b) Mastered (sub-) tasks (c) Learning process**		
Outside the game	(d) Overall assumptions	(a) Learning product	(e) Transfer to the workplace	(f) Targeted organizational outcomes

Source: Own depiction

With regard to (a) the learning product, we suggest counting the achieved points for each task. Each correct response earns one point. The points are distributed according to the different steps of the game structure (Figure 4): 1. Questioning: Task 1 (maximum 3 points), Task 2 (maximum 3 points); 2. Analysis: Task 3 (maximum 1 point), Task 4 (maximum 8 points), Task 5 (maximum 3 points), Task 6 (maximum 5 points); 3. Developing measures and prioritizing: Task 7 (maximum 4 points); 4. Examining selected measures: Task 8 (maximum 14 points); 5. Implementing the new measures: Task 9 (maximum 3 points); Task 10 (maximum 3 points).

In total, 47 points are relevant for exiting the EER respectively escaping the culture shock phase and establishing a benchmark. For a second trial, there will be a penalty of –0.5 points and –1 point for using the pass card. As everyone will ultimately use a pass card, all players will eventually escape. Comparing the individual points achieved with the maximum of 47, players can broadly evaluate their intercultural competence. Players scoring less than 30% of the maximum points are suggested to pursue additional training.

With regard to (b) measuring intercultural competence (in the context of culture shock), we refer to ECgD (Mislevy et al., 2014, pp. 34–39), which proposes triangulating three models for assessment: the student model, the task model, and the evidence model (see Figure 1). The *student model* defines and operationalizes the intended competencies, such as using intercultural communication skills or Hofstede's tool (Figure 7). These competencies are observed through specific player behavior respectively responses in the game and matched with the learning goals integrated into the game's learning features. The *task model* represents the challenges within the game that prompt player behavior reflecting their competencies. Game features such as mechanics (story, rules, and feedback), dynamics (types of actions on different levels), and aesthetics (game design appealing to all senses) guide players toward the intended outcomes. The *evidence model* connects the task and student models by matching observed player behaviors with the expected competencies. Scoring guides and advanced statistical methods (e.g., classical test theory, item response theory, Bayesian networks) are used to evaluate performance (Mislevy et al., 2014, pp. 51–53; 136). This evidence model represents the assessment features.

Additional considerations in the broader assessment context include producing and prototyping the EER (e.g., authoring content, finalizing rubrics, setting up automated scoring, piloting the game for usability and cognitive load, and evaluating its quality regarding validity and reliability) as well as assessment delivery (e.g., player interaction with the game, task selection, presentation formats [multiple-choice, open-ended], and how and where responses are collected). Responses are scored using a transparent guide, synthesized across the game, and matched with the student model to determine if the intended competencies are achieved.

Our suggested EER has a linear sequential structure, so analyzing the pathway (c) is less relevant. The assessment area (d) can be covered by a 360-degree survey focusing on players' impressions, feelings, and experiences. Areas (e) and (f) are important but can only be carried out once the EER has been implemented.

DISCUSSION

In today's rapidly changing world, firms find themselves navigating an increasingly tense intersection of economic demands, emerging technological opportunities, and shifting employee expectations. According to Deloitte's 2025 report (Flynn et al., 2025), businesses are challenged to organize work in ways that are both efficient and future-ready, to attract, develop, and retain global talents over the long term, and to ensure they have the right organizational culture, support, and structures in place to enable sustainable performance.

Within the context of global mobility, a significant transformation is underway. Organizations are moving beyond managing only strategic assignments and are now addressing a broader spectrum of mobility types. These include international remote workers, self-initiated expatriates, digital nomads, and more fluid and diverse forms of global movement (Krogmann & Zinner, 2023; Bozzi, 2023). The expatriate population itself has become increasingly heterogeneous—not limited to single professionals from industrialized nations working in high-income tech sectors with strong passports—but encompassing a variety of professions, family statuses, travel patterns, motivations, and expectations. This shift has rendered global mobility a complex ecosystem where cross-border collaboration and cultural integration influence both corporate culture and talent acquisition strategies (Bozzi, 2023).

Yet, despite the increasing digitalization of work, relatively little attention has been paid to how digital technologies can support the daily lives of expats (Bucher & Deller, 2021), and global mobility management remains insufficiently connected to digital solutions (Hausberg et al., 2019). This paper responds to recent calls for innovative approaches to support global work (Selmer et al., 2022) by proposing the use of an EER as a flexible, digital method for developing intercultural competence—a key factor in facilitating successful cross-cultural adjustment (Canhilal et al., 2022; Wang et al., 2024).

To be educationally effective, EERs must be built with curricular validity (Veldkamp et al., 2020b) and designed according to the principles of evidence-centered game design (ECgD) (Mislevy et al., 2014, 2016; Li et al., 2024; Weber et al., 2021a). This means beginning with an analysis of real intercultural encounters (here: the culture shock phase), identifying typical challenges as well as the competencies required to manage them effectively (Ting-Toomey & Dorjee, 2019; Blömeke et al.,

2015), and translating these into clearly defined learning objectives (*student model*). These objectives are then operationalized into game tasks (mechanics) that are able to evoke the intended learning processes by solving the domain-specific tasks (dynamics) and engage the player by an exciting authentic story, layout and user interior (aesthetics) (*task model*). By analyzing the observed performance with a coherent assessment, inferences can be made from the players' responses and task solutions to the underlying, non-directly observable latent competence constructs (*evidence model*). Hence, the learner may acquire the intended competence by achieving the EER game goals (Veldkamp et al., 2020a).

However, designing such serious games is no simple matter. There is still a lack of concrete guidelines for creating EERs that also include competence-oriented assessment features (Fotaris & Mastoras, 2022; Veldkamp et al., 2020b). To address this, we developed a detailed blueprint for an EER designed to promote intercultural competence (according to Ting-Toomey & Chung, 2022), with a particular focus on helping expats overcome the critical phase of culture shock. Given the diversity of global mobility experiences, culture shock presents itself in many ways. Nevertheless, nearly every expatriate encounters corresponding moments of frustration and disorientation. Successfully navigating this adjustment period is essential not only for personal well-being but also for effective task and job performance (Setti et al., 2022; Wang & Varma, 2019).

Our approach also draws attention to a broader issue: while digital formats are increasingly being adopted in education and training, many fail to align with sound instructional design and learning theory. Developing an EER that integrates learning theory, game design, and assessment strategies effectively is a major challenge. Empirical testing is essential to ensure quality. Small changes—such as altering the storyline, switching media formats, or using other technologies like virtual reality—can influence how learners engage with and respond to the content.

Once the learner model is fully aligned with the task model and embedded in a coherent evidence model, reliable conclusions can be drawn from observed behaviors about the learners' latent intercultural competencies—in the sense of a so-called „evidence-based reasoning" (Brown et al., 2010; Pellegrino et al., 2016).

From an Human Resource and organizational development perspective, the use of EERs opens up several promising possibilities. The game tasks can be expanded to address (a) a broader range of critical encounters also related to other types of global mobility as e.g., digital nomads, (b) additional intercultural competence facets especially collaboration when playing in groups, but (c) also various proficiency levels. Thereby, our "canvas" and its blueprint serve as a useful guideline. Such EERs can also be strategically integrated into broader support and training programs, especially within online or blended-learning environments. Learning experiences can be flexibly combined across synchronous and asynchronous formats, digital and analog methods, and formal, non-formal, and informal learning approaches reflecting various situations, phases, and needs of global staff mobility (Lee, 2020).

Moreover, selected elements of the game—or the game in its entirety—can be adapted to other instructional formats, such as mobile microlearning. This approach targets learners who value mobility and flexibility, enabling them to learn in short bursts using portable devices like smartphones, for instance while waiting for a coffee or commuting (Georgiadou et al., 2024; Grant, 2019).

SUMMARY AND OUTLOOK

In summary, our contribution proposes EERs as an innovative, theory-based solution that not only addresses the growing complexity of global mobility and cross-cultural adjustment but also aligns with current trends in digital learning and strategic human resource development.

Future research could explore the potential of AI to address these challenges, offering support in analyzing the different needs of the employees, the design, refinement, assessment, and delivery of EERs, thereby enhancing their effectiveness and applicability in educational settings.

REFERENCES

Alfaro, L., & Chen, M. X. (2014). The global agglomeration of multinational firms. *Journal of International Economics*, *94*(2), 263–276. DOI: 10.1016/j.jinteco.2014.09.001

Anderson, L. W., & Krathwohl, D. R. (2001). *A taxonomy for learning, teaching, and assessing*. Longman.

Ang, S., & Van Dyne, L. (2015). *Handbook of cultural intelligence: Theory, measurement, and applications*. Routledge. DOI: 10.4324/9781315703855

Ang, S., Van Dyne, L., Koh, C., Ng, K. Y., Templer, K. J., Tay, C., & Chandrasekar, N. A. (2007). Cultural Intelligence: Its Measurement and Effects on Cultural Judgment and Decision Making, Cultural Adaptation and Task Performance. *Management and Organization Review*, *3*(3), 335–371. DOI: 10.1111/j.1740-8784.2007.00082.x

Aprea, C., & Ifenthaler, D. (Eds.). (2021). *Game-based learning across the disciplines*. Springer., DOI: 10.1007/978-3-030-75142-5

Binkley, M., Erstad, O., Herman, J., Raizen, S., Ripley, M., Miller-Ricci, M., & Rumble, M. (2012). Defining twenty-first century skills. In Griffin, P., McGaw, B., & Care, E. (Eds.), *Assessment and teaching of 21st century skills* (pp. 17–66). Springer., DOI: 10.1007/978-94-007-2324-5_2

Black, S. J., Mendenhall, M., & Oddou, G. (1991). Toward a comprehensive model of international adjustment: An integration of multiple theoretical perspectives. *Academy of Management Review*, *16*(2), 291–317. DOI: 10.2307/258863

Bley, S. (2017). Developing and validating a technology-based diagnostic assessment using the evidence-centered game design approach: An example of intrapreneurship competence. *Empirical Research in Vocational Education and Training*, *9*(1), 6. DOI: 10.1186/s40461-017-0049-0

Blömeke, S., Gustafsson, J. E., & Shavelson, R. J. (2015). Beyond dichotomies: Competence viewed as a continuum. *Zeitschrift für Psychologie*, *223*(1), 3–13. DOI: 10.1027/2151-2604/a000194

Bloom, B. S., Engelhart, M. D., Furst, E. J., Hill, W. H., & Krathwohl, D. R. (1956). *Taxonomy of educational objectives: The classification of educational goals. Handbook I: Cognitive domain*. David McKay.

Bonache, J., Brewster, C., & Froese, F. J. (2024). Global mobility: Reasons, trends, and strategies. In Bonache, J., Brewster, C., & Froese, F. J. (Eds.), *Global mobility and the management of expatriates* (pp. 1–28). Cambridge University Press., DOI: 10.1017/9781108679220.001

Börsch-Supan, A. (2003). Labor market effects of population aging. *Labour*, *17*(1), 5–44. DOI: 10.1111/1467-9914.17.specialissue.2

Bozzi, A. (2024). Digital nomadism from the perspective of places and mobilities: A literature review. *European Transport Research Review*, *16*(1), 50. DOI: 10.1186/s12544-024-00663-z

Brown, N. J. S., Furtak, E. M., Timms, M., Nagashima, S. O., & Wilson, M. (2010). The Evidence-Based Reasoning Framework: Assessing Scientific Reasoning. *Educational Assessment*, *15*(3-4), 123–141. DOI: 10.1080/10627197.2010.530551

Bucher, J., & Deller, J. (2021). Digital technologies and expatriation - a systematic literature review. *Proceedings - Academy of Management*, *21*(1), 11–27. DOI: 10.5465/AMBPP.2021.11027abstract

Bucher, J., Lazarova, M., & Deller, J. (2024). Digital technology and global mobility: Narrative review and directions for future research. *International Business Review*, *102294*. Advance online publication. DOI: 10.1016/j.ibusrev.2024.102294

Canhilal, S. K., Canboy, B., & Bakici, T. (2022). Social support for expatriates through virtual platforms: Exploring the role of online and offline participation. *International Journal of Human Resource Management*, *33*(5), 1005–1036. DOI: 10.1080/09585192.2020.1752283

Cascio, J. (2020, April 29). *Facing the age of chaos*. Medium. https://medium.com/@cascio/facing-the-age-of-chaos-b00687b1f51d

Chao, M. M., Takeuchi, R., & Farh, J. L. (2017). Enhancing cultural intelligence: The roles of implicit culture beliefs and adjustment. *Personnel Psychology*, *70*(1), 257–292. DOI: 10.1111/peps.12142

Clarke, S. J., Peel, D. J., Arnab, S., Morini, L., Keegan, H., & Wood, O. (2017). EscapED: A framework for creating educational escape rooms and interactive games to for higher/further education. *International Journal of Serious Games*, *4*(3), 73–86. DOI: 10.17083/ijsg.v4i3.180

DeBruijn, E., & Baartman, L. K. J. (2011). Integrating knowledge, skills and attitudes: Conceptualising learning processes towards vocational competence. *Educational Research Review*, *6*(2), 125–134. DOI: 10.1016/j.edurev.2011.03.001

Dochy, F., Engeström, Y., Sannino, A., & van Meeuwen, N. (2022). Inter-organisational expansive learning at work. In Dochy, F., Gijbels, D., Segers, M., & van den Bossche, P. (Eds.), *Theories of workplace learning in changing times* (2nd ed., pp. 209–231). Routledge., DOI: 10.4324/9781003187790-12

Enatto, H. E. (2024). Cross-Cultural Training and the Performance of American Expatriates in Nigeria. *European Journal of Business and Innovation Research, 12*(1), 29–41. DOI: 10.37745/ejbir.2013/vol12n12941

Escobar Borruel, I. (2022). Repatriate social capital: An untapped resource at the individual and organizational levels. In Andresen, M., Anger, S., Al Ariss, A., Barzantny, C., Brücker, H., Dickmann, M., Mäkelä, L., Muhr, S. L., Saalfeld, T., Suutari, V., & Zølner, M. (Eds.), *Wanderlust to wonderland? Exploring key issues in expatriate careers: Individual, organizational, and societal insights* (pp. 39–57). Bamberg University Press. DOI: 10.20378/irb-55766

Evseeva, S., Evseeva, O., & Rawat, P. (2022). Employee development and digitalization in BANI world. In Rodionov, D., Kudryavtseva, T., Skhvediani, A., & Berawi, M. A. (Eds.), *Innovations in digital economy. SPBPU IDE 2021* (pp. 253–264). Springer., DOI: 10.1007/978-3-031-14985-6_18

Flynn, J., Commisso, C., Mallon, D., Van Durme, Y., Harrington, S., & Lahiri, G. (2025). *Deloitte's 2025 Human Capital Trends - Turning tensions into triumphs: Helping leaders transform uncertainty into opportunity*. Deloitte. Online: 02.05.2025: https://www2.deloitte.com/content/dam/insights/articles/glob187692_global-human-capital-trends/DI_2025-Global-Human-Capital-Trends.pdf

Fotaris, P., & Mastoras, T. (2022). Room2Educ8: A framework for creating educational escape rooms based on design thinking principles. *Education Sciences, 12*(11), 768. DOI: 10.3390/educsci12110768

Frick, N. R. J., & Marx, J. (2021). Integrating Digital Nomads in Corporate Structures: Managerial Contemplations. *Proceedings of the 54th Hawaii International Conference on System Sciences.* DOI:DOI: 10.24251/HICSS.2021.260

Genkova, P. (2021). Interkulturelle Trainings: eine kritische Betrachtung. [Intercultural training: A critical view] In Ringeisen, T., Genkova, P., & Leong, F. T. L. (Eds.), *Handbuch Stress und Kultur* [Handbook on stress and culture]. (pp. 585–602). Springer Fachmedien., DOI: 10.1007/978-3-658-27789-5_47

Genkova, P., & Kruse, L. (2020). Do stays abroad increase intercultural and general competences, affecting employability? *Leadership, Education, Personality. An Interdisciplinary Journal, 2*(2), 81–89. DOI: 10.1365/s42681-020-00014-1

Genkova, P., & Kruse, L. (2021). Auslandsaufenthalt als Kompetenzschule? Eine empirische Untersuchung der Auswirkungen von Auslandsaufenthalten auf die berufsbezogenen Kompetenzbereiche [Can we consider stays abroad as competence schools? The relationship of stays abroad with job related competences]. *Gruppe. Interaktion. Organisation.* [GIO]. *Zeitschrift für Angewandte Organisationspsychologie*, *52*(1), 135–146. DOI: 10.1007/s11612-021-00553-1

Georgiadou, A., Amari, A., Swalhi, A., & Hofaidhllaoui, M. (2024). How does perceived organizational support improve expatriates' outcomes during global crises? The mediating role of the ethical organizational climate in global organizations. *Journal of International Management*, *30*(3), 101131. DOI: 10.1016/j.intman.2024.101131

Grant, M. M. (2019). Difficulties in defining mobile learning: Analysis, design characteristics, and implications. *Educational Technology Research and Development*, *67*(2), 361–388. DOI: 10.1007/s11423-018-09641-4

Gronlund, N. E. (2000). *How to write and use instructional objectives*. Prentice-Hall Inc./Pearson Education.

Hartig, J., Klieme, E., & Leutner, D. (Eds.). (2008). *Assessment of competencies in educational context*. Hogrefe & Huber.

Hausberg, J. P., Liere-Netheler, K., Packmohr, S., Pakura, S., & Vogelsang, K. (2019). Research streams on digital transformation from a holistic business perspective: A systematic literature review and citation network analysis. *Journal of Business Economics*, *89*(2), 931–963. DOI: 10.1007/s11573-019-00956-z

Hensellek, S., & Puchala, N. (2021). The emergence of the digital nomad: A review and analysis of the opportunities and risks of digital nomadism. In M. Orel, O. Dvoulety, & V. Ratten (Eds.), *The Flexible Workplace* (pp. 195–214). Springer. 11DOI: 10.1007/978-3-030-62167-4_11

Hertting, K., Holmquist, M., & Parker, J. (2020). Ping pong for health: The meaning of space in a sport based health intervention at the workplace. *International Journal of Qualitative Studies on Health and Well-being*, *15*(sup1), 1689602. DOI: 10.1080/17482631.2019.1689602 PMID: 33103634

Hofstede, G., Hofstede, G. J., & Minkov, M. (2010). *Cultures and organizations: Software of the mind: Intercultural cooperation and its importance for survival* (3rd ed.). McGraw Hill.

Ifenthaler, D., & Kim, Y. J. (Eds.). (2019). *Game-based assessment revisited*. Springer., DOI: 10.1007/978-3-030-15569-8

Jenkin, I., & Fairfurst, N. (2019). Escape room to operating room: A potential training modality? *Medical Teacher*, *42*(5), 596. DOI: 10.1080/0142159X.2019.1657821 PMID: 31448990

Kapp, K. M. (2012). *The gamification of learning and instruction: Game-based methods and strategies for training and education*. Pfeiffer.

Kapp, K. M., Blair, L., & Mesch, R. (2014). *The gamification of learning and instruction fieldbook: Ideas into practice*. Wiley.

Kirkpatrick, J. D., & Kayser Kirkpatrick, W. (2016). *Kirkpatrick's four levels of training evaluation*. Association for Talent Development.

Kirshenblatt-Gimblett, B. (1978). Culture shock and narrative creativity. In Dorson, R. (Ed.), *Folklore in the modern world* (pp. 109–122). De Gruyter Mouton., DOI: 10.1515/9783110803099.109

Kirste, L., & Holtbrügge, D. (2019). Experiential Learning in the Digital Context: An Experimental Study of Online Cultural Intelligence Training. *Journal of Teaching in International Business*, *30*(2), 147–174. DOI: 10.1080/08975930.2019.1663775

Knocke, J., & Schuster, T. (2017). Repatriation of international assignees: Where are we and where do we go from here? A systematic literature review. *Journal of Global Mobility*, *5*(3), 275–303. DOI: 10.1108/JGM-01-2017-0001

Kour, S., & Jyorti, J. (2022). Cross-cultural training and adjustment through the lens of cultural intelligence and type of expatriates. *Employee Relations*, *44*(1), 1–36. DOI: 10.1108/ER-07-2020-0355

Kraimer, M., Bolino, M., & Mead, B. (2016). Themes in expatriate and repatriate research over four decades: What do we know and what do we still need to learn? *Annual Review of Organizational Psychology and Organizational Behavior*, *3*(1), 83–109. DOI: 10.1146/annurev-orgpsych-041015-062437

Krogmann, P., & Zinner, D. (Hosts). (2023). Evolution from HR Tech to People Tech [Audio podcast episode]. In *Global People Mobility Insights Podcast*. Podigee. https://people-mobility.org/the-evolution-from-hr-tech-to-people-tech/

Kutz, A. (2018). *Double-Bind-Kommunikation als Burnout-Ursache: Ein Theorie-Vorschlag zu Auswirkungen toxischer Kommunikation in Organisationen* [Double bind communication as a cause of burnout: A theory proposal on the effects of toxic communication in organizations]. 2nd ed.). Springer., DOI: 10.1007/978-3-658-21917-8

Larson, K. (2020). Serious games and gamification in the corporate training environment: A literature review. *TechTrends*, *64*(1), 319–328. DOI: 10.1007/s11528-019-00446-7

Lee, J. (2010). Design of blended training for transfer into the workplace. *British Journal of Educational Technology*, *41*(2), 181–198. DOI: 10.1111/j.1467-8535.2008.00909.x

Lessle, A., Haslberger, A., & Brewster, C. (2024). Expatriate adjustment. In Bonache, J., Brewster, C., & Froese, F. J. (Eds.), *Global mobility and the management of expatriates* (pp. 57–79). Cambridge University Press., DOI: 10.1017/9781108679220.003

Leutner, D., Fleischer, J., Grünkorn, J., & Klieme, E. (2017). *Competence assessment in education: Research, models and instruments (Methodology of educational measurement and assessment)*. Springer., DOI: 10.1007/978-3-319-50030-0

Li, J., Bai, J., Zhu, S., & Yang, H. H. (2024). Game-based assessment of students' digital literacy using evidence-centered game design. *Electronics (Basel)*, *13*(2), 285. DOI: 10.3390/electronics13020385

Lindemann, V., Mauer, R., Schulte, B., & Zimmermann, R. (2013). *Personaleinsatz im Ausland: Personalmanagement, Arbeitsrecht, Sozialversicherungsrecht, Steuerrecht* (2nd ed.). C.H. Beck. [Personnel assignment abroad: Personnel management, labor law, social security law, tax law. (2nd ed.)]

López-Pernas, S., Gordillo, A., Barra, E., & Quemada, J. (2019). Examining the use of an educational escape room for teaching programming in a higher education setting. *IEEE Access : Practical Innovations, Open Solutions*, *7*, 31723–31737. DOI: 10.1109/ACCESS.2019.2902976

Makri, A., Vlachopoulos, D., & Martina, R. A. (2021). Digital escape rooms as innovative pedagogical tools in education: A systematic literature review. *Sustainability (Basel)*, *13*(8), 45–87. DOI: 10.3390/su13084587

Mary, R. (2024). An essential approach to mitigating expatriate challenges: Examining effective selection and training strategies for expatriates. *International Journal of Advanced Research in Commerce. Management and Social Science*, *7*(3), 141–148.

Marzano, R. J., & Kendall, J. S. (2007). *The new taxonomy of educational objectives* (2nd ed.). Corwin Press.

Menon, D., & Romero, M. (2020). Game mechanics supporting a learning and playful experience in educational escape games. In Tomei, L., & Farber, M. (Eds.), *Global perspectives on gameful and playful teaching and learning* (pp. 143–162). IGI Global., DOI: 10.4018/978-1-7998-2015-4.ch007

Mislevy, R., Oranje, A., Bauer, M. I., von Davier, A., Hao, J., Corrigan, S., Hoffman, E., DiCerbo, K., & John, M. (2014). *Psychometric considerations in game-based assessment*. GlassLab.

Mislevy, R. J., Corrigan, S., Oranje, A., DiCerbo, K., Bauer, M. I., von Davier, A., & John, M. (2016). Psychometrics and game-based assessment. In Drasgow, F. (Ed.), *Technology and testing: Improving educational and psychological measurement* (pp. 23–48). Routledge., DOI: 10.4324/9781315871493-2

Morrell, B., & Eukel, H. N. (2021). Shocking escape: A cardiac escape room for undergraduate nursing students. *Simulation & Gaming*, *52*(1), 72–78. DOI: 10.1177/1046878120958734

Mulder, M. (Ed.). (2017). *Competence-based Vocational and Professional Education. Bridging the Worlds of Work and Education*. Springer. DOI: 10.1007/978-3-319-41713-4

Nederveen Pieterse, A., van Knippenberg, D., & van Dierendonck, D. (2013). Cultural diversity and team performance: The role of team member goal orientation. *Academy of Management Journal*, *56*(3), 782–804. DOI: 10.5465/amj.2010.0992

Oberg, K. (1960). Culture shock and the problems of adjustment to new cultural environments. *Practical Anthropology*, *7*(4), 177–182. DOI: 10.1177/009182966000700405

Peleg, R., Yayon, M., Katchevich, D., Moria-Shipony, M., & Blonder, R. (2019). A lab-based chemical escape room: Educational, mobile, and fun! *Journal of Chemical Education*, *96*(5), 955–960. DOI: 10.1021/acs.jchemed.8b00406

Pellegrino, J. W., DiBello, L. V., & Goldman, S. R. (2016). A framework for conceptualizing and evaluating the validity of instructionally relevant assessments. *Educational Psychologist*, *51*(1), 59–81. DOI: 10.1080/00461520.2016.1145550

Schell, J. (2020). *The art of game design: A book of lenses* (3rd ed.). CRC Press.

School of Creative Thinking. (2024). *COCD-Box*. https://schoolofcreativethinking.nl/en/cocd-box/

Selmer, J., Dickmann, M., Froese, F. J., Lauring, J., Reiche, B. S., & Shaffer, M. (2022). The potential of virtual global mobility: Implications for practice and future research. *Journal of Global Mobility*, *10*(1), 1–13. DOI: 10.1108/JGM-07-2021-0074

Setti, I., Sommorigo, V., & Argentero, P. (2022). Enhancing expatriates' assignments success: The relationship between cultural intelligence, cross-cultural adaptation and performance. *Current Psychology (New Brunswick, N.J.)*, *41*(7), 42914311. DOI: 10.1007/s12144-020-00931-w

Shavelson, R. J. (2012). Assessing business planning competence using the Collegiate Learning Assessment as a prototype. *Empirical Research in Vocational Education and Training*, *4*(1), 77–90. DOI: 10.1007/BF03546509

Sternberg, R. J., & Detterman, D. K. (Eds.). (1986). *What is intelligence? Contemporary viewpoints on its nature and definition*. Praeger.

Stoermer, S., Froese, F. J., & Peltokorpi, V. (2024). Self-initiated expatriates. In Bonache, J., Brewster, C., & Froese, F. J. (Eds.), *Global mobility and the management of expatriates* (pp. 181–203). Cambridge University Press., DOI: 10.1017/9781108679220.008

Tharenou, P. (2015). Researching expatriate types: The quest for rigorous methodological approaches. *Human Resource Management Journal*, *25*(2), 149–165. DOI: 10.1111/1748-8583.12070

The Culture Factor Group. (2024). *Country comparison tool*. Retrieved May 10, 2025, from https://www.hofstede-insights.com/country-comparison-tool?countries=germany%2Cunited+states

Thomas, A. (2022). *Praxisbuch Interkulturelle Handlungskompetenz* [Practical guide to intercultural competence]. Springer., DOI: 10.1007/978-3-662-63671-8

Ting-Toomey, S., & Chung, L. C. (2022). *Understanding intercultural communication* (3rd ed.). Oxford University Press.

Ting-Toomey, S., & Dorjee, T. (2019). *Communicating across cultures* (2nd ed.).

Urgun, D., Seidel, J., Vangeli, E., Borges, M., & de Oliveira, R. F. (2025). Exploring the impact of cross-cultural training on cultural competence and cultural intelligence: A narrative systematic literature review. *Frontiers in Psychology*, *16*, 1511788. DOI: 10.3389/fpsyg.2025.1511788 PMID: 40260004

van Bakel, M. (2019). It takes two to tango: A review of the empirical research on expatriate-local interactions. *International Journal of Human Resource Management*, *30*(21), 2993–3025. DOI: 10.1080/09585192.2018.1449763

van Bakel, M., van Oudenhoven, J. P., & Gerritsen, M. (2017). Expatriate contact with a local host: An intervention to increase social support. *Human Resource Development International*, *20*(3), 215–235. DOI: 10.1080/13678868.2016.1248720

van Merrienboer, J. J. G., & Kirschner, P. A. (2018). *Ten steps to complex learning* (3rd ed.). Routledge., DOI: 10.1007/s11528-018-0254-0 van Rosmalen, P., & Westera, W. (2014). Introducing serious games with Wikis: Empowering the teacher with simple technologies. *Interactive Learning Environments, 22*(5), 564–577. DOI: 10.1080/10494820.2012.707128

Veldkamp, A., Daemen, J., Teekens, S., Koelewijn, S., Knippels, M.-C. P. J., & Joolingen, W. R. (2020a). Escape boxes: Bringing escape room experience into the classroom. *British Journal of Educational Technology, 51*(4), 1220–1239. DOI: 10.1111/bjet.12935

Veldkamp, A., van de Grint, L., Knippels, M.-C. P., & van Joolingen, W. R. (2020b). Escape education: A systematic review on escape rooms in education. *Educational Research Review, 15*(31), 1–18. DOI: 10.1016/j.edurev.2020.100364

Verghese, T. (2013). *The invisible elephant: Exploring cultural awareness* (2nd ed.). Synergistic Press.

Vromans, P., van Engen, M., & Mol, S. T. (2013). Presumed cultural similarity paradox: Expatriate adjustment and performance across the border or over the globe. *Journal of Global Mobility, 1*(2), 219–238. DOI: 10.1108/JGM-02-2013-0011

Wang, C. H., & Varma, A. (2019). Cultural distance and expatriate failure rates: The moderating role of expatriate management practices. *International Journal of Human Resource Management, 30*(15), 2211–2230. DOI: 10.1080/09585192.2017.1315443

Wang, Y., Lockett, M., & Zhou, A. J. (2024). Digitalization and expatriate cross-cultural adjustment: The role of mobile apps. *Journal of Global Mobility: The Home of Expatriate Management Research, 10*. Advance online publication. DOI: 10.1108/JGM-04-2024-0041

Ward, C., Bochner, S., & Furnham, A. (2020). *Psychology Culture Shock*. Routledge., DOI: 10.4324/9781003070696

Waxin, M.-F., & Brewster, C. (2024). The recruitment, selection, and preparation of expatriates. In Bonache, J., Brewster, C., & Froese, F. J. (Eds.), *Global Mobility and the Management of Expatriates* (pp. 31–56). Cambridge University Press., DOI: 10.1017/9781108679220.002

Weber, S., & Achtenhagen, F. (2017). Competence domains and vocational-professional education in Germany. In Mulder, M. (Ed.), *Competence-based vocational and professional education* (pp. 337–359). Springer., DOI: 10.1007/978-3-319-41713-4_16

Weber, S., Draxler, C., Achtenhagen, F., Bley, S., Wiethe-Körprich, M., Kreuzer, C., & Gürer, C. (2021b). Measuring apprentices' intrapreneurship competence in vocational education and training (VET): An interdisciplinary model-based assessment. In E. Kuusisto, M. Ubani, P. Nokelainen & A. Toom (Eds.), *Good teachers for tomorrow's schools* (pp. 257–279). Brill, Sense. DOI: 10.1163/9789004465008_014

Weber, S., Off, M., Hackenberg, T., Schumann, M., & Achtenhagen, F. (2021a). Serious games as assessment tool: Visualizing sustainable creative competence in the field of retail. In Aprea, C., & Ifenthaler, D. (Eds.), *Game-based learning across the disciplines* (pp. 109–140). Springer., DOI: 10.1007/978-3-030-75142-5_6

Wittek, B. H. (2021). Where are we today in understanding the role of the firm as a driver of international flows of highly skilled migrants? Reviewing the status of the literature on direct and indirect host country meso-level influences. *International Journal of Human Resource Management*, *32*(20), 4253–4286. DOI: 10.1080/09585192.2019.1651378

Zaharna, R. S. (1989). Self-shock: The double-binding challenge of identity. *International Journal of Intercultural Relations*, *13*(1), 501–525. DOI: 10.1016/0147-1767(89)90026-6

Zimmermann, J., Greischel, H., Jonkmann, K., & Neyer, F. J. (2021). Growth all along the road? Personality development and international contacts of (in) experienced sojourners. *European Journal of Personality*, *35*(4), 581–597. DOI: 10.1177/0890207020988439

ADDITIONAL READING LIST

Bonache, J., Brewster, C., & Froese, F. J. (Eds.). (2024). *Global mobility and the management of expatriates*. Cambridge University Press.

Bucher, J., Lazarova, M., & Deller, J. (2025). Digital technology and global mobility: Narrative review and directions for future research. *International Business Review*, *102294*(1), 102294. Advance online publication. DOI: 10.1016/j.ibusrev.2024.102294

Fotaris, P., & Mastoras, T. (2022). Room2Educ8: A framework for creating educational escape rooms based on design thinking principles. *Education Sciences*, *12*(11), 768. DOI: 10.3390/educsci12110768

Ting-Toomey, S., & Chung, L. C. (2022). *Understanding intercultural communication* (3rd ed.). Oxford University Press.

Weber, S., Off, M., Hackenberg, T., Schumann, M., & Achtenhagen, F. (2021a). Serious games as assessment tool: Visualizing sustainable creative competence in the field of retail. In Aprea, C., & Ifenthaler, D. (Eds.), *Game-based learning across the disciplines* (pp. 109–140). Springer., DOI: 10.1007/978-3-030-75142-5_6

KEY TERMS AND DEFINITIONS

BANI: The BANI framework describes the complex, unstable nature of today's world. Introduced by Cascio (2020), it reflects a shift from the earlier VUCA model and emphasizes the fragility of systems (brittle), widespread unease (anxious), unpredictable cause-effect relationships (nonlinear), and the difficulty in making sense of events (incomprehensible). In such a climate, organizations must rethink and adapt their approaches to global talent mobility and workforce management.

Cultural-oriented training: Education and training programs to develop intercultural competence, support the adjustment process to the aligned culture and promote task or job performance. It includes both "hard facts" (e.g., bureaucratic assistance, housing, legal aid) and "soft facts" such as cultural training, coaching, and mentoring. A belief that one's own culture is superior to other cultures.

Culture shock: Culture shock refers to a profound sense of disorientation and alienation of individuals—a feeling of not being "at home," of not belonging, and of being an outsider. The familiar cues and behavioral scripts they once relied on suddenly no longer function in the new cultural context. The belief that family is central to well-being and that family members and family issues take precedence over other aspects of life.

Digital Nomads: Digital nomads are professionals who use digital technologies to work remotely from various global locations. Unlike traditional expatriates, they are not assigned by employers but choose a mobile lifestyle for reasons such as autonomy, lower living costs, or personal growth. The COVID-19 pandemic accelerated this trend, expanding the demographic to include not only freelancers but also salaried employees, families, and individuals from diverse backgrounds.

Educational Escape Room (EER): An Educational Escape Room (EER) is an instructional method requiring learners to engage in individual or collaborative playful activities specifically designed to promote domain knowledge acquisition, skill development, or behavioral change. Participants work alone or together to achieve a defined goal—such as escaping a physical or virtual room, solving a mystery, or preventing a simulated disaster—by completing puzzles tied to clear learning objectives within a set time limit.

Evidence-centered game design (ECgD): ECgD is a game-based design and assessment that simultaneously is addressing three different perspectives within the same artifact, namely learning features, game features, and assessment features.

Expats: Expats are individuals who temporarily relocate abroad for work, either assigned by their employers or self-initiated. Motivations include career growth, personal development, and cultural interest. In today's flexible global work landscape, mobility includes also digital nomads.

Integrative Identity Negotiation Theory: A communication theory developed by Ting-Toomey that emphasizes the co-creation of shared meanings in intercultural interactions. It posits that individuals—such as expatriates—must continually negotiate three dimensions of meaning: content (factual information), relational (social expectations and nonverbal cues), and identity (personal identity needs). Successful negotiation relies on intercultural communication competence, which includes awareness, knowledge, skills, and responsive attitudes. The theory highlights that identity negotiation occurs across various life domains (e.g., work, social, personal) and is shaped by the broader sociocultural and historical context.

APPENDIX 1

Table 2. Solutions to the ten tasks

Tasks	Correct answers	Maximum amount of points
1	3 answers out of 5 correct answers: 1, 4, 7, 8, 10	3
2	1, 5, 6	3
3	Indulgence	1
4	(a) a3, a2, a1, a4; (b) b2, b3, b4, b1	8
5	3, 7, 10	3
6	Amy (1-B), Brain (2-E), Cathy (3-A), Lin (4-D), Pit (5-C)	5
7	Do: III, Move: IV, Limit: I, Avoid: II	4
8	Type of contacts: 1 (C,b), 2 (A, C, a, b, c), 3 (C, b), 4 (A, B, a, b), 5 (C, a, b), 6 (A, B, a), 7 (-, d)	14
9	2, 6, 8	3
10	3 answers out of 5 correct answers: 2, 3, 5, 6, 9	3
	Total:	**47**

Source: Own depiction

Chapter 11
Digital Accessibility in the Professional Workplace

Laura Hopkins
The University of Texas at Arlington, USA

ABSTRACT

Navigating the global workforce includes understanding digital accessibility and how it impacts people. The chapter begins by defining digital accessibility and its relevance in the modern workplace, dispelling some myths about those with disabilities. The chapter dives into the legal requirements of electronic accessibility and provides step-by-step instructions on electronic accessibility. The chapter ends with a review of common challenges, key take aways and a list of on-line resources. Accessibility must become habit so that it is part of what you do every day in everything that you do.

INTRODUCTION

Over 70 million people - that is how many adults in the United States have reported having a disability (CDC 2024a). This number doesn't include those that chose not to report, those that have "slowed down" due to age, or many that have temporary disabilities such as broken bones, pregnancy, medical treatments with serious side effects, or disabilities that do not often require medical attention such as having colorblindness.

Whether an employee is responsible for communicating internally within an organization or externally to the public or to customers, understanding how to provide barrier-free communications is crucial. In other words, be sure that employees are not discriminating against those with disabilities. Failure to be accessible can impact

DOI: 10.4018/979-8-3373-5322-7.ch011

the growth/retention of customers and, for those legally required to be accessible, can expose the business or agency to legal action.

What is Digital Accessibility?

Let's break this down into what is "digital" and what is "accessibility".

Digital Resources: A resource is digital if it is shared electronically. Digital resources require the use of a computer, smart phone, tablet or other equipment with a graphic user interface. Different states have different acronyms for digital resources. The Texas Administrative Code uses the acronym EIR – Electronic and Information Resources while the federal government uses the acronym ICT – Information and Communication Technology. For this textbook, we will use the phrase "digital resources" and it is synonymous with EIR and ICT.

Common examples of digital resources in the workplace include:

- Websites
- Emails (including Outlook)
- PDFs
- PowerPoint, Word or Excel files
- Social Media Postings
- On-line Advertising, including job postings
- On-line Platforms; and
- Software, including Software as a Service.

Accessibility: Equal access to information, without barriers.

It really is just that simple. When an email is sent, provide all the information in that email to everyone. Some items to consider are:

- If someone has colorblindness, is there sufficient color contrast so they can also see all the information?
- If someone is blind, is the content formatted so that a screen reader will provide all the same information?
- If someone is deaf, will they see all the same information?
- If someone doesn't use a mouse, can they navigate the content?

The good news is that being accessible isn't difficult. But good habits must be developed and always keep accessibility a priority.

This chapter will help the reader start thinking about accessibility in the workplace but one should continue to learn more about digital accessibility. Refer to the Resources section at the end of this chapter for many on-line resources to grow knowledge, skills, and habits.

DISPEL THE MYTH

28.7% adults in the United States and an estimated 1.3 billion people worldwide (1 in 6) experience a significant disability (CDC 2024b, WHO 2023). If this isn't a high enough number to draw attention, consider this: almost everyone is expected to experience at least a temporary disability at some point in their lives. Examples of temporary disabilities:

- An ear infection that impacts one's hearing,
- An eye infection that impacts one's vision,
- Illness that impacts sleep and cognitive skills,
- Brain injury such as a concussion that impacts cognitive skills,
- Faltering vision or hearing due to age, or
- An injury that impedes use of a computer mouse such as a broken finger.

As this publication specifically targets the workplace, be cautious to not fall into one of these falsehoods:

a) No one on my team has a disability.

When someone suggests that they do not have any team members with disabilities, remember these two important details:

- You do not have any team members with disabilities **that you know of.**
  - Do not ever ask an employee/co-worker if they have a disability. This could be a violation of the ADA and should be handled by your business or agency ADA Coordinator. Most workers choose to not disclose disabilities, and the law does not require them to do so. The law does however require businesses/agencies to be accessible.
- You do not have any team members with a disability **today**.
  - Certainly, it is reasonable to anticipate with such a large percentage of the population having disabilities that your team could have someone join in the future that has a disability. To suggest otherwise would be to admit to discrimination.

b) No one with a disability could understand this content.

- o Having a disability does not usually correlate to someone's level of intelligence. Do not let your own bias towards those with disabilities lull you into believing that you know what someone else can or cannot understand.

c) This graphic is too hard to explain with alt text.

- o If your graphic is too hard to explain with alt text, there are other options:
  - ■ Use body text in your document to explain the information in the graph and the key takeaways from the image.
  - ■ If you cannot convey the meaning or purpose of the graph, that usually means that the graph is either too complicated (divide it into multiple graphs) or it is poorly designed.
  - ■ Particularly if you are using the graph as a visual aid during a presentation with only a limited amount of viewing time, you must be able to concisely explain the graph.
  - ■ Writing alt text is an excellent tool in evaluating graphs provided by a vendor. If you cannot look at the graph and explain it, then the vendor needs to redesign the graph. Pay attention to the details. Does the graph have an X and a Y axis? You may be surprised how often marketing companies use a "graph" that isn't a graph but only decoration.

d) There isn't enough time to make my email (webpage, PDF, PowerPoint) accessible.

- o If you don't have time to make it accessible, then you don't have time to make it. Deciding to exclude a quarter of the population because you don't have time is not only a failure to the public, but it exposes your business or agency to legal exposure. If you are limited on time, make the presentation shorter but make it accessible.
- o Cultivating good accessibility habits will benefit you when time is of the essence. If you are already short on time, pushing out an inaccessible presentation because you have time to remediate it later doesn't sound reasonable. Remember that it will always take more time (time is money) to remediate a website/file than to make it accessible in the first place.
- o When you assign tasks to a web developer, a graphic designer or an author, ensure that they all understand that accessibility is everyone's responsibility – unless you are also going to hire a remediation professional that will be required to rebuild the content from scratch, extending both the budget and the timeline.

In addition to disabilities, often environmental settings can cause barriers if resources are not accessible:

- A student needs to watch a video as part of a class assignment while in the library where computer speakers are not allowed to be broadcasted. Unfortunately, the student failed to bring their headphones. If the video does not have captions, they cannot complete the assignment.
- An employee needs to finish continuing education to renew their certification. They are trying to complete the required courses while staying up with an ill relative. Unfortunately, their headphones are broken. If the videos do not have captions, they are unable to complete their renewal on time.
- An employee's mouse stops working but they are still on a work deadline to complete a task. If the interface is not operable by a keyboard, they will not complete the task on time.

Being accessible benefits everyone, not only those with disabilities. In fact, having an accessible website is directly related to succeeding with Search Engine Optimization (SEO). If the webpage is formatted with proper heading structure and all elements are properly tagged, the SEO will be improved. If the webpage is not accessible, does not have good tag structure, the SEO will be poor.

We must all be on the lookout for electronic communications that were designed solely because "they look great"! They look great, but are they accessible? If they aren't accessible, it doesn't matter how great they look. Making the conscious decision to discriminate against over a quarter of the population is never the right answer morally and is likely to open the business up to legal action.

ACCESSIBILITY IS A LEGAL REQUIREMENT

Not only is being accessible the right thing to do, ensuring electronic communications are barrier-free is a requirement in the United States under the Americans with Disabilities Act (ADA) for the following sectors (DOJ, n.d.):

- Federal Agencies, and all those receiving federal funds
- State Agencies, including schools
- Restaurants
- Hotels/Motels
- Shops
- Movie Theaters
- Private Schools (including housing)

- Doctors' Offices and Private Hospitals
- Day Care Centers
- Gyms
- Organizations Offering Courses or Examinations related to Applications, Licensing, Certifications, or Credentialing for Professional or Trade Purposes
- Privately Operated Transit and
- Commercial Facilities

NOTE: This chapter is not providing legal advice.

Although not all-encompassing, these are the main U.S. federal laws that specify the requirement to be accessible:

§ **Federal Law 29 U.S.C.,** Title 29, Chapter 16, Subchapter V, Sec. 794d - Electronic and Information Technology
§ **Rehabilitation Act of 1973**, Section 503, Section 504 and Section 508
§ **Americans with Disabilities Act** of 1990, as amended
§ Justice Department **Rule Nondiscrimination on the Basis of Disability**; Accessibility of Web Information and Services of State and Local Government Entities, published 4/24/24; effective date 6/24/24.

While not all states in the U.S. have the same requirements as the federal laws, if federal funds are received or if the business is listed by the ADA as a place requiring public accommodations, compliance to the federal standards is required.

These requirements are also important to understand a company provides services to any federal or state agencies. Government contracts will include language requiring the deliverables to comply with all state/federal laws. This means that the contracts will demand electronic communications to be accessible to those with disabilities – in everything from bid submissions to marketing services, to IT development services.

Many workplaces today are international work environments. Governments around the world have similar laws to the U.S. regarding digital accessibility. While businesses are required to complete their own research, the Web Accessibility Laws and Policies webpage from W3C provides an overview table by country and it may be a good place to start investigating requirements in other countries (W3C, 2023a).

The Legal Standard for Digital Accessibility

The U.S. government, and many governments around the world, have specified that digital accessibility will be measured by compliance to the Web Content Accessibility Guidelines[a] (WCAG).

Don't let the name of the standards cause confusion. While the word "web" is included in the name of the standard, the WCAG standards are also used to define accessibility in other electronic communications such as documents, emails and social media postings. There is a valid argument that PDFs should be measured against PDF/UA[a] standards instead of WCAG but this chapter addresses legal compliance to the U.S. standards (Drümmer et al., 2012). Today, Section 508 of the Rehabilitation Act (USAB, 2024), Chapter E205.4, and the ADA requires compliance to the WCAG standard.

In April 2024, the U.S. Department of Justice (DOJ) issued a new rule (Federal Register, 2024a) related to web and mobile application accessibility. At that time, the DOJ had the opportunity to change the standard for PDF accessibility from WCAG to PDF/UA but declined to make such a change.

The Rehabilitation Act cites WCAG as the standard for electronic documents. In the Act, Chapter E205.4 has two additional passages that are applicable to our course content. Here is the passage in full (USAB, 2024):

1. E205.4 Accessibility Standard. Electronic content shall conform to Level A and Level AA Success Criteria and Conformance Requirements in WCAG 2.0 (incorporated by reference, see 702.10.1).
2. EXCEPTION: Non-Web documents shall not be required to conform to the following four WCAG 2.0 Success Criteria: 2.4.1 Bypass Blocks, 2.4.5 Multiple Ways, 3.2.3 Consistent Navigation, and 3.2.4 Consistent Identification.
3. E205.4.1 Word Substitution when Applying WCAG to Non-Web Documents. For non-Web documents, wherever the term "Web page" or "page" appears in WCAG 2.0 Level A and AA Success Criteria and Conformance Requirements, the term "document" shall be substituted for the terms "Web page" and "page".

Passage 1 above sets the compliance standard as WCAG 2.0AA.

Passage 2 indicates that non-web documents must also conform to the standards except for four Success Criteria.

The author of this text suggests you read that last sentence again.

Passage 2 brings into scope for the accessibility requirements **non-web documents.** Examples of non-web documents are documents shared with others even though they are not posted on a website.

One cannot avoid the accessibility requirements by claiming that these are "only internal" documents. The rules apply equally to internal documents, even those that are not publicly posted.

Passage 3 explains how to apply WCAG standards to electronic documents. To paraphrase the passage, one simply replaces the word "web page" or "page" in the WCAG standard with "document".

Update to Compliance Standard April 2024

As mentioned earlier, in April 2004 the DOJ issued a new rule regarding electronic accessibility. The rule has an effective date of June 2026 or 2027, depending on the agency's size. The rule only pertains to web sites and mobile applications. But, for those resources, the WCAG standard is increased from WCAG 2.0 AA to WCAG 2.1AA.

While each workplace will make their own policy decisions regarding compliance, it would make sense to keep the web and electronic document standards synchronized. It would likely cause confusion to allow compliance to WCAG 2.0 for electronic documents but require WCAG 2.1 for websites. Moving all aspects of the office's digital resources to WCAG 2.1 will cause less confusion not only with employees but also with vendors regarding expectations of compliance.

Table 1. Version of WCAG and the corresponding standards

WCAG Version	Date Published	Standard
WCAG 2.2	October 2023	Not in U.S. federal standard
WCAG 2.1	September 2023	U.S. DOJ Rule April 2024
WCAG 2.0	December 2008	U.S. Sec508 and ADA

As of September 2024, the current version of WCAG is 2.2. It is expected that the federal standards will continue to be increased over time but will always lag the most recently published version of WCAG.

Businesses may always set their internal policy at a higher level than the minimum required by the federal government. For example, the state of Pennsylvania has already adopted WCAG 2.2 as their minimum state requirement (Commonwealth of Pennsylvania, n.d.).

Legal Risk

Most legal risk for digital accessibility appears through one of four avenues:

- An Office of Civil Rights complaint filed with the Department of Justice against a government agency, a business required to be accessible per the ADA, or institution.
- An Office of Civil Rights complaint filed with the Department of Education against an institution.
- A lawsuit (the claimant hires an attorney and sues the business for discrimination)
- A class-action lawsuit

Figure 1. Per UsableNet (UsableNet Inc., 2024), ADA lawsuit rates have increased from 2,314 in 2018 to 4,630 in 2023

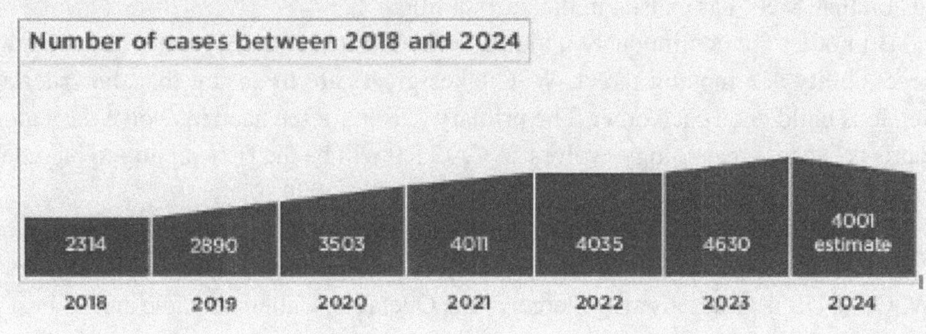

In 2020, Harvard University was decreed to pay $1.5M in "reasonable attorneys' fees, costs and expenses" because of a class action lawsuit brought by those impacted by the lack of captions on Harvard's online video content and online audio content without transcripts (Disability Law Center, 2020).

In May 2023, the Civil Rights Division of the U.S. Department of Justice and the Office of Civil Rights of the U.S. Department of Education sent a joint "Colleague" letter indicating that in May 2022, OCR proactively launched 100 compliance reviews regarding digital accessibility.

What does "proactively launch" mean? It means that even without a compliant being filed, the federal government is selecting 100 institutions to review for compliance of digital accessibility to the standards.

The legal risks of choosing to not be accessible is real. Each day a business has an inaccessible webpage, shares inaccessible files, or posts inaccessible social media content on- line, their exposure to legal risk grows.

Web Content Accessibility Guidelines © (WCAG)

The World Wide Web Consortium (W3C) publishes the Web Content Accessibility Guidelines to provide the world with common accessibility standards to ensure communications are accessible to those with disabilities. Per W3C (W3C. Org, 2024), the standards "enable developers to build rich interactive experiences that can be available on any device."

Because we understand that WCAG also applies to electronic documents, we could also update this statement to include authors, as well as developers.

The guidelines are continuously updated. **NOTE**: When WCAG 3.0 is published, the name will be changed from WCAG (Web Content Accessibility Guidelines) to "WCAG (W3C Accessibility Guidelines). The name change will remove the confusion that 'web' has caused in the current title.

Do not let the continuously updated WCAG criteria make you feel as though accessibility is a moving target. W3C takes great care to ensure that the criteria versions build upon each other. The primary reason for the need to evolve the standards is because technology evolves. WCAG 3.0 will be the first version to include criteria involving Artificial Intelligence (AI) (W3C, 2024a).

The WCAG standards are a list of Success Criteria (SC). The list is divided into "the Four Principles of Accessibility", referred to as POUR (W3C, 2023b). Per W3C, POUR is an acronym for Perceivable, Operable, Understandable and Robust.

P -*Perceivable*
O -*Operable*
U -*Understandable*
R –*Robust*

If the digital resource cannot be perceived, operated, understood by those with disabilities, or is not robust enough to be used by assistive technologies and a variety of technologies, then it is not accessible.

The WCAG Success Criteria (SC) are divided into three levels: A, AA and AAA. A is the base level of accessibility. When a standard specifics WCAG AA, the "AA" indicates that all Level A and all Level AA are required.

Visit WCAG 2.1 to review the list of Success Criteria (SC) required by the U.S. federal government. Each is explained and each SC has two additional links: 1) Understanding the Criteria and 2) How to Meet the Criteria.

The WCAG criteria must be followed for all content posted online, both internal to the organization and externally to customers and/or the public.

Here is a summary of three examples of Success Criteria from WCAG 2.1 AA:

- 1.1.1 Non-text Content – Ensure alt text is added to non-text content
- 1.4.1 Use of Color – Color is not used as the only visual means of conveying information
- 2.1.3 Keyboard (No Exception) – All functionality of the content is operable through a keyboard interface without requiring specific timings for individual keystrokes.

Review the full list of requirements at W3.org.

VPAT©

VPAT is an acronym for Voluntary Product Accessibility Template. It is a form, most often completed by a vendor, that lists the WCAG criteria. Vendors are expected to provide a response for each criterion. Response options are: Supports, Partially Supports, Does Not Support, N/A, or Not Evaluated. VPATs are created by the Information Technology Industry (ITI) Council© and are available from the Information Technology Industry Council (2023).

VPATs are quite useful as each Success Criteria is hyperlinked directly to the W3C page that will offer additional information on the specific criteria.

Be careful to not confuse versions of VPATs with versions of WCAG. While the current version of WCAG is 2.2, the current version of VPAT is 2.5.

Those that have roles in procurement, electronic accessibility, ADA compliance, or accessibility services will need to complete additional research on VPATs and how to conduct business with vendors to ensure that resources procured are accessible. ITI offers VPAT training on their website at www.itic.org/policy/accessibility.

WEBSITE ACCESSIBILITY

Website accessibility begins before the webpage is ever created. Ensure that all decisions made from the very beginning will result in an accessible, compliant, webpage when completed.

Important steps to take prior to beginning work is to include specifying a color palette and which color combinations will provide sufficient color contrast, setting the heading styles as part of the CSS (Cascading Style Sheet), and establishing the procedures to ensure compliance to WCAG 2.1. If the business is using a vendor to provide the website development, ensure that the vendor understands the compliance requirements and complete thorough testing prior to payment of services.

The right decisions must be made continuously as the webpage is created and updated, including:

- Ensure sufficient color contrast for text, graphics, buttons and links.
- Never rely on color as a single identifier.
- All images and hyperlinks have alt text.
- All elements (e.g., headings, tables, graphs) are properly tagged.
- The page is navigable via keyboard controls.
- All elements receive visible focus when reached.
- All videos have accurate and complete captions.
- Refer to WCAG 2.1 AA for a complete list of required Success Criteria.

Institute a regular internal review to ensure the website remains compliant to the standards.

In the past, the U.S. government had indicated that providing telephone support might offset having an inaccessible website. It is important to note that the DOJ rule published in April 2024 states that "the Department does not now believe that a staffed telephone line – even if it is offered 24/7 – provides equal opportunity in the way that an accessible website can" (Federal Register, 2024b). The law is that websites are to be accessible – by complying with WCAG 2.1 AA. Failure to provide an accessible website cannot be resolved by offering phone support. Phone support does not offer the user equal access to information.

Don't let people fool you! Sometimes people will complain that demanding "full compliance" is asking too much. Remind those people that the requirement to meet WCAG 2.1 AA is reaching only "minimum compliance" with the legal requirement. The law is not new. In 1998, the Rehabilitation Act of 1973 was amended to include an electronic accessibility requirement (General Services Administration, 2024a).

Overlays

Website overlays is a booming industry. Overlay companies sometimes claim that by using an overlay, the website is made accessible.

This is misleading or at least only partially true. We've already explained that our legal requirement means compliance with the Success Criteria of WCAG 2.1 AA. Using an overlay does not remediate the html code to comply with the standards. Overlays attempt to offer tools that users may be able to use to more easily navigate the website.

Unfortunately, these overlays also tend to require the user to learn how to use the overlay tool. As there are many of these tools in the marketplace, requiring users to learn a different tool as they visit different websites is not compliant with the WCAG standards.

The use of overlays tools may also introduce a security concern because some of these products may store information.

Perhaps artificial intelligence will, someday, make tools that will remediate websites so that the site complies to the standards. Until that time arrives, remember that compliance to the law requires compliance to the WCAG Success Criteria – businesses cannot force a user to learn an additional tool to reach the content.

Per Siteimprove, Inc., "Apart from the legal risks involved, overlays can create barriers for people with disabilities and how they experience a website" (Siteimprove, Inc., 2024).

Accessibility Testing for Websites

Testing a website for accessibility issues involves automated and manual testing. There are many free, automated testing tools available. Some of the most common are Siteimprove, Silktide, WAVE from WebAIM, and IBM Equal Access Accessibility Checker. Note, there are many to choose from. Businesses are encouraged to use several automated checkers as each has their own forte. Some tools are designed for developers while others are targeted more towards content contributors.

No matter what automated tools are used, manual testing is still required. Harvard University provides an excellent resource of items that should be manually reviewed to ensure accessibility. The list of testing steps addresses three areas: Content Review, Keyboard Testing, and Screen Reader Review. Learn more at Harvard University's Manual Testing for Accessibility webpage.

FOUNDATIONS OF ELECTRONIC ACCESSIBILITY

Color

It is estimated that 1 in 12 men and 1 in 200 women have some type of colorblindness (National Eye Institute, 2024). Worldwide, there are more than 367 million people with colorblindness (ColorWillOrg, n.d.). In order to share information equally with those that have colorblindness, never rely on color as a single identifier and always provide sufficient color contrast between the font color and the background color.

Sometimes those that have colorblindness have difficulty seeing the difference between two colors but other times, the colorblindness causes the person to see only in grayscale.

This requirement applies to all electronic communications, including webpages, emails, electronic documents, videos, and social media posts.

Never Use Color as a Single Identifier (WCAG 1.4.1)

Never rely on color as a single identifier. For example, never ask someone to check a red box or a green box to provide a response – because not everyone can determine which box is red and which is green (W3C, 2023c).

Graphs

Also, never rely on a color as a single identifier for graphs. Below is a sample line graph that was made using Microsoft Excel©. It has three solid lines representing three datasets. Each line is a different color: blue, orange and gray.

Figure 2. A graph with three different colored, solid lines showing cookie sales for four quarters

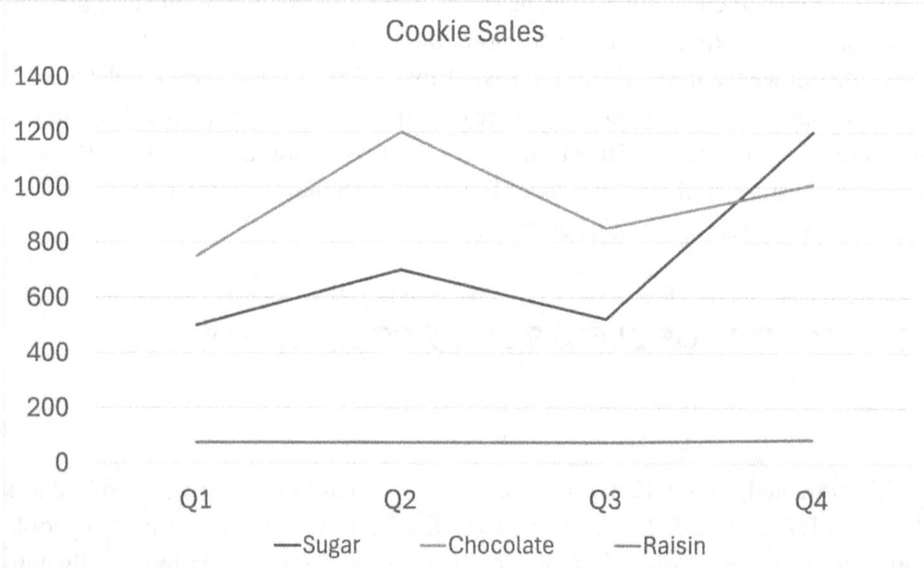

An easy way to test a graph is to print the graph in black and white. Are you able determine which data set is which?

Figure 3. The same graph as above except without three different colored lines. The three data sets use a gray scale

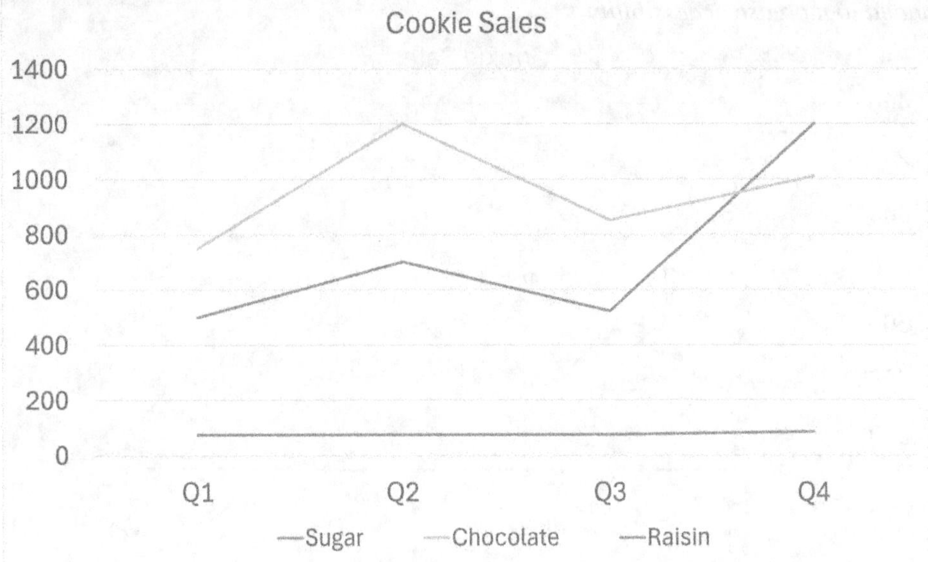

When the graph is printed in black and white, it is impossible to understand which dataset is which. And particularly if someone is presenting this type of graphic and providing people only a limited amount of time to study the figure, it is not accessible.

The graph does not provide the same information to everyone. The graph does not provide equal access. The graph discriminates against those that have colorblindness.

By pairing sufficient colors that contrast against the background with patterns, the graph becomes accessible. Adding additional details, such as data labels can also be helpful. The graph below uses a dashed, dark blue line; a dotted, purple line; and a solid, dark red line to represent the three data sets. Even if this were printed on a gray scale, it would be clear which line represented which data set because of the patterns used.

Figure 4. Each of the three data sets has a unique pattern and a color that contrasts sufficiently against the white background. Additionally, data set numbers have been added to increase accessibility

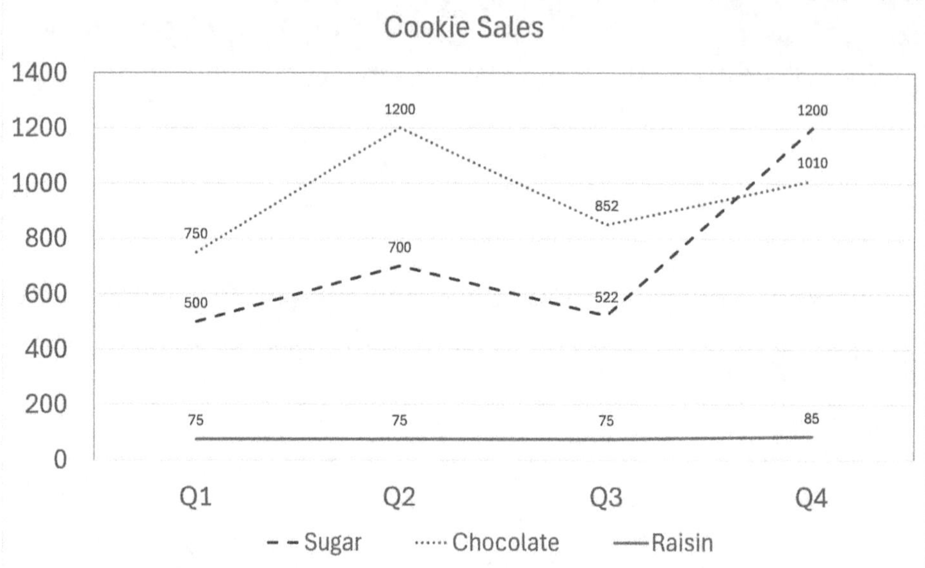

And of course, just like images, all graphs must have alt text attached. The alt text description must provide the pertinent information that is being conveyed. If the actual numbers are critical, it would be best to also present the data as a table.

Table 2. Graph example for alt text

Flavor	**Q1**	**Q2**	**Q3**	**Q4**
Sugar	500	800	500	1200
Chocolate	600	2050	690	1200
Raisin	250	250	250	300

Suggested alt text for the graph above:

A line graph showing data sets of Sugar, Chocolate and Raisin Cookies for quarters 1, 2, 3 and 4. Chocolate peaked in Q 2 at 2,050 but stayed between 600 and 800 for the other 3 quarters. Sugar cookies ran 500 – 800 for the first three quarters then peaked at 1200 for Q4. Raisin was steady at 250 for the first three quarters and peaked at 300 in Q4.

When referring to the graph, do not refer to a specific data set by the color but by the data set name.

"Look how that purple line peaked out in Q2!"
"Look how the Chocolate sales peaked out in Q2!"

Hyperlinks

Another common use of color is setting apart hyperlinked text. Here are two examples of hyperlinked text as it may appear in Word:

1) Not an accessible hyperlink because the hyperlinked text is not underlined:
   Visit W3C for Accessibility Fundamentals Overview
2) An accessible hyperlink because the hyperlinked text **is** underlined.
   Visit W3C for Accessibility Fundamentals Overview.

The first example has sufficient color contrast against the white background. However, the color of the black text leading up to the blue of the hyperlinked text is so slight of a change that many of those with colorblindness would not be able to perceive a difference.

Without an underline, if someone doesn't understand that the color has changed, there would be nothing to indicate that the text is hyperlinked. An underline of hyperlinked text is required, and it must not wait until the link receives mouse or keyboard focus. This is true in PDFs, in emails, on webpages – in all digital resources.

Sufficient Color Contrast

Per WCAG 2.1 AA, the minimum contrast required for normal font is 4.5:1. Or, for 14pt bold or larger fonts, the minimum contrast required is 3:1.

Consider that the contrast between black and white is 21:1. Therefore, requiring a minimum contrast of 4.5:1 is not that high of a bar. Meeting the minimum required by law will not provide enough contrast for everyone to see text. While meeting the minimum may protect a business from legal action, everyone is encouraged to strive for a higher minimum contrast, such as 7:1, which is recommended by WCAG AAA. Remember that 4.5:1 is the floor, not the ceiling! Businesses can always do more than the minimum required by law.

If a business/agency has brand colors that do not contrast well with white, they will need to relegate the lighter colors to decorative elements only and not use them for text on a white background. Some of the most problematic colors used with white include orange, green, pink, and yellow. If trying to use these colors on white, ensure the shade has a sufficient amount of brown included and always check the contrast!

There are many free contrast checking tools available. When using a Microsoft product, they have made it simple to use colors with strong contrast against white. In the color palette option, stay on the bottom row to choose strong contrast options. Also, use the first or last three options of the Standard Color Options.

Figure 5. Microsoft Word Toolbar. Click on the color palette button to see the Theme Colors and Standard Colors options

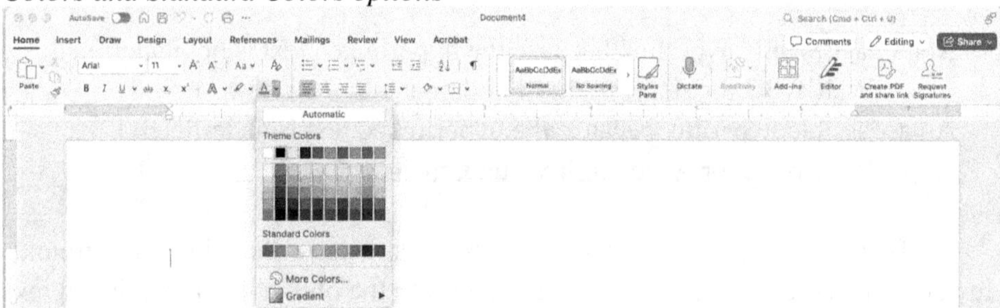

Always run the <u>Accessibility Checker</u> in Word. If the Accessibility Checker reports a color contrast warning, increase the color contrast until the error clears.

The Accessibility Checker is found under the Review menu.

Figure 6. Microsoft Word Toolbar. Select Review in the main menu and then Check Accessibility

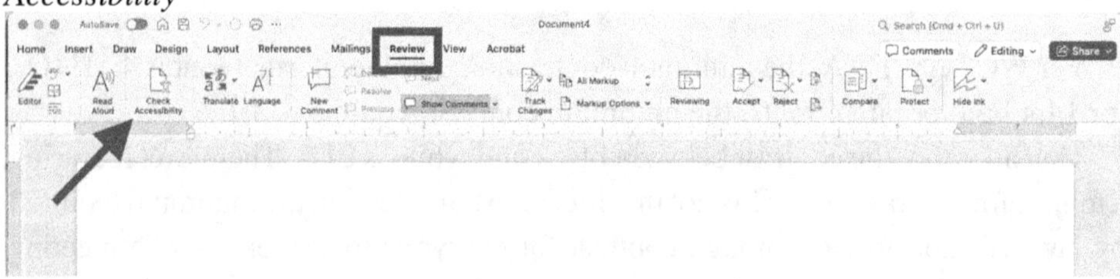

One area often overlooked for contrast concerns is text presented in videos. Always ensure that the text being communicated has sufficient contrast, no matter the medium being used.

Styles

When looking at a newspaper, either on-line or in real life, do you start reading at the beginning of the paper and read all the way through to the end? No, of course not! Readers glance at the headings to decide which parts of the newspaper they want to read. That is how headings work and they are very important. Headings have a unique visual appearance to draw one's attention.

Unfortunately, many people use fake headings instead of real headings. A fake heading is text that is formatted to look like a heading but isn't styled (or tagged) as a heading. This is particularly egregious against those that use a screen reader because the screen reader's only option is to read the entire document/webpage top to bottom, without the ability to navigate to a specific article or section. Screen readers are used by those with blindness or those with severe low vision. The use of fake headings discriminates against this part of the population.

The Microsoft format options such as font size, font color, underline or bold are visual formats only. If these are used to change the text so that it appears to be a heading – this is a fake heading.

When using Microsoft products, avoid using the manual formatting options located on the left-end of the Home toolbar.

Figure 7. Microsoft Toolbar with the formatting buttons for font, font size, bold, italics, underlined, strike, subscript and superscript are highlighted

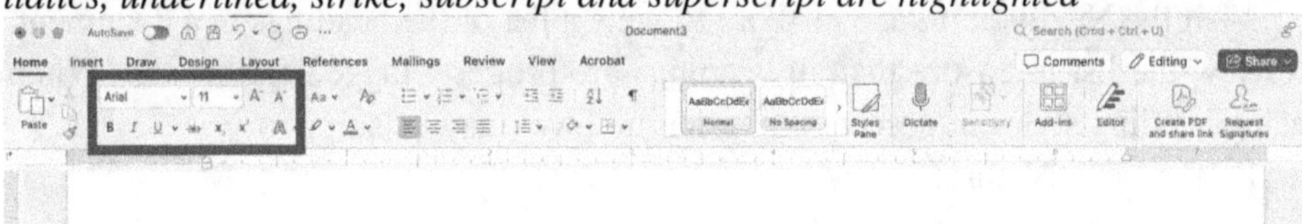

Instead, use the Styles buttons to properly format text.

Figure 8. Microsoft Toolbar with the Styles buttons highlighted

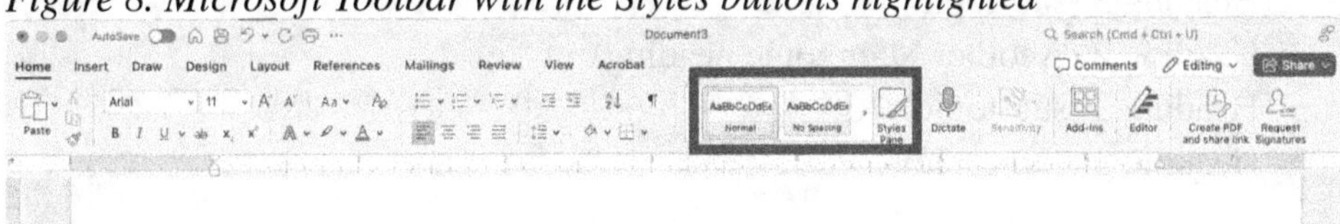

Use of the Styles format buttons have several important purposes:

a) Headings are tagged appropriately and can be used for navigation purposes by those that use screen readers.
b) The Heading tags are saved if the document is saved as a PDF. This will ensure that the headings are tagged appropriately as a PDF document.

c) If a change to a particular Heading style is needed, update the Style and all text formatted with that heading style is updated automatically.
d) By using Styles, this allows a Table of Contents to be created by the software.

The use of proper Styles (also called Heading Tags) is a foundational accessibility issue and applies to all electronic communications, including:

- Word
- PowerPoint
- Excel
- Outlook
- InDesign©
- Webpages
- Surveys

Navigation Pane

Visit the Navigation Pane in Word to view a list of the headings in a document. Review the list to ensure that all headings are properly tagged and nested. When using heading styles in descending order, no level may be skipped.

Proper tag structure:

Heading 1 (The main title, only used once)
Heading 2 (Main topic heading)
Heading 2 (Another Main topic heading)
Heading 3 (sub-topic)
Heading 3 (sub-topic)
Heading 2 (Another Main topic heading)
Heading 3 (sub-topic)
Heading 3 (sub-topic)

Improper tag structure:

Heading 1 (The main title, only used once)
Heading 5 (used improperly)
Heading 2 (Main topic heading)
This is 'normal' text only visually formatted (improper)
Heading 2 (Another Main topic heading)
Heading 3 (sub-topic)
Heading 3 (sub-topic)

Heading 5 (used improperly)
Heading 2 (Another Main topic heading)
Heading 3 (sub-topic)
Heading 3 (sub-topic)

Sometimes people will use a specific heading style because they like the visual appearance of the style without regard for the structure of the page/document. This breaks accessibility because it breaks navigation and structure of the page/document.

Alternative Text

Alternative Text, or alt text, is text describing an element so that those using a screen reader can understand the element. Screen readers are most often used by those with blindness or with severely low vision.

When a screen reader reaches an image, it knows that the image is present and will announce the image. Because we do not want to confuse the listener, all images must either have appropriate alt text or be marked as decorative.

If the image is marked as decorative, the screen reader will not announce that the image is present. This feature must only be used when the image is decorative and does not provide any content not otherwise provided. If the image is only decorative, mark it as decorative. Failure to mark decorative items as decorative will cause those that use screen readers to waste their time.

If working on a holiday greeting card and there is a dark night sky background covered in snowflakes, do not add alt text to every snowflake indicating that it is a snowflake. That would take a great deal of time and most people would give up listening to it before reaching the message. Instead, add alt text to the first snowflake that describes the dark night sky and glistening snowflakes. Then, mark all the other snowflakes as decorative.

Always be conscientious of how long it will take someone to listen to the alt text of the image. Be concise and clear. Avoid unnecessary punctuation as all punctuation will be announced by the screen reader. However, do not leave out any text contained in the graphic unless the text is repeated as normal text elsewhere on the page or in the document.

Exception: For graphics that include a word cloud, if the specific words are not important, those words are not required to be part of the alt text.

If using acronyms, understand how they will be announced by the screen reader. If the image is a logo for the Office of Information Technology, type the alt text as o i t so that it will be read properly and not as 'oit'.

Either adding alt text or marking the image as decorative is required for every image, every time. This is true for images in emails, on webpages, in electronic documents, and even those posted on social media.

Alt text is an accessibility best practice that needs to become habit so that it becomes second nature. The good news is that Microsoft makes it easy to add alt text. Simply right click on the image and select add/edit alt text to open the alt text pane. Or select the image and then select the Picture Format menu and select the button labeled Alt Text.

Figure 9. Microsoft Toolbar which an image is selected, Select Picture Format to reach the Alt Text button

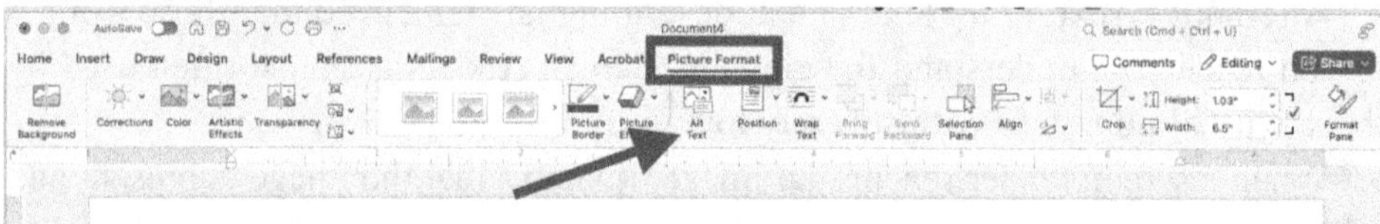

Images are not the only items that require alt text. Alt text must also be added to:

- Buttons
- Charts
- Graphs
- Tables

Applying alt text to images in Word and PowerPoint will also be included if the document is saved as a PDF.

Caution:

- SmartArt is not accessible because it cannot be reached via keyboard navigation.
- WordArt is only accessible if alt text is added to the element.

Lists and Bullets

It is best practice to use the bullet and list formatting buttons whenever they are available.

Figure 10. Microsoft Word Toolbar shows the bulleted lists buttons highlighted

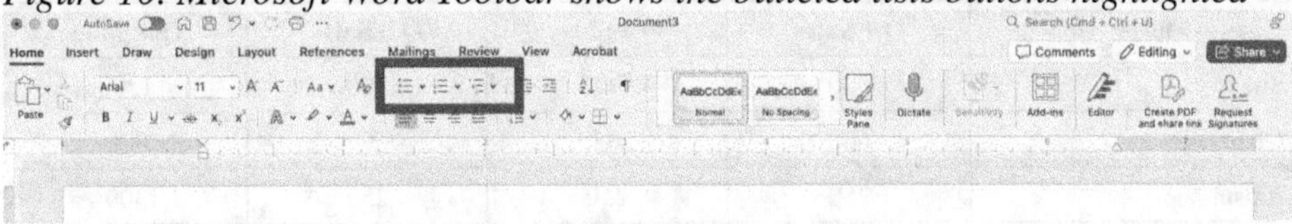

Use of these formatting tools will apply the appropriate list tags to the document so that a screen reader will know a list is present. This is true in electronic documents, emails and webpages.

The bullet format will be read as an unordered list while the numbered bullets are announced as an ordered list. Below is a sample list followed by how the list will be read by a screen reader.

A list of accessibility best practices already introduced:

1. Web accessibility
2. Color as a single identifier
3. Sufficient color contrast
4. Alt text

A screen reader will read the list above as:

A list of accessibility best practices already introduced. A list of four items. Item 1 web accessibility. Item 2 Color as a single identifier. Item 3 Sufficient color contrast. Item 4 Alt text. End of List.

Just like alt text, the list formats will also be carried forward if the document is saved as a PDF.

Tables

Microsoft Word

It is crucial to understand that Table formatting must only be used for tables and tables are used to provide data.

It is an improper use of table formatting to provide a visual representation of a form.

Table 3. Example A – Table of data with a header row and data in each cell

Cookie Flavor	Q 1 Sales	Q 2 Sales	Q 3 Sales	Q 4 Sales
Sugar	500	800	500	1200
Chocolate	600	2050	690	800
Raisin	250	250	250	300

Table 4. Example B – Table formatting used improperly because data is not being presented

A Sample Form			
First Name:		**Email:**	
Last Name:		Phone Number:	

When Table formatting is used, specific table tags are created and those using screen readers will be confused by the lack of an actual table.

Sample Table tagging:

```
<Table>

<TR> (Table Row)

<TH> (Table Header)

<TH> (Table Header)

<TH> (Table Header)

<TH> (Table Header)

<TH> (Table Header)
```

<TR> (Table Row)

<TD> (Table Data)

<TD> (Table Data)

<TD> (Table Data)

<TD> (Table Data)

<TD> (Table Data)

If the intention is to share the document as a PDF - unless the employee is prepared to remediate the PDF in Adobe Acrobat Pro - do not include any split or merged cells in the Table.

If a form is needed, instead of using a Table format, draw lines and indicate each line as decorative. Please note that the "developer" tool in Word does not create accessible form fields and should be avoided.

Microsoft Excel

There are just a few things to remember to ensure Excel files are accessible to everyone.

Cell A1 must include text or instructions so those that use a screen reader will understand how the file is designed.

Always ensure that the cursor in cell A1 when the file is saved. This ensures that when the file is opened, the screen reader will first announce the text located in cell A1.

If the file has multiple worksheets, the information in cell A1 should explain how the file is designed and provide any important information to navigate the file.

As in all digital resources, pay close attention if using red fonts for negative numbers to ensure that sufficient contrast is maintained.

There must be at least one heading (not part of a table). Format the heading by selecting Cell Styles from the Home row of menu options and then select the appropriate Heading level. Heading levels must always start with 1. There should only be one Heading 1 per worksheet or document.

Figure 11. Microsoft Excel. Cell Styles highlighted in menu bar displays a drop-down box that allows one to select heading styles

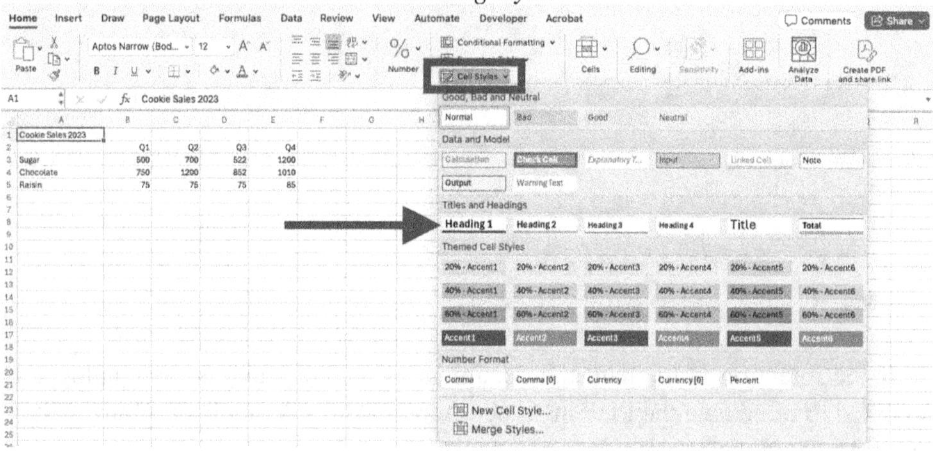

Select the cells of the table, including the header row, and select Format as Table from the Home menu bar.

Figure 12. Microsoft Excel. Select the cells of the table and then select Format as a Table from the menu bar

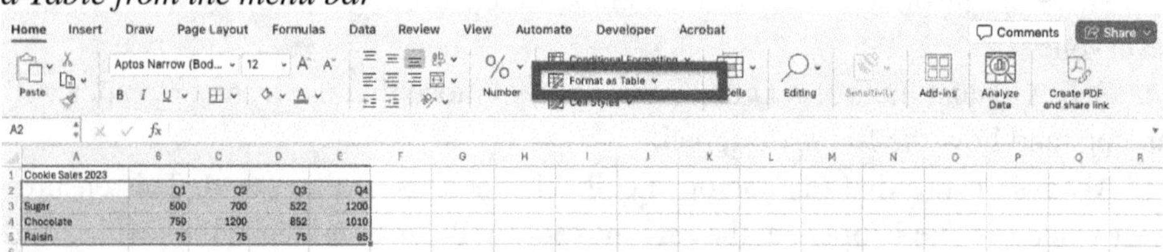

When the cells are formatted as a table, the Table menu will be visible. Enter a Table Name and decide whether to remove the Filter Buttons from the header row by unchecking the Filter Button checkbox.

Figure 13. Microsoft Excel. Once the table is formatted, provide a Table Name and decide whether the "filter button" should be part of the header row

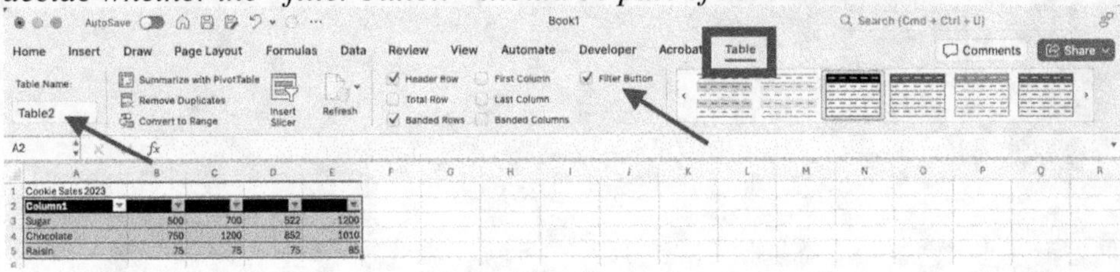

Please note that the Table Name may not contain any spaces. While multiple tables may be present on a single worksheet, each table must have a unique name and must be explained in the directions.

Figure 14. Microsoft Excel. Once a table is formatted, provide a Table Name. The Table Name may not have any spaces

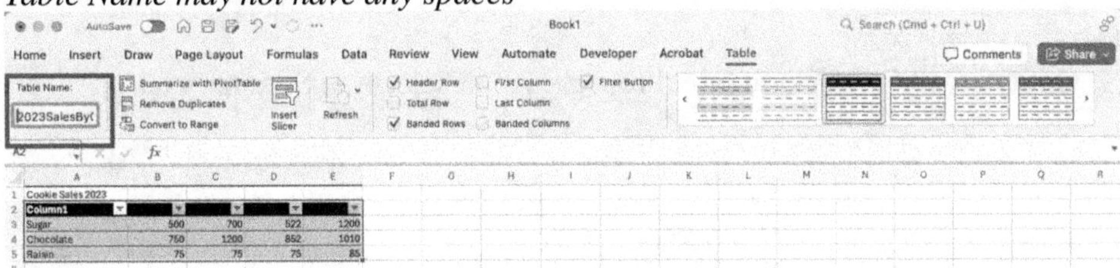

Document Title

Each Microsoft Office document has a file title set under Properties.

In most versions of Windows, click on File, Info, and type a title into the field named "Add A Title".

Figure 15. Microsoft, File, Save As, Under Properties, enter a Title for the file

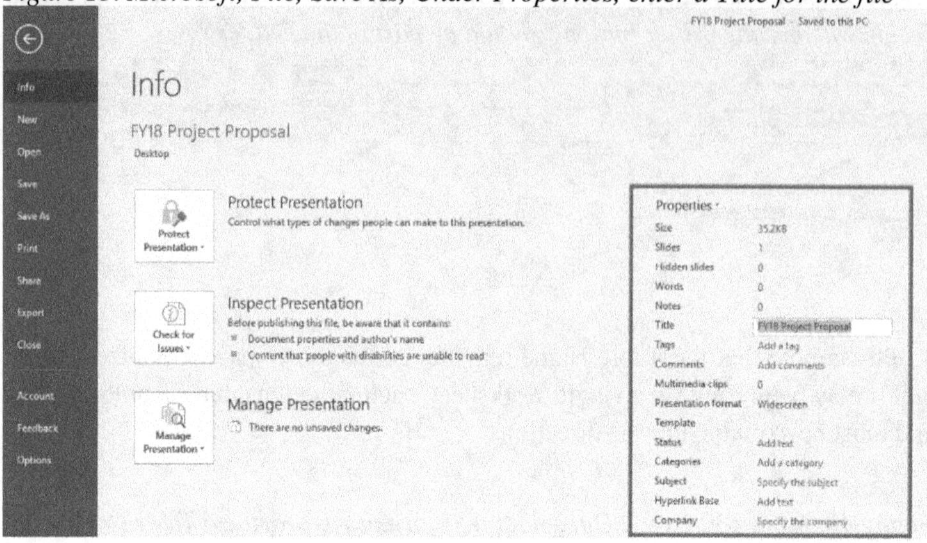

On iOS (MAC), click on File, Properties, and select the Summary tab

Figure 16. Microsoft on a MAC, File, Properties, Under the Summary Tab, type in a Title for the file

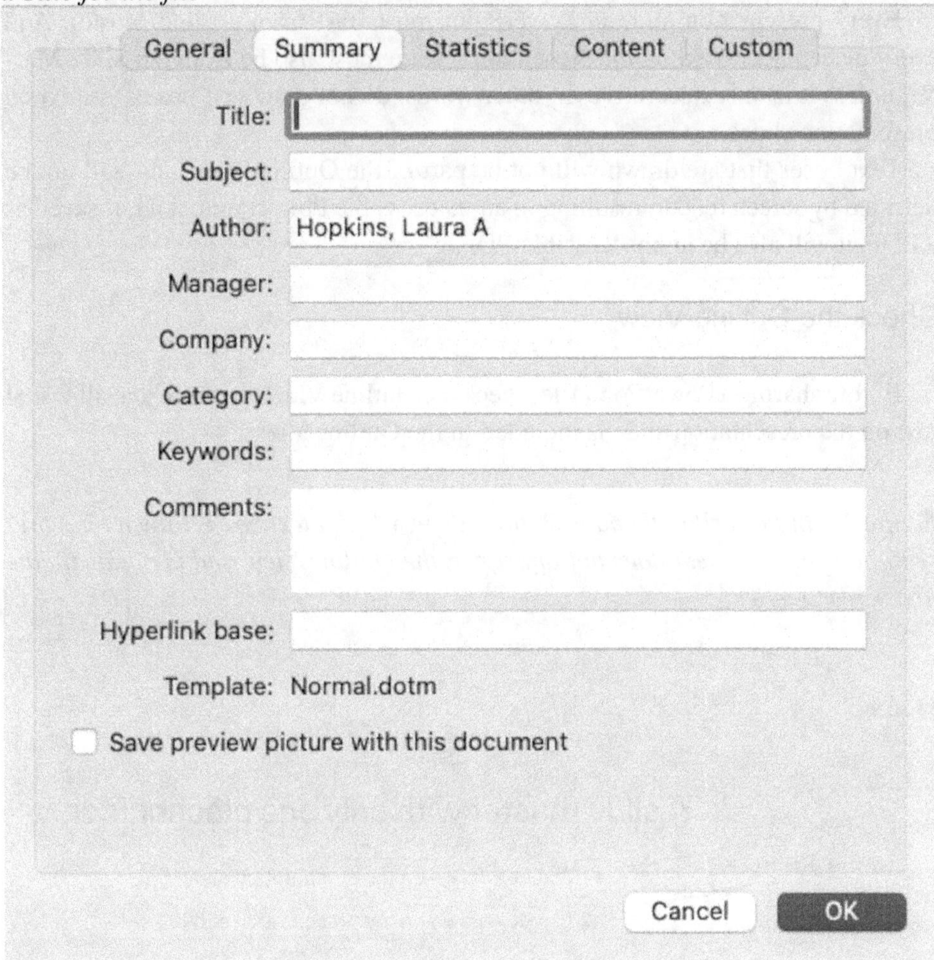

For support, visit Microsoft Support and select the specific operating system for step by step instructions. Note that when saving a Word or PowerPoint file as a PDF, the text entered as the Document Title under properties will be displayed in the document tab in Adobe Acrobat. The Document Title does not need to match the file name. It should include normal spacing and capitalization.

PowerPoint Files

When creating documents with PowerPoint, as opposed to Word, there are two critical accessibility practices that must be used: Slide Masters and Reading Order

Slide Master

Every presentation slide in PowerPoint must start from a Slide Master. And every placeholder used on the presentation slide must also be from the Slide Master, unless it is only decorative. In other words, do not draw text boxes for text on presentation slides.

Text boxes that are drawn will not be part of the Outline View and will not be detected by screen reader, resulting in an inaccessible PowerPoint. And, if saved as a PDF, it will also be an inaccessible PDF.

Check the Outline View

Before sharing a PowerPoint file, check the Outline View to ensure that all visual text on the presentation slide is included in the Outline View.

Figure 17. In PowerPoint, under Outline View, when a text box is drawn on a presentation slide, the text does not appear in the Outline View and is not available to a screen reader

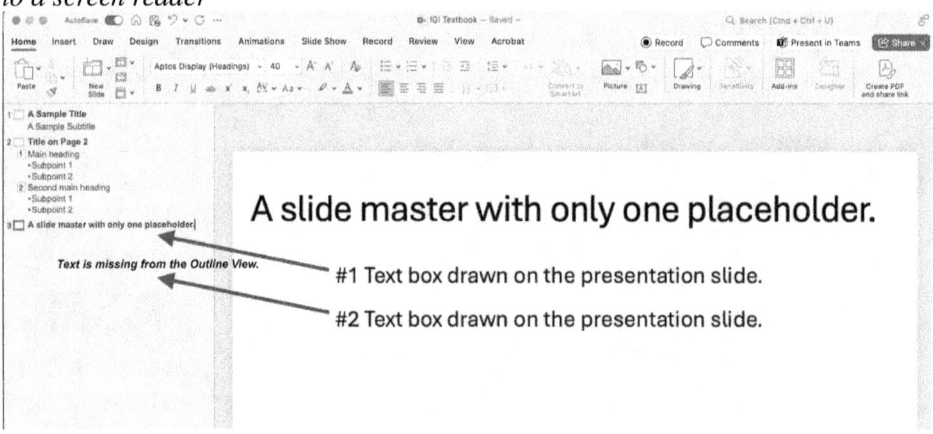

If text is missing from the Outline View (View, Outline View), the file is not accessible. To remediate, insert a new slide master with enough placeholders to hold all the slide's content. Copy and paste the **contents** from placeholders on the original slide to the new slide that has placeholders from a Slide Master. Do not copy the entire placeholder. Copy only the content from inside the placeholder.

Adding New Slides

Each time a new slide is added to a presentation file, it must be a Slide Master that has enough placeholders to hold all the content that will be on the slide. If unsure how many placeholders will be needed, select a slide master that has several placeholders. Placeholders can always be deleted.

Once it is determined that there are not enough placeholders on a presentation slide, it will be necessary to start over with a new slide master that has more placeholders. It may be necessary for you to create your own Slide Masters.

On the "New Slide" button, select the down arrow to reach a list of Slide Master options.

The down arrow on the New Slide button is highlighted to draw attention to its location.

Figure 18. Microsoft PowerPoint Toolbar with the down arrow beside the New Slide button highlighted

This presents the current Slide Master options. By default, there are 9 options to choose from.

Figure 19. Microsoft PowerPoint, Options displayed after selecting the down arrow beside the New Slide button

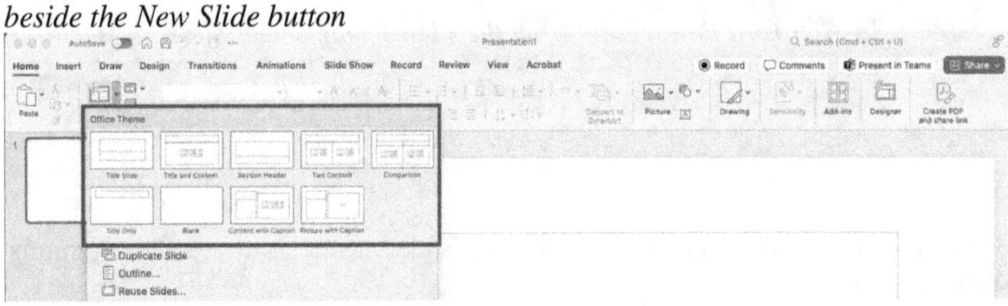

The most versatile placeholder type is the universal placeholder.

Figure 20. The Universal Placeholder in PowerPoint Slide Masters will accept a variety of input including text, pictures and graphs

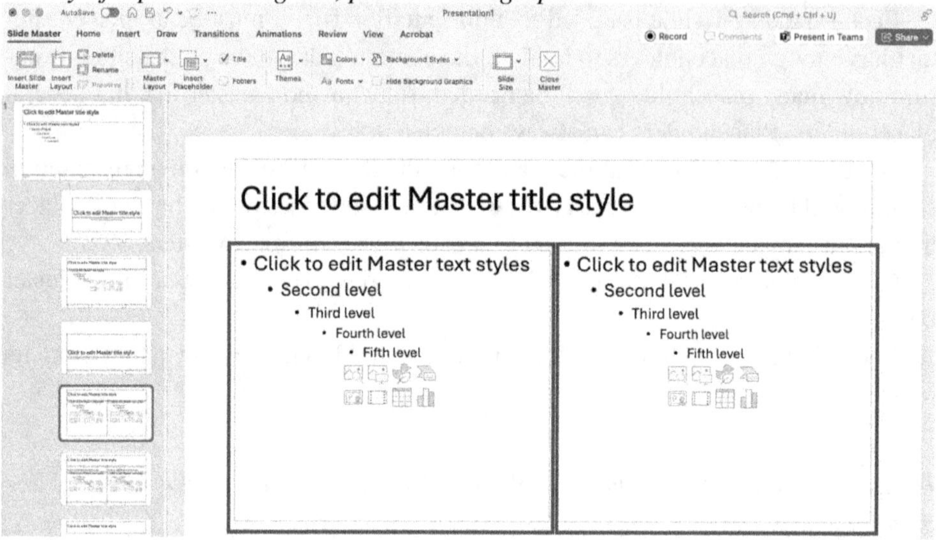

Universal placeholders may be used for text, pictures, videos, tables, or charts and graphs.

Creating Slide Masters

From the main tool bar, click on View, then Slide Master to select a Slide Master:

Figure 21. In Microsoft PowerPoint from the View menu, select Slide Master

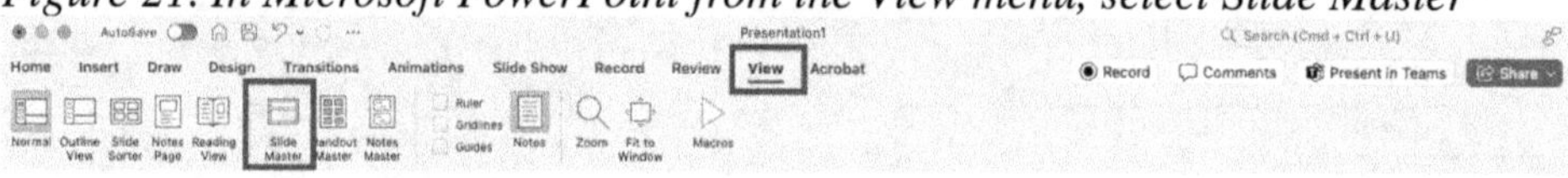

Once Slide Master is selected, notice that "Slide Master" is now at the beginning of the tool bar.

Figure 22. Once Slide Master has been selected, it will be displayed at the beginning of the menu bar until Close Master is selected

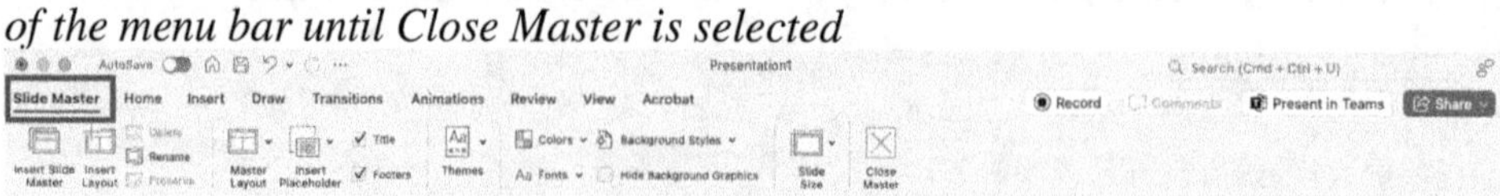

The toolbar will remain in Slide Master mode until the "Close Master" button at the end of the menu is selected. When working in Slide Master mode, only templates are being created. Presentation slides are not created while in Slide Master mode.

When entering Slide Master mode, the left pane will display the Masters Slides that already exist. These Master Slides are numbered, left justified and followed by a set of slides nested beneath it. These nested slides are referred to as Layout slides.

Each Master Slide controls the formatting of the Layout slides nested beneath it. For example, if the background color is changed on the Master Slide to blue, all the layout slides beneath that Master Slide will experience the same update.

Many companies use Slide Masters developed by their Marketing Team to ensure proper use of brand colors, proper fonts, logos and color contrast.

Figure 23. A Slide Master has layout slides. A change to the Slide Master migrates the same change to all the nested layout slides. For instance, changing the background color from white to navy on the Slide Master, made the same change to the nested Slide Layouts.

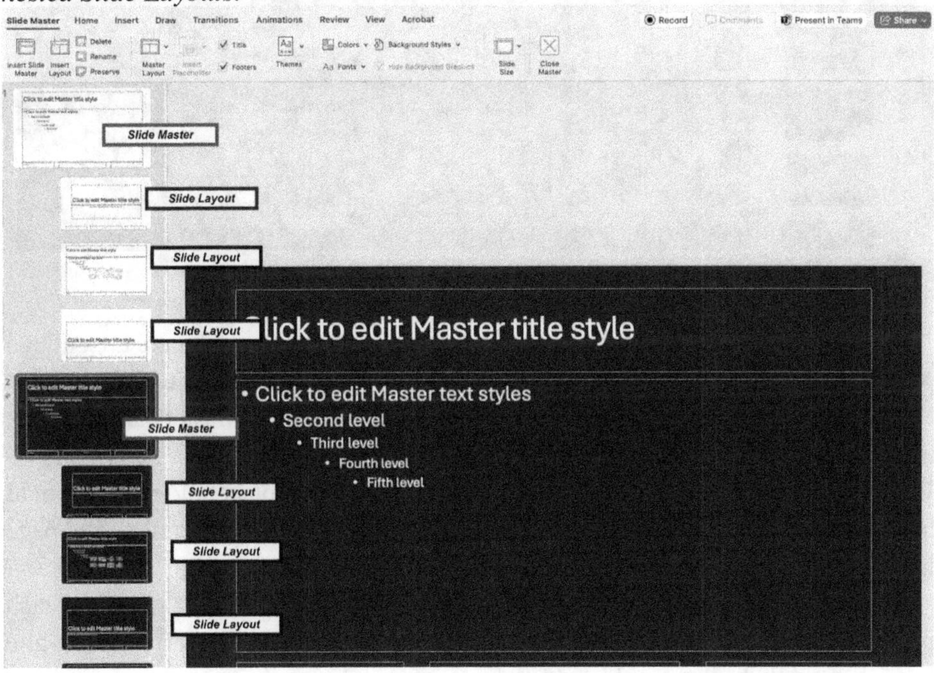

Keep the default Slide Masters to build a Slide Master library. Simply select the #1 Slide Master, copy and paste it and then there will be a second set of slides to edit.

If a Slide Master with four universal placeholders is needed, use an existing slide master that already has at least one universal placeholder.

Figure 24. Select any slide layout that has a universal placeholder and copy/paste it to have a new slide. In the new slide, copy/paste the universal placeholder to create as many placeholders as you need. Resize and lay out the placeholders so that the template is easy to use

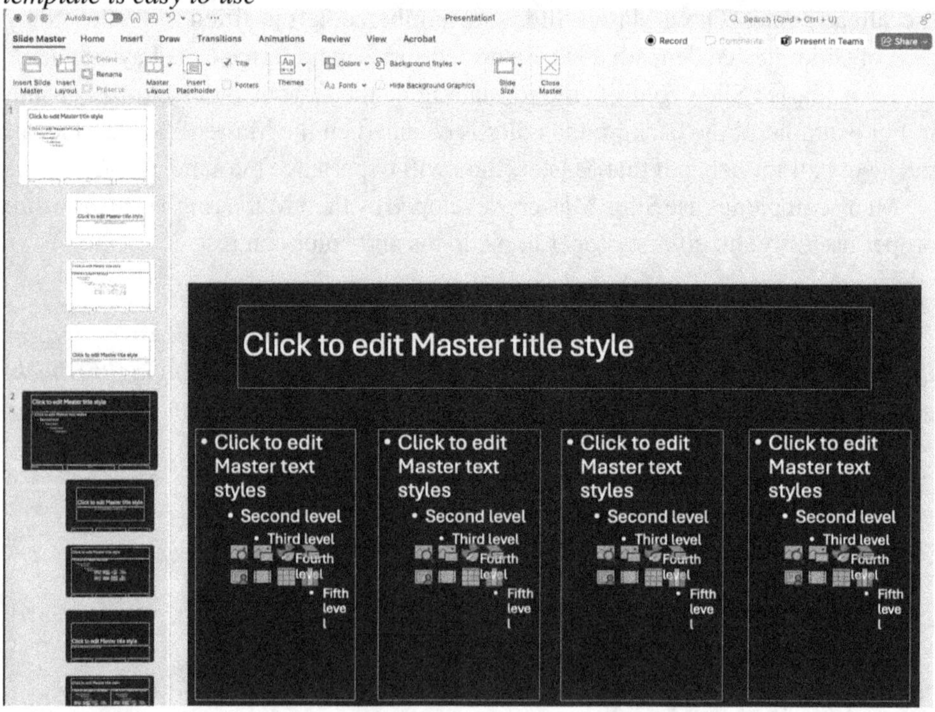

Select one of the universal placeholders, then copy/paste until there are enough placeholders on the slide. Resize the placeholders so they are easy to use.

Text can be typed into placeholders, but the text on Slide Masters is **not** actual text, it is only a tip or reminder.

In the example below, I copy and pasted the universal placeholders so I would have 8 boxes for text, in addition to the title field. I deleted the footer, date and page number fields because I don't intend to use them.

I typed text in each field so my employee would know what data goes into each placeholder. Also, I formatted the quarterly heading placeholders to have a white font on a purple background.

When this Slide Master is inserted into the Presentation file, it appears as:

Figure 25. When a Slide Master is brought into a presentation file, the text from the Slide Master is visual text only. It is not real text

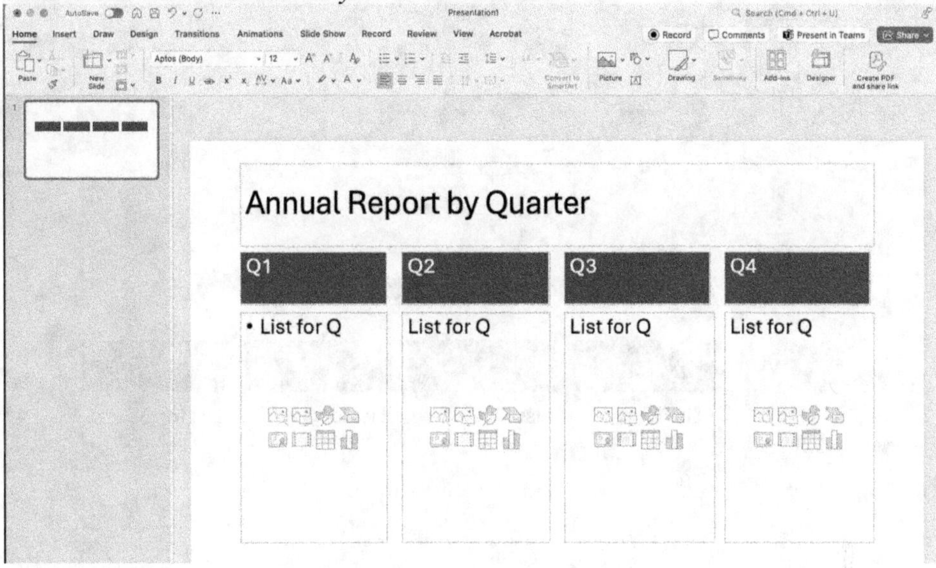

As previously stated, none of the text presented visually from the slide master is real text. This is apparent when reviewing the Outline View.

Figure 26. The Outline View shows that the presentation slide does not have any real text

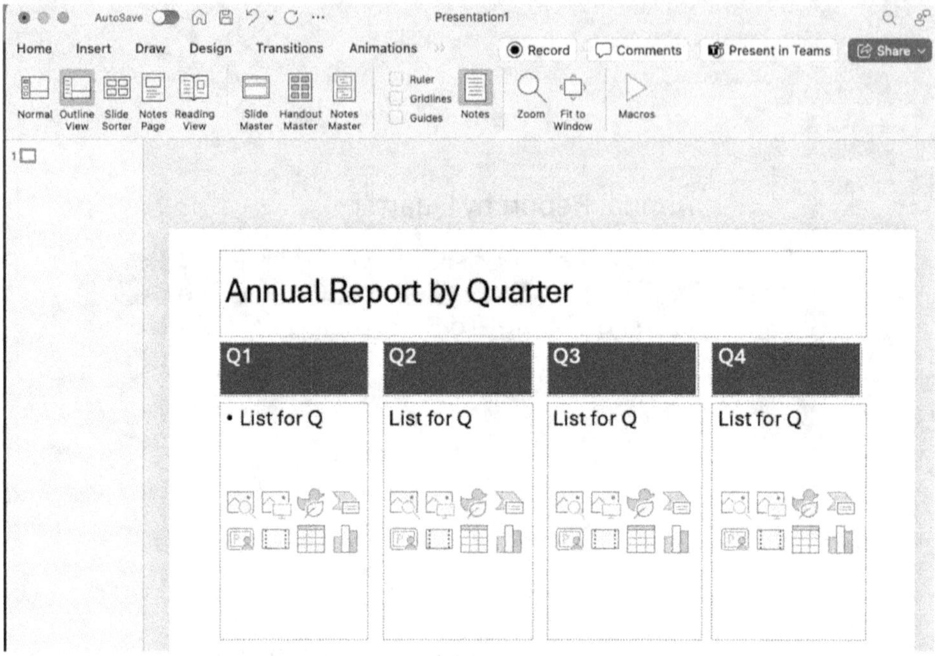

Text will only appear in the Outline View once text is typed into the placeholders on the presentation slide.

Ensure that every presentation slide has a title placeholder. When creating Slide Masters, simply check the box for "Title"

Figure 27. Every PowerPoint Slide Master must have a title placeholder by checking the Title checkbox

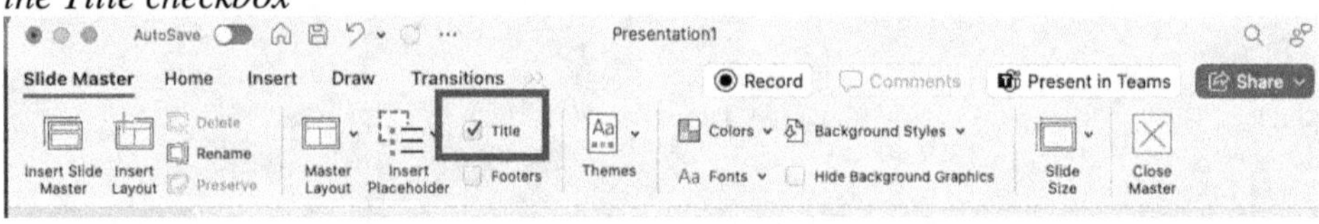

It is a requirement to have a Title placeholder. However, on the presentation slide, if the visual title is not wanted, once the title text is typed into the placeholder, the placeholder may be slid off the presentation slide.

A screen reader will still identify the title text as a title. This will also be important if the file is saved as a PDF.

The image below shows a title placeholder that was slid off the top of the presentation slide. The title text will be read by a screen reader but will not be visible during a Slide Show presentation.

Figure 28. The Title placeholder has been slid off the presentation area into the background area

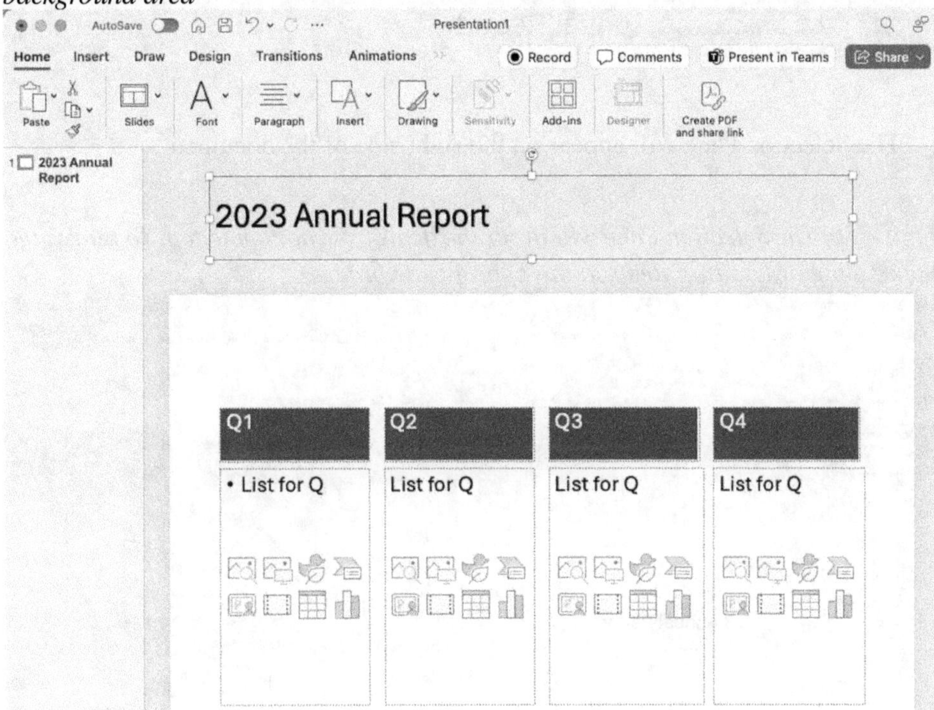

Reading Order

Ensure that the reading order is set properly on every presentation slide. The easiest way to check the reading order is to simply tab through the slide. If the placeholders highlight in the proper order, then the reading order is correct. However, if placeholders are not presenting in the proper order, then the reading order must be set.

Click on Review, then select the down arrow on the Accessibility Checker button and choose Selection Pane on a MAC or Reading Order pane on Windows.

Figure 29. Under Review, Check Accessibility, select Selection Pane

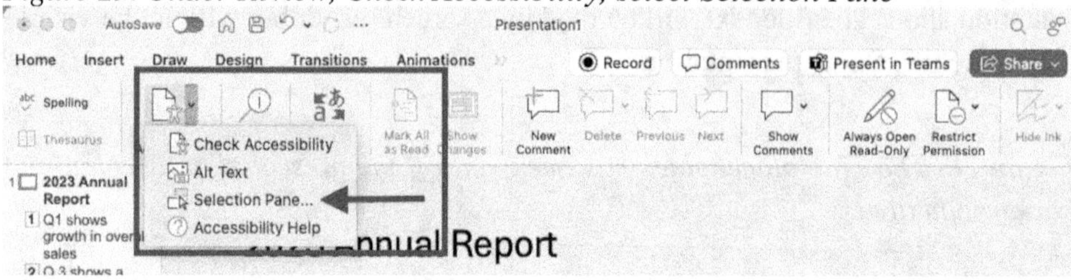

The Selection Pane will appear on the right side of the document.

Figure 30. The Selection Pane will order the items from bottom to top. To rearrange the reading order, drag items to the appropriate order

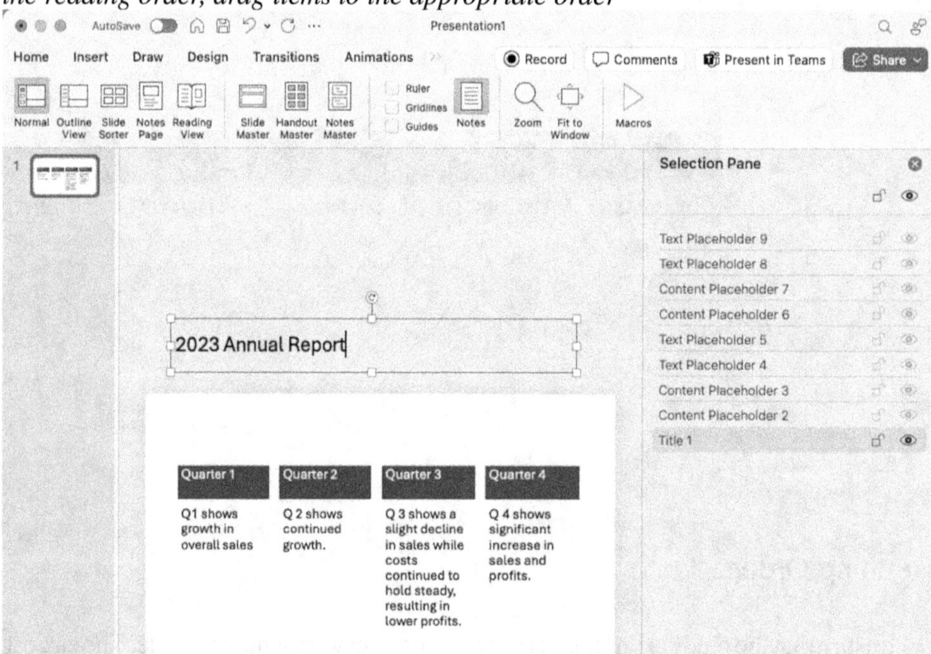

The items in the Selection Pane are read from the bottom to the top on MAC and the Reading Order pane is read top to bottom on PCs. Notice that the "title" placeholder is at the bottom of the list. That is a hint that the list reads from the bottom to the top. If placeholders are not in the proper order, simply drag and drop them into the proper order inside the Selection Pane.

TIP: Set the reading order on the Slide Masters. Then, check the reading order of every presentation slide because placeholders may be rearranged while creating/editing the presentation slides.

Flyers

Many organizations like to email flyers to make big announcements such as the Annual Company Picnic. To "make it look great", the graphic designer may elect to use a tool such as Canva or Prezi. These types of tools almost never save a PDF as an accessible PDF. The PDFs do not meet the WCAG criteria of having alt text, headings and proper reading order.

Unless there is a remediator tasked with resolving the issues in Adobe Acrobat Pro prior to distribution, do not use these tools to create PDFs.

However, these tools (e.g., Prezi, Canva) may be used to create graphics that are then inserted into accessible Word or PowerPoint files – following all the rules reviewed so far in this chapter to make accessible PDFs.

PDFs

Saving Word Files as PDFs

In Word, content included in header and footer panes will not be announced by a screen reader except for page numbers. The same is true when the file is saved as a PDF. Best practice is to include the header content on page one as actual body text, outside of the header pane, so that it is announced once by the screen reader. For footer text that is repeated throughout the document, it is recommended that it be placed as body text on the last page of the document.

Footnotes, not footers, are accessible and tagged appropriately in PDF.

Saving PowerPoint Files as PDFs

From Windows, PowerPoint files save properly as PDFs if the file was created using accessibility best practices (e.g., slide masters, reading order, alt text, contrast).

From iOS, the PowerPoint file will not save properly to a PDF. Instead, upload the file to Microsoft Office 365 and then save it as a PDF. If this is not an option available, remediation in Adobe Acrobat Pro will be required to make the file accessible.

After saving a file as a PDF, run the Adobe Accessibility Checker understand if there are accessibility issues that require remediation. The Adobe Accessibility Checker is only available in Adobe Acrobat Pro©, not Adobe Reader©.

Visit Adobe.Com to learn how to create and verify PDF accessibility in Acrobat Pro.

Important fact about Reading Order in PDFs: Reading Order is controlled by the tag tree. This is an important fact to understand. Sometimes people believe that reading order is controlled by the “reading order pane” – but that is false. So again, reading order is only controlled by the tag tree.

Sample tag tree in Adobe Acrobat PDF:

Figure 31. Sample of an Accessibility Tag tree from Adobe Acrobat Pro

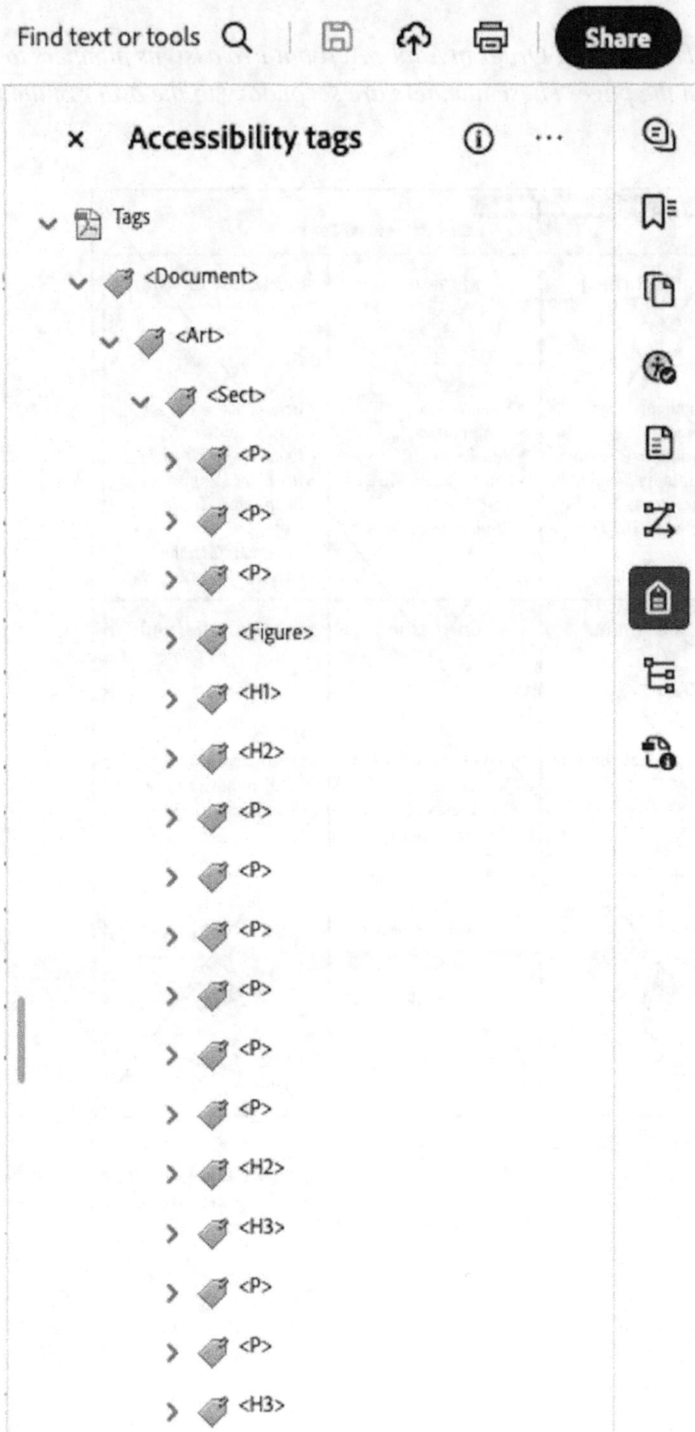

Sample of the Reading Order view in Adobe Acrobat PDF:

Figure 32. The Reading Order in Adobe Acrobat Pro assigns numbers to difference segments on the page. These numbers are secondary to the order of the tags in the tag tree

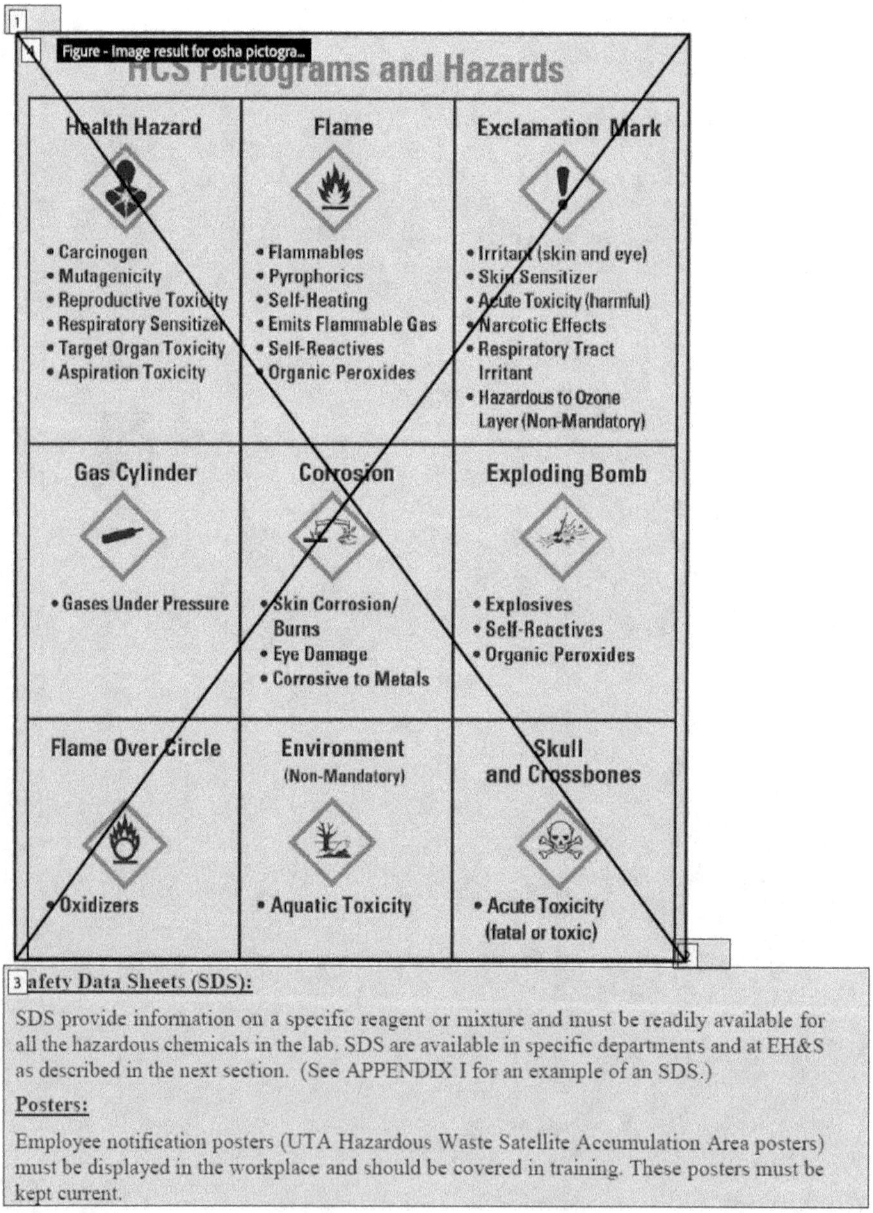

Social Media Posts

Different social media companies have different options for accessibility. The key things to remember are:

- Always provide sufficient color contrast, even in images/videos.
- Images must have alt text or the image must be described in the post.
- Videos must have captions or a transcript in the post.

Helpful Social Media Links

- Facebook – Alt Text - https://www.facebook.com/help/android-app/214124458607871?_rdr
- Facebook – Add or Remove Captions - https://www.facebook.com/help/261764017354370/?helpref=related_articles
- Instagram – Alt Text - https://help.instagram.com/503708446705527
- Instagram – Add a Caption - https://help.instagram.com/236245819849257/?helpref=related_articles
- Instagram – Manage Reels and Video Captions on Instagram - https://help.instagram.com/225479678901832
- X – Alt Text - https://help.x.com/en/using-x/add-image-descriptions
- X – Captions - https://help.x.com/en/using-x/upload-caption-srt-file
- YouTube – Captions - https://support.google.com/youtube/answer/2734796?hl=en
- LinkedIn – Alt Text - https://www.linkedin.com/help/linkedin/answer/a519856/adding-alternative-text-to-images-for-accessibility?lang=en
- LinkedIn – Captions - https://www.linkedin.com/help/linkedin/answer/a552177?hcppcid=search

Digital Signage

Letter Height and Density

Digital signage is generally presented in public areas and is expected to be viewed as someone walks past the sign. In addition to electronic accessibility rules, one must also be aware of the physical ADA signage requirements. The ADA requires letter height on signs to be at least 1" high for every 10' of viewing distance (U.S. Access Board, 2022). Depending on the program used to create the digital content, testing may need to be performed to ensure that the broadcasted image meets the minimum letter height requirement.

The letter height requirement will limit the amount of text that can be displayed. When testing how the graphic displays, also understand if there is sufficient time lapse before the image is replaced with the next image. Read slowly through the text and add 10 seconds (for those that walk up after the slide has loaded or for those that read more slowly) to ensure there is enough display time for text on the slide to be read.

Remind content contributors that they are designing for a billboard, not a brochure! Feel free to provide a hyperlink to a webpage that provides more information.

Color Contrast and Flashing Images

Ensure that the display image provides sufficient color contrast as discussed at the beginning of this chapter.

Ensure that there are no flashing images or animations that flash faster than three times a second (W3C, 2024b). Failure to meet this important requirement may result in the sign causing an epileptic seizure.

Videos

Common uses of videos in the workplace are training sessions, social media postings, and sharing marketing information.

The most obvious accessibility requirement of a video is captions. While captions are crucial, there are more accessibility items that need to be addressed other than only captions. The Bureau of Internet Accessibility has an excellent Video Accessibility Checklist that would help ensure all videos are accessible (Bureau of Internet Accessibility, n.d.).

Captions

1 in 8 people (13%) ages 12 or older have hearing loss in both ears (National Institute of Health, 2024). When videos are presented without captions, that discriminates against this large part of the population. People often prefer captions over sound due to environmental or hardware constraints. Captions also help those that are listening to a language that is not their native language. Remember – accessibility helps many, not only those with disabilities!

Captions are required to be accurate and have proper sentence capitalization and punctuation (General Services Administration, 2024b). Platforms such as YouTube and Adobe.com offer free, auto-captioning services. The auto-captions generally do not have proper sentence capitalization or punctuation and will require remediation prior to sharing the video.

Captions are also required to be synchronized with the content and include any audio descriptions that are relevant to the user experience.

Video Content

Review the content of the video to ensure that there is always sufficient color contrast.

Ensure that there are no images in the presentation that fail Success Criteria 2.3.1 Three Flashes or Below Threshold (Level A). Failure to comply with this SC could cause those with photosensitivity to have a seizure. Learn more about flashing and blinking items in WCAG 2.1 2.3.1.

Transcript

Provide a transcript of the video. The transcript document must be an accessible document. Remember that accessible documents must have proper heading structure to ensure navigation by those that use a screen reader, have sufficient color contrast, and be in a format that is free to access. Keep in mind that only those that have purchased a Microsoft Word license can open a Word file.

If the business provides every employee with a Word license, then sharing transcripts as Word files to only employees is allowed. If, however, the business wants to share a file publicly, the format of the file must be publicly available (e.g. PDF, html) unless the business is willing to purchase a Word license for everyone that wants it.

Podcasts

For audio-only recordings, a transcript must be available for those that cannot hear. This will also benefit those that need to read instead of listening due to environmental reasons. And of course, the transcript must be an accessible file!

Use People First Language

When writing about those with disabilities, always use "people first" language. This article, "Communicating With and About People with Disabilities" from the Center for Disease Control has an excellent article explaining the best practices for people first language.

The premise is that text should always begin by addressing the person and then the disability. Examples:

- Do not use “deaf person”. Use “a person with deafness”.
- Do not use “epileptic”. Use “a person with epilepsy”.
- Do not use “normal person”. Use “a person without disabilities”.

Important Reminders

- Word: Do not use the Developer tool, as they are not accessible.
- Word: Text contained in the header and footer panes are not reached by a screen reader.
- PowerPoint: Remove all animations prior to saving the PowerPoint as a PDF. Animated objects will not present properly in PDF.
- PowerPoint: When using PowerPoint on a MAC iOS, it will not save properly as a tagged PDF. Instead, upload the PPT file to Microsoft Office 365 and download it as a PDF. This will result in a properly tagged PDF if slide masters were used to create the presentation slides.

THE CHALLENGES

There are two main roadblocks to businesses providing accessible communications:

1. Lack of knowledge
    a. Many people are simply unaware that their communications are not accessible. It never crossed their mind that they may be blocking people from accessing information by using insufficient contrast or not adding alternative text to images.
    b. Lack of knowledge is solved by completion of training. The good news is that there are many, free accessibility training resources available. However, it may be necessary for companies to mandate employee training to ensure everyone knows that they are each responsible for their part of electronic accessibility.
2. Lack of desire
    a. Unfortunately, some people simply do not care whether their work product is accessible. They most often claim either there isn't enough time to make it accessible or it isn't their job to be accessible. A frequent example of this scenario is for graphic designers. Some graphic designers feel their only obligation is to design a graphic that is visually pleasing and easy to understand (from their own viewpoint).

b. Companies must have a published policy that explains every employee's output is required to be accessible. This equally applies to graphics designed for marketing materials, employee training videos, PowerPoints shared internally/externally and company websites.
c. The expectation is that every deliverable is accessible every time. If there is a pressing reason that an inaccessible resource must be shared, it should be remediated as quickly as possible and reshared through the same channels as the original. If you don't have time (and money) to make it accessible, then you must have the time (and money) to remediate it. This will always be a business decision – but it comes with real legal risks.
d. Creating accessible electronic resources should be habit for all employees. Following the foundational accessibility best practices should be the way that all employees conduct themselves, from the President to the temporary employee.

KEY TAKEAWAYS

Over 70 million people - now you know the foundations of electronic accessibility and can start ensuring that you do not leave out any of the 70 million people in the U.S. that have disabilities (CDC 2024a). Whether communicating internally within an organization or externally to the public or to customers, use these best practices to provide barrier-free communications.

- Accessibility is everyone's responsibility!
- There is a legal standard to follow: WCAG 2.1 AA
- Share your knowledge!
- As with most topics - the more one learns, the more one understands there is much more yet to learn!

In organizations, it is imperative that the requirement to be accessible must flow from the top of the organizational chart to the very last rung of the ladder. Being accessible is not optional. Each individual employee impacts the accessibility of the organization – each individual employee can put the entire organization at risk of legal exposure.

Be sure that you are an accessibility champion at your organization. You know the foundations of electronic accessibility. You can serve as a source of information and may even step into a full-time electronic accessibility role at your organization. If you see something that isn't accessible, say something! You may be the reason that your organization does not get sued. You may be the reason that your organization is awarded a contract or gains a new customer – because the communications are accessible.

CHECKLIST

- Color
    - Never use color as a single identifier
    - Ensure sufficient color contrast
- Use Styles (headings)
- Add Alt Text to all images, charts, graphs and tables
- Use Tables for data (not forms)
- Add a Document Title
- PowerPoints
    - Use Slide Masters
    - Set the reading order
- Excel
    - Instructions start in cell A1
    - Format the data as a table
    - Add a table name
- Videos must have captions with proper sentence capitalization and punctuation
- Podcasts must have a transcript

RESOURCES

Web Accessibility Resources

- Section508.gov Training: *Accessibility Training for Developers.*https://www.section508.gov/create/developer-training/
- Section 508 Trusted Tester Conformance Test Process. https://www.dhs.gov/trusted-tester
- W3C – Web Accessibility Initiative. Digital Accessibility Foundations Free Online Course. https://www.w3.org/WAI/courses/foundations-course/
- W3C (July 2024). *Developing for Web Accessibility.* https://www.w3.org/WAI/tips/developing/
- Google – Web Accessibility Course. Free. https://www.udacity.com/course/web-accessibility--ud891?ranMID=53187&ranEAID=SAyYsTvLiGQ&ranSiteID=SAyYsTvLiGQ-xW0IO_b4KqiyBnCQfrzTyw&utm_source=affiliates

Alt Text Resources

- Microsoft. (Date Unknown). *Everything You Need to Know to Write Effective Alt Text.*https://support.microsoft.com/en-us/office/everything-you-need-to-know-to-write-effective-alt-text-df98f884-ca3d-456c-807b-1a1fa82f5dc2
- W3C (December 2021). Good Alt Text, Bad Alt Text – *Making Your Content Perceivable.*https://www.wcag.com/blog/good-alt-text-bad-alt-text-making-your-content-perceivable/
- W3C (May 2024). *An alt Decision Tree.* https://www.w3.org/WAI/tutorials/images/decision-tree/
- Meta Facebook. (Date Unknown). *How do I Edit the Alternative Text for a Photo on Facebook?*https://www.facebook.com/help/214124458607871
- Meta Instagram. (Date Unknown). *Edit the Alternative Text for a Post on Instagram.*https://help.instagram.com/503708446705527
- X (Date Unknown). *How to Make Images Accessible for People.* https://help.x.com/en/using-x/picture-descriptions

Color Contrast

- Adobe Inc. (Unknown). *Color Contrast in Photography.* https://www.adobe.com/creativecloud/photography/hub/guides/what-is-color-contrast.html
- WebAIM. (January 2021). *Contrast and Color Accessibility.* https://webaim.org/articles/contrast/

Styles

- Microsoft, Inc. (Unknown). *Customize or Create New Styles.* https://support.microsoft.com/en-us/office/customize-or-create-new-styles-d38d6e47-f6fc-48eb-a607-1eb120dec563
- Microsoft, Inc. (Unknown). *Apply Styles.* (Video) https://support.microsoft.com/en-us/office/apply-styles-f8b96097-4d25-4fac-8200-6139c8093109

Navigation Pane

- Microsoft., Inc. (Unknown). *What is the Navigation Pane?*https://support.microsoft.com/en-us/office/what-is-the-navigation-pane-24fcad76-7604-4ab0-80ed-18d65fcc9dc3
- Microsoft, Inc. (Unknown). *Use the Navigation Pane in Word.*https://support.microsoft.com/en-us/office/use-the-navigation-pane-in-word-394787be-bca7-459b-894e-3f8511515e55

Writing Effective Alt Text

- Microsoft, Inc. (Unknown). *Everything You Need to Know to Write Effective Alt Text.*https://support.microsoft.com/en-us/office/everything-you-need-to-know-to-write-effective-alt-text-df98f884-ca3d-456c-807b-1a1fa82f5dc2
- WebAIM. (October 2021). *Alternative Text.*https://webaim.org/techniques/alttext/
- The American Foundation for The Blind. (Unknown). *Writing Effective Image Descriptions for "Alt Text".*https://www.afb.org/digital-inclusion/accessibility-resources/writing-effective-image-descriptions

Tables

- Perkins School for the Blind. (Unknown). *Creating an Accessible Table in Word.*https://www.perkins.org/resource/creating-accessible-table-word/
- Microsoft, Inc. (Unknown). *Create More Accessible Tables in Excel.* (Video) https://support.microsoft.com/en-us/office/video-create-more-accessible-tables-in-excel-86e50f77-0f15-4537-ab1d-62d0e4cd5645

PowerPoint

- Section508.Gov. (June 2021). *Create Accessible Presentations.*https://www.section508.gov/create/presentations/
- Perkins School for the Blind. (September 2023). *How to Create Accessible PowerPoints.*https://www.perkins.org/resource/how-create-accessible-powerpoints/

PDFs

- Adobe.com. (August 2024). *Create and Verify PDF Accessibility (Acrobat Pro).*https://helpx.adobe.com/acrobat/using/create-verify-pdf-accessibility.html

Captions

- Harvard University. (Unknown). *Technique: Writing Captions.* (Video) https://accessibility.huit.harvard.edu/technique-writing-captions

REFERENCES

W3C (2023a). Web Accessibility Laws and Policies. https://www.w3.org/WAI/policies/

W3C. (2023b). W3C introduction to understanding WCAG. https://www.w3.org/WAI/WCAG21/Understanding/intro#understanding-the-four-principles-of-accessibility

W3C. (2023c). Understanding SC 1.4.1: Use of color (Level A). W3.org. https://www.w3.org/WAI/WCAG21/Understanding/use-of-color.html

W3C. (2024a). W3C accessibility guidelines. https://www.w3.org/TR/wcag-3.0/

W3C. (2024b). Understanding SC 2.3.1: Three flashes or below threshold (Level A). https://www.w3.org/WAI/WCAG22/Understanding/three-flashes-or-below-threshold.html

Bureau of Internet Accessibility. (n.d.). Video accessibility checklist. BOIA.org. https://www.boia.org/video-accessibility-checklist?utm_adgroup=Video-Accessibility-Checklist&utm_source=google&utm_medium=paidsearch&utm_campaign=Generic-Checklists-Guides-Content-Downloads-97F&utm_term=video%20accessibility%20checklist&utm_content=checkl

Centers for Disease Control and Prevention (CDC). (2024a). CDC data shows over 70 million U.S. adults reported having a disability. Centers for Disease Control and Prevention. https://www.cdc.gov/media/releases/2024/s0716-Adult-disability.html

Centers for Disease Control and Prevention (CDC). (2024b). Disability Impacts All of Us. U.S. Center for Disease Control. https://www.cdc.gov/ncbddd/disabilityandhealth/infographic-disability-impacts-all.html

ColorWillOrg. (n.d.). Colorblind guide. Colorblindguide.com. https://www.colorblindguide.com/post/colorblind-people-population-live-counter

Commonwealth of Pennsylvania. (n.d.). Accessibility best practices. WCMS Author Guide. https://wcmauthorguide.pa.gov/en/accessibility-best-practices.html

Disability Law Center. (2020, January 1). Notice of settlement of class action relating to captioning of Harvard's public web content. Disability Law Center. https://www.dlc-ma.org/2019/12/13/notice-of-settlement-of-class-action-relating-to-captioning-of-harvards-public-web-content/

Drümmer, O., Erle, M., Zagler, W., Karshmer, A., Penaz, P., & Miesenberger, K. (2012). PDF/UA – A New Era for Document Accessibility: Understanding, Managing and Implementing the ISO Standard PDF/UA (Universal Accessibility): Introduction to the Special Thematic Session. *Lecture Notes in Computer Science*, *585–586*, 585–586. Advance online publication. DOI: 10.1007/978-3-642-31522-0_88

Federal Register (2024a). Nondiscrimination on the Basis of Disability; Accessibility of Web Information and Services of State and Local Government Entities. https://www.federalregister.gov/documents/2024/04/24/2024-07758/nondiscrimination-on-the-basis-of-disability-accessibility-of-web-information-and-services-of-state

Federal Register. (2024b). Nondiscrimination on the basis of disability; Accessibility of web information and services of state and local government entities. FederalRegister.gov. https://www.federalregister.gov/documents/2024/04/24/2024-07758/nondiscrimination-on-the-basis-of-disability-accessibility-of-web-information-and-services-of-state

General Services Administration. (2024a). IT accessibility laws and policies. www.Section508.gov. https://www.section508.gov/manage/laws-and-policies/#:~:text=In%201998%2C%20Congress%20amended%20the,accessible%20to%20people%20with%20disabilities

General Services Administration. (2024b). General guidelines for captions. Section508.gov. https://www.section508.gov/create/captions-transcripts/#:~:text=General%20Guidelines%20for%20Captions&text=The%20text%20and%20the%20speech,99%25%20accuracy%20to%20be%20readable

Information Technology Industry Council. (2023, November). Accessibility. ITIC.org. https://www.itic.org/policy/accessibility

National Eye Institute. (2024, August 1). Color blindness. NEI.NIH.gov. https://www.nei.nih.gov/learn-about-eye-health/eye-conditions-and-diseases/color-blindness

National Institute of Health. (2024, March). Quick statistics about hearing, balance & dizziness. NIH.gov. https://www.nidcd.nih.gov/health/statistics/quick-statistics-hearing

Siteimprove, Inc. (2024). A guide to accessibility overlays. Siteimprove.com. https://www.siteimprove.com/glossary/accessibility-overlays/

U. S. Department of Justice. (n.d.). Businesses That Are Open To the Public. ADA.Gov. https://www.ada.gov/topics/title-iii/

U.S. Access Board. (2022). Guide to the ADA accessibility standards, Chapter 7: Signs (Character height). Access-Board.gov. https://www.access-board.gov/ada/guides/chapter-7-signs/#technical-requirements-for-characters

U.S. Access Board (USAB). (2024). Information and Communication Technology, Revised 508 Standards and 255 Guidelines. https://www.access-board.gov/ict/

UsableNet Inc. (2024). Get the 2024 midyear report on digital accessibility lawsuits. UsableNet.com. https://usablenet.com/resources?contentType=Reports

World Health Organization (WHO). (2023). Disability. https://www.who.int/news-room/fact-sheets/detail/disability-and-health#:~:text=An%20estimated%201.3%20billion%20people,earlier%20than%20those%20without%20disabilities

Chapter 12
Next-Gen Learning: Gamification Strategies for Engaging Diverse Workforces and Advancing DEI

Hazel Gruenewald
https://orcid.org/0000-0003-2044-3696
Reutlingen University, Germany

Lena Riha
https://orcid.org/0009-0003-1018-363X
Reutlingen University, Germany

ABSTRACT

Despite widespread efforts, traditional Diversity, Equity, and Inclusion (DEI) training often falls short of driving meaningful change. This chapter explores how gamification can improve DEI initiatives by integrating features like interactivity, feedback loops, and tailored challenges into workplace learning. A transformative tool, gamification offers engaging and scalable learning experiences. However, its success hinges on thoughtful contextual design, leadership commitment, and measurable outcomes. Building on Meiman et al.'s (2019) framework, which integrates Universal Design for Learning (UDL), growth mindset, and design thinking, this chapter provides insights for designing gamified training that advance DEI. UDL ensures accessibility through multiple means of engagement, representation, and expression, while a growth mindset fosters continuous learning. Design thinking prioritizes user experience. The chapter draws on research and practical examples to illustrate how gamification can create equitable learning environments and outlines strategies for effective implementation.

DOI: 10.4018/979-8-3373-5322-7.ch012

INTRODUCTION

In today's rapidly evolving work environment, the demand for effective workplace learning has skyrocketed as industries grapple with pervasive skills shortages driven by factors like climate change, digitalization, artificial intelligence, and demographic shifts (Li, 2022; Müller & Gruenewald, 2024; World Economic Forum, 2020). These challenges have prompted a significant push for upskilling and reskilling initiatives to help employees continuously adapt to new technological, economic, and social developments (Autor et al., 2022; Bersin, 2022; Brynjolfsson & McAfee, 2018; Krath et al. 2021; Müller & Gruenewald, 2024; World Economic Forum, 2020). At the same time, organizations face mounting pressure to ensure that their learning strategies not only meet these challenges but also embody the tenets of **Diversity**, **Equity**, and **Inclusion** (DEI).[1]

This situation presents learning and development (L&D) professionals with a complex dual mandate. Rather than treating DEI as a separate initiative, there is a growing call to integrate DEI principles into the design, delivery, and accessibility of broader training frameworks. This requires that learning programs provide marginalized employees with equal opportunities for development and success, on par with their peers. As DEI becomes a cornerstone of sustainable organizational growth, it is essential that training programs are not only inclusive and equitable but also actively respond to the diverse needs of participants (Dobbin & Kalev, 2018, 2022; Roberson et al., 2020; Vardeman, 2024; Zheng, 2022). In addition, there is increasing momentum to align training efforts more closely with overarching DEI initiatives and to rigorously measure their true impact in driving meaningful and enduring change (Dobbin & Kalev, 2018; Paluck et al., 2021; Roberson et al., 2020; Zheng, 2022).

Still, significant challenges persist, particularly in the realm of DEI training. Pamela Newkirk (2019), in her book *Diversity, Inc: The Failed Promise of a Billion-Dollar Business*, argues that despite the widespread implementation of DEI training programs, they often fall short of achieving their intended objectives and have minimal impact on creating lasting workplace transformation—an argument supported by numerous researchers (Bezrukova et al., 2016; Dobbin & Kalev, 2018, 2022; Kulik & Roberson, 2008; Nathoo, 2021; Paluck & Green, 2009; Paluck et al., 2021; Read, 2021; Roberson et al., 2020; Zheng, 2022).

The challenges with DEI training have been further compounded by the impact of the COVID-19 pandemic, which forced many organizations to shift to online training. Although digital solutions offer timely, flexible, and scalable options for reaching large numbers of learners across various devices, they also introduce new complexities. L&D professionals now face the added difficulty of delivering effective online training that resonates with employees who are geographically dispersed and working in hybrid environments, all while ensuring learners are not overwhelmed by training or that their well-being is compromised. Indeed, the transition to remote and hybrid work arrangements has introduced new challenges for employees, leading to increased feelings of isolation, anxiety, and disconnection from colleagues and the organization (Buonomo et al., 2023). These changes have not only intensified existing mental health issues including heightened anxiety, depression, and physical health concerns but have also contributed to diminished motivation levels overall (Caligiuri et al., 2020; Hamouche, 2020; Koekemoer et al., 2021).

As the workforce evolves, researchers have identified gamification as a potential solution to address some of the aforementioned challenges (Gatheral, 2022; Humanoo, n.d.). The concept has gained significant popularity, particularly in the context of remote learning, as it provides an employee-centric approach that can boost engagement and foster a sense of community—often seen as an effective counter to declining attention spans[2]. By incorporating gamified elements into DEI-driven training programs, organizations can potentially transform mundane learning experiences into immersive and impactful journeys, equipping employees with the skills and resilience needed to navigate the complexities of a dynamic, global work environment.

In a 2019 survey conducted by TalentLMS (Apostolopoulos, 2019), 33% of respondents expressed a desire for more game-like features in their employee training software. The survey also revealed a strong correlation between gamification and employee engagement: Incorporating game-like elements into training boosted motivation to 83% and reduced boredom to just 10%. These findings highlight the potential of gamification to significantly enhance employee motivation and engagement during training sessions. However, despite these compelling results, many organizations have yet to adopt gamification practices. Notably, 43% of respondents admitted to being unaware of any gamification elements in their workplace. This gap in adoption is particularly concerning in the context of DEI initiatives, where, according to Zheng (2022), practitioners are often tasked with managing extensive projects and measures without the necessary support, budget, or tools to effectively carry out their responsibilities.

In this chapter, we will explore how gamification might be leveraged to bolster DEI efforts within learning and development, helping to engage and prepare employees from diverse backgrounds for the demands of a future-ready global workforce. We start by outlining the necessity for DEI and examining the limitations of traditional DEI training. Subsequently, we investigate the common challenges organizations face when implementing gamification without thorough preparation or customization to user needs. In the concluding section, we apply the framework proposed by Meiman et al. (2019) to examine and suggest strategies for designing gamified training that effectively supports DEI objectives. The discussion is intended to equip HR professionals, corporate trainers, organizational leaders, and education innovators with actionable insights to harness the transformative power of gamification in supporting DEI and broader sustainability goals.

BACKGROUND: THE GROWING IMPERATIVE FOR DEI

Over the past few decades, the demand for DEI initiatives, including training, has surged, driven by changing workforce demographics, globalization, ongoing litigation, and other significant factors (Dobbin & Kalev, 2022; Zheng, 2022). However, as Carucci (2024) points out, attitudes toward workplace diversity often swing dramatically, much like a pendulum. He notes that in just the past year, many companies have scaled back their DEI investments in response to politicized push-back and backlash from call-out culture. This reduction in investment is occurring despite evidence from some studies showing moderate improvements in key areas like the representation of women and people of color.

Carucci presents a strong, evidence-based case for the benefits of diversity, emphasizing the substantial returns from well-implemented DEI strategies. He references the latest McKinsey *Diversity Matters* report (Dixon-Fyle et al., 2023), which shows that companies committed to diversity substantially outperform those that are not. When employees perceive that their unique contributions are recognized and that they belong in an inclusive workplace, their commitment and morale increase markedly. This heightened sense of belonging leads to a more engaged and productive workforce, ultimately driving overall business success. Carucci (2024) further emphasizes, "Promoting diversity and inclusion helps everyone on your team feel included and safe. When employees know that their opinions are respected and valued, they become more willing to speak their minds. This encourages everyone to maximize their contributions."

A recent Forbes article asserts that while DEI efforts should not focus solely on retention, the benefits in this area are undeniable (Fayad, 2022). Data from the Society for Human Resource Management (Lynchburg Regional SHRM, 2017) shows that replacing an employee earning $60,000 annually can cost between $30,000 and $45,000—50% to 75% of the departing employee's annual salary. For highly skilled workers, this cost can rise to as much as 213% of their annual salary. Effective DEI policies allegedly help lower these costs by reducing turnover.

Moreover, companies that embrace DEI are better positioned to attract top talent and tap into a broader customer base, leading to increased market share and profitability (Carucci, 2024; Fayad, 2022). DEI measures also drive innovation, creativity and problem-solving by bringing together diverse perspectives. Diversity, in this context, includes both inherent traits (e.g., race, gender, age, sexual orientation, socioeconomic background, religion, disability, nationality) and acquired diversity (e.g., global mindsets, language skills, cross-functional knowledge, cultural fluency). A Harvard Business Review study (Lorenzo & Reeves, 2018) found that organizations with diversity scored 19% higher in innovation and 9% higher in financial performance. This clearly demonstrates the direct positive impact that workforce diversity has on a company's financial success. Thus, integrating DEI initiatives is not only a moral and social imperative but also essential for financial sustainability and growth.

Given this background, it is unsurprising that DEI training has become a staple in global workplace learning. This trend is evident across a broad spectrum of organizations, from Fortune 500 companies to smaller enterprises and higher education institutions (Dobbin & Kalev, 2018, 2022; Nathoo, 2021). Nonetheless, while there is substantial evidence that DEI training can be beneficial under certain conditions (Anand & Winters, 2008; Rudman et al., 2001; Smith et al., 2006), a significant body of research has questioned the genuine effectiveness of DEI training programs (Dobbin & Kalev, 2018, 2022; Kaplan, 2006; Nathoo, 2021; Newkirk, 2019; Read, 2021; Robb & Doverspike, 2001; Zheng, 2022). In the following section, we will explore these criticisms in greater detail before considering how gamification can be utilized to enhance the effectiveness of DEI training programs.

TRADITIONAL DEI TRAINING: WHY THE OLD PLAYBOOK FAILS

While DEI training has evolved into a lucrative and booming industry, concerns have been raised that it often serves as low-hanging fruit for organizations eager to showcase their commitment to diversity and inclusion (Nathoo, 2021; Newkirk, 2019; Read, 2021; Zheng, 2022). Critics argue that its prevalence is driven more by the desire to project a responsible corporate image and to mitigate potential legal risks than by a genuine commitment to fostering diversity (Dobbin & Kalev, 2018, 2022; Nathoo, 2021; Zheng, 2022). For instance, in response to high-profile incidents of racial insensitivity, companies like Sephora and Starbucks publicly announced racial bias education for employees, seemingly using these initiatives to deflect criticism and protect their corporate reputation. While such measures may help to calm public outrage and shield companies from litigation, it remains questionable whether they lead to meaningful and lasting change within the workplace.

To address these concerns, Bezrukova et al. (2016) conducted a meta-analysis of 40 years of research on diversity training, synthesizing results from 260 independent studies to provide a comprehensive evaluation of its effectiveness. The authors note that "little has been done to reconcile the opposing effects of diversity training to understand when and how diversity training promotes positive changes in trainees' learning outcomes" (p. 5).

Diversity Training Context

Bezrukova et al. (2016) highlight that the effectiveness of DEI training is highly dependent on contextual factors. Their study emphasizes that diversity training embedded within the organizational culture is more likely to be perceived by employees as meaningful and impactful. Such integration demonstrates a strong organizational commitment to DEI, which in turn enhances participant motivation and improves training outcomes. Other key contextual factors identified include the level of endorsement and support from senior management, differences between educational and organizational settings, and the impact of voluntary versus mandatory attendance. Table 1 summarizes the main findings from the study in relation to these contextual factors, enriched by additional critical insights from other academic sources.

Table 1. Contextual issues to be considered in diversity training

Context Factor	Key Issues Addressed by Bezrukova et al. (2016)	Further Scholarly Perspectives
Institutional endorsement and support	• "Authority sanction" condition: Interactions between different groups need to be endorsed by higher authorities.	• Institutional support is critical in shaping the effectiveness of such interactions (Paluck, 2006). • The business need has to be clearly identified and explained by leadership (Morley, 2018). • Active commitment from senior leadership to DEI sends a strong message and encourages employees to take DEI initiatives seriously (Bhaduri, 2023; Dobbin & Kalev, 2018, 2022; Morley, 2018; Roberson et al., 2020; Zheng, 2022).
Organizational versus educational settings	• Diversity training is generally more effective in educational settings than in organizational ones, as it is less likely to be seen as disruptive to work tasks. • Diversity training in organizations is often viewed as an 'add-on' rather than a core part of the mission. • The perceived difference between settings may be overstated; the key issue in organizations is how well diversity training is integrated with other initiatives that complement and reinforce its goals.	• Educational environments focus on deepening understanding of diversity and addressing prejudice through experiential learning and intergroup interactions (Avery & Thomas, 2004; King et al., 2010). • In contrast, organizations aim to foster an inclusive workplace culture that strengthens internal and external relationships (Cox & Blake, 1991; Mor-Barak, 2005).
Standalone versus integrated approach	• Embedded programs that combine awareness and skills components within broader diversity initiatives are shown to have a higher overall impact than standalone sessions. • Ongoing support and reinforcement mechanisms are essential for translating knowledge and attitudes into sustained actions that align with organizational goals and practices.	• So-called 'piecemeal' interventions sessions often check diversity boxes without driving meaningful or lasting changes in participants' habits or long-term behaviors (Dobbin & Kalev, 2018, 2022; Lai, 2023; Roberson et al., 2020; Zheng, 2022). • Low cost often correlates with low payoffs. While short, one-time sessions may raise awareness of implicit biases, motivate participants to address them, and provide some basic strategies, they are unlikely to create substantial change. Instead, these sessions serve to initiate conversations and open the door to deeper engagement (Hemphill, 2018). • Evidence suggests that standalone interventions may inadvertently reinforce the very stereotypes they are designed to dismantle (Egan & Bendick, 2008; Galinsky & Moskowitz, 2000; Kulik et al., 2000; Macrae et al., 1994).

continued on following page

Table 1. Continued

Context Factor	Key Issues Addressed by Bezrukova et al. (2016)	Further Scholarly Perspectives
Mandatory versus voluntary attendance	• The overall impact of diversity training shows little difference between mandatory and voluntary participation. • Mandatory training proved more effective in promoting behavioral and cognitive learning • Voluntary training is generally perceived more positively by participants.	• Comprehensive research by Dobbin and Kalev (2018, 2022), analyzing 800 American firms over three decades, reveals that 80% of U.S. corporations require diversity training—a factor that may contribute to its unpopularity compared to voluntary participation. • Despite the preference for voluntary training (Dobbin & Kalev, 2022; Kaplan, 2006), it may not yield the most significant changes and be less impactful. Those who choose to participate often already hold pro-diversity views and are not necessarily the ones who need the most improvement in cognitive, attitudinal, or behavioral outcomes (Ellis & Sonnenfeld, 1994; Pettigrew and Tropp, 2006). • Mandatory courses often provoke anger and resistance, particularly among young white men, who may view the training as a career threat, leading to increased hostility toward other groups (Dobbin & Kalev, 2018, 2022). • Compliance-driven initiatives may be seen as an attempt to control behavior, resulting in resistance and disengagement. It can reinforce biases compared to a reduction in biases when participants feel ownership over their decisions (Kulik et al., 2007). • Voluntary diversity training has been shown to produce more favorable outcomes, such as an increase in the number of ethnic minorities in management positions (Dobbin & Kalev, 2018, 2022). In contrast, mandatory training failed to improve minority representation and even reduced the proportion of Black women and Asian Americans in management roles. • Mandatory training can create false confidence in anti-discrimination efforts, fostering complacency about personal biases. Castilla and Benard (2010) found that gender biases persisted when participants believed their employers were non-discriminatory. Similarly, Kaiser et al. (2013) showed that pro-diversity measures, like training, led employees to assume workplaces were bias-free and dismiss discrimination claims.

Diversity Training Design

A second key focus of Bezrukova et al.'s (2016) study is training design. Effective DEI training should accommodate diverse learning styles, schedules, and levels of technological access to ensure broad participation and engagement. By prioritizing inclusivity in training design, organizations can maximize the impact of DEI initiatives and foster a more inclusive workplace culture.

The authors identify several factors that influence the effectiveness of diversity training programs, which include the choice between group-specific versus inclusive approaches, training duration, training type, single versus multiple-method formats, and group composition. Table 2 presents an overview of these critical findings, supplemented by insights from other academic studies.

Table 2. Design issues to be considered in diversity training

Design Factor	Key Issues Addressed by Bezrukova et al. (2016)	Further Scholarly Perspectives
Focus: Group specific versus inclusive	• No significant differences in outcomes were found based on whether diversity training focused on broad inclusivity or targeted specific demographic groups.	• Recent studies indicate a growing trend among organizations toward adopting a 'colorblind' approach, which downplays initiatives aimed at specific demographic groups in favor of broader inclusion strategies that promote cooperation and reduce intergroup tensions (Emerson, 2017). While this approach aims to foster unity, it may paradoxically undermine inclusion efforts, leaving some employees feeling excluded or marginalized. • On the other hand, group-specific approaches may inadvertently exacerbate intergroup differences, leading to attitude polarization (Stratton et al., 2006).
Duration	• A strong correlation was found between longer diversity training programs and their effectiveness. • While cognitive knowledge remains stable, attitudinal and behavioral effects decay over time. This finding reinforces the need for long-term strategies, such as periodic refresher courses and continuous engagement initiatives, to sustain the benefits of training.	• Zheng (2022) observes that the practical implementation of DEI training means it is typically a one-off event and usually too brief to have a durable effect. For instance, while many forms of allyship training intend to boost bystander intervention, truly effective training for bystander intervention often requires at least five hours. Yet, many allyship training sessions may last only about an hour.
Training Type: Awareness, behavior-based or combined	• Awareness-based diversity training tends to have the least impact on both attitudinal/affective and behavioral learning outcomes. • Training programs, which combine both awareness and behavioral components, are more effective than those that address these elements separately. • Diversity training shows the strongest impact on participants' immediate reactions and cognitive learning. However, initial positive reactions or knowledge retention do not necessarily translate into to long-term behavioral or attitudinal changes.	• Zheng (2022) discusses a broad range of training programs designed to tackle issues related to identity and inequity, including "Courageous Conversations," "Sensitivity Training," "Allyship Training," and "Unconscious Bias Training." However, she points out that the effectiveness and approach of these trainings can differ significantly based on how they are executed. If not handled with care, these programs risk simplifying complex issues, causing resentment, or inducing emotional distress among participants. This can lead to outcomes that are not only ineffective but also counterproductive. • Fujimoto and Härtel (2017) argue that diversity training promotes understanding and respect among employees from varied backgrounds by enabling them to share values and perspectives. However, the authors claim that the effectiveness of attitudinal training is limited if it does not involve a diverse participant group or if it targets specific groups, preventing wider attitudinal and behavioral changes (see section on trainee characteristics).

continued on following page

Table 2. Continued

Design Factor	Key Issues Addressed by Bezrukova et al. (2016)	Further Scholarly Perspectives
Instruction: Many methods versus one method	• While diversity training based on many instructional methods had larger effect sizes for reactions, the results were not significant for cognitive or behavioral learning.	• Gill & Olson (2023) advise against a "one size fits all" approach. Lindsey et al. (2017) found that perspective-taking benefits participants with low empathy, while goal-setting promotes more pro-diversity behaviors after three months and enhances pro-diversity attitudes after nine months.

continued on following page

Table 2. Continued

Design Factor	Key Issues Addressed by Bezrukova et al. (2016)	Further Scholarly Perspectives
Trainee characteristics	• The study found no significant impact of trainees' demographic characteristics on the outcomes, with one exception: Training groups with a higher proportion of women tended to respond more favorably to the training.	• Roberson et al. (2001) found that the composition of training groups does not influence the effectiveness of training for participants with limited prior experience. These individuals may actually benefit from the diversity within heterogeneous groups. In contrast, trainees with extensive experience developed more tailored strategies for applying the training content to their work when trained in homogenous groups. The authors propose that the choice between homogeneous and heterogeneous training groups should be based on evaluating the organization's training objectives and the participants' prior experience with diversity training. They also state that familiarity between group members may have a moderating effect. • Personality traits may influence training effectiveness, with certain strategies benefiting specific employees. For example, perspective-taking exercises are more effective for individuals with low empathy, as highly empathetic people naturally engage in this behavior, while those with lower empathy need structured activities to develop it (Lindsey et al., 2017). • Gill and Olson (2023) point out that intergroup interactions can lead to both conflict and prejudice reduction. Allport's (1954) contact hypothesis highlights that cooperative interactions with equality and shared goals improve attitudes toward outgroups. Positive and meaningful contact fosters empathy, reduces anxiety, promotes perspective-taking (Tropp & Barlow, 2018; Pettigrew & Tropp, 2008), and shifts perceptions from "them" to an inclusive "we" (Gaertner & Dovidio, 2000). Repeated interactions and friendships humanize outgroup members, encourage acceptance, and reduce stereotypes, creating space for individuals to connect as people rather than as group representatives. • Various studies (Dobbin & Kalev, 2018, 2022; Gill & Olson, 2023) demonstrate that majority group members may react defensively to diversity training, viewing diversity initiatives, for example, as "anti-White" or as minority gains at their expense. Efforts perceived as punitive, targeting specific groups, or threatening autonomy often lead to resentment and resistance.

While the findings outlined above may be shaped by contextual limitations or the scope of variables analyzed, they nonetheless offer valuable insights for designing effective training programs. Some of the highlighted challenges reinforce the need for a thoughtful, integrated approach to diversity training—one that prioritizes long-term development and leverages intrinsic motivators to foster genuine inclusivity and acceptance.

With these considerations in mind, the next section will explore how training design might be reimagined to address and overcome some of the challenges mentioned.

Designing Training to be More Equitable and Inclusive for Diverse Learners

We propose utilizing the conceptual framework of Meiman et al. (2019) as a foundation for designing training programs that are more accessible and widely accepted. Although originally developed to enhance accessibility within library settings, the framework holds significant potential for DEI training and any instructional program informed by DEI principles. It integrates Universal Design for Learning (UDL) principles (CAST, 2024) with three contemporary learning models: the ACRL Framework (2016), growth mindset theory (Dweck, 2006), and design thinking (Miller, 2015).

By combining UDL principles with instructional design (ID) strategies, this model offers a flexible, learner-centered approach to training, allowing materials and programs to adapt to diverse needs and environments. This holistic integration not only ensures inclusivity but also fosters deeper engagement and meaningful progress toward DEI objectives.

Three Core Guidelines Emphasized in the UDL Framework:

1. **Multiple means of engagement** – Sustaining learners' interest and motivation through varied instructional methods.
2. **Multiple means of representation** – Presenting information in diverse formats to ensure accessibility.
3. **Multiple means of action and expression** – Allowing learners to demonstrate understanding through varied methods.

The **ACRL framework** reimagines informational literacy as a series of interconnected concepts supported by learning goals, positioning learners as active, reflective participants who develop critical abilities over time. Its emphasis on dispositions such as curiosity, motivation, confidence, and persistence acknowledges the emotional dimensions of learning—especially relevant for those who may begin with uncertainty or anxiety. These foundational traits are equally important for DEI-informed training, where fostering psychological safety and engagement is critical. Trainers and instructional designers must critically examine how their own positionality and mindset shape their facilitation methods and, consequently, participants' learning experiences.

This reflective approach aligns with **Dweck's (2006)growth mindset theory**, which contrasts fixed (entity) and growth (incremental) perspectives on intelligence. Applying this to the training environment underscores the importance of fostering a mindset that encourages continuous learning, openness, and adaptability. Trainers working with diverse groups must not only re-evaluate their practices but also ensure representation in training materials by incorporating contributions and narratives from underrepresented communities, including Black, Indigenous, LGBTQ+, disabled, and other marginalized voices. Training activities should encourage participants to explore the intersectionality of their identities, highlighting the richness and complexity of lived experiences. Cultivating a growth mindset creates a supportive environment where participants from marginalized communities feel seen, valued, and heard. Conversely, neglecting this approach risks reinforcing exclusion, undermining the effectiveness of DEI initiatives, and missing opportunities to drive transformative change within organizational cultures.

Design thinking further enhances this approach by providing a structured, user-centered framework for innovation. Defined by principles such as *Show Don't Tell*, *Focus on Human Values*, *Embrace Experimentation*, and *Radical Collaboration* (Miller, 2015), design thinking fosters creative problem-solving. Its five key steps—empathize, define, ideate, prototype, and test—fall within broader phases of hear, create, deliver, emphasizing iterative development and collaboration. Applied to DEI training, design thinking enables trainers to identify barriers to learning and develop dynamic, engaging, and inclusive learning environments. One promising application is gamification, which integrates game-based elements into training to enhance motivation, engagement, and retention.

Before applying the framework proposed by Meiman et al. (2019), it is essential to discuss the concept of gamification and its relevance to DEI initiatives. The next section will explore the definition of gamification, review its various applications, and evaluate its potential to transform DEI efforts. By strategically incorporating gamification into DEI training and broader instructional programs, it can serve as a powerful tool for tackling DEI-related challenges while simultaneously supporting sustainable development goals.

Capitalizing on Gamification to Advance Inclusive and Sustainable Workforce Development

The term 'gamification' was coined by British computer programmer Nick Pelling in 2002 to describe his initiative to develop a 'game-like' user interface for electronic transactions, with the goal of making them both enjoyable and efficient (Ahmadi, 2020; Grünewald et al., 2019). Today, the widely accepted definition proposed by Deterding et al. (2011, p. 11) describes gamification as the "use of game elements in non-game contexts." Its popularity as a tool for increasing engagement has been well-documented in business literature (Ahmadi, 2020; Burke, 2014; Grünewald et al., 2019; Hamari et al. 2013; Larson, 2020; Rahiman et al., 2023; Robson et al., 2015; Seaborn & Fels, 2015; Werbach & Hunter, 2012; Zichermann & Linder, 2013).

Over recent decades, gamification has transitioned from a novel concept to a major industry with widespread adoption across various business contexts. In 2019, educational gamification was associated with up to a 60% increase in employee engagement in organizational programs and up to a 50% improvement in employee productivity (finances online, 2024). Current projections suggest the global gamification market will grow from $15.4 billion in 2024 to $48.7 billion by 2029 (Afzal, 2024; Gupta, 2024). These figures highlight that investing in gamification is not merely about embracing new technologies; it is about remaining competitive in the global economy.

To fully capitalize on this trend, organizations must stay attuned to evolving EdTech developments and align these innovations with their overarching goals and key drivers. When implemented wisely and effectively, gamified learning can yield substantial benefits across the **triple bottom line—people, planet, and profit**—while tapping into the growing interest in environmental and social activism, particularly prevalent among younger generations. This approach supports sustainable and profitable business practices (Chan & Lee, 2023; Rahiman et al., 2023). The transformative potential of gamification lies in driving engagement and productivity, fostering skill development, and promoting organizational success. This makes gamification a powerful catalyst for achieving individual and collective goals, including the Sustainable Development Goals (SDGs) outlined by the United Nations (2015) in the 2030 Agenda for Sustainable Development. These 17 SDGs, introduced in 2015, emphasize a vision of development that is inclusive, participatory, and environmentally sustainable, underscoring the importance of DEI in fostering a holistic approach to global progress. (*Diversity and inclusion*, n.d.).

The development of gamification applications that address economic, societal, and environmental sustainability is gaining momentum (Spanellis et al., 2024). This trend includes initiatives that center on DEI content, which play a crucial role in promoting decent work and economic growth (SDG 8). However, the impact of gamified DEI extends beyond content alone; it is essential to explore how gamified approaches can support sustainable development by creating more engaging and inclusive learning environments. By integrating DEI principles into these gamified learning strategies, organizations can enhance the quality of education (SDG 4) and ensure that their training programs not only meet current challenges but also align with broader goals of inclusivity and equity, contributing to sustainable organizational growth. This is a daunting, yet vital task in today's dynamic workplace.

In the subsequent sections, we will explore the strategic application of gamification to DEI initiatives, expanding on the earlier discussion about related challenges and opportunities. Initially, we will examine common pitfalls that must be avoided to ensure effectiveness. Following that, we will focus on specific design and contextual considerations essential for successfully integrating gamification into DEI efforts. This approach will help us understand how to tailor gamification techniques to enhance inclusivity and engagement while avoiding common missteps that could undermine these objectives.

Navigating the Pitfalls of Gamified DEI to Achieve Impact and Lasting Results

Given the enduring presence of DEI training in organizational settings, it is crucial to explore strategies for achieving greater impact. A suggested approach to gaining traction is the use of gamification in DEI training (Gatheral, 2022). Daphne Forbes, Assistant General Counsel at Microsoft and advisor to the DEI gamification specialists Conscious Inclusion Company, has witnessed these benefits firsthand. In an interview with *Law Journal Newsletters (LJN)* (2021), she noted that traditional diversity training often leads participants to merely memorize facts to check off a box. In contrast, gamification encourages learning through active participation rather than rote memorization, thereby deepening understanding and retention of DEI principles.

Even when training content does not explicitly address DEI, applying gamified learning principles tailored to diverse needs might significantly advance DEI objectives (Vardeman, 2024). Gamification's scalability enables broader outreach, but as research increasingly demonstrates, training programs must still address the distinct emotional, psychological, and cultural characteristics of today's diverse workforce (Joshi et al., 2010; Larson, 2020; Urick, 2017). This can potentially be achieved by offering personalized and adaptive learning pathways that cater to varying learning styles, requirements and abilities.

As previously noted, traditional DEI training often faces criticism for its lack of engagement and limited effectiveness in fostering empathy or driving lasting change among learners. While gamified learning can potentially mitigate some of these shortcomings through experiential methods, such as interactive scenarios, role-playing games, and simulations, it is not a 'silver bullet' for the industry's challenges (Gatheral, 2022). Numerous potential pitfalls must be carefully considered, and the success of these initiatives ultimately depends on a range of factors, which will be examined more closely in the following section.

Gamified Training: The Importance of Context and Design

DEI initiatives, while broadly applicable across various companies, need to be tailored to each organization's unique context and stage in its DEI journey (Bhaduri, 2023). Organizations are encouraged to conduct self-assessments of their progress toward DEI goals and customize training programs to align with their unique needs (Coffman et al., 2021). This process involves identifying key competencies required to achieve business objectives, understanding the target audience, and recognizing factors that will effectively engage and motivate participants.

Careful attention should be given to instructional design, context, and objectives to ensure relevance and lasting change. As Werbach and Hunter (2012) stress, selecting the appropriate game mechanics is a significant, yet final step, in a carefully planned roadmap. Moreover, technology, rewards, and competition, often overemphasized components, should not dominate the learning experience, but rather complement and enhance the content and design. Furthermore, the learning materials must be grounded in reliable sources and independent research to ensure credibility and effectiveness.

The framework proposed by Meiman et al. (2019) offers a robust structural lens for designing effective gamified DEI training programs. By integrating the Universal Design for Learning (UDL) principles with growth mindset theory and design thinking, organizations can create dynamic, inclusive, and learner-centered training experiences that resonate with diverse audiences. The framework provides a coherent structure to guide effective gamified DEI training.

Designing Gamified Training for Diverse Learners: UDL Principles in Action

The UDL principle of **engagement** emphasizes the need to motivate and sustain learner interest through strategies that account for diverse preferences and emotional needs. One effective approach is the use of interactive games, which integrate enjoyment, deep engagement, structured experiences, creativity, and social interaction (Haaland, 2023). Simulations, role-playing scenarios, and team challenges help connect training content to real-world applications, making learning more immersive and impactful. However, while gamification is well-suited to addressing serious issues, it is often misunderstood and undervalued in discussions about diversity, equity, and inclusion (Turner, 2021). To maximize its effectiveness, designers must carefully balance engagement with education, ensuring that the gravity of the subject matter remains intact within a gamified approach.

The success of DEI-focused gamified training programs further hinges on the organizational setting and level of support provided. Leadership backing plays a pivotal role in ensuring that DEI-focused gamified training programs achieve their full potential. Roberson et al. (2020) argue that training programs emphasizing their organizational value and visibly reflecting leadership's commitment to diversity are more likely to engage participants and produce meaningful learning outcomes. When leaders actively support and reinforce these initiatives, they help create an environment where DEI principles are not just taught but embedded into the organization's culture. Additionally, sufficient budget and resources must be allocated to sustain and enhance the effectiveness of these programs.

In the following, we apply Universal Design for Learning (UDL) principles to provide recommendations for designing gamified training interventions that promote DEI advancement. Our approach is informed by further scholarly discourse on the key areas identified by UDL, allowing for a more critical and structured analysis of the proposed strategies and issues. While not exhaustive, this approach offers valuable insights and starting points for further exploration.

Application of UDL Principles to Gamified Training

1. Multiple Means of Engagement

Access: Welcoming Interests and Identities

- **Optimize choice and autonomy** in training programs to enhance engagement. Research shows that many DEI training programs, particularly those centered on compliance, are often delivered as mandatory exercises with a heavy emphasis on formal regulations and grievance procedures. This 'comply or face consequences' messaging can contribute to a sense of 'DEI fatigue' among participants, framing the training in a negative light and diminishing its overall effectiveness (seppo, 2023).
    - Given the inevitability of compliance training, it is important to integrate stimulating features to counteract negative perceptions of mandatory training. The 2019 TalentLMS gamification survey found that 30% of respondents ranked gamification in corporate compliance training as their top choice (Apostolopoulos, 2019).
    - Balancing "mandatory fun" with consent can help maximize positive outcomes. Mollick and Rothbard (2014) highlight an inherent paradox

in this approach: "Management imposition of games, no matter how well meaning, changes what was an organic worker-generated process and makes it a required activity". The authors argue that this creates "a double-edged sword." When employees willingly embrace the gamified activity, there is a notable increase in positive affect. Conversely, without this consent, not only does positive affect decrease, but there is also a marginal decline in job performance. Even if participation is required, the design should ensure that learners engage with the content willingly, without feeling coerced or manipulated (Mollick & Rothbard, 2014; Werbach, 2014).

    - Ensure transparency and fairness in gamified training design. Willingness to consent is closely tied to understanding the rules, perceiving fairness and justice, and the degree of control learners have over the gamification process. When employees view gamified activities as legitimate and feel a sense of control agency, their positive emotions and motivation are likely to increase (Laine & Lindberg, 2020; McGonigal, 2011; Mollick & Rothbard, 2014).
    - Offer choice in gamification mechanics to accommodate diverse learning styles and motivations. Research suggests that intergenerational workplaces, for example, benefit from allowing employees to select the game elements they find most engaging (Foxman, cited in Haaland, 2023).
    - Ensure meaningful choices throughout the training process. Providing learners with autonomy enhances motivation and increases the likelihood of internalizing DEI principles.
- **Optimize relevance, value and authenticity** by leveraging narrative, imagery, and music to create immersive experiences. Research highlights that a well-crafted game narrative can effectively capture players' interest when structured appropriately (Doney, 2019; Oliveira et al., 2021).
    - Develop compelling and relevant scenarios to educate employees about the experiences and perspectives of diverse individuals. The combination of staging and storyline creates opportunities for players to make more informed decisions, fostering understanding and empathy for different viewpoints. Studies confirm that scenarios with realistic settings, multidimensional characters, and structured storytelling significantly enhance learning outcomes (Laine & Lindberg, 2020; Oliveira et al., 2021; North-Samardzic & de Witt, 2019).
    - Key components such as events, characters, settings, structure, and timing immerse players in the game's environment, boosting motivation and deepening learning (Domínguez et al., 2013; Jackson et al., 2018;

Laine & Lindberg, 2020). However, fictional elements must resonate with the target audience (Doney, 2019), ensuring the gamified environment remains intrinsically motivating and aligned with DEI principles. Inclusive language and imagery throughout the training materials further reinforce this alignment.

- Adopt a multidimensional approach for a nuanced understanding of DEI issues. Conventional programs often present limited perspectives, overlooking critical workplace realities. Dobbin and Kalev (2022) highlight the exclusion of key scenarios in sexual harassment training, which predominantly focuses on men harassing women while neglecting cases involving other gender identities and orientations e.g. trans and gay workers, who experience disproportionately high rates of harassment. Gamified training must address these gaps to ensure that content authentically mirrors the real-world complexities of workplace dynamics.
- Adapt gamification strategies for different age demographics. Research on age and gamification acceptance is still limited (Eikelboom, 2016; Larson, 2020), though existing studies suggest that younger users tend to embrace gamification more readily than their older counterparts, who may have lower technology acceptance or associate 'play' with frivolity, in other words, something disconnected from 'real work' (Chung et al., 2010; Haaland, 2023; Koivisto & Hamari, 2014). Older adults' lower familiarity with advanced technologies can diminish their self-confidence when navigating these systems (Haaland, 2023) and cause them to feel discomfort and tension (Algashami et al. 2018; Shahri et al. 2014; Stefanidis et al. 2018).
- Offering multiple modes of engagement—such as simplified interfaces, clear instructional support, or analog alternatives that integrate game mechanics without relying on complex digital interactions—can help bridge technological gaps. Additionally, embedding familiar workplace elements into gamified experiences can reinforce their relevance, making them feel purposeful rather than purely recreational. Providing opportunities for gradual skill-building and emphasizing the tangible benefits of gamification, such as improved learning retention and engagement, can further support acceptance across age groups.
- Incorporate familiar competitive structures to increase engagement across generations and recognized shared preferences. A recent SalesScreen survey (Haaland, 2023) found that leaderboards appeal to both Boomers (57%) and Gen Z (64%), while physical prizes hold nearly equal appeal (Haaland, 2023). Design elements should reflect intergenerational preferences. For example, "streaks" (ongoing interactions

similar to those on Snapchat) might appeal to Gen Z participants who enjoy social gaming elements ; status badges could offer Millennials an opportunity to showcase their status or skills ; and competition-based incentives might attract older workers.

  - Balance competition to ensure inclusivity. Attitudes toward competition can vary significantly across different demographics, particularly between genders (Hong et al., 2012; Oliveira, 2021; Niederle & Vesterlund, 2008). Gender-based differences in competitive engagement, for example, require careful consideration. Coppens (2018) observes that gamification often aligns with a linear, goal-oriented designs, which typically resonate more with male preferences that emphasize speed and efficiency in reaching objectives. This competitive framework, however, can inadvertently disadvantage female players, who may feel sidelined. Coppens' research reveals that 45% of women are less likely to engage in competitive settings if they perceive a low likelihood of success. Moreover, while men prioritize goal achievement, meeting deadlines, and initiative, women often value balance, respect, intuition, and collaboration. Being mindful of these differences is crucial when designing gamified systems to ensure inclusivity and engagement for all participants.

- **Nurture joy and play** to counteract fatigue and inspire engagement.
  - With Millennials and Gen Z reporting high burnout rates (Deloitte, 2024), incorporating elements of fun and levity in workplace learning becomes essential. These digital-native generations, who drive the global gaming industry, expect interactive and immersive experiences (Garcia-Cabot et al., 2019; Gruenewald et al., 2019; Oliveira et al., 2021).
  - Replace monotonous DEI training with interactive gamified experiences. Traditional compliance-focused sessions, often perceived as rigid, prescriptive, or "preachy," fail to engage employees and promote meaningful discussions (Seppo, 2023). As a result, employees may complete these sessions without truly internalizing key lessons, leaving workplace culture and behaviors largely unchanged. Gamified training leverages simulations, team challenges, and role-playing games to create emotional and cognitive investment, ensuring employees connect with real-world DEI issues.
  - Align gamification with cognitive science and motivation theories to enhance engagement. Research from neuroscience, behavioral economics, and motivation theory supports gamification as a tool for fostering learning. Effective game mechanics satisfy core psychological needs

such as recognition, status, achievement, self-expression, competition, and altruism (Richter et al., 2015). Motivation theories—including self-determination theory, reinforcement theory, expectancy theory, and flow theory—provide valuable insights into how games leverage intrinsic and extrinsic rewards to encourage specific behaviors (Laine & Lindberg, 2020; Krath et al., 2021; Richter et al., 2015; Sailor et al., 2013).

- **Address biases, threats, and distractions** to create a supportive learning culture.
    - o Ensure fairness and transparency in game mechanics to promote trust and voluntary engagement. A recent LinkedIn blog (2024) warns against coercive or misleading tactics in gamification, emphasizing the importance of clear rules, accessible feedback mechanisms, and opt-out options to safeguard user autonomy (Doney, 2019). Offering customizable controls allows participants to align the experience with their preferences and values, increasing their willingness to engage (Laine & Lindberg, 2020; Mollick & Rothbard, 2014).
    - o Prioritize accessibility by addressing diverse abilities, cultural norms, and digital literacy levels. Gamified solutions should account for different abilities, disabilities, cultural norms, digital literacy levels and language barriers etc. (Dingari, 2023). Organizations could, for example, offer solutions that support older employees adapting to new technologies, assist non-native speakers with language proficiency, and implement accessible learning modules for employees with disabilities (Andrews, 2024; Baltzar, 2023; Scope, n.d.).
    - o Leverage adaptive learning technologies to enhance inclusivity. Personalized support and real-time feedback improve training effectiveness by tailoring experiences to individual needs.
    - o Acknowledge gender-based differences in gaming engagement. Research has historically found that male gamers exhibit higher visuospatial processing efficiency (Bonanno & Kommers, 2010; Oliveira et al., 2021; Paaßen et al., 2017), but this landscape is evolving. Women now constitute 46% of the gaming population (Skwarczek, 2024), and studies indicate that they download and interact with apps more frequently than men (Coppens, 2018). It is important to account for these shifting trends in demographics and not base design on outdated or inaccurate assumptions.

Support: Sustaining Effort & Persistence

- **Optimize challenge and support** to promote individual performance.

- Establish a continuous learning environment to reinforce DEI principles over time. Traditional DEI training often lacks follow-up, making its impact short-lived. Gamified training should integrate repetitive loops and peer-to-peer learning to create sustained engagement (Oliveira et al., 2021; Gatheral, 2022).
- Implement structured, ongoing challenges that encourage real-world application of DEI concepts. Weekly or monthly tasks, insights, exercises, and quizzes help employees internalize key lessons and apply inclusive behaviors in their daily routines. Recognition systems, such as badges for inclusion champions, further motivate participation.
- Use nudges and push notifications to sustain engagement. Timely reminders prompt learners to reflect, adjust behaviors, and integrate DEI principles into their workplace interactions.
- Utilize serious games and simulations to create immersive learning experiences. Research highlights the importance of realistic and relevant scenarios in helping employees build confidence in applying DEI knowledge to everyday situations in their professional lives (Doney, 2019; Gruenewald et al., 2019).
- Assign decision-making roles in simulations to deepen engagement. Role-based exercises, such as developing diversity and inclusion policies or navigating workplace conflicts, provide a safe space for learners to practice complex problem-solving while fostering autonomy, competence, and relatedness (Deci & Ryan, 1980, 1985).
- Promote healthy competition while ensuring inclusivity. While competition can drive performance, it must align with DEI values. Some employees thrive in competitive environments, while others may find them discouraging (Domínguez et al., 2013; Oliveira et al., 2021). Gamification experts caution against leaderboards that exclusively highlight top performers, as they can alienate average participants. Deloitte, for example, resets leaderboards weekly to maintain motivation across all employees (Meister, 2013; Rimon, 2016).
- Accommodate for diverse motivational factors. Research suggests that women are more engaged by social interaction, relatable narratives, and social sharing, while men are often driven by competition, challenge, and novelty (Coppens, 2018; Codish & Ravid, 2017; Koivisto & Hamari, 2014; Kotsopoulos et al., 2017).
- Harness IoT and AI-driven personalization to enhance DEI initiatives. The rapid expansion of IoT-connected devices, ranging from smartphones and smart watches to virtual reality devices, enables more interactive and adaptive learning environments (Afzal, 2024). AI-powered

algorithms further refine gamified learning by dynamically tailoring content, identifying potential disengagement, and offering real-time support (Blurton, 2024). Chatbots simulate human interaction, providing instant feedback and clarification to improve learning outcomes.

- Ensure AI-driven gamification tools promote equity. While personalization enhances engagement—particularly for Millennials and Gen Z, who prefer customized learning experiences (Chan & Lee, 2023)—AI also carries risks, such as amplifying biases or exacerbating accessibility challenges (Cachat-Rosset & Klarsfeld, 2023). Companies must carefully balance innovation with ethical considerations to prevent unintended inequalities.

- **Foster collaboration and community** to enhance belonging, shared learning, responsibility and problem-solving.
    - Incorporate forums for open and respectful discussions to create an inclusive learning environment. Gamified DEI-oriented training should provide structured spaces where employees can share perspectives, challenge biases, and engage in constructive dialogue. These interactions help learners navigate cognitive dissonance and better grasp complex problems and diverse viewpoints (Gatheral, 2022; Griffin, 2022; Seppo, 2023). Moreover, they provide opportunities for employees to find common ground, fostering a cohesive organizational culture that reinforces a sense of community.
    - Encourage social accountability through gamification. Constructivist learning theory highlights the importance of experiential learning through social interactions (Haaland, 2023; York & deHaan, 2018). Gamification strengthens peer accountability by making DEI efforts visible and collaborative, reinforcing inclusion as a shared responsibility (Dobbin & Kalev, 2024). Team-based gamified activities further promote a sense of collective responsibility, as employees work together to achieve shared goals.
    - Integrate leaderboards, team challenges, and public recognition to drive engagement. Gamified training should reward employees for active participation in DEI initiatives, reinforcing positive behaviors and motivating broader involvement. At the same time, including gamification elements that emphasize collaboration over competition ensure that all employees feel valued in their learning journey.
- **Offer action-oriented feedback** to sustain motivation and support progress.
    - Deliver immediate and delayed feedback to reinforce learning and behavior change. Gamified DEI training should provide employees with real-time responses and long-term performance insights, helping them

understand the impact of their actions. Feedback can be delivered through the game itself, peer interactions, or facilitators, depending on the training format (Doney, 2019).
  - Leverage reinforcement theory to strengthen behavioral change. Consistent with Skinner's (1953) reinforcement theory, gamification fosters a direct link between training and action. Timely rewards and feedback increase the likelihood that employees will adopt and sustain inclusive behaviors (Krath et al., 2021).
  - Deliver meaningful feedback. Move beyond binary right-or-wrong answers. Use summative and formative feedback to explain decisions, providing context and reinforcing learning rather than penalizing mistakes (Doney, 2019). This can contribute to creating a more inclusive, equitable and trust-based learning environment.Formularende

Executive Function: Emotional Capacity

- **Recognize expectations, beliefs, and motivations** to accommodate the emotional capacity of learners.
  - Encourage self-directed learning through gamification. Transform employees into active consumers of information. This approach is especially effective when DEI principles are seamlessly embedded into the training to create programs that resonate with the diverse needs of participants, while achieving utilitarian goals (Hamari & Koivisto, 2014).
  - Leverage gamification to promote purpose-driven work. Emerging workforce trends indicate that younger employees prioritize social responsibility and sustainability (Baer, 2022). Scientometric research highlights the increasing use of gamification in environmental awareness, well-being, and corporate responsibility initiatives (Bassanelli et al., 2022).
  - Incorporate reward systems to reinforce learning and motivation. Certificates, badges, and emblems serve as strong motivators, particularly for achievement-oriented learners (Deterding et al., 2011; Learning Everest, 2024). Publicly recognizing these achievements—via office channels, social media, or LMS dashboards—enhances engagement by adding a social dimension (Capatina et al., 2024; Garcia-Cabot et al., 2019; Haaland, 2023; Hajarian et al., 2019).
  - Balance extrinsic rewards with intrinsic motivation. Tying rewards to tangible outcomes helps embed accountability into DEI initiatives. Connecting achievements to performance reviews or career development opportunities ensures that DEI efforts translate into meaningful workplace impact.

Nonetheless, over-reliance on rewards and poorly designed metrics can undermine the learning objectives (Doney, 2019; Rimon, 2016). Studies show that when rewards emphasize speed over accuracy or short-term performance, employees may misrepresent achievements or focus excessively on short-term gains at the expense of long-term success (Callan et al., 2015; Landers et al., 2019). Excessive use of extrinsic motivators often leads to superficial engagement, where employees revert to previous behaviors once incentives are removed. This phenomenon, known as the undermining or overjustification effect (Lepper et al., 1973; Rheinberg, 2010), occurs when individuals shift from learning for intrinsic enjoyment to pursuing external rewards, such as leaderboard positions, which ultimately diminishes intrinsic motivation (Deci & Ryan, 1980, 1985).

While tangible rewards effectively motivate extrinsically driven learners, long-term success depends on cultivating a genuine desire to learn. This involves creating an environment where learning is valued not merely as a means to an end but as a rewarding experience in itself. Offering internal rewards such as enjoyment, personal growth, and happiness aligns with DEI principles by actively promoting learner well-being and fostering an inclusive and positive learning culture (Brull et al., 2017).

- o Mitigate emotional stress linked to gamification. An over-reliance on extrinsic rewards may also provoke stress or backlash. This draws attention to the principal role of emotions in gamification, as noted by Robson et al. (2015). Gamified experiences can evoke a range of emotions from positive feelings such as happiness, surprise, wonder, and euphoria to negative ones like stress, anger, or disappointment. Although frustration can sometimes spur positive learning behaviors, maintaining a predominance of positive emotions is essential to ensure an engaging and motivating learning experience.
  - **Develop awareness of self and others** to help learners understand their strengths and weaknesses and to appreciate why others tick the way they do.
- o Incorporate branching scenarios to foster critical thinking and empathy. Present learners with diverse choices at various stages, encouraging them to reflect on their values, preferences, and goals. Rather than using simple binary options, integrate opt-in, opt-out, or customized choices to deepen engagement and participation.
- o Personalize learning experiences through avatars and narratives. Immersive storytelling makes training more relatable, allowing employees to see the real-world impact of their decisions in a controlled environment.
- o Design consequence-driven learning pathways that provide tangible feedback based on user choices. This structured approach helps learners grasp the

complexities of diversity-related issues while reinforcing the importance of informed decision-making.

- **Promote individual and collective reflection** to develop emotional capacity.
  - o Create a safe space for reflection and practical application. By allowing employees to explore different perspectives in a risk-free environment, gamified DEI training encourages behavioral change and prepares participants to navigate diverse workplace interactions more effectively. Gamified learning can significantly enhance accountability in this way, allowing employees to practice new skills and reflect on their behaviors without fear of judgment or failure (Bhaduri, 2023; Gatheral, 2022; Oliveira et al., 2021).
  - o Implement interactive simulations and role-playing games that require employees to navigate complex social situations, and experiment with different approaches. These exercises not only build confidence in applying DEI principles in daily work but also empower employees to take ownership of their growth and development.
  - o Design reflection activities to be engaging. Integrating opportunities. Practices such as journaling, self-assessment exercises, and active participation in diversity forums can encourage employees to explore and challenge their biases in a structured yet dynamic manner (Griffin, 2022). These reflective activities transform potentially tedious tasks into more engaging and impactful experiences, making the learning process both meaningful and motivating. They can also enhance personal accountability.
  - o Ensure challenge levels are appropriately matched to learners' needs. Poorly calibrated activities can induce anxiety or boredom, reducing effectiveness (Doney, 2019). Training programs must align difficulty levels with participants' readiness to maximize engagement.
  - o Support employees in resolving cognitive dissonance. By addressing conflicts between beliefs and behaviors, reflection exercises help employees align their actions with DEI values, fostering meaningful personal and organizational growth (Griffin, 2022; Seppo, 2023).
  - o Provide scaffolds and constructive feedback for those learners who need more external support.

2. Multiple Means of Representation:

Access: Perception

- **Support multiple ways to perceive information** to ensure maximum accessibility. By offering multiple ways to perceive and interact with information, gamification ensures that learners can engage with the material in a way that best suits their preferences and needs.

- Ensure all users can access and engage with information by incorporating multiple ways to perceive content. Leverage gamification's strength in delivering material through diverse modalities to accommodate different learning styles and cognitive abilities. Use videos, infographics, interactive narratives, and simulations to reach visual, auditory, and kinesthetic learners effectively.
- Make content dynamic—use videos and animations to break down complex concepts visually. Simplify data with infographics for quick comprehension. Build emotional connections through storytelling, helping learners empathize with diverse perspectives. Engage users directly with interactive elements like quizzes, role-playing games, and decision-based scenarios, allowing them to test their understanding in a risk-free environment.
- Design gamified DEI training to be inclusive at its core. Structure content delivery to support varied learning preferences, ensuring all employees can actively participate and benefit. This approach not only drives engagement but also strengthens knowledge retention and real-world application.

- **Represent a diversity of perspectives and identities in authentic ways** to foster a sense of validation, affirmation, and belonging and to increase exposure to other perspectives.
  - Represent diverse perspectives and identities authentically. Ensure participants see themselves reflected in training materials by integrating inclusive language and imagery. Use content that represents diversity across gender, race, age, abilities, and cultural backgrounds to foster belonging and engagement. These identities should be featured in non-tokenizing ways.
  - Use inclusive language. Eliminate stereotypes and biases by prioritizing neutrality and respect. Choose gender-neutral terms, avoid cultural assumptions, and incorporate terminology that reflects the evolving landscape of diversity and inclusion.
  - Incorporate diverse and authentic imagery. Avoid generic or homogeneous stock photos. Instead, showcase real-world diversity—feature individuals of varying abilities collaborating, team members from different age groups and ethnic backgrounds solving problems, and workplace interactions that reflect genuine inclusivity.
  - Craft narratives that reflect lived experiences. Design gamified DEI scenarios that highlight varied perspectives, ensuring learners connect with

the content on a personal level. Make DEI training a reflection of real-world experiences, reinforcing that diversity, equity, and inclusion are not just theoretical concepts but integral to the workplace culture.

Support: Language & Symbols

- **Cultivate understanding and respect across languages, dialects and cultures** to promote cross-linguistic and cross-cultural understanding.
    - o Ensure gamified DEI solutions account for cultural nuances, especially in multinational organizations (Larson, 2020). Recognize that individuals from different cultures interpret achievement in different ways and are driven by varying motivations, goals, and approaches (Salili & Hoosain, 2007).
    - o Prioritize cultural sensitivity in design. Avoid the common oversight of neglecting cultural differences—only 50% of gamified solutions currently do so (Guhl, 2017a).
    - o Measure impact and refine strategies. Conduct thorough cultural assessments to understand employees' values, norms, and communication styles and to guide decision-making (Bhaduri, 2023). Use these insights to create inclusive learning experiences that foster cross-cultural dialogue and collaboration and track progress.
    - o Adapt training to diverse cultural contexts. Integrate localized narratives, culturally relevant examples, and language options to make learning relatable and accessible. Consider formal and structured communication styles in cultures like China, while embracing more open, expressive approaches in regions like Brazil and Sweden (Guhl, 2017b).

3. Multiple Means of Action & Expression:

Access: Interaction

- **Use accessible materials and assistive and accessible technologies and tools to** enhances opportunities for all learners to engage, participate, and advance in the learning process.
    - o Ensure all learners can engage fully. While multimedia elements like animations, images, and audio enhance learning, be mindful of cognitive load constraints. Limit simultaneous auditory and visual demands, recognizing that information processing capacities vary across demographic groups (Doney, 2019). Capatina et al. (2024) emphasize that aligning learning materials with a learner's preferred style can not only

reduce cognitive load but also support knowledge retention and the practical application of content.

- o Integrate key accessibility features. Provide subtitles, adjustable text sizes, and flexible difficulty settings to remove barriers for neurodivergent and disabled learners. Improve text readability, optimize visual clarity, refine color schemes, and integrate visual cues for audio elements. Implement assistive technologies such as screen readers, customizable interfaces, and adaptive controllers to enable full participation (Andrews, 2024; Scope, n.d.).
- o Design inclusive game mechanics. Offer controller sensitivity adjustments and simplified navigation to improve accessibility. Acknowledge that disabled gamers engage with games more frequently than their non-disabled counterparts, yet 66% still face accessibility barriers (Scope, n.d.). Research shows that disabled gamers often view gaming as a primary hobby, engaging with games more frequently and for longer sessions than their non-disabled counterparts (Scope, n.d.). However, 66% of gamers with disabilities report facing barriers to accessing games. Address these gaps by creating inclusive experiences that allow all users to interact meaningfully.
- o Establish accessibility as a priority. The gaming industry has yet to fully standardize accessibility features (Andrews, 2024; Baltzar, 2023). Unlike other media that have made strides in inclusivity, accessible gaming remains underdeveloped. Take the lead by embedding accessibility into gamified DEI training, ensuring all learners—regardless of ability—can engage, reflect, and grow.

Support: Expression & Communication

- **Build fluencies with graduated support for practice and performance** to help learners explore, experiment, practice, and develop confidence.
    - o Engage digital-native learners. Millennials and Gen Z thrive in technology-enabled, interactive learning environments. Deliver gamified training that aligns with their expectations—offering challenge, feedback, recognition, and opportunities for growth. Make learning self-paced, on-demand, and hands-on to support independent exploration and real-world application (Chan & Lee, 2023).
    - o Design adaptable, credible training. Recognize that Gen Z learners quickly question outdated or inconsistent content. Avoid rigid, prescriptive instruction—opt instead for flexible, up-to-date material that accommodates self-directed learning while maintaining credibility.

- Implement personalized learning pathways. Use interactive scenarios and adaptive difficulty levels to tailor training to individual progress. Introduce graduated support mechanisms, such as scaffolding exercises and guided practice, to help learners build fluency incrementally—starting with basic tasks and advancing to complex challenges. Provide clear, actionable feedback throughout to foster a sense of achievement and continuous improvement.

Executive Function: Strategy Development

- **Set meaningful goals** that reflect the vision and complexity of the learning process while remaining clear, objective, and measurable.
  - Ensure gamified DEI training drives real change. Do not allow gamification to become a tool for box-checking. Design training to challenge biases rather than reinforce them (Dobbin & Kalev, 2018, 2022; Kulik et al., 2007; Roberson et al., 2020; Zheng, 2022). Prioritize learning experiences that build awareness, encourage reflection, and translate into sustained behavioral change.
  - Integrate DEI training with broader organizational practices. Align gamified DEI training with equitable recruitment, career development, and workplace policies. Ensure transparency in how training influences these areas, reinforcing a culture of accountability that is both strategic and effective.
  - Ensure accountability. Bridge the gap between raising awareness and driving measurable, actionable behavior in DEI training (Dobbin & Kalev, 2018, 2022; Roberson et al., 2020; Zheng, 2022). While many DEI programs successfully increase knowledge and understanding, they often fall short in translating these lessons into tangible, measurable actions for which employees can be held accountable (Coffman et al., 2021). Move beyond intent—establish rigorous quality control measures to ensure training delivers tangible outcomes for stakeholders (Zheng, 2022).
  - Avoid superficial gamification. Do not implement gamification simply because it is fashionable. Abrahamson (1996) and Burke (2014) caution that while adopting popular practices can enhance legitimacy—by signaling alignment with societal expectations and appearing progressive—it is essential to ensure these solutions are contextually appropriate and effectively implemented. Grünewald et al. (2019) echo this sentiment, stressing the importance of tailoring interventions to specific organizational needs and objectives.

- Align gamified DEI training with strategic business objectives. Require employees to take concrete actions that advance DEI goals, such as participating in diversity-focused discussions, mentoring underrepresented colleagues, or integrating inclusive practices into daily work. Track and measure these actions to ensure impact, accountability, and alignment with broader business strategies (Callan et al., 2015).

- **Anticipate and plan for challenges** to minimize obstacles and create more opportunities for individuals to achieve their goals.
  - Be cautious when implementing accountability mechanisms in DEI initiatives. Some may be counterproductive and carry the risk of unintended consequences. Strict diversity targets may push managers toward superficial, quick-fix solutions rather than fostering genuine inclusion and equity (Kalinoski et al., 2013; Roberson et al., 2020). Prevent this by emphasizing meaningful, process-driven approaches rather than rigid quotas.
  - Design game mechanics strategically. Align mechanics with learning objectives—reward progression, incentivize collaboration, and reinforce key behaviors (Robson et al., 2015). Anticipate unexpected interactions, as players may engage with mechanics in unpredictable ways, influencing learning outcomes.
- **Organize information and resources** to improve working memory.
  - Leverage gamification to enhance learning and retention. Design training experiences that tap into the brain's natural reward system. Use gameplay elements that trigger dopamine release to boost motivation and improve memory formation (Lazzaro, 2004). Foster positive emotions during learning to strengthen both short-term and long-term knowledge retention. When learners experience positive emotions during the learning process, they are better able to absorb and commit information to short-term, but more importantly, long-term memory. Various studies have demonstrated that learners trained in a gamified environment retain and apply more knowledge compared to those taught through traditional didactic methods or non-gamified online learning (Brull et al., 2017; Kapp, 2012; Putz and Treiblmaier, 2019).
  - Structure content for maximum engagement. Break down training modules into manageable chunks with individual challenges, prompts, and immediate feedback to maintain learner focus and encourage active participation (Capatina et al., 2024). Implement spaced repetition and progressive difficulty to reinforce concepts effectively.
  - Distinguish between surface-level and deep learning. In today's era of information overload, gamification emerges as a potential strategy to

enhance knowledge retention (Turan et al., 2016). Nonetheless, organizations should avoid relying solely on basic gamified exercises like flashcards, multiple-choice questions, and drag-and-drop tasks. While these can reinforce foundational knowledge, they fall short in fostering deeper understanding—especially in DEI training. Integrate immersive scenarios, interactive discussions, and problem-solving exercises to encourage critical thinking and meaningful application of DEI principles.

- **Enhance capacity for monitoring progress** to enable learners to become more self-sufficient in assessing their effort and practice.
  - o Embrace AI-driven personalization in training models by utilizing dynamic feedback mechanisms and differentiated self-assessment tools. Modern gamification techniques adapt to individual skill levels, interests, and learning styles, promoting continuous engagement through progress trackers, badges, and performance-based rewards (Afzal, 2024; Blurton, 2024; Oliveira et al., 2021; Rodrigues et al., 2023). However, it's crucial to balance personalization with standardization to maintain consistency, comparability, and replicability across different populations. Standardized elements help mitigate the risks of over-personalization, which can diminish the generalizability of training effects and complicate the assessment of effectiveness (Oliveira et al., 2021).

Further, adopt data-driven personalization strategies that go beyond mere preferences to include a range of multidimensional factors like demographics, learning styles, and game preferences. This approach can optimize engagement and performance, tailored to individual needs (Hallifax et al., 2019; Hamari et al., 2014; Hajarian et al., 2019; Rodrigues et al., 2023). For instance, Rodrigues et al. (2023) found that while personalization maintained motivation as effectively as a one-size-fits-all approach, it did not consistently enhance performance. Notably, the effectiveness of personalization varied with individual characteristics—females and technically-educated students saw greater benefits, whereas those who favored adventure games or single-player modes had diminished motivation. This suggests that a nuanced approach, possibly supported by a cost-benefit analysis, could determine the optimal level of personalization based on learner demographics, training objectives, and available resources.

- **Challenge exclusionary practices** to be more inclusive.
  - o Ensure ethical integrity and oversight. Integrating oversight from ethics committees can help avoid unintentionally exploiting vulnerabilities and ensure that the training is ethically sound and compliant with data

protection regulations and other relevant principles, such as respect, beneficence, justice, honesty, and accountability.

- o Educate participants to enable them to engage in informed decision-making and better understand the implications of their choices. This reinforces their autonomy and can increase their commitment to DEI. Use transparent communication—eliminate jargon and technical terms to ensure clarity and accessibility.
- o Work both individually and collectively to identify, examine, and tackle practices that exclude others.

While incorporating the above-mentioned principles into design, it is essential to acknowledge the challenge of predicting real-world dynamics. Players may engage with the mechanics of a gamified learning intervention in unforeseen ways, leading to unintended behaviors. This unpredictability is further compounded by the diverse backgrounds and preferences of players. Limited research exists on the distinct emotional and psychological needs of different demographic groups within gamified environments (Larson, 2020).

Mike Brennan, president and chief service officer at Leapgen, emphasizes that understanding and considering the diverse characteristics, motivators, compensation models, and job roles of employees during the design phase is crucial for creating effective gamified DEI programs (Lewis, 2019). He advocates for actively engaging individuals from the target population to ensure the training resonates with their unique experiences and needs. Brennan argues that this involvement not only fosters empathy among learners but also serves as the most reliable indicator of the program's effectiveness, with the success or failure of gamification largely depending on the input gathered during this phase.

Utilizing focus groups, pre- and post-learning surveys, and interviews can provide valuable insights into which mechanics and content might best meet the needs of diverse participants or resonate with their values (Bhaduri, 2023; Coppens, 2018). Pre-learning surveys establish a baseline by identifying knowledge gaps and misconceptions, while post-learning surveys measure the impact by evaluating changes in knowledge, attitudes, and behaviors. Comparing these responses allows organizations to gauge the training's success, identify areas for improvement, and quantify the knowledge gained, attitude shifts, and behavioral changes resulting from the program.

Additionally, interviews can offer valuable qualitative insights, complementing quantitative data to give a more personalized understanding of participants' perspectives and helping to uncover emerging themes. By analyzing this data, organizations can refine and tailor their gamified systems to better align with individual learner preferences and needs. It is also crucial to test designs with diverse user groups.

While differences exist between social groups, there are also overlapping preferences shaped by intersectionality—the way various aspects of a person's identity, such as race, gender, socioeconomic status and educational background, interact to create unique experiences and perspectives. It is, therefore, advisable to test gamified solutions with both separate and mixed social groups to identify overlapping needs, minimize bias, and ensure broad appeal (Coppens, 2018). Applying data-driven insights from users helps ensure the content remains relevant and impactful.

In the next section, we will explore how the ACRL Framework can be leveraged to design gamified training experiences that promote DEI by fostering critical information literacy, encouraging reflective learning, and supporting inclusive knowledge creation.

Leveraging Dispositions from the ACRL Framework

The Framework for Information Literacy in Higher Education (2015) marked a significant shift from a skills-based approach to information literacy toward a more holistic, conceptual model. It emphasizes interconnected learning goals rather than isolated competencies and redefines the learner's role as active and critical in engaging with information. This shift aligns well with applying DEI principles to training in both educational and organizational settings, which similarly requires participants to actively engage with concepts, challenge assumptions, and develop awareness through continuous reflection.

A key element of the Framework is its focus on affective learning, addressing attitudes, emotions, and values in the learning process. These aspects are critical in DEI training, where confidence, persistence, and curiosity play a central role in fostering empathy and encouraging individuals to challenge biases. Just as the Framework recognizes that novice learners often begin with uncertainty and anxiety, they may also experience discomfort when confronting issues of privilege, systemic inequality, and cultural differences.

One effective instructional strategy derived from the Framework is peer-driven inquiry, which can be adapted for gamified training, whether it focuses on DEI content or aims to be more accessible to diverse communities. Meiman et al. (2019) present a "gallery walk" activity in library instruction that allows students to generate and refine research questions collaboratively. A similar approach can be applied in gamified training to encourage dialogue, active participation, and perspective-taking.

Example: "Perspectives Exchange" Activity

- **Setup:** Each participant writes a personal reflection or experience related to diversity, equity, or inclusion with regard to the gamified initiative.

- **Exchange & Expansion:** Participants pass their reflections around, and others add comments, questions, or alternative perspectives.
- **Iteration & Gamification:** To enhance engagement, a **time limit** (e.g., one or two minutes per response) can be set, creating an element of **urgency and excitement** akin to a game.
- **Reflection & Synthesis:** After several rounds, participants review the collective input, gaining new insights into how others perceive the same issue.

Fostering a Growth Mindset

In designing gamified training with DEI in mind, it is essential to consider how mindset influences learning. Having drawn from the ACRL Framework for Information Literacy, it becomes clear that educators and trainers must not only encourage learners to develop inclusive habits of mind and knowledge practices but also critically examine their own perspectives. Integrating Carol Dweck's theories of intelligence—particularly the concepts of fixed and growth mindsets—into DEI training design can help facilitators cultivate more effective, inclusive learning environments.

Dweck's theories suggest that individuals with a fixed mindset see intelligence and abilities as static, while those with a growth mindset believe that skills and knowledge can be developed over time. This distinction is crucial in DEI training, where implicit biases, privilege, and systemic inequalities must be addressed in a way that fosters reflection, openness, and long-term engagement.

For DEI-informed learning to be impactful, facilitators must recognize how their own teaching practices either encourage or hinder growth.

Applying a Growth-Oriented Approach to Training Initiatives:

- **Recognize and address systemic barriers** (e.g., how access to knowledge is shaped by privilege, socioeconomic status, and institutional structures).
- **Highlight diverse voices and perspectives to challenge dominant narratives** (e.g., addressing whose experiences and contributions are historically centered or marginalized).
- **Encourage persistence and reflection among learners**, helping them work through discomfort and uncertainty.

Incorporating Design Thinking into Gamified DEI Training

To create engaging, impactful DEI training, integrating design thinking principles alongside growth mindset strategies and the ACRL Framework offers a holistic, user-centered approach. Design thinking—while fluid in definition—provides a structured yet flexible process that encourages experimentation, problem-finding, and iteration, making it ideal for gamified learning experiences informed by DEI principles.

Design thinking focuses on human needs as the starting point for problem-solving and learning. This mindset aligns with DEI efforts, which require empathy, adaptability, and a commitment to addressing systemic barriers. Miller's (2015) definition of design thinking highlights core principles that are particularly relevant to DEI training:

- **"Focus on Human Values"** → Center diverse perspectives and lived experiences.
- **"Embrace Experimentation"** → Encourage learners to explore and challenge biases through iterative exercises.
- **"Mindful of Process"** → Acknowledge that DEI learning is nonlinear and requires reflection and ongoing engagement.
- **"Radical Collaboration"** → Foster inclusive dialogue by involving diverse voices in problem-solving.

These principles align with the five core stages of design thinking:

1. **Empathize** → Understand the perspectives, barriers, and challenges learners face in DEI contexts.
2. **Define** → Identify key issues related to inclusivity, bias, and systemic inequities.
3. **Ideate** → Generate innovative, interactive ways to engage learners in these discussions.
4. **Prototype** → Design gamified learning exercises, test them in real-world settings, and refine them based on feedback.
5. **Test** → Gather insights from participants and iterate on the training experience to maximize impact.

To make this more tangible, we provide the following example of how design thinking could be applied to gamified training.

Ways to Apply Design Thinking to Gamified DEI Training

1. Gamifying Empathy

Empathy is foundational in DEI training. A role-playing simulation can immerse participants in diverse perspectives, encouraging perspective-taking and emotional intelligence. Example activity:

- **Walk in Their Shoes:** Participants are assigned fictional identities with different social, economic, and cultural backgrounds. Through a decision-based game, they navigate real-world DEI challenges, experiencing the impact of privilege, discrimination, and bias.

2. Problem-Finding Instead of Just Problem-Solving

Instead of jumping to solutions, design thinking emphasizes identifying systemic barriers first. In DEI training, this means addressing root causes rather than just reacting to surface-level issues. Example activity:

- **Equity Puzzle:** Learners are given scenarios of institutional bias (e.g., hiring discrimination, lack of accessibility, microaggressions). Instead of proposing solutions immediately, they must map out the systemic structures that contribute to these inequities, reinforcing critical thinking and systemic awareness.

3. Prototyping and Iteration in DEI Learning

Gamification allows trial-and-error learning, where participants refine their approaches over multiple rounds. Example activity:

- **Bias Detection Lab:** A game-based simulation where learners analyze workplace policies or media representations, identifying hidden biases. Through multiple iterations, they refine strategies for addressing these biases, reinforcing growth mindset principles.

4. Fostering Radical Collaboration

Design thinking prioritizes collaboration across disciplines and perspectives—essential in DEI training. Example activity:

- **Diverse Team Challenge:** Participants work in mixed-background teams to redesign a hiring process, onboarding program, or corporate DEI policy. Each team member plays a different stakeholder (e.g., HR manager, job applicant from an underrepresented group, executive leader), fostering perspective-sharing and problem-solving.

By incorporating design thinking into gamified DEI training, organizations can create immersive, adaptable learning experiences that encourage reflection, experimentation, and real-world problem-solving. The iterative, user-centered nature of design thinking ensures that DEI training is not a one-time exercise but a continuous process of learning, adapting, and improving.

CONCLUSION

Successfully implementing DEI gamified approaches training requires more than just careful planning and thoughtful design—it demands a sustained commitment to evaluation, adaptation, and alignment with the organization's broader sustainability and DEI goals. This holistic approach ensures that DEI principles permeate every aspect of training, fostering a truly inclusive environment. In this context, DEI should be seen not merely as content to be delivered, but also as a guiding principle to be seamlessly integrated into existing training programs across the organization.

While gamification can significantly boost short-term engagement, its true potential lies in driving sustained behavioral change This can only be achieved when game design is strategically aligned with the unique context of the organization. Hastily adopted strategies, if not meticulously executed, not only risk long-term disengagement but also the undermining of DEI initiatives (Laine & Lindberg, 2020; Landers et al., 2019; Rodrigues et al., 2024; Tondello & Nacke, 2020). Given the widespread criticism of traditional DEI training, it is imperative that gamified approaches deliver measurable value and contribute meaningfully to advancing the organization's DEI and sustainable development objectives.

Thorough testing and evaluation are crucial to achieving lasting results. By rigorously analyzing collective data, organizations can uncover valuable insights into learners' perceptions, such as whether they feel they have equal access to development opportunities, if additional training is required, or if the training effectively addresses and mitigates discrimination within the organization. These insights are essential for refining and personalizing gamified systems to meet the diverse needs of learners, ensuring that DEI initiatives resonate across different demographic groups and cultural contexts. Gamification is not a one-time fix; it is a dynamic, evolving process that must continuously adapt to shifts in user expectations, organizational goals, and technological advancements. A data-driven approach is, therefore, critical to maintaining the relevance and effectiveness of gamified systems over time.

To truly assess the impact of DEI training, organizations must track a comprehensive set of key metrics. These should include learners' understanding, satisfaction, and skills development. However, as Coffman et al. (2021) emphasize, it is also essential to evaluate broader outcomes, such as retention, engagement, and promotion rates among the direct reports of managers who have completed DEI training. By comparing these outcomes with historical data and control groups, organizations can gain deeper insights into the effectiveness of their DEI initiatives in fostering an inclusive culture. Sharing such findings with employees, researchers, and other organizations is vital for ensuring accountability and contributing to the expanding body of knowledge in the field of DEI.

Finally, it is essential to remain vigilant in identifying and adopting good practices in gamified DEI training. Many of the studies reviewed in this article offer compelling insights, yet also underscore the inherent complexities involved in addressing DEI issues through gamification. By learning from current research and integrating these insights into gamified DEI training, organizations can better navigate the challenges of creating meaningful and lasting change, ultimately driving progress toward a more inclusive and equitable workplace.

REFERENCES

A Complete Guide to Diversity Training Gamification and its Strategies (2024, March 1). Learning Everest. https://www.learningeverest.com/diversity-training-gamification/#content

Abrahamson, E. (1996). Management Fashion. *Academy of Management Review*, *21*(1), 254–285. DOI: 10.2307/258636

Accessibility in gaming report. (n.d.). Scope. https://www.scope.org.uk/campaigns/research-policy/accessibility-in-gaming

Afzal, M. (2024, May 13). *Top Gamification Trends To Look Out For In 2024.* eLearning Industry. https://elearningindustry.com/top-gamification-trends-to-look-out-for-in-2024

Ahmadi, M. M. (2020, August). Managing the New Gamified World: How Gamification Changes Businesses. *International Journal of Management. Accounting and Economics*, *7*(7), 305–325.

Algashami, A., Cham, S., Vuillier, L., Stefanidis, A., Phalp, K. T., & Ali, R. (2018). Conceptualising gamification risks to teamwork within enterprise. In Buchmann, R., Karagiannis, D., & Kirikova, M. (Eds.), *The Practice of Enterprise Modeling. PoEM 2018. Lecture Notes in Business Information Processing* (Vol. 335). Springer., DOI: 10.1007/978-3-030-02302-7_7

Allport, G. W. (1954). *The Nature of Prejudice*. Addison-Wesley.

Anand, R., & Winters, M.-F. (2008). A retrospective view of corporate diversity training from 1964 to the present. *Academy of Management Learning & Education*, *7*(3), 356–372. DOI: 10.5465/amle.2008.34251673

Andrews, S. (2024, May 30). *Accessibility in Gaming*. bcs: The Chartered Institute for IT. https://www.bcs.org/articles-opinion-and-research/accessibility-in-gaming/

Apostolopoulos, A. (2019, August 19). The 2019 Gamification at Work Survey [Blog]. *TalentLMS*. https://www.talentlms.com/blog/gamification-survey-results/

Association of College & Research Libraries (ACRL). (2016). *Framework for Information Literacy for Higher Education.*https://www.ala.org/acrl/standards/ilframework

Autor, D., Mindell, D. A., & Reynolds, E. B. (2022). *The Work of the Future: Building better Jobs in an Age of intelligent Machines*. MIT Press. DOI: 10.7551/mitpress/14109.001.0001

Avery, D. R., & Thomas, K. M. (2004). Blending content and contact: The role of diversity curriculum and campus heterogeneity in fostering diversity management competency. *Academy of Management Learning & Education, 3*(4), 380–396. DOI: 10.5465/amle.2004.15112544

Baer, S. (2022, April 14). *Gamification: Turning Corporate Responsibility Into An Authentic And Fun Experience*. Forbes. https://www.forbes.com/councils/forbeshumanresourcescouncil/2022/04/05/gamification-turning-corporate-responsibility-into-an-authentic-and-fun-experience/

Baltzar, P. (2023, May 17). Accessibility in Digital Learning Games – Why Is It Relevant? [Blog]. *seppo*. https://seppo.io/blog/accessibility-digital-learning-games/?

Bassanelli, S., Vasta, N., Bucchiarone, A., & Marconi, A. (2022). Gamification for Behavior Change: A Scientometric Review. *Acta Psychologica, 228*(103657), 103657. https://www.sciencedirect.com/science/article/pii/S000169182200172X. DOI: 10.1016/j.actpsy.2022.103657 PMID: 35767927

Bersin, J. (2022). *Irresistible: The Seven Secrets of the World's most enduring employee-Focused organizations*. Ideapress Publishing.

Bezrukova, K., Spell, C. S., Perry, J. L., & Jehn, K. A. (2016). A meta-analytical integration of over 40 years of research on diversity training evaluation. *Psychological Bulletin, 142*(11), 1227–1274. DOI: 10.1037/bul0000067 PMID: 27618543

Bhaduri, S. (2023, July 12). *How to Measure the Effectiveness and Impact of DEI Training*. Training Industry. https://trainingindustry.com/articles/measurement-and-analytics/how-to-measure-the-effectiveness-and-impact-of-dei-training/

Blurton, D. (2024, January 23). Hyper-personalization in iGaming: A trend taking the industry by storm [Blog]. *Ciklum*. https://www.ciklum.com/resources/blog/hyper-personalization-in-igaming-a-trend-taking-the-industry-by-storm

Bonanno, P., & Kommers, P. A. M. (2010). Gender differences and styles in the use of digital games. *Educational Psychology, 25*(1), 13–41. DOI: 10.1080/0144341042000294877

Brull, S., Finlayson, S., Kostelec, T., Macdonald, R., & Krenzischeck, D. (2017). Using Gamification to Improve Productivity and Increase Knowledge Retention During Orientation. *The Journal of Nursing Administration, 47*(9), 448–453. DOI: 10.1097/NNA.0000000000000512 PMID: 28834805

Brynjolfsson, E., & McAfee, A. (2018). *The Second Machine Age: Wie die nächste digitale Revolution unser aller Leben verändern wird*. Plassen.

Buonomo, I., Ferrara, B., Pansini, M., & Benevene, P. (2023). Job Satisfaction and Perceived Structural Support in Remote Working Conditions—The Role of a Sense of Community at Work. *International Journal of Environmental Research and Public Health, 20*(13), 6205. DOI: 10.3390/ijerph20136205 PMID: 37444053

Burke, B. (2014). *Gamify: How Gamification Motivates People to Do Extraordinary Things*. Gartner Inc.

Cachat-Rosset, G., & Klarsfeld, A. (2023). Diversity, Equity, and Inclusion in Artificial Intelligence: An Evaluation of Guidelines. *Applied Artificial Intelligence, 37*(1), 2176618. Advance online publication. DOI: 10.1080/08839514.2023.2176618

Caligiuri, P., De Cieri, H., Minbaeva, D., Verbeke, A., & Zimmermann, A. (2020). International HRM insights for navigating the COVID-19 pandemic: Implications for future research and practice. *Journal of International Business Studies, 51*(5), 697–713. DOI: 10.1057/s41267-020-00335-9 PMID: 32836500

Callan, R. C., Bauer, K. N., & Landers, R. N. (2015). How to avoid the dark side of gamification: ten business scenarios and their unintended consequences. In Reiners, T., & Wood, L. (Eds.), *Gamification in education and business* (pp. 553–568). Springer. DOI: 10.1007/978-3-319-10208-5_28

Capatina, A., Juarez-Varon, D., Micu, A., & Micu, A. E. (2024). Leveling up in corporate training: Unveiling the power of gamification to enhance knowledge retention, knowledge sharing, and job performance. *Journal of Innovation & Knowledge, 9*(3), 100530. DOI: 10.1016/j.jik.2024.100530

Carucci, R. (2024, January 24). *One More Time: Why Diversity Leads To Better Team Performance*. Forbes. https://www.forbes.com/sites/roncarucci/2024/01/24/one-more-time-why-diversity-leads-to-better-team-performance/

CAST. (2024). *Universal design for learning guidelines version 3.0* [graphic organizer]. Author. https://udlguidelines.cast.org/

Castilla, E. J., & Benard, S. (2010). The Paradox of Meritocracy in Organizations. *Administrative Science Quarterly, 55*(4), 543–576. DOI: 10.2189/asqu.2010.55.4.543

Chan, C. K. Y., & Lee, K. K. W. (2023). The AI generation gap: Are Gen Z students more interested in adopting generative AI such as ChatGPT in teaching and learning than their Gen X and millennial generation teachers? *Smart Learning Environments, 10*(60), 60. Advance online publication. DOI: 10.1186/s40561-023-00269-3

Codish, D., & Ravid, G. (2017). Gender moderation in gamification: Does one size fit all? In *Proceedings of the 50th Hawaii international conference on system sciences*. https://doi.org/DOI: 10.24251/HICSS.2017.244

Coffman, J., Rosenblum, E., D'Arcy, A., & Thompson Love, L. (2021, August 11). *10 Proven Actions to Advance Diversity, Equity, and Inclusion* [Report]. Bain & Company. https://www.bain.com/insights/10-proven-actions-to-advance-diversity-equity-and-inclusion/

Coppens, A. (2018, October 22). Gamification for diversity and inclusion [Blog]. *Gamification Nation.* https://gamificationnation.com/blog/gamification-for-diversity-and-inclusion/

Cox, T., & Blake, S. (1991). Managing cultural diversity: Implications for organizational competitiveness. *The Academy of Management Perspectives*, *5*(3), 45–56. DOI: 10.5465/ame.1991.4274465

Deci, E. L., & Ryan, R. M. (1980). The empirical exploration of intrinsic motivational processes. In Berkowitz, L. (Ed.), (pp. 39–80). Advances in experimental social psychology. Academic Press. DOI: 10.1016/S0065-2601(08)60130-6

Deci, E. L., & Ryan, R. M. (1985). *Intrinsic motivation and self-determination in human behaviour*. Plenum.

Deterding, S., Dixon, D., Khaled, R., & Nacke, L. (2011, September). From game design elements to gamefulness: defining gamification. In *Proceedings of the 15th international academic MindTrek conference: Envisioning future media environments* (pp. 9-15). ACM. DOI: 10.1145/2181037.2181040

Dingari, S. (2023, April 26). Gamification for Diversity and Inclusion: The Challenges and Opportunities in Training [Blog]. *CommLab India*. https://blog.commlabindia.com/elearning-design/gamification-diversity-inclusion-training

Diversity and inclusion. (n.d.). Sustainable Development Goals - Resource Centre. https://sdgresources.relx.com/diversity-and-inclusion

Diversity, Equity, and Inclusion Definitions. (2021, September 23). UW Research. https://www.washington.edu/research/or/office-of-research-diversity-equity-and-inclusion/dei-definitions/

Dixon-Fyle, S., Huber, C., & del Mar Martínez Márquez, M. Thomas. A. & Hunt, V. (2023, December 5). *Diversity matters even more: The case for holistic impact*. McKinsey & Company. https://www.mckinsey.com/featured-insights/diversity-and-inclusion/diversity-matters-even-more-the-case-for-holistic-impact

Dobbin, F., & Kalev, A. (2018). Why Doesn't Diversity Training Work? The Challenge for Industry and Academia. *Anthropology Now*, *10*(2), 48–55. DOI: 10.1080/19428200.2018.1493182

Dobbin, F., & Kalev, A. (2022). *Getting to Diversity. What works and what doesn't.* The Belknap Press of Harvard University Press.

Domínguez, A., Saenz-De-Navarrete, J., De-Marcos, L., Fernández-Sanz, L., Pagés, C., & Martínez-Herráiz, J.-J. (2013). Gamifying learning experiences: Practical implications and outcomes. *Computers & Education, 63*, 380–392. DOI: 10.1016/j.compedu.2012.12.020

Doney, I. (2019). Research into effective gamification features to inform e-learning design. *Research in Learning Technology, 27*(0). Advance online publication. DOI: 10.25304/rlt.v27.2093

Dweck, C. S. (2006). *Mindset: The new psychology of success.* Random House.

Egan, M. L., & Bendick, M.Jr. (2008). Combining multicultural management and diversity into one course on cultural competence. *Academy of Management Learning & Education, 7*(3), 387–393. DOI: 10.5465/amle.2008.34251675

Eikelboom, J. J. (2016). *Engagement, gamification, and workplace satisfaction: A convergent study of user indicators.* University of South Maine.

Ellis, C., & Sonnenfeld, J. A. (1994). Diverse approaches to managing diversity. *Human Resource Management, 33*(1), 79–109. DOI: 10.1002/hrm.3930330106

Emerson, J. (2017, September 11). *Colorblind Diversity Efforts Don't Work.* Harvard Business Review. https://hbr.org/2017/09/colorblind-diversity-efforts-dont-work

Essential Elements of Employee Retention. (2017, October 29) [Blog]. *Lynchburg Regional SHRM.* https://lrshrm.shrm.org/blog/2017/10/essential-elements-employee-retention

Fayad, A. (2022, October 11). *The Importance Of Diversity And Inclusion Training.* Forbes. https://www.forbes.com/sites/theyec/2022/10/11/the-importance-of-diversity-and-inclusion-training/

Fujimoto, Y., & Härtel, C. E. (2017). Organizational diversity learning framework: Going beyond diversity training programs. *Personnel Review, 46*(6), 1120–1141. DOI: 10.1108/PR-09-2015-0254

Gaertner, S. L., & Dovidio, J. F. (2000). *Reducing intergroup bias: The common ingroup identity model.* Psychology Press.

Galinsky, A. D., & Moskowitz, G. B. (2000). Perspective-taking: Decreasing stereotype expression, stereotype accessibility, and in-group favoritism. *Journal of Personality and Social Psychology, 78*(4), 708–724. DOI: 10.1037/0022-3514.78.4.708 PMID: 10794375

Gamification in DEI: The Golden Nugget? (2023, June 19) [Whitepaper]. seppo. https://seppo.io/dei-whitepaper/

Gamification Trends for 2024: Current Forecasts You Should Be Thinking About (2024, August 2). Finances Online. https://financesonline.com/gamification-trends/

Garcia-Cabot, A., Garcia-Lopez, E., Caro-Alvaro, S., Gutierrez-Martinez, J., & De-Marcos, L. (2019). Measuring the effects on learning performance and engagement with a gamified social platform in an MSc program. *Computer Applications in Engineering Education, 28*(1), 207–223. DOI: 10.1002/cae.22186

Gatheral, J. (2022, July 14). *Using Gamification Techniques for More Effective DEI Training*. Training Industry. https://trainingindustry.com/articles/diversity-equity-and-inclusion/using-gamification-techniques-for-more-effective-dei-training/

Gausby, A. (2015). *Attention spans: Consumer Insights, Microsoft Canada*. Microsoft. https://sherpapg.com/wp-content/uploads/2017/12/MAS.pdf

Gill, L. J., & Olson, M. A. (2023). A dual-process framework for diversity training to reduce discrimination in organizational settings. *Social Issues and Policy Review, 17*(1), 79–103. DOI: 10.1111/sipr.12094

Griffin, S. R. (2022, May 7). *Where Diversity Training Goes Wrong, Part II. Underdeveloped Theories of How People Learn & Change*. Medium. https://medium.com/@shaylargriffin/where-diversity-training-goes-wrong-part-ii-7a5e946a2022

Guhl, A. (2017a). *Gamification across borders: The importance of culture* (Master's thesis). University of Gothenburg.

Guhl, A. (2017b). *National culture in gamification design: A conceptual approach* (Doctoral dissertation). University of Gothenburg.

Gupta, S. (2024, August 20). Gamification Statistics and Future Trends [Blog]. *Nudge*. https://www.nudgenow.com/blogs/gamification-stats-enhancing-learning#

Haaland, S. (2023. November 14). You think older generations don't respond to gamification? The data says differently [Blog]. *SalesScreen*. https://www.salesscreen.com/blog/older-generations-and-gamification/

Hajarian, M., Bastanfard, A., Mohammadzadeh, J., & Khalilian, M. (2019). A personalized gamification method for increasing user engagement in social networks. *Social Network Analysis and Mining, 9*(1), 47. DOI: 10.1007/s13278-019-0589-3

Hallifax, S., Serna, A., Marty, J. C., & Lavoué, É. (2019). Adaptive Gamification in Education: A Literature Review of Current Trends and Developments. In M. Scheffel, J. Broisin, V. Pammer-Schindler, A. Ioannou & J. Schneider (Eds.), *Transforming Learning with Meaningful Technologies*. EC-TEL 2019. Lecture Notes in Computer Science, vol 11722. Springer. https://doi.org/DOI: 10.1007/978-3-030-29736-7_22

Hamari, J., Koivisto, J., & Sarsa, H. (2014). Does Gamification Work? - A Literature Review of Empirical Studies on Gamification. In *Proceedings of the 47th Annual Hawaii International Conference on System Sciences* (pp. 3025–3034). https://doi.org/DOI: 10.1109/HICSS.2014.377

Hamouche, S. (2020, April 20). COVID-19 and employees' mental health: Stressors, moderators and agenda for organizational actions. *Emerald Open Research*. Advance online publication. DOI: 10.1108/EOR-02-2023-0004

Hemphill, E. (2018, May 29). *A look at the research behind implicit biases with Wash U professor Calvin Lai.* St. Louis Public Radio. https://www.stlpr.org/show/st-louis-on-the-air/2018-05-29/a-look-at-the-research-behind-implicit-biases-with-wash-u-professor-calvin-lai

Hong, J., Hwang, M., & Peng, Y. (2012). Gender Difference of Social Behavior in the Cooperative-Competitive Game. *Procedia: Social and Behavioral Sciences*, *64*, 244–254. DOI: 10.1016/j.sbspro.2012.11.029

How do you avoid coercion and manipulation in gamified consent processes? (2024, June, 26). LinkedIn. https://de.linkedin.com/advice/0/how-do-you-avoid-coercion-manipulation-gamified-consent?lang=en

Jackson, L. C., O'Mara, J., Moss, J., & Jackson, A. C. (2018). A Critical Review of the Effectiveness of Narrative-Driven Digital Educational Games. [IJGBL]. *International Journal of Game-Based Learning*, *8*(4), 32–49. DOI: 10.4018/IJGBL.2018100103

Joshi, A., Dencker, J. C., Franz, G., & Martocchio, J. J. (2010). Unpacking generational identities in organizations. *Academy of Management Review*, *35*(3), 392–414. DOI: 10.5465/AMR.2010.51141800

Kaiser, C. R., Major, B., Jurcevic, I., Dover, T. L., Brady, L. M., & Shapiro, J. R. (2013). Presumed fair: Ironic effects of organizational diversity structures. *Journal of Personality and Social Psychology*, *104*(3), 504–519. DOI: 10.1037/a0030838 PMID: 23163748

Kalinoski, Z. T., Steele-Johnson, D., Peyton, E. J., Leas, K. A., Steinke, J., & Bowling, N. A. (2013). A meta-analytic evaluation of diversity training outcomes. *Journal of Organizational Behavior*, *34*(8), 1076–1104. DOI: 10.1002/job.1839

Kaplan, D. M. (2006). Can Diversity Training Discriminate? Backlash to Lesbian, Gay, and Bisexual Diversity Initiatives. *Employee Responsibilities and Rights Journal, 18*(1), 61–72. DOI: 10.1007/s10672-005-9005-4

Kapp, K. M. (2012). *The Gamification of Learning and Instruction: Game-Based Methods and Strategies for Training and Education*. Pfeiffer.

King, E. B., Gulick, L. M. V., & Avery, D. R. (2010). The divide between diversity training and diversity education: Integrating best practices. *Journal of Management Education, 34*(6), 891–906. DOI: 10.1177/1052562909348767

Koekemoer, L., de Beer, L. T., Govender, K., & Brouwers, M. (2021). Leadership behaviour, team effectiveness, technological flexibility, work engagement and performance during COVID-19 lockdown: An exploratory study. *SA Journal of Industrial Psychology, 47*. Advance online publication. DOI: 10.4102/sajip.v47i0.1829

Koivisto, J., & Hamari, J. (2014). Demographic differences in perceived benefits from gamification. *Computers in Human Behavior, 35*, 179–188. DOI: 10.1016/j.chb.2014.03.007

Kotsopoulos, D., Bardaki, C., Lounis, S., Papaioannou, T. G., & Pramatari, K. (2017). Designing an IoT-enabled gamification application for energy conservation at the workplace: Exploring personal and contextual characteristics. In *Bled eConference* (p. 25). https://doi.org/DOI: 10.17083/ijsg.v5i2.225

Krath, J., Schürmann, L., & von Korflesch, H. F. O. (2021, December). Revealing the theoretical basis of gamification: A systematic review and analysis of theory in research on gamification, serious games and game-based learning. *Computers in Human Behavior, 125*, 106963. DOI: 10.1016/j.chb.2021.106963

Kulik, C. T., Pepper, M. B., Roberson, L., & Parker, S. K. (2007). The rich get richer: Predicting participation in voluntary diversity training. *Journal of Organizational Behavior, 28*(6), 753–769. DOI: 10.1002/job.444

Kulik, C. T., Perry, E. L., & Bourhis, A. C. (2000). Ironic evaluation processes: Effects of thought suppression on evaluations of older job applicants. *Journal of Organizational Behavior, 21*(6), 689–711. DOI: 10.1002/1099-1379(200009)21:6<689::AID-JOB52>3.0.CO;2-W

Kulik, C. T., & Roberson, L. (2008). Common Goals and Golden Opportunities: Evaluations of Diversity Education in Academic and Organizational Settings. *Academy of Management Learning & Education, 7*(3), 7. DOI: 10.5465/amle.2008.34251670

Lai, C. K., & Lisnek, J. A. (2023). The impact of implicit-bias-oriented diversity training on police officers' beliefs, motivations, and actions. *Psychological Science*. https://journals.sagepub.com/doi/10.1177/09567976221150617

Laine, T. H., & Lindberg, R. S. N. (2020). Designing Engaging Games for Education: A Systematic Literature Review on Game Motivators and Design Principles. *IEEE Transactions on Learning Technologies*, *13*(4), 804–821. https://ieeexplore.ieee.org/stamp/stamp.jsp?tp=&arnumber=9173738. DOI: 10.1109/TLT.2020.3018503

Landers, R. N. (2019). Gamification misunderstood: How badly executed and rhetorical gamification obscures its transformative potential. *Journal of Management Inquiry*, *28*(2), 137–140. DOI: 10.1177/1056492618790913

Larson, K. (2020). Serious Games and Gamification in the Corporate Training Environment: A Literature Review. *TechTrends*, *64*(2), 319–328. DOI: 10.1007/s11528-019-00446-7

Lazzaro, N. (2004). *The 4 Keys 2 Fun* [Whitepaper]. XEODesign. http://www.xeodesign.com/category/the-4-keys/

Lepper, M. R., Greene, D., & Nisbett, R. E. (1973). Undermining children's intrinsic interest with extrinsic reward: A test of the "overjustification" hypothesis. *Journal of Personality and Social Psychology*, *28*(1), 129–137. DOI: 10.1037/h0035519

Lewis, N. (2019, February 28). *Be Careful: Gamification at Work Can Go Very Wrong*. SHRM. https://www.shrm.org/topics-tools/news/technology/careful-gamification-work-can-go-wrong

Li, L. (2022). Reskilling and Upskilling the Future-ready Workforce for Industry 4.0 and Beyond. *Information Systems Frontiers*. Advance online publication. DOI: 10.1007/s10796-022-10308-y PMID: 35855776

Lindsey, A., King, E., Membere, A., & Cheung, H. K. (2017, July 28). *Two Types of Diversity Training That Really Work*. Harvard Business Review. https://hbr.org/2017/07/two-types-of-diversity-training-that-really-work

Lorenzo, R., & Reeves, M. (2018, January 30). *How and Where Diversity Drives Financial Performance*. Harvard Business Review. https://hbr.org/2018/01/how-and-where-diversity-drives-financial-performance

Macrae, C. N., Bodenhausen, G. V., Milne, A. B., & Jetten, J. (1994). Out of Mind but Back in Sight: Stereotypes on the Rebound. *Journal of Personality and Social Psychology*, *67*(5), 808–817. DOI: 10.1037/0022-3514.67.5.808

McGonigal, J. (2011). *Reality is broken: why games make us better and how they can change the world*. Penguin Press.

Meiman, M., Brown, N. E., & Hodges, A. (2019). Diversity, Equity, and Inclusion: A Conceptual Framework for Instruction. ACRL *19th National Conference, "Recasting the Narrative", Cleveland, Ohio. April 10-13, 2019*, 675-682.

Meister, J. C. (2013, January 2). *How Deloitte Made Learning a Game*. Harvard Business Review. https://hbr.org/2013/01/how-deloitte-made-learning-a-g

Mental health today. A deep dive based on the 2024 Gen Z and Millennial survey. (2024). Deloitte. https://www2.deloitte.com/content/dam/Deloitte/fr/Documents/human-capital/Publications/deloitte_genz-millennial-survey_mental-health-deep-dive.pdf

Miller, P. N. (2015, March 26). Is 'Design Thinking' the New Liberal Arts? *The Chronicle of Higher Education*. https://www.chronicle.com/article/is-design-thinking-the-new-liberal-arts/

Mollick, E. R., & Rothbard, N. (2014, September 30). *Mandatory fun: Consent, gamification and the impact of games at work*. The Wharton School Research Paper Series. https://doi.org/DOI: 10.2139/ssrn.2277103

Mor-Barak, M. (2005). Managing diversity: Toward a globally inclusive workplace. *Sage (Atlanta, Ga.)*.

Morley, T. (2018). Making the business case for diversity and inclusion: Short case studies and research papers that demonstrate best practice in HR. *Strategic HR Review*, *17*(1), 58–60. DOI: 10.1108/SHR-10-2017-0068

Müller, M., & Gruenewald, H. (2024). *Upskilling und Reskilling für die Personalentwicklung: Kompetenzen der Zukunft erkennen und Personal erfolgreich qualifizieren*. Springer Nature. https://link.springer.com/book/9783658444037

Nathoo, Z. (2021, June 17). *Why ineffective diversity training won't go away*. BBC worklife. https://www.bbc.com/worklife/article/20210614-why-ineffective-diversity-training-wont-go-away

Newkirk, P. (2019). *Diversity, Inc.: The Failed Promise of a Billion-Dollar Business*. Bold Type Books.

Niederle, M., & Vesterlund, L. (2008). Gender Differences in Competition. *Negotiation Journal*, *24*(4), 447–463. DOI: 10.1111/j.1571-9979.2008.00197.x

North-Samardzic, A., & de Witt, M. (2019). Designing a Human Resource Management Simulation to Engage Students. *Journal of Management Education*, *43*(4), 359–395. DOI: 10.1177/1052562919841411

Oliveira, R. P., Souza, C. G., Reis, A. C., & Souza, W. M. (2021). Gamification in E-Learning and Sustainability: A Theoretical Framework. *Sustainability (Basel)*, *13*(21), 11945. DOI: 10.3390/su132111945

Paaßen, B., Morgenroth, T., & Stratemeyer, M. (2017). What is a True Gamer? The Male Gamer Stereotype and the Marginalization of Women in Video Game Culture. *Sex Roles*, *76*(7-8), 421–435. DOI: 10.1007/s11199-016-0678-y

Paluck, E. L. (2006). Diversity training and intergroup contact: A call to action research. *The Journal of Social Issues*, *62*(3), 577–595. DOI: 10.1111/j.1540-4560.2006.00474.x

Paluck, E. L., & Green, D. P. (2009). Prejudice Reduction: What Works? A Critical Look at Evidence from the Field and the Laboratory. *Annual Review of Psychology*, •••, 60.

Paluck, E. L., Porat, R., Clark, C. S., & Green, D. P. (2021). Prejudice reduction: Progress and challenges. *Annual Review of Psychology*, *72*(1), 533–560. DOI: 10.1146/annurev-psych-071620-030619 PMID: 32928061

Pettigrew, T. F., & Tropp, L. R. (2006). A meta-analytic test of intergroup contact theory. *Journal of Personality and Social Psychology*, *90*(5), 751–783. DOI: 10.1037/0022-3514.90.5.751 PMID: 16737372

Pettigrew, T. F., & Tropp, L. R. (2008). How does intergroup contact reduce prejudice? Meta-analytic tests of three mediators. *European Journal of Social Psychology*, *38*(6), 922–934. DOI: 10.1002/ejsp.504

Phillips, B. N., Deiches, J., Morrison, B., Chan, F., & Bezyak, J. L. (2016). Disability diversity training in the workplace: Systematic review and future directions. *Journal of Occupational Rehabilitation*, *26*(3), 264–275. DOI: 10.1007/s10926-015-9612-3 PMID: 26519035

Promoting Mental Health at Work: The Impact of Gamification. (n.d,). Humanoo. https://humanoo.com/en/magazin/promoting-mental-health-at-work-the-impact-of-gamification/

Putz, L.-M., & Treiblmaier, H. (2019, January 21). Increasing Knowledge Retention through Gamified Workshops: Findings from a Longitudinal Study and Identification of Moderating Variables. *Proceedings of the 52nd Hawaii International Conference on System Sciences*.

Rahiman, H. U., Kodikal, R., & Suresh, S. (2023). Game on: Can gamification enhance productivity? *F1000Res*. https://doi.org/DOI: 10.12688/f1000research.131579.2

Read, B. (2021, May 26). *Doing the Work at Work What are companies desperate for diversity consultants actually buying?* The Cut. https://www.thecut.com/article/diversity-equity-inclusion-industrial-companies.html

Rheinberg, F. (2010). Intrinsic Motivation and Flow. In Heckhausen, J., & Heckhausen, H. (Eds.), *Motivation and Action* (4th ed., pp. 365–388). Cambridge University Press.

Richter, G., Raban, D. K., & Rafaeli, S. (2014). Studying Gamification: The Effect of Rewards and Incentives on Motivation. In Reiners, T., & Woods, L. (Eds.), *Gamification in Education and Business* (pp. 21–46). Springer International Publishing., DOI: 10.1007/978-3-319-10208-5

Rimon, G. (2016, June 7). *Sales Gamification: 5 Leaderboard Mistakes to Avoid.* eLearning Industry. https://elearningindustry.com/sales-gamification-5-leaderboard-mistakes-avoid

Robb, L. A., & Doverspike, D. (2001). Self-reported proclivity to harass as a moderator of the effectiveness of sexual harassment-prevention training. *Psychological Reports*, *88*(1), 85–88. DOI: 10.2466/pr0.2001.88.1.85 PMID: 11293058

Roberson, L., Kulik, C. T., & Pepper, M. B. (2001). Designing effective diversity training: Influence of group composition and trainee experience. *Journal of Organizational Behavior*, *22*(8), 871–885. DOI: 10.1002/job.117

Roberson, Q., King, E. B., & Hebl, M. R. (2020). Designing more effective practices to address workplace inequality. *Behavioral Science & Policy*, *6*(1), 39–49. DOI: 10.1177/237946152000600104

Robson, K., Plangger, K., Kietzmann, J. H., McCarthy, I., & Pitt, L. (2015). Is it all a game?: Understanding the principles of gamification. *Business Horizons*, *58*(4), 411–420. DOI: 10.1016/j.bushor.2015.03.006

Rodrigues, L., Palomino, P. T., Toda, A. M., Klock, A. C. T., Pessoa, M., Pereira, F. D., Oliveira, E. H. T., Oliveira, D. F., Cristea, A. I., Gasparini, I., & Isotani, S. (2023). How Personalization Affects Motivation in Gamified Review Assessments. *International Journal of Artificial Intelligence in Education*, *34*(2), 147–184. DOI: 10.1007/s40593-022-00326-x PMID: 36685293

Rudman, L. A., Ashmore, R. D., & Gary, M. L. (2001). "Unlearning" automatic biases: The malleability of implicit prejudice and stereotypes. *Journal of Personality and Social Psychology*, *81*(5), 856–868. DOI: 10.1037/0022-3514.81.5.856 PMID: 11708562

Ryan, M., Sleigh, A., Soh, K. W., & Li, Z. (2013). Why gamification is serious business. *Outlook–The Journal of High-Performance Business (Accenture), 1*, 1-6. https://www.accenture.com/us-en/insight-outlook-why-gamification-is-serious-business

Ryan, R. M., & Deci, E. L. (2000). Self-determination theory and the facilitation of intrinsic motivation, social development and well-being. *The American Psychologist, 55*(1), 68–78. DOI: 10.1037/0003-066X.55.1.68 PMID: 11392867

Sailer, M., Hense, J., Mandl, H., & Klever, M. (2013). Psychological Perspectives on Motivation through Gamification. *Interaction Design and Architecture(s). Journal, 19*, 28–37.

Salili, F., & Hoosain, R. (Eds.). (2007). *Culture, motivation and learning: A multicultural perspective*. IAP.

Seaborn, K., & Fels, D. I. (2015). Gamification in theory and action: A survey. *International Journal of Human-Computer Studies, 74*, 14–31. DOI: 10.1016/j.ijhcs.2014.09.006

Shahri, A., Hosseini, M., Phalp, K., Taylor, J., & Ali, R. (2014). Towards a code of ethics for gamification at enterprise. In Frank, U., Loucopoulos, P., Pastor, Ó., & Petrounias, I. (Eds.), *IFIP working conference on the practice of enterprise modeling* (pp. 235–245). Springer. DOI: 10.1007/978-3-662-45501-2_17

Skinner, B. F. (1953). *Science and human behavior*. Pearson Education, Inc., DOI: 10.1016/B978-012370509-9.00087-5

Skwarczek, B. (2024, June 26). *Breaking Boundaries: How Diversity, Equity And Inclusion Initiatives Are Reshaping The Gaming Industry*. Forbes. https://www.forbes.com/councils/forbestechcouncil/2024/06/26/breaking-boundaries-how-diversity-equity-and-inclusion-initiatives-are-reshaping-the-gaming-industry/

Smith, T. B., Constantine, M. G., Dunn, T. W., Dinehart, J. M., & Montoya, J. A. (2006). Multicultural education in the mental health professions: A meta-analytic review. *Journal of Counseling Psychology, 53*(1), 132–145. DOI: 10.1037/0022-0167.53.1.132

Spanellis, A., Harviainen, J. T., Fernández Galeote, D., & Thibault, M. (2024). Gamification for Sustainable Development. *Simulation & Gaming, 55*(3), 361–365. DOI: 10.1177/10468781241249324

Stefanidis, A., Phalp, K., & Ali, R. (2018). Conceptualising gamification risks to teamwork within enterprise. In *The practice of enterprise modeling: 11th IFIP WG 8.1. Working conference*, PoEM 2018, Vienna, Austria, October 31–November 2, 2018 (Vol. 335, p. 105). Springer.

Stratton, J., Canales, C., Armas, V., & Miller, N. (2006). Positive stereotyping: Influence tactic for prejudice reduction? *Social Influence*, *1*(4), 265–287. DOI: 10.1080/15534510601008882

Tondello, G. F., & Nacke, L. E. (2020). Validation of User Preferences and Effects of Personalized Gamification on Task Performance. *Frontiers of Computer Science*, *2*, 29. Advance online publication. DOI: 10.3389/fcomp.2020.00029

Tropp, L. R., & Barlow, F. K. (2018). Making advantaged racial groups care about inequality: Intergroup contact as a route to psychological investment. *Current Directions in Psychological Science*, *27*(3), 194–199. DOI: 10.1177/0963721417743282

Turan, Z., Avinc, Z., Kara, K., & Goktas, Y. (2016). Gamification and Education: Achievements, Cognitive Loads, and Views of Students. [iJET]. *International Journal of Emerging Technologies in Learning*, *11*(07), 64–69. DOI: 10.3991/ijet.v11i07.5455

Turner, H. (2021, September 28). *How Gamification Leads To Meaningful Workplace DEI Changes*. Law Journal Newsletters. https://www.lawjournalnewsletters.com/2021/09/01/how-gamification-leads-to-meaningful-workplace-dei-changes/?slreturn=20220606054104

United Nations. Department of Economic and Social Affairs Sustainable Development (2015.). *The 17 Goals | Sustainable Development*. https://sdgs.un.org/goals

Urick, M. (2017). Adapting training to meet the preferred learning styles of different generations. *International Journal of Training and Development*, *21*(1), 53–59. DOI: 10.1111/ijtd.12093

Vardeman, C. (2024, March 20). Rethinking Diversity, Equity, and Inclusion (DEI) training: From good vs. Bad to integrated respect and understanding [Blog]. *LinkedIn*. https://www.linkedin.com/pulse/rethinking-diversity-equity-inclusion-dei-training-from-vardeman-xp2rc/

Werbach, K. (2014). (Re)defining gamification: A process approach. In A. Spagnolli, L. Chittaro, & L. Gamberini (Eds.), *Persuasive Technology:9th International Conference, PERSUASIVE 2014* (pp. 266-272). Springer.

Werbach, K., & Hunter, D. (2012). *For the Win: How Game Thinking Can Revolutionize Your Business*. Wharton Digital Press.

World Economic Forum. (2020). *The future of jobs report 2020*. https://www3.weforum.org/docs/WEF_Future_of_Jobs_2020.pdf

York, J., & deHaan, J. W. (2018). A Constructivist Approach to Game-Based Language Learning: Student Perceptions in a Beginner-Level EFL Context. [IJG-BL]. *International Journal of Game-Based Learning*, *8*(1), 19–40. DOI: 10.4018/IJGBL.2018010102

Young Entrepreneur Council (YEC). (2022, 11 October). *The Importance of Diversity and Inclusion Training*. Forbes. https://www.forbes.com/councils/theyec/2022/10/11/the-importance-of-diversity-and-inclusion-training/

Zheng, L. (2022). *DEI Deconstructed: Your No-Nonsense Guide to Doing the Work and Doing It Right*. Berrett-Koehler Publishers.

ENDNOTES

[1] For current definitions, refer to UW Research (2005) and Zheng (2022).

[2] A study from Microsoft Corp. (Gausby, 2015) indicates that since the onset of the mobile revolution around the year 2000, the average human attention span has declined from 12 seconds to just eight seconds, in other words lower than that of a goldfish.

Compilation of References

A Complete Guide to Diversity Training Gamification and its Strategies (2024, March 1). Learning Everest. https://www.learningeverest.com/diversity-training-gamification/#content

Abrahamson, E. (1996). Management Fashion. *Academy of Management Review*, *21*(1), 254–285. DOI: 10.2307/258636

Accenture. (2022). *The business value of play: How gaming initiatives drive organizational performance*. Accenture Research.

Accessibility in gaming report. (n.d.). Scope. https://www.scope.org.uk/campaigns/research-policy/accessibility-in-gaming

Activision Blizzard. (2021). *Corporate culture and employee engagement report.* Activision Blizzard, Inc.

Adachi, P. J. C., & Willoughby, T. (2013). More than just fun and games: The longitudinal relationships between strategic video games, self-reported problem-solving skills, and academic grades. *Journal of Youth and Adolescence*, *42*(7), 1041–1052. DOI: 10.1007/s10964-013-9913-9 PMID: 23344653

Afzal, M. (2024, May 13). *Top Gamification Trends To Look Out For In 2024.* eLearning Industry. https://elearningindustry.com/top-gamification-trends-to-look-out-for-in-2024

Aggarwal, S., Gupta, S., Mittal, A., & Rastogi, S. (2022). Gen Z entering the workforce: Restructuring HR policies and practices for fostering the task performance and organizational commitment. *Journal of Public Affairs*, *22*(3), e2535. Advance online publication. DOI: 10.1002/pa.2535

Ahmadi, M. M. (2020, August). Managing the New Gamified World: How Gamification Changes Businesses. *International Journal of Management. Accounting and Economics*, *7*(7), 305–325.

Ahmed, A., Aziz, S., Abd-alrazaq, A., Farooq, F., & Sheikh, J. (2022). Overview of Artificial Intelligence–Driven Wearable Devices for Diabetes: Scoping Review. *Journal of Medical Internet Research*, *24*(8), e36010–e36010. DOI: 10.2196/36010 PMID: 35943772

Ahmed, A., Aziz, S., Alzubaidi, M., Schneider, J., Irshaidat, S., Abu Serhan, H., Abd-alrazaq, A. A., Solaiman, B., & Househ, M. (2023). Wearable devices for anxiety & depression: A scoping review. *Computer Methods and Programs in Biomedicine Update*, *3*, 100095. DOI: 10.1016/j.cmpbup.2023.100095 PMID: 36743720

Ahuja, A., Agrawal, S., Acharya, S., Batra, N., & Daiya, V. (2024). Advancements in Wearable Digital Health Technology: A Review of Epilepsy Management. *Cureus*, *16*(3), e57037–e57037. DOI: 10.7759/cureus.57037 PMID: 38681418

al Akimov, N. (2023). Components of education 4.0 in open innovation competence frameworks: Systematic review. *Journal of Open Innovation*, *9*(2), 100037. DOI: 10.1016/j.joitmc.2023.100037

Al Kuwaiti, A., Nazer, K., Al-Reedy, A., Al-Shehri, S., Al-Muhanna, A., Subbarayalu, A. V., Al Muhanna, D., & Al-Muhanna, F. A. (2023). A Review of the Role of Artificial Intelligence in Healthcare. *Journal of Personalized Medicine, 13*(6), 951-. https://doi.org/DOI: 10.3390/jpm13060951

Aldao, A., Nolen-Hoeksema, S., & Schweizer, S. (2010). Emotion-regulation strategies across psychopathology: A meta-analytic review. *Clinical Psychology Review*, *30*(2), 217–237. DOI: 10.1016/j.cpr.2009.11.004 PMID: 20015584

Alfaro, L., & Chen, M. X. (2014). The global agglomeration of multinational firms. *Journal of International Economics*, *94*(2), 263–276. DOI: 10.1016/j.jinteco.2014.09.001

Algashami, A., Cham, S., Vuillier, L., Stefanidis, A., Phalp, K. T., & Ali, R. (2018). Conceptualising gamification risks to teamwork within enterprise. In Buchmann, R., Karagiannis, D., & Kirikova, M. (Eds.), *The Practice of Enterprise Modeling. PoEM 2018. Lecture Notes in Business Information Processing* (Vol. 335). Springer., DOI: 10.1007/978-3-030-02302-7_7

Alhejaili, R., & Alomainy, A. (2023). The Use of Wearable Technology in Providing Assistive Solutions for Mental Well-Being. *Sensors (Basel)*, *23*(17), 7378. DOI: 10.3390/s23177378 PMID: 37687834

Ali, M. (2023). Strategic leadership in the digital age: Navigating uncertainty. *Journal of Management & Social Science*, *1*(1), 1–8.

Allen, T. D., Merlo, K., Lawrence, R. C., Slutsky, J., & Gray, C. E. (2021). Boundary management and work-nonwork balance while working from home. *Applied Psychology*, *70*(1), 60–84. DOI: 10.1111/apps.12300

Alleway, H. K., Klein, E. S., Cameron, L., Douglass, K., Govia, I., Guell, C., Lim, M., Robin, L., & Thurstan, R. H. (2023). The shifting baseline syndrome as a connective concept for more informed and just responses to global environmental change. *People and Nature*, *5*(4), e10473. Advance online publication. DOI: 10.1002/pan3.10473

Allport, G. W. (1954). *The Nature of Prejudice*. Addison-Wesley.

American Psychological Association. (2022, October 31). How stress affects your health. https://www.apa.org/topics/stress/health

Anand, R., & Winters, M.-F. (2008). A retrospective view of corporate diversity training from 1964 to the present. *Academy of Management Learning & Education*, *7*(3), 356–372. DOI: 10.5465/amle.2008.34251673

Anderson, C. A., & Dill, K. E. (2000). Video games and aggressive thoughts, feelings, and behavior in the laboratory and in life. Journal of personality and social psychology, 78(4), 772.DOI: 10.25035/jade.02.01.03

Anderson, L. W., & Krathwohl, D. R. (2001). *A taxonomy for learning, teaching, and assessing*. Longman.

Andrews, S. (2024, May 30). *Accessibility in Gaming*. bcs: The Chartered Institute for IT. https://www.bcs.org/articles-opinion-and-research/accessibility-in-gaming/

Ang, S., & Van Dyne, L. (2015). *Handbook of cultural intelligence: Theory, measurement, and applications*. Routledge. DOI: 10.4324/9781315703855

Ang, S., Van Dyne, L., Koh, C., Ng, K. Y., Templer, K. J., Tay, C., & Chandrasekar, N. A. (2007). Cultural Intelligence: Its Measurement and Effects on Cultural Judgment and Decision Making, Cultural Adaptation and Task Performance. *Management and Organization Review*, *3*(3), 335–371. DOI: 10.1111/j.1740-8784.2007.00082.x

Apostolopoulos, A. (2019, August 19). The 2019 Gamification at Work Survey [Blog]. *TalentLMS*. https://www.talentlms.com/blog/gamification-survey-results/

Aprea, C., & Ifenthaler, D. (Eds.). (2021). *Game-based learning across the disciplines*. Springer., DOI: 10.1007/978-3-030-75142-5

Associated Press. (2017). *AP Stylebook 2017*. https://www.apstylebook.com/blog_posts/7

Association for Career and Technical Education. (2022, March 7). *Academic esports: Engage in the future*. ACTE. https://www.acteonline.org/tech-academic-esports/

Association of College & Research Libraries (ACRL). (2016). *Framework for Information Literacy for Higher Education.* https://www.ala.org/acrl/standards/ilframework

Atherton, G., & Cross, L. (2021). The use of analog and digital games for autism interventions. *Frontiers in Psychology*, *12*, 669734. DOI: 10.3389/fpsyg.2021.669734 PMID: 34447328

Autor, D., Mindell, D. A., & Reynolds, E. B. (2022). *The Work of the Future: Building better Jobs in an Age of intelligent Machines*. MIT Press. DOI: 10.7551/mitpress/14109.001.0001

Avery, D. R., & Thomas, K. M. (2004). Blending content and contact: The role of diversity curriculum and campus heterogeneity in fostering diversity management competency. *Academy of Management Learning & Education*, *3*(4), 380–396. DOI: 10.5465/amle.2004.15112544

Babu, M., Lautman, Z., Lin, X., Sobota, M. H., & Snyder, M. P. (2023). Wearable Devices: Implications for Precision Medicine and the Future of Health Care. *Annual Review of Medicine*. Advance online publication. DOI: 10.1146/annurev-med-052422-020437 PMID: 37983384

Baer, S. (2022, April 14). *Gamification: Turning Corporate Responsibility Into An Authentic And Fun Experience*. Forbes. https://www.forbes.com/councils/forbeshumanresourcescouncil/2022/04/05/gamification-turning-corporate-responsibility-into-an-authentic-and-fun-experience/

Baicker, K., Cutler, D., & Song, Z. (2022). Workplace wellness programs can generate savings. *Health Affairs*, *29*(2), 304–311. DOI: 10.1377/hlthaff.2009.0626 PMID: 20075081

Bajwa, J., Munir, U., Nori, A., & Williams, B. (2021). Artificial intelligence in healthcare: Transforming the practice of medicine. *Future Healthcare Journal*, *8*(2), e188–e194. DOI: 10.7861/fhj.2021-0095 PMID: 34286183

Bakker, D., Kazantzis, N., Rickwood, D., & Rickard, N. (2018). Mental health smartphone apps: Review and evidence-based recommendations for future developments. *JMIR Mental Health*, *5*(1), e7. DOI: 10.2196/mental.4984 PMID: 26932350

Baltzar, P. (2023, May 17). Accessibility in Digital Learning Games – Why Is It Relevant? [Blog]. *seppo*. https://seppo.io/blog/accessibility-digital-learning-games/?

Bamela, U., Kumar, S., Lim, W. M., Bamelf, N., & Meyer, N. (2022). Managing the dark side of digitalization in the future of work: A fuzzy TISM approach. *Journal of Innovation & Knowledge*, *7*(4), 100275. DOI: 10.1016/j.jik.2022.100275

Banerjee, S., Hemphill, T., & Longstreet, P. (2018). [PDF] wearable devices and Healthcare: Data sharing and privacy ... Semantic SCHOLAR. https://www.semanticscholar.org/paper/Wearable-devices-and-healthcare:-Data-sharing-and-Banerjee-Hemphill/93adc384700d2b5ba5a0a76b9287ce16d5dfa351

Banyai, F., Griffiths, M. D., Demetrovics, Z., & Kiraly, O. (2019). Online gaming and gaming disorder: More than just a trivial pursuit. *Current Addiction Reports*, *6*(3), 1–13. https://www.researchgate.net/publication/334846962_Online_gaming_and_gaming_disorder_more_than_just_a_trivial_pursuit PMID: 31366420

Baptista, N. T., Dessalles, R., Illner, A.-K., Ville, P., Ribet, L., Anton, P. M., & Durand-Dubief, M. (2024). Harnessing the power of resistant starch: A narrative review of its health impact and processing challenges. *Frontiers in Nutrition*, *11*, 1369950–1369950. DOI: 10.3389/fnut.2024.1369950 PMID: 38571748

Barr, M. (2018). Student attitudes to games-based skills development: Learning from video games in higher education. *Computers in Human Behavior*, *80*, 283–294. DOI: 10.1016/j.chb.2017.11.030

Bassanelli, S., Vasta, N., Bucchiarone, A., & Marconi, A. (2022). Gamification for Behavior Change: A Scientometric Review. *Acta Psychologica*, *228*(103657), 103657. https://www.sciencedirect.com/science/article/pii/S000169182200172X. DOI: 10.1016/j.actpsy.2022.103657 PMID: 35767927

Baumann, N. A. (2017). The importance of effective communication: Some food for thought. *The Journal of Applied Laboratory Medicine: An AACC Publication*, *1*(4), 460–461. DOI: 10.1373/jalm.2016.021865 PMID: 33636815

Bavelier, D., Green, C. S., Han, D. H., Renshaw, P. F., Merzenich, M. M., & Gentile, D. A. (2011). Brains on video games. *Nature Reviews. Neuroscience*, *12*(12), 763–768. DOI: 10.1038/nrn3135 PMID: 22095065

Bawden, D. (2008). Origins and concepts of digital literacy. In Lankshear, C., & Knobel, M. (Eds.), *Digital literacies: Concepts, policies and practices* (pp. 17–32). Peter Lang.

Bella, K. M. J. (2023). The role of flexibility: Balancing work and personal needs. *International Journal of Scientific Research in Modern Science and Technology*, *2*(2), 25–30.

Bellanca, J. A., & Brandt, R. (2010). *21st Century Skills: Rethinking How Students Learn*. Solution Tree Press.

Benítez-Márquez, M. D., Valverde-Berrocoso, J., Morales-Cevallos, M. B., & Sánchez-Santillán, M. (2021). Generation Z in the Workplace through the Lenses of Human Resource Professionals - A Qualitative Study. *ResearchGate*. Retrieved from https://www.researchgate.net/publication/352374489_Generation_Z_in_the_Workplace_through_the_Lenses_of_Human_Resource_Professionals_-_A_Qualitative_Study

Bennerstedt, U., Ivarsson, J., & Linderoth, J. (2012). How gamers manage aggression: Situating skills in collaborative computer games. *International Journal of Computer-Supported Collaborative Learning*, *7*(2), 251–269. DOI: 10.1007/s11412-011-9136-6

Bennett, E. E., & McWhorter, R. R. (2021). Virtual HRD's role in crisis and the post Covid-19 professional lifeworld: Accelerating skills for digital transformation. *Advances in Developing Human Resources*, *23*(1), 5–25. DOI: 10.1177/1523422320973288

Beňo, M. (2023). Re-establishing home and work boundaries by pseudo-commuting whilst working from home. *Central European Business Review*, *12*(4), 123–134. DOI: 10.18267/j.cebr.335

Berger, P., Bitsch, F., Bröhl, H., & Falkenberg, I. (2018). Play and playfulness in psychiatry: A selective review. *International Journal of Play*, *7*(2), 210–225. DOI: 10.1080/21594937.2017.1383341

Bersin, J. (2022). *Irresistible: The Seven Secrets of the World's most enduring employee-Focused organizations*. Ideapress Publishing.

Bezrukova, K., Spell, C. S., Perry, J. L., & Jehn, K. A. (2016). A meta-analytical integration of over 40 years of research on diversity training evaluation. *Psychological Bulletin*, *142*(11), 1227–1274. DOI: 10.1037/bul0000067 PMID: 27618543

Bhaduri, S. (2023, July 12). *How to Measure the Effectiveness and Impact of DEI Training*. Training Industry. https://trainingindustry.com/articles/measurement-and-analytics/how-to-measure-the-effectiveness-and-impact-of-dei-training/

Bhatt, P., & Muduli, A. (2023). Artificial intelligence in learning and development: A systematic literature review. *European Journal of Training and Development*, *47*(7/8), 677–694. DOI: 10.1108/EJTD-09-2021-0143

Binkley, M., Erstad, O., Herman, J., Raizen, S., Ripley, M., Miller-Ricci, M., & Rumble, M. (2012). Defining twenty-first century skills. In Griffin, P., McGaw, B., & Care, E. (Eds.), *Assessment and teaching of 21st century skills* (pp. 17–66). Springer., DOI: 10.1007/978-94-007-2324-5_2

Birje, A. (2024). How AI has transformed the Learning and Development L&D Program, https://www.airmeet.com/hub/blog/how-ai-has-transformed-the-learning-and-development-ld-program/

Birla, R. (2023). The Challenges of Media Education in the Digital Era. *Journal of Communication Management (London)*, *2*(04), 281–288.

Black, S. J., Mendenhall, M., & Oddou, G. (1991). Toward a comprehensive model of international adjustment: An integration of multiple theoretical perspectives. *Academy of Management Review*, *16*(2), 291–317. DOI: 10.2307/258863

Bleakley, C. M., Charles, D., Porter-Armstrong, A., McNeill, M. D., McDonough, S. M., & McCormack, B. (2015). Gaming for health: A systematic review of the physical and cognitive effects of interactive computer games in older adults. *Journal of Applied Gerontology*, *34*(3), NP166–NP189. DOI: 10.1177/0733464812470747 PMID: 24652863

Bley, S. (2017). Developing and validating a technology-based diagnostic assessment using the evidence-centered game design approach: An example of intrapreneurship competence. *Empirical Research in Vocational Education and Training*, *9*(1), 6. DOI: 10.1186/s40461-017-0049-0

Blömeke, S., Gustafsson, J. E., & Shavelson, R. J. (2015). Beyond dichotomies: Competence viewed as a continuum. *Zeitschrift für Psychologie*, *223*(1), 3–13. DOI: 10.1027/2151-2604/a000194

Bloom, B. S., Engelhart, M. D., Furst, E. J., Hill, W. H., & Krathwohl, D. R. (1956). *Taxonomy of educational objectives: The classification of educational goals. Handbook I: Cognitive domain*. David McKay.

Blumenstein, M. (2020). Synergies of learning analytics and learning design: A systematic review of student outcomes. *Journal of Learning Analytics*, *7*(3), 13–32. DOI: 10.18608/jla.2020.73.3

Blurton, D. (2024, January 23). Hyper-personalization in iGaming: A trend taking the industry by storm [Blog]. *Ciklum*. https://www.ciklum.com/resources/blog/hyper-personalization-in-igaming-a-trend-taking-the-industry-by-storm

Bodily, R., Graham, C. R., & Bush, M. D. (2017). Online learner engagement: Opportunities and challenges with using data analytics. *Educational Technology*, •••, 10–18.

Bonache, J., Brewster, C., & Froese, F. J. (2024). Global mobility: Reasons, trends, and strategies. In Bonache, J., Brewster, C., & Froese, F. J. (Eds.), *Global mobility and the management of expatriates* (pp. 1–28). Cambridge University Press., DOI: 10.1017/9781108679220.001

Bonanno, P., & Kommers, P. A. M. (2010). Gender differences and styles in the use of digital games. *Educational Psychology*, *25*(1), 13–41. DOI: 10.1080/0144341042000294877

Börner, K., Scrivner, O., Gallant, M., Ma, S., Liu, X., Chewning, K., Wu, L., & Evans, J. A. (2018). Skill discrepancies between research, education, and jobs reveal the critical need to supply soft skills for the data economy. *Proceedings of the National Academy of Sciences of the United States of America, 115*(50), 12630–12637. DOI: 10.1073/pnas.1804247115 PMID: 30530667

Börsch-Supan, A. (2003). Labor market effects of population aging. *Labour*, *17*(1), 5–44. DOI: 10.1111/1467-9914.17.specialissue.2

Bozkurt and Sharma. (2020). Emergency remote teaching in the time of global crisis due to corona virus pandemic. *Asian Journal of Distance Education, 15*(1), 1–6. DOI: 10.5281/zenodo.3778083

Bozkurt, A., Jung, I., Xiao, J., Vladimirschi, V., Schuwer, R., Egorov, G., & Paskevicius, M. (2020). A global outlook to the interruption of education due to COVID-19 pandemic: Navigating in a time of uncertainty and crisis. *Asian Journal of Distance Education, 15*(1), 1–126.

Bozzi, A. (2024). Digital nomadism from the perspective of places and mobilities: A literature review. *European Transport Research Review*, *16*(1), 50. DOI: 10.1186/s12544-024-00663-z

Brancheverenigning Esports Nederland. (2023). *Dutch esports ecosystem* [Infographic]. https://www.esportsnederland.com/infographic_esports_nederlandse_ecosysteem

Brinson, N. H., & Rutherford, D. N. (2020). Privacy and the quantified self: A review of U.S. health information policy limitations related to wearable technologies. *The Journal of Consumer Affairs*, *54*(4), 1355–1374. DOI: 10.1111/joca.12320

Bronnimann, J., West, D., Huijser, H., & Heath, D. (2018). Applying learning analytics to the scholarship of teaching and learning. *Innovative Higher Education, 43*(5), 353–367. DOI: 10.1007/s10755-018-9431-5

Brown, N. J. S., Furtak, E. M., Timms, M., Nagashima, S. O., & Wilson, M. (2010). The Evidence-Based Reasoning Framework: Assessing Scientific Reasoning. *Educational Assessment*, *15*(3-4), 123–141. DOI: 10.1080/10627197.2010.530551

Brull, S., Finlayson, S., Kostelec, T., Macdonald, R., & Krenzischeck, D. (2017). Using Gamification to Improve Productivity and Increase Knowledge Retention During Orientation. *The Journal of Nursing Administration*, *47*(9), 448–453. DOI: 10.1097/NNA.0000000000000512 PMID: 28834805

Brunetti, F., Matt, D. T., Bonfanti, A., De Longhi, A., Pedrini, G., & Orzes, G. (2020). Digital transformation challenges: Strategies emerging from a multi-stakeholder approach. *The TQM Journal*, *32*(4), 697–724. DOI: 10.1108/TQM-12-2019-0309

Brynjolfsson, E., & McAfee, A. (2018). *The Second Machine Age: Wie die nächste digitale Revolution unser aller Leben verändern wird*. Plassen.

Bucher, J., & Deller, J. (2021). Digital technologies and expatriation - a systematic literature review. *Proceedings - Academy of Management*, *21*(1), 11–27. DOI: 10.5465/AMBPP.2021.11027abstract

Bucher, J., Lazarova, M., & Deller, J. (2024). Digital technology and global mobility: Narrative review and directions for future research. *International Business Review*, *102294*. Advance online publication. DOI: 10.1016/j.ibusrev.2024.102294

Buonomo, I., Ferrara, B., Pansini, M., & Benevene, P. (2023). Job Satisfaction and Perceived Structural Support in Remote Working Conditions—The Role of a Sense of Community at Work. *International Journal of Environmental Research and Public Health*, *20*(13), 6205. DOI: 10.3390/ijerph20136205 PMID: 37444053

Bureau of Internet Accessibility. (n.d.). Video accessibility checklist. BOIA.org. https://www.boia.org/video-accessibility-checklist?utm_adgroup=Video-Accessibility-Checklist&utm_source=google&utm_medium=paidsearch&utm_campaign=Generic-Checklists-Guides-Content-Downloads-97F&utm_term=video%20accessibility%20checklist&utm_content=checkl

Burke, B. (2014). *Gamify: How Gamification Motivates People to Do Extraordinary Things*. Gartner Inc.

Burleigh, T. L., Griffiths, M. D., Sumich, A., Wang, G. Y., Stavropoulos, V., Kannis-Dymand, L., & Kuss, D. J. (2022). Co-Occurrence of Gaming Disorder and Other Potentially Addictive Behaviours between Australia, New Zealand, and the United Kingdom. International Journal of Environmental Research and Public Health, 19(23), 16078–. https://doi.org/DOI: 10.3390/ijerph192316078

Burr, M. (2024), The Rapidly Evolving Role of L&D in an AI-Powered World, https://nomadiclearning.com/blog/2024/04/the-rapidly-evolving-role-of-l-and-d-in-an-ai-powered-world

Cachat-Rosset, G., & Klarsfeld, A. (2023). Diversity, Equity, and Inclusion in Artificial Intelligence: An Evaluation of Guidelines. *Applied Artificial Intelligence*, *37*(1), 2176618. Advance online publication. DOI: 10.1080/08839514.2023.2176618

Cai, L., Huang, Z., Feng, Q., Chang, X., & Yan, K. (2022). Co-Transformation of Digital Health and eSport in Metaverse: Moderating Effects of Digital Personality on Mental Health in Multiplayer Online Battle Arena (MOBA). *International Journal of Environmental Research and Public Health,* 20(1), 760–. https://doi.org/DOI: 10.3390/ijerph20010760

Caligiuri, P., De Cieri, H., Minbaeva, D., Verbeke, A., & Zimmermann, A. (2020). International HRM insights for navigating the COVID-19 pandemic: Implications for future research and practice. *Journal of International Business Studies*, *51*(5), 697–713. DOI: 10.1057/s41267-020-00335-9 PMID: 32836500

Callan, R. C., Bauer, K. N., & Landers, R. N. (2015). How to avoid the dark side of gamification: ten business scenarios and their unintended consequences. In Reiners, T., & Wood, L. (Eds.), *Gamification in education and business* (pp. 553–568). Springer. DOI: 10.1007/978-3-319-10208-5_28

Canali, S. Schiaffonati, V., & Aliverti, A. (2022). Challenges and recommendations for wearable devices in Digital Health: Data Quality, interoperability, health equity, fairness. PLOS Digital Health. https://journals.plos.org/digitalhealth/article?id=10.1371%2Fjournal.pdig.0000104

Canhilal, S. K., Canboy, B., & Bakici, T. (2022). Social support for expatriates through virtual platforms: Exploring the role of online and offline participation. *International Journal of Human Resource Management*, *33*(5), 1005–1036. DOI: 10.1080/09585192.2020.1752283

Capatina, A., Juarez-Varon, D., Micu, A., & Micu, A. E. (2024). Leveling up in corporate training: Unveiling the power of gamification to enhance knowledge retention, knowledge sharing, and job performance. *Journal of Innovation & Knowledge*, *9*(3), 100530. DOI: 10.1016/j.jik.2024.100530

Caravan, S. (2024), AI and its Role in Talent Management, https://www.skillscaravan.com/post/ai-and-its-role-in-talent-management#:~:text=AI%20in%20Talent%20Management%20refers,performance%20management%2C%20and%20workforce%20planning

Carucci, R. (2024, January 24). *One More Time: Why Diversity Leads To Better Team Performance*. Forbes. https://www.forbes.com/sites/roncarucci/2024/01/24/one-more-time-why-diversity-leads-to-better-team-performance/

Cascio, J. (2020, April 29). *Facing the age of chaos*. Medium. https://medium.com/@cascio/facing-the-age-of-chaos-b00687b1f51d

CAST. (2024). *Universal design for learning guidelines version 3.0* [graphic organizer]. Author. https://udlguidelines.cast.org/

Castilla, E. J., & Benard, S. (2010). The Paradox of Meritocracy in Organizations. *Administrative Science Quarterly*, *55*(4), 543–576. DOI: 10.2189/asqu.2010.55.4.543

Centers for Disease Control and Prevention (CDC). (2024a). CDC data shows over 70 million U.S. adults reported having a disability. Centers for Disease Control and Prevention. https://www.cdc.gov/media/releases/2024/s0716-Adult-disability.html

Centers for Disease Control and Prevention (CDC). (2024b). Disability Impacts All of Us. U.S. Center for Disease Control. https://www.cdc.gov/ncbddd/disabilityandhealth/infographic-disability-impacts-all.html

Cesar, P., & Geerts, D. (2011). Past, present, and future of social TV: A categorization. In *Proceedings of the 2011 IEEE Consumer Communications and Networking Conference (CCNC)* (pp. 347–351). IEEE. DOI: 10.1109/CCNC.2011.5766487

Cès, P., Duflos, M., Tricard, E., Jhean-Larose, S., & Giraudeau, C. (2024). Playing board games to increase emotional competencies in school-age children and older people: A systematic review. *Leisure Sciences*, •••, 1–24. DOI: 10.1080/01490400.2024.2373415

Chaaban, Y., Al-Thani, H., & Du, X. (2021). A narrative inquiry of teacher educators' professional agency, identity renegotiations, and emotional responses amid educational disruption. *Teaching and Teacher Education*, *108*, 103522. DOI: 10.1016/j.tate.2021.103522

Chan, C. K. Y., & Lee, K. K. W. (2023). The AI generation gap: Are Gen Z students more interested in adopting generative AI such as ChatGPT in teaching and learning than their Gen X and millennial generation teachers? *Smart Learning Environments*, *10*(60), 60. Advance online publication. DOI: 10.1186/s40561-023-00269-3

Chandel, T.A (2023) Reshape the Sustainable State-of the-Art Development of Smart Cities, e book Convergence of IoT, Blockchain and Computational Intelligence in Smart Cities, 58-82, CRC Press, Taylor & Francis Group, DOI: 10.1201/9781003353034-4

Chandel, T. A. (2022). *Green Entrepreneurship and Sustainable Development" "International Perspectives on Value Creation and Sustainability through Social Entrepreneurship." 173-208*. Global publisher., DOI: 10.4018/978-1-6684-4666-9.ch009

Chandel, T. A. (2023). *Hybrid Energy Storage Systems for Renewable Energy Integration and Application: Artificial Intelligence Applications in Battery Management Systems and Routing Problems in Electric Vehicles*. GI Global., DOI: 10.4018/978-1-6684-8816-4.ch011

Chandel, T. A.. (2023). *Green and Clean Energy: Current Global Scenario, Renewable Energy and AI for sustainable Developments* (Vol. 1-30). CRC Press, Taylor & Francis., DOI: 10.1201/9781003369554-1

Chao, M. M., Takeuchi, R., & Farh, J. L. (2017). Enhancing cultural intelligence: The roles of implicit culture beliefs and adjustment. *Personnel Psychology*, *70*(1), 257–292. DOI: 10.1111/peps.12142

Chen, K., Zdorova, M., & Nathan-Roberts, D. (2017). Implications of Wearables, Fitness Tracking Services, and Quantified Self on Healthcare. Proceedings of the Human Factors and Ergonomics Society Annual Meeting, 61, 1066 1070.DOI: 10.1177/1541931213601871

Chen, M., Ma, Y., Song, J., Lai, C. F., & Hu, B. (2016). Smart Clothing: Connecting Human with Clouds and Big Data for Sustainable Health Monitoring. *Mobile Networks and Applications*, *21*(5), 825–845. DOI: 10.1007/s11036-016-0745-1

Chevtaeva, E., Neuhofer, B., Egger, R., & Rainoldi, M. (2024). Travel while working remotely: A topological data analysis of well-being in remote work trip experiences. *Journal of Travel Research*, *63*(2), 466–480. DOI: 10.1177/00472875231151923

Chiauzzi, E., Rodarte, C., & DasMahapatra, P. (2015). Patient-centered activity monitoring in the self-management of chronic health conditions. *BMC Medicine*, *13*(1), 77. Advance online publication. DOI: 10.1186/s12916-015-0319-2 PMID: 25889598

Chidambaram, S., Maheswaran, Y., Patel, K., Sounderajah, V., Hashimoto, D. A., Seastedt, K. P., Mcgregor, A. H., Markar, S. R., & Darzi, A. (2022). Using Artificial Intelligence-Enhanced Sensing and Wearable Technology in Sports Medicine and Performance Optimisation. *Sensors (Basel)*, *22*(18), 6920. Advance online publication. DOI: 10.3390/s22186920 PMID: 36146263

Chiu, T. K. F., Xia, Q., Zhou, X., Chai, C. S., & Cheng, M. (2023). Systematic literature review on opportunities, challenges and future research recommendations of artificial intelligence in education. *Journal of Computers and Education: Artificial Intelligence*, *4*, 100118. DOI: 10.1016/j.caeai.2022.100118

Choi, C., Hums, M. A., & Bum, C.-H. (2018). Impact of the Family Environment on Juvenile Mental Health:eSports Online Game Addiction and Delinquency. *International Journal of Environmental Research and Public Health, 15*(12), 2850–. https://doi.org/DOI: 10.3390/ijerph15122850

Choi, L., & Chung, S. (2021). Navigating online language teaching in uncertain times: Challenges and strategies of EFL educators in creating a sustainable technology-mediated language learning environment. *Sustainability (Basel), 13*(14), 7664. DOI: 10.3390/su13147664

Chow, D. H. K., & Mann, S. K. F. (2023). Exergaming and education: A relational model for games selection and evaluation. *Frontiers in Psychology, 14*, 1197403. Advance online publication. DOI: 10.3389/fpsyg.2023.1197403 PMID: 37484077

Chung, A. T., Lenci, L. T., Wang, K., Collins, T. E., Griess, M. D., Oetting, T. A., & Shriver, E. M. (2017). Effect of fine-motor-skill activities on surgical simulator performance. *Journal of Cataract and Refractive Surgery, 43*(7), 763–768. https://europepmc.org/article/MED/28823438. DOI: 10.1016/j.jcrs.2017.05.024 PMID: 28823438

Cigdem, H., & Öncü, S. (2023). Leveraging Learning Analytics to Improve Student Engagement. In *Perspectives on Learning Analytics for Maximizing Student Outcomes* (pp. 64–88). IGI Global. DOI: 10.4018/978-1-6684-9527-8.ch004

Cisco. (2020). *Esports as a tool for leadership development*. Cisco Systems, Inc.

Claned, (2024/04/12), The Role of AI in Personalized Learning, https://claned.com/the-role-of-ai-in-personalized-learning/

Clarke, S. J., Peel, D. J., Arnab, S., Morini, L., Keegan, H., & Wood, O. (2017). EscapED: A framework for creating educational escape rooms and interactive games to for higher/further education. *International Journal of Serious Games, 4*(3), 73–86. DOI: 10.17083/ijsg.v4i3.180

Clarke, T. (2019). Creative destruction, technology disruption, and growth. In *Oxford Research Encyclopedia of Economics and Finance*. Oxford University Press. DOI: 10.1093/acrefore/9780190625979.013.393

Codish, D., & Ravid, G. (2017). Gender moderation in gamification: Does one size fit all? In *Proceedings of the 50th Hawaii international conference on system sciences*. https://doi.org/DOI: 10.24251/HICSS.2017.244

Coffman, J., Rosenblum, E., D'Arcy, A., & Thompson Love, L. (2021, August 11). *10 Proven Actions to Advance Diversity, Equity, and Inclusion* [Report]. Bain & Company. https://www.bain.com/insights/10-proven-actions-to-advance-diversity-equity-and-inclusion/

Colbert, A., Yee, N., & George, G. (2016). The digital workforce and the workplace of the future. *Academy of Management Journal*, *59*(3), 731–739. DOI: 10.5465/amj.2016.4003

ColorWillOrg. (n.d.). Colorblind guide. Colorblindguide.com. https://www.colorblindguide.com/post/colorblind-people-population-live-counter

Colvonen, P. J., DeYoung, P. N., Bosompra, N., & Owens, R. L. (2020). Limiting racial disparities and bias for wearable devices in health science research. *Sleep (Basel)*, *43*(10), zsaa159. Advance online publication. DOI: 10.1093/sleep/zsaa159 PMID: 32893865

Commonwealth of Pennsylvania. (n.d.). Accessibility best practices. WCMS Author Guide. https://wcmauthorguide.pa.gov/en/accessibility-best-practices.html

Connelly, F. M., & Clandinin, D. J. (1990). Stories of Experience and Narrative Inquiry. *Educational Researcher*, *19*(5), 2–14. DOI: 10.3102/0013189X019005002

Coppens, A. (2018, October 22). Gamification for diversity and inclusion [Blog]. *Gamification Nation*. https://gamificationnation.com/blog/gamification-for-diversity-and-inclusion/

Cox, T., & Blake, S. (1991). Managing cultural diversity: Implications for organizational competitiveness. *The Academy of Management Perspectives*, *5*(3), 45–56. DOI: 10.5465/ame.1991.4274465

Danesi, M. (2018). *Ahmes' legacy: Puzzles and the mathematical mind*. Springer. DOI: 10.1007/978-3-319-93254-5

Daniau, S. (2016). The transformative potential of role-playing games: From play skills to human skills. *Simulation & Gaming*, *47*(4), 423–444. DOI: 10.1177/1046878116650765

Datta, S., Sehgal, S., Bhattacharya, B., & Satgunam, P. N. (2023, May). pattern and associations with asthenopic symptoms. *Indian Journal of Ophthalmology*, *71*(5), 2071–2075. DOI: 10.4103/ijo.IJO_2056_22 PMID: 37203083

Davis, T., & Higgins, J. (2013). A blockbuster failure: How an outdated business model destroyed a giant. In *Chapter 11 bankruptcy case studies* (Vol. 11). https://ir.law.utk.edu/utk_studlawbankruptcy/11

Dawson, S., Joksimovic, S., Poquet, O., & Siemens, G. (2019, March). Increasing the impact of learning analytics. In *Proceedings of the 9th international conference on learning analytics & knowledge* (pp. 446-455). DOI: 10.1145/3303772.3303784

De Ramón Fernández, A., Ruiz Fernández, D., Gilart Iglesias, V., & Marcos Jorquera, D. (2022). Analyzing the use of artificial intelligence for the management of chronic obstructive pulmonary disease (COPD). *International Journal of Medical Informatics, 158*, 104640–104640. DOI: 10.1016/j.ijmedinf.2021.104640 PMID: 34890934

De Rosa, A. S., Mannarini, T., Gil de Montes, L., Holman, A., Lauri, M. A., Negura, L., & Lubinga, E. (2021). Sensemaking processes and social representations of COVID-19 in multi-voiced public discourse: Illustrative examples of institutional and media communication in ten countries. *Community Psychology in Global Perspective*, *7*(1), 13–53.

DeBruijn, E., & Baartman, L. K. J. (2011). Integrating knowledge, skills and attitudes: Conceptualising learning processes towards vocational competence. *Educational Research Review*, *6*(2), 125–134. DOI: 10.1016/j.edurev.2011.03.001

Deci, E. L., & Ryan, R. M. (1980). The empirical exploration of intrinsic motivational processes. In Berkowitz, L. (Ed.), (pp. 39–80). Advances in experimental social psychology. Academic Press. DOI: 10.1016/S0065-2601(08)60130-6

Deci, E. L., & Ryan, R. M. (1985). *Intrinsic motivation and self-determination in human behaviour*. Plenum.

Dekker, S., & Slotboom, C. (2023). Benefits of recreational gaming. *International Journal of Esports*, *1*(1). https://www.ijesports.org/article/96/html

Delanghe, P. (2023), 1956: The official birth of AI, Generative AI strategy consultant, https://www.linkedin.com/pulse/1956-official-birth-ai-philippe-delanghe-couac/

Delello, J. A., McWhorter, R. R., Roberts, P., Dockery, H. S., De Giuseppe, T., & Corona, F. (2021). The rise of esports: Insights into the perceived benefits and risks for college students. [IJER]. *International Journal of eSports Research*, *1*(1), 1–19. DOI: 10.4018/IJER.20210101.oa5

Deloitte. (2020). *The millennial survey: Understanding the next generation of talent*. Deloitte Touche Tohmatsu Limited.

Deming, D. J. (2018). *The value of soft skills in the labor market*. National Bureau of Economic Research. https://www.nber.org/reporter/2017number4/value-soft-skills-labor-market

Deterding, S., Dixon, D., Khaled, R., & Nacke, L. (2011, September). From game design elements to gamefulness: defining gamification. In *Proceedings of the 15th international academic MindTrek conference: Envisioning future media environments* (pp. 9-15). ACM. DOI: 10.1145/2181037.2181040

Deterding, S., & Zagal, J. P. (2018). *Role-Playing Game Studies: Transmedia Foundations*. Routledge., DOI: 10.4324/9781315637532-1

Devine, J. K., Schwartz, L. P., & Hursh, S. R. (2022). Technical, Regulatory, Economic, and Trust Issues Preventing Successful Integration of Sensors into the Mainstream Consumer Wearables Market. National Library of Medicine. https://www.ncbi.nlm.nih.gov/pmc/articles/PMC9002880/

Dichev, C., & Dicheva, D. (2017). Gamifying education: What is known, what is believed, and what remains uncertain: A critical review. *International Journal of Educational Technology in Higher Education*, *14*(1), 9. DOI: 10.1186/s41239-017-0042-5

DiFrancisco-Donoghue, J., Balentine, J., Schmidt, G., & Zwibel, H. (2019, January). Managing the health of the eSport athlete: An integrated health management model. *BMJ Open Sport & Exercise Medicine*, *5*(1), e000467–e000467. DOI: 10.1136/bmjsem-2018-000467 PMID: 30792883

Dingari, S. (2023, April 26). Gamification for Diversity and Inclusion: The Challenges and Opportunities in Training [Blog]. *CommLab India*. https://blog.commlabindia.com/elearning-design/gamification-diversity-inclusion-training

Dinh-Le, C., Chuang, R., Chokshi, S., & Mann, D. (2019). Wearable Health Technology and Electronic Health Record Integration: Scoping Review and Future Directions. *JMIR mHealth and uHealth*, *7*(9), e12861–e12861. DOI: 10.2196/12861 PMID: 31512582

Disability Law Center. (2020, January 1). Notice of settlement of class action relating to captioning of Harvard's public web content. Disability Law Center. https://www.dlc-ma.org/2019/12/13/notice-of-settlement-of-class-action-relating-to-captioning-of-harvards-public-web-content/

Diversity and inclusion. (n.d.). Sustainable Development Goals - Resource Centre. https://sdgresources.relx.com/diversity-and-inclusion

Diversity, Equity, and Inclusion Definitions. (2021, September 23). UW Research. https://www.washington.edu/research/or/office-of-research-diversity-equity-and-inclusion/dei-definitions/

Dixon-Fyle, S., Huber, C., & del Mar Martínez Márquez, M. Thomas. A. & Hunt, V. (2023, December 5). *Diversity matters even more: The case for holistic impact.* McKinsey & Company. https://www.mckinsey.com/featured-insights/diversity-and-inclusion/diversity-matters-even-more-the-case-for-holistic-impact

Dobbin, F., & Kalev, A. (2018). Why Doesn't Diversity Training Work? The Challenge for Industry and Academia. *Anthropology Now*, *10*(2), 48–55. DOI: 10.1080/19428200.2018.1493182

Dobbin, F., & Kalev, A. (2022). *Getting to Diversity. What works and what doesn't.* The Belknap Press of Harvard University Press.

Dochy, F., Engeström, Y., Sannino, A., & van Meeuwen, N. (2022). Inter-organisational expansive learning at work. In Dochy, F., Gijbels, D., Segers, M., & van den Bossche, P. (Eds.), *Theories of workplace learning in changing times* (2nd ed., pp. 209–231). Routledge., DOI: 10.4324/9781003187790-12

Docles, E. (2023). Healthcare Artificial Intelligence: Transforming the Future of Medicine. *Health Science Journal*, *17*(6), 1–3. DOI: 10.36648/1791-809X.17.6.1033

Domínguez, A., Saenz-De-Navarrete, J., De-Marcos, L., Fernández-Sanz, L., Pagés, C., & Martínez-Herráiz, J.-J. (2013). Gamifying learning experiences: Practical implications and outcomes. *Computers & Education*, *63*, 380–392. DOI: 10.1016/j.compedu.2012.12.020

Doney, I. (2019). Research into effective gamification features to inform e-learning design. *Research in Learning Technology*, *27*(0). Advance online publication. DOI: 10.25304/rlt.v27.2093

Drape, J. (2021, December 19). Step Aside, LeBron and Dak, and Make Room for Banjo and Kazooie. *The New York Times*. https://www.nytimes.com/2021/12/19/sports/esports-fans-leagues-games.html

Drümmer, O., Erle, M., Zagler, W., Karshmer, A., Penaz, P., & Miesenberger, K. (2012). PDF/UA – A New Era for Document Accessibility: Understanding, Managing and Implementing the ISO Standard PDF/UA (Universal Accessibility): Introduction to the Special Thematic Session. *Lecture Notes in Computer Science*, *585–586*, 585–586. Advance online publication. DOI: 10.1007/978-3-642-31522-0_88

Duignan, P. A. (2020). Navigating the future of learning: The role of smart technologies. In *Leading educational systems and schools in times of disruption and exponential change: A call for courage, commitment and collaboration* (pp. 125–137). Emerald Publishing Limited. DOI: 10.1108/978-1-83909-850-520201012

Duterte, J. P. (2024). Technology-Enhanced learning environments: Improving engagement and learning. *International Journal of Research and Innovation in Social Science*, *8*(10), 1305–131. DOI: 10.47772/IJRISS.2024.8100111

Dutra, M. J. (2021). What is the gaming lifestyle? An exploratory investigation. *Journal of Games, Game Art, and Gamification*, *6*(2), 44–55. Advance online publication. DOI: 10.21512/jggag.v6i2.7891

Dweck, C. S. (2006). *Mindset: The new psychology of success*. Random House.

Dwivedi, Y.K. et al (2022). Climate change and COP26: Are digital technologies and information management part of the problem or the solution? An editorial reflection and call to action. International Journal of Information Management, 63(2022)102456, 1-39 https://doi.org/.DOI: 10.1016/j.ijinfomgt.2021.102456

Dye, M. W. G., Green, C. S., & Bavelier, D. (2009). Increasing speed of processing with action video games. *Current Directions in Psychological Science*, *18*(6), 321–326. DOI: 10.1111/j.1467-8721.2009.01660.x PMID: 20485453

Ebermann, C., Piccinini, E., Brauer, B., Busse, S., & Kolbe, L. (2016). The impact of gamification-induced emotions on in-car IS adoption – The difference between digital natives and digital immigrants. In *Proceedings of the 49th Hawaii International Conference on System Sciences (HICSS)* (pp. 1307–1316). IEEE. DOI: 10.1109/HICSS.2016.169

Edwards, C. (2003). Wearable computing struggles for social acceptance. *IEE Review*, *49*(9), 24–25. https://digital-library.theiet.org/content/journals/10.1049/ir_20030904. DOI: 10.1049/ir:20030904

Egan, M. L., & Bendick, M.Jr. (2008). Combining multicultural management and diversity into one course on cultural competence. *Academy of Management Learning & Education*, *7*(3), 387–393. DOI: 10.5465/amle.2008.34251675

Eichenbaum, A. B. (2014). Video games: Play can do serious good. *American Journal of Play*, *71*(1), 50–72.

Eikelboom, J. J. (2016). *Engagement, gamification, and workplace satisfaction: A convergent study of user indicators*. University of South Maine.

Elias, T. (2011). Learning analytics. *Learning*, *1*, 22.

Ellis, C., & Sonnenfeld, J. A. (1994). Diverse approaches to managing diversity. *Human Resource Management*, *33*(1), 79–109. DOI: 10.1002/hrm.3930330106

Emerson, J. (2017, September 11). *Colorblind Diversity Efforts Don't Work*. Harvard Business Review. https://hbr.org/2017/09/colorblind-diversity-efforts-dont-work

Enatto, H. E. (2024). Cross-Cultural Training and the Performance of American Expatriates in Nigeria. *European Journal of Business and Innovation Research, 12*(1), 29–41. DOI: 10.37745/ejbir.2013/vol12n12941

Entertainment Software Association. (2024). *Essential facts about the computer and video game industry*. https://www.theesa.com/wp-content/uploads/2024/05/Essential-Facts-2024-FINAL.pdf

Escobar Borruel, I. (2022). Repatriate social capital: An untapped resource at the individual and organizational levels. In Andresen, M., Anger, S., Al Ariss, A., Barzantny, C., Brücker, H., Dickmann, M., Mäkelä, L., Muhr, S. L., Saalfeld, T., Suutari, V., & Zølner, M. (Eds.), *Wanderlust to wonderland? Exploring key issues in expatriate careers: Individual, organizational, and societal insights* (pp. 39–57). Bamberg University Press. DOI: 10.20378/irb-55766

Esports Wales. (2024). *Esports Wales set to inspire at BETT 2024*. Esports Wales. https://esportswales.org/esports-wales-set-to-inspire-at-bett-2024/\

Essential Elements of Employee Retention. (2017, October 29) [Blog]. *Lynchburg Regional SHRM*. https://lrshrm.shrm.org/blog/2017/10/essential-elements-employee-retention

European Games Developer Federation. (2022). *2022 European video games industry insight report*.https://www.egdf.eu/wp-content/uploads/2024/06/2022-European-video-games-industry-insight-report.pdf

European Parliament & Council of the European Union. (2019). Directive (EU) 2019/770 of 20 May 2019 on certain aspects concerning contracts for the supply of digital content and digital services. *Official Journal of the European Union, L, 136*, 1–27. https://eur-lex.europa.eu/eli/dir/2019/770/oj

European Parliament. (2022). *Report on esports and video games (2022/2027(INI)) [A9-0244/2022]*. Committee on Culture and Education. https://www.europarl.europa.eu/doceo/document/A-9-2022-0244_EN.html

Evseeva, S., Evseeva, O., & Rawat, P. (2022). Employee development and digitalization in BANI world. In Rodionov, D., Kudryavtseva, T., Skhvediani, A., & Berawi, M. A. (Eds.), *Innovations in digital economy. SPBPU IDE 2021* (pp. 253–264). Springer., DOI: 10.1007/978-3-031-14985-6_18

Ewers, M., & Kangmennaang, J. (2023). New spaces of inequality with the rise of remote work: Autonomy, technostress, and life disruption. *Applied Geography (Sevenoaks, England), 152*, 152. DOI: 10.1016/j.apgeog.2023.102888

Ewoldsen, D. R., Eno, C. A., Okdie, B. M., Velez, J. A., Guadagno, R. E., & DeCoster, J. (2012). Effect of playing violent video games cooperatively or competitively on subsequent cooperative behavior. *Cyberpsychology, Behavior, and Social Networking*, *15*(5), 277–280. DOI: 10.1089/cyber.2011.0308 PMID: 22489544

Fadda, D., Pellegrini, M., Vivanet, G., & Zandonella Callegher, C. (2022). Effects of digital games on student motivation in mathematics: A meta-analysis in K-12. *Journal of Computer Assisted Learning*, *38*(1), 304–325. DOI: 10.1111/jcal.12618

Falkenthal, E., & Byrne, A. M. (2021). Distributed leadership in collegiate esports. *Simulation & Gaming*, *52*(2), 185–203. DOI: 10.1177/1046878120958750

Farrell, M., Spender, A., Bullen, C., Altmann-Richer, L., Cripps, J., Duffy, R., Falkous, C., Horn, T., Wigzell, J., & Yeap, W. (2018, September 1). Wearables and the internet of things - considerations for the life and health insurance industry. Queen's University Belfast. https://pure.qub.ac.uk/en/publications/wearables-and-the-internet-of-things-considerations-for-the-life-

Fayad, A. (2022, October 11). *The Importance Of Diversity And Inclusion Training*. Forbes. https://www.forbes.com/sites/theyec/2022/10/11/the-importance-of-diversity-and-inclusion-training/

Federal Register (2024a). Nondiscrimination on the Basis of Disability; Accessibility of Web Information and Services of State and Local Government Entities. https://www.federalregister.gov/documents/2024/04/24/2024-07758/nondiscrimination-on-the-basis-of-disability-accessibility-of-web-information-and-services-of-state

Federal Register. (2024b). Nondiscrimination on the basis of disability; Accessibility of web information and services of state and local government entities. FederalRegister.gov. https://www.federalregister.gov/documents/2024/04/24/2024-07758/nondiscrimination-on-the-basis-of-disability-accessibility-of-web-information-and-services-of-state

Feng, J. (2024). *University students' participation and opinions on esports in China: An empirical research. Asian Journal of Sport History & Culture*. DOI: 10.1080/27690148.2024.2395954

Ferguson, C. J. (2015). Everything in moderation: Moderate use of screens unassociated with child behavior problems. *The Psychiatric Quarterly*, *86*(1), 1–8. DOI: 10.1007/s11126-014-9326-5 PMID: 25270895

Ferguson, R. (2012). Learning analytics: Drivers, developments and challenges. *International Journal of Technology Enhanced Learning*, *4*(5-6), 304–317. DOI: 10.1504/IJTEL.2012.051816

Flynn, J., Commisso, C., Mallon, D., Van Durme, Y., Harrington, S., & Lahiri, G. (2025). *Deloitte's 2025 Human Capital Trends - Turning tensions into triumphs: Helping leaders transform uncertainty into opportunity*. Deloitte. Online: 02.05.2025: https://www2.deloitte.com/content/dam/insights/articles/glob187692_global-human-capital-trends/DI_2025-Global-Human-Capital-Trends.pdf

Ford, E. S., & Caspersen, C. J. (2012, October). review of prospective studies. *International Journal of Epidemiology*, *41*(5), 1338–1353. DOI: 10.1093/ije/dys078 PMID: 22634869

Fotaris, P., & Mastoras, T. (2019). Escape rooms for learning: A systematic review. *Educational Technology Research and Development*, *67*(2), 123–145. DOI: 10.1007/s11423-018-9612-5

Fotaris, P., & Mastoras, T. (2022). Room2Educ8: A framework for creating educational escape rooms based on design thinking principles. *Education Sciences*, *12*(11), 768. DOI: 10.3390/educsci12110768

Freeman, G., & Wohn, D. Y. (2017). Social support in eSports: Building emotional connections with teammates in competitive gaming. *Computers in Human Behavior*, *75*, 23–31.

Frick, N. R. J., & Marx, J. (2021). Integrating Digital Nomads in Corporate Structures: Managerial Contemplations. *Proceedings of the 54th Hawaii International Conference on System Sciences.* DOI:DOI: 10.24251/HICSS.2021.260

Fujimoto, Y., & Härtel, C. E. (2017). Organizational diversity learning framework: Going beyond diversity training programs. *Personnel Review*, *46*(6), 1120–1141. DOI: 10.1108/PR-09-2015-0254

Fuller, J., McKittrick, K., Seibel, S., Wilson, J., Dash, V., & Epstein, A. (2023). Unlocking economic prosperity: Career navigation in a time of rapid change.

Gaertner, S. L., & Dovidio, J. F. (2000). *Reducing intergroup bias: The common ingroup identity model.* Psychology Press.

Gajardo Sánchez, A. D., Murillo-Zamorano, L. R., López-Sánchez, J., & Bueno-Muñoz, C. (2023). Gamification in Health Care Management: Systematic Review of the Literature and Research Agenda. *SAGE Open*, *13*(4), 21582440231218834. Advance online publication. DOI: 10.1177/21582440231218834

Galinsky, A. D., & Moskowitz, G. B. (2000). Perspective-taking: Decreasing stereotype expression, stereotype accessibility, and in-group favoritism. *Journal of Personality and Social Psychology*, *78*(4), 708–724. DOI: 10.1037/0022-3514.78.4.708 PMID: 10794375

Gallup. (2021). *State of the global workplace*. Gallup, Inc.

Gamification in DEI: The Golden Nugget? (2023, June 19) [Whitepaper]. seppo. https://seppo.io/dei-whitepaper/

Gamification Trends for 2024: Current Forecasts You Should Be Thinking About (2024, August 2). Finances Online. https://financesonline.com/gamification-trends/

Gandolfi, E. (2016). To watch or to play, it is in the game: The game culture on Twitch.tv among performers, players, and audiences. *Journal of Gaming & Virtual Worlds*, *8*(1), 63–82. DOI: 10.1386/jgvw.8.1.63_1

Gao, Z., & Chen, S. (2014). Are field-based exergames useful in preventing childhood obesity? A systematic review. *Obesity Reviews*, *15*(8), 676–691. DOI: 10.1111/obr.12164 PMID: 24602072

Garcia-Cabot, A., Garcia-Lopez, E., Caro-Alvaro, S., Gutierrez-Martinez, J., & De-Marcos, L. (2019). Measuring the effects on learning performance and engagement with a gamified social platform in an MSc program. *Computer Applications in Engineering Education*, *28*(1), 207–223. DOI: 10.1002/cae.22186

Gardner, P. (2017). Flourishing in the face of constant disruption: Cultivating the T-professional or adaptive innovator through WIL. In *Work-integrated learning in the 21st century: Global perspectives on the future* (pp. 69–81). Emerald Publishing Limited. DOI: 10.1108/S1479-367920170000032004

Gartner, Inc. (2024, October 3). Gartner says generative AI will require 80 percent of engineering workforce to upskill through 2027 [Press release]. https://www.gartner.com/en/newsroom/press-releases/2024-10-03-gartner-says-generative-ai-will-require-80-percent-of-engineering-workforce-to-upskill-through-2027

Gasevic, D., Paul, P. R. I. N. S. L. O. O., Chen, B., Fan, Y., Rodrigo, M. M., Cobo, C., & Cecilia, A. G. U. E. R. R. E. B. E. R. E. (2018). Learning analytics for the global south.

Gatheral, J. (2022, July 14). *Using Gamification Techniques for More Effective DEI Training*. Training Industry. https://trainingindustry.com/articles/diversity-equity-and-inclusion/using-gamification-techniques-for-more-effective-dei-training/

Gausby, A. (2015). *Attention spans: Consumer Insights, Microsoft Canada*. Microsoft. https://sherpapg.com/wp-content/uploads/2017/12/MAS.pdf

Gazis, A., & Katsiri, E. (2023). *Serious games in digital gaming: A comprehensive review of applications, game engines, and advancements*. WSEAS Transactions on Computer Research., DOI: 10.37394/232018.2023.11.2

General Services Administration. (2024a). IT accessibility laws and policies. www.Section508.gov. https://www.section508.gov/manage/laws-and-policies/#:~:text=In%201998%2C%20Congress%20amended%20the,accessible%20to%20people%20with%20disabilities

General Services Administration. (2024b). General guidelines for captions. Section508.gov. https://www.section508.gov/create/captions-transcripts/#:~:text=General%20Guidelines%20for%20Captions&text=The%20text%20and%20the%20speech,99%25%20accuracy%20to%20be%20readable

Genkova, P. (2021). Interkulturelle Trainings: eine kritische Betrachtung. [Intercultural training: A critical view] In Ringeisen, T., Genkova, P., & Leong, F. T. L. (Eds.), *Handbuch Stress und Kultur* [Handbook on stress and culture]. (pp. 585–602). Springer Fachmedien., DOI: 10.1007/978-3-658-27789-5_47

Genkova, P., & Kruse, L. (2020). Do stays abroad increase intercultural and general competences, affecting employability? *Leadership, Education, Personality. An Interdisciplinary Journal*, *2*(2), 81–89. DOI: 10.1365/s42681-020-00014-1

Genkova, P., & Kruse, L. (2021). Auslandsaufenthalt als Kompetenzschule? Eine empirische Untersuchung der Auswirkungen von Auslandsaufenthalten auf die berufsbezogenen Kompetenzbereiche [Can we consider stays abroad as competence schools? The relationship of stays abroad with job related competences]. *Gruppe. Interaktion. Organisation.* [GIO]. *Zeitschrift für Angewandte Organisationspsychologie*, *52*(1), 135–146. DOI: 10.1007/s11612-021-00553-1

Gennari, R., Matera, M., Morra, D., Melonio, A., & Rizvi, M. (2023). Design for social digital well-being with young generations: Engage them and make them reflect. *International Journal of Human-Computer Studies*, *173*(103006), 1–21. DOI: 10.1016/j.ijhcs.2023.103006

Gentile, D. A., Anderson, C. A., Yukawa, S., Ihori, N., Saleem, M., Lim, K. M., Shibuya, A., Liau, A. K., Khoo, A., Bushman, B. J., Huesmann, L. R., & Sakamoto, A. (2009). The effects of prosocial video games on prosocial behaviors: International evidence from correlational, longitudinal, and experimental studies. *Personality and Social Psychology Bulletin*, *35*(6), 752–763. DOI: 10.1177/0146167209333045 PMID: 19321812

George, G., Merrill, R. K., & Schillebeeckx, S. J. D. (2021). Digital sustainability and entrepreneurship: How digital innovations are helping tackle climate change and sustainable development. *Entrepreneurship Theory and Practice*, *45*(5), 999–1027. https://commonslibrary.parliament.uk/climate-change-solutions-the-role-oftechnology/. DOI: 10.1177/1042258719899425

Georgiadou, A., Amari, A., Swalhi, A., & Hofaidhllaoui, M. (2024). How does perceived organizational support improve expatriates' outcomes during global crises? The mediating role of the ethical organizational climate in global organizations. *Journal of International Management*, *30*(3), 101131. DOI: 10.1016/j.intman.2024.101131

Gill, L. J., & Olson, M. A. (2023). A dual-process framework for diversity training to reduce discrimination in organizational settings. *Social Issues and Policy Review*, *17*(1), 79–103. DOI: 10.1111/sipr.12094

Ginda, M., Richey, M. C., Cousino, M., & Börner, K. (2019). Visualizing learner engagement, performance, and trajectories to evaluate and optimize online course design. *PLoS One*, *14*(5), e0215964. DOI: 10.1371/journal.pone.0215964 PMID: 31059546

Goetzel, R. Z., & Ozminkowski, R. J. (2020). The health and cost benefits of work site health-promotion programs. *Annual Review of Public Health*, *29*(1), 303–323. DOI: 10.1146/annurev.publhealth.29.020907.090930 PMID: 18173386

Gomes, N., Pato, M., Lourenço, A. R., & Datia, N. (2023). A Survey on Wearable Sensors for Mental Health Monitoring. *Sensors (Basel)*, *23*(3), 1330. DOI: 10.3390/s23031330 PMID: 36772370

Grace, K., & Maher, M. (2021). Towards computational co-creation in modding communities. *Proceedings. AAAI Artificial Intelligence and Interactive Digital Entertainment Conference*, *10*(3), 15–20. Advance online publication. DOI: 10.1609/aiide.v10i3.12750

Grand View Research. (2024). *Digital therapeutics market size, share & trends analysis report by product, by application (oncology, respiratory, diabetes), by end-use (patients, providers, payers), by region, and segment forecasts, 2023–2030.* https://www.grandviewresearch.com/industry-analysis/digital-therapeutics-market

Granic, I., Lobel, A., & Engels, R. C. (2014). The benefits of playing video games. *The American Psychologist*, *69*(1), 66–78. DOI: 10.1037/a0034857 PMID: 24295515

Grant, M. M. (2019). Difficulties in defining mobile learning: Analysis, design characteristics, and implications. *Educational Technology Research and Development*, *67*(2), 361–388. DOI: 10.1007/s11423-018-09641-4

Green, C. S., & Bavelier, D. (2007). Action-video-game experience alters the spatial resolution of vision. *Psychological science, 18(*1), 88-94. https://www.jstor.org/stable/40064582

Green, C. S., & Bavelier, D. (2012). Learning, attentional control, and action video games. *Current Biology*, *22*(6), 197–206. DOI: 10.1016/j.cub.2012.02.012 PMID: 22440805

Green, E. C., & Murphy, E. M. (2014). *The Health Belief Model.* The Wiley Encyclopedia of Health Psychology., DOI: 10.1002/9781118410868.wbehibs410

Greller, W., & Drachsler, H. (2012). Translating learning into numbers: A generic framework for learning analytics. *Journal of Educational Technology & Society*, *15*(3), 42–57.

Griffin, S. R. (2022, May 7). *Where Diversity Training Goes Wrong, Part II. Underdeveloped Theories of How People Learn & Change.* Medium. https://medium.com/@shaylargriffin/where-diversity-training-goes-wrong-part-ii-7a5e946a2022

Gronlund, N. E. (2000). *How to write and use instructional objectives.* Prentice-Hall Inc./Pearson Education.

Guevara, M. (2023), The future of L&D: How AI is revolutionizing talent development, https://www.chieflearningofficer.com/2023/03/20/the-future-of-ld-how-ai-is-revolutionizing-talent-development/

Guhl, A. (2017a). *Gamification across borders: The importance of culture* (Master's thesis). University of Gothenburg.

Guhl, A. (2017b). *National culture in gamification design: A conceptual approach* (Doctoral dissertation). University of Gothenburg.

Gui, H., & Liu, J. (2018). Latest Progresses in Developing Wearable Monitoring and Therapy Systems for Managing Chronic Diseases. arXiv: Medical Physics. https://doi.org//arXiv.1802.01747DOI: 10.48550

Gupta, S. (2024, August 20). Gamification Statistics and Future Trends [Blog]. *Nudge*. https://www.nudgenow.com/blogs/gamification-stats-enhancing-learning#

Haaland, S. (2023. November 14). You think older generations don't respond to gamification? The data says differently [Blog]. *SalesScreen*. https://www.salesscreen.com/blog/older-generations-and-gamification/

Hajarian, M., Bastanfard, A., Mohammadzadeh, J., & Khalilian, M. (2019). A personalized gamification method for increasing user engagement in social networks. *Social Network Analysis and Mining*, *9*(1), 47. DOI: 10.1007/s13278-019-0589-3

Hall, M. M. D. (2021). *Fortnite, Screenagers, and Student Resistance: A Correlational Analysis of Video Game Performance and Critical Thinking Levels.* ProQuest Dissertations & Theses, Regent University.

Hallifax, S., Serna, A., Marty, J. C., & Lavoué, É. (2019). Adaptive Gamification in Education: A Literature Review of Current Trends and Developments. In M. Scheffel, J. Broisin, V. Pammer-Schindler, A. Ioannou & J. Schneider (Eds.), *Transforming Learning with Meaningful Technologies*. EC-TEL 2019. Lecture Notes in Computer Science, vol 11722. Springer. https://doi.org/DOI: 10.1007/978-3-030-29736-7_22

Hamari, J., Koivisto, J., & Sarsa, H. (2014). Does gamification work? A literature review of empirical studies on gamification. In *Proceedings of the 47th Hawaii International Conference on System Sciences* (pp. 3025-3034). IEEE. DOI: 10.1109/HICSS.2014.377

Hamari, J., & Sjöblom, M. (2017). What is eSports and why do people watch it? *Internet Research*, *27*(2), 211–232. DOI: 10.1108/IntR-04-2016-0085

Hamari, J., & Sjöblom, M. (2017). *What is eSports and why do people watch it?* Internet.

Hamouche, S. (2020, April 20). COVID-19 and employees' mental health: Stressors, moderators and agenda for organizational actions. *Emerald Open Research*. Advance online publication. DOI: 10.1108/EOR-02-2023-0004

Harney, B., & Collings, D. G. (2021). Navigating the shifting landscapes of HRM. *Human Resource Management Review*, *31*(4), 100824. DOI: 10.1016/j.hrmr.2021.100824

Harteveld, C., & Bekebrede, G. (2016). A frame-reflective discourse analysis of serious games. *Simulation & Gaming*, *47*(5), 632–654. DOI: 10.1177/1046878116662959

Hartig, J., Klieme, E., & Leutner, D. (Eds.). (2008). *Assessment of competencies in educational context*. Hogrefe & Huber.

Hausberg, J. P., Liere-Netheler, K., Packmohr, S., Pakura, S., & Vogelsang, K. (2019). Research streams on digital transformation from a holistic business perspective: A systematic literature review and citation network analysis. *Journal of Business Economics*, *89*(2), 931–963. DOI: 10.1007/s11573-019-00956-z

Hemphill, E. (2018, May 29). *A look at the research behind implicit biases with Wash U professor Calvin Lai*. St. Louis Public Radio. https://www.stlpr.org/show/st-louis-on-the-air/2018-05-29/a-look-at-the-research-behind-implicit-biases-with-wash-u-professor-calvin-lai

Henke, R. M., Goetzel, R. Z., McHugh, J., & Isaac, F. (2019). Recent experience in health promotion at Johnson & Johnson: Lower health spending, strong return on investment. *Health Affairs*, *30*(3), 490–499. DOI: 10.1377/hlthaff.2010.0806 PMID: 21383368

Hensellek, S., & Puchala, N. (2021). The emergence of the digital nomad: A review and analysis of the opportunities and risks of digital nomadism. In M. Orel, O. Dvoulety, & V. Ratten (Eds.), *The Flexible Workplace* (pp. 195–214). Springer. 11DOI: 10.1007/978-3-030-62167-4_11

Hernández-de-Menéndez, M., Morales-Menendez, R., Escobar, C. A., & Ramírez Mendoza, R. A. (2022). Learning analytics: State of the art. [IJIDeM]. *International Journal on Interactive Design and Manufacturing*, *16*(3), 1209–1230. DOI: 10.1007/s12008-022-00930-0 PMID: 40478020

Hertting, K., Holmquist, M., & Parker, J. (2020). Ping pong for health: The meaning of space in a sport based health intervention at the workplace. *International Journal of Qualitative Studies on Health and Well-being*, *15*(sup1), 1689602. DOI: 10.1080/17482631.2019.1689602 PMID: 33103634

Hickey, B. A., Chalmers, T., Newton, P., Lin, C.-T., Sibbritt, D., McLachlan, C. S., Clifton-Bligh, R., Morley, J., & Lal, S. (2021). Smart Devices and Wearable Technologies to Detect and Monitor Mental Health Conditions and Stress: A Systematic Review. *Sensors (Basel)*, *21*(10), 3461. DOI: 10.3390/s21103461 PMID: 34065620

Hitt, K. (2020, January 31). *Pittsburgh Knights and Coco-Cola partner to help launch Coke Energy*. The Esports Observer. https://esportsobserver.com/pittsburgh-knights-coca-cola-deal

Hofstede, G., Hofstede, G. J., & Minkov, M. (2010). *Cultures and organizations: Software of the mind: Intercultural cooperation and its importance for survival* (3rd ed.). McGraw Hill.

Holden, J. T., Rodenberg, R. M., & Kaburakis, A. (2017). Esports corruption: Gambling, doping, and global governance. *SSRN*, *32*, 236–273. DOI: 10.2139/ssrn.2831718

Hong, J., Hwang, M., & Peng, Y. (2012). Gender Difference of Social Behavior in the Cooperative-Competitive Game. *Procedia: Social and Behavioral Sciences*, *64*, 244–254. DOI: 10.1016/j.sbspro.2012.11.029

Hooda, M., & Rana, C. (2020). Learning analytics lens: Improving quality of higher education. *International Journal of Emerging Trends in Engineering Research*, *8*(5), 1626–1646. DOI: 10.30534/ijeter/2020/24852020

Horn, M. B., & Staker, H. (2017). *Blended: Using disruptive innovation to improve schools*. John Wiley & Sons.

How do you avoid coercion and manipulation in gamified consent processes? (2024, June, 26). LinkedIn. https://de.linkedin.com/advice/0/how-do-you-avoid-coercion-manipulation-gamified-consent?lang=en

Howard, K. S., Tondeur, J., Siddiq, F., & Scherer, R. (2021). Ready, set, go! Profiling teachers' readiness for online teaching in secondary education. *Technology, Pedagogy and Education, 30*(1), 141–158. DOI: 10.1080/1475939X.2020.1839543

Hubert-Wallander, B., Green, C. S., & Bavelier, D. (2010). Stretching the limits of visual attention: The case of action video games. *Wiley Interdisciplinary Reviews: Cognitive Science, 1*(1), 1–9. DOI: 10.1002/wcs.44 PMID: 26302012

Huss, J. A. (2023). *Gen Z students are filling our online classrooms: Do our teaching methods need a reboot?* InSight: A Journal of Scholarly Teaching, 18, 101-110. https://files.eric.ed.gov/fulltext/EJ1407503.pdf

IBM. (2018). *Innovation jam: Collaborative problem-solving through gaming*. IBM Corporation.

IBM. (2019). *Virtual onboarding: Using gaming to enhance the employee experience*. IBM Corporation.

Ifenthaler, D., & Kim, Y. J. (Eds.). (2019). *Game-based assessment revisited.* Springer., DOI: 10.1007/978-3-030-15569-8

Information Technology Industry Council. (2023, November). Accessibility. ITIC.org. https://www.itic.org/policy/accessibility

International Telecommunication Union. (2023). *Universal and meaningful connectivity by 2030.*https://www.itu.int/en/mediacentre/Pages/PR-2023-09-12-universal-and-meaningful-connectivity-by-2030.aspx

Internet and Videogaming Addiction on Adolescent Vision: A Review of the Literature. Frontiers in Public Health, 8, 63–63. https://doi.org/DOI: 10.3389/fpubh.2020.00063

J. (2023, July 18). *The Hidden Struggles of Esports: LoL pros in a mental health crisis.* Esports.net. https://www.esports.net/news/industry/hidden-struggles-of-esports-athletes-mental-health-crisis/#:~:text=A%20study%20by%20Psychology%20Today

Jackson, L. A., Witt, E. A., Games, A. I., Fitzgerald, H. E., von Eye, A., & Zhao, Y. (2012). Information technology use and creativity: Findings from the Children and Technology Project. *Computers in Human Behavior, 28*(2), 370–376. DOI: 10.1016/j.chb.2011.10.006

Jackson, L. C., O'Mara, J., Moss, J., & Jackson, A. C. (2018). A Critical Review of the Effectiveness of Narrative-Driven Digital Educational Games. [IJGBL]. *International Journal of Game-Based Learning*, *8*(4), 32–49. DOI: 10.4018/IJGBL.2018100103

Jacobides, M. G., Ma, M. D., Trantopoulos, K., & Vassalos, V. (2024). The business value of gamification. *California Management Review*, *66*(2), 91–107. https://lbsresearch.london.edu/id/eprint/3621/1/jacobides-et-al-2024-the-business-value-of-gamification.pdf. DOI: 10.1177/00081256231218469

Jaramillo-Mediavilla, L., Basantes-Andrade, A., Cabezas-González, M., & Casillas-Martín, S. (2024). Impact of gamification on motivation and academic performance: A systematic review. *Education Sciences*, *14*(6), 639. DOI: 10.3390/educsci14060639

Javed, I., & Arham, R. (2023). Technological Disruption and Change Management: Navigating Uncertainty in the Digital Age. *The Management Science Letter*, *1*(01), 65–75.

Jenkin, I., & Fairfurst, N. (2019). Escape room to operating room: A potential training modality? *Medical Teacher*, *42*(5), 596. DOI: 10.1080/0142159X.2019.1657821 PMID: 31448990

Jenny, S. E., Besombes, N., Brock, T., Cote, A. C., & Scholz, T. M. (2024). *Routledge handbook of esports*. Taylor & Francis. DOI: 10.4324/9781003410591

Jenny, S. E., Manning, R. D., Keiper, M. C., & Olrich, T. W. (2017). Virtual(ly) athletes: Where esports fit within the definition of "sport.". *Quest*, *69*(1), 1–18. DOI: 10.1080/00336297.2016.1144517

Jenny, S., Gawrysiak, J., & Besombes, N. (2021). Esports.edu: An inventory and analysis of global higher education esports academic programming and curricula. *International Journal of Esports*, *1*(1). https://www.ijesports.org/article/59/html

Jiahong, S., & Weipeng, Y. (2022). Artificial intelligence in early childhood education: A scoping review, Computers and Education: Artificial Intelligence. 2022,100049 DOI: 10.1016/j.caeai.2022.100049

John Dian, F., Vahidnia, R., & Rahmati, A. (2020). Wearables and the Internet of Things (IoT), Applications, Opportunities, and Challenges: A Survey. *IEEE Access : Practical Innovations, Open Solutions*, *8*, 69200–69211. DOI: 10.1109/ACCESS.2020.2986329

John McCarthy et al. (1955), Dartmouth workshop/Summer Research Project on Artificial Intelligence, held at Dartmouth College, Hanover, New Hampshire, 1-13, http://jmc.stanford.edu/articles/dartmouth/dartmouth.pdf

Jones, C. M., Scholes, L., Johnson, D., Katsikitis, M., & Carras, M. C. (2014). Gaming well: Links between videogames and flourishing mental health. *Frontiers in Psychology*, *5*. Advance online publication. DOI: 10.3389/fpsyg.2014.00260 PMID: 24744743

Joshi, A., Dencker, J. C., Franz, G., & Martocchio, J. J. (2010). Unpacking generational identities in organizations. *Academy of Management Review*, *35*(3), 392–414. DOI: 10.5465/AMR.2010.51141800

Junaid, S. B., Imam, A. A., Abdulkarim, M., Surakat, Y. A., Balogun, A. O., Kumar, G., Shuaibu, A. N., Garba, A., Sahalu, Y., Mohammed, A., Mohammed, T. Y., Abdulkadir, B. A., Abba, A. A., Iliyasu Kakumi, N. A., & Hashim, A. S. (2022). Recent Advances in Artificial Intelligence and Wearable Sensors in Healthcare Delivery. *Applied Sciences, 12*(20), 10271-. https://doi.org/DOI: 10.3390/app122010271

Kaiser, C. R., Major, B., Jurcevic, I., Dover, T. L., Brady, L. M., & Shapiro, J. R. (2013). Presumed fair: Ironic effects of organizational diversity structures. *Journal of Personality and Social Psychology*, *104*(3), 504–519. DOI: 10.1037/a0030838 PMID: 23163748

Kalinoski, Z. T., Steele-Johnson, D., Peyton, E. J., Leas, K. A., Steinke, J., & Bowling, N. A. (2013). A meta-analytic evaluation of diversity training outcomes. *Journal of Organizational Behavior*, *34*(8), 1076–1104. DOI: 10.1002/job.1839

Kane, D., & Spradley, B. D. (2017). Recognizing ESports as a Sport. *The Sport Journal*.

Kang, H. S., & Exworthy, M. (2022). Wearing the Future—Wearables to Empower Users to Take Greater Responsibility for Their Health and Care: Scoping Review. *JMIR mHealth and uHealth, 10*(7), e35684. Advance online publication. DOI: 10.2196/35684 PMID: 35830222

Kaplan, D. M. (2006). Can Diversity Training Discriminate? Backlash to Lesbian, Gay, and Bisexual Diversity Initiatives. *Employee Responsibilities and Rights Journal*, *18*(1), 61–72. DOI: 10.1007/s10672-005-9005-4

Kapp, K. M. (2012). *The gamification of learning and instruction: Game-based methods and strategies for training and education*. Pfeiffer.

Kapp, K. M. (2012). *The Gamification of Learning and Instruction: Game-Based Methods and Strategies for Training and Education*. Pfeiffer.

Kapp, K. M., Blair, L., & Mesch, R. (2014). *The gamification of learning and instruction fieldbook: Ideas into practice*. Wiley.

Kapur, V. K., Olson, E. J., Rosen, C. L., Rowley, J. A., Shelgikar, A. V., & Trotti, L. M. (2021). Sleep is essential to health: An American Academy of Sleep Medicine position statement. *Journal of Clinical Sleep Medicine : JCSM : Official Publication of the American Academy of Sleep Medicine*, *17*(10), 2115–2119. DOI: 10.5664/jcsm.9476 PMID: 34170250

Kasemsap, K. (2016). The role of learning analytics in global higher education. In *Developing effective educational experiences through learning analytics* (pp. 282–307). IGI Global. DOI: 10.4018/978-1-4666-9983-0.ch012

Kato, P. M. (2010). Video games in health care: Closing the gap. *Review of General Psychology*, *14*(2), 113–121. DOI: 10.1037/a0019441

Kaytoue, M., Silva, A., Cerf, L., Meira, W.Jr, & Raïssi, C. (2012, April). Watch me playing, I am a professional: A first study on video game live streaming. In *Proceedings of the 21st International Conference on World Wide Web* (pp. 1181–1188). DOI: 10.1145/2187980.2188259

Ketelhut, S., Martin-Niedecken, A. L., Zimmermann, P., & Nigg, C. R. (2021). Physical Activity and Health Promotion in Esports and Gaming-Discussing Unique Opportunities for an Unprecedented Cultural Phenomenon. *Frontiers in Sports and Active Living*, *3*, 693700. DOI: 10.3389/fspor.2021.693700 PMID: 34604743

Keykhosravi, A., Neamatshahi, M., Mahmoodi, R., & Navipour, E. (2018). Radiation Effects of Mobile Phones and Tablets on the Skin: A Systematic Review. *Advances in Medicine*, *2018*, 1–5. Advance online publication. DOI: 10.1155/2018/9242718 PMID: 29850642

Khandelwal, M. (2022) AI Based Adaptive Learning, https://www.linkedin.com/pulse/ai-based-adaptive-learning-mudit-khandelwal/

Khan, I. A., & Al-Shibami, A. H. (2019). Generation Z's learning preferences: Impact on organizational learning and development-a study conducted in a vocational institute in UAE. *International Journal of Learning and Change*, *11*(4), 379–399.

Khesht-Masjedi, M. F., Shokrgozar, S., Abdollahi, E., Habibi, B., Asghari, T., Ofoghi, R. S., & Pazhooman, S. (2019). The relationship between gender, age, anxiety, depression, and academic achievement among teenagers. *Journal of Family Medicine and Primary Care*, *8*(3), 799–803. DOI: 10.4103/jfmpc.jfmpc_257_19

Kimathi, K. (2024). *Strategic Communication in Esports: Predictive analysis and Optimization for team Performance* (Master's thesis, University of Twente).

Kimmig, A.-C. S., Andringa, G., & Derntl, B. (2018). Potential Adverse Effects of Violent Video Gaming: Interpersonal- Affective Traits Are Rather Impaired Than Disinhibition in Young Adults. *Frontiers in Psychology, 9*, 736–736. DOI: 10.3389/fpsyg.2018.00736 PMID: 29867689

King, E. B., Gulick, L. M. V., & Avery, D. R. (2010). The divide between diversity training and diversity education: Integrating best practices. *Journal of Management Education, 34*(6), 891–906. DOI: 10.1177/1052562909348767

Kirk, M. A., Amiri, M., Pirbaglou, M., & Ritvo, P. (2019). Wearable Technology and Physical Activity Behavior Change in Adults With Chronic Cardiometabolic Disease: A Systematic Review and Meta-Analysis. *American Journal of Health Promotion, 33*(5), 778–791. DOI: 10.1177/0890117118816278 PMID: 30586996

Kirkpatrick, J. D., & Kayser Kirkpatrick, W. (2016). *Kirkpatrick's four levels of training evaluation*. Association for Talent Development.

Kirshenblatt-Gimblett, B. (1978). Culture shock and narrative creativity. In Dorson, R. (Ed.), *Folklore in the modern world* (pp. 109–122). De Gruyter Mouton., DOI: 10.1515/9783110803099.109

Kirste, L., & Holtbrügge, D. (2019). Experiential Learning in the Digital Context: An Experimental Study of Online Cultural Intelligence Training. *Journal of Teaching in International Business, 30*(2), 147–174. DOI: 10.1080/08975930.2019.1663775

Knocke, J., & Schuster, T. (2017). Repatriation of international assignees: Where are we and where do we go from here? A systematic literature review. *Journal of Global Mobility, 5*(3), 275–303. DOI: 10.1108/JGM-01-2017-0001

Koekemoer, L., de Beer, L. T., Govender, K., & Brouwers, M. (2021). Leadership behaviour, team effectiveness, technological flexibility, work engagement and performance during COVID-19 lockdown: An exploratory study. *SA Journal of Industrial Psychology, 47*. Advance online publication. DOI: 10.4102/sajip.v47i0.1829

Koivisto, J., & Hamari, J. (2014). Demographic differences in perceived benefits from gamification. *Computers in Human Behavior, 35*, 179–188. DOI: 10.1016/j.chb.2014.03.007

Kolovos, P. (2020). Wearable Technologies in Post-Operative Recovery: Clinical Applications and Positive Impacts. *International Journal of Caring Sciences, 13*(2), 1474–1479.

Kotsopoulos, D., Bardaki, C., Lounis, S., Papaioannou, T. G., & Pramatari, K. (2017). Designing an IoT-enabled gamification application for energy conservation at the workplace: Exploring personal and contextual characteristics. In *Bled eConference* (p. 25). https://doi.org/DOI: 10.17083/ijsg.v5i2.225

Kour, S., & Jyorti, J. (2022). Cross-cultural training and adjustment through the lens of cultural intelligence and type of expatriates. *Employee Relations*, *44*(1), 1–36. DOI: 10.1108/ER-07-2020-0355

Kraimer, M., Bolino, M., & Mead, B. (2016). Themes in expatriate and repatriate research over four decades: What do we know and what do we still need to learn? *Annual Review of Organizational Psychology and Organizational Behavior*, *3*(1), 83–109. DOI: 10.1146/annurev-orgpsych-041015-062437

Krath, J., Schürmann, L., & von Korflesch, H. F. O. (2021, December). Revealing the theoretical basis of gamification: A systematic review and analysis of theory in research on gamification, serious games and game-based learning. *Computers in Human Behavior*, *125*, 106963. DOI: 10.1016/j.chb.2021.106963

Kraus, S., Jones, P., Kailer, N., Weinmann, A., Chaparro-Banegas, N., & Roig-Tierno, N. (2021). Digital transformation: An overview of the current state of the art of research. *SAGE Open*, *11*(3). Advance online publication. DOI: 10.1177/21582440211047576

Krogmann, P., & Zinner, D. (Hosts). (2023). Evolution from HR Tech to People Tech [Audio podcast episode]. In *Global People Mobility Insights Podcast*. Podigee. https://people-mobility.org/the-evolution-from-hr-tech-to-people-tech/

Kulik, C. T., Pepper, M. B., Roberson, L., & Parker, S. K. (2007). The rich get richer: Predicting participation in voluntary diversity training. *Journal of Organizational Behavior*, *28*(6), 753–769. DOI: 10.1002/job.444

Kulik, C. T., Perry, E. L., & Bourhis, A. C. (2000). Ironic evaluation processes: Effects of thought suppression on evaluations of older job applicants. *Journal of Organizational Behavior*, *21*(6), 689–711. DOI: 10.1002/1099-1379(200009)21:6<689::AID-JOB52>3.0.CO;2-W

Kulik, C. T., & Roberson, L. (2008). Common Goals and Golden Opportunities: Evaluations of Diversity Education in Academic and Organizational Settings. *Academy of Management Learning & Education*, *7*(3), 7. DOI: 10.5465/amle.2008.34251670

Kutz, A. (2018). *Double-Bind-Kommunikation als Burnout-Ursache: Ein Theorie-Vorschlag zu Auswirkungen toxischer Kommunikation in Organisationen* [Double bind communication as a cause of burnout: A theory proposal on the effects of toxic communication in organizations]. 2nd ed.). Springer., DOI: 10.1007/978-3-658-21917-8

Kwak, H., Blackburn, J., & Han, S. (2015). Exploring Cyberbullying and Other Toxic Behavior in Team Competition Online Games. *Proceedings of the 33rd Annual ACM Conference on Human Factors in Computing Systems*, 3739–3748. DOI: 10.1145/2702123.2702529

Lafrenière, M. A., Bureau, J. S., Vallerand, R. J., & Ntoumanis, N. (2013). On passion and moral behavior in achievement settings: The mediating role of pride. *Motivation and Emotion*, *37*(1), 121–133. DOI: 10.1007/s11031-012-9292-7

Lai, C. K., & Lisnek, J. A. (2023). The impact of implicit-bias-oriented diversity training on police officers' beliefs, motivations, and actions. *Psychological Science*. https://journals.sagepub.com/doi/10.1177/09567976221150617

Laine, T. H., & Lindberg, R. S. N. (2020). Designing Engaging Games for Education: A Systematic Literature Review on Game Motivators and Design Principles. *IEEE Transactions on Learning Technologies*, *13*(4), 804–821. https://ieeexplore.ieee.org/stamp/stamp.jsp?tp=&arnumber=9173738. DOI: 10.1109/TLT.2020.3018503

Lamarre, E., Chheda, S., Riba, M., Genest, V., & Nizam, A. (2023, July 31). The value of digital transformation. *Harvard Business Review*.

Landers, R. N. (2019). Gamification misunderstood: How badly executed and rhetorical gamification obscures its transformative potential. *Journal of Management Inquiry*, *28*(2), 137–140. DOI: 10.1177/1056492618790913

Lara, J. S. (2023). Spotting k-TriCaps in SPOT IT! *Senior Projects Spring 2023*, 349. https://digitalcommons.bard.edu/senproj_s2023/349

Larson, K. (2020). Serious games and gamification in the corporate training environment: A literature review. *TechTrends*, *64*(1), 319–328. DOI: 10.1007/s11528-019-00446-7

Lazzaro, N. (2004). *The 4 Keys 2 Fun* [Whitepaper]. XEODesign. http://www.xeodesign.com/category/the-4-keys/

Lee, B. C., Ajisafe, T., Vo, T. V., & Xie, J. (2019). Understanding Long-Term Adoption and Usability of Wearable Activity Trackers Among Active Older Adults. Interacción. https://link.springer.com/chapter/10.1007/978-3-030-22012-9_18

Lee, D., & Yeo, S. (2022). Developing an AI-based chatbot for practicing responsive teaching in mathematics. *Computers & Education*, *191*, 104646. DOI: 10.1016/j.compedu.2022.104646

Lee, J. (2010). Design of blended training for transfer into the workplace. *British Journal of Educational Technology*, *41*(2), 181–198. DOI: 10.1111/j.1467-8535.2008.00909.x

Lejuez, C. W., Read, J. P., Kahler, C. W., Richards, J. B., Ramsey, S. E., Stuart, G. L., Strong, D. R., & Brown, R. A. (2002). Evaluation of a behavioral measure of risk-taking: The Balloon Analogue Risk Task (BART). *Journal of Experimental Psychology. Applied*, *8*(2), 75–84. DOI: 10.1037/1076-898X.8.2.75 PMID: 12075692

Lemmens, J. S., Valkenburg, P. M., & Peter, J. (2011). Psychosocial causes and consequences of pathological gaming. *Computers in Human Behavior*, *27*(1), 144–152. DOI: 10.1016/j.chb.2010.07.015

Lenhart, A., Kahne, J., Middaugh, E., Macgill, A. R., Evans, C., & Vitak, J. (2008). *Teens, video games, and civics: Teens' gaming experiences are diverse and include significant social interaction and civic engagement.* Pew Internet & American Life Project. https://files.eric.ed.gov/fulltext/ED525058.pdf

Leonardi, P. M., Parker, S. H., & Shen, R. (2023). How remote work changes the world of work. *Annual Review of Organizational Psychology and Organizational Behavior*, *11*(1), 193–221. DOI: 10.1146/annurev-orgpsych-091922-015852

Lepper, M. R., Greene, D., & Nisbett, R. E. (1973). Undermining children's intrinsic interest with extrinsic reward: A test of the "overjustification" hypothesis. *Journal of Personality and Social Psychology*, *28*(1), 129–137. DOI: 10.1037/h0035519

Leutner, D., Fleischer, J., Grünkorn, J., & Klieme, E. (2017). *Competence assessment in education: Research, models and instruments (Methodology of educational measurement and assessment)*. Springer., DOI: 10.1007/978-3-319-50030-0

Lewis, N. (2019, February 28). *Be Careful: Gamification at Work Can Go Very Wrong*. SHRM. https://www.shrm.org/topics-tools/news/technology/careful-gamification-work-can-go-wrong

Li, J., Bai, J., Zhu, S., & Yang, H. H. (2024). Game-based assessment of students' digital literacy using evidence-centered game design. *Electronics (Basel)*, *13*(2), 285. DOI: 10.3390/electronics13020385

Li, L. (2022). Reskilling and Upskilling the Future-ready Workforce for Industry 4.0 and Beyond. *Information Systems Frontiers*. Advance online publication. DOI: 10.1007/s10796-022-10308-y PMID: 35855776

Li, M., Ma, S., & Shi, Y. (2023). Examining the effectiveness of gamification as a tool promoting teaching and learning in educational settings: A meta-analysis. *Frontiers in Psychology*, *14*, 1253549. DOI: 10.3389/fpsyg.2023.1253549 PMID: 37876838

Lindemann, V., Mauer, R., Schulte, B., & Zimmermann, R. (2013). *Personaleinsatz im Ausland: Personalmanagement, Arbeitsrecht, Sozialversicherungsrecht, Steuerrecht* (2nd ed.). C.H. Beck. [Personnel assignment abroad: Personnel management, labor law, social security law, tax law. (2nd ed.)]

Lindsey, A., King, E., Membere, A., & Cheung, H. K. (2017, July 28). *Two Types of Diversity Training That Really Work.* Harvard Business Review. https://hbr.org/2017/07/two-types-of-diversity-training-that-really-work

Li, R. W., Ngo, C., Nguyen, J., & Levi, D. M. (2011). Video-game play induces plasticity in the visual system of adults with amblyopia. *PLoS Biology*, *9*(8), e1001135. DOI: 10.1371/journal.pbio.1001135 PMID: 21912514

Li, Y., Chen, D., & Deng, X. (2024). The impact of digital educational games on student's motivation for learning: The mediating effect of learning engagement and the moderating effect of the digital environment. *PLoS One*, *19*(1), e0294350. DOI: 10.1371/journal.pone.0294350 PMID: 38206923

Lobelo, F., Kelli, H. M., Tejedor, S. C., Pratt, M., McConnell, M. V., Martin, S. S., & Welk, G. J. (2016). The Wild Wild West: A Framework to Integrate mHealth Software Applications and Wearables to Support Physical Activity Assessment, Counseling and Interventions for Cardiovascular Disease Risk Reduction. *Progress in Cardiovascular Diseases*, *58*(6), 584–594. DOI: 10.1016/j.pcad.2016.02.007 PMID: 26923067

Loncar-Turukalo, T., Zdravevski, E., Machado da Silva, J., Chouvarda, I., & Trajkovik, V. T., Trajkovik, V., Chouvarda, I., Machado da Silva, J., & Zdravevski, E. (2019). Literature on wearable technology for Connected Health: Scoping Review of research trends, advances, and barriers. Journal of medical Internet research. https://pubmed.ncbi.nlm.nih.gov/31489843/

López-Pernas, S., Gordillo, A., Barra, E., & Quemada, J. (2019). Examining the use of an educational escape room for teaching programming in a higher education setting. *IEEE Access : Practical Innovations, Open Solutions*, *7*, 31723–31737. DOI: 10.1109/ACCESS.2019.2902976

Lorenzo, R., & Reeves, M. (2018, January 30). *How and Where Diversity Drives Financial Performance.* Harvard Business Review. https://hbr.org/2018/01/how-and-where-diversity-drives-financial-performance

Lu, L., Zhang, J., Xie, Y., Gao, F., Xu, S., Wu, X., & Ye, Z. (2020). Wearable Health Devices in Health Care: Narrative Systematic Review. *JMIR mHealth and uHealth*, *8*(11), e18907. DOI: 10.2196/18907 PMID: 33164904

Lumbreras, A. G., Hurwitz, J. T., Liang, X., Schippers, S., Phillip, K., Bhattacharjee, S., Waters, H. C., & Malone, D. C. (2024). Insights into insurance coverage for digital therapeutics: A qualitative study of US payer perspectives. *Journal of Managed Care & Specialty Pharmacy*, *30*(4), 313–320. DOI: 10.18553/jmcp.2024.30.4.313 PMID: 38555623

lUNESCO (2020). Global Education Coalition. COVID-19 Education Response. Retrieved from: https://en.unesco.org/covid19/educationresponse/globalcoalition

Macfadyen, L. P., Dawson, S., Pardo, A., & Gašević, D. (2014). Embracing big data in complex educational systems: The learning analytics imperative and the policy challenge. *Research & Practice in Assessment*, *9*, 17–28.

Macrae, C. N., Bodenhausen, G. V., Milne, A. B., & Jetten, J. (1994). Out of Mind but Back in Sight: Stereotypes on the Rebound. *Journal of Personality and Social Psychology*, *67*(5), 808–817. DOI: 10.1037/0022-3514.67.5.808

Makri, A., Vlachopoulos, D., & Martina, R. A. (2021). Digital escape rooms as innovative pedagogical tools in education: A systematic literature review. *Sustainability (Basel)*, *13*(8), 45–87. DOI: 10.3390/su13084587

Mao, E. (2021). The structural characteristics of esports gaming and their behavioral implications for high engagement: A competition perspective and a cross-cultural examination. *Addictive Behaviors*, *123*, 107056. DOI: 10.1016/j.addbeh.2021.107056 PMID: 34332273

Marques, C., Bachega, S. J., & Tavares, D. M. (2019). Framework proposal for the environmental impact assessment of universities in the context of Green IT. *Journal of Cleaner Production*, *241*(118346), 118346. DOI: 10.1016/j.jclepro.2019.118346

Mary, R. (2024). An essential approach to mitigating expatriate challenges: Examining effective selection and training strategies for expatriates. *International Journal of Advanced Research in Commerce. Management and Social Science*, *7*(3), 141–148.

Marzano, R. J., & Kendall, J. S. (2007). *The new taxonomy of educational objectives* (2nd ed.). Corwin Press.

Maseleno, A., Sabani, N., Huda, M., Ahmad, R., Jasmi, K. A., & Basiron, B. (2018). Demystifying learning analytics in personalised learning. *IACSIT International Journal of Engineering and Technology*, *7*(3), 1124–1129.

Maslow, A. H. (1954). *Motivation and personality*. Harpers. https://psycnet.apa.org/record/1955-02233-000

Mathur, S., & Modani, U. S. (2016) Smart city a gateway for artificial intelligence in India. *2016 IEEE Student Conference on Electrical, Electronics and Computer Science (SCEECS)*, 1–3 DOI: 10.1109/SCEECS.2016.7509291

Matthews, D. (n.d.). DIY adaptive gaming: Game control for people with upper limb disabilities (Bachelor's thesis, University of Twente).

Mayer, I. S. (2009). The gaming of policy and the politics of gaming: A review. *Simulation & Gaming*, *40*(6), 825–862. DOI: 10.1177/1046878109346456

McGonigal, J. (2011). *Reality is broken: why games make us better and how they can change the world*. Penguin Press.

McGuire, R. (2021). What Is Adaptive Learning And How Does It Work To Promote Equity In Higher Education?. Everylearnereverywhere. org.

McNulty, C., Jenny, S. E., Leis, O., Poulus, D., Sondergeld, P., & Nicholson, M. (2022). Physical exercise and performance in esports players: An initial systematic review. *Journal of Electronic Gaming and Esports*. DOI: 10.1123/jege.2022-0014

Meehirr, K. (2023), How AI Is Personalizing Education for Every Student, https://elearningindustry.com/how-ai-is-personalizing-education-for-every-student

Meiman, M., Brown, N. E., & Hodges, A. (2019). Diversity, Equity, and Inclusion: A Conceptual Framework for Instruction. ACRL *19th National Conference, "Re-casting the Narrative", Cleveland, Ohio. April 10-13, 2019*, 675-682.

Meister, J. C. (2013, January 2). *How Deloitte Made Learning a Game*. Harvard Business Review. https://hbr.org/2013/01/how-deloitte-made-learning-a-g

Meister, J. C. (2015). *Future of work: Using gamification for human resources*. Forbes Media LLC.

Menon, D., & Romero, M. (2020). Game mechanics supporting a learning and playful experience in educational escape games. In Tomei, L., & Farber, M. (Eds.), *Global perspectives on gameful and playful teaching and learning* (pp. 143–162). IGI Global., DOI: 10.4018/978-1-7998-2015-4.ch007

Mental health today. A deep dive based on the 2024 Gen Z and Millennial survey. (2024). Deloitte. https://www2.deloitte.com/content/dam/Deloitte/fr/Documents/human-capital/Publications/deloitte_genz-millennial-survey_mental-health-deep-dive.pdf

Meticulous Research. (2023). *Gamification market by type (structural, content), offering, organization size, deployment mode, application (HRM, CRM, customer engagement), end-use industry (BFSI, retail & e-commerce, education & research), and geography - Global forecast to 2030 (Report ID: MRICT - 104314).* Meticulous Research. https://www.meticulousresearch.com/product/gamification-market-5015

Mettler, T., & Wulf, J. (2020). Health promotion with physiolytics: What is driving people to subscribe in a data-driven health plan. *PLoS One*, *15*(4), e0231705–e0231705. DOI: 10.1371/journal.pone.0231705 PMID: 32294126

Miami University. (2023, October 14). *Miami University eSports Panel* [Video]. YouTube. https://youtu.be/b2jN8SBQ9Ig

Microsoft. (2020). *Xbox Academy: Gaming for skill development*. Microsoft Corporation.

Microsoft. (2021). *Gaming for everyone: Diversity and inclusion in gaming*. Microsoft Corporation.

Migliore, L., McGee, C., & Moore, M. N. (2021). *Handbook of esports medicine: Clinical aspects of competitive video gaming*. Springer., DOI: 10.1007/978-3-030-73610-1

Miller, J. (2020). Climate change solutions: The role of technology, House of Commons Library,

Miller, P. N. (2015, March 26). Is 'Design Thinking' the New Liberal Arts? *The Chronicle of Higher Education*. https://www.chronicle.com/article/is-design-thinking-the-new-liberal-arts/

Miller, C. H. (2004). *Digital storytelling: A creator's guide to interactive entertainment*. Focal Press.

Minea-Pic, A. (2020). Innovating teachers' professional learning through digital technologies.

Mislevy, R. J., Corrigan, S., Oranje, A., DiCerbo, K., Bauer, M. I., von Davier, A., & John, M. (2016). Psychometrics and game-based assessment. In Drasgow, F. (Ed.), *Technology and testing: Improving educational and psychological measurement* (pp. 23–48). Routledge., DOI: 10.4324/9781315871493-2

Mislevy, R., Oranje, A., Bauer, M. I., von Davier, A., Hao, J., Corrigan, S., Hoffman, E., DiCerbo, K., & John, M. (2014). *Psychometric considerations in game-based assessment*. GlassLab.

Mitsea, E., Drigas, A., & Skianis, C. (2024). Well-being technologies and positive psychology strategies for training metacognition, emotional intelligence and motivation meta-skills in clinical populations: A systematic review. *Psych*, *6*(1), 305–344. DOI: 10.3390/psych6010019

Mizumoto, A., & Eguchi, M. (2023). Exploring the potential of using an AI language model for automated essay scoring. *Research Methods in Applied Linguistics*, *2*(2), 1–13. DOI: 10.1016/j.rmal.2023.100050

Mollick, E. R., & Rothbard, N. (2014, September 30). *Mandatory fun: Consent, gamification and the impact of games at work.* The Wharton School Research Paper Series. https://doi.org/DOI: 10.2139/ssrn.2277103

Mollick, E., & Mollick, L. (2023). Using AI to Implement Effective Teaching Strategies in Classrooms: Five Strategies, Including Prompts, Wharton School of the University of Pennsylvania & Wharton Interactive, March 16, https://ssrn.com/abstract=4391243

Moore, G. E. (1998). Cramming More Components Onto Integrated Circuits. *Proceedings of the IEEE*, *86*(1), 82–85. DOI: 10.1109/JPROC.1998.658762

Mor-Barak, M. (2005). Managing diversity: Toward a globally inclusive workplace. *Sage (Atlanta, Ga.).*

Morley, T. (2018). Making the business case for diversity and inclusion: Short case studies and research papers that demonstrate best practice in HR. *Strategic HR Review*, *17*(1), 58–60. DOI: 10.1108/SHR-10-2017-0068

Moroianu, N., ... 2023 Artificial Intelligence in Education: a Systematic Review, The 6 th International Conference on Economics and Social Sciences, 906-921 https://www.icess.ase.ro/wp-content/uploads/2024/07/Artificial-Intelligence-in-Education.pdf

Morrell, B., & Eukel, H. N. (2021). Shocking escape: A cardiac escape room for undergraduate nursing students. *Simulation & Gaming*, *52*(1), 72–78. DOI: 10.1177/1046878120958734

Motti, V. G. (2019). Wearable Health: Opportunities and Challenges. Proceedings of the 13th EAI International Conference on Pervasive Computing Technologies for Healthcare. https://dl.acm.org/doi/10.1145/3329189.3329226

Mould, S. (2022, October 27). *Mechanical circuits: Electronics without electricity* [Video]. YouTube. https://www.youtube.com/watch?v=QrkiJZKJfpY

Mulder, M. (Ed.). (2017). *Competence-based Vocational and Professional Education. Bridging the Worlds of Work and Education.* Springer. DOI: 10.1007/978-3-319-41713-4

Müller, M., & Gruenewald, H. (2024). *Upskilling und Reskilling für die Personalentwicklung: Kompetenzen der Zukunft erkennen und Personal erfolgreich qualifizieren*. Springer Nature. https://link.springer.com/book/9783658444037

NACE StarLeague. (2023, July 22). *Dunwoody Hawks vs Fort Lewis College Skyhawks | COD: Modern Warfare 3 | NACE StarLeague Playoffs* [Video]. YouTube. https://youtu.be/bEoFcijlR78

Nadar, S. (2024), The Role of AI in Personalized Learning for Students, https://blog.shivnadarfoundation.org/educational-empowerment/the-role-of-ai-in-personalized-learning-for-students/

Naeem, M., Ozuem, W., Howell, K. E., & Ranfagni, S. (2023). A step-by-step process of thematic analysis to develop a conceptual model in qualitative research. *International Journal of Qualitative Methods*, *22*, 16094069231205789. Advance online publication. DOI: 10.1177/16094069231205789

Nahavandi, D., Alizadehsani, R., Khosravi, A., & Acharya, U. R. (2022). Application of artificial intelligence in wearable devices: Opportunities and challenges. *Computer Methods and Programs in Biomedicine*, *213*, 106541–106541. DOI: 10.1016/j.cmpb.2021.106541 PMID: 34837860

Nakamura, L. (2002). *Cybertypes: Race, ethnicity, and identity on the Internet.* Routledge. DOI: 10.4324/9780203953365

Narbariya, S. (n.d.). Navigating the future of work: Challenges and strategies. In *Digital paradigm shift: Unravelling technological disruption in business* (p. 193).

Nathoo, Z. (2021, June 17). *Why ineffective diversity training won't go away*. BBC worklife. https://www.bbc.com/worklife/article/20210614-why-ineffective-diversity-training-wont-go-away

National Academies of Sciences, Engineering, and Medicine. (2018). *How people learn II: Learners, contexts, and cultures*. The National Academies Press.

National Association of Colleges and Employers (NACE). (2021). *NACE Report 2021*. https://www.naceweb.org/about-us/

National Association of Colleges and Employers. (2021). *Career readiness defined.* NACE https://www.naceweb.org/docs/default-source/default-document-library/2024/resources/nace-career-readiness-competencies-revised-apr-2024.pdf?sfvrsn=1e695024_3

National Eye Institute. (2024, August 1). Color blindness. NEI.NIH.gov. https://www.nei.nih.gov/learn-about-eye-health/eye-conditions-and-diseases/color-blindness

National Institute of Health. (2024, March). Quick statistics about hearing, balance & dizziness. NIH.gov. https://www.nidcd.nih.gov/health/statistics/quick-statistics-hearing

National Soft Skills Association. (2023). *Research and best practices in soft skills.* National Soft Skills Association. https://www.nationalsoftskills.org

Nayak, B., & Bhattacharyya, S. S. (2020). The Changing Narrative in the Health Insurance Industry: Wearables Technology in Health Insurance Products and Services for the COVID-19 World. *Journal of Health Management*, *22*(4), 550–558. DOI: 10.1177/0972063420983112

Nederveen Pieterse, A., van Knippenberg, D., & van Dierendonck, D. (2013). Cultural diversity and team performance: The role of team member goal orientation. *Academy of Management Journal*, *56*(3), 782–804. DOI: 10.5465/amj.2010.0992

Network of Academic and Scholastic Esports Federation. (2024). About NASEF. NASEF. https://www.nasef.org/about

Newkirk, P. (2019). *Diversity, Inc.: The Failed Promise of a Billion-Dollar Business.* Bold Type Books.

Newzoo. (2021). *Newzoo's global esports & live streaming market report 2021 (free version).* https://newzoo.com/resources/trend-reports/newzoos-global-esports-live-streaming-market-report-2021-free-version

Newzoo. (2023). *Global games market report 2023.* https://newzoo.com/resources/trend-reports/newzoo-global-games-market-report-2023-free-version

Newzoo. (2023). *Global games market report*. Newzoo.

Newzoo. (2024). *Global games market report 2024.* https://newzoo.com/resources/trend-reports/newzoos-global-games-market-report-2024-free-version

Nguyen, C. T., Bang, H., Manogaran, G., Athota, V., & Tavares, J. M. R. S. (2020). Internet-of-Things (IoT) technologies for healthcare: Opportunities, challenges, and management. In Nguyen, C. T., Bang, H., Manogaran, G., Athota, V., & Tavares, J. M. R. S. (Eds.), *Internet of Things (IoT) Technologies for Healthcare* (pp. 3–24). Springer.

Niederle, M., & Vesterlund, L. (2008). Gender Differences in Competition. *Negotiation Journal*, *24*(4), 447–463. DOI: 10.1111/j.1571-9979.2008.00197.x

Nielson, R., & Hanghoj, T. (2019). *Esports skills are people skills*. ResearchGate., DOI: 10.34190/GBL.19.041

Nikolić, J. L., & Lazarević, S. (2022). Employer Branding and Employee Value Proposition for Generation Z in Digital Economy. Marketing (0354-3471), 53(3).OpenAI. (2024). Response generated by ChatGPT (July 21, 2024).https://chat.openai.com/

North-Samardzic, A., & de Witt, M. (2019). Designing a Human Resource Management Simulation to Engage Students. *Journal of Management Education*, *43*(4), 359–395. DOI: 10.1177/1052562919841411

Oakman, J., Kinsman, N., Stuckey, R., Graham, M., & Weale, V. (2020). A rapid review of mental and physical health effects of working at home: How do we optimise health? *BMC Public Health*, *20*(1), 1–13. DOI: 10.1186/s12889-020-09875-z PMID: 33256652

Oberg, K. (1960). Culture shock and the problems of adjustment to new cultural environments. *Practical Anthropology*, *7*(4), 177–182. DOI: 10.1177/009182966000700405

Occupational Safety and Health Administration. (n.d.). Radiofrequency and Microwave Radiation—Health Effects. https://www.osha.gov/radiofrequency-and-microwave-radiation/health-effects

Oliveira, R. P., Souza, C. G., Reis, A. C., & Souza, W. M. (2021). Gamification in E-Learning and Sustainability: A Theoretical Framework. *Sustainability (Basel)*, *13*(21), 11945. DOI: 10.3390/su132111945

Olyanasab, A., & Annabestani, M. (2024). Leveraging Machine Learning for Personalized Wearable Biomedical Devices: A Review. *Journal of Personalized Medicine, 14*(2), 203-. https://doi.org/DOI: 10.3390/jpm14020203

Ometov, A., Shubina, V., Klus, L., Skibińska, J., Saafi, S., Pascacio, P., Flueratoru, L., Gaibor, D. Q., Chukhno, N., Chukhno, O., Ali, A., Channa, A., Svertoka, E., Qaim, W. B., Casanova-Marqués, R., Holcer, S., Torres-Sospedra, J., Casteleyn, S., Ruggeri, G., & Lohan, E. S. (2021). A Survey on Wearable Technology: History, State-of-the-Art and Current Challenges. *Computer Networks*, *193*, 108074. DOI: 10.1016/j.comnet.2021.108074

Paaßen, B., Morgenroth, T., & Stratemeyer, M. (2017). What is a True Gamer? The Male Gamer Stereotype and the Marginalization of Women in Video Game Culture. *Sex Roles*, *76*(7-8), 421–435. DOI: 10.1007/s11199-016-0678-y

Padyab, A. M., & Habibipour, A. (2021). Issues and Adoption Barriers in Wearable Technologies. *International Journal of Technology Diffusion*, *12*(1), 75–89. https://ideas.repec.org/a/igg/jtd000/v12y2021i1p75-89.html. DOI: 10.4018/IJTD.2021010104

Palanichamy, T., Sharma, M. K., Sahu, M., & Kanchana, D. M. (2020). Influence of Esports on stress: A systematic review. *Industrial Psychiatry Journal*, *29*(2), 191. DOI: 10.4103/ipj.ipj_195_20 PMID: 34158701

Paluch, S., & Tuzovic, S. (2019). Persuaded self-tracking with wearable technology: Carrot or stick? *Journal of Services Marketing*, *33*(4), 436–448. DOI: 10.1108/JSM-03-2018-0091

Paluck, E. L. (2006). Diversity training and intergroup contact: A call to action research. *The Journal of Social Issues*, *62*(3), 577–595. DOI: 10.1111/j.1540-4560.2006.00474.x

Paluck, E. L., & Green, D. P. (2009). Prejudice Reduction: What Works? A Critical Look at Evidence from the Field and the Laboratory. *Annual Review of Psychology*, •••, 60.

Paluck, E. L., Porat, R., Clark, C. S., & Green, D. P. (2021). Prejudice reduction: Progress and challenges. *Annual Review of Psychology*, *72*(1), 533–560. DOI: 10.1146/annurev-psych-071620-030619 PMID: 32928061

Pamela McCorduck & Cli Cfe. (2004) Machines Who Think, A K Peters/CRC Press, Second Edition, 2004, https://doi.org/DOI: 10.1201/9780429258985

Pamula, A., & Zalewska-Turzyńska, M. (2023). Internal communication satisfaction while remote work: The organizational culture perspective. *European Research Studies*, *26*(2), 30–48. DOI: 10.35808/ersj/3137

Panda, S., & Kaur, N. (2023). Crafting sustainable careers in a dynamic professional terrain. In Panda, S., & Kaur, N. (Eds.), *Crafting sustainable careers in a dynamic professional terrain* (pp. 77–87).

Parekh, R. (2024). The Future of Business Leadership: Navigating Technological Disruption. *Management Science Research Archives*, *1*(4), 35–46.

Pasmore, W., Lafferty, K., & Spencer, S. (2014). Developing a leadership strategy: A critical ingredient for organizational success. Center for Creative Leadership, 1-28.

Patel, M. S., Asch, D. A., & Volpp, K. G. (2015). Wearable devices as facilitators, not drivers, of health behavior change. *Journal of the American Medical Association*, *313*(5), 459–460. DOI: 10.1001/jama.2014.14781 PMID: 25569175

Pauly, D. (1995). Anecdotes and the shifting baseline syndrome of fisheries. *Trends in Ecology & Evolution*, *10*(10), 430. https://hdl.handle.net/20.500.12348/2785. DOI: 10.1016/S0169-5347(00)89171-5 PMID: 21237093

Peleg, R., Yayon, M., Katchevich, D., Moria-Shipony, M., & Blonder, R. (2019). A lab-based chemical escape room: Educational, mobile, and fun! *Journal of Chemical Education*, *96*(5), 955–960. DOI: 10.1021/acs.jchemed.8b00406

Pellegrino, J. W., DiBello, L. V., & Goldman, S. R. (2016). A framework for conceptualizing and evaluating the validity of instructionally relevant assessments. *Educational Psychologist*, *51*(1), 59–81. DOI: 10.1080/00461520.2016.1145550

Pellis, S. M., & Pellis, V. C. (2007). Rough-and-tumble play and the development of the social brain. *Current Directions in Psychological Science*, *16*(2), 95–98. DOI: 10.1111/j.1467-8721.2007.00483.x

Penders, J., Altini, M., Hoof, C. V., & Dy, E. (2015). Wearable Sensors for Healthier Pregnancies. *Proceedings of the IEEE*, *103*(2), 179–191. DOI: 10.1109/JPROC.2014.2387017

Pentland, A. P. (2004). Healthwear: Medical technology becomes wearable. *Computer*, *37*(5), 42–49. https://pubmed.ncbi.nlm.nih.gov/16301769/. DOI: 10.1109/MC.2004.1297238

Perkins, K.M, et al (2018). International perspectives on the pedagogy of climate change. Journal of Cleaner Production, 200, 1043-1052, https://doi.org/. 2018.07.296. DOI: 10.1016/j.jclepro

Pettigrew, T. F., & Tropp, L. R. (2006). A meta-analytic test of intergroup contact theory. *Journal of Personality and Social Psychology*, *90*(5), 751–783. DOI: 10.1037/0022-3514.90.5.751 PMID: 16737372

Pettigrew, T. F., & Tropp, L. R. (2008). How does intergroup contact reduce prejudice? Meta-analytic tests of three mediators. *European Journal of Social Psychology*, *38*(6), 922–934. DOI: 10.1002/ejsp.504

Phillips, B. N., Deiches, J., Morrison, B., Chan, F., & Bezyak, J. L. (2016). Disability diversity training in the workplace: Systematic review and future directions. *Journal of Occupational Rehabilitation*, *26*(3), 264–275. DOI: 10.1007/s10926-015-9612-3 PMID: 26519035

Pluss, M. A., Novak, A. R., Bennett, K. J. M., Panchuk, D., Coutts, A. J., & Fransen, J. (2023, April). The reliability and validity of mobalytics proving ground as a perceptual-motor skill assessment for esports. *International Journal of Sports Science & Coaching*, *18*(2), 470–479. DOI: 10.1177/17479541221086793

Polkinghorne, D. (1988). *Narrative knowing and the human sciences*. State University of New York Press.

Ponzo, S., Morelli, D., Kawadler, J. M., Hemmings, N. R., Bird, G., & Plans, D. (2020). Efficacy of the Digital Therapeutic Mobile App BioBase to Reduce Stress and Improve Mental Well-Being Among University Students: Randomized Controlled Trial. *JMIR mHealth and uHealth*, *8*(4), e17767. DOI: 10.2196/17767 PMID: 31926063

Prensky, M. (2001). Digital natives, digital immigrants. *On the Horizon*, *9*(5), 1–6. DOI: 10.1108/10748120110424816

Promoting Mental Health at Work: The Impact of Gamification. (n.d,). Humanoo. https://humanoo.com/en/magazin/promoting-mental-health-at-work-the-impact-of-gamification/

Purcell, W. M., & Lumbreras, J. (2021). Higher education and the COVID-19 pandemic: Navigating disruption using the sustainable development goals. *Discover Sustainability*, *2*(1), 6. DOI: 10.1007/s43621-021-00013-2 PMID: 35425919

Putz, L.-M., & Treiblmaier, H. (2019, January 21). Increasing Knowledge Retention through Gamified Workshops: Findings from a Longitudinal Study and Identification of Moderating Variables. *Proceedings of the 52nd Hawaii International Conference on System Sciences*.

PwC. (2020). *Game-based learning: Transforming professional development*. PricewaterhouseCoopers.

PwC. (2024). *Global Workforce Hopes and Fears Survey 2024*.https://www.pwc.com/gx/en/issues/workforce/hopes-and-fears.html

Rachmad, Y. E. (2021). Disruptive dynamics: Navigating the tech-led business boom. In *Book of the Association for Information Systems Publishing*. Professional Book Atlanta Special Issue.

Rad, D., Roman, A., Runcan, R., Toderici, O., Stoian, C. D., Sinaci, M., & Arion, F. (2024). Adapting to the unseen: Understanding workplace learning disruptions in educational counseling during COVID-19. *Migration Letters : An International Journal of Migration Studies, 21*(S8), 1236–1255.

Rahiman, H. U., Kodikal, R., & Suresh, S. (2023). Game on: Can gamification enhance productivity? *F1000Res*. https://doi.org/DOI: 10.12688/f1000research.131579.2

Raith, L., Bignill, J., Stavropoulos, V., Millear, P., Allen, A., Stallman, H. M., Mason, J., De Regt, T., Wood, A., & Kannis-Dymand, L. (2021). Massively multiplayer online games and well-being: A systematic literature review. *Frontiers in Psychology, 12*, 698799. DOI: 10.3389/fpsyg.2021.698799 PMID: 34276523

Ra, S., Jagannathan, S., & Maclean, R. (2021). *Powering a learning society during an age of disruption*. Springer Nature. DOI: 10.1007/978-981-16-0983-1

Ray, P. P. (2023). ChatGPT: A comprehensive review on background, applications, key challenges, bias, ethics, limitations and future scope. *Internet of Things and Cyber-Physical Systems, 3*, 121–154. DOI: 10.1016/j.iotcps.2023.04.003

Read, B. (2021, May 26). *Doing the Work at Work What are companies desperate for diversity consultants actually buying?* The Cut. https://www.thecut.com/article/diversity-equity-inclusion-industrial-companies.html

Reich, J. (2020). *Failure to disrupt: Why technology alone can't transform education*. Harvard University Press.

Reid, C. R., Schall, M. C.Jr, Amick, R. Z., Schiffman, J. M., Lu, M., Smets, M., Moses, H. R., & Porto, R. (2017). Wearable Technologies: How Will We Overcome Barriers to Enhance Worker Performance, Health, And Safety? *Proceedings of the Human Factors and Ergonomics Society Annual Meeting, 61*(1), 1026–1030. DOI: 10.1177/1541931213601740

Rheinberg, F. (2010). Intrinsic Motivation and Flow. In Heckhausen, J., & Heckhausen, H. (Eds.), *Motivation and Action* (4th ed., pp. 365–388). Cambridge University Press.

Riatti, P., & Thiel, A. (2021). The societal impact of electronic sport: A scoping review. *German Journal of Exercise and Sport Research*. Advance online publication. DOI: 10.1007/s12662-021-00784-w PMID: 40477796

Rich, E., Knight, K., & Nair, S. B. (2010). *Artificial Intelligence* (3rd ed.). Tata McGraw Hill India., https://pubhtml5.com/ning/enwh/

Richter, G., Raban, D. K., & Rafaeli, S. (2014). Studying Gamification: The Effect of Rewards and Incentives on Motivation. In Reiners, T., & Woods, L. (Eds.), *Gamification in Education and Business* (pp. 21–46). Springer International Publishing., DOI: 10.1007/978-3-319-10208-5

Rimon, G. (2016, June 7). *Sales Gamification: 5 Leaderboard Mistakes to Avoid.* eLearning Industry. https://elearningindustry.com/sales-gamification-5-leaderboard-mistakes-avoid

Riot Games. (2019). *Team building through gaming: A case study*. Riot Games, Inc.

Robb, L. A., & Doverspike, D. (2001). Self-reported proclivity to harass as a moderator of the effectiveness of sexual harassment-prevention training. *Psychological Reports*, *88*(1), 85–88. DOI: 10.2466/pr0.2001.88.1.85 PMID: 11293058

Roberson, L., Kulik, C. T., & Pepper, M. B. (2001). Designing effective diversity training: Influence of group composition and trainee experience. *Journal of Organizational Behavior*, *22*(8), 871–885. DOI: 10.1002/job.117

Roberson, Q., King, E. B., & Hebl, M. R. (2020). Designing more effective practices to address workplace inequality. *Behavioral Science & Policy*, *6*(1), 39–49. DOI: 10.1177/237946152000600104

Robertson, J. (2014). Learner-Centric Learning Analytics. *Recuperado el, 24.*

Robertson, M. M., Ciriello, V. M., & Garabet, A. M. (2013). Office ergonomics training and a sit-stand workstation: Effects on musculoskeletal and visual symptoms and performance of office workers. *Applied Ergonomics*, *44*(1), 73–85. DOI: 10.1016/j.apergo.2012.05.001 PMID: 22727324

Robson, K., Plangger, K., Kietzmann, J. H., McCarthy, I., & Pitt, L. (2015). Is it all a game?: Understanding the principles of gamification. *Business Horizons*, *58*(4), 411–420. DOI: 10.1016/j.bushor.2015.03.006

Rodrigues, L., Palomino, P. T., Toda, A. M., Klock, A. C. T., Pessoa, M., Pereira, F. D., Oliveira, E. H. T., Oliveira, D. F., Cristea, A. I., Gasparini, I., & Isotani, S. (2023). How Personalization Affects Motivation in Gamified Review Assessments. *International Journal of Artificial Intelligence in Education*, *34*(2), 147–184. DOI: 10.1007/s40593-022-00326-x PMID: 36685293

Rosell Llorens, M. (2017). eSport Gaming: The Rise of a New Sports Practice. *Sport, Ethics and Philosophy*, *11*(4), 464–476. DOI: 10.1080/17511321.2017.1318947

Roth, E. (2017, April 6). *It's official: The AP style guide spells it esports, not eSports, e-sports or eSports*. Yahoo! Sports. https://sports.yahoo.com/its-official-the-ap-style-guide-spells-it-esports-not-esports-e-sports-or-esports-233434245.html

Rothwell, G., & Shaffer, M. (2019). eSports in K-12 and Post-Secondary schools. *Education Sciences*, *9*(2), 105. DOI: 10.3390/educsci9020105

Roy, S. N., Srivastava, S. K., & Gururajan, R. (2018). Integrating wearable devices and recommendation system: Towards a next generation healthcare service delivery. AIS Electronic Library (AISeL). https://aisel.aisnet.org/jitta/vol19/iss4/2/

Rudman, L. A., Ashmore, R. D., & Gary, M. L. (2001). "Unlearning" automatic biases: The malleability of implicit prejudice and stereotypes. *Journal of Personality and Social Psychology*, *81*(5), 856–868. DOI: 10.1037/0022-3514.81.5.856 PMID: 11708562

Rudolf, K., Bickmann, P., Froböse, I., Tholl, C., Wechsler, K., & Grieben, C. (1870). K., Bickmann, P., Froböse, I., Tholl, C., Wechsler, K., & Grieben, C. (2020). Demographics and Health Behavior of Video Game and eSports Players in Germany: The eSports Study 2019. *International Journal of Environmental Research and Public Health*, *17*(6), 1870. Advance online publication. DOI: 10.3390/ijerph17061870

Russell, S. J., & Novig, P. (2021). *Artificial Intelligence: A modern Approach* (4th ed.)., https://en.wikipedia.org/wiki/Artificial_intelligence#CITEREFRussellNorvig2021

Ryan, M., Sleigh, A., Soh, K. W., & Li, Z. (2013). Why gamification is serious business. *Outlook–The Journal of High-Performance Business (Accenture)*, *1*, 1-6. https://www.accenture.com/us-en/insight-outlook-why-gamification-is-serious-business

Ryan, R. M., & Deci, E. L. (2000). Self-determination theory and the facilitation of intrinsic motivation, social development and well-being. *The American Psychologist*, *55*(1), 68–78. DOI: 10.1037/0003-066X.55.1.68 PMID: 11392867

Rykov, Y., Thach, T.-Q., Bojic, I., Christopoulos, G., & Car, J. (2021). Digital Biomarkers for Depression Screening With Wearable Devices: Cross-sectional Study With Machine Learning Modeling. *JMIR mHealth and uHealth*, *9*(10), e24872. DOI: 10.2196/24872 PMID: 34694233

Saeed, S. A., & Masters, R. M. (2021). Disparities in health care and the digital divide. *Current Psychiatry Reports*, *23*(9), 61. DOI: 10.1007/s11920-021-01274-4 PMID: 34297202

Sailer, M., Hense, J., Mandl, H., & Klever, M. (2013). Psychological Perspectives on Motivation through Gamification. *Interaction Design and Architecture(s). Journal*, *19*, 28–37.

Salili, F., & Hoosain, R. (Eds.). (2007). *Culture, motivation and learning: A multicultural perspective*. IAP.

Santhakumar, S. (2024), 6 Ways AI is Personalizing Education for Every Student, https://www.quixl.ai/blog/6-ways-ai-is-personalizing-education-for-every-student/

Santo, R. (2021). Making public policy fun: How political aspects and policy issues are found in video games. *Journal of Political Science Education*, *17*(3), 389–406. DOI: 10.1080/15512169.2019.1696880

Sanz-Matesanz, M., Gea-García, G. M., & Martínez-Aranda, L. M. (2023). Physical and psychological factors related to player's health and performance in esports: A scoping review. *Computers in Human Behavior*, *143*, 107698. DOI: 10.1016/j.chb.2023.107698

SAP. (2021). *Esports and employee engagement*. SAP SE.

Saquib, N., Saquib, J., Wahid, A., Ahmed, A. A., Dhuhayr, H. E., Zaghloul, M. S., Ewid, M., & Al-Mazrou, A. (2017). Video game addiction and psychological distress among expatriate adolescents in Saudi Arabia. *Addictive Behaviors Reports*, *6*, 112–117. DOI: 10.1016/j.abrep.2017.09.003 PMID: 29450245

Schary, D. P., Jenny, S. E., & Koshy, A. (2022). Leveling up esports health: Current status and call to action. *International Journal of Esports*, *3*(3).

Schell, J. (2020). *The art of game design: A book of lenses* (3rd ed.). CRC Press.

Schmierbach, M. (2010). "Killing spree": Exploring the connection between competitive game play and aggressive cognition. *Communication Research*, *37*(2), 256–274. DOI: 10.1177/0093650209356394

Schmitz, M., Van Limbeek, E., Greller, W., Sloep, P., & Drachsler, H. (2017). Opportunities and challenges in using learning analytics in learning design. In *Data Driven Approaches in Digital Education: 12th European Conference on Technology Enhanced Learning, EC-TEL 2017, Tallinn, Estonia, September 12–15, 2017* [Springer International Publishing.]. *Proceedings*, *12*, 209–223.

School of Creative Thinking. (2024). *COCD-Box*. https://schoolofcreativethinking.nl/en/cocd-box/

Schroder, A., Prockl, G., & Constantiou, I. (2021). How Digital Platforms with a Social Purpose Trigger Change towards Sustainable Supply Chains, *Proceedings of the 54th Hawaii International Conference on System sciences*, DOI: 10.24251/HICSS.2021.580

Seaborn, K., & Fels, D. I. (2015). Gamification in theory and action: A survey. *International Journal of Human-Computer Studies*, *74*, 14–31. DOI: 10.1016/j.ijhcs.2014.09.006

Seffah, K. D., Salib, K., Dardari, L., Taha, M., Dahat, P., Toriola, S., Satnarine, T., Zohara, Z., Adelekun, A., Ahmed, A., Gutlapalli, S. D., Patel, D., & Khan, S. (2023). Health Benefits of Esports: A Systematic Review Comparing the Cardiovascular and Mental Health Impacts of Esports. *Cureus*, *15*(6), e40705. DOI: 10.7759/cureus.40705 PMID: 37485153

Selmer, J., Dickmann, M., Froese, F. J., Lauring, J., Reiche, B. S., & Shaffer, M. (2022). The potential of virtual global mobility: Implications for practice and future research. *Journal of Global Mobility*, *10*(1), 1–13. DOI: 10.1108/JGM-07-2021-0074

Sengupta, D. (2016). *A mathematical analysis of Spot It!* http://deepusengupta.com/projects/mathematical_analysis_spot_it.pdf?i=1

Sequeira, L., Perrotta, S., LaGrassa, J., Merikangas, K., Kreindler, D., Kundur, D., Courtney, D., Szatmari, P., Battaglia, M., & Strauss, J. (2020). Mobile and wearable technology for monitoring depressive symptoms in children and adolescents: A scoping review. *Journal of Affective Disorders*, *265*, 314–324. DOI: 10.1016/j.jad.2019.11.156 PMID: 32090755

Setti, I., Sommorigo, V., & Argentero, P. (2022). Enhancing expatriates' assignments success: The relationship between cultural intelligence, cross-cultural adaptation and performance. *Current Psychology (New Brunswick, N.J.)*, *41*(7), 42914311. DOI: 10.1007/s12144-020-00931-w

Shahri, A., Hosseini, M., Phalp, K., Taylor, J., & Ali, R. (2014). Towards a code of ethics for gamification at enterprise. In Frank, U., Loucopoulos, P., Pastor, Ó., & Petrounias, I. (Eds.), *IFIP working conference on the practice of enterprise modeling* (pp. 235–245). Springer. DOI: 10.1007/978-3-662-45501-2_17

Shajari, S., Kuruvinashetti, K., Komeili, A., & Sundararaj, U. (2023). The Emergence of AI-Based Wearable Sensors for Digital Health Technology: A Review. *Sensors (Basel, Switzerland)*, *23*(23), 9498-. https://doi.org/DOI: 10.3390/s23239498

Sharma, H. K., Kumar, A., Pant, S., & Ram, M. (2022). Role of Artificial Intelligence, IoT and Blockchain in Smart Healthcare. In *Artificial Intelligence, Blockchain and IoT for Smart Healthcare* (1st ed., pp. 25–36). Routledge. https://doi.org/DOI: 10.1201/9781003333050-3

Shavelson, R. J. (2012). Assessing business planning competence using the Collegiate Learning Assessment as a prototype. *Empirical Research in Vocational Education and Training*, *4*(1), 77–90. DOI: 10.1007/BF03546509

Shaw, A. (2015). *Gaming at the edge: Sexuality and gender at the margins of gamer culture*. University of Minnesota Press., DOI: 10.5749/minnesota/9780816693153.001.0001

Shaw, A. (2022). Creative Minecrafters: Cognitive and personality determinants of creativity, novelty, and usefulness in Minecraft. *Psychology of Aesthetics, Creativity, and the Arts*. Advance online publication. DOI: 10.1037/aca0000310

Shopify. (2021). *Shopify Gaming League: Building community through play*. Shopify Inc.

Siddiq, F., Hatlevik, O. E., Olsen, R. V., Throndsen, I., & Scherer, R. (2016). Taking a future perspective by learning from the past: A systematic review of assessment instruments that aim to measure primary and secondary school students' ICT literacy. *Educational Research Review*, *19*, 58–84. DOI: 10.1016/j.edurev.2016.05.002

Sidhu, P., Carter, M., & Zagal, J. P. (Eds.). (2024). *Fifty years of Dungeons & Dragons*. MIT Press. DOI: 10.7551/mitpress/15175.001.0001

Siemens, G. (2013). Learning analytics: The emergence of a discipline. *The American Behavioral Scientist*, *57*(10), 1380–1400. DOI: 10.1177/0002764213498851

Singer, J. A. (2004). Narrative identity and meaning making across the adult lifespan: An introduction. *Journal of Personality*, *72*(3), 437–460. DOI: 10.1111/j.0022-3506.2004.00268.x PMID: 15102034

Singh, R. (2025). Revamping Employee Experience for the Next Generation Workforce. In *Approaching Employee Experience Management With Data Science* (pp. 65–94). IGI Global Scientific Publishing. DOI: 10.4018/979-8-3693-7848-9.ch003

Sissine, M., Segan, R., Taylor, M., Jefferson, B., Borrelli, A., Koehler, M., & Chelvayohan, M. (2014). Cost comparison model: Blended eLearning versus traditional training of community health workers. *Online Journal of Public Health Informatics*, *6*(3). Advance online publication. DOI: 10.5210/ojphi.v6i3.5533 PMID: 25598868

Siteimprove, Inc. (2024). A guide to accessibility overlays. Siteimprove.com. https://www.siteimprove.com/glossary/accessibility-overlays/

Skinner, B. F. (1953). *Science and human behavior*. Pearson Education, Inc., DOI: 10.1016/B978-012370509-9.00087-5

Skwarczek, B. (2024, June 26). *Breaking Boundaries: How Diversity, Equity And Inclusion Initiatives Are Reshaping The Gaming Industry*. Forbes. https://www.forbes.com/councils/forbestechcouncil/2024/06/26/breaking-boundaries-how-diversity-equity-and-inclusion-initiatives-are-reshaping-the-gaming-industry/

Sliwinski, J., Katsikitis, M., & Jones, C. M. (2017). A review of interactive technologies as support tools for the cultivation of mindfulness. *Mindfulness*, *8*(5), 1150–1159. DOI: 10.1007/s12671-017-0698-x

Sloan, K. (2020). E-Learning: How the coronavirus has changed education forever. Cybint, retrieved from: https://www.cybintsolutions.com/e-learning-how-the-coronavirus-has-changed-education-forever/

Slotboom, C. (2024). *The new gaming & esports pyramid 2024*. Team Locktree. https://www.teamlocktree.com/news/business/the-new-gaming-esports-pyramid-2024/

Slotboom, C. (2024). *Locktree Gaming Quadrant*. Team Locktree.

Smith, M., Sharpe, B., Arumuham, A., & Birch, P. (2022). Examining the Predictors of Mental Ill Health in Esport Competitors. Healthcare (Basel), 10(4), 626–. https://doi.org/DOI: 10.3390/healthcare10040626

Smith, M. J., Birch, P. D., & Bright, D. (2019). Identifying stressors and coping strategies of elite esports competitors. [IJGCMS]. *International Journal of Gaming and Computer-Mediated Simulations*, *11*(2), 22–39. DOI: 10.4018/IJGCMS.2019040102

Smith, T. B., Constantine, M. G., Dunn, T. W., Dinehart, J. M., & Montoya, J. A. (2006). Multicultural education in the mental health professions: A meta-analytic review. *Journal of Counseling Psychology*, *53*(1), 132–145. DOI: 10.1037/0022-0167.53.1.132

Society for Human Resource Management. (2022). *Human capital benchmarking report*. SHRM.

Soliño-Fernandez, D., Ding, A., Bayro-Kaiser, E., & Ding, E. L. (2019). Willingness to adopt wearable devices with behavioral and economic incentives by health insurance wellness programs: Results of a US cross-sectional survey with multiple consumer health vignettes. *BMC Public Health*, *19*(1), 1649–1649. DOI: 10.1186/s12889-019-7920-9 PMID: 31839006

Song, Z., & Baicker, K. (2019). Effect of a workplace wellness program on employee health and economic outcomes: A randomized clinical trial. *Journal of the American Medical Association*, *321*(15), 1491–1501. DOI: 10.1001/jama.2019.3307 PMID: 30990549

Spanellis, A., Harviainen, J. T., Fernández Galeote, D., & Thibault, M. (2024). Gamification for Sustainable Development. *Simulation & Gaming*, *55*(3), 361–365. DOI: 10.1177/10468781241249324

Srinivasa, K. G., & Kurni, M. (2021). *A beginner's guide to learning analytics*. Springer.

Staiano, A. E., & Calvert, S. L. (2011). Exergames for physical education courses: Physical, social, and cognitive benefits. *Child Development Perspectives*, *5*(2), 93–98. DOI: 10.1111/j.1750-8606.2011.00162.x PMID: 22563349

Statista. (2023). *Gaming industry - Statistics & facts*. Statista.

Statista. (2024). *Frequency of using smartphones to play games in the U.S.* Statista. https://www.statista.com/statistics/248892/frequency-of-using-smartphones-to-play-games-in-the-us/

Stefanidis, A., Phalp, K., & Ali, R. (2018). Conceptualising gamification risks to teamwork within enterprise. In *The practice of enterprise modeling: 11th IFIP WG 8.1. Working conference*, PoEM 2018, Vienna, Austria, October 31–November 2, 2018 (Vol. 335, p. 105). Springer.

Steinkuehler, C., & Duncan, S. (2008). Scientific habits of mind in virtual worlds. *Journal of Science Education and Technology*, *17*(6), 530–543. DOI: 10.1007/s10956-008-9120-8

Sternberg, R. J., & Detterman, D. K. (Eds.). (1986). *What is intelligence? Contemporary viewpoints on its nature and definition*. Praeger.

Stewart, J. B. (2013). *Looking for a lesson in Google's perks*. The New York Times.

Stratton, J., Canales, C., Armas, V., & Miller, N. (2006). Positive stereotyping: Influence tactic for prejudice reduction? *Social Influence*, *1*(4), 265–287. DOI: 10.1080/15534510601008882

Student Affairs Administrators, N. A. S. P. A. (2019, June 5). *Esports: Promoting student success in and out of the classroom* [Video]. YouTube. https://www.youtube.com/watch?v=FTaJuqV1bJs

Susilo, T. (2024). The impact of talent management, employee well-being initiatives, and remote work policies on workforce productivity. *The Journal of Academic Science*, *1*(2), 81–90.

Taborda Mosquera, J. P., Arango-López, J., Gutiérrez Vela, F. L., & Padilla Zea, N. (2021). Analyzing effectiveness and fun through metrics applied to pervasive gaming experiences. *Universal Access in the Information Society*, *20*(3), 545–554. DOI: 10.1007/s10209-020-00768-x

Tackett, T., & Lemon, L. L. (2025). A balanced approach: Remote employees' experiences with employee engagement and well-being. *Corporate Communications: An International Journal*. Vol. ahead-of-print No. ahead-of-print. https://doi.org/ DOI: 10.1108/CCIJ-08-2024-0154

Taguimdje, W.. (2020). Influence of artificial Intelligence on form performance: The business value of AI-based transformation projects. *Business Process Management Journal*, *26*(7), 1893–1924. DOI: 10.1108/BPMJ-10-2019-0411

Tahiru, F. (2021). AI in Education: A Systematic Literature Review [JCIT]. *Journal of Cases on Information Technology*, *23*(1), 1–20. DOI: 10.4018/JCIT.2021010101

Tallat, R., Hawbani, A., Wang, X., Al-Dubai, A., Zhao, L., Liu, Z., & Alsamhi, S. H. (2023). Navigating industry 5.0: A survey of key enabling technologies, trends, challenges, and opportunities. *IEEE Communications Surveys and Tutorials*, *26*(2), 1080–1126. DOI: 10.1109/COMST.2023.3329472

Tam, G., & El-Azar, D. (2020). 3 ways the coronavirus pandemic could reshape education. World Economic Forum, https://www.weforum.org/stories/2020/03/3-ways-coronavirus-is-reshaping-education-and-what-changes-might-be-here-to-stay/

Tariq, F., Islam, S. M. R., & Mostefaoui, G. K. (2023). Future Challenges in Artificial Intelligence for Smart Healthcare. In *Artificial Intelligence for Disease Diagnosis and Prognosis in Smart Healthcare* (1st ed., Vol. 1, pp. 305–310). CRC Press., DOI: 10.1201/9781003251903-17

Tariq, M. U. (2025). AI and Work-Life Balance: Transforming Employee Wellbeing in the Modern Workplace. In Ahmed, E., Babar, A., Samad, A., Ahmed, R., & Beydoun, G. (Eds.), *Strengthening Human Relations in Organizations With AI* (pp. 85–110). IGI Global Scientific Publishing., DOI: 10.4018/979-8-3693-6507-6.ch004

Tariq, M. U. (2025). AI-Powered Business Process Automation: Revolutionizing Firm Management. In Derbali, A. (Ed.), *AI, Economic Perspectives, and Firm Business Management* (pp. 199–224). IGI Global Scientific Publishing., DOI: 10.4018/979-8-3693-7357-6.ch010

Tariq, M. U. (2025). Innovative Business Models: Integrating Social, Economic, and Environmental Goals in Rural Manufacturing. In Prabhakar, A., Yu, P., & Erokhin, V. (Eds.), *Rural Social Entrepreneurship Development: Network-Based Manufacturing System Model* (pp. 147–174). IGI Global Scientific Publishing., DOI: 10.4018/979-8-3693-7515-0.ch005

Tariq, M. U. (2025). Navigating Public Administration 5.0: Embracing AI for Smarter Governance. In Wongmahesak, K., Ahmad, J., & Mustanir, A. (Eds.), *Public Governance Practices in the Age of AI* (pp. 167–186). IGI Global Scientific Publishing., DOI: 10.4018/979-8-3693-9286-7.ch008

Tariq, M. U. (2025). Revitalizing Pedagogy: Integrating Indigenous Knowledge and Practices Into Higher Education Disciplines. In Kgari-Masondo, M. (Ed.), *Indigenous Teaching Disciplines and Perspectives for Higher Education* (pp. 379–400). IGI Global Scientific Publishing., DOI: 10.4018/979-8-3693-9296-6.ch018

Tavinor, G. (2009). *The art of videogames*. Wiley-Blackwell. DOI: 10.1002/9781444310177

Taylor, T. L. (2015). *Raising the stakes: E-sports and the professionalization of computer gaming*. Mit Press.

Technologies, T. (2023), The role of artificial intelligence in personalized https://www.trigyn.com/insights/role-artificial-intelligence-personalized-learning

Techopedia. (n.d.). *What is location-aware?* https://www.techopedia.com/definition/29929/location-aware

Tharenou, P. (2015). Researching expatriate types: The quest for rigorous methodological approaches. *Human Resource Management Journal*, *25*(2), 149–165. DOI: 10.1111/1748-8583.12070

The Culture Factor Group. (2024). *Country comparison tool*. Retrieved May 10, 2025, from https://www.hofstede-insights.com/country-comparison-tool?countries=germany%2Cunited+states

The List Show TV. (2019, May 29). *How esports is changing the world* [Video]. YouTube. https://www.youtube.com/watch?v=OAiCjNg3pZY

Tholl, C., Bickmann, P., Wechsler, K., Froböse, I., & Grieben, C. (2022, December). disorders in video gamers – a systematic review. *BMC Musculoskeletal Disorders*, *23*(1), 1–678. DOI: 10.1186/s12891-022-05614-0

Thomas, A. (2022). *Praxisbuch Interkulturelle Handlungskompetenz* [Practical guide to intercultural competence]. Springer., DOI: 10.1007/978-3-662-63671-8

Ting-Toomey, S., & Chung, L. C. (2022). *Understanding intercultural communication* (3rd ed.). Oxford University Press.

Ting-Toomey, S., & Dorjee, T. (2019). *Communicating across cultures* (2nd ed.).

T-Mobile. (2020). *Employee engagement and retention report.* T-Mobile US, Inc.

Tondello, G. F., & Nacke, L. E. (2020). Validation of User Preferences and Effects of Personalized Gamification on Task Performance. *Frontiers of Computer Science*, *2*, 29. Advance online publication. DOI: 10.3389/fcomp.2020.00029

Tondello, G. F., Wehbe, R. R., Diamond, L., Busch, M., Marczewski, A., & Nacke, L. E. (2016). The gamification user types hexad scale. In *Proceedings of the 2016 Annual Symposium on Computer-Human Interaction in Play* (pp. 229-243). ACM.

Trammell, A., Loring-Albright, G., & Boluk, S. (2017). Mechanics of trauma in *The Grizzled. Analog Game Studies, 4*(1). https://analoggamestudies.org/2017/01/mechanics-of-trauma-in-the-grizzled/

Tremblay, M. S., Aubert, S., Barnes, J. D., Saunders, T. J., Carson, V., Latimer-Cheung, A. E., Chastin, S. F. M., Altenburg, T. M., & Chinapaw, M. J. (2017). Sedentary behavior research network (SBRN)–terminology consensus project process and outcome. *The International Journal of Behavioral Nutrition and Physical Activity*, *14*(1), 75. DOI: 10.1186/s12966-017-0525-8 PMID: 28599680

Tropp, L. R., & Barlow, F. K. (2018). Making advantaged racial groups care about inequality: Intergroup contact as a route to psychological investment. *Current Directions in Psychological Science*, *27*(3), 194–199. DOI: 10.1177/0963721417743282

Turan, Z., Avinc, Z., Kara, K., & Goktas, Y. (2016). Gamification and Education: Achievements, Cognitive Loads, and Views of Students. [iJET]. *International Journal of Emerging Technologies in Learning*, *11*(07), 64–69. DOI: 10.3991/ijet.v11i07.5455

Turel, O., Romashkin, A., & Morrison, K. M. (2017, August). A model linking video gaming, sleep quality, sweet drinks consumption and obesity among children and youth. *Clinical Obesity*, *7*(4), 191–198. DOI: 10.1111/cob.12191 PMID: 28320073

Turner, H. (2021, September 28). *How Gamification Leads To Meaningful Workplace DEI Changes*. Law Journal Newsletters. https://www.lawjournalnewsletters.com/2021/09/01/how-gamification-leads-to-meaningful-workplace-dei-changes/?slreturn=20220606054104

Turner, M., & Javed, A. (2023). Technological disruption and change management: Navigating uncertainty in the digital age. *The Management Science Letter*, *1*(01), 65–75.

U. S. Department of Justice. (n.d.). Businesses That Are Open To the Public. ADA. Gov. https://www.ada.gov/topics/title-iii/

U.S. Access Board (USAB). (2024). Information and Communication Technology, Revised 508 Standards and 255 Guidelines. https://www.access-board.gov/ict/

U.S. Access Board. (2022). Guide to the ADA accessibility standards, Chapter 7: Signs (Character height). Access-Board.gov. https://www.access-board.gov/ada/guides/chapter-7-signs/#technical-requirements-for-characters

United Nations. (2018). *E-government survey 2018: Gearing e-government to support transformation towards sustainable and resilient societies.*https://publicadministration.un.org/egovkb/en-us/Reports/UN-E-Government-Survey-2018

United Nations. Department of Economic and Social Affairs Sustainable Development (2015.). *The 17 Goals | Sustainable Development*. https://sdgs.un.org/goals

Urgun, D., Seidel, J., Vangeli, E., Borges, M., & de Oliveira, R. F. (2025). Exploring the impact of cross-cultural training on cultural competence and cultural intelligence: A narrative systematic literature review. *Frontiers in Psychology*, *16*, 1511788. DOI: 10.3389/fpsyg.2025.1511788 PMID: 40260004

Urick, M. (2017). Adapting training to meet the preferred learning styles of different generations. *International Journal of Training and Development*, *21*(1), 53–59. DOI: 10.1111/ijtd.12093

UsableNet Inc. (2024). Get the 2024 midyear report on digital accessibility lawsuits. UsableNet.com. https://usablenet.com/resources?contentType=Reports

Uttal, D. H., Meadow, N. G., Tipton, E., Hand, L. L., Alden, A. R., Warren, C., & Newcombe, N. S. (2013). The malleability of spatial skills: A meta-analysis of training studies. *Psychological Bulletin*, *139*(2), 352–402. DOI: 10.1037/a0028446 PMID: 22663761

Valdez, V. B., & Javier, S. P. (2021). Digital divide: From a peripheral to a core issue for all SDGs. In *Reduced inequalities* (pp. 88–101). Springer International Publishing. DOI: 10.1007/978-3-319-95882-8_107

van Bakel, M. (2019). It takes two to tango: A review of the empirical research on expatriate-local interactions. *International Journal of Human Resource Management*, *30*(21), 2993–3025. DOI: 10.1080/09585192.2018.1449763 van Bakel, M., van Oudenhoven, J. P., & Gerritsen, M. (2017). Expatriate contact with a local host: An intervention to increase social support. *Human Resource Development International*, *20*(3), 215–235. DOI: 10.1080/13678868.2016.1248720

van Dijk, J. (2020). *The digital divide* (2nd ed.). Polity Press.

van Merrienboer, J. J. G., & Kirschner, P. A. (2018). *Ten steps to complex learning* (3rd ed.). Routledge., DOI: 10.1007/s11528-018-0254-0

van Rosmalen, P., & Westera, W. (2014). Introducing serious games with Wikis: Empowering the teacher with simple technologies. *Interactive Learning Environments*, *22*(5), 564–577. DOI: 10.1080/10494820.2012.707128

van Zoest, V. (2015). *Relationship between video gaming and spatial thinking skills of children 8 to 10 years old* (Bachelor's thesis). Wageningen University and Research Centre. https://edepot.wur.nl/351159

Vardeman, C. (2024, March 20). Rethinking Diversity, Equity, and Inclusion (DEI) training: From good vs. Bad to integrated respect and understanding [Blog]. *LinkedIn*. https://www.linkedin.com/pulse/rethinking-diversity-equity-inclusion-dei-training-from-vardeman-xp2rc/

Vaughn, M. (2023) The Rise of Artificial Intelligence in L&D: New Opportunities and Challenges, https://www.openlms.net/blog/insights/rise-ai-learning-development-opportunities-challenges/

Veldkamp, A., Daemen, J., Teekens, S., Koelewijn, S., Knippels, M.-C. P. J., & Joolingen, W. R. (2020a). Escape boxes: Bringing escape room experience into the classroom. *British Journal of Educational Technology*, *51*(4), 1220–1239. DOI: 10.1111/bjet.12935

Veldkamp, A., van de Grint, L., Knippels, M.-C. P., & van Joolingen, W. R. (2020b). Escape education: A systematic review on escape rooms in education. *Educational Research Review*, *15*(31), 1–18. DOI: 10.1016/j.edurev.2020.100364

Velez, J. A., Mahood, C., Ewoldsen, D. R., & Moyer-Gusé, E. (2012). Ingroup versus outgroup conflict in the context of violent video game play: The effect of cooperation on increased helping and decreased aggression. *Communication Research*, *39*(8), 1–20. DOI: 10.1177/0093650212456202

Verghese, T. (2013). *The invisible elephant: Exploring cultural awareness* (2nd ed.). Synergistic Press.

Video Game Insights. (2024). *Global PC Games Market Report 2024*. https://vginsights.com/assets/reports/VGI_Global_PC_Games_Market_Report_2024.pdf

Viltz-Emerson, M. A. (2021). *Forward solutions in digital learning transformation: A study in navigating 21st-century organizational learning for learning & development professionals*. Pepperdine University.

Vink, P. (2009). *Creating supportive environments for workplace well-being*. CRC Press. https://books.google.nl/books?id=2RYNDgAAQBAJ

Vinyals, O., Babuschkin, I., Czarnecki, W. M., Mathieu, M., Dudzik, A., Chung, J., Choi, D. H., Powell, R., Ewalds, T., Georgiev, P., Oh, J., Horgan, D., Kroiss, M., Danihelka, I., Huang, A., Sifre, L., Cai, T., Agapiou, J. P., Jaderberg, M., & Silver, D. (2019). Grandmaster level in StarCraft II using multi-agent reinforcement learning. *Nature*, *575*(7782), 350–354. Advance online publication. DOI: 10.1038/s41586-019-1724-z PMID: 31666705

Vlada, I. P., Galina, A. M., Elena, A. P., & Yuliya, V. M. (2019). Features of mental activity of students-Esport players. *International Journal of Cognitive Research in Science. Engineering and Education*, 7(2), 67–76.

Vlasova, H. (2022, March 21). *Online education statistics—How COVID-19 changed the way we learn*. Admissionsly. https://admissionsly.com/online-education-statistics/

Von der Heiden, J. M., Braun, B., Müller, K. W., & Egloff, B. (2019). The association between video gaming and psychological functioning. *Frontiers in Psychology*, *10*, 1731. DOI: 10.3389/fpsyg.2019.01731 PMID: 31402891

Vromans, P., van Engen, M., & Mol, S. T. (2013). Presumed cultural similarity paradox: Expatriate adjustment and performance across the border or over the globe. *Journal of Global Mobility*, *1*(2), 219–238. DOI: 10.1108/JGM-02-2013-0011

Vygotsky, L. (1978). *Mind in society*. Harvard University Press.

W3C (2023a). Web Accessibility Laws and Policies. https://www.w3.org/WAI/policies/

W3C. (2023b). W3C introduction to understanding WCAG. https://www.w3.org/WAI/WCAG21/Understanding/intro#understanding-the-four-principles-of-accessibility

W3C. (2023c). Understanding SC 1.4.1: Use of color (Level A). W3.org. https://www.w3.org/WAI/WCAG21/Understanding/use-of-color.html

W3C. (2024a). W3C accessibility guidelines. https://www.w3.org/TR/wcag-3.0/

W3C. (2024b). Understanding SC 2.3.1: Three flashes or below threshold (Level A). https://www.w3.org/WAI/WCAG22/Understanding/three-flashes-or-below-threshold.html

Wagner, M. G. (2006). On the scientific relevance of eSports. In *Proceedings of the 2006 International Conference on Internet Computing & Conference on Computer Games Development* (pp. 437-442). CSREA Press.

Wai, J., Cacchio, M., Putallaz, M., & Makel, M. C. (2010). Sex differences in the right tail of cognitive abilities: A 30 year examination. *Intelligence*, *38*(4), 412–423. DOI: 10.1016/j.intell.2010.04.006

Walmart. (2019). *Safety training through gamification*. Walmart Inc.

Wand, X.. (2023). Preparing for AI-enhanced education: Conceptualizing and empirically examining teachers' AI readiness. *Computers in Human Behavior*, *146*, 107796. DOI: 10.1016/j.chb.2023.107798

Wang, C. H., & Varma, A. (2019). Cultural distance and expatriate failure rates: The moderating role of expatriate management practices. *International Journal of Human Resource Management*, *30*(15), 2211–2230. DOI: 10.1080/09585192.2017.1315443

Wang, Y., Lockett, M., & Zhou, A. J. (2024). Digitalization and expatriate cross-cultural adjustment: The role of mobile apps. *Journal of Global Mobility: The Home of Expatriate Management Research*, *10*. Advance online publication. DOI: 10.1108/JGM-04-2024-0041

Ward, C., Bochner, S., & Furnham, A. (2020). *Psychology Culture Shock*. Routledge., DOI: 10.4324/9781003070696

Ward, C., Henderson, S. M., & Metcalfe, N. H. (2013). A short history on pacemakers. *International Journal of Cardiology*, *169*(4), 244–248. DOI: 10.1016/j.ijcard.2013.08.093 PMID: 24083883

Wattanapisit, A., Wattanapisit, S., & Wongsiri, S. (2020). Public Health Perspectives on eSports. *Public health reports (Washington, D.C.: 1974)*, *135*(3), 295–298. https://doi.org/DOI: 10.1177/0033354920912718

Waxin, M.-F., & Brewster, C. (2024). The recruitment, selection, and preparation of expatriates. In Bonache, J., Brewster, C., & Froese, F. J. (Eds.), *Global Mobility and the Management of Expatriates* (pp. 31–56). Cambridge University Press., DOI: 10.1017/9781108679220.002

Weaver, J. B.III, Mays, D., Sargent Weaver, S., Kannenberg, W., Hopkins, G. L., Eroĝlu, D., & Bernhardt, J. M. (2009). Health-Risk Correlates of Video-Game Playing Among Adults. *American Journal of Preventive Medicine*, *37*(4), 299–305. DOI: 10.1016/j.amepre.2009.06.014 PMID: 19765501

Weber, S., Draxler, C., Achtenhagen, F., Bley, S., Wiethe-Körprich, M., Kreuzer, C., & Gürer, C. (2021b). Measuring apprentices' intrapreneurship competence in vocational education and training (VET): An interdisciplinary model-based assessment. In E. Kuusisto, M. Ubani, P. Nokelainen & A. Toom (Eds.), *Good teachers for tomorrow's schools* (pp. 257–279). Brill, Sense. DOI: 10.1163/9789004465008_014

Weber, S., & Achtenhagen, F. (2017). Competence domains and vocational-professional education in Germany. In Mulder, M. (Ed.), *Competence-based vocational and professional education* (pp. 337–359). Springer., DOI: 10.1007/978-3-319-41713-4_16

Webster-Wright, A. (2009). Reframing professional development through understanding authentic professional learning. *Review of Educational Research*, *79*(2), 702–739. DOI: 10.3102/0034654308330970

Weigand, K., Flanagan, T., Dye, K., & Jones, P. (2014). Collaborative foresight: Complementing long-horizon strategic planning. *Technological Forecasting and Social Change*, *85*, 134–152. DOI: 10.1016/j.techfore.2013.08.016

Werbach, K. (2014). (Re)defining gamification: A process approach. In A. Spagnolli, L. Chittaro, & L. Gamberini (Eds.), *Persuasive Technology:9th International Conference, PERSUASIVE 2014* (pp. 266-272). Springer.

Werbach, K., & Hunter, D. (2012). *For the win: How game thinking can revolutionize your business*. Wharton Digital Press.

Werbach, K., & Hunter, D. (2012). *For the Win: How Game Thinking Can Revolutionize Your Business*. Wharton Digital Press.

Wheless, E. (2021). The top gaming partnerships of 2021; Gaming and esports got a popularity

Wiegard, R., Guhr, N., Krylow, S., & Breitner, M. H. (2019). Analysis of wearable technologies' usage for pay-as-you-live tariffs: Recommendations for insurance companies. *Zeitschrift Für Die Gesamte Versicherungs-Wissenschaft*, *108*(1), 63–88. DOI: 10.1007/s12297-019-00431-2

Williams, W. M., & Ayres, C. G. (2020). Can active video games improve physical activity in adolescents? A review of RCT. *International Journal of Environmental Research and Public Health*, *17*(2), 669. DOI: 10.3390/ijerph17020669 PMID: 31968642

Willis Towers Watson. (2022). *Global benefits attitudes survey*. Willis Towers Watson.

Wilmink, G., Dupey, K., Alkire, S., Grote, J., Zobel, G., Fillit, H. M., & Movva, S. (2020). Artificial Intelligence–Powered Digital Health Platform and Wearable Devices Improve Outcomes for Older Adults in Assisted Living Communities: Pilot Intervention Study. *JMIR Aging*, *3*(2), e19554–e19554. DOI: 10.2196/19554 PMID: 32723711

Wilson, A., Watson, C., Thompson, T. L., Drew, V., & Doyle, S. (2017). Learning analytics: Challenges and limitations. *Teaching in Higher Education*, *22*(8), 991–1007. DOI: 10.1080/13562517.2017.1332026

Wittek, B. H. (2021). Where are we today in understanding the role of the firm as a driver of international flows of highly skilled migrants? Reviewing the status of the literature on direct and indirect host country meso-level influences. *International Journal of Human Resource Management*, *32*(20), 4253–4286. DOI: 10.1080/09585192.2019.1651378

World Economic Forum. (2020). *The future of jobs report 2020*. https://www3.weforum.org/docs/WEF_Future_of_Jobs_2020.pdf

World Health Organization (WHO). (2023). Disability. https://www.who.int/news-room/fact-sheets/detail/disability-and-health#:~:text=An%20estimated%201.3%20billion%20people,earlier%20than%20those%20without%20disabilities

World Health Organization. (2017). *Protecting workers' health.*https://www.who.int/news-room/fact-sheets/detail/protecting-workers'-health

World Health Organization. (2020). *Mental health in the workplace*. WHO.

World Health Organization. (2022). Mental disorders. https://www.who.int/news-room/fact-sheets/detail/mental-disorders

World Health Organization. (2023). Depressive disorder (depression). https://www.who.int/news-room/fact-sheets/detail/depression

Woźniak, J. (2020). Gamification for sales incentives. *Contemporary Economics*, *14*(2), 144–161. DOI: 10.5709/ce.1897-9254.337

Xie, Y., Lu, L., Gao, F., He, S., Zhao, H., Fang, Y., Yang, J., An, Y., Ye, Z., & Dong, Z. (2021). Integration of Artificial Intelligence, Blockchain, and Wearable Technology for Chronic Disease Management: A New Paradigm in Smart Healthcare. *Current Medical Science*, *41*(6), 1123–1133. DOI: 10.1007/s11596-021-2485-0 PMID: 34950987

Yağanoğlu, M. (2021). Real time wearable speech recognition system for deaf persons. *Computers & Electrical Engineering*, *91*, 107026. DOI: 10.1016/j.compeleceng.2021.107026

Yee, N. (2006). Motivations for play in online games. *Cyberpsychology & Behavior*, *9*(6), 772–775. DOI: 10.1089/cpb.2006.9.772 PMID: 17201605

Yee, N. (2014). *The Proteus paradox: How online games and virtual worlds change us—and how they don't*. Yale University Press.

Yelne, S., Chaudhary, M., Dod, K., Sayyad, A., & Sharma, R. (2023). Harnessing the Power of AI: A Comprehensive Review of Its Impact and Challenges in Nursing Science and Healthcare. *Cureus*, *15*(11), e49252–e49252. DOI: 10.7759/cureus.49252 PMID: 38143615

Yin, K., Zi, Y., Zhuang, W., Gao, Y., Tong, Y., Song, L., & Liu, Y. (2020). Linking Esports to health risks and benefits: Current knowledge and future research needs. *Journal of Sport and Health Science*, *9*(6), 485–488. DOI: 10.1016/j.jshs.2020.04.006 PMID: 32417192

York, J., & deHaan, J. W. (2018). A Constructivist Approach to Game-Based Language Learning: Student Perceptions in a Beginner-Level EFL Context. [IJGBL]. *International Journal of Game-Based Learning*, *8*(1), 19–40. DOI: 10.4018/IJGBL.2018010102

Young Entrepreneur Council (YEC). (2022, 11 October). *The Importance of Diversity and Inclusion Training*. Forbes. https://www.forbes.com/councils/theyec/2022/10/11/the-importance-of-diversity-and-inclusion-training/

Yu, E. (2020). Student-inspired optimal online learning design for Generation Z. *The Journal of Educators Online*, *17*(1). https://files.er

Zaharna, R. S. (1989). Self-shock: The double-binding challenge of identity. *International Journal of Intercultural Relations*, *13*(1), 501–525. DOI: 10.1016/0147-1767(89)90026-6

Zahrt, O. H., Evans, K. M., Murnane, E. L., Santoro, E., Baiocchi, M. T., Landay, J. A., Delp, S. L., & Crum, A. J. (2022). Effects of Wearable Fitness Trackers and Activity Adequacy Mindsets on Affect, Behavior, and Health: Longitudinal Randomized Controlled Trial. *Journal of Medical Internet Research*, *25*, e40529. Advance online publication. DOI: 10.2196/40529 PMID: 36696172

Zheng, L. (2022). *DEI Deconstructed: Your No-Nonsense Guide to Doing the Work and Doing It Right*. Berrett-Koehler Publishers.

Zhong, Y., Guo, K., Su, J., & Chu, S. K. W. (2022). The impact of esports participation on the development of 21st-century skills in youth: A systematic review. *Computers & Education, 191*, 104640. Advance online publication. DOI: 10.1016/j.compedu.2022.104640

Zhu, L., Wang, Y., Wu, Y., Wilson, A., Zhou, H., Li, N., & Wang, Y. (2024). Longitudinal associations between the frequency of playing Mahjong and cognitive functioning among older people in China: Evidence from CLHLS, 2008–2018. *Frontiers in Public Health, 12*, 1352433. Advance online publication. DOI: 10.3389/fpubh.2024.1352433 PMID: 38550318

Zimmermann, J., Greischel, H., Jonkmann, K., & Neyer, F. J. (2021). Growth all along the road? Personality development and international contacts of (in)experienced sojourners. *European Journal of Personality*, *35*(4), 581–597. DOI: 10.1177/0890207020988439

About the Contributors

Vanessa Hammler Kenon, Ed.D., is the Associate Vice President Technology Compliance and Community Engagement and oversees the audit, compliance, and risk services sections of the University Technology Solutions (UTS) department. She also supervises the department's experiential learning Bold Careers Ambassadors and Interns Program and acts as the department liaison for UTS' internal and external community outreach and engagement. Dr. Kenon is an important UTS connection to UTSA (The University of Texas at San Antonio) students, professors, and staff. She is a member of several UTSA committees and task forces that support technology, student success, community engagement, eSports and game design student programs, audit and compliance, and the UTSA annual United Way SECC (State Employee Charitable Campaign). She also serves as an EDUCAUSE Ambassador and is on the state TASSCC Board. She is also a member of the American Education Research Association. Dr. Kenon has over 30 years of experience in higher education positions of instruction, leadership, and management in both private and public higher education programs, with 28 of those years spent overseeing technology-related departments and initiatives. She also serves on various boards and committees in the San Antonio and surrounding communities.

James E. Bartlett, II, Ph.D., has 24 years of Teaching Experience. He is currently working as Associate Professor of Postsecondary and Workforce Development at Old Dominion University and Director of the Community College Leadership Ph.D. program. He also worked as Executive Director for the Association for Career and Technical Education Research. He has published research streams, including topics of postsecondary career and technical education, business partnerships, community college improvement, doctoral education, and improving individual and organizational performance. He has published over 40 referred journals and presented research methods and other topics at over 200 national and international conferences. He has also edited numerous professional research journals, including special editions on research methods, and chaired over 75 dissertations. In addition, he has taught and developed business courses, including business communications, management, human resource development, entrepreneurship, and human resource management. Dr. Bartlett regularly presents his research at national conferences such as the Council for the Study of Community Colleges (CSCC), the Association for Career and Technical Education Research (ACTER), and the American Education Research Association (AERA).

***

Frank Achtenhagen (fachten@uni-goettingen.de) graduated 1963 as Diplom-Handelslehrer (MSc) (Business Education and Management) (Free University Berlin). Following professional positions: 1965 Assessor (Senate of Berlin), 1966–1969 Assistant (Free University Berlin), 1969 Dr. rer. pol. Free University Berlin, 1969–1971 Research Assistant (University Münster), 1971–2007 Full University Professor and Director (Institute for Business Education and Human Resources Development, Georg-August-University Göttingen), 2007—Full Professor Emeritus. He received Honorary Doctorates (1991: St. Gallen, CH; 2000: Helsinki). He is Fellow of the AERA. His research outcomes include more than 470 publications, he is an active member in national and international projects and research routines.

Keren Asgodom is a graduate of the University of Texas at San Antonio where she studied public health and has since pursued a Graduate degree in Health, Community & Policy. During her internship with the UTS Bold Careers Program, she researched how technology - in specific wearable technology - impacted public health.

Michelle Bartlett, Assistant Professor at Old Dominion University, received her Ph.D. at Clemson University in Higher Education Leadership with a cognate in statistics. Michelle was the past editor for the Career and Technical Education Research (CTER) Journal. She currently serves as the Professional Development Trustee for the Association for Career and Technical Education Research where she leads initiatives to help the membership learn new research skills. Michelle shares her passion for inclusive training design as the co-founder of the UNITE Design Lab.

Ajay Chandel is working as an Associate Professor at Mittal School of Business, Lovely Professional University, Punjab. He has 14 years of teaching and research experience. He has published papers in SCOPUS, WOS, and UGC listed Journals in areas like Social Media Marketing, E-Commerce, and Consumer Behaviour. He has published cases on SMEs and Social Entrepreneurship in The Case Centre, UK. He also reviews The Case Journal, Emerald Group Publishing, and International Journal of Business and Globalisation, Inderscience. He has authored and developed MOOCs on Tourism and Hospitality Marketing under Epg-Pathshala- A gateway to all postgraduate courses (a UGC-MHRD project under its National Mission on Education Through ICT (NME-ICT).

Tarana Afrin Chandel has received her Ph.D. degree from Integral University, Lucknow, M. Tech degree from UP Technical University, U.P and B. Tech degree from Magadha University, Bihar Presently she is working as an Associate Professor in Integral University, Lucknow, U.P. She is invited for distinguished speaker on Annual International Congress on Renewable Energy, United Kindom, UK,to be held on September 2024. She has published three patents i.e. "LOW COST MICRO CRACK MEASURING INSTRUMENT FOR DETECTION OF FAULTS ON SITE IN SOLAR PANELS", published on 02/06/2023; "SYSTEMATIC APPROACH TO UNLOCK THE FULL POTENTIAL OF PEROVSKITE, published on 01/09/2023 and "LOW-COST INSTRUMENT TO DETECT THE DEGRADATION OF PHARMACEUTICAL FORMULATIONS BASED MEDICINES SOLAR CELL TECHNOLOGY THROUGH MACHINE LEARNING", published on 24/06/2022. She is Principal Investigator of the project title "Performance Analysis of 1MW Grid Connected Solar Photovoltaic System using Image Analysis, sanctioned by Institute of Engineer, Kolkata-700020, West Bengal, India. She is recently honored as Indo Asian – Best Researcher Award 2022 in Renewable Energy & VLSI Design by Ratna Prasad Multidisciplinary Research & Educational Society on 28 February 2022, International Teaching Excellence Award 2021 on the occasion of Global Annual Education & Research Excellence Summit on 18 December 2021, Incredible Academician of INDIA-21 by Record Owner, Home of World Record on 25 September 2021. She is also honoured as Excellence in Research by 'Global & Research Development Award-21' on 30, June 2021. She has been honored as Recognition of Academic Excellence (Faculty-National) and Recognition of Research Excellence Ph.D. by IEI and Fr. C. Rodrigues Institution of Technology, Vashi on 16 January 2021. She has been honored as Excellence in Reviewing in recognition of an outstanding contribution to the quality of journal on 21 September 2020, Best Research Award 2020 for The Contribution and Honourable Achievements in Innovative on New Science Invention NESIN 2020, on 18 November 2020. She is honoured as Pride of India by International House on 12 September 2018. She is honored with Excellent Teaching award in Higher Education for AIRF-International Women Research and Connect Award 2018 on 8 March 2018, Best Faculty award in Rural Institution, AIRFA- National Conference on Exploring Science and Technology for the Future Developments held on 25

November 2017, She is awarded Best Paper Award: Paper title "Efficient Address Generator for WiMAX Deinterleaver" in 4 National conference on Challenges & opportunities for Technical Innovation on 19th & 20th February 2016 held at Ambalika Institute of Management and Technology, Lucknow, U.P. She has achieved "Rashtriya Gaurav Award" And Certificate of Excellence for Meritorious Services, Outstanding Performance and Remarkable Role by Dr. Bhishma Naraian Singh (Former Governor of Assam and Tamil Nadu) at the Seminar on Global Participation of India's Economic Development at New Delhi on 24 May 2010. She has published 8 book chapters on IGI and Taylor & Francis publication & one is in process, 28 research articles in International Journals and has presented 38 papers in International and National conference and also had poster presentation in IEEE conference. She is "Life member of Solar Energy Society of India, Indian Society for Technical Education", Life member of The Institution of Engineers (India), Indian Society for Technical Education and CPACE (Center for Professional Advancement). She is President and Life member of Robotic Society, Integral University, Lucknow, U.P. She also serves as reviewer in national and international journals. Indexed in Scopus

Autumn Garcia grew up along the border of Texas and Mexico in Brownsville. Here, in the face of healthcare inequities, her passion for community health advocacy began. Fueled by a commitment to address health disparities and promote preventative measures, Autumn earned a Bachelor of Science in Public Health from the University of Texas at San Antonio, where she also committed to extensive public health research as part of the UTS Bold Careers Program. Since graduating, she has chosen to continue schooling to channel her passion into dental hygiene. As a pre-dental hygiene student at Palo Alto College, she aspires to integrate her expertise in oral health with broader public health strategies.

Anthony Mark Gray Jr. is a dedicated scholar originally from Cape Hatteras, North Carolina. He completed his undergraduate studies at Elizabeth City State University and earned a Master's degree from East Carolina University. He holds a Ph.D. in Education with a concentration in Workforce and Organizational Development from Old Dominion University's Darden School of Education. His research focuses on soft skill development through nontraditional learning platforms such as esports. Anthony is married to his amazing wife, Paula, and together they have two grown sons.

Hazel Gruenewald is a professor of Organisational Behaviour at ESB Business School, Reutlingen University, Germany, where she headed International Relations for over a decade. She has been a visiting lecturer at multiple universities abroad including Universiti Malaysia Pahang, Malaysia, SBM ITB, Indonesia, EMLV, France, MCI Innsbruck, Austria and ZSEM, Croatia. Awarded a fellowship for innovation in teaching by the Baden-Württemberg Stiftung 2013 - 2016, she developed an innovative simulation game Quest 3C for undergraduate and MBA students, which has been deployed internationally. (b44b0a13-884e-48a9-8ab3-1b4b2a41025f

Sebastian Gutierrez is a graduate of the University of Texas at San Antonio where he studied public health. During his internship with the UTS Bold Careers Program, he researched how technology - in specific wearable technology - impacted public health.

Laura Hopkins holds a Masters of Information Technology Management and a Bachelors of Business Administration degrees as well a the Certified Professional in Accessibility Core Competencies (CPACC) certification from the International Association of Accessibility Professionals (IAAP) and the Certified Associate in Project Management (CAPM) certification from the Project Management Institute (PMI). Also, Ms. Hopkins holds two procurement certifications from the State of Texas: 1) Certified Texas Contract Manager (CTCM) and 2) Certified Texas Contract Developer (CTCD).

Mahrukh Khan is a graduate of the University of Texas at San Antonio, where she earned her degree in Public Health and served as a former UTS Bold Careers intern. She has conducted research on the impact of wearable technology in public health.

|**Lena Riha** is an instructor of Business Communication at ESB Business School, Reutlingen University, Germany. She got her start in the Department of Modern Languages, Literature, and Linguistics teaching at the University of Oklahoma, USA and Oklahoma City Community College, USA. During this time, she received several awards for outstanding work and integration of interactive supplementary activities for adult learners of foreign languages, as well as holding lectures on didactic integration of such assignments. Thereafter she received a Fulbright Assistantship in Austria, where she began teaching English as a Second Language. Since then she has taught at multiple language institutes and private companies with a focus on scientific writing and healthcare.

Chris Slotboom is a passionate advocate for gaming and esports. He co-founded Gaming@Work, a startup aimed at making everyone digitally skilled by 2030. Chris is a frequent speaker and moderator on gaming and esports-related topics. Chris shows how Game-derived skills can bridge the digital gap between generations. Leveraging his background in cloud services, high-end gaming systems, and published work, he explains how playing videogame software enhances problem-solving, teamwork, and digital literacy in the workplace. As Vice-Chair of the Dutch Esports Association (BEN), Chris is deeply involved in the esports community, driving its growth and influence. BEN, a collective of 70 esports-related businesses, emphasizes digital transformation in Education and Sports. Chris strives to unite ecosystem stakeholders and build collaboration to drive positive societal and economic change through the esports industry. During his previous tenure at Dell Technologies, Chris generated a total revenue of $129M with his team. He has also co-established the global Esports Research Collaborative, and fostered international videogaming partnerships that generated $400K revenue. Chris's career journey began in hospitality event management before transitioning into recruitment consulting, followed by business development for IT advisory services. Drawing from his diverse background, Chris offers unique perspectives on technology and societal solutions, aiding organizations and employees to thrive in today's digital landscape. He is a passionate speaker and collaborator, who frequently discusses future tech trends, innovation, gaming culture, and diversity. In his free time, Chris enjoys multiplayer games, ethical chocolates, and Dungeons & Dragons.

Muhammad Usman Tariq has more than 16+ year's experience in industry and academia. He has authored more than 200+ research articles, 100+ case studies, 150+ book chapters and several books other than 4 patents. He is founder and CEO of The Case HQ, a unique repository for courses, narrative and video case studies. He has been working as a consultant and trainer for industries representing six sigma, quality, health and safety, environmental systems, project management, and information security standards. His work has encompassed sectors in aviation, manufacturing, food, hospitality, education, finance, research, software and transportation. He has diverse and significant experience working with accreditation agencies of ABET, ACBSP, AACSB, WASC, CAA, EFQM and NCEAC. Additionally, Dr. Tariq has operational experience in incubators, research labs, government research projects, private sector startups, program creation and management at various industrial and academic levels. He is Certified Higher Education Teacher from Harvard University, USA, Certified Online Educator from HMBSU, Certified Six Sigma Master Black Belt and has been awarded PFHEA, SMIEEE, and CMBE.

Alina Vadsariya is a driven and compassionate individual whose journey is marked by dedication with a dream to become a veterinarian one day. Alina recently graduated from the University of Texas at San Antonio with a magna cum laude Bachelor of Science degree in Public Health, with a minor in Biology. Throughout her time at UTSA, Alina demonstrated an exceptional talent for learning and a deep-rooted passion for promoting the well-being of both humans and animals. In her free time she likes to spend time with her 4 year old Siberian husky and her family. As she continues on her path towards fulfilling her dream of becoming a veterinarian, Alina remains steadfast in her commitment to making a difference in the lives of animals and the communities she serves.

Susanne Weber (s.weber@lmu.de) studied Human Resource Education and Management at Georg-August University, Göttingen, from 1985 to 1990 and worked as a senior researcher. She holds a doctoral degree (Dr. rer. pol. 1994) from the Georg-August University, Göttingen, and fulfilled her Habilitation at Humboldt University of Berlin in 2004. Since 2005, she has been a Full Professor and Director of the Institute of Human Resource Education and Management, Munich School of Management, Ludwig-Maximilians-University in Munich | LMU. Her main reseach areas are intercultural leaning, entre-/intrapreneurship education, sustainability and digitalization. She runs governmental projects and publishes nationally and internationally.

Johnny L Williams is a dynamic leader and visionary entrepreneur, known for his innovative approach to integrating gaming, esports, and wellness into corporate environments. As the driving force behind Player Epic Inc, Johnny leverages his unique background as a gamer, former NFL athlete, and University of Kentucky alum to create groundbreaking solutions that address the evolving needs of the modern workforce. With a degree in Economics and a successful career in professional sports, Johnny understands the importance of teamwork, discipline, and continuous improvement. His passion for gaming and commitment to promoting a healthy work-life balance have led him to develop a platform that merges the excitement of gaming with the benefits of corporate wellness programs. Johnny's experience in both the sports and tech industries gives him a unique perspective on how to motivate and engage individuals. Under his leadership, Player Epic Inc has become a pioneer in using gaming and esports to enhance employee wellness, boost productivity, and foster a positive corporate culture.

Mohit Yadav is an Associate Professor in the area of Human Resource Management at Jindal Global Business School (JGBS). He has a rich blend of work experience from both Academics as well as Industry. Prof. Mohit holds a Ph.D. from Department of Management Studies, Indian Institute of Technology Roorkee (IIT Roorkee) and has completed Master of Human Resource and Organizational Development (MHROD) from prestigious Delhi School of Economics, University of Delhi. He also holds a B.Com (Hons.) degree from University of Delhi and

UGC-JRF scholarship. He has published various research papers and book chapters with reputed publishers like Springer, Sage, Emerald, Elsevier, Inderscience etc. and presented research papers in national and International conferences both in India and abroad. He has many best paper awards on his credit too. He is reviewer of various international journals like Computers in Human Behavior, Policing etc. His areas of interest are Organizational Behavior, HRM, Recruitment and Selection, Organizational Citizenship Behavior, Quality of work life and role.

Index

A

B

C

D

H

I

L

M

N

P

R

S

T

V

W

www.ingramcontent.com/pod-product-compliance
Lightning Source LLC
LaVergne TN
LVHW080351011026
849161LV00009B/2264
9798337353227